THE REAL THING

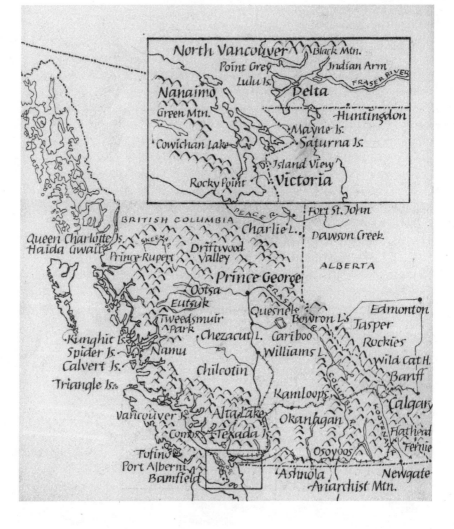

the real thing

The Natural History
of Ian McTaggart Cowan

by BRIONY PENN

RMB

RMB | Rocky Mountain Books Ltd.
rmbooks.com
@rmbooks
facebook.com/rmbooks

Cataloguing data available from Library and Archives Canada
ISBN 978-1-77160-070-5 (pbk.)
ISBN 978-1-77160-071-2 (epub)

Printed and bound in Canada

Distributed in Canada by Heritage Group Distribution and in the U.S. by Publishers Group West

For information on purchasing bulk quantities of this book, or to obtain media excerpts or invite the author to speak at an event, please visit rmbooks.com and select the "Contact Us" tab.

RMB | Rocky Mountain Books is dedicated to the environment and committed to reducing the destruction of old-growth forests. Our books are produced with respect for the future and consideration for the past.

We acknowledge the financial support of the Government of Canada through the Canada Book Fund and the Canada Council for the Arts, and of the province of British Columbia through the British Columbia Arts Council and the Book Publishing Tax Credit.

Nous reconnaissons l'aide financière du gouvernement du Canada par l'entremise du Fonds du livre du Canada et le Conseil des arts du Canada, et de la province de la Colombie-Britannique par le Conseil des arts de la Colombie-Britannique et le Crédit d'impôt pour l'édition de livres.

Canada Council
for the Arts

Conseil des arts
du Canada

BRITISH COLUMBIA
ARTS COUNCIL
An agency of the Province of British Columbia

CONTENTS

Preface   vii

Part 1
The Early Years: 1910–1920   1
Chapter 1   3
Chapter 2   19
Chapter 3   31
Chapter 4   43

Part 2
The Formative Years: 1927–1929   61
Chapter 5   63
Chapter 6   75
Chapter 7   81

Part 3
Gathering Skills: 1929–1932   89
Chapter 8   91
Chapter 9   103
Chapter 10   121
Chapter 11   131
Chapter 12   147
Chapter 13   155
Chapter 14   163

Part 4
The Berkeley Years: 1932–1935   175
Chapter 15   177
Chapter 16   193

Part 5
The Museum Years: 1935–1940   201
Chapter 17   203
Chapter 18   215
Chapter 19   219

Chapter 20   231
Chapter 21   247
Chapter 22   265
Chapter 23   283
Chapter 24   297

Part 6

The Early University Years: 1941–1950   307
Chapter 25   309
Chapter 26   329
Chapter 27   351
Chapter 28   373
Chapter 29   393

Part 7

Travel, Television and Advocacy: 1952–2010   409
Chapter 30   411
Chapter 31   425
Chapter 32   439

Afterword   461

Acknowledgements   462

Table of Species   465

Notes   473

Bibliography   515

Index   541

About the author   558

PREFACE

"All my life I have tried to explain to colleagues, family, students – anyone
who will listen to me – the beautiful, fascinating things that I see! It is
not all sweetness and light but this world is absolutely fascinating."[1]

In the opening pages of his 1956 handbook *The Mammals of British Columbia*,
Ian McTaggart Cowan encouraged us, his readers, to join him in "unraveling
the innermost secrets of the lives of mammals."[2] This book is a continuing invitation to reveal the innermost secrets not only of the lives of animals but of the
man himself and the lives of his gentle, paradoxical and radical cohort of naturalists who influenced British Columbia in more ways than I ever imagined before
starting this project.

Ian McTaggart Cowan first came into my life, as he did for many of us, through
this small, pocket-companion guide. The handbook series put out by the BC
Provincial Museum half a century ago (some of which are now updated through
the Royal BC Museum), which Cowan was to have such an important hand in, explained in encouraging language the mammals, birds, reptiles, amphibians, shells,
ferns and more. Species by species, we all learned the names of our fellow British
Columbians and became members of a fascinating community. On the cover of the
handbooks were the names that became as familiar as the large, charismatic mammals featured within: Ian McTaggart Cowan, Charlie Guiguet, Clifford Carl and
many more. It was hard to imagine that something as innocuous as a field guide or
handbook could be perceived by some as such a dangerous political weapon.

Ian McTaggart Cowan would have been only halfway through his life when
I first came under his enthusiastic spell, but by then that influence had already
spread around the province like mycelia – the fine roots of underground fungi that
feed the forest and the next generation – and I was one of its many beneficiaries.
As a budding naturalist growing up in Victoria, I was introduced to the subversive
Vancouver Island Rock and Alpine Garden Society by a horticulturalist, Mr. Raven.
Under his instruction we made magical native moss gardens for the annual show,
cultivating wild Shooting Stars and Easter Lilies. For my school field trips, park
naturalist Freeman (Skipper) King, who loomed like the giant Western Redcedar
at Goldstream Provincial Park, explained the spectacle of a salmon spawn. First
Bristol Foster, then Yorke Edwards, headed up the sparkling new provincial museum that overshadowed even the provincial legislature. They reassured a generation of us that where we lived was exciting, beautiful and important, inhabited by a
diverse showcase of creatures and cultures. All of these men had been supported in

their pursuits either directly or indirectly through institutions touched by Cowan. These vibrant people appeared everywhere: on the trails in the Rocky Mountains, in the intertidal zone at Long Beach, up in the grasslands above Kamloops and on university field trips at UBC. If there was no one around, I always had the pocket companions from the provincial museum to guide me.

These naturalists used a language that was reassuring for a child. They were interested in small things, in the natural world, in sharing their knowledge, and they cared enough to speak out to protect that world. These were the broad shoulders upon which many of us cobbled our careers and vocations, and Ian McTaggart Cowan's name was ever present. In the course of those years, I got interested in the culture of these naturalists and started to collect their stories on the side. They came from all ecological niches: the expected – biologists, native elders, environmental educators, raging grannies; but also the unexpected – nuns, cowboys, hunters, trappers and shopkeepers. Most were regular Canadians. Some were prominent scientist–activists such as Bristol Foster, Yorke Edwards and David Suzuki; political leaders with strong environmental interests like David Anderson and Elizabeth May; and activists and artists on the edge like Paul Watson, Roy Henry Vickers, Colleen and Wayne McCrory and Robert Bateman. All of them had a connection back to Ian McTaggart Cowan.

In 1999 I decided to try to put the stories of this group together in a book proposal with the working title *Beautiful British Columbians*. The criteria for inclusion were a love of the province, a will to defend the landscape and a desire to share their knowledge. A Canada Council grant bought me a couple of months to come up with a list, do some longer interviews and tie down this idea that had been burrowing away in my brain like Cowan's famous moles of the Fraser Delta.

Book publishers posed the question why anyone should care about these naturalists. I have had time to hone my response, the first ending in a rejected book proposal. First of all, these scientists were funny and curious – almost radical qualities these days. These were people that hadn't adopted the prevailing pioneer mentality to go out and conquer the landscape. They liked what was already here, and that included the indigenous cultures and the wildlife. Their story might throw some light on how to encourage this. It is an important question of the 21st century. It may be the only question our grandchildren will thank us for trying to answer.

I also knew people were feeling despair at the state of the world and would want to hear how others coped. It was heartbreaking being an environmental journalist documenting the changes. Surely there were many of us watching the constant destruction and suffering – looking for hope, given that extinctions have a certain finality about them. Only mythological phoenix species ever rise from ashes. I was interested in a question that deserves the best minds we can find to answer it: What would be a useful thing to do, given the extraordinary challenges we face today? While conducting interviews in 2000, I was told repeatedly, "You have to talk to Dr. Cowan." After nearly a century of witnessing and contemplating these issues, he had an influence that was legendary. In the parlance of the biologist, he was the alpha male. He was a keystone species unto himself, upon which an entire ecosystem relied. It was time to interview this man.

Ian McTaggart Cowan had been described to me as "the father of wildlife conservation and ecology" and "one of the world's leading mammalogists and ornithologists." Others mentioned his expertise in rodents, molluscs, ungulates, alpine flowers and revenue stamps. More accolades: "the ultimate Renaissance man" and "Canada's pioneer of natural history television programming" (his shows were being broadcast around the world before I was even born). He was an academic who had received more distinctions (including Officer of the Order of Canada and Order of British Columbia) than any other Canadian scientist. He was the namesake of two professorships and three scholarships, and a trusted mentor for at least three generations of students, colleagues, activists and policy-makers.

When I first contacted him, in 2000, he was 90 years old. I was a half century behind him. A rather rigorous exchange of emails ensued, during which, I gather, he was testing my resolve. He was interested in the type of questions I would be asking and how I would use the material. He was in the middle of co-writing the last volume of what would be his final collaborative venture, the magnum opus that is *Birds of BC*. His wife, Joyce, wasn't well, and (as he later told me) he only had so much energy to give in a day. He felt it was essential that there be an educational purpose to my book. I obviously passed the test and was invited to come over.

The Victoria city bus left me at a sandy beach in Cadboro Bay, which offered up a flock of American Wigeon and a River Otter family. I followed a Nootka rose and snowberry trail up towards Sea View Road, which led to the dappled shade of Woodhaven Terrace – I was arriving at some kind of fabled destination. Hidden from view behind large Douglas-firs and an array of alpine species, his house was an unassuming bungalow buzzing with hummingbirds and chickadees. I had arrived at the door of a Canadian legend.

I was nervous when I knocked; legends are either terrifying or disappointing. A tall, lean, handsome man, attired as though for the trail or garden, swung the door open with a flourish and gave me a warm welcome. He insisted I call him Ian. It was easy to imagine why he had been one of UBC's most popular professors ever – students crowding his lecture theatre until the fire department had to come. A Columbian Black-tailed Deer buck, with some exceptionally fine antlers, the subject of his PhD dissertation at Berkeley in 1935, had just crossed in front of me seconds earlier as I arrived in the garden. Ian's love of deer both alive and in his freezer was also legendary. We watched it saunter off to the next-door garden before he ushered me in.

We entered his study packed with books and wildlife paraphernalia: shells, skulls, casts of tracks, horns, duck decoys, sculptures and paintings. A desk and computer, with statistical software currently in use, marked the inner den of Ian McTaggart Cowan. He invited me to browse the shelves: a row of early children's books by authors like Ernest Thompson Seton; an entire bookshelf of his own publications, both academic and popular, including the original editions of *Mammals of* BC and *Birds of* BC; his cloth-bound field journals taking up at least two rows; a shelf of publications by his graduate students, numbering more than a hundred; a row of wildlife guides from around the world; and an entire wall of academic journals. In every patch of spare space hung his own exquisite black and white photographs: Mountain Goats on rocky crags; Great Horned Owls mantling prey; Pikas, or rock rabbits, next to a famous portrait of his friend and mentor Jimmy Simpson at a mountain camp – each individual comfortable in their habitat. Photos of his family – Joyce; their children, Garry and Ann; their grandchildren; their first great-grandchild – alternated with paintings of birds by Fenwick Lansdowne, Frank Beebe, Allan Brooks, Roy Henry Vickers and Glen Smith – renowned wild-life artists who were also friends, mentors or students.

Awards lay everywhere, dozens of them, propping up the books, acting as door-stops. I picked up randomly a bronze Haida carving of an orca for his contributions to the international conservation of marine mammals; a stone humpback fluke for his contributions to the Society of Conservation Biologists; a plaque from the BC Field Ornithologists for contributions to the study of birds; a carved wooden bowl presented by the Lieutenant-Governor of BC for his pioneering work on parks; a whooping crane for being named International Conservationist of the Year by the US National Wildlife Federation; a chunk of Precambrian rock for service as a fel-low of the Arctic Institute of Canada; a gold certificate from the Alpine Garden Club of BC for his alpine azaleas; and a gold medal for his collection of Yukon rev-enue stamps. After tea with Joyce, Ian's wife of over 60 years, we wandered round the rock garden, where his greatest enthusiasm of the day was reserved for the tiny alpine *Scilla* that had just won another prize. We sat down and negotiated the terms of the interviews: we would start with three half-days staggered over a month, and the notes would be for educational use only.

It was clear that the timeline provided was one of Ian's little jokes. After the first round of interviews, we hadn't gotten much beyond 1926. He was in a category of his own – a global category, not just among the "beautiful British Columbians." Unbeknownst to me, the groundwork for a much larger work was being laid. The time required was not just in trying to record a century of a life packed full, but also due to the man's phenomenal ability to accurately recall places, names and details. He could recount, for example, the size of a Bighorn Sheep herd on a particular day on a particular mountain slope fifty years earlier. When I discussed my own re-search project into Sandhill Cranes on the Central Coast, he recalled instantly that he had seen nesting cranes in the back lagoon of Spider Island in the spring of 1939.

Our conversations leapt seamlessly from his biography to zoology and from an-ecdote to science. Sporadically over the next five years, I ended up with about 20 hours of interviews, on both audio- and videotapes, completed with the help of his close friends and students Bristol Foster, Val Geist and Rod Silver, as well as Bob Weeden, Don Eastman and Peter Ommundsen.[3] I didn't yet know at that stage that I was going to write his biography (oh, the questions I would ask now!). My last in-terview with Ian was in 2005 – three years after his stroke and Joyce's death, both of which had diminished but not extinguished his incredible enthusiasm for all forms of life.

In these interviews I got a privileged glimpse into his century – and what a century. In mathematical terms, the population-savvy Cowan would have noted that 1910 to 2010 represents one of the steepest trajectories in rates of extinction the world has ever experienced, rivalling the late Cretaceous. In his lifetime the number of humans had escalated from 1.75 billion to just under 7 billion, consuming proportionally more resources than in the past ten millennia to achieve a rising standard of living but also an obscene inequity. In poetic terms, Cowan the photographer and writer had captured the beauty and diversity of the wildlife and landscapes devoured. The loss of them was profound. What captured my imagination was that he was both early witness to and participant in these changes. He was the last of the naturalist–hunters and the first of the alarmed scientists. He also had the experience of an immigrant Canadian in search of that rising standard of living – having left a ravaged European country with its forests and native wildlife long decimated to come to one of the richest places in North America. He could be as hungry as anyone for wild game, a load of wood to build his house and a trip on a plane to Baja. He could also articulate the impacts of development and express his gratefulness to the activist who could point out the destruction and the tragicomic irony of our lives. As an educator of some three generations of students, he had observed first-hand the downward slide of knowledge about and connection to the natural world, and he worried about the children who had no relations with nature.

It was his empathy for the forces at work in the world that most intrigued me. The son of a market gardener, he supplemented the family protein, as many Canadians of that era did, through good marksmanship. It was a skill that served him well in his career as wildlife biologist and museum curator, when shooting specimens and handling skins were part of the job. Having experienced poverty, he had an appreciation for the people who subsisted on wildlife, whether native trapper or local hunter. It was this very crossing of boundaries that caught the respect of most who met him. Cowan, during my generation, had skirted the factionalism and politics of environmentalism in a way that few have since. He was as well respected by female urban activists as by male rural hunters.

One of the lectures he delivered in the mid-1970s was called "A Whimsical and Slightly Irreverent Look at Environment in Canada." In typical style, Cowan had carefully observed, catalogued and mapped out this colourful community in which he lived and worked, the "varied fauna of vertebrates exhibiting some of the strangest behaviour patterns I have detected in a lifetime of research." He characterized the various groups who lobbied for the environment as being different species of crows that inhabited "rough country featuring many isolated hills." Their raucous calls were "so varied and unique to each peak that it inhibited effective genetic exchange." Observing that some feed off others while others forge links that cross disciplines and support one another, he concluded that "relationships with the other biota range from symbiotic to parasitic." Their greatest predator was *Gymnogyps rapinus*, or the Corporate Buzzard, "a continent-wide, resource-hungry raptor that is semi-solitary and territorial, with a sex-ratio highly biased to males; with a high rate of consumption but low energetic efficiency, leading to an abnormally high defecation rate. Areas of activity, therefore, are marked by high accumulations of waste products." Then there was *Canis parliamentarius*, "frequently harried by crows and courted by *Gymnogyps*."

In these lecture notes, which looked much like his guides to fauna, lies the essence of Cowan the scientific observer and educator. The man who had studied the ecosystem of Canadian society, and his own niche in it – which he told me was to make whatever contribution he could best make at the time. Fortified by his societal distinctions, bolstered with his voluminous research and clad in his camouflage garb of museum curator, professor, chair of committees, dean or chancellor, Cowan was able to express his passions and legitimize the protection of the natural world in a way that few other advocates for nature can. His contributions helped build a supportive ecosystem in which my generation flourished. He had helped put in place the curriculum, teachers, books, museums, programs, parks, jobs and cultural milieu that enabled a "Super, Natural BC" culture to thrive.

Cowan at age 90 was still very much on top of his game and had allocated some of his diminishing energy to sharing his stories with an activist–journalist quite raucous in tone. I produced several articles and a short television episode on his life but couldn't find a publisher for my original book idea. At the time, Ian had said he'd like to write his autobiography after the completion of *Birds of BC*. His intention: "I want to document what we are losing, with this book." But that wasn't to be. Meanwhile, two projects emerged that involved colleagues and students (he had over 100 grad students alone). The first was a book that began as a collection of 100 memories of Cowan, to coincide with his 100th birthday;[4] and a tribute article documenting the more than 300 papers and books he produced over his lifetime.[5] Neither publication, however, was primarily focused on documenting the losses.

After Ian Cowan died in 2010, just before his 100th birthday, his surviving daughter, Ann Schau, and student–colleague Rod Silver began a conversation about a biography of sorts based on the collection of his field journals, photographs, correspondence, lecture materials and interviews. In true Cowan fashion, his instructions were that they could only be used for public educational purposes. In 2012 I was brought into the project, and we spent the next ten months assessing and cataloguing the collection with the assistance of archivist Walter Meyer zu Erpen and the many who are named in the acknowledgements. We worked our way through filing cabinets and boxes of material, digitizing the most relevant. It was obvious that these were journals and correspondence saved precisely for the public's eyes. We didn't have to look far for evidence of this. Cowan had pasted his intentions right in the back of an early field journal from 1933. It was the instructions of Joseph Grinnell, his much-admired academic supervisor at Berkeley, to his students:

> Ascertain everything possible in regard to the natural history of the
> vertebrate life of the regions traversed and to make careful record

of the facts gathered in the form of specimens and notes, to be preserved for all time. All this is for the *information of others*; strive to make your record in all respects clearly intelligible. Remember that the value of our manuscripts increases as the years go by and faunal changes take place. Some of our earlier notebooks describe conditions now vanished in the localities they dealt with.

— J. Grinnell, September 12, 1933

In many cases, the fauna of the localities Cowan worked in have indeed vanished and the journals are poignant reminders of what we have destroyed. The field notes for the Okanagan grasslands describe the quiet diggings of badgers under a full moon amongst the Antelope Brush, much of which now lies under strip malls and vineyards. The journals describing the Ootsa, the Kootenay and the Peace River valleys are ghost landscapes. Much now lies underwater. Field notes from the Mackenzie Delta or the forests of Vancouver Island tell us what was there before dams, highways, pipelines, logging and mining carved up the landscape. The journal of the fauna of Point Grey or Richmond points to a Vancouver that is almost unrecognizable. The journals also give us some sense of what could be restored should we have the inclination. In some cases, like the islands off the central coast, we have a benchmark that hasn't changed so drastically, accentuating the importance of these last intact ecosystems, allowing us to celebrate the restoration of populations like the Humpback Whales. Revisiting these landscapes today as part of my research formed a vital part of telling this story.

According to Cowan, the simple explanation of landscape and wildlife doesn't make a story sufficiently engaging for readers. He developed his own art of storytelling – at which he was a master – through simple observation of his students:

> Most textbooks start with a discussion of anatomy, then start with protozoa and work up to mammals. That is not what students are interested in. I started talking about humans ... Then you can start telling them about the other categories of creatures, because you have them."[6]

My favourite example of his technique is his opening for a 1961 Vancouver Institute lecture on population ecology, "Of Mice and Men," where his first reference to scientific data starts: "I have a friend who decided to breed a pair of mice and see how many there would be after a year." In the background of that early reel-to-reel recording, you hear the audience laugh and audibly relax into a good evening of entertainment and education as the revered dean takes the audience from his friend's mice-infested basement to the marvels of evolution through his example of mouse speciation on the islands of BC's coast and then to the thornier and more difficult territory of human consumption and overpopulation. In writing this biography, I've attempted to emulate Cowan's technique and use stories from his long life to springboard into the behaviour of unusual animals or the peculiarities of places. In the process, there is always that didactic moment to throw in the mechanisms of evolution or the tools of conservation.

Because Cowan had seen more flora and fauna around British Columbia than virtually any human being could have before or will again, his stock of stories was almost inexhaustible. He also witnessed the impacts of overhunting, pollution, pesticides, logging, dam construction, oil and gas development and climate change that pointed to an increasingly impoverished future. Not surprisingly, he was always one of the first – if not *the* first – to raise the alarm. As Canadians we haven't done a very good job of crediting our scientists as leaders, prophets or innovators of ideas. As one of my interviewees noted, if Cowan had been born in the United States, he would have been a household name.

That isn't to say his accomplishments have gone unnoticed. Ten months of assembling his folio of papers gives us just a glimpse of the outward accomplishments of the man. They are so extensive that few can wade through his progression of honours without getting a little weary and casting about for some peccadillo or personal skeleton in a closet. There are indeed lots of skeletons, an entire museum (or two or three), such as the Cowan Tetrapod Collection in the Beaty Biodiversity Museum at UBC. That is the most interesting paradox for modern eyes – Cowan's intense love of hunting, coupled with an equally intense desire to see wildlife survive. The scale of his hunting animals as a young man is matched only by the scale of his saving animals as a middle-aged administrator. It is no wonder he felt protective of the predators, being one himself. This biography teases out the intertwined and paradoxical relationship between the two activities.

Other than some youthful blood lust, there was little to dislike in Cowan, and for a biographer that is always a problem. Writing about Ian McTaggart Cowan can border on hagiography at times. I looked hard for some kind of tragic flaw. He may have had an overly fond regard for regalia and was very competitive, but so are many male pheasants. We love them for it. He liked his group of male friends, but so do Mule Deer. This might have suggested a fatal streak of chauvinism in Cowan, but on closer inspection of his papers and of interviews with his oldest colleagues and students, I found little evidence of such. Instead, a much more fascinating and complex picture emerged. Cowan's early invitation to "unravel the innermost secrets of the lives of mammals", was what I found myself doing in perusing his own life.

The most revealing find in this large collection was a slim file enigmatically called the 'B.' It was there that we discover the broader historical context for Cowan's life path: a secret, underground network of scientists and naturalists that threaded the continent like root filaments. This society was a veritable who's who of ecology that included such well-known names as Aldo Leopold, and it embodied a centuries-long history of determined struggle against political forces intent on discrediting voices like theirs that spoke up for the sanctity of the wild.

This biography starts with Ian McTaggart Cowan's origins and follows his early years from 1926 to 1961 as captured in his field journals. The story is told largely in his own words, drawn from those journals and from correspondence, articles and books. Some of his earliest students, who spent time with him in the field, have filled in the gaps. They are themselves Beautiful British Columbians. Interspersed are the descriptions of species as Cowan encountered them in the field – using selected excerpts from his various field guides (tabled alphabetically at p.465). The excerpts serve two purposes: they educate the reader in a little natural history (which Cowan insisted on); and they hint at what was going on in his life, from courtship to flourishing career to dying, through metaphor (which he did not suggest).

The observations of Cowan in his habitat by friends, students and family, and the evidence from his biographies of species, were mostly all I had to go on, since he kept very few personal letters. The reader can use inference and metaphor drawn from the lives of Northern Flying Squirrels, Black-tailed Deer or Red-legged Frogs for the innermost life of Cowan. I don't think he would have disapproved. In truth, his accounts of a young Mountain Goat's first steps or the breeding habits of the Northern Flying Squirrel are some of the most compelling expressions of parenthood and love that I have read. Cowan had many personal sorrows, but he pragmatically slotted them into the natural cycles of birth, growth, death and decay.

This is a book that essentially wrote itself, with a natural synchronicity. Invariably I'd wonder about some aspect in Cowan's life and he'd mention an animal in a journal whose description provided a clue to his own life. Sometimes that same animal would suddenly turn up outside my window and I would be reminded of Cowan's observation that when you pay attention to your own landscape, a rich life pervades.

When he considered my interview question about coping with despair, he initially responded with a question in return: "I would ask, Is [despair] that useful?" This was quintessential Cowan. Within his story lies the secret to how he stayed buoyant through a century of change. The answer is to follow him into the mountains and through the arid grasslands, sail with him over the seas, sleep under the stars, stalk prey, cook it over an open fire and eat it in the company of good friends, revelling in the freedom, the beauty and the space that humans everywhere once experienced as the seasons cycled through and that Cowan wished for everyone to experience. He had good teachers and you will meet them in this book. They have fur and feathers, scales and skin. All of them I found "fascinating" and they have reinforced what I had suspected as a child, that nature has an exceptional ability to produce "the real thing."

Reader's notes

The book uses standard conventions for the scientific names and the English, or common, names of animals. All species' Common Names have been capitalized, which is not conventional with mammals, though it is with birds. Older scientific and English names used by Cowan in his publications are cited as he described them at the time, followed by [the contemporary name in square brackets]. Common regional names (in round brackets) have been included for clarity. All the variations of a name are included only at first mention of the species; otherwise the name is as Cowan cited it in his journal at the time. For example:

Franklin Grouse (Fool Hen) [Spruce Grouse]
Canachites franklinii [*Canachites canadensis franklinii*]

In addition to mentions in the text, dozens of species are highlighted in magazine-style "sidebars" throughout, with descriptive text by Cowan as author or co-author in recognized reference works. All sources are duly cited of course, but because these descriptions and archival photos were compiled separately, and long before the book was in layout, their endnote numbers will not necessarily track the sequence of note numbers in the adjacent text. Neither will they necessarily be consecutive. In other words, wherever note numbers appear to be missing in action or out of order, you'll find them loyally serving in sidebars located somewhere nearby.

There are two more elements to consider as you navigate the book, which in part require a crash course on the colonial history of the naming of animals. The first is that taxonomies have changed over the decades. Subspecies have become species and vice versa. For example, the Franklin Grouse has been downlisted to a subspecies of the Spruce Grouse. Keen's Mouse was elevated from a subspecies of the Deer Mouse to a species unto itself. The other complicating element is that in the early 20th century, when splitting into subspecies was more in vogue, subspecies would get their own standard English names. That tradition is not as robust today – which is sad, I think – and the subspecies are often lumped together under the common species name, which is captured in the square brackets of the common name:

Olympic Meadow Mouse [Long-tailed Vole]
Microtus mordax macrurus [*Microtus longicaudus macrurus*]

All of these elements of nomenclature have cultural and political ramifications. When we give a name to a distinctive animal (a subspecies or even a population) that is special to one's region, it enters our culture as a valued thing. For example, the Southern Resident Orca or the Kermode (Spirit) Bear have won a place in the hearts and culture of British Columbians. Our biggest industry, tourism, thrives on this "Super, Natural" branding. When our common names take in the various subspecies, some of which are locally endangered, some not, it is possible that this makes us less able to express our concern and rally support. Take for example the Horned Lark. It is common on the prairies, but around the Fraser lowlands it is nearly extirpated. How much better to have "Vancouver Horned Lark" as a name so that residents can embrace it as their own? Surely one of the big casualties of globalization and efficiency is the standardization of names. (The sources relied on for the current common and scientific names of species are listed in the Bibliography under "Taxonomy authorities.")

Having argued against this homogenization, however, there is one name that I have standardized for this book: that of Ian McTaggart Cowan himself. Throughout his century he signed himself variously as Ian Cowan, Ian McTaggart Cowan, I.M. Cowan, I. McT. Cowan, I. McTaggart-Cowan and Ian McTaggart-Cowan. The hyphenation of his name doesn't really start appearing in his published works until after 1982, which is when the field journals, the main source of material, end. An added confusion was that his father's first name was McTaggart, last name Cowan. To make it easy for the reader, all references to Ian are simply "Cowan." In the bibliography he is "Cowan, Ian McTaggart." This is purely to keep it simple and focus the reader's attention on more important things like the ability of Pocket Gophers to detect subtle changes in carbon dioxide, which we might find useful one day.

Finally, many readers who knew Ian may be disappointed not to find references here to particular events, people or places. The gaps in this account are as large as those in the evolutionary record. It is a life that bears far more examination. The Jakimchuk, Campbell and Demarchi book fills in many of these, especially as to Cowan's students and teaching career. I have relied heavily on others but take full responsibility for any errors or omissions. Cowan's journals, correspondence and the specimens are now all in the public realm for others to help reconstruct not only a life well lived but also the story of ecosystems that have suffered. I have just tried to do what he always hoped to do: to tell the story of beautiful British Columbia and encourage people to conserve it, for there will be no biographies on a dead planet.

PART 1
THE EARLY YEARS:
1910–1920

CHAPTER 1

"Something inside you brings out the interest track."

Edinburgh, 1910–1913

Ian McTaggart Cowan's birthplace, Edinburgh, Scotland, is an elegant university city of granite spires and cobbled streets at the edge of a once rich inland sea. It was built around an extinct volcano that had been left untamed by virtue (or not) of a thousand years of monarchs demanding an exclusive place to hunt. Ironically, this wild heart of the city became the wellspring of a scientific and humanistic renaissance that inspired the likes of Charles Darwin, pioneer geologists James Hutton and Charles Lyell, botanists Joseph Hooker, John Hutton Balfour and David Douglas and naturalist and early environmentalist John Muir, who grew up just south of the city at Dunbar. Teeming with naturalists and pioneering scientists, Edinburgh was the habitat of the Scottish Enlightenment that began in the 18th century. Its inhabitants had a profound impact on western science and thought, as they, their progeny and their ideas disseminated around the world like the down of the ubiquitous Scottish Thistle.[7]

Cowan was born into the lineage of these scientists and their tradition in a city – dubbed the Modern Athens – which already boasted a Museum of Natural History, a Zoological Gardens and a Botanical Gardens, all popular institutions within walking distance of the Cowan family home on Great King Street. Natural history museums were attracting more families like the Cowans than even attended football (soccer) games at the time.[8] Pubs were probably the only institution that still surpassed museums for attendance amongst the burgeoning 19th century middle class. By the turn of that century, natural history societies, such as the Botanical Society, the Royal Society of Edinburgh, the Wernerian Society and the Plinian Society (most of which were started or attended by Cowan's ancestors), were approaching their 100th anniversaries. In these societies lay the intellectual origins of western modern ecology and conservation biology, which Cowan was to embrace and expand upon.

It was also a place impoverished by human mismanagement of wildlife and ecosystems and by social inequity. By 1910 the North Sea populations of herring that underpinned the marine life were collapsing through overfishing. The hills, once covered in temperate rainforest, had long been deforested. Enclosures of large estates by elite landowners, who overstocked them with sheep or deer, ensured little chance of forest regeneration. The once extensive Caledonian pine forests of Scotland were down to a few scanty patches of compromised trees in the northern parts of the country. Intensive farming in the lowlands and nearly two centuries of gamekeeping on the vast private estates, where every predator found was shot, had left a greatly simplified fauna and flora.

In his infamous autobiography, naturalist and hunter Osgood Mackenzie writes approvingly of the lethal efforts of his family to kill "vermin" during the mid-19th century when many of the extirpations were underway.

> The vermin consisted of all kinds of beasts and birds, a good many of which are now extinct ... The last kite had disappeared before my time. ... The pine martens, the polecats, and the badgers are all quite extinct with us now, but they were all still in existence when I bought Inverewe [northwest Scotland.[9]

European Rabbit

Oryctolagus cuniculus

The European Rabbit is a medium to large rabbit with variable fur colour and markings depending on the breed ... The original range of this rabbit was probably southern France, the Iberian Peninsula of Spain and north Africa. In historical times, feral populations were introduced to all the continents and many oceanic islands.[12]

The last wolf in Scotland had been shot dead in the Findhorn Valley by the 18th century, while introduced plants like Broom, Gorse and Bracken dominated the hills. Mackenzie's family is credited with moving feral rabbits into the northwest of Scotland. "My grandfather introduced them ... from England..."[10] Cowan attributed the impoverishment to "the land-grabbing aristocracy of Britain, who had already taken to themselves one acre of every seven in the nation."[11] Scotland in 1913 was, in modern terms, a wildly unbalanced ecosystem that was most memorable to a child for its plague of rabbits.

It was this introduced species that captured Ian McTaggart Cowan's imagination as a 3-year-old, prior to his own "introduction" into North America. Two feral populations of the European Rabbit have persisted in BC and curiously were linked to Cowan until the end of his life. One feral colony survived on remote Triangle Island (now an ecological reserve) in competition with a subspecies of Townsend's Vole, *Microtus townsendii cowani*, unique to the island and named after Cowan by his student Charles Guiguet. The other feral colony reached plague proportions on the campus of the University of Victoria, where Cowan as chancellor would trip over them on the walk to his office, not unlike his childhood memories from Holyrood Park.

Cowan attributed early expeditions with his mother and uncle, with rabbits popping in and out of their burrows on either side of the track, to igniting his curiosity as a budding naturalist and stimulating a lifelong fascination with wildlife. From the family's elegant Georgian townhouse flat one can see the extinct volcano of Arthur's Seat, which dominates the park. A rare example, even then, of unploughed native grasslands, the park is a pocket wilderness in the midst of a city. In 1913, rabbit populations were exploding in the park due to the indiscriminate shooting of their predators – golden eagles and other raptors – by the Queen's gamekeepers, who, according to Osgood Mackenzie, "were in reality only game-killers."[13] The introduced European Hare (*Lepus europaeus*) was also occupying the park, while the native Mountain Hare, or Blue Hare (named *timidus* after its temperament), had long been driven back to the summits of the remotest mountainous regions of Scotland.

Mountain Hare

Lepus timidus

Inhabits tundra and taiga, particularly pine, birch and juniper … Moors and bogland are the preferred habitats for this species in Ireland and Scotland….[14]

Eastern Cottontail Rabbit
[Eastern Cottontail]

Sylvilagus floridanus mearnsi
[s.f. *alacer*]

Nothing is known of the life history of the species in British Columbia. It is a recent arrival from introduced populations.[17]

The Scottish landscape became imprinted on Cowan from these early forays, as did the tragic history of the extirpations of species and ecosystems. Forty years later he would return on sabbatical to the city of his birth to write *The Mammals of British Columbia*, as well as to introduce scientific concepts of wilderness and wildlife management developed in British Columbia to Scottish policy-makers and landowners. Scotland, besides exporting enlightened ideas, had been exporting some of the most lethal methods for exploitation of resources, from clear-cutting of forests to bounties on wild animals. Cowan was a fierce critic of Scotland's indiscriminate killing of predators, the privatization of wildlife, unscientific wildlife management, failure to conserve natural ecosystems, introduction of invasive species and the impacts all of this had on animal, and ultimately human, health. "The Scottish–German philosophy is quite different [from the North American]. That is, an elitist take on it: if you own an estate, you own the wildlife on it."[15]

Artificial manipulation of animal populations by introducing diseases was also well underway the year he returned to Scotland in 1952. Myxomatosis – with its characteristic suppurating tumours around rabbits' eyes – had just been introduced into Europe, wiping out 95 per cent of the invasive rabbit population but also adversely impacting the native lynx and Spanish Imperial eagle. The disease would reach Scotland the following spring, with similar effects. Cowan was to hold a critical view of simplified human interventions with pathogens, arguing for maintaining complex ecosystems. That same December of 1952, the first specimen of an introduced Eastern Cottontail Rabbit in BC was caught and prepared by Cowan's mentor and father-in-law Kenneth Racey with his son Alan at their farm at Huntingdon on the BC–Washington border.[16] Hares and rabbits were to leap in and out of burrows along Cowan's track for his entire life.

Cowan claimed that his memories of rabbits also started him on his interest in population ecology. In one of his first published articles, he looked at the accounts of fur trappers and compared them to his own observations in the field, linking the economic cycle of fur-bearing animals like foxes with their choicest prey, the Snowshoe Hare. He wrote:

Snowshoe Hare

Lepus americanus

Of typical hare form with disproportionately long legs ... The snowshoe hare does not burrow; its resting place consists of a small depression or "form" situated in a thicket beneath the lower branches of a small tree, within the roots of a stump or in a similarly sheltered location. The young number from two to four in a litter and there may be four litters per year.[21]

> In 1932, ... in 4 miles along the Cariboo Highway ... I counted upwards of 150 rabbits [Snowshoe Hares] feeding on the edge of the road. ... Two years later, in the same district, not a rabbit was to be seen. ... It so happens that rabbit conditions have been recorded over a period of 174 years in Canada; and it has been shown ... that they reach a period of abundance on the average every 9.7 years.[18]

The cycles of small prey mammals would feature strongly not only in his formulation of prey–predator relationships but also in his innovative attempts to stop human persecution of predators, whether eagles, lynxes or wolves. The continuing survival of many predator species in BC has a great deal to do with Cowan's early observations of boom–bust cycles of rabbits and hares. It was a topic which connected into the pioneering work of population ecologist Charles Elton, whom Cowan would meet back in Scotland 40 years later. Cowan's national campaign to stop the bounty system in Canada wouldn't start until the 1940s, but the groundwork was already being laid in his childhood.

He lightheartedly enlisted rabbits in the opening remarks of his 1961 public lecture "Of Mice and Men," to chuckles from his audience:

> Mr. Chairman, ladies and gentlemen, this business of animal numbers is an interesting and important one. It is one of certain rather dramatic complexities. I am always amused by the little story that came to me some years ago about two little rabbits on a fine spring morning that were chased into a hollow log by two hunting dogs on

a spree. It is reported that the rabbits said to one another: "Say, let's stay here until we outnumber them." This they're very well equipped to do.[19]

The topic of that lecture was the diversity of ways that populations of animals regulate and/or are regulated by their environment, leading to the inevitable discussion of the question of human populations – a subject that was to increasingly interest him as the world's population doubled during each generation he lived through. Fittingly, he would name a subspecies of one of BC's native Snowshoe Hares (also called "Varying Hare" then) (*Lepus americanus pallidus* Cowan).[20] Cowan's subspecies was a pale-reddish-brown hare with a darker-reddish face and long legs that inhabits the mountain ranges on the west side of the Rockies, a not inaccurate description of the man himself.

His second published work, at the age of 20, included his notes on another subspecies, the Washington Hare, which he described as the darkest of the hares, a "rich chestnut brown, or sayal brown liberally blended with black hair-tips."[22] Cowan's

American Pipit

Anthus rubescens

In British Columbia, the American Pipit nests in alpine habitats throughout mountainous areas of the interior, and to a lesser extent in coastal alpine habitats ... Habitat occupied during the breeding season includes sparsely vegetated alpine tundra heath meadows and more richly vegetated alpine meadows ... Nest sites are usually situated on sloping hillsides where solifluction and erosion leave overhanging clumps of vegetation, sod and stones as cover for the nest.[27]

aesthetic eye for discerning the details of animals distinguished him to all his students and colleagues. The Washington Hare population had briefly exploded on the UBC campus during the years he studied zoology there. He noted in a 1930 article that there were plenty of hares as a direct result of their predators being exterminated.[23] He would later return to UBC, as a professor, and it was there that his crusade against the bounty system was launched.[24]

Mountains were Cowan's second earliest memory and they captivated his imagination. His mother, a keen naturalist (and occasional naturist), had taken him up into the Scottish hills, and he remembers her shedding her clothes to dip into a burbling, chilly mountain stream, which "set him howling."[25] His third memory is of picking up a bird's egg. At the time, the heathlands of Holyrood Park would have had healthy populations of pipits, skylarks, partridges and corncrakes, all ground nesters.[26] Even today, Meadow Pipits can be seen providing their exceptional spring aerial displays and distinctive *pip pip pip* calls to any curious child wandering the grassy slopes of Arthur's Seat. Cowan was to enjoy these attractive birds right until his death. The North American cousin of the Meadow Pipit, the American Pipit, nests in the Rocky Mountains he loved and migrates through the low-lying fields close to his homes, first in Vancouver, then Vancouver Island.

When he described these earliest memories at the age of 90, he commented on the fact that they were all about nature, "which makes me think there must be something built in that starts you on an interest track."[28] Mammals, birds and mountains did indeed dominate Cowan's career. The impressionable early childhood experiences also led him to become a strong advocate for childhood immersion in nature. This became a recurring theme in his popular writing, lecturing, television programs, leading of student expeditions and with his own children. Not surprisingly, his first television program, *Fur and Feathers*, was aimed at children and involved bringing live animals and a child together in a studio and filming their interaction.

Cowan's precocious observational skills and interest as an educator were right in keeping with the lineage of Scots academics and naturalists into which he was born. This included the elite of the scientific establishment stretching back to the 18th century and the start of the Scottish Enlightenment. Through his father's line he was related to both James Hutton, the father of modern geology and first western thinker to conceive of the earth as millions of years old, and John Hutton Balfour, a major figure in botany and evolution and part of the Hooker–Darwin naturalist cohort.

James Hutton, born in Edinburgh in 1726, was one of the city's leading lights. He attended Edinburgh, Paris and Leiden universities, studying medicine and chemistry, and had a wide range of interests – not least his great curiosity about how the world worked. This led Hutton first to a life as a gentleman farmer so he could pursue his naturalist studies. He was a collector of fossils, and his observational skills were legendary. In the course of rambles on his land in and around Edinburgh, he was able to develop a comprehensive theory of the history of the earth from the geological evidence he saw at places like Salisbury Crags in Holyrood Park and Siccar Point just south of Edinburgh along the coast. Salisbury Crags is a section of old seabed through which the volcanic rock of Arthur's Seat has oozed or intruded. It triggered a theory which a subsequent expedition to Siccar Point proved. Hutton took two gentlemen from the Royal Society, John Playfair and Sir James Hall, to view "a rock exposure on the battered cliffs that would prove one of the most stunning claims in the history of science – that the [age of the] earth was beyond calculation."[29]

Siccar Point is a heavily eroded cliff headland with exposed layers of two distinct types of sedimentary rock. At the bottom of the cliff were layers of shale standing straight up like books on a shelf and on top were horizontal layers of younger red sandstone sandwiching a middle layer of muddled rock and sand. Wrote Playfair:

> We felt ourselves necessarily carried back to the time when the schistus on which we stood was yet at the bottom of the sea, and when the sandstone before us was only beginning to be deposited, in the shape

of sand or mud, from the waters of a superincumbent ocean … The mind seemed to grow giddy by looking so far into the abyss of time…[30]

Cowan too developed an expertise in fossils and the intimate interplay of geology and evolution. He was to stand gazing at the same geological features in 1953 with some of the leading evolutionary thinkers of the time, pondering that relationship.

Hutton expounded his theories of deposition and erosion in his famous address to the newly formed Royal Society of Edinburgh in 1788. Close to 200 years later Cowan would deliver a lecture to the same society on the evolutionary history of vertebrate fauna in western North America. Hutton identified the processes that drove the shaping of landscape, from the role of rain to the force of heat from the earth's centre, as an explanation for volcanoes, mountain building, hot springs and metamorphic rocks. He presented his findings under the concepts of "actualism" and "uniformitarianism," proposing that, contrary to the biblical interpretations by the theologians, these earth processes had been going on for millions of years and were still at work shaping the present-day landscape. Cowan identified the processes of ice sheets sweeping down the continent and changing sea levels shaping the landscape, separating populations of animals and plants, creating refugia on islands, mountaintops and coastal plains. He described how new species were emerging after isolation of just 5,000 years before the great repopulation of the glaciated landscape. Both men were storytellers in their own new scientific paradigm.

The audience at Cowan's 1952 Royal Society lecture would have been entertained by the tale he told of the "age-old migration routes" of small birds such as wheatears that still flew 30,000-kilometre routes which had been shaped and deflected by the old ice sheets. He described witnessing the elegant little birds breeding in the Mackenzie Delta of Canada, migrating through Scotland and landing on the ship in which he was travelling off Denmark the week before, to rest on their way to Africa for the winter.

Hutton's successors were Thomas Hope and Charles Lyell (who largely was given the credit for Hutton's ideas, although he himself credited Hutton). Lyell mentored Darwin, and Darwin's imagination around biological evolution was triggered by Hutton's narrative of an ancient earth and a set of processes that could shape the landscape – and its inhabitants as well. In his later work of 1794, Hutton proposed a form of natural selection for animals.[32] Darwin was exposed to this work during his natural history and medical studies in Edinburgh 35 years later. It was in this intertidal zone of fecund intellectual activity that Cowan was spawned.

While these ideas, like the species that accompanied the colonizers, were being broadcast across Europe and into the colonies, the bastion of conservatism

Northern Wheatear

Oenanthe oenanthe

Breeds in North America from northern Alaska, northern Yukon and northwestern Mackenzie south to western and south-coastal Alaska and southern Yukon … Winters in the Old World. Most of the distribution of the species is in Eurasia.[31]

was showing no signs of crumbling. Even more impenetrable than Castle Rock in Edinburgh (another geological feature that helped armies defend the castle for millennia), the orthodox sects of the Scottish Presbyterian church were still entrenched in their belief that the earth was 6,000 years old, fortified by their 17th century religious scholars who had declared that fossils were animals lost during a "recent" biblical flood. Hutton sidestepped accusations of heresy by a combination of good humour and a more moderate strain of Presbyterian faith that inoculated him from the worst of the Scottish witch hunts. It was a family tradition to skirt religious orthodoxy through a scientific approach that incorporated conventional societal beliefs.

Two centuries later, Cowan was to encounter cyclical revivals of the 6,000-year-old-earth story during his own career. He handled these challenges with the same dexterity as Hutton. The last decade of his life saw the election of a Canadian prime minister who was a member of a creationist, "young earth" evangelical church. Approaching his 100th birthday, Cowan nevertheless received a letter of congratulation from that same prime minister, although their beliefs couldn't have varied more widely, nor could they have disagreed more on the value of scientists. Cowan carried a historical sensibility of the tension between the creationists and the humanists that provided credibility in his profession and opportunities for humour. Among the marginalia of his journal during the 1952 trip to Scotland, he wrote a note-to-self: "The display leks [breeding grounds] of some grouse are not matrimonial bureaus, but revival meetings."

Cowan's relationship to Hutton was through his great grandmother, Margaret Balfour. She was related to Sarah Balfour, Hutton's mother. Margaret was also John Hutton Balfour's sister. Balfour founded the Botanical Society of Edinburgh in 1836 – coincidentally one block away from Cowan's birthplace on Great King Street – and helped build up a vast botanical collection and herbarium. Balfour was cut from the same cloth as Hutton, tromping through the countryside with an indefatigable enthusiasm. Rising to become chair of botany at Glasgow, succeeding William Hooker, Darwin's mentor, Balfour eventually beat out William's son Joseph Hooker for the botany chair at Edinburgh in 1845, and finished his career as the Queen's Botanist (Regius Keepership) for the Royal Botanic Gardens in Edinburgh.[33] The battle between Balfour and Joseph Hooker for the chair was famous, and instructive, as it played against a backdrop of political and religious schisms that would be reenacted in various permutations in Cowan's own career.

The Hooker–Balfour battle would also involve a betrayal of friendship and determine the value placed on mentorship by society. Balfour and Hooker had been fellow students and friends and shared many expeditions together. As Hooker once wrote to Balfour:

> … many a time do I think over our excursions in the Highlands together & to the W. of Ireland – Do you remember sleeping under the old blanket in Glen Isla? When you would not go to sleep for asking me whether I was warm, & getting heather for my feet.[34]

The fight over the position became acrimonious and the eventual decision by the board that awarded Balfour the position of chair and keepership over Hooker involved two qualities that were upheld above all: his sense of justice and his support of students even above research.[35]

Like his ancestor Hutton, Balfour didn't limit himself to a narrow specialty but developed an extraordinary breadth of interests, from medicine to molluscs. The similar range of Cowan's interests was entirely on par with this indefatigable family. In a testimonial written by William Carpenter, a fellow of the Botanical Society and former president of the Royal Medical Society, Edinburgh, promoting his colleague for an appointment as professor in 1841 at Edinburgh, a portrait of Balfour emerges that eerily resembles the testimonial for Cowan almost exactly 100 years later for his first position as professor at the University of British Columbia. In this description of Cowan's ancestor, one can simply substitute zoology for botany and the portrait is the same:

> Dr. Balfour has cultivated both systematic and physiological botany during many years with great assiduity. He has always appeared to me to possess a peculiar natural aptitude for the pursuit, combining great quickness of observation with a retentive memory, and both these with intellectual powers which have been most advantageously cultivated by previous education, and with that ardent desire for truth which thinks no amount of labour in the search for it too great. These talents he has employed with a zeal, originating alike in natural temperament, and in earnest attachment to his object; and his attainments in botanical science have thus become of a very high order – such as, in fact, would do great credit to any one who had made it his sole pursuit during a long life ... I feel confident that by his own evident enthusiasm, he would do much to excite the ardour of his pupils whilst his pleasure in witnessing their improvement would lead him to do all in his power to promote it.[36]

Peter Ommundsen, a student of Cowan's for many years, recalled the qualities of Cowan in the field:

> I think something about Ian that would strike me in any circumstance was going the extra mile and encouraging us to go the extra mile ... He could see things that other people didn't see, patterns that others didn't see. I remember, for example, we were down at Mount Baker [Washington] one day and he saw a mountain sheep in the distance, and this was absolutely phenomenal because at that time there was no record of mountain sheep anywhere near there. I think that's the type of thing – in that case, a fairly spectacular example. When I mentioned it to one of the Washington State biologists, on a subsequent occasion, as to where we'd seen the sheep, he simply refused to believe it.

> And [Ian] had a great sense of humour ... I remember when we
> were ... looking at mountain goats for some time and the weather
> was not good and he was getting tired ... I was surprised to hear him
> say, "Okay, let's get going – they're just goats on a hill." That's sort of
> the antithesis of what you would expect, but that sort of always stuck
> in my mind.[37]

Balfour, like Cowan, was a skilled speaker and believed in accessible education, service and hard work. As personal qualities, they manifested as cheerful reliance on good science, common sense and encouragement of the young, which the
Balfour family had in spades. The Scottish universities and their selection committees distinguished themselves from the English institutions in this important facet,
avoiding the rarified atmosphere of the English university tradition at institutions
like Cambridge and Oxford. Balfour was at the forefront of maintaining public access to lands and initiated the famous Battle of Glen Tilt, which was on par with the
great battles led by Cowan in the Rocky Mountain national parks against privatization interests one hundred years later.

In August of 1847, Balfour tried to lead his students into Glen Tilt for a natural history expedition. Glen Tilt was one of the huge estates owned by the Duke of
Atholl, who had converted his estate into a private deerhunting consortium and
blocked the traditional rights of way to the land. In the legal action brought against
Atholl the court examined the right of the public to sue if a public right of way was
blocked.[38] This led to the establishment of the Scottish Rights of Way Society and
a period of legal reform with bills like Access to the Mountains proposed in the
House of Commons at the turn of the century. The increasing conflicts between the
landowning elite and the rest of the population during the enclosures of the 17th
and 18th centuries had led to these landmark legal cases. They established important precedents and principles of rights of access to land and to view wildlife even
if it was on private land. The other important case, *Winans v. Macrae*,[39] was between an American lessee, William Louis Winans, who had restricted public access to a 200,000-acre deer-hunting estate, and crofter Murdoch Macrae, whose pet
lamb had wandered into the plaintiff's unfenced deer forest. The appellate Court of
Session ruled in the defendant's favour, and no longer could the Scottish elite block
public access to land if no damage was done.

Balfour was at the forefront of these reforms. He published limited editions of
his journals, sharing with the people his findings on his expeditions. On one such
trip to the Isle of Arran in the summer of 1869, he recounts:

> An evening was spent in dredging Lamlash Bay and in visiting St.
> Molio's Cave. A number of interesting Echinodermata and Molluscs
> were brought up by the dredging party. Among the animals obtained
> were *Comatula rosacea, Echinus miliaris* and *sphaera, Goniaster temple-
> toni, Ophiocoma bellis, Opiura texturata, Spatangus purpureus, Solaster
> papposus, Uraster glacialis, Adamsia palliata, Pagurus bernhardus...*"[40]

Balfour's later-life interest in marine invertebrates was echoed by Cowan's interest in molluscs during the 1960s and '70s. Both men pursued a sideline in malacology to the point of becoming leading experts in this diverse phylum. In molluscs lie important clues to understanding evolution, since there are few animals or plants that leave such a binding impression in the rock – or in naturalists' hearts – as hard-shelled molluscs. Cowan became particularly interested in them at a time when he could combine collecting molluscs on the weekends and holidays with mucking around in boats with his son Garry and Garry's friend William (Bill) Merilees, both of whom carried on his passion.

Garry Cowan became a marine biologist at Memorial University in Newfoundland, and together father and son sorted out some of the little-known molluscs on both the east and the west coasts. As Cowan Sr. wrote to James McLean at Stanford University in 1963, "The real treasures are among the chitons."[41] Chitons were of special interest to the Cowans for the clues they held to the history of the landscape. These small univalve animals demonstrate a phenomenon that occurs when a major environmental event splits a population up, whether by glacial barriers or faults caused by oceanic earthquakes. When conditions change and the two populations reunite, they may be reproductively isolated. If so, they would be considered two different species, in what is called "sympatric speciation." They look the same and occupy the same geographic area but are different. It was a metaphor that wasn't lost on Cowan with regard to many aspects of a father–son relationship. After a decade of collecting, Cowan and Cowan named a colourful, new-to-science chiton:

Cowan also had a chiton named after him by his malacologist friend Roger Clark: *Tripoplax cowani*.[43] The Balfour–Hutton men would have easily recognized their descendants' spirit of inquiry and adventure, the systematist's competitive pursuit of a new species and their great enthusiasm for exploring the world. As Balfour wrote:

> I have often thought amidst all my wanderings over mountains and valleys, and plains, travelling by sea and land in quest of plants, with large parties, how grateful I should be that there has not occurred any untoward event, involving serious consequences to life or health.[44]

Red-flecked Mopalia

Mopalia spectabilis Cowan & Cowan

A large chiton, mature specimens approximately 55 mm × 45 mm in preserved state. Colour distinctive and diagnostic. General colour of valves bright blue, brightest in young specimens and on lateral areas, which are conspicuously marked with orange red in zigzag bands ...[42]

The tying of health to nature was well established in the Scottish universities. Medical and botanical degrees were integrated and professors taught in both faculties. This was to continue with Cowan's expertise in botany, comparative anatomy and parasitology that led him to publish on the relationship of wildlife health and indigenous people's health.

Balfour's curriculum for his introductory course on botany included the following lecture topics:

> The adaptation of plants to particular climates and localities and their mode of distribution. Importance of botany as a branch of study to the admirer of natural scenery, to the moralist and divine, to the geologist, zoologist, agriculturalist and medical man. Historical view of the science. Knowledge of plants possessed by the Chaldeans, Egyptians, Greeks and Romans. Revival of botany in the sixteenth century and its subsequent progress. Discovery of the microscope and the important influence exercised by it on the progress of botanical science. Chief promoters of botany. Origin of botanic gardens and their importance.[45]

Cowan throughout his life delivered similar courses and popular lectures that integrated science with stories and included enthusiastic promotion of public access to wildlife and wild areas, like the national parks. He also followed his ancestor in an interest in microscopic images. He described the innovation in one of his television series, *Web of Life*:

> I had a photographer who really knew his camera, and he knew the physics of photography. I remember showing him some paramecia and amoebae under the microscope and he said, "That's fascinating, why can't we do that?" Next week, he came back and said, "We can do that." He had taken the front lens off his camera and constructed a gadget of cardboard which fitted over the top of the microscope, and you looked straight down the microscope. You could show all sorts of things, like an amoeba dividing. It was fascinating! You could slow it down as much as you liked and people began to see there was a whole new world. We were the first people in the world to show microscopic animals on television.[46]

In one episode, Cowan peered down the microscope and pointed out the skeleton of a copepod. In the Cowans' library was a children's book from 1829 called *The Wonders of the Microscope* with the long subtitle "*or, an explanation of the wisdom of the Creator in objects comparatively minute adapted to the understanding of young persons*."[47] It had an exquisite fold-out rendering of an enlarged view of a louse. It was the 19th century equivalent of high definition television, bringing the wonder of science to a lay audience. Then it delved anatomically into every part of its lousy body, from blood to reproductive parts. At the end, the anonymous author concludes that the "works of nature plainly prove that the hand which formed them was absolute master of the materials upon which it acted…."[48] The book ends in the realm of spirituality, which for Cowan is where his scientific self left off and his naturalist self began. Cowan's student Bob Weeden explained the distinction between the scientist and the naturalist:

> The naturalist comes into the natural environment with everything open; the naturalist doesn't leave anything behind. The scientist goes there with a job to do, which is to reveal truths that in the scientific sense can be proved. The scientist is supposed to leave his self behind and only engage that part of the mind that is a computer. Whereas the naturalist is open to a spiritual dimension, is open to being emotionally moved and can say so, and is open to being reminded of the metaphors that are all around us in nature of the non-human world and this veneer of artifact that we live in.[49]

The spiritual dimension of nature had undoubtedly survived scrutiny under the Victorian scientific microscopes, as exemplified by John Muir, but it also exposed the naturalist to being hijacked by detractors on all sides of the political and religious spectrums. The freedom to be openly moved and say so was not available at all times – then or now. Political and religious interests that were served by keeping nature subdued also sought to subdue the scientist–naturalist. There was enough behavioural polymorphism in Cowan's family to provide that range of interests.

The Hutton–Balfour line was just one of Cowan's Scots lineages. He had several files on his family history, as would have been typical of Scots families of that time keenly interested in clans. Sir Walter Scott had firmly established, some say invented, the "romantic" Scots Highlander as a highly desirable literary character and therefore a worthy ancestor. Clippings of births, obituaries, family trees and clan crests filled a whole drawer in Cowan's filing cabinet and had contributions of relatives from all over the world. Personal pedigrees even spilled into his professional life; he placed the family trees of the Rocky Mountain wolves in the same file as his Mackenzie family lineage. One sensed that Cowan's distinctions between carnivores and other mammalian orders were not as great as others would draw. Not surprisingly either, with his biologist's genetic interest, he annotated his family trees with some additional data on heights of ancestors. Males six feet and over seemed to occur commonly through one branch of the family. Cowan's sister Joan noted in her memoirs that "the Cowan family came from Ayrshire, a district of Scotland that was originally a Norse colony and you can still see the Norse strain in the long-legged Cowans"[50] This hare-like quality he inherited from his father, McTaggart, nicknamed "Garry" by his family, whom Cowan described as a "big gentle soul with reddish hair and moustache."[51] At 6'6" he was an imposing man but gentle in his ways, preferring botany and badminton to his son's more robust hunting habits. He played goal for the Scottish national field hockey team and latterly played for the Canadian national badminton team.

Cowan's great-great-grandfather, Hugh Cowan, was a banker from Ayr. Hugh Cowan had written up his own "pedigree" (sometime after 1841) that pointed to another trait of the family, captured in the Gaelic meaning of "Cowan," which signified "to serve or to minister." Another family story that was "handed down at the fireside"[52] was about their direct descendant Sir James Douglas (not the first BC premier), devoted friend of Robert the Bruce, who established the Douglas family motto: "Never behind: always the leader." It was Hugh Cowan who had married Elizabeth McTaggart, prompting the first joining of the McTaggart and Cowan names (although the name was never originally hyphenated, simply incorporated into the names). The earliest picture of the young Ian Cowan in Edinburgh was taken in 1911 with his paternal grandfather, Peter McTaggart Cowan, whiskered, cravatted and bowler-hatted as would befit a professional gentleman of the day, having just plucked the child from a large pram in the gardens nearest Great King Street in Edinburgh. Their son, Ian's father, born in 1883, was (somewhat confusingly) McTaggart Cowan.

McTaggart (Garry) Cowan married Laura Alice Mackenzie on September 13, 1911. Laura came from an esteemed Highland line of judges, military leaders and bishops. Clan Mackenzie (Seaforth) portrays the crest of a "Rock in Flames" with the motto *Luceo non uro*, meaning "I shine not burn." Cowan also identified with his maternal Mackenzie clan, which included notable Scottish personages like his great-great-grandfather Sir Archibald Campbell (1769–1843), an early Lieutenant-Governor of New Brunswick who had commanded British forces in the first Anglo-Burmese War (1824–1826). Another ancestor admired by Cowan was Colonel Kenneth Douglas Mackenzie (1811–1873), a lieutenant general in Wellington's time. The colonel was described in his obituary as the archetypal "honest, gallant Highlander who will ever be remembered with affection by those whom he served in every quarter of the globe."[53] Lord Donald Mackenzie (1818–1875), his maternal great-grandfather, was a Judge of the Court of Session and of the six sons he sired, all won scholarships to Oxford – the oldest of whom, Donald Mackenzie, served an equally distinguished career as a barrister and was Cowan's maternal grandfather. The barrister's daughter Laura was Ian's mother, and it was to his mother that Cowan attributed his greatest influence.

From her Mackenzie lineage, Laura acquired the interest in what many upper-middle-class families with military traditions pursued: skilled marksmanship and a penchant for filling the pot with game. Cowan's maternal grandparents lived in Great Stuart Street in Edinburgh and regularly travelled to the countryside to fish and shoot. His uncle Daniel lived in a country house in Perth latterly. They were members of consortiums who fished on the Dee and shot grouse in places like Lochbuie on the Isle of Mull, which wasn't without its paradoxes for the Balfour line. "Mackenzies were born with guns in their hands,"[54] according to Hilary Mackenzie, daughter of Cowan's closest first cousin, Brian Mackenzie (Daniel's son), with whom he would stay in Perthshire when he returned to Scotland. Brian Mackenzie was a naturalist, a silversmith, a boat builder, spoke nine languages and had spent much of his life travelling the world "in service to his country." He had killed his first rabbit at the age of 5.

The influence of Scottish shooting culture – the sportsman in his tweeds, the gillie and the "glorious 12th of August" when the gentry and aspiring gentry headed to those estates to shoot red grouse at the opening of the season – was evident in his Mackenzie family line. The family would also have been well aware of the "romantic" Scottish characters such as the Earl of Southesk, who in Edinburgh had published his journal of "one of the most remarkable and ambitious hunting trips undertaken in North America."[55] In his book *Empire of Nature*, author John Mackenzie argues that imperialist hunters like Southesk, coming from the upper-class British hunting elite, used their interest in natural history and pursuit of science to rationalize the killing of game and collecting of trophy heads.[56] However, the McTaggart Cowan family traditions in natural history and shooting in Scotland were far more complex than just a foil for the hunting elite.

When Cowan returned to Edinburgh in 1952, he dug up, after "a bit of sleuthing," the original 1875 volume of Southesk's journal, *Saskatchewan and the Rocky Mountains*, which he had followed in his own research in the Rockies. In one of his unpublished essays, called "In the Steps of Southesk," Cowan writes:

> The Earl of Southesk, on his first visit to North America, left Fort Garry, now Winnipeg, on June 15, 1859, on horseback, with a small group of guides and packers. They rode across the limitless prairies and fought their way up steep, narrow, heavily timbered valleys into the Rocky Mountains. There, on September the 3rd, 1859, the Earl and his party reached the height of land between the head of the Medicine Tent (now Rocky River) and the Cairn River, and was the first European to enter the magnificent bighorn ranges of the unnamed peak that bears his name. He had crossed the Atlantic and ridden for 2 months to take specimens of the wild sheep and mountain goat of the Rockies.[57]

Cowan's influences and experiences over his first 40 years had taken him in a very different direction than the lordly Southesk. He was clearly not immune to Scots romanticism, but his early boyhood experiences in Canada were far from his comfortable, upper-middle-class roots, as poverty made hunting a necessity to feed their family. Cowan demonstrated no appetite for big game trophy hunting. In fact, he fought against elitist interests and upheld the humanist principles of a public right of access to land and wildlife until the day he died.

Conflicted values around conservation in Scotland were reflected in the McTaggart Cowan lineages. Cowan himself, however, seems to have embodied an amalgam of family mottoes to become a well-educated, inquiring scientist and naturalist with a duty to enthuse and not just to serve well but to shine and lead. It was to this cultural influence and early "interest track" in nature that Cowan attributed his vocation. It was also an opportune mindset to be bringing to a far-flung colonial outpost – "I brought my parents out at the age of three"[58] – to British Columbia, a place brimming with wild animals, wide vistas and the possibility of adventure.

CHAPTER 2

"You get a feel for these creatures and you feel like these creatures."

Vancouver, 1913–1919

T he decision for the family to come out to British Columbia in 1913 was propelled by Cowan Sr.'s desire to abandon the stockbroking profession in which he had been trained. His real passion was for botany, a pursuit he had also received training in and which had strong family precedents. He had set his hopes on forestry, which, if not directly, at least indirectly, would connect him to plants and the outdoors. The only place to study forestry in those days was in Germany, and according to his son, his family "wouldn't hear of it." Political tensions in Germany at the time had much to do with their discouragement.

When Cowan Sr.'s brother developed tuberculosis and was sent to Wyoming for the drier climate, he wrote enthusiastically about the opportunities in North America. Laura and McTaggart Cowan left their two young children, Ian and his younger brother, Patrick, with an aunt and travelled across North America looking for somewhere to settle. They landed in Vancouver but there was little in the way of training for foresters. The BC Forest Service had only just been created. With a young family to support, Cowan Sr. found a job as superintendent of the Pacific Lime Company on Texada Island, still operating today, which provided lime for the Powell River pulp and paper mills. The family followed across the Atlantic by ship, then crossed the continent in the old "colonist cars" of the Canadian Pacific Railway. Cowan remembers little of the trip except the arrival in Vancouver and moving into their first house at the foot of Nicola and Beach in the west end. "The garden went right to the beach. It was a beautiful place but the heating was primitive. It had 13 fireplaces and no furnace. Again, my memory is of seeing – what my mother helped me to identify as – a Sharp-tailed Grouse in the garden and turned out to be a hen pheasant, of course. There were almost no bird books in those days."[59]

Ian's mother was quick to resolve the problem of not having a bird book by discovering the first pocket guide on western birds of North America. It was written and illustrated by a young American, Chester A. Reed, and was published the very year they arrived. "It was bound in green morocco. I treasured it, but it fell apart. It had illustrations of each species. It was a good start."[60] It was written for the western US reader but provided the first pocket guide of its kind for British Columbians and fuelled Cowan's interest in birds. Laura Cowan was quick to follow up with other books, like *Our Bird Friends*, by George F. Burba.[61]

> As soon as I showed an interest, then my Christmas presents turned out to be books on the topics. I've still got them. *Heart of the Rockies*, by G.A. Henty; *More Kindred of the Wild* [and] *Feet of the Furtive*, by Charles Roberts; *The Last of the Mohicans, The Gorilla Hunters, The Swan, The Young Lion Hunters, The Last of the Plains Men, Animal Heroes*, by Ernest Thompson Seton. I read them and read them and re-read them when I was going to bed at night. Tremendous fun. You got a *feel* for these creatures and feel *like* these creatures.[62]

One of Seton's animal heroes, a Grey Wolf that tried to take on a bounty hunter, came alive under its author's pen: "A Gray-wolf can glance over the morning wind as a man does over his newspaper, and get all the latest news."[63] The influence of these colonial stories on the young boy's imagination was profound and indoctrinated him into a culture of natural historians that he would never really abandon. Seton and Roberts, both Canadians, became guiding lights of that generation. As Alexander Burnett put it in his book *A Passion for Wildlife*:

Sharp-tailed Grouse

Pedioecetes phasianellus

At an earlier time, the distribution of this form was more or less continuous through the Osoyoos and the Dry Forest and Cariboo Parklands, west into the Chilcotin and north to the Vanderhoof region. It is now extirpated over much of its former range.[64]

Ring-necked Pheasant

Phasianus colchicus

Introduced, fairly common to common resident in southeastern Vancouver Island, the Fraser Lowlands, the Okanagan Valley and the vicinities of Salmon Arm and Creston.[65]

> By combining first-hand observation of animal behaviour with some latitude in attributing human emotional and intellectual responses to their animal subjects, they found a formula for bestselling success.[66]

It was a literary formula that for Seton married his scientific observations with influences (some would argue cultural appropriations) from an indigenous oral tradition of animal stories that he had gathered in his travels. But like Sir Walter Scott, whose romanticization of Highlanders seized the imagination of his generation, he knew good stories when he heard them. Seton was an active lobbyist for conservation and a serious scientist–naturalist who published scientific work as well, such as his massive, two-volume *Mammals of Manitoba* and, barely two years later, *The Arctic Prairies*.[67] In 1902 Seton had reined in a group of disenfranchised white youth and formed the Woodcraft Indians, a forerunner of Outward Bound. Four years into the experiment, he wrote a manifesto for the group, *The Birch Bark Roll of the Woodcraft Indians*,[68] which captured Lord Baden-Powell's attention and brought the two men together. Eventually their youth movements morphed into what became the Boy Scouts.

Cowan's link to Seton came directly through one of his first mentors, Hamilton Mack Laing, who also had come under the spell of Seton. Growing up in Manitoba, Laing had honed his boyhood woodcraft skills before following the author to New York, where he came under the mentorship of G.O. Shields, publisher of *Recreation* magazine, who had discovered Seton fifteen years earlier.[69]

Other books of the time that had travelled out with and influenced the Cowan family included those by John Buchan, a Scots minister's son who would later become the first Baron Tweedsmuir, the 15th Governor General of Canada and the namesake for what would become BC's largest provincial park. Cowan would meet Buchan just before the Second World War, while working at the provincial museum, for it was he who had done the biological inventory and reconnaissance prior to Buchan's celebrated visit to the park in 1937. Buchan had written his first adventure story the year Cowan was born and had gone on to capture a wide readership with tales of Scots abroad.

Rudyard Kipling too was standard bedtime reading, captivating young Cowan with the laws of the jungle and the oriental splendour of the empire experienced by great aunts and uncles. "I grew up on Mowgli and *The Jungle Book* and *Just So Stories*. We always read to each other. When I got old enough to read it myself, I did. That sort of thing colours the way you construct your own language."[70]

Cowan's interest was also exploding with the variety of the wildlife around Vancouver. Like Edinburgh, it was at the edge of the sea and in the shadow of volcanoes. But unlike Scotland, these oceans and mountains were still very much active – tectonically and biologically. Vancouver's mountains were still mostly forested and BC's herring industry hadn't decimated stocks to the same degree as Scotland's fishery had done. The herring spawns and salmon runs still brought on the full spring and autumn cacophony of seabirds and marine mammals within walking distance of the Cowan house. "People have forgotten what it was like. I can remember looking out across the sea and there were salmon jumping everywhere, as far as you could see..."[71] This was a memory he frequently conjured up through his tenure on the national Fisheries Research Board when spawning events were diminishing in size and intensity.

Photographs from the family album show an idyllic Vancouver existence for a child. In one picture, a 4-year-old Ian is standing barefoot on a sandstone outcrop pointing excitedly, probably at a bird, out to sea. The photo was possibly taken on Texada Island, where the family joined Cowan Sr. for a summer in Ian's fifth year. This idyllic prewar existence would end all too quickly, however. In a stroke of bad timing, just as Cowan Sr. had taken over the management of a company, it went into debt and he had to return to Scotland to arrange refinancing through his family connections. But with the outbreak of the First World War, the money was cancelled, the company was reorganized and Cowan Sr. lost his job. He resisted signing up for France and returned to BC and his botanist–horticulturalist roots to set up a market garden.

When Ian was 7, the family, with new sister Joan in tow, moved to North Vancouver, settling into a more modest house at 25th and Jones, four blocks west of Lonsdale on the side of Grouse Mountain – a good address for a budding ornithologist. It was a dirt road then, with open ditches, and except for a couple of houses, it backed on to forest and mountain. Today the Upper Levels Highway roars past the front door, but back then it was wild and remote, opening up a world of possibilities:

> We had a beautiful swimming hole in one of the creeks, and there
> was a mill on Queen's Road. We had a river through our property
> and the salmon used to come up through it. And there was a skid
> row within a block of our house. No one remembers what a skid row
> really is – now it is tied to the east side of town.[72]

The real skid rows/roads were made with logs laid transversally every couple of metres along a trail, on top of which large sleds built of slab wood skidded logs off the mountain. The skids were dragged up and down by a team of Clydesdales. The horses dragged the empty sleds up to the landing stages, where the timber was loaded on. At that time, the loggers were harvesting burntwood. The fires at the turn of the century had left towering dead trees of clear wood up to 10 metres tall standing on the mountain, which was harvested for firewood. The Cowan house was heated with a wood-fired furnace and it was Ian's job to ensure the cord of four-foot billets delivered got cut, split, wheelbarrowed down to the basement and stacked, and to keep the furnace stoked.

> That was my chore, and we all had chores. I feel sorry for the kids
> now because you can't have chores if you live in an apartment. We
> all had something that you were not paid for. This was our contribu-
> tion to the family welfare.[73]

This was the time when Cowan bonded with mountains and their inhabitants – including the loggers and their horses. He had a natural gift for befriending everyone, of whatever species or segment of society. "My parents were Scots and I had respect for my elders and the ability to listen."[74] The lanky, inquisitive boy hanging around the loggers was nicknamed "butterfly boy" for his keenness on catching butterflies. It was an excellent nickname, presaging his future role as a cross-pollinator of disciplines, a role that earned him the more prosaic title "last of the Renaissance men" used in newspaper headlines at his death in 2010. "They knew me well. I was up there every few days right to where they were working, chatting to them. They were nice fellows. I think that way, too, you get a better appreciation for the different levels of your society."[75]

While hunting up in the Hollyburn Ridge area, he met a local game warden who encouraged his interests. Cowan described one memorable time when the warden took him up to the logging camp, the lights of which he could see from his house. They went up the railway, as it ran from the camp to the shoreline at Mosquito Creek by the shipyards. "We had our dinner at the logging camp. Boy, was I impressed with the amount of food they had."[76] Where the logging roads ended, the trail up to Grouse Mountain started. On that trail he was to meet the Mundays, pioneering alpinists, who built a cabin on Grouse, hauling everything up that trail on their backs. Known as "the royal family of mountaineers," both Phyllis and Don Munday did the first documented ascent of Mount Waddington (or Mystery Mountain as they called it) and many of the other coastal mountains. They spared time on the way up Grouse Mountain to chat and share the young boy's interests. Their mountaineering skills and self-sufficiency would have been yet another benchmark by which Cowan could measure his own. Their trails continued to cross over the years, culminating in 1983, when Cowan as chancellor of the University awarded Phyllis an honorary degree for her contributions to "the conservation of our natural heritage."[77]

Blue Grouse [now split into Dusky Grouse (*D. obscurus*) and Sooty Grouse (*D. fuliginosus*)][80]

[Dendragapus fuliginosus]

The Blue Grouse is widely distributed throughout British Columbia, including Vancouver Island and the Queen Charlotte Islands. Its distribution is closely associated with mountains throughout its range. Logging can in some cases bring about rapid population increases by creating favorable breeding habitat. Usually, however, densities increase to a lesser degree and only for a short while, then stabilize at a moderate rate until the tree canopy begins to close; then they decline to a low density or disappear altogether.[81]

With not much money in the family there was another good reason to be roaming around – namely, to obtain protein:

> This is the way we were living. We were very nearly self-sufficient, but not quite. There was a little money from investments coming in but we lived pretty frugally. My dad was a gardener. We had a big garden that we cultivated. We had chickens. We had raspberries, which we sold. We sold eggs; eggs after the First World War were

terribly expensive. We couldn't afford to eat the darn eggs, we had
to sell them.[78]

One of the ways Cowan supplemented the family diet was to go down the hill to
the wharf and catch crabs in the intertidal – red rock and Dungeness. That started
him on the pursuit of bigger and larger prey.

On his 12th birthday, his mother gave him a .22 rifle and taught him how to use
it. "Probably her brother had taught her, because she had two brothers in the army
and one of them was a crack shot. Anyway I still have that rifle. She made me a case
so I could carry it around on my back."[79] He devised a way of concealing the rifle
in his trouser legs, stock down one, barrel down the other, so he could stroll non-
chalantly around the neighbourhood shooting dinner and riding buses without being discovered. He started off shooting grouse for the pot. His choice spot was an
inactive quarry two streets down from the Cowans', where 23rd Street ended. It had
become a booming ground, or lek, for Blue Grouse in the spring. If there was one
thing a young male Scotsman was trained to do, it was shoot grouse.

Grouse were one of the first birds Cowan studied in depth, in 1940.[82] A half century later, when *Birds of BC* was written, the research had advanced on every level:
genetic, behavioural and ecological. Where Cowan left off, his students picked
up – from his first grad student, Jim Hatter, who became BC's first game biologist,[83]
to Fred Zwickel and James Bendell, who wrote the definitive tome on the Blue
Grouse.[84] In the 70 years that Cowan had observed grouse, he had seen them go
from an expanding population to a species at risk in the province (Blue Listed). In
1947 he wrote, "Following removal of the conifer forest ... Perhaps the most spectacular change as viewed by the layman has been the increase in the blue grouse
accompanying this floral revolution. From a primitive population close to nil, this
bird now exists in uncountable numbers..."[85] *Vancouver Sun* outdoor columnist
Lee Straight cited him in his column (as he did frequently over the years) with the
headline "Game Likes Its Logging Patchy."[86] However, Cowan's seven decades of
observation and research also represented one industrial timber harvest cycle. He
lived long enough to observe first-hand that the fortunes of grouse and logging
were inextricably and inversely linked.

By the 1950s it was obvious that opening up "patches" of old-growth forest
only offered temporary benefits to grouse, and that the loss of old-growth coastal
Douglas-fir as winter habitat was lethal. Cowan witnessed the closing in of the
even-aged forests and the subsequent declines – in some cases complete crashes –
of many populations of birds and mammals. At an international congress of zoology in 1963, he told the audience that "almost none of the threatened species is being menaced through direct killing by man (our earlier problem) [i.e., hunting].
Almost all that are presently in danger of extinction are now experiencing the consequences of alteration in their habitats arising from human activity."[87] "Lumbering"
was the first activity on his list.

Part of Cowan's credibility for both students and policy-makers came not only
from his first-hand observations but from his ability to change his mind with

evidence. He observed the animals trying to adapt – or not – to these drastically altered landscapes over time. He and his students, such as Zwickel and Bendell,[88] documented the important concept of a wildlife "sink" (where clear-cuts created an abundance of habitat for certain animals for a short period, but as forest structure changed, contributed to declines in those populations).[89] Fluctuations in the Blue Grouse populations started Cowan on his lifelong critique of industrial clear-cutting practices in BC and the need for protected areas to include different ages of a forest and critical winter habitat, which for grouse was old-growth.

Franklin Grouse
(Fool Hen) [Spruce Grouse]

Canachites franklinii
[*Canachites canadensis franklinii*]

Resident in the subalpine forest, the Columbia forest and southern portions of the Boreal Forest biotic area.[93]

Tom Bergerud, another of Cowan's students and later a popular wildlife professor at the University of Victoria, conducted experiments on declining Blue Grouse populations of the Gulf Islands in the early 1970s. Specifically, he and a colleague, R.E. Page, were interested in testing an hypothesis proposed by Dennis H. Chitty, a population ecologist Cowan had brought out to UBC from Oxford in 1961. Chitty had developed a theory that populations regulate themselves genetically through something called behavioural polymorphism. This was an observation that within any population of animals there are different types of morphs (different alleles of a gene) that become dominant or "fit" at different times, depending on whether the population is increasing or decreasing in the environmental conditions prevailing at the time. Bergerud found that Chitty's theory held, at least in the case of Blue Grouse.[90]

In any given population of Blue Grouse, the theory posited, the potential to be either a "stay-putter" or a "disperser" lurked in the genes. Stay-putters were aggressive in holding territory and typically more interested in fighting off territorial challengers than even mating. The other morph, the "dispersers," or pioneers, expanded into new territory and were less competitive and more adaptable, but their pioneering ways were assumed to be a real disadvantage when territory was not expanding. As the population or the environmental conditions changed, each genotype would come into its own as the dominant type, or morph. The metaphor for human adaptations, especially in a competitive university in an era when so many males returning from mortal conflict were facing a time of economic ebullience, was not lost on Cowan. Behavioural work was to blossom under his departmental leadership and no one could have been more encouraging for this type of research than someone with an early predisposition for being a "disperser," or pioneer.

Part of Cowan's long affection for grouse stemmed from his summer holidays at Grace Harbour on Gambier Island, where his mother, Laura, took her children camping. They would set up tents on a friend's ten-acre parcel by the sea. "I was an expert with the slingshot and the Blue Grouse population suffered badly with me there. I think about enforcing the law now; I was an arrant poacher!"[91]

In 1941 he wrote up a description of the grouse species in Hamber Provincial Park in the Rocky Mountains, now part of the Canadian Rocky Mountain Parks World Heritage Site, one of the largest protected areas in the world. His style of popular writing for the museum continued with its Setonesque ring:

> Three species of ptarmigan can be found leading their broods across the alpine snowbanks: the ventriloquial booming of the Dusky Grouse is as characteristic of spring in the high timberland as the drum toll of the Ruffed Grouse in the river bottoms and aspen woods, while throughout the wooded areas the Franklin Grouse, or fool hen, is as trusting as its name implies.[92]

Now considered a subspecies of the Spruce Grouse, the Franklin Grouse at the time was of special interest to Cowan. The holotype for the Franklin had been taken in the Rockies by the Edinburgh naturalist David Douglas in 1827, but the specimen had been lost to science. (A holotype is the single physical example of a species, used when the species is formally named.) Cowan, more than a century later, had been following Douglas's journals for his research and unearthed an important clue which eventually led him to discover the lost holotype through some serendipitous sleuthing.[94] While travelling up the Columbia River to the Canoe River and over Athabasca Pass, Cowan notes,

> We came out at the head of a whirlpool. It must have been an Indian route ... the Whirlpool River in Jasper Park. There was a beautiful pond there called the Committee Punchbowl. [Douglas] camped there and he records that he shot a partridge ... He wrote, "One of its legs got broken by the shot, but it is an interesting bird. I'd never seen it before so I made a specimen of it and ate the rest."[95]

The specimen did make it back to Britain (although Douglas the disperser did not), but it disappeared into the dusty vaults of the University of Edinburgh. The last clue was a paper published in 1829 confirming the Franklin as a new species. Cowan describes what happened 123 years later:

> I was doing some work in 1952... and in the Royal Scottish Museum I stumbled on the lost specimen. Douglas's label was still on it and it had its left leg broken with his shot just as he recorded it. It was fun. When you go to museums in Europe, you can go hunting in the museum and find all sorts of treasures.[96]

In 1940 Cowan was also the first researcher to draw attention to new fatal diseases of the Ruffed Grouse and the Sooty Grouse and the relationships between wild birds and domesticated ones infecting each other with viruses transmitted through mites or flies. With recent outbreaks of avian flu, this has become a major source of epidemiological research, with health implications for humans as well as birds. In 1942, Cowan would also do a study for the BC Game Commission of the economic status of the introduced pheasant. This mastery of a subject matter, whether through the lens of pathology, systematics, behaviour, economics, recreation or conservation – just in the grouse/pheasant family – placed Cowan in a rank of his own.

At age 15 he was definitely a disperser, but it was a trait shared more by his mother. His father, McTaggart Cowan, was neither a hunter nor a camper. "My father hated camping. Everything out there was too small for him and too uncomfortable, so he just came and spent the weekends with us."[97] What young Ian got from his father was a passion for plants and for challenging conventional wisdom – not surprising given the Hutton–Balfour legacy. McTaggart Cowan Sr. had already caused a few ripples in the scientific community back in 1916 when he claimed that Garry oak were not native to British Columbia in the true sense of the word. In a letter to the editor of *The Daily Province*, commenting on a book by professor J.K. Henry entitled *Flora of British Columbia*, Cowan Sr. wrote: "In the introduction, the author gives some short description of what he considers ecological divisions of British Columbia, and we read with surprise that the oak is the characteristic tree of Vancouver Island."[98]

The director of the museum, Francis Kermode (who would hire Ian in 1935), wrote to Cowan Sr. asking for further clarification. The elder Cowan's reply (which is the only written record of his botanical ideas) points to a line of enquiry about the movement of flora around the landscape that his son would later adapt to the movement of fauna:

> The oak is present in the Fraser River Valley also, and here, owing to its surroundings, the fact that none of the trees are of any great age and that it does not flourish in a way in which it would, provided it was in its natural surroundings, lead to the conclusion that it was introduced at some time by Indians. In southern Vancouver Island, I think you will find that there are no oaks of the very great age attained by such trees as Douglas-fir and "Cedar" and that the oldest trees are to be found round Victoria – an old Indian settlement and Hudson's Bay fort. These facts together with a careful consultation of the writings of early observers, such as [Robert] Brown ... lead us to believe that the oak there also, has been introduced at a very early date by the Indians. There are many other plants still looked upon as indigenous that are not so, although they have found conditions suitable to their increase, enabling them to flourish even at the expense of the true native flora; such plants will undoubtedly become a powerful ecological factor, but when dividing a country into ecological divisions it is a mistake to

use a doubtfully indigenous plant as the typical species of the division – hence my remark.[99]

Cowan Sr. wasn't too far off in his assumptions. Western science has since caught up with indigenous cultural knowledge of Garry oak ecosystems, that these were cultivated landscapes – gardened, burned and weeded just like other cultivated gardens.[100] It is in the realm of possibility that the oaks, and the edible bulbs of the Camas Lily, *Camassia quamash*, and the Chocolate Lily, *Fritillaria lanceolata,* were at least assisted in their movement north into the coastal grasslands by indigenous peoples as they resettled the glaciated landscape, carrying their favourites with them. And who better to know this than a gardener? "My father owned a commercial garden, so as a teenager I had spent my summers in the pursuit of weeds, defending our plant treasures from disaster."[101] Cowan learned the skills from his dad and remained a skilled gardener for both food and ornamental alpine species until he died, winning countless medals for his alpine specimens.

Cowan Sr. was also a gifted photographer and recorded his children in various situations, including haunting silhouettes of the three siblings in a Peter Pan-like tableau. In later life he worked in the photography section of Woodward's department store in Vancouver and no doubt passed on his photographic skills to his son. Another insight into the senior Cowan is seen in a sequel to *Mary had a little lamb* that he penned for one of his granddaughters, whose independence he strongly encouraged:

> Now Mary's teacher had a rule:
> "No animals allowed in school."
> But Mary did not give a hoot.
> She took her lamb and mice to boot.[102]

Cowan noted, "My parents, particularly my mother, believed in encouraging every interest that their young ones showed."[103] When Ian was 13, Laura bought him a second-hand bike, on which he travelled alone to get farther afield for his expeditions. He used to ride as far as Steveston in the Fraser Delta, about 30 kilometres. Besides summer camping, every Easter weekend Laura would take the three children to Victoria to visit provincial institutions like the museum, library and archives. During one visit, Ian was encouraged to talk to the librarian, having exhausted his own bird book collection:

> To my amazement, he invited me into the stacks to see what was available in terms of bird books. We went in and one of the things I discovered was a full set of Gould's *Birds of Australia* – all hand coloured, it was gorgeous. What it was doing in the legislative library I cannot imagine. It would have been worth a fortune today. The only one I could find was Chapman's *Birds of North America* [*Colour Key to North American Birds*] and I was allowed to take it out of the

library, although I had to take it back before we went home. But that started me, and all my life I've been a book lover.[104]

It wasn't surprising he went on to co-edit and co-write the full set of *Birds of British Columbia* from his 70s into his 90s.

Ian's brother, Patrick, who was only two years younger, had less interest in natural history or hunting. He was a mathematician who won a Rhodes scholarship to Oxford. He trained in meteorology and was the research meteorologist in Newfoundland at the time of the early experimental trans-Atlantic flights. He later became the chief meteorologist for Canada as well as the first president of Simon Fraser University. Cowan was amused at the difference in their pursuits. "It's that nature versus nurture."[105] The relationship between the two brothers was good, though, despite the differences in their interests; and although geographically separated all their working lives, they kept each other professionally abreast of their respective disciplines.

Patrick was one of the first Canadian meteorologists to alert policy-makers about climate change, as early as 1975. When he was executive director of the Science Council, he started a program called *Living with Climatic Change* and organized a conference for scientists and government officials from North America to alert them to the dangers.[106] It would be another quarter of a century before the public and governments would even begin to grasp the significance of the situation. Patrick's brother attended these gatherings and was quick to corroborate the impacts emerging in the biotic community:[107]

> There is growing evidence that the world is entering a new climate regime. Both the rate of change of the climate and the amplitude of short-period climatic variations will be much more pronounced.
>
> Those of us concerned with science policy became aware of the almost total absence of communication between the meteorologists with the knowledge of climate change and the economic and social decision-makers and planners. These latter groups seemed to be going about their business blissfully using meteorological statistics drawn from the past 25 years when the weather on the whole had been rather benign and quiescent...[108]

Joan (Zink), Ian and Patrick's older sister, was a successful botanist and landscape architect, one of the first women to graduate in agriculture at UBC. Their younger sister, Pamela (Charlesworth), who wasn't born until Ian was 17, similarly excelled in her field, starting off as one of just two women in the first class in architecture at UBC after the war. She was a maverick in the discipline, with a progressive environmental and artistic sensibility and heading up professional and public service institutions like her brothers.[109] It was a highly successful family which fostered independence in both the girls and the boys. Given such a modest income, the family's dedication to supporting each of their children's interests seems to have paid off handsomely.

CHAPTER 3

"Dear Sir, I am keenly interested in birds."

North Vancouver, 1923–1925

By 1923, at the age of 13, "butterfly boy" was skillfully navigating solo the difficult terrain of the North Shore mountains. These adventures would lead him to his future mentors. Stumbling upon a Scout troop in the forest was the first step. In the imperial tradition of Seton, Baden-Powell and Kipling, the North Shore troop had been set up by Kingsley School, one of the first boarding schools for boys on that side of Burrard Inlet, modelled on the British public school system.[110] Kingsley School built a four-room log cabin clubhouse in the woods (now 27th Street) as their headquarters for weekend camping. Cowan didn't attend the school – he was at Lonsdale School, there being few resources in the family for a private-school education – but he struck up friendships with the Scouts and their masters and joined the troop.

One of the masters was Reverend Sykes, an expat British colleague of Albert H. Scriven, the school's founder and a renowned Scouter with a long history of "Kiplingesque" instruction of boys. As was the custom in those days, scoutmasters would sometimes adopt orphans and Cowan's troop leader was a young man called Dalziel, who had been adopted and raised by Sykes. Sykes had taught him to trap and the older boy shared those finer arts with Cowan:

> He had a trapline that started at Point Atkinson and ran along the shore almost out to Horseshoe Bay. He was trapping mink and raccoons. We used to go out on our bicycles and cycle from North Vancouver, which was a long way, nine miles or so, and run his traps. Later, I had my own trapline.[111]

Mink furs generated much-needed income at that time. Many early naturalists started their careers as boys trapping mink, gophers or muskrat for pocket money. Their skills in skinning stood them in good stead for the preparation of scientific specimens. Cowan also loved the rapid acquisition of survival skills from his scoutmasters:

> … putting up a bridge with just some rope and twigs. All the square lashing and diagonal lashing that I've used all my life. The batteries

of knots you learned, all had a purpose. I would never have tied a slipknot around a horse's neck, because you always tie a bowline when you don't want it to close up. A bowline was one of our competition knots and I could tie it like a whizz.[113]

Cowan later admitted that Scouts also provided him with an opportunity to develop his highly competitive nature and love of insignia, which never left him: "I had the whole set [of scout badges] – a whole armful – my pioneer's badge, ambulance first aid badge, laundryman's badge, carpenter's badge."[114] His favourite was the naturalist's badge, and while working on it at the age of 15 he stumbled into the second opportunity that was to alter the course of his life. An advertisement had come out from the Dominion Parks Branch that any Scout who kept a diary of birds for a year and submitted it would receive a field guide to the birds of Canada.[115]

Mink

Mustela vison [Neovison vison]

A dark-brown, weasel-like animal. Males weigh up to three pounds. Females about half that. The male measures two feet in length ... Coastal mink subsist largely upon marine crustaceans, notably crabs.[112]

A letter to the curator of the BC Provincial Museum, Francis Kermode, sent by the young Ian Cowan, suggests his journal was well under way with observations in October of 1925.

> Dear Sir,
> As I cannot see any record in your catalogue of British Columbia Birds of *Xanthocephalus xanthocephalus* being found in this district, I am writing to tell you that on October 22, 1925, while I was walking up a road beside a big meadow which is surrounded by low scrub bush and dead stumps in which a colony of blackbirds nest every year, I heard a clucking noise coming from a bunch of grass. On getting closer I was able to clearly discern this bird, it had a yellow head and neck and dark-brown body. I was so close to it (being only about 15 ft. from it) that I could not fail to recognize it as the Yellow-headed Blackbird. When I showed myself it flew straight up and then headed straight south. If I can be of any help to you by observing birds in this district I will be more than pleased to do it.
> Yours truly,
> Ian Cowan[116]

Cowan recalled the next exchange of correspondence:

Within a matter of a few weeks after I sent in that diary I got a letter from Jim Munro. He said that he was interested in my diary, that there were one or two things he wanted to correct, a few misidentifications. And that if I had any questions, I should drop him a line. So I did. And I got another letter [from Munro]. Here was the chief federal migratory bird officer writing to this kid, and not off-handedly; he was writing to me as a scientist! I remembered that all my life and who would have guessed that he and I [one day] would be co-authors of [A Review of the] Bird Fauna of BC.[118]

The budding young naturalist couldn't have guessed the background events that had led to this simple exchange of correspondence, a correspondence and friendship that would continue until Munro's death in 1959. Nor could he have guessed that Munro was part of a larger secret brotherhood that would extend its influence into virtually every wildlife and conservation institution of North America and guide Cowan through his formative years. Nor did he learn until much later, when he himself joined the brotherhood, that Munro, like his fellow naturalists and scientists, had vowed to mentor the next generation to strengthen conservation and legitimize their vocation. The reasons for the secrecy reached back into the historic struggle in Europe between the Darwinists and the creationists–dominionists, that is, those that defended the wild and public access to it versus those that wanted no obstacles in the pursuit of resources. The struggle had crossed the Atlantic and an invitation to join it had arrived in Cowan's mailbox.

Outwardly, Munro was simply a generous public servant who himself had once been an enthusiastic young ornithologist starved for mentorship. To the young Cowan, he was from a familiar genus. Munro was born to Scottish immigrants and had grown up prowling the wilder margins of Toronto looking for food and refuge from a family of 10. His first egg collection was of a Swamp Sparrow in 1898 at the age of 14.[119] Swamp Sparrows too prowl the wilder margins – of swampy habitat all the way to the Rockies.

Yellow-headed Blackbird

Xanthocephalus xanthocephalus

Abundant local summer visitant to cattail and tule marshes in the Osoyoos-arid, Dry forest and Cariboo Parklands biotic areas, north to, but much less common in, the Chilcotin, the Vanderhoof region and Ootsa Lake. Casual in the Puget Sound lowlands and Gulf Islands biotic areas.[117]

Munro himself had been encouraged and employed by early naturalists with the Ontario Provincial Museum (called the Royal Ontario Museum as of 1912) before marrying. His wife, Isabella Darby, suffered from tuberculosis and so they had sought the dry air of the Okanagan, moving to Okanagan Landing in 1910. It was a hot spot for naturalists as well as wildlife, as was Comox on Vancouver Island, to which the couple migrated seasonally. (Isabella died in 1919 and Munro married Alice Olive Bunting in 1921.) Like many naturalists, he eked out a living on the land as an orchardist to give him an excuse to be outside, supplementing his income with his real love of ornithology by collecting specimens for the national and BC provincial museums.

....

Swamp Sparrow

Melospiza georgiana

Munro and Cowan (1947) describe the Swamp Sparrow as a summer visitant to the Peace River Parklands and the Vanderhoof Region ... Since then the status of this "eastern" species has changed markedly. The Swamp Sparrow is now known to be a common summer visitant well north of the Peace River in the Taiga Plains ...[120]

....

Having established a good reputation throughout the museum world, Munro was hired as the chief federal migratory bird officer for the western provinces, where he flourished in his roles as both ornithologist and educator. At the time he was first corresponding with Cowan, he was beginning his work on a guide for teachers, *An Introduction to Bird Study in British Columbia*. In the preface, he hints at the change in public attitudes toward naturalists:

> There was a time, not so many years ago, when the ornithologist was looked upon as a more or less harmless person engaged upon a purposeless and childish career ... To know birds is to love them, and a love for birds may well prove the deciding factor in the creation of a love for humanity and point the way toward ideal citizenship.[121]

Cowan would meet Munro the following year at the home of another member of the brotherhood, Kenneth Racey. Racey was to become Cowan's most important mentor and his father-in-law. In their first exchanges, Munro's intent to instruct is as clear as Cowan's desire to be instructed:

May 3, 1926

Dear Mr. Munro,
I have just received my Scout diary back from the Canadian National Parks Board at Ottawa. You were kind enough to make some comments in the margin, which I would like to discuss with you. The book from which I identify birds is "Western Bird Guide" by Chester A. Reed ... [Cowan then proceeds to discuss over the next four pages detailed field identification clues, beginning with Buffleheads and ending with Horned Grebes. He finishes ...] I am very keenly

interested in birds but it is very hard to identify some birds just at the first sight without an expert to refer to. It is very kind indeed of you to help me and if there is any way in which I can be of help to you, you must of course let me know. My home is really in the bush right at the foot of the mountains and I have every opportunity of observing birds.

Yours truly,

Ian McTaggart Cowan, Troop Leader with North Van. Scouts.[122]

One of the species the two took up correspondence about was a finch that Cowan had called House Finch but Munro had corrected as Purple Finch. The two species are easily confused: the House Finch is redder and slighter, but back in 1926 there would have been no comparison possible for Cowan around Vancouver. House Finches weren't yet present in BC, and Cowan's first field guide, by Reed, was written for audiences in the US, where the species was common. Unbeknownst to both Cowan and Munro at the time, however, the House Finch was extending its range northward due to warming temperatures. Coincidentally, it was Cowan who recorded the first House Finch sighting in BC and the first nest record for both the interior and the coast, in 1935. He had just returned to Victoria after completing his doctorate in Berkeley, California, where the birds were a prominent feature, "and the House Finch song was still echoing in my mind. I was

Purple Finch (top)

Carpodacus purpureus

On the coast, there appears to be a spring movement in the Georgia Depression as small numbers pass through in April, about the same time that resident birds are beginning to establish breeding territories ... The breeding distribution of the Purple Finch in British Columbia is poorly known.[126]

House Finch (bottom)

Carpodacus mexicanus

The House Finch was migratory during the decade following its first appearance in BC. In the Okanagan Valley it did not begin to overwinter until at least 1945 and it was not reported as a wintering bird on the coast until 1951... Through the 1950s, the House Finch rapidly expanded its range...[125]

walking to work past the Crystal Pool [in downtown Victoria] and there it was. Its nest was within my reach and they raised three broods that summer."[123]

Later, in the Rockies, he was to record the species' first appearance in Alberta:

We walked from Blue Creek up Topaz; we were having lunch in front of the warden cabin ... We were sitting on the only piece of bare ground in the country, the rest was all snow. The flagpole was right behind us, and I looked up and there was a House Finch. So I collected it. Then I collected its mate.[124]

By 1947, when their book came out, the House Finch had become a local summer visitant in Victoria and the Okanagan. Cowan frequently used the House Finch expansion as an example of witnessing the effects of climate change first-hand.

In 1926 Munro had the new field guide, *Birds of Western Canada* – hot off the press – to offer the Scouts that responded. It was written by his colleague Percy Algernon Taverner, the chief ornithologist of the National Museum of Natural Sciences (later Museum of Nature) and illustrated by his neighbour, artist–naturalist Major Allan Brooks, at Okanagan Landing. Munro advised Cowan: "When you are able to refer to the *Birds of Western Canada*, there will be much less difficulty in the matter of identification."[127] According to Cowan at 90, the book never lost its attraction: "I still use it but the cover's coming loose."[128] "It was a really beautiful book and it was accurate. It was the first good manual for identifying birds that I had as a youngster. It made a big difference. When I was older I met the man [Taverner], big tall fellow with a beard, with a terrible stammer. He couldn't lecture. He was a good bird man."[129]

Teaching specimens including the **Yellow Warbler**

Dendroica aestiva
[*Setophaga petechia*]

This is the commonest breeding Warbler in southern Canada. It shares with the Goldfinch the popular name of Wild Canary, but the lack of black anywhere will determine it at a glance. It is found in shrubby localities in open country along stream or marsh edges. It is a common visitor to the garden and its cheery little song is very pleasing.[132]

Taverner was also a member of the brotherhood. More than just a bird man, he was one of the old-school generalists, "intelligent, passionately dedicated, eclectic, in their scientific interests, but largely self-taught."[130] Taverner and Munro were close-knit friends. Declared Munro:

> He had a genius for friendship. There was in him a warmth and an understanding to which men responded and many confided in him. He had in him a zest for life – a life which he saw in broad and tolerant perspective … He laughed often, at life, at himself, at sacred cows and noisy mountebanks. But at sincerity he did not laugh and he spoke ill of no man.[131]

John Cranmer-Byng's extensive biography of Taverner describes his subject's early interest in birds, which persisted through a challenging childhood, a father that deserted the family, and his own shyness, which brought on the stammer.

Taverner's first entry in his own field journals records a Yellow Warbler. He later wrote this description of the species in *Birds of Western Canada*.

Cranmer-Byng characterizes Taverner as a spiritual man: "Although not "religious" in the usual human use of the term, he felt a sense of mystery about the complex interactions of the universe of which the human species was a part."[133] Taverner had been encouraged by a series of friendships with early ornithologists, especially James H. Fleming, who in 1911 was instrumental in Taverner's appointment as curator of birds at the Victoria Memorial Museum of Ottawa (later the National Museum of Canada).

In 1926, when Cowan received his copy of the *Birds of Western Canada*, Taverner was well on his way to becoming a household name, encouraging a new generation of birdwatchers and enthusiasts for nature through his popular guides. (The western guide followed *Birds of Eastern Canada*, and the two were later amalgamated as *Birds of Canada*.) When, that same year, the annual meeting of the revered American Ornithologists' Union was held for the first time in Canada – hosted in Ottawa by the Canadian government and the National Museum – each attendee was given a copy of the western book and a greeting from the government as a souvenir. One of the excursions for the continent's top ornithologists, including luminaries like Ernest Thompson Seton, Cowan's childhood hero, was to climb nearby King's Mountain clutching their new books from which to identify passing species.

For his scouting prowess, Cowan received at the same time a companion book, *The Conservation of the Wild Life of Canada*, written by Dominion Entomologist Gordon Hewitt. "This was my first introduction to wildlife conservation. I still have the volume, with its congratulations signed by J.B. Harkin, director of National Parks of Canada. I was impressed."[134] As an introduction to conservation, Hewitt's writing was impressive. He was one of the "new breed in a public service, university trained"[135] who had married a vocation for the natural world with a skill at influencing the public on the issue of wildlife on both sides of the border. Hewitt had died tragically in 1920, of influenza and pleural pneumonia at the age of 36, and his wife Elizabeth released the book posthumously.[136] Duncan Campbell Scott of the Royal Society of Canada had expressed at his memorial:

> His gifts were varied, and his sympathies deep and general. He touched life at so many points that one cannot think that his interest ever flagged. His knowledge and appreciation of the arts and *belles lettres* were finely balanced by a warm love of nature, and this led him into enthusiasms for our wild life ... There was in all his work a rare combination of earnestness, with lightness of touch. Highly characteristic, too, was a fine sense of humour, which kept all things in their proper relation.[137]

Hewitt in his introduction called on the young to take up the challenge for conservation. "A young country enjoys the advantage of being able to profit by the mistakes of older countries. It lies within our power to preserve for ourselves, but more particularly for posterity for whom we hold it in trust, the wild life of this country."[138]

The book was an omnibus of facts about the national parks and wildlife. One of the birds Hewitt wrote about was the Wood Duck, which endeared itself to many Canadians with its resplendent regalia.

The other autograph on the second book given to Cowan was that of James B. Harkin. Harkin was one of the key instigators of the secret brotherhood with his colleague Hoyes Lloyd. He was also the head of the new Dominion Parks Branch. As commissioner, Harkin brought to his job what historian J. Alexander Burnett has called a "commitment to a philosophy of parks that bordered on the mystical. He was deeply influenced by the writings of the American conservationist John Muir and he believed fervently in the recreational, aesthetic, and spiritual values of unspoiled wilderness."[140]

Wood Duck

Aix sponsa

Of all our wild ducks this species is by far the most gorgeous in its colouring; in fact, it is not excelled in beauty of colouration by any other wild duck in the world.[139]

Harkin's vocation came to him one night around a campfire in 1912, the same year he was made administrator of the national parks.[141] He had just completed a strenuous hike over Vermilion Pass to an Alpine Club of Canada camp in the Rockies, which he describes this way:

> ... watching the firelight play upon the faces of the climbers who were, like myself, luxuriating in the sense of physical well-being and the spiritual peace which comes from a day spent in hard exercise in the clean, life-giving air of the mountains, when I heard the gaiety of the conversation and experienced the comradeship which grows out of dangers and pleasures shared in common, culminating in the subtle fraternity of the camp fire, I realized very strongly the uses of the wilderness.[142]

The ubiquitous Whisky Jack, or Canada Jay, was also there that day in camp. Harkin's friend and colleague Taverner's description of this member of the Jay family could have described any of these men [see sidebar opposite].

Harkin identified with animals seeking refuge; his childhood had been deeply troubled. He was the youngest son of a doctor from eastern Ontario who died prematurely. The young James was sent to his uncle's farm and he escaped into nature. First, as a young journalist and later as private secretary to two successive federal ministers, he rapidly embraced the popular "back to nature" idea proselytized by his bosses under Prime Minister Laurier.

Laurier needed no convincing regarding conservation. His philosophy was fairly clear from a pamphlet published by the Canadian Forestry Association, *The Forests and the People*, which quoted his remarks to the association's 1906 convention:

> It is not fair to the country – it is not fair to us who are living and still less is it fair to the generations to come after us – that we should allow the destruction of the forest to go on year by year ... and make no effort whatever to replace what is thus taken away.[144]

Laurier had been much influenced by the spirit of conservation coming from the leading Canadian and US foresters who had been raising the alarm to their political masters for many years. G.O. Buchanan, a forester and president of the Associated Boards of Trade of Southeastern British Columbia, had delivered "an Exhaustive Address on Fearful Waste of Natural Resources – Worst Danger that Threatens Any Nation," which was given a full page of the Victoria *Daily Times* in the spring of 1908. Buchanan quotes John Muir and then goes on prophetically to say: "Let us consider the general consequences of the destruction of the forest. With the extirpation of the forest, the climate of a country is partially changed."[145]

Buchanan and others were building on the fraternal leadership initiated by the Supreme Chief Ranger of the Foresters of Canada, Dr. Oronhyatekha (Burning Cloud, also baptized Peter Martin). Born on the Six Nations Reserve near Brantford, Ontario, Oronhyatekha was a remarkable and little-celebrated Canadian: an Oxford graduate, medical doctor, forester and Mohawk chief, as well as the first Canadian Indian to get a degree from a Canadian university. He was the driving force behind the Independent Order of the Foresters, another fraternal organization – though not secret – that traced its roots back to 14th century English origins of the early foresters. In 1903 the

Canada Jay
(Whiskey Jack) [Gray Jay]

Perisoreus canadensis

If the other Jays are clownish, one scarcely knows how to characterize the Canada Jay. It has all the family characteristics in an exaggerated form, but seems to lack the keen appreciation of its own humour that the others possess. Its entire lack of self-consciousness or poise is notable and it does the most impudent things with an air of the most matter-of-fact innocence ... Lonely places are its favourite haunts, and as soon as the temporary camp becomes a permanent settlement, it deserts the neighbourhood and retires to more secluded localities, or possibly suffers the fate resultant on too great confidence, for often civilized man is more intolerant of wild life than are more primitive hunters and trappers.[143]

IOF were a going concern, drawing a big headline in the *Toronto Globe*: "Ottawa Welcomes Dr. Oronhyatekha. Seven Hundred and Fifty New Foresters Initiated."[146] When Oronhyatekha died in 1907, Bernard Fernow, who had laid the foundations for the United States Forest Service, picked up the gauntlet in Canada when he was appointed dean of the Faculty of Forestry at Toronto. It was Fernow who had cautioned Canadians that "if you have any conception that Canada is capable of enduring as a nation for a thousand years, do not be in a hurry to dispose of your resources."[147]

There was appetite for change on both sides of the border. In 1909, Theodore Roosevelt's call to action "to consider the mutual interests of the countries in the conservation of their natural resources," prompted the first North American Conservation Conference, with representatives from the US, Canada (plus Newfoundland) and Mexico addressing the conservation of the extensive public forests, especially those with shared boundaries. Harkin was well placed to take a senior role in setting up the Canadian delegation, providing ample opportunity to share his interests with like-minded men, including Roosevelt.

Harkin was influenced by the policy of Roosevelt – not surprising given they were both naturalists.[148] Roosevelt too had been a "butterfly boy." He had dreamt of becoming another Audubon, preparing his own student collection of bird and mammal skins. His connection to the open prairie had been deepened by the premature death of his young wife and mother on the same day, which had led him to his own retreat into the wilds of North Dakota. It had also led him to a natural friendship with John Muir. The laboratory part of a scientific training bored him, but he became deeply interested in influencing policy on conservation, so he entered politics. By the time he was governor of New York, he was closing down factories that made hats from endangered bird feathers. He was supportive of the work of William Hornaday, head of the New York Zoological Society and the instigator of protection for the last of the bison through his American Bison Society. Hornaday wrote in his book *Our Vanishing Wild Life*:

> The rage for wild-life slaughter is far more prevalent to-day throughout the world than it was in 1872, when the buffalo butchers paved the prairies of Texas and Colorado with festering carcasses. ... I have been shocked by the accumulation of evidence showing that all over our country and Canada fully nine-tenths of our protective laws have practically been dictated by the killers of the game ... And yet, the game of North America does not belong wholly and exclusively to the men who kill! The other ninety-seven per cent of the People have vested rights in it, far exceeding those of the three per cent. Posterity has claims upon it that no honest man can ignore.[149]

Both Hornaday and Roosevelt had controversial elements to their conservationist views, dabbling in early eugenics and how to address burgeoning human populations. Roosevelt and his milieu were to exert a great influence – but also exhibit a great vulnerability – to the next generation of scientists/naturalists and conservationists.

Cowan had inadvertently stumbled into the collective fold of this next generation. Jim Munro, Percy Taverner, Hoyes Lloyd, James Harkin, Kenneth Racey and Hamilton Mack Laing were some of the Canadian members of the Brotherhood of Venery, or the 'B' as they were known amongst themselves. Started in 1925, the 'B' drew from wildlife and conservation professions and non-profit societies on both sides of the border. One of their goals was to shape, guide and foster the interests and vocations of the generation that followed after them – and Cowan was a prime candidate. The nationwide contest for young naturalists by the Dominion scientists, to which Cowan the young Scout had responded, was just part of a larger strategy.

CHAPTER 4

"We have adopted a ritual for extending our brotherhood and for teaching the sacredness of game and the proper protection of it."

Vancouver, 1925–1927

When Cowan set about "unravelling the innermost secrets of the lives of mammals" in *Mammals of BC*, he probably wasn't anticipating his own life being put under the same microscope. The handbooks of the 'B', however, provide an essential guide to the natural history of Cowan. The founding members were a tribe. They were uniformly unassuming, practical and intensely spiritually driven men. They pledged to adopt and advocate what member Aldo Leopold (described as the most influential conservation thinker of the 20th century[150]) coined for the group: a "conservation ethic,"[151] later called the "land ethic." Other US members included T. Gilbert Pearson, president of the Audubon Society; John Burnham, president of the American Game Protective and Propagation Association; Herbert L. Stoddard, ecologist and conservationist; and George Bird Grinnell, naturalist, author and advocate for native cultures and the bison. The lives and aspirations of many of the members became so intrinsically intertwined with Cowan's that one might suspect some behavioural polymorphism among the human population.

Leopold, Pearson and Grinnell are all well-known American figures and have had extensive biographies written about them, as have the Canadians Taverner, Harkin and Laing. Others, though, are virtually unknown today. Herbert L. "Larry" Stoddard was typical of the lesser-known US members. Like all the others, he had developed a deep love of birds as a child, exploring the ancient Florida swamps in the 1890s. He was known as a kindly man and a mentor. In his autobiography, *Memoirs of a Naturalist*, he finishes with this thought:

> I have learned that without Nature man has nothing, and my greatest desire would be satisfied if I could know that my grandchildren, and their children after them, will develop a love, an understanding, and an appreciation of the natural world. They can find no greater satisfaction in life.[152]

Stoddard, like Cowan, pointed to his first memory as one of discovering a bird's nest, in his case a ground dove. Professionally, he is recognized as one of the most important conservationists of the American South. An ornithologist and expert on grasslands, he recognized the role of fire and cultural burning practices in the ecology of dry forest and grassland communities. Stoddard advocated changes in the management of wildfire and was among the first to critique industrialized agriculture for its impact on wildlife. His seminal work was on the native American quail, the Bobwhite. Students of Stoddard's became close colleagues of Cowan.

In the constitution of the 'B,' the conservation ethic is laid out very clearly:

> Article II. The object of the Brotherhood shall be to advance wildlife knowledge and wildlife protection, and the spread of the ideals of sportsmanship through friendship, education and the reviving of the old art of the venery.
>
> Article III. Membership shall be open to those who are deemed to have advanced the objects of the Brotherhood by contributing constructively to the cause of conservation with particular reference to the woods, waters, and wilderness, and the inhabitants thereof, and whose friendly co-operative attitude toward others similarly engaged is an assurance of their worthiness as members of the Brotherhood of Venery.[154]

The rules of the 'B' were modelled on the English Charter of the Forest, established in 1299, which decrees that "No Waste ... shall be made in Forests ... Rangers shall make their Range in the Forest ... Freemen may use his Land in the Forest ... No nobleman may kill a Deer in the Forest."[155] The first book outlining these traditions was *Le livre de la chasse*, by Gaston Phébus, comte de Foix, ca. 1387. Sometime after 1406, Edward, Second Duke of York, translated the work and added chapters to it as *The Master of Game*. A modern-English edition was published in 1904 with a foreword by Theodore Roosevelt which was included in a 1909 2nd edition.[156]

Members passed on their ideas through "Lessons," which were prepared and read by different members at the annual meeting (the bracketed dates show when the lessons were read). The lessons included historical accounts of the rituals of the hunt, tributes to wilderness, aboriginal "messages," personal elegies of place, animals or trees and intimations of political support (or not) for their objectives. Aldo Leopold's five contributions – "Marshland Elegy"[157] (1937), "Song of the Gavilan"[158] (1940), "Clandeboye" (1941), "The Geese Return" (1943) and "On a Monument to the Pigeon" (1947), all of which later appeared in *A Sand County Almanac* (1949) – were first heard a decade earlier by the 'B'. Leopold was, in fact, building on the brotherhood's established tradition of conservation essays that were written by one member each year and read at the start of meetings. Hoyes Lloyd's First Lesson, called "Cave Men and Their Ritual,"[159] covers four pages of early rituals of hunting described in the writing of l'Abbé Henri Breuil. The "Men of the Reindeer Age" were evoked through their figures of animals on the cave walls of Perigord, as were "the Eskimos ... and the order of the Great Spirit who rules all the cosmic forces."[160]

Lloyd had addressed the small group at their first meeting, in 1925, in a hotel room in Denver after the scientific presentations were over:

> We thus find that a ritual of venery was connected with the chase long, long ago and as ritual, like venery, is one of the most primitive and hence powerful of human instincts, we have adopted a ritual for extending our Brotherhood of Venery and for teaching the sacredness of game and the proper protection of it, which is necessary if all are to enjoy that which is now no longer a necessity, but a very great privilege.[161]

Lloyd identified winter solstice as the time they would hold their annual meetings, because "this was also the time for initiating younger members of the tribe who had reached into the proper age, into their sexual and social obligations and to teach them the tribal mysteries and the traditional "catechism" treating of all man needed to know of the world, visible and invisible."[162] It also happened to coincide with the timing of the annual North American Wild Life Conferences. Cowan was being recruited as one of the younger members of the tribe while the elders teaching the tribal mysteries and catechism were circling around him like Muskoxen defending their young.

The key instigators of the 'B' in 1925 were Lloyd and Harkin. Historian and documentary filmmaker Janet Foster first traced their legacy in her seminal 1978 book, *Working for Wildlife*.[164] At that time, Canada's environmental history was largely unexplored and was deemed the work of an industrious but rather dull group of Canadian bureaucrats. Historian Alan MacEachern has termed their contribution "a distinctly Canadian tale: bureaucrat as hero."[165] But these were far more than dull bureaucrats with a nine to five duty of service. In the preface to Gordon Hewitt's book, his widow Elizabeth drew attention to the circle of scientists that worked in the various roles of wildlife conservation: "Indeed, the relation that existed between my husband and his associates was like that which animates a group of friends, where each one gives the best that is in him and looks for the best in others – a bright record in Civil Service history of loyalty…"[166]

British Columbia historian Lorne Hammond writes: "Far out of proportion to their numbers, the achievements of this small group have given us a remarkable legacy."[167] Leading up to 1925, these men had "brought our national parks into

---

Bob-white [Northern Bobwhite]

Colinus virginianus

A very small partridge or quail-like bird … Eastern North America, from just north of the Canadian boundary along Lake Erie … It has been introduced in southern Vancouver Island, Fraser Valley and Ashcroft and Vernon districts, British Columbia.[153]

Musk-ox [Muskox or Musk Ox]

Ovibos moschatus

… an animal allied to the sheep family that is particularly distinctive of our region of the world, ranging as it does over the barren grounds and arctic regions of the north and eastward to Greenland.[163]

---

existence, preserved bison herds, regulated hunting over large areas of this country, protected nesting areas, and put in place an international convention to protect migratory birds."[168] During the interwar period, the political latitude to create this legacy was possible, but with the instability of the minority governments led by Mackenzie King and challenges by the provinces to the natural resources in national parks, progress was hampered. Funding and interest dried up, and worse still, their good work was being unravelled, leading inexorably to a strategy for survival.

Hoyes Lloyd documented the discussion within the Brotherhood:

> A year and a month ago, ten or eleven of us met at Denver, Colorado, and founded this order. Its basis is friendship; – it has a creed for guidance; – its aim is to bring back as much as possible the old art of venery; – to make education a fundamental reason for its existence; – to teach that the enjoyment of wildlife is a great privilege; – to link existing conservation efforts by friendship bonds.[169]

The year 1925 was a challenging time for conservation on many fronts – for politicians and scientists but most of all for bison, that archetypal North American symbol of the wild and conservation. The bison were a rallying point for the conservation movement, as their survival hung in the balance. That struggle continued to be a strong symbolic presence throughout Cowan's career.[170]

Wood Bison cow and calves **[a subspecies of American Bison, *Bison bison*]**

Bison bison athabascae

Formerly occupied the extreme northern parts of the province. One skull of recent origin was taken from the muskeg near Atlin ... Larger and darker than the plains bison.[171]

Plains Bison [a subspecies of American Bison, *Bison bison*]

Bison bison bison

One specimen from the British Columbia side of Howse Pass.

The election faceoff between Liberal Prime Minister Mackenzie King and Conservative Arthur Meighen had heightened Canadians' sensitivities – one of them being to the culling of the Plains Bison, which had outgrown the paltry reserve set aside for them. A politically expedient proposal was to ship two thousand of the Plains Bison to Wood Buffalo National Park in Alberta, which had just been established for a completely different subspecies of bison. The Wood Bison themselves were only just recovering from perilously low numbers and were still near extinction. There was concern about the mixing of the two subspecies and the potential for disease.[172] The advice of the government's own scientists, Hoyes Lloyd and Harrison Lewis, had gone unheeded, so Lloyd, in his other capacity as president of the Ottawa Field-Naturalists' Club, all "young turks" like himself, blew the whistle.

Eastern Kingbird

Tyrannus tyrannus

The Eastern Kingbird is a versatile and adaptable species that selects a wide variety of situations in which to build its nest.[179]

A more unassuming "Master of Game" and whistleblower would have been hard to find. Like the rest of the tribe, Hoyes Lloyd was a "butterfly boy" who had tramped the same still-wild periphery of Toronto as J.A. Munro. In Lloyd's obituary, Munro's son David characterized his father's friend as "a warm and friendly person, unfailingly courteous … always generous with his time and knowledge, particularly with younger people."[173] His accomplishments "rested upon his thorough knowledge of wildlife, his keen sense of what was possible and practical and, perhaps most importantly, his ability to pick a path through political and bureaucratic tangles with calmness, diligence and humour."[174]

Described as "a chemist by profession and ornithologist by vocation," Lloyd "found himself in a small group of like-minded men who shared a strong sense of mission."[175] While overseeing the Migratory Bird Treaty of 1916 in Ottawa, he connected with veteran naturalists like Taverner and Laing, who supplied him with sightings of birds from remote military training stations. Lloyd's official position, chief ornithologist for the Dominion Parks Service, was created after the war. Inspired by Gordon Hewitt, he joined him as a "tireless spokesman for wildlife conservation."[176]

Lloyd didn't just write articles. He also organized radio lecture series, held essay and photographic competitions in schools and led countless field trips and workshops for building bird boxes. He kept a daily field journal for 70 years and in the early entries, written as a romantic 18-year-old paddling through Algonquin Park as a deputy game warden, there is an essence of the passion that never left him. "The moon is shining full as I write alone by the campfire and the hooting of a nearby owl, combined with the weird howling of the wolves in the distance makes an impression not soon to be forgotten. Now I feel, at last, that we are well away from civilization …"[177]

Historian Daniel Brunton, as a young boy, once met the elderly Lloyd on a field trip to see a solar eclipse. As Brunton relates:

> [Lloyd] prepared a study skin of an Eastern Kingbird my father had struck with the car on the way up; Lloyd did so with a pocket knife on the hood of the car; little conversation during this, though I believe he explained why he was doing this – very quick and skilled.[178]

In 1922 Lloyd organized the inaugural Federal–Provincial Wildlife Conference, which showcased his "capacity for unobtrusive but effective group leadership."[180] He went on to organize and lead gatherings of many intergovernmental, international and non-profit organizations, including the North American Wildlife Conference, which became the venue for dovetailing with the meeting of the 'B' each year.

When the bison issue flared up in 1925, Lloyd called on his friends to help. He asked an American colleague to pen a letter to the editor critical of the proposed transfer, which he printed in the February 1925 issue of *The Canadian Field-Naturalist*, his club's journal.[181] According to Brunton, the letter was "an excellent, scientifically correct (and prescient) assessment of the issue."[182] Then he took the bolder step of sending the letter *and* the journal issue directly to the Interior Minister, Charles Stewart, a former Alberta premier charged with looking after Alberta interests in the King cabinet. Brunton notes:

> King didn't like how Stewart was handling things "out there," so raising an Alberta problem with him was probably not good thinking in that atmosphere of political discomfort – especially being openly critical of his department's stated plans for an iconic feature like the bison in that region.[183]

On the front of the journal were the names of not just Lloyd and Lewis but many of Stewart's own prominent scientists and civil servants: botanist William Macoun of the Department of Agriculture, J.P. Wright of the Geological Survey, Percy Taverner, R.M. Anderson of the National Museum and Francis Kermode in BC. The covering letter would have been signed by the president of the club, his "loyal" senior civil servant Hoyes Lloyd.

Lloyd and journal editor Harrison Lewis were given clear instructions from their political masters to publicly dissociate themselves from the club immediately or be sacked.[184] At the April 11, 1925, council meeting, held at Macoun's house, Lewis and Lloyd announced their immediate resignations as directors with no recorded reason. As Brunton notes,

> Can you imagine someone today surviving openly criticizing their elected bosses like that? Notwithstanding that the present paranoid government won't even allow scientists to state basic facts gathered by programs supported with public money, let alone give an informed opinion. Frankly, it is amazing that Lewis and Lloyd escaped very serious career damage.[185]

Instead they kept their jobs. Lloyd stayed on the board but their vocations went underground.

Across the border, the United States had their own conservation disaster brewing. The western droughts of past years had dried out 60 per cent of the migratory bird feeding grounds, adding enormous stress to bird populations on top of pressures such as development and hunting. The major conservation organizations, like the Audubon Society, headed up by T. Gilbert Pearson, and the American Game Protective and Propagation Association, led by John Burnham, had been lobbying the US government to bring in federal game refuges – no-shooting areas as refuges for birds. The game refuge issue was fiercely debated in Congress over several years, against Republican anti-tax interests.[186] Funding new refuges without raising additional taxes was the challenge before the conservation lobbyists and scientists. The "Denver Committee" was appointed by the International Association of Game, Fish and Conservation Commissioners to draft a new bill that would provide the details of a workable funding formula using game licences or the existing ammunition tax.[187] It was brewing up to be a fist fight with industry. (Cowan would help launch a similar funding formula for habitat protection, the Habitat Conservation Trust Foundation, nearly 50 years later.) Lloyd attended the Denver Committee meeting in November of 1925, and it was there that he gathered recruits for the 'B' from among the directors and scientists, setting out their tasks and the reasons for them.

In their own history, the 'B' reported that

> After much thought and discussion, Hoyes Lloyd proposed a new approach to forestall the serious situation which threatened to damage the cause of wildlife conservation in United States and Canada. It called for banding together, in secret, a group of individuals who could be counted upon under all circumstances and who could be depended upon absolutely ... With this concurrence a draft Constitution was prepared by Hoyes Lloyd.[188]

The *Lessons* reflect the range of risks on the political and social landscape of the time. One risk certainly was clear: a fear of having their legitimacy undermined by the political forces encountered in the fight to preserve wildlife and public lands and the right to subsistence hunting. The bison and bird refuge issues were symptomatic of the continuing pressures that wildlife and wilderness had been experiencing all across North America since the late 19th century. The other political challenges were coming from big game hunting lobbies, which were increasingly a threat to the national parks, then and into the 1940s. The club's adopted Charter of the Forest decreed that "no nobleman shall kill a deer in the [Crown] forest," and this became a principle to govern their actions. They began recruiting members from all the non-profit conservation societies and government scientists across North America, who had been responding to external threats to wilderness and wildlife for years.

The Ottawa Field-Naturalists' Club's journal (February 1925) touches on the mood of the time in an editorial titled "Wilderness": "More than anything else, it is the fact that Canada possesses an abundance of wilderness that renders it desirable, above countries less fortunate in this respect...."[189] The editorial points to the "sad condition" of places like Indiana, quoting the director of the Department of Conservation of a state which, in little more than a century, had lost ninety-five per cent of its forests and witnessed diminished soil fertility, lowered lakes, drained marshes and disappearing native plants and animals. It was a state, the director wrote, which had "converted sparkling rivers into muddy streams." The editorial concludes that "the progress of mechanical invention, the increase of the world's human population and the lust for money are constantly at work to destroy our wilderness, as those of other nations have been destroyed in the past."[190] With millions of hectares of public land on both sides of the border in the sights of large corporate interests hungry for ownership, with failing political leadership, with threats to their jobs, these men were struggling to strengthen their efforts and weather the political storms.

Their values were not new. As documented in the editorial, they pointed straight back to Darwin and Roosevelt, while the emphasis on education, mentoring, science and social equity echoed the Scottish Muir tradition – bound by the common desire to maintain access to wilderness and food. The movement had also weathered the divisive 1896 debate between the preservationist stance taken by Muir and the conservationist stance of Gifford Pinchot, a professional forester who promoted the "wise use" approach, characterized as more "pragmatic." Pinchot was regarded by Muir and others as being "too political, too opportunistic, too ready to compromise on principle to win support in the Congress and state capitals, too indifferent to aesthetics and to wildlife protection."[191] Being alert to compromise that put biological systems at risk was clearly one of the functions identified by the 'B'. This debate was to sunder not only Pinchot and Muir's friendship and the movement itself, but downplay the much greater threat that Roosevelt, during his presidency, faced from large corporate interests in seeing the millions of acres of state lands privatized.

By 1909 Roosevelt had skillfully negotiated (with some concessions) 16 national parks, in places like Yosemite through his collaboration with Muir, and 51 federal wildlife refuges and had protected 150 million acres in forest reserves. He set up the new US Forest Service, appointing Pinchot to the helm with the mandate that "the forest reserves should be set apart forever for the use and benefit of our people as a whole and not sacrificed to the shortsighted greed of a few."[192] Canada, under Prime Minister Wilfrid Laurier, who was sympathetic to the same ideals, was to follow suit a year later, as did provinces such as BC, which set up its Forest Service in 1912.

A *Lesson* of the 'B' recalls the earlier Roosevelt era, when naturalists and scientists were still in the political ascendancy. The essay captures the British Viscount Grey's meetings with Roosevelt in 1910, the year after his presidency ended and the year Cowan was born. Grey describes two "sacred moments." First, when they share the pleasure of the song of one of two similar birds: the old world Goldcrest, which reminds Roosevelt of the New World Gold-crowned Kinglet. And second when the two men take off their shoes to wade along a flooded path together like boys. "Cultivate the enjoyment of the beauty of nature," says Lord Grey, "because it costs nothing and is everywhere for everybody."[193]

It is hard to imagine contemporary leaders discussing kinglets, taking off their shoes to wade in a puddle together and celebrating beauty. Grey goes on to remark, "Two of the greatest experts in natural history told me the other day that Colonel Roosevelt could hold his own with experts."[195] One of those experts was C. Hart Merriam, the chief of the US Biological Survey, a friend and colleague whom Roosevelt acknowledged as "one of the most knowledgeable field naturalists of his generation."[196] Merriam's patron was the pioneering zoologist Annie Alexander. She was also the patron of Joseph Grinnell, who, along with Merriam, was instrumental in supporting Cowan's academic career; Alexander financed Cowan's post-graduate degree. Cowan named them all in the acknowledgements of his dissertation.

Cowan was coming into a tribe whose expertise had been recognized and valued by leaders of three nations. Roosevelt had set in place new standards of stewardship in public lands that spilled north over the border through institutions spawned by the North American Conservation Conference, like the Canadian Commission of Conservation.[197] His scientific interests recognized the importance of wardens and scientists in the forest and he passed budgets to enable them to do research and live the life he himself would have chosen had he been able to. Roosevelt opened the doors to legitimizing a way of life that Lloyd, Taverner, Munro, Leopold and Cowan all eventually enjoyed. However, their hold on these ideals was tenuous and the 'B' worked hard to maintain legitimacy. As David Munro wrote in 1979, "For anyone of Hoyes Lloyd's generation, there was scant opportunity for a professional career in wildlife conservation. Almost all of those who broke into the field before 1930 were first obliged to seek means of livelihood less closely matched to their real interests."[198]

Roosevelt was never a member of the 'B' and was distant from them in most respects, overriding them in time, privilege and power. Later in life he was prone to excesses such as big game sport hunting, which the 'B' didn't condone. Roosevelt also had another dark element to him that would rise up and bite the very scientists who were working in the various fields associated with him: he was an early proponent of eugenics. The term, which came to mean the application of agricultural techniques of breeding to humans, had been coined among the same heady intellectual confraternity that gave rise to evolutionary theory and humanism. Francis Galton, cousin of Charles Darwin, reasoned that "the improvement of the breed of mankind is no insuperable difficulty."[199] Roosevelt was attracted to the idea. In a

---

Golden-crowned Kinglet

Regulus satrapa

This kinglet occurs in every ecoprovince, but its centre of winter abundance is in the Fraser Lowland and throughout southeastern Vancouver Island and the Sunshine Coast ... Two geographic races of Golden-crowned Kinglets occur in British Columbia. Cowan found the subspecies R. s. satrapa in the Peace Lowland.[194]

1913 letter to Charles Davenport, a US eugenicist and founder of something called the Eugenics Record Office, Roosevelt wrote:

> It is really extraordinary that our people refuse to apply to human beings such elementary knowledge as every successful farmer is obliged to apply to his own stock breeding. Any group of farmers who permitted their best stock not to breed, and let all the increase come from the worst stock, would be treated as fit inmates for an asylum.[200]

It was a dangerous idea, but many people from across the political spectrum on both sides of the Atlantic adopted it. In British Columbia, eugenics was taught in schools and entrenched in law with the Sexual Sterilization Act (1933), which wasn't repealed until 1973; Alberta too had a sterilization statute, in force from 1928 to 1972.[201] The Second World War brought harrowing revelations about the most perverse consequences of the idea. Hundreds of thousands of people were sterilized against their will during the war. With these disclosures, eugenics would become irrevocably linked to proponents like Roosevelt and Darwin and, by association, to evolution, conservation and population ecologists. It became the ecologists' Achilles heel, applied to biologists by some of the Christian right. It also became another political means to discredit scientists. The two-century-long ideological war between creationists and Darwinists, in which eugenics plays a role, is well covered by historians today and demonstrates the minefields that Cowan seemed adept at navigating.

Cowan tackled eugenics head-on. There is no evidence that he subscribed to these ideas; in fact, the opposite is true. Cowan didn't begin to write about human populations until 1955, when he revealed his position very clearly at one of the annual general meetings of wildlife managers that the 'B' attended. He pointed out that although human population pressures are a huge problem, "the various trappings that we call our way of life" are a bigger one and that "the wildlife dollar is the same as the automobile dollar and the whiskey dollar and we must compete for it with all our imagination.[202] There was only one solution as far as he understood: "So as I began [this talk] with education, I end with it."[203]

In 1957, in an address to the Royal Society of Canada called "The Penalties of Ignorance of Man's Biological Dependence," he made the following observations:

> Our national policy is directed toward increasing the number of men in Canada as rapidly as possible without much regard to the biological forces involved. Even if desired it is doubtful that we could control the increase in our population. We must plan for much larger populations before we learn to control our enthusiasm for unbridled procreation ... a wider public understanding of the biological forces at work in man's environment is urgent ... Our fishes, birds and mammals in their native habitat have as much to give to our future as have any of our other resources; the are a perpetual source of

the energy that is life, but they are dependent upon our wisdom and foresight for their survival.[204]

In his "Of Mice and Men" lecture in 1961, Cowan recounted to his audience Charles Darwin's famous 1858 Linnaean Society lecture when Darwin unveiled his theory of evolution and suggested that a nation which undertook planned parenthood would gradually diminish in population relative to nations which had not opted for "a world of luxury and not of numbers." Cowan argued, however, that modern circumstances are different and that mere numbers are no longer the absolute criterion for survival. "Survival today – and even more, to me, in the future – depends upon the effectiveness of social organization, the breadth and depth of our education that can lead to the most ingenious and the most effective use of men and human environment."[205] As for Galton, the only reference Cowan appears to have made to the early statistician was to his prospective son-in-law, Mikkel Schau, as a kind of pre-nuptial test. Cowan gave Schau a Galton paper to review, called "Statistical Inquiries into the Efficacy of Prayer," which had found no evidence that prayer works. Schau believes his response to the paper must have passed Cowan's test, as he married Ann with her father's approval.

The 16-year-old Scout interested in the natural history of Vancouver couldn't have been farther away from the political forces that would lead to acts of genocide, but he was about to enter a profession that would hold some of the most controversial ideas of the 20th century. His influences from the philosophical framework of the 'B' may well have helped him negotiate these contentious ideas despite the powerful voices he encountered. At 90, Cowan had this to say about human population:

> What is the right amount of resources that we should consume and the right number of children we should have? The basic minimum? We don't want to judge. Who wants to judge? Who wants to regulate? There are no answers that are acceptable to humans. Those of us who are biologists can do the arithmetic and predict, but we also realize that there is not a damn thing we can do about it. Populations crash.[206]

For Cowan, and as expressed in the 'B' essays, consumption and greed were the most egregious issues. Of course, this attitude was also the issue that sat least well with industrial magnates such as J.P. Morgan, Frederick Weyerhaeuser, the Rockefeller brothers and E.H. Harriman, who had designs on public land. With Roosevelt's passing, industry had certainly come close to swaying public opinion towards privatizing US public lands, and the Canadians were seeing the implications down the line for Canadian federal lands. The 1935 'B' *Lesson*, by Ernest Thompson Seton, "Message of the Indian," tackled the age-old issue of privatization:

> He [the Indian] solved one great economic problem that vexes us today. By his life and tribal constitution, he has shown us that nationalization of all natural resources and national interests puts a stop

at once equally to abject poverty and to monstrous wealth.[207]

The backbone and public face of the forest service for both countries were the government scientists and the forest and park rangers. One of the ways of undermining Roosevelt's legacy was to claim that his "green rangers" were "google-eyed, bandy-legged dudes, sad-eyed, absent-minded professors and bugologists."[208] The absent-minded professors were the 'B' from south of the border: Aldo Leopold, T. Gilbert Pearson, John Burnham and George Bird Grinnell, among others.

The key to credibility for these men was to publicly emphasize the use of science and to educate people about it, whether assessing the impact of predator control on wildlife populations or introducing concepts of ecology or land use policy. Leopold biographer Susan Flader tracked this emergence of the scientific approach through

California Quail brooding

Callipepla californica

Established through introductions in southern British Columbia, Washington, western Idaho and Utah as well as Chile, Australia, New Zealand and Germany. California Quail were first introduced to British Columbia near Victoria in the early 1860s.[215]

Leopold's work on the ecology of deer, wolves and the forest habitat.[209] Leopold highlighted, as did Cowan, the contrast between North America's large tracts of public forests where complex prey–predator systems still existed, versus the traditional, private, enclosed European game reserves where game animals were farmed, predators were exterminated and forests were reduced to simplified plantations. Leopold's seminal textbook *Game Management* (1933) was, according to Flader, "a plea for ecological understanding, for the extension of ethics from the realm of human social relations to the whole land community of which man was an interdependent member."[210] Leopold's papers from his visit to Germany in 1935 would solidify his thinking about the potential loss if the vast tracts of North American wilderness and complex wild ecosystems were to become fragmented, enclosed, privatized and reduced to places for the privileged few. Cowan reiterated these ideas after his study tour of Europe in 1952.

Cowan would meet Leopold several times during his academic career before Leopold's premature death in 1948.[211] They referred to each other's work, which is not surprising given their overlapping specialties of deer and wolves. In addition to the 'B', they were both members of the Wildlife Society, the Ecologists' Union (formed in 1946; Cowan was on the study committee) and the US National Deer Committee. They also met at the annual North American Wildlife Conferences, although there is no extant correspondence. Cowan spoke of being considered for a faculty position at the University of Wisconsin where Leopold reigned,[212] although according to Stanley Temple, emeritus professor of conservation at Wisconsin, there is no evidence of this. There is, however, a 1947 letter to Leopold from Leonard Wing at the State College of Washington mentioning Cowan among candidates being considered for a position there.[213] According to Cowan, an invitation to go to the US did come during the war and a response had to be delayed until after the conflict was over. By that time, though, he was already entrenched at UBC. "I didn't want to go to the United States, really, and if I had I would have gone to Berkeley."[214]

Berkeley was a second home to Cowan after his graduate work there, and that is where he met Leopold's eldest son, zoologist A. Starker Leopold, a contemporary of Cowan's who became a friend and colleague. Starker Leopold became an expert on the California Quail, a sociable bird which gathers in coveys and has an extraordinary ability to disappear into the bush. It was also a species that had strong links back to Cowan's childhood.

The Leopold and Cowan families were intertwined through the years, culminating professionally in 1968 when Ian and Starker sat on two committees together. The first panel took a "hard, critical look"[216] at the wildlife refuges in North America set up by Roosevelt (starting with Pelican Island, Florida, in 1903 and now numbering 250). The following year, the two men sat on the steering committee for a Conservation Foundation conference on "Future Environments of North America," presided over by Frank Fraser Darling, Scotland's most influential naturalist, ecologist and conservationist of that time. Cowan's introductory remarks began, "We face in the long run probably the most difficult problem of all in a democratic society: the constant collision between public benefit versus private gain in the use of resources. We are making poor headway in resolving this one."[217]

Cowan's final link to Leopold was winning the Aldo Leopold Award of the Wildlife Society in 1970. In the award ceremony he was honoured for being "understanding and tolerant" and for having "enlarged our understanding of wildlife of his homeland – and far beyond."[218]

Bob Weeden, a student of Cowan's who went on to teach environmental policy, ethics, planning and philosophy at the University of Alaska, Fairbanks, reflected on the historical importance of the 'B' and its guidance in the development of the profession generally:

> In our working life, we [wildlife managers] would be directed to do things that weren't in the best interests of wildlife. The 'B' provided a safe place to say "my boss is wrong and I don't know how to stop them." As scientists trained to protect wildlife, we were focused on the long term. Our bosses had political pressures to make decisions in the short term. With the division in the conservation movement between the short-term pragmatism of Pinchot and the spiritual aspects of Muir, the pragmatism typically won out. The 'B' allowed senior people in the profession to express themselves frankly and safely in the context of an ideal for looking after the natural world; externally we called it "the resource." Stewardship needed to be based on

science but there was also an almost spiritual belief in the relationship of humans with wildlife – more of the Muir tradition. The fear
of discovery is what made the society secret.[219]

Secrecy was well understood by Cowan. Through years of observing the hidden world of small mammals like the shrew, he had a deep understanding of the
benefits of staying hidden. "… the more than 200 kinds of small fry, that make up
the mammal fauna of the province, live their fascinating lives unseen and unsus-
pected."[220] The 'B' had many other reasons to maintain their secrecy, as the greatest challenge to their group was looming over Europe. Hoyes Lloyd writes about it
in the fifth *Lesson* in 1930:

> Some primordial instincts are worthy of encouragement; some,
> while they cannot be escaped at once, may be controlled in time,
> and here I am thinking of war. We do not need to kill men to eat,
> nor to get their field or hunting grounds … Bertrand Russell rec-
> ommends Alpine climbing *as a substitute for war* [author empha-
> sis added]. Both require risk and hardihood … Even to be alone in
> the wilderness and to depend on one's own resources may satisfy the
> instinct of hunting, of overcoming nature by existing with it, yet in
> spite of it. This is becoming difficult because the wilderness is so rare.
> In the wilderness man has time to think.[221]

Harkin had masked these same sentiments in a public address he made to an
American audience on national parks in 1917:

> Mr. Chairman, I think you recognize that national parks are a much
> bigger question than a mere getting of tourist revenue or a mere
> matter of carrying passengers. In Canada we who are charged with
> parks matters believe they concern the very life of the nation. We
> claim it is our first duty to see that every person is given an opportu-
> nity to gather some of these "coins of life." At present one of the most
> important matters in connection with national parks … is the ne-
> cessity of more and still more parks … particularly parks nearer the
> large cities…. I want to refer briefly to what the Canadian soldiers
> are doing in France … there seems reason to believe that to a consid-
> erable extent, …the resourcefulness and courage and energy which
> they have shown on the battlefields of Europe have been due to the
> habits of the outdoor life which they lived in Canada. …[222]

Shell shock (now diagnosed as post-traumatic stress disorder) left thousands of
First World War veterans less able to deal with ordinary life. Harkin speaks in pa-
triot's language, but the *Lessons* of the 'B' extol the value of time spent in the wilderness – a sanctuary – ideas that couldn't be publicly articulated. The wild provided
members of the 'B' with freedom from the conventions of a society that ridiculed
lovers of nature, scientists with spirituality or critics of capitalist values and war,

a society that didn't recognize damaged psyches. Similar fraternities, such as the "brotherhood of the rope," emerged within the alpine clubs.[223] This solidarity, and nature itself, afforded companionship, sanctuary, even the possibility, however remote, that members' robust activities in the wild could actually prevent war.

Secret societies were common during this period in Canada, and scholarly works have attributed to them a wide variety of functions, from enabling administrators to do their job, to, as Jessica Harland-Jacobs notes, creating a vibrant community "off-limits to women ... and jealously guarded by its denizens."[224] There was also the desire for shared relationships mirroring those of biological brothers. "Bound by ritual and often ideology, members of fraternal associations were pledged to privilege one another's interests over those who did not belong to the brotherhood."[225] Moreover, organizations such as Freemasonry played an influential role in aiding British imperialism throughout its far-flung colonies:

> ... belonging to the fraternity made life easier for Britons who ran, defended and lived in the empire ... The brotherhood was thus instrumental in the making of a colonial middle class and defining its boundaries ... The brotherhood ... was ... dominated by loyalist, Protestant, respectable white men.[226]

The writings and actions of Munro, Taverner or Lloyd don't place their fraternity squarely within a more typical elite, white-male British colonial stock who, thanks to indigenous assistance, did rather well. In his essay "The Empire's Eden," Greg Gillespie alludes to this type of British sporting gentlemen who

> used their upper-class hunting code to tie their sport to issues of conservation and natural history. This connection of hunting to the advancement of natural history rationalized and legitimized hunting by highlighting the educated, civilized and imperial nature of their sport.[227]

Virtually none of the 'B' came from this class, though they may have aspired to it at times. The Canadian members were largely sons of farmers or immigrants with humanist values who could be more characteristically described as those who hunted to eat. Far from advocating private game reserves, they were advocating for the commons, for civility and the calming nature of a subsistence lifestyle. They were also looking for kindness and friendship. For these men, conventional power and privilege was not something they experienced. As mostly aspiring professionals, they strove to maintain a way of life that had more to do with freedom to practise their love of the outdoors and hunting. Preserving the place to do it was the motivation for conservation.

With regard to gender, they appeared to be a society far more preoccupied with remaining hidden from a class of men that threatened their occupations and freedom than with blocking access to women that didn't. In fact there is no evidence that barring women was a primary objective. Jim Munro's second wife, Olive, was a member, as was Pearl McGahey of Ottawa, probably by virtue of their interests – and perhaps their secretarial skills. It is difficult to assign Harkin to any conventional box when he asks at their meeting in 1938 at a Baltimore hotel: "Are we today any more just towards these rights [of animals]? And why our attitude? Is it not because we have lost the old idea that the world was made for all living things and not for man alone?"[228]

Tina Loo's book *States of Nature*, which explores the early days of saving Canada's wildlife, argues that Harkin and his colleagues were of "the more aloof and scientific approach to state-sponsored environmentalism."[229] She describes the pivotal time of Laurier's government as "Canada's push to systematize, centralize, and bureaucratize wildlife conservation."[230] She rightfully raises the possibility of "imperial eyes"[231] in wildlife conservation that would overlook the dispossession of aboriginal lands and a way of life, positing that "making a place for wildlife involved pushing some people out of the way."[232]

However, with closer observation at the individual level, as Cowan would have encouraged, it is difficult to equate the loving attention to nature demonstrated by the stammering Percy Taverner to an aloof state-sponsored environmentalism. The small kindnesses and voluminous correspondence of Munro to the young naturalists don't feel bureaucratic or centralized. The sensitivity of Joseph Grinnell to indigenous dispossession that he witnessed first-hand suggests that in fact these were the earliest critics of the "imperial eye." Harkin's advocacy for the rights of animals was hardly narrowing a world view. The subsistence hunters were banding together to protect the natural world. The destruction had been immense, profound and incessant, and those who loved nature had to defend it in whatever small ways they could. The armour of this group was science, their weapon, education. Without these tools they had no protection and their small advances to protect wild refuges would be lost.

The secrecy of the members of the 'B' has kept them unexamined for nearly a century. No historian has yet investigated their role under the various lenses of gender, race and class. A zoological lens would turn up a fascinating niche in the ecosystem. The 'B' vie with some of the small mammals for supremacy in secrecy. Also like the small mammals, the brotherhood were constantly under predation from Cowan's raptors of industry. His observation with regard to different marmot adaptations to the threat of winter in the alpine – a similar formidable threat to oil interests – may provide some insight here as to the thinking of the 'B.' "In general there were three avenues of attack open to the early mammal colonizers of this rugged habitat. The winter could be avoided, anticipated or ignored. Each has been successfully applied by one group or another of the hardy fraternity."[233]

Cowan never spoke publicly about the 'B' in interviews or even to his family, but when talking about his own career, he always credited the men who had guided him. "You know, the people who influenced the way you go are very important."[234] He wrote up their many biographies in the first volume of *Birds of BC*.[235] When

Starker Leopold died in 1983, his university's eulogy of him concluded with these words:

> Starker will no doubt be remembered longest by students, colleagues and friends for his personal qualities. Love of the outdoors, great personal warmth, sensitivity to others, profound appreciation and respect for the intricate beauty of nature: these were characteristics which knit his life to those of his legions of friends in intimately personal ways.[236]

It could have been the eulogy for any of them.

Cowan left the files containing the privately published *Lessons* and correspondence as part of his personal collection, appropriately labelled 'B'. The 'B's network was widespread and they built upon already existing societies, fraternities, professional associations and friendships around North America to extend and strengthen their influence. Cowan landed right into their circle from his teenage years onwards. For an impressionable and expansive young mind, gaining entry to this cohort at a formative time was critical in every way.

The experiences of the 'B' guided Cowan through his own life. Attacks on scientists had come from highly influential corporate interests for a century and were to continue for the rest of his life. His response would echo his mentors: work quietly through networks. In 1984 he was still active in challenging a round of serious budget cuts to the Canadian Wildlife Service. In a letter to a colleague, he writes, "I understand that the assistant deputy minister is the man responsible. His background is agriculture and he looks upon wildlife as a nuisance value at best."[237]

That same year, his student and close friend Bristol Foster made a big splash on the front page of the provincial capital newspaper when he resigned his post as director of the Ecological Reserves Unit after a decade. The headline read "B.C.-muzzled Expert Quits Ecology Post." A change in government to conservative interests had brought a sea change to the unit, and Foster, a mammalogist and PhD student of Cowan's, wrote: "We're told no more public speaking ... no more proselytizing – that's the word they're using – no more promoting ecological reserves ... But they really want bureaucrats – grey, clawless pussycats – who just do quietly what they're told..."[238]

In a 2001 interview, Cowan detected another cycle of suppression of scientists:

> At the moment we are going through a swing and I don't see where that swing is going to end, because the boundary is getting farther and farther to the ultraconservative. Those are the sort of people who will say: What value is a grizzly anyway? If you ask that question you are certainly labelling yourself as totally without knowledge of the world in which you live.[239]

Cowan was responding this time to a wave of new attacks sparked by material such as *Off Limits: How Radical Environmentalists Are Stealing Canada's National Parks*,[240] which had just been published by right-wing "think tank" the Fraser Institute. In it, the authors attacked Leopold, Muir and contemporary colleagues of Cowan like his friend Monte Hummel. The Fraser was using language almost identical to that used by their forebears from the previous century:

> One can certainly acknowledge the right of Monte Hummel or of anyone else to hold whatever eccentric beliefs they wish in exactly the same way that people can pronounce lakes, rivers, mountains, and caves to be sacred. The question of concern in this analysis, however, is that some of these eccentric opinions, which may or may not be held by individual environmentalists, do not provide a sound foundation for the development and implementation of sensible public policy concerning Canada's national parks. We will see that efforts to formulate a coherent parks policy on the basis of a kind of mystic ecocentrism introduces several additional and unnecessary constraints.[241]

The "unnecessary constraints" were any species, ecosystem or culture that may stand in the way of resource extraction. The exposure of any kind of emotional connection to the natural world was and continues to be the first line of attack by those interested in removing the obstacles to resources. The attacks on credibility were only too well known by traditional subsistence hunters as well. The desire by the 'B' to protect subsistence economies laid the groundwork for upholding constitutional rights of indigenous people to hunt. In his work in the Mackenzie Delta in 1947, and in his subsequent projects in the North as oil and gas began impacting hunter lifestyles, Cowan would be a strong advocate along with his colleague Justice Thomas Berger and close friend Tom Beck. He met Beck through the Arctic Land Use Research Advisory Committee and later the Canadian Environmental Advisory Council, which he chaired for a while. As Beck notes:

> [Cowan] had a perspective to identify with the issues of whoever he was dealing with, whether it was a rancher, a bureaucrat or northern people. He had an obvious primary interest in wildlife but it didn't stop him from being objective ... so that the social concerns of other people were alleviated and at the same time the wildlife would prosper.[242]

Cowan had time for anyone who had knowledge of the land, regardless of training or tribe. He was indoctrinated into a tribe bound by an allegiance to the land and an ancient relationship with it forged by hunting. As Hoyes Lloyd wrote in his First Lesson: "Lest I be accused of romancing, let me close with the thought that imagination supplies the bond in historical enquiries that link together the broken fragment of tradition."[243]

PART 2
THE FORMATIVE YEARS: 1927–1929

CHAPTER 5

"You couldn't just go out with a pair of field glasses and see the things. You had to really get at it and study them."

Vancouver, 1927

Cowan's correspondence with J.A. Munro sparked a much greater scientific bent. His trapping and shooting skills (for food) had given him the opportunity to see in his hands the subtle differences of the animals he was observing. Now he started to notice not just the differences between species of mice and shrew, but the even more subtle differences between the same species up the mountain, on an island or at sea level, something that was nearly impossible to do without having them together for comparison. "At this time, I had been setting out little traps mostly for mice and shrews and I began to realize the extraordinary wealth of small mammals that there were. One of the things that attracted me was they were more difficult. You couldn't just go out with a pair of field glasses and see the things. You had to really get at it and study them."[244]

At the time the young Cowan was collecting mice, only one species was recognized, but it was obvious to him that there was more to the evolutionary story than that. His early conjecture on "undescribed" deer mouse species was proven correct by later DNA testing; but obviously a lab can't come anywhere close to replicating the experience of crawling through dense bush on islands up the BC coast. Cowan developed a mouse's-eye view of life in the species' highly volatile environment. When he was a budding scientist back in 1927, there was a dearth of teachers to encourage him on his path. Cowan had entered North Vancouver High School, which, though new, had no biology teacher. The school (now gone) was in a pastiche building on 23rd Street East, with around 300 students divided into 11 classes. As one of the students wrote in 1927, "For the recreation of the student the high school possesses a very fine and extensive library consisting of two pocket dictionaries and one edition of *Mother Goose Tales* and other tragedies."[246] There was, however, a physics teacher, D.L. Shaw:

> A fellow that was one of the worst teachers (there were plenty of them), as he could not keep order in his class. It was slightly hidden chaos in his classroom. But if he sensed that you were slightly interested in his topic there was nothing that he wouldn't help you

with. I found physics fascinating, it was the world I was living in … So he got the idea I was interested and I was. So after the first exam when I made a first class mark on it, he encouraged me to stay after school and he'd look up other topics, other questions, other problems for me and we would work them out on the blackboard. I got the top mark in the province in the exams for physics. I could have gone into physics but I was in first year biology in university and I found that you could make a living at this beautiful stuff – biology.[247]

What it lacked in resources, however, the school made up in its own literary, sporting and outdoor pursuits. The annual is full of natural history essays, poems, jokes and photos of class picnics to Horseshoe Bay, Kennedy Lake and waterfalls on the North Shore and sledding and skiing on Grouse Mountain. In his graduating year, Ian Cowan was described in his high school annual this way:

White-footed Mouse, or Deer Mouse nursing four young

Peromyscus maniculatus

This mammal is perhaps the most plastic of all North American species and has given rise to many subspecies with very easily appreciated external and internal differences. Most of the islands along the coast of the province are inhabited by the species, and the isolation so achieved has fostered the development of new forms. Several of these have already been described and named but it is known that undescribed forms remain.[245]

> I may be tall, I may be thin,
> But I'm a blame good fellow for the state I'm in.
>
> Ian is one of our well-known students. He is a faithful worker and sure to succeed in his future occupation. Sickness has kept Ian from taking an active part in school athletics but he has shown his splendid school spirit by aiding us in our literary societies. Even from first year he has been seen on the platform on many occasions. Ian has a kindly disposition and a keen sense of humour and his hearty laugh may be often heard in Room 1.
>
> Favourite occupation: Trying to prove a point in literature without laughing.
>
> Pet expression: "I can't do the bally thing."[248]

Cowan's illness – most probably a lingering chest infection, as he later tested TB positive – which kept him from rugby or basketball, kept his energy on his naturalist activities. The school had little capacity or resources to meet his zoological interests, so Laura Cowan was tracking down her own prey: the serious researchers of birds and mammals to meet her son's insatiable appetite for information. She was also about to give birth to her last daughter, Pamela, and anxious to launch her eldest son on a secure "interest track."

The Vancouver Natural History Society had been started in 1918 under the leadership of UBC botanist John Davidson, another Scotsman with roots in the Aberdeen Working Man's Natural History and Scientific Society. The VNHS had provided a good venue for Vancouverites, but by 1927 a rift had developed in the group. According to both Cowan and his long-time friend Bert Brink (a plant scientist whose rarely used full name was Dr. Vernon Cuthbert Brink), the society was not friendly to the zoologists and "collectors" of specimens. Recalls Brink:

Olympic Phenacomys
[Heather Vole] runway and nest

Phenacomys intermedius olympicus

The phenacomys is the rarest mouse in the Alta Lake region. It is known to us from two specimens – a subadult male, No. 678 I. McT. C., taken August 3rd 1928 in Avalanche Pass altitude 5,500 feet, and an adult male, No. 1064 K.R., taken at the same locality July 21st 1932.[251]

> [Davidson's] focus was on botany, first and foremost. He tolerated birders, like [J.D.] Turnbull; he tolerated the microscopists … And he distanced himself to some degree from the zoology people as well … I'm very well aware of the considerable disaffection with John in many quarters; but at the same time, the people on that side did not in fairness recognize John's pre-eminent qualities as well. A little bit of disaffection on both sides, if I might say.[249]

For Cowan, the rift was opportune, as it led to a smaller covey of "serious" students and collectors of birds, mammals and insects who had broken off from the society and formed the Burrard Field-Naturalists. They met at the provincial museum in the old Carnegie Building at Main and Hastings. Probably it was Munro who tipped off the boy about the brand new group and that there was going to be a fellow named Kenneth Racey (another member of the 'B') giving a talk on the small mammals of British Columbia. Cowan would have encountered Racey then as a very fit man with close-cropped dark hair, a dapper moustache and wire spectacles.

The lecture that night covered the landscapes Racey had been trekking through and the wide variety of small mammals he had been trapping, preparing and identifying for the national and provincial museums. He was presenting findings on his mammal work from around the coast, into the dry interior around Kamloops and up Howe Sound, where, as he and Cowan would write in a paper seven years later, "the fauna of Alta Lake contains several kinds of mammals that reflect in their external and cranial characters a transition from conditions usually associated with coastal races to conditions that characterize the dry-belt races of the same mammals."[250] This "transition zone" was the very stuff of evolution. (In 1935 subspecies were given their own common names in the spirit of diversity, but this fashion has changed in most cases to just one common species name, which is included in square brackets for clarity.)

Cowan, himself still a "subadult male," was riveted by Racey. "I listened to this lecture with great interest and afterwards went up to talk to him. He sensed that I was quite serious and said: 'Look I have a large collection, why don't you come up sometime and see it?'"[252] Cowan went to his house at 1st Avenue and Point Grey in Vancouver, one of the tall houses lining the avenue with a clear view out over English Bay. Racey took him up to his attic in which there were three rooms full of "beautifully prepared specimens and beautifully cared for."[253] There was no looking back for Cowan. Amongst Racey's artifacts was also an extensive bird collection on which he had published scientific articles, providing the ornithological authority for Cowan. Racey was probably the first role model that captured all Cowan's interests, including his sharp marksmanship and mountain savvy.

Kenneth Racey immediately took the young Cowan under his ornithological wing. The Racey family had similar interests and background to the Cowans. Although a businessman, Racey came from an old Montreal medical family with connections to Edinburgh and naturalist roots. His great-grandfather John Racey had studied at the University of Edinburgh in 1829, taking courses in botany and what was then called natural philosophy besides attending lectures on medical subjects. Cowan's ancestor John Hutton Balfour was doing botany and medicine at Edinburgh at exactly the same time, between 1824 and 1832. Undoubtedly the two would have met or at least been moving in the same societies, enjoying the same heady atmosphere and attending professor Robert Graham's botany classes.[255] John Racey had been a keen naturalist and spent time walking in the Highlands during his studies, the descriptions of which had been recorded and passed down to his progeny by his wife Suzanna after his premature death.

Having served as house surgeon of the Cholera Hospital in Edinburgh during the outbreak of that disease in 1832, John Racey returned to Montreal, where he was appointed professor of anatomy and surgery at McGill College. He had developed a specialty in treating infectious diseases, both in Scotland and Montreal, during the

---

**Olympic Meadow Mouse
[Long-tailed Vole]**

Microtus mordax macrurus
[*Microtus longicaudus macrurus*]

This species penetrates the mountains along the watercourses at low elevations. In the Alta Lake region ... in 1922 it was taken in small numbers; in 1924 it had reached abundance; since then there has been a return to approximately the former status.[254]

epidemics in the 1830s, eventually succumbing to typhoid himself in 1847. This elevated him to a high rank in the family annals, and a line of Racey physicians followed, all having attended McGill.

Kenneth Racey was born in 1882 in Montreal and was one of four brothers who had attended McGill, but "hard times had followed and Kenneth was the one who went out to work."[256] He continued the scientific tradition as a keen amateur scientist–naturalist and borrowed his physician-father's surgical kit to prepare his first specimens, the very first being a Ruby-throated Hummingbird. Racey had moved to Vancouver in 1909 as a purchasing agent in the logging and mining industries, mindful of the opportunities to travel as a naturalist in a new territory with undescribed species. He married (Kathleen) Eileen Louise Stewart in the fall of 1911.

Eileen's family came from the Maritimes. She too would be a strong influence on Cowan. She was a musician who had played in the Halifax Symphony Orchestra before marrying Racey and moving west. She was also a keen outdoorswoman, especially adept at fly-fishing. The Raceys had three children, all born in Vancouver: Joyce in 1912, (Kenneth) Alan in 1914 and (Robert) Stewart in 1918. By 1920 the family had acquired a summer retreat at Alta Lake, four acres west of what is now Whistler Village. Here Kenneth Racey did most of his collecting of birds and small mammals, Eileen pursued her passion for fly-fishing and the entire family used their cabin as a base for their extensive camping expeditions into the mountains.

Cowan was adopted into the family; the Raceys' house on 1st Avenue and their Alta Lake cabin became second homes. Racey taught the young Cowan all the finer arts of taxonomy and museum collecting, including the preparation of specimens to the highest standards. Specimen collecting perforce involved killing the animal, but rarely if ever was it described as such. Instead, euphemisms such as "taken" or "secured" were used. The relationship a collector had with his specimens was complex and scientific, but also intimate, as it didn't end with the killing or the eating. What ensued was the laborious and detailed work of preparing the skins. This had to be attended to quickly after the kill to prevent decay and ensure the specimen stayed in top condition. Out in the field in the 1920s, there were no easy options such as freezers.

The art of preparing research specimens (also known as voucher specimens or museum study skins) is very different from the taxidermic art of preparing display mounts for exhibitions. It has its own set of protocols and objectives for the taxonomic uses that are made of them. There have been some refinements to the process to ensure that specimens will last longer and can be used for modern evolutionary research. These include keeping tissue for future DNA analysis and avoiding the use of chemicals, but the basic techniques have not changed much in two hundred years. The art of bird specimen preparation continues with the curators of natural history collections like the Royal British Columbia Museum, the Royal Ontario Museum and the Beaty Biodiversity Museum. Skilled preparators can detect the signature styles of the early collectors, like Cowan.

It is no mean feat to prepare a specimen, even in a laboratory with all the right conditions. The author's first attempt, preparing just one bird wing, with limited tissue to deal with and no fat, took three hours. Out in the field, with mixed weather, mosquitoes and a race against time, temperature and fading light, the job requires speed, skill, steady hands and much stamina. The fatter the animal, the harder the task. A mouse would take about half an hour to prepare, according to Cowan's student Bristol Foster, who did his doctorate on small mammals. Foster is a scientist who bridged the worlds of the old collectors or alpha taxonomists and the DNA lab scientists: "…all you need now is a hair to determine right down to individual."[257] The ethics of the killing were not a big concern in the early days. There were few other options at that time. "Killing another mouse was never thought of as being cruel; the trap killed them pretty quickly."[258] Foster describes mouse specimen preparation with Cowan, an activity that occupied every second of their time when not collecting, sleeping or eating. Sometimes they ate and skinned at the same time. Cowan, according to Foster, was a master at skinning:

> Skinning is like taking off a zip-sweater. You zip down the front and pull it back. You pull it off one leg and cut at the elbow, then the other one and cut at that elbow. Finally you pull down the rear end and pull off the tail leaving the tailbone sticking out, and cut the skin off at the knees. When you have the body out, you go back to the skin and take any meat off the calf and arms and rub on hardwood dry sawdust and wrap a bit of cotton around the bone here and there – the tibia/fibula. Then you take a wad of cotton outside the body and start poking it into the head and turning the skin right side out over the cotton. You take your needle and thread and sew it up and make sure you can see the cotton inside the head with Orphan Annie eyes looking out at you. You pin it nicely to a piece of cardboard so its legs are in the front and hind legs out the back and tweak it so there is a smile on its face. You put a label on one foot with date, time, location, stuff like that. Finally you take the measurements. It takes about half an hour per mouse.[259]

The collector's specimen kit looks like the outfit of an early medic crossed with that of a fly-fisher: lots of scissors, both straight and curved, forceps, scalpels, paintbrush, calipers, scales, dissecting probes, hooks, bottles of powdered borax and alum, bone-crunching tools, string, air pumps, hypodermics, needles and thread, tape measures, pen and ink, wooden sticks and pins for mounting, dust shot, charcoal, canvas bags full of shot, cotton and sawdust, and labels preprinted with the names of the institutions the collector was working for. Racey's kit was passed on to Cowan – a green tin box with several trays, more than 20 pounds to pack, which held labels from both men.

If skeletons were required the biologist would have to debone the animal. Jim Hatter, one of Cowan's first grad students, recalls his initiation by fire: deboning a moose during a pack trip in the Rockies after directions from Cowan to do so for the university collection. Hatter was left for the day to carry it out and describes his tutor's encouragement:

> As he rode up [at the end of the day] he began to laugh at the sight of a small pile of bones and huge mound, 1.5 metres high of moose parts, of which no piece would be more than 12 kilos, the capacity of our small scale. I had weighed the blood, contents of the paunch, intestines and everything else. I will never forget how much that moose weighed.[260]

At the same time as preparing the specimens, the biologists would typically inspect the animal for infestations, toxicological damage, irregular features and disease. They would look through the intestines, inspect what it had been eating and whether it had intestinal worms. They would also explore the reproductive organs and determine the stage of reproduction, and look at the teeth and horns for signs of illness. At the end of all this work, Cowan rarely wasted an opportunity to eat the flesh if the animal was on his list of edible species. He admitted to having eaten most. After that, what remained from the field preparation could be left for the other meat eaters of the natural world. The entire experience of stalking, trapping, preparing and eating provided the field biologist with a visceral sense of the animal and its life. Working on specimens imprints the animal irrevocably on the preparer. Cowan could recall specimens that he had prepared 75 years earlier, remembering the species, the sex, even measurements like one particular pack rat's record long tail.

Zoologists today have a very different relationship with animals. They are either remotely looking at their DNA in labs, tracking them remotely (in which case they need to attach radio transmitters) or making long-term observations on live individuals in a natural setting, which Cowan had started doing in the 1940s with wolves. Given the declining numbers of many species, not collecting these rare specimens is a good thing. Cowan over the years was the first to identify and draw attention to the pressures that collectors put on already threatened populations. He was part of the new generation of scientists that challenged the old collectors. Conversely, there was no argument amongst any of them that the impacts of habitat destruction vastly outweighed pressures from collectors. Cowan staunchly advocated the continuing role of field biologist–taxonomists monitoring what was happening on the ground. "I'm not very encouraged about the situation. Mammalogists need a lot of training, and there is no one being trained. That is one of my biggest worries, that we don't have people out there."[261] Cowan latterly was highly supportive of a new hybrid type of science where the researcher still went out in the field to observe but collected scat and hair for DNA instead of specimens.

His concerns were not only for the diminution of scientific knowledge about what is out there, but also for the loss of the intimate connection which fieldwork affords between the biologist and the animal, its habitat and its health. "There are not a lot of people doing work on the whole animal. I am very concerned about that. The museum [RBCM] now has got a sort of a basic pittance from the government and is trying to run on what they earn."[262] He also was an advocate of collections for the wealth of information they held for population baselines and genetic information for modern evolutionary and conservation biology.

Today, specimens such as Cowan's can be a source of material for new molecular or genetic techniques, zoogeography, anatomy, morphology and, most importantly, planning for conservation.[263] According to David Nagorsen, mammalogist and past curator of mammals at the Royal BC Museum, who took on a major role in the revision of *The Mammals of BC*, "Historic specimens such as Cowan's provide the basis for small rodent range maps and handbooks which are based almost entirely on museum specimens."[264] To be able to determine ranges and critical habitat of species at risk is critical to questions of where public money is going to be spent on conservation efforts and which areas are going to be set aside for conservation. The most dramatic example of this is in the protection of unique populations, whether at the subspecies level (coastal subspecies of the Snowshoe Hare, Cowan's "Washington Hare") or the species level, such as the Vancouver Island Marmot. Scientists have to provide accurate information on the range and genetics of these animals; it provides the legal framework towards protection of their habitat. This is also what leads to the politicization of scientists and collections, when resource interests are competing with species at risk for the same territory.

In 1990 Cowan voiced these concerns for the future of the provincial and national collections:

> Effective curating is a first responsibility of museums of natural history. I fear that in Canada we are forgetting this. Where today can we look for permanent care of valuable collections that can no longer be nurtured locally? We are not alone. The Museum of Comparative Zoology in Harvard is huge and it's got a lot of British Columbia stuff. We could not get at it for the bird book. There was nobody there to answer the letters and look out the specimens.[265]

Today most of Cowan's specimens are at UBC in the Beaty Biodiversity Museum, but a sizable collection is also housed in the RBCM, from the period when he was employed there. There are small numbers of his specimens scattered in half a dozen other North American museums. The entire Racey collection is housed at the Beaty

Purple Martin

Progne subis

The Purple Martin has never been a common species on the south coast of British Columbia; as with most peripheral species, its numbers fluctuate from year to year. Kermode (1923) noted it was a "common summer resident" in Victoria in the late 1890s but was quite rare by the 1920s, with only 2 or 3 pairs reported for several years.[267]

except for his type specimens, which are at the Museum of Nature in Ottawa. Today anyone can visit these collections and see them with their tags connecting the observer with an animal, a place, a time, the conditions and a relationship. People can also access collections digitally through searchable databases, some of them attached to the institutions, or on international databases such as Vertnet.

When Cowan met Racey, back in 1927, Racey was five years into a major initiative of setting up another club, the short-lived British Columbia Ornithologists Union, with 19 fellow pioneer bird men and an ambitious agenda: the advancement of the study of ornithology and "to work towards the preservation of Bird Life."[266] Their unusual form of communication was "The Migrant," a three-ring binder that "migrated" by post to members scattered around the province, to which they added birding notes, readings and proposals. Occasionally "The Migrant" would "moult"

Belted Kingfisher

Ceryle alcyon

The Belted Kingfisher breeds throughout the province, including Vancouver Island and the Queen Charlotte Islands, wherever breeding sites, in the form of natural or man-made cutbanks, are near foraging areas.[272]

when the binder got too full. Only one original copy remains. The influences on Cowan's thinking about various issues are evident in this collection. The notes to Munro from Francis Kermode, who was the first president of the organization, give some insight into what was grabbing their attention: a commitment to end the bounty on birds of prey (the raven gets special attention for being a bird needing protection); the need to protect habitat; educating the public on the impacts of cats on bird populations; ensuring that all science and collections are shared for public use; and lobbying to halt the introduction of invasive birds like starlings and house sparrows, which had impacted native populations like Western Bluebirds and Purple Martins.

In the opening pages is the pledge "to endeavor to have legislation passed whereby the young students who are interested in the study of bird life should receive some encouragement ... by giving them permits to collect migratory birds for study."[268] Those collectors who had collecting permits under the Migratory Birds Convention Act were rare breeds themselves and in "The Migrant" the distinction was made between the two subspecies of "systematic" ornithologist that "collected, identified and catalogued,"[269] and the ornithologist who simply "observed and noted." Each was deemed as necessary "as the arms of a pair of forceps"[270] and both types were found in the membership, but the "observer must be prepared to have his statement doubted; as the bird in the hand was the only certain evidence."[271] Theed Pearse was one of "The Migrant" contributors who was not a collector but had built up a strong reputation as an observer/naturalist and conservationist. The tensions between the observers and the collectors in the Vancouver Natural History Society had driven their two arms of the forceps apart, albeit temporarily, with the branching into the Burrard Field-Naturalists led by Racey and Reuter Stinson Sherman in 1926. Racey was the ultimate systematist and Cowan became his acolyte.

The Burrard Field-Naturalists lasted only five years but their lecture offerings were impressive. Both Cowan and his father were members, as were other naturalists such as the lepidopterist L.E.R. Glendenning from the Department of Agriculture in Agassiz; J.C. Bennett, a Victoria botanist; G.H. Wailes from the Pacific Biological Station at Nanaimo; Fred Perry, who monitored impacts of logged slopes on salmon habitat; and the club's secretary, A.R. Snowball, who bravely tried to keep the wide range of interests of the membership met by inviting stimulating guest lecturers. Over the years, they held sessions on fairy flies, small mammals (Racey's lecture described earlier), bacteria, alpine flowers and aphids, fish boils and phosphate impacts on plankton, food relations of the sockeye salmon, the life of the ant, and kingfishers (the club wrote a letter to the Attorney General to protect this species).

The club had no more records after October 5, 1931. Archival materials for the Burrard Field-Naturalists contain correspondence with James Harkin about collecting, material about Fred Perry's expeditions, a "land ethic" and a letter from Snowball to Racey pointing out that he hadn't paid membership dues for three years. But the society was just one of many similar organizations that were mushrooming from the fertile soil that was British Columbia natural history at the time – there was a vast array of issues that keen naturalists were observing and a wide divergence of political and practical approaches to the solutions.

The British naturalists and historians Barbara Mearns and Richard Mearns, in their book *The Bird Collectors*, explore the shifting relationship between the collectors and the observers as ornithology matured and populations (of birds) became more threatened. Although "the study of living birds became increasingly more important and collectors became a mistrusted minority,"[273] the contributions of this fraternity throughout the western world were critical.

> Writing, lecturing, lobbying, serving on committees, founding societies, shaping new laws, undertaking biological research, establishing reserves and getting involved in practical habitat management, they challenge the modern perception of the collecting fraternity as a self-centred, destructive and objectionable subculture. While they do not fit the popular image of the dastardly bird collector, it has to be said that they do not fit into the new mould of green activists either. All of them were dedicated collectors for at least part of their lives and some of them were enthusiastic wildfowlers or big game

hunters to the end of their lives. *Some readers will regard this fusion of interests as natural – to others if will seem at best paradoxical, at worst hypocritical. It is, however, an unavoidable fact that many of the most important pioneering conservationists learned to respect and value wildlife through hunting for science or sport.*[274] [Emphasis added by present author.]

The scientific tradition Cowan was inducted into can easily be traced through the journals of the American Society of Mammalogists, of which Racey was also a founding member. The society published an historical monograph about their founders, who were said to have been "preoccupied with faunal surveys and documenting the occurrences and distribution of species and subspecies of mammals."[275] The preoccupation stemmed from a common philosophy "that if a specimen were demonstrably different from 'typical' individuals, it should be given a formal scientific name so that the fact of its uniqueness would not be lost to the scientific community."[276] Within their recognition of uniqueness lay their declaration of value and the foundations for conservation biology. It was this tradition that Cowan embraced throughout his life. As part of the 'B', he was supported in his relentless contributions to conservation.

Although no field journals by Cowan exist for the pre-1929 period, the Racey journals and the family albums for the late 1920s document a full outdoor life of camping and collecting expeditions which included the young Ian. Eileen Racey and her children would spend summers up at Alta Lake, and Kenneth Racey would join them as much as he could after a week in the city, often bringing his young acolyte with him. The trip to Alta Lake consisted of catching a boat from Vancouver up to the head of the Sound near Squamish, then boarding the steam train, riding it up to Mons Station next to the Alta Lake Hotel, and walking the short distance to the small family cabin on the lake, nestled amongst the mountains of Garibaldi to the southeast and Mount Callaghan to the northwest. In Cowan and Racey's 1935 article on the mammals of Alta Lake, they describe what Cowan would have encountered as he stepped off the train and explored that region for the first time:

> The main valley is narrow, presenting little arable land and only small areas of natural marsh. On either side, the peaks rise abruptly to heights of from 7,000 to 8,000 feet. On many of the highest peaks snow persists in patches throughout the summer. In some of the hanging valleys, small glaciers still exist. Timberline is reached at approximately 5,500 feet and on some of the mountains, noticeably Garibaldi and London, the succeeding 2,000 feet present large areas of alpine meadow, in July and August clothed in a growth of flowers not equalled in North American ranges other than the Cascades.[277]

CHAPTER 6

"Clad in her one blouse, she often travels hundreds of miles through the dense wild-animal infested forest, to warn her lover of a plot..."[278]

Alta Lake, 1928

A full set of summer correspondence from Eileen Racey to her husband Kenneth in the early 1920s provides an intimate look into the comings and goings of this isolated summer community that became the present-day international destination resort of Whistler. Much of the valley today is altered beyond recognition, although Alta Lake hasn't changed as much and the small cabin is still there and enjoyed by the family. The days then were filled with fly-fishing, bird watching, hikes to waterfalls, berry gathering, swimming in the chilly lake, wood chopping, trips to the hotel to deliver letters (and "swipe" more ink) and domestic chores. Eileen also shared her husband's interests and provided updates, a role that Joyce would also play for Cowan throughout their lives. "August 23, 1923. The lake was covered with divers [loons] yesterday and they went off in the evening with the greatest of noise you have ever heard. I have never seen so many up here before."[279]

Joyce, as the eldest of the clutch of three, appears to have acquired her mother's taste for fishing expeditions as well as her father's interest in birds and small mammals. "Dear Daddy, I caught lots of mice after you went in ... Yesterday I saw a blue grouse and her children."[281] Eileen Racey writes:

> Alan's little mouse escaped this afternoon ... I saw it coming out from under the china cupboard and it seemed quite at home, so Alan caught it and put it back in its box. It seemed quite pleased and started to eat at once. Imagine it coming back after getting away like that.[282]

When Cowan first meets Joyce, she is an attractive 15-year-old, a skilled markswoman, camper, hiker and naturalist in her own right. From her childhood letters to her father, which accompanied her mother's, she demonstrates her growing adeptness at fly-fishing, berry gathering and birdwatching. In an account of a nest, she describes it for her father this way: "The nest was made of sticks, straw, mud, pieces of bark, string and leaves. The bird itself had a ring around its neck, a black head, and the breast was the same as a robin."[284]

Ten years later, Joyce would accompany her family on a backpacking trip along the Cheakamus River and her fiancé, Cowan, would note:

> Several pairs of Varied Thrush are encountered and one of them evidently had young in the vicinity as they flew around making quite an outcry. The female uttered repeatedly a cry I have never heard before. Two or three long drawn metallic whistles, then a series of *chuk-chuk-chuk* like the alarm of a robin but pitched higher. The musical combination was quite pleasant as was also vouched for by the ladies of the party.[286]

The cabin was a small, wooden, largely one-room affair with living, dining and kitchen space in one, with a large, enamelled, wood-burning stove as the hub and hearth. There was a screened veranda in which visitors could bunk. Cowan easily fit into the family routine and joined the women fly-fishing on the lake. He liked to attribute his learning of these finer arts of fishing to his future mother-in-law, whom he admired enormously. From the photographs and Racey's field notes, it appears the family expeditions between 1927 and 1929 to Mount Garibaldi, Black Tusk, Mount Overlord, Red Mountain and Cheakamus Canyon, Lake and Glacier were a formative time – both for learning and for his developing affection for Joyce.

Cowan wrote of his father-in-law: "He welcomed a shy young enthusiast to his study and his fireside, introduced me to the arts of bird study and the collecting of specimens of birds and mammals and took me on frequent weekend field trips with his family."[287] The photographs of the family[288]

Common Loon

Gavia immer

Autumn migration begins in late August and is still evident in southern areas in late November ... Sizes for clutches ranged from 1–3 eggs. Apparently, one female was responsible for the nest with three eggs.[280]

Mount Baker Chipmunk [Yellow-pine Chipmunk]

Eutamias amoenus felix [*Neotamias amoenus felix*]

These attractive little animals are abundant in all suitable localities. At Alta Lake they favour the rocky bluffs where wild raspberries, blackcaps, brambles, snowberries and bearberries provide an abundant summer food-supply.[283]

with Cowan catch them at the different elevations where they were collecting specimens, from valley bottoms to glaciers. For the growing scientific community, mountains were pivotal at this time for throwing light on evolution. The remarkable adaptations and speciation in the flora and fauna as one moves up the mountain were the focus for many of the pioneering taxonomists – Racey being no exception. He had introduced the young Cowan to the new concept of Transcontinental Life Zones – the landscape classification system developed by C. Hart Merriam in 1889 that took into account not only longitude and latitude but altitude – and by proxy, temperature and precipitation. Cowan was later to meet his hero Merriam in Berkeley when he went to do his PhD, and he was much taken with the great scientist's conceptualizing of the landscape:

> [Merriam] got that idea when he was doing some fieldwork in Arizona, and he was looking at San Francisco Mountain. You stand in the desert, then you've got brush and then trees and then no trees. So on that mountain, he could see the transition zones. There were hundreds of people that looked at that mountain but he was the first one to say: "Wow, I could draw lines along them. What's going on here?" That vision is exactly the same vision that led to the discovery of antibiotics. You look at the world from what's behind it – your mind is looking through your eyes.[289]

Varied Thrush

Ixoreus naevius

The nest is a bulky cup of grass, moss and rootlets, on a base of twigs. It is usually lined with fine grass, although leaves and shredded red-cedar bark are also frequent components ... In mountainous areas the Varied Thrush occurs from sea level to near 2000 m elevation.... Noteworthy records: Whistler Mountain, 24 June 1924 – many nesting.[285]

Merriam's ideas were to ignite Cowan's appreciation for the diversity of fauna lurking within the complex zones of the Coast Mountains – Joyce being by no means minor fauna in his life. One set of photographs captures the family and Cowan perched on large, river-rounded boulders by a creek amongst the thickets of salmonberry and salal, dwarfed by the old-growth Douglas-fir and Western Redcedar forests of Cheakamus – in what was called the Canadian Zone. Joyce and Ian are on adjacent boulders and the two young people are clearly enjoying their budding courtship.

Another photograph is taken of a camp at 4,000 feet on Black Mountain in North Vancouver, where the Mountain Hemlock and Yellow-cedar have started to thin out into clumps – the Hudsonian Zone. Their makeshift camp in a clearing consists of canvas tarps thrown over a single line, with preparations in full swing for the ubiquitous billycan of tea over a fire. Daughter Ann recalls her father's stories about the family hiking in the mountains and being overtaken by darkness, so they would just bed down together because they all carried a blanket and a rifle.[291]

Sixty years later, Joyce and Ian were at a rhododendron conference in Whistler and taking a break from the proceedings to venture up Whistler Mountain's new express gondola to have brunch at the Pika Patio. Joyce writes in a letter to her daughter Ann, "What a devastation has taken place to the whole area. It is hard to believe this is where we had so many happy summers when we were growing up and when you were small."[293] Another photograph shows the young Joyce in an alpine meadow at the treeline, above 5,000 feet – the Alpine Arctic Zone. She is studiously examining a freshly trapped Hoary Marmot while Cowan waits patiently beside her with two additional ones for her inspection.

Exploring the edges of the glaciers and the volatile zones of glacial outwash was another species bonanza for Racey and his assistants. One photograph captures them all lined up on a glacier en route to tracking down signs of the maze of tunnels and burrows of the Wrangell Bog-Lemming (also called the Lemming Mouse).

Seventy years later, David Nagorsen, in his update of *Mammals of BC*, noted there had been little advancement in the understanding of this small creature, "...the

---

Red-backed Mouse
[Southern Red-backed Vole]

Clethrionomys caurinus [Myodes gapperi caurinus, now a subspecies]

A characteristic inhabitant of the forests, this species is found from timberline to lake level under fallen logs, moss-grown rocks and in the timber-encircled rock slides of the lower mountain-slopes. The thick, mossy carpet provides adequate cover for large numbers of red-back mice.[290]

Wrangell Bog-Lemming
[Northern Bog Lemming]

Synaptomys borealis wrangeli [*S. b. truei*]

In 1924, Mr. Racey found this scarce and elusive mouse abundant in Avalanche Pass at altitudes of 5,500 to 6,500 feet. By 1927, lemming mice were extremely scarce ... It would seem, then, that the lemming mice have rather more pronounced breeding seasons than is usual in the Microtinae.[295]

least-known rodent in BC. Virtually every aspect of its biology, including distribution, taxonomy and ecology, needs more research."[296]

In every photograph, it is hard not be struck by the Raceys' jaunty style of expedition wear. Joyce and Eileen sport wool jodhpurs, sleeveless white V-necked cotton shirts with a red bandana tied loosely around their necks, and large floppy hats – regardless of weather. The men wear check shirts and canvas trousers cinched high with a leather belt. The choice of footwear is the laced leather boot for men and plimsolls for the women. Tucked amongst the photos for this period is a clue to their fashion source. The outfits are modelled on the 1923 *Montreal Daily Star* cartoons of the Young Canadian Girl and Man from a series called "Canada According to the American Movies" – probably sent out west by aunts. The cartoons were popular at the time for satirizing Hollywood's portrayal of Canadians: "Clad in her one blouse, she often travels hundreds of miles through the dense, wild-animal-infested forest to warn her lover of a plot …"[297] The Canadian Male is "endowed with superhuman strength … rescuing a Canadian Girl and making sloppy love to her, sometime under a pine tree and sometimes when they are drenching wet hanging on a log in the middle of a roaring rocky rapid, near the brink of a high thundering fall with death staring them in the face."[298]

A great sense of camaraderie and playfulness comes through the pictures. It appears that Cowan had found his Canadian Girl, although anything serious was a long way off; a post-secondary education and the depression were looming on the mountainous horizon. He had also found the perfect future father-in-law in Racey. Through

A darker Selkirk whistler peers from its burrow entrance.

Cascade Hoary Marmot (Whistler) [Hoary Marmot]

Marmota caligata cascadensis

The Hoary Marmot, or Whistler, is an abundant resident of the higher altitudes and sometimes even descends into the valley.[294]

Rock Rabbit [American Pika]

Ochotona princeps brunnescens

Rock rabbits, or pikas as they are often called, are among the common small mammals of the Alta Lake region. They are found in nearly all suitable rock slides from 2,000 to 6,000 feet.[292]

Racey he was also to meet many local trappers and naturalists, all of whom provided knowledge and skills. They included Alex Philip, Alfred Barnfield, P.D. Lineham, Mrs. Burbridge, J.W. "Billy" Bailiff, Fred Woods and Dr. and Mrs. Naismith. Bailiff was the trapper Cowan later worked with along his trapline,[300] collecting specimens like the Bobcat for the provincial museum. On one winter expedition in 1935 along Fitzsimmons Creek to Lost Lake, "The tracks of a bobcat followed the trail down from mile 40. It was interesting to notice that the bobcat had not gone through the light crust on the snow while coyote + squirrels, even the rabbits, went through at each step."[301]

Today the section of Fitzsimmons Creek he was walking is heavily diked and rip-rapped as it flows through the resort of Whistler. Bailiff's traplines are long gone and the light tracks of a Bobcat are less likely to be seen, but the legacy of Cowan and Racey's biological inventory is still evident today.[303] Back in 1926 Cowan was developing his insatiable appetite for acquiring local knowledge, and this would stand him in good stead as he entered his first year at UBC.

Small mammals, including *Zapus*

Northwest Jumping Mouse [Pacific Jumping Mouse]

Zapus trinotatus trinotatus

The jumping mice of the region ... are readily distinguished from Lillooet specimens by their more brilliantly coloured sides and sharper contrast with the dark dorsal area, the presence usually of a buff patch on the chest...[299]

Bobcat

Lynx rufus

A medium-sized cat resembling the Lynx but smaller, with shorter hair and more prominent markings. The feet are small and black underneath; the tip of the tail is black only on top and is preceded by one or two black bars.[302]

CHAPTER 7

*"It was only after I went to university that I discovered
you could make a living at biology."*

UBC, 1927–1929

U BC in 1927–28 was a new, small university in the northwest part of Point
Grey. Cowan would be publishing his second refereed scientific article on
the fauna of this campus two years later. In his first, he described the place
and denizens he came to know intimately:

> Point Grey is the name given to the point of land that lies to the west
> of the City of Vancouver.... On the west, the point ends abruptly and
> drops off in sheer sand cliffs; in between these cliffs the steep banks
> are of a rather moist nature and support a heavy growth of salmon
> berry, devil's club and sword fern, with numerous Douglas-fir, cedar,
> maple and alder trees ...
>
> So far as mammals are concerned Point Grey is rather peculiarly
> situated in that it is completely shut off, by the city, from all commu-
> nication with other areas of wild land.
>
> Civilization is fast encroaching on the remaining wild areas,
> so that in a few years hardly any of the more timid species will be
> found here. On the northwest corner are the lands and building of
> the University of British Columbia; on the east and south, building
> and road-making are going on apace.[304]

Starting as a student in this virtual island of biodiversity within the sea of the
city provided a unique opportunity for Cowan to witness and document the phenomenon of the disappearance of "the more timid species" as the islands of wild
land were cut off. He was aware of the early observations first put forward by scientists like Alfred Wallace for the delineation of species by geography, i.e., the Wallace
Line. The Wallace Line is a faunal boundary dividing Australian and Asian species that is also geographical in terms of deep continental shelf contours. But it
was the next generation of scientists like Cowan who really emphasized how human modification could be as effective and disruptive to distribution of species as
the edge of a sea, a mountain range or a major river. A sea of suburbia may in some
cases be even more daunting than a sea of saltwater for some species. It wouldn't

be until 1967 that Edward O. Wilson and Robert McArthur at Harvard would quantify and predict these rates of change and coin the term "island biogeography" for the next generation of ecologists.

Today the study of island biogeography has became critical in the study of conservation biology, since islands of natural areas within seas of modified and urbanized landscapes create the fundamental conceptual framework for thinking about species and ecosystem conservation – how much land, and where, needs to be conserved to protect species. The smaller the parks and the less connected they are to other natural areas, the greater the chance for extirpations of native flora and fauna. Streator's Weasel and the Puget Sound Spotted Skunk are two species Cowan observed on what were the UBC Endowment Lands between 1927 and 1929 (now reduced in size but conserved as Pacific Spirit Park) and both today are extirpated from the Point Grey region. Both species are dependent on forests and so disappeared with the carving up of their habitat and isolation from a larger population.

Streator's Weasel
[Ermine or Short-tailed Weasel]

Mustela streatori
[Mustela erminea fallenda]

Rare, single specimen, a male, no. 1028, was taken by Mr. A.S. Walker on March 24, 1923, and is now in the collection of Mr. K. Racey. Since that time I do not know of any specimens being seen or taken.[305]

As with Darwin, the study of islands became a central focus throughout Cowan's life. Islands not only provoked questions about evolution at work but also evolution in reverse – the simplification of biological diversity by human modification. His studies of island insularity of mice and shrews on BC's coast continued for another 40 years.[307] The long duration of his stay on campus allowed him to witness first-hand the swinging fortunes of other species with the arrival of humans. The Washington Hare [Snowshoe] population he had commented when he arrived in 1929, for example, had a brief expansion following the eradication of all its predators, but today this subspecies is on BC's Red (endangered) list. Conversely, the raccoon at that time was elusive and rarely seen, compared to today, when it is the ubiquitous top predator in the city with the disappearance of top predators and the prevalence of garbage cans.

When Cowan started at UBC, the biology, botany and zoology departments were very small and located in a few of the scattered buildings. The student registration for the whole university was only 2,000 and the entire graduating class from all faculties was just 300. His first-year biology course was taught out of the botany department and Cowan sailed through it with a first class. The zoology department had been set up by Charles McLean Fraser, Cowan's second-year professor, whom he counted amongst his most influential teachers:

> Fraser had a mind like a rat trap. When the bell rang he started talking. He didn't look at you, he just looked out over the class and started talking. When the bell rang [at the end] he stopped talking. But what he said in between was amazing. He had it all down pat, all in order. There was nothing exciting about it, except for the intellectual content. So a lot of people thought he was dull. He was brilliant.[309]

Fraser was a marine biologist, but he is best known as one of the pioneers of fisheries biology and oceanography on the Pacific Coast of Canada and the classification of hydroids.[310] Hydroids are tiny and very diverse predatory marine animals that come in every possible colour and shape and that have both planktonic and colonizing phases. From a lifetime of trying to sort out the amazing array of shapes and sizes of this one tiny animal, Fraser would have thought long and hard about evolution.

Fraser had first come to British Columbia in 1903 from the Atlantic coast, making the long pilgrimage out to

Puget Sound Spotted Skunk [Western Spotted Skunk]

Spilogale phenax olympica [Spilogale gracilis]

Most abundant representative of the weasel family.... This skunk seems to prefer damp places, and its tracks are frequently seen beside a small river that runs through the Indian Reserve.[306]

Pacific Raccoon [Northern Raccoon]

Procyon lotor pacifica

Rare, known only from its tracks which the writer observed on the beach in the fall of 1927.[308]

the unique women's research camp at Botany Bay on Vancouver Island (known as the Minnesota Seaside Station, established by a pioneering botanist from the University of Minnesota named Josephine Tilden). Fraser made his first collection of hydroids there, which established his reputation in that field. In 1908, when the federal Pacific Biological Station was established at Nanaimo, Fraser was called down from his teaching position in Nelson, BC, to take a research post. He wrote the first life history of the Pacific herring, did extensive work on all five species of salmon and researched the interdependencies of herring, salmon and sea lions at a time when bounties on the latter were prevalent and in Fraser's opinion not useful. It wasn't the first time government ignored the scientists, nor would it be the last.

In 1920 Fraser was appointed to head up the new zoology department at UBC and wrote his treatise on hydroids in both the Pacific and Atlantic. According to Robert Scagel, a seaweeds expert who became a colleague of Fraser upon joining the botany department, he was one of the last classical zoologists at UBC, from the time before genetic studies negated the need for such painstaking and elegant taxonomic skills of distinguishing one species from another.[312]

It would have been hard to feign disinterest in the emerging research into these hydroids, even with a dull lecturer. But Cowan tapped into Fraser's inclination to reward the interested students with his time. "He liked individual students, anyone that showed interest. The good ones he never forgot. He'd write you on your birthday. If you were going away on graduate work you'd go and see him if you were home at Christmas time."[313] In his third and fourth years, there were only seven students and Cowan had the almost undivided attention of one of the world's experts on a difficult taxa. He also benefited from Fraser's unusual lab style, which was to come in at the beginning of the term with a pile of books and these instructions:

**Northern Sea Lion
[Steller's Sea Lion]**

Eumetopias jubatus

During summer months, on and around certain rocky islets along the entire Pacific Coast of North America from California northwards. In winter months, often seen in littoral waters from the south end of Vancouver Island northwards. During periods of eulachon, herring and salmon runs, sea lions tend to concentrate in the river estuaries and often forage a short distance up some of the larger systems.[311]

> This is what we have to cover by Christmas. Here's the information, here are your slides … your cats, dogfish and so on for dissections. Here is one of the best lab books from last year and I'll be in the next room if you need me.[314]

Fraser would expect students to be improving each year on the previous year's work, notching it up another degree in elegance. "It was a great way to teach. I learned a lot from him.[315]

Another huge influence on Cowan was entomologist and naturalist George J. Spencer. Today at the Beaty Biodiversity Museum, one can wander from the Cowan Tetrapod Collection to the Spencer Entomological Collection. Spencer, like Cowan, was another colonial boy-naturalist, although he had been raised in southern India, immersed in insects, snakes and the real Kiplingesque stuff of boyhood dreams. After fighting in the First World War (having first completed an MSc at the University of Illinois), Spencer retreated to the undamaged landscape of BC, which was full of insects waiting to be described. When he was hired by Fraser in 1924, the collection consisted of "less than a handful" of unlabelled specimens.[316] Over the next 30 years, Spencer would build it up to over 300,000 specimens, wandering many continents to find them. The impact of the war on Spencer had been profound, and according to his daughter, Ann Taylor, entomology afforded him a reason to "set off in May and be away from the world and people until September."[317]

Cowan admired Spencer for taking an interest in the personality of his students as well as their knowledge:

> I remember him saying to me, "You've got one problem you need to correct. You're bright and you're going to go a long way. But you don't need to tell people about it. When we're talking you are too apt to say, 'I know, yeah, I know that,' and that gets a little galling."[318]

Spencer's contribution in pointing out his young student's idiosyncrasies was critical. He was a war veteran who had lived and travelled all over the world. He had great respect for people with practical and local knowledge, so he carried with him little of the arrogance of academia. This would be an essential key to Cowan's later success as a communicator:

> Those personal twists make a difference in how you come across later, how you relate to people. You run into all sorts of people back in the hinterland – old-timers. If you think you know it all, you're not going to get much information out of them. Just get them talking. If you doubt it, go and search it out.[319]

Spencer was also to have a very practical influence on Cowan. As a member of the Burrard Field-Naturalists Society and a friend of Racey, he was able to get Cowan his first summer job as a biologist working for his colleague and friend Ronald Buckell, a Cambridge-educated entomologist (who had also survived the First World War) and retreated from the world by collecting in the "undescribed" grasslands for the Dominion Entomological Branch.

In an interview at age 90, Cowan was asked how he had earned the praise of zoologists and botanists alike, including his colleague the eminent forest ecologist Vladimir Krajina, who described him as "a glowing example of the zoologist that knew more about plants than the bloody foresters he was teaching."[320] Cowan's response was, "Well you didn't have to know much. The rest of the foresters were trained as forest engineers. Their specialty was How fast can you take a beautiful tree and convert it into garbage?"[321]

Frank Dickson, another botanist and collector at UBC, introduced Cowan to plant physiology. Dickson had been conducting forest pathology research at the newly created Aleza Lake Forest Experiment Station and probably liked having a zoologist in his course who was interested in more than just Douglas-fir. As a collector, Dickson built up the early fungal collection, now in the Beaty Biodiversity Museum, from a single case.[322]

Cowan was also taught by the head of the biology department, Andrew H. Hutchinson, who had come from back east with extensive fieldwork experience and a broad background in botany, both terrestrial and marine.[323] His pioneering work in marine biology laid the foundations for UBC's Institute of Oceanography.[324]

Cowan was heavily influenced by these field scientists with less conventional research paths, at a time when they had more freedom to pursue whatever ignited their curiosity. "Those were the men that I studied with. I learned a lot about teaching techniques from these men."[325]

It was also apparent that Cowan had an extraordinary capacity to be enthusiastic about just about everything and everyone. He describes his student cohort as energetic and keen, and credited lots of his learning to his fellow students:

> We'd go to lab in the morning, hang up our coats and work there all day. If we had lectures to go to we'd go and then come back to the lab. In that way it was more like a graduate environment that I grew up in. For that reason the University of British Columbia was producing some of the best trade scientists in North America in that time. They were just ready to go on into graduate schools, and they did well no matter where they went.[326]

In the laboratory, Cowan was to develop his skills for dissection, anatomy and taxonomy and to augment his burgeoning skills as a field biologist and alpha taxonomist, which required collecting specimens. This was to extend over the next twenty years.

Trevor Goward, the current lichenologist and curator at the UBC herbarium, speaking about Cowan's legacy as a collector, described the personal significance of being a collector:

> In the simple act of collecting a species – by which I mean the act of gathering it, curating it, accessioning it, depositing it as a "specimen" into a collection – in that simple act, collectors "internalize" it,

Coast Mole

Scapanus orarius

In winter pelage, upper parts deep mouse grey with a velvety sheen sometimes imparting a silvered appearance. The Coast Mole inhabits a wide variety of soil types. It is most abundant in cultivated ground and in pastures but found also in second-growth forests and even in mature conifer forests.[328]

Mountain Beaver

Aplodontia rufa

Of the general size of a muskrat (12 inches) but distinguished by having almost no tail; head broad and flat with small eyes and ears and long whiskers; forefeet with strong claws. The mountain beaver constructs long, complicated burrows, 6–8 inches in diameter, opening to the surface here and there.[331]

transform it into part of who they are. It becomes part of their biography, part of the ever-enlarging past that they carry around inside of them. Should I happen later, even decades later, to come upon a specimen, I'm often and instantly returned to the moment of my first encounter with it: a whiff of fresh air, a Varied Thrush calling, who I used to be at the time, a good friend laughing uproariously. Specimen by specimen, you assemble a kind of internalized biography, legible, except for the dates and coordinates, to yourself alone. To the laboratory-based scientist who later studies it, it's doubtless just another specimen, one among hundreds or thousands. But to the collector, it's the most legible embodiment they'll ever have of a particular moment in their life's unfolding.[327]

Cowan's biography is laid out in the specimens lying today in the various museums, from his earliest in 1929 until his last specimens prepared in the winter of 1977, collected from his garden on Acadia Road at UBC for a Creeping Vole and Coast Mole.

Cowan's descriptions of animals were always elaborate but precise. He had an artist's eye for the subtlety of the animal's appearance. On the subject of communication he said, "If you want to be influential, use good vocabulary. If you only know red and not the whole host of hues from pale pink to crimson you can't be effective."[329] For every one of his specimens, Cowan also remembered an autobiographical detail. For example, he and his future father-in-law travelled out to naturalist J.W. Winson's farm at Huntingdon on a blustery March day in 1929 and trapped a Mountain Beaver, an elusive creature famous for harbouring the world's largest flea, at a third of an inch.[330]

No doubt discussions were had, as the two men crawled their way through the thickets of Thimbleberries and Vine Maple, on the subject of where Cowan should aim for postgraduate studies and his intentions regarding Joyce. Racey being well-connected through the 'B' and familiar with the scholarship going on at Berkeley, would have directed him to the door of the director of the Museum of Vertebrate Zoology, Joseph Grinnell, cousin of George Bird Grinnell of the 'B.'

PART 3
GATHERING SKILLS:
1929–1932

CHAPTER 8

*"The things you see on your first exposure are going to
be the most vivid, probably the most detailed."*

Kamloops, 1929

At the end of Cowan's second year, in April of 1929, his professor George
Spencer, through his friendship with entomologist Ronald Buckell at the
Dominion Entomological Branch, got Cowan a job collecting small mammals for Rocky Mountain tick research in the Kamloops region. Kamloops, which
sits at the confluence of the North and South Thompson rivers, is right in the heart
of the interior grasslands where the rain shadow effects of the mountain ranges to
the west and east create arid open savannahs of bunchgrass. These grasslands are
well-loved by browsing ungulates, burrowing small mammals and their once ample
predators. The town of Kamloops, at the time, occupied a small area of the southern
bank of the South Thompson; tall stands of cottonwood still lined the other banks
of the rivers. The northeast corner was the Thompson Indian Reserve and the flood
land between the rivers was grabbed by ranchers for hay meadows. Gently rolling
hills of grasslands and ponderosa pine cut up by gullies and draws filled with aspen
stretched out from the town, the heart of cattle and cowboy country.

Ranches like Monte Creek and the Douglas Lake Cattle Company, which, at
half a million acres, is now the largest working ranch in Canada, stretched to the
west and south. Because most of these lands were actually publicly owned, with the
ranches holding only grazing leases, the government retained a proprietary interest
in the issues of grassland and animal health. Grazing pressures in some areas had
converted the rich bunchgrass communities into dusty needle grass and tumble-
weed patches, so erosion and grazing patterns were one area of concern. Ticks and
grasshopper plagues were another. The Department of Agriculture had appointed
Buckell to investigate the myriad issues concerning grasslands and insects. Buckell,
like his colleague Spencer, was a naturalist too, and Cowan was much taken with
him:

> Ronald Buckell lived in a little shack on the north side of Sumas
> Lake. He had two horses and he'd just take off. He became a special-
> ist on the grasshoppers and bumblebees of Western Canada. He had
> collecting gear in the saddlebags on the packhorse. This was the life

these men lead. It was kind of a golden era. He was interested in the grasslands, so he would go all over and document them. He was a very nice, very quiet man. When I got to know him we would chat.[332]

Buckell was a Cambridge University scholar who had emigrated to BC in 1911 after finishing his degree in entomology. His contributions to BC's ecological health were as an early advocate against DDT in the mid-1940s, not long after this synthetic pesticide had been introduced – and decades before Rachel Carson drew national attention to the issue in the US with her book *Silent Spring* in 1962. His shyness prevented him from speaking publicly, so he would accompany Spencer to lectures in rural communities around British Columbia, warning against the dangers of DDT on the chief pollinators, the bees. At a Farmers Institute meeting in the Cariboo during the spring of 1946, Spencer, "delegated to do the talking" on behalf of the two men, stressed the beneficial uses of the vast majority of the two and a half million insects and "the menace of DDT."[333]

Buckell was definitely of the naturalist–scientist mould: a boy-naturalist, he started keeping a field journal of birds and an egg collection at the age of 8; the collection still resides in the British Museum. Having only just arrived on Shuswap Lake to help his family on their fruit farm, he had to return to Europe to fight in the First World War, during which he was badly wounded. He became a provincial expert on bumblebees and grasshoppers but also had a deep understanding of their relationship to avian predators. As Spencer, a lifelong friend and colleague, wrote in an obituary for Buckell in 1963: "Ronald was a man's man, passionately fond of the outdoors and adept at camping, hunting and fly-fishing. His love of nature began early."[334] The wisdom gleaned from this quiet man certainly meant that Cowan himself became an early advocate warning of the dangers of DDT, publicly condemning them in a lecture and paper in 1955.[335] Although not a specialist in toxicology, he decried the use of DDT and pesticides all his life. In a memorable address to students at the University of Alberta in 1971, he was no doubt thinking of scientists like Buckell when he said:

> Many dozens of men throughout the populous and especially the technologically advanced nations have been decrying our course for at least 50 years and seeing in it the seeds of human disaster. But their ideas came as tiny, almost insignificant sparks of light against the gathering darkness.[336]

A newspaper reporter wrote up that 1971 lecture under the headline "Put Ecology First U Grads Are Told" and recounted Cowan's historical analysis of how those concerned with the environment in the past two years had increased from these few individuals to a "conflagration of international dimension."[337] According to Cowan, leading the way were the naturalists, but also politicians, engineers, economists and student radicals. "Confrontation is clearly not the answer. This is based on naive, simplistic attitudes and upon an assumption that society falls neatly into the 'good guys' and the 'bad guys.' Many, in fact most of us, fall awkwardly into both camps"[338] He cited several examples: a chief executive officer of the top manufacturer of DDT who wrote a sensitive book on hummingbirds; protesters against polluting who also voted against tax increases to pay for sewage treatment; and students at anti-pollution rallies leaving behind large amounts of litter.

That summer of 1929, Buckell introduced the young Cowan to grassland ecology. For his part, Buckell was happy to leave his skilled young assistant, vetted by his colleagues, to get on with the task of quantifying the highest-risk candidates for small-mammal vectors that the ticks used before jumping onto the cattle. The Rocky Mountain woodtick would have proved a really interesting challenge for any mammalogist of the time. As a three-host tick, it starts its life feeding on the blood of small grassland mammals like mice before moulting into the nymph stage, which feeds on slightly larger mammals such as hares and marmots. The nymphs then moult into adults, which jump onto large mammals for their final feed before dropping to the ground with thousands of eggs to start the process all over again. Traditionally, the final host would have been deer, but the introduction of cattle had created a veritable feeding frenzy for the tick.

Yellow-bellied Marmot

Marmota flaviventris avara

This marmot inhabits the hotter, more arid parts of the province, where it is most abundant in regions providing an abundance of broken rock, low cliffs, or stone piles. Along the edge of the grasslands it invades the forest edge where suitable rocky den sites occur ... This species is one of the favoured hosts of the tick *Dermacentor andersoni*, the transmitter of Rocky Mountain spotted fever and the cause of the paralysis in man and domestic animals.[339]

For the cattleman, the ticks were a nuisance because the toxins left by the tick led to a paralysis of their cows which, if unmonitored or left too long by the cowboys, could lead to death. The cure was simple and quite miraculous when witnessed for the first time: once the tick on the cow was removed, within minutes the cow would be back on its feet and grazing away. Cowan's job was to locate the smaller hosts for the first two feedings of the tick and understand a little more about the different species' roles as vectors. To do his research he had to trap the animals and extract the ticks. In the course of his Kamloops research, he trapped most of the grassland rodents and prepared specimens from them. This was his first introduction to those species close at hand, and with the aid of these pioneer entomologists, the exercise gave him a classic introduction to grassland ecology.

Cowan started the job and his first journal entries on May 23 at Peterson Creek, which flows north through Kamloops into the Thompson. Temperatures were already reaching 96°F in the treeless grasslands, but Cowan scarcely paused. In his first 24 hours, he caught two dozen Yellow-bellied Marmots (commonly called "groundhogs" in those days).

It was the Yellow-bellied Marmot that was to be the subject of Cowan's first published article in 1929.[340]

> The females occupied the burrows away from the road and among the trees. The burrows in the open were invariably occupied by males or yearlings without families. One young one, surprised away from home, elevated its tail over its back and walked about on its tip toes until it maneuvered about so that it got me out of its way; it then dashed for its burrow and immediately put out its head to have a look at me. The young were very inquisitive and not frightened by bullets fired at them.[341]

He worked from May until September, and while he was doing his tick research he also put together, at the behest of Racey,

Red Squirrel

Tamiasciurus hudsonicus

Upper parts from grey to olive brown with a reddish wash heaviest along midline. Underparts white or greyish-white; tail as along as body, flattish but bushy ... Tips of tail hairs black ... Large quantities of food stored for winter use, usually consist of cones buried in or heaped upon the ground, or dry mushrooms placed in the fork of a branch near the base of a tree.[350]

a guide to the mammals of Kamloops. His unpublished manuscript of that name had a list of the 28 species he saw or trapped that summer, an identification key he worked out and a picture of 11 prepared specimens of small mammals. His photograph captures the small mammal diversity in just one small region around Kamloops. In a later piece for the popular magazine *Canadian Geographic*, he wrote: "From one barren-looking plot of land in the woods near Kamloops, I set out mousetraps on an area of 100 square yards and took thirty animals of eight different species. Nor was this unusual."[342]

From the larger marmots and weasels to the tiny Wandering Shrew, you can see the diversity in pelts, coloration, length of tails, whiskers, claws and body shape, all adapted to different niches of the prairie – all of which Cowan explored. For example, on June 4 he scrambled up 1,800 feet above Rayleigh on the north side of the Thompson to the sage flats and bunchgrass meadows, where he observed a subspecies of the Northwestern Chipmunk [Yellow-pine Chipmunk] descending 500 feet down a cliff to get water from a stream. The chipmunk got away but he was to spend considerable time over the years sorting out the large variation in chipmunks at the species and subspecies level.[343]

By June 16 he's on Schiedam Flats –
open, rolling country covered in flowering plants and bordered by forests of pine
and fir – noting that "a great many microtus [vole] burrows were to be seen, particularly on the lupine-covered slopes where
the land was honeycombed."[344] On top of
Mount Paul, he writes, "life is very scarce,
vegetation sparse, except where the wild
cherry and poison ivy are abundant."[345] On
July 1 at Pemberton Lake, he watched an
open area covered with orange lilies, where
ten shrews chased each other in groups of
two or three. "Occasionally one would out-
distance its pursuers and then stop and emit
a loud, shrill squeal, whereupon another
one would come and chase it again."[346]

By July 4 the mosquitoes were intensify-
ing enough to be mentioned, and the ticks
were starting to appear in numbers, most
of them occurring on marmots in sheep
pastures. While searching for marmots at
Monte Creek Ranch – the creatures proved
elusive – Cowan runs into a Long-tailed
Weasel which "wanders into camp while I
was eating my supper. It ran around making a thumping sound with its feet much
like a rabbit and finally took one of my squirrels."[347] He shot it and counted 208
ticks on it.

Long-tailed Weasel

Mustela frenata nevadensis

The long-tailed weasel is a versatile animal, found from sea level to mountain-
top in almost every terrestrial habitat.
In British Columbia it frequents river
banks, lakeshores, rockslides, forest
edge and prairie lands where ground
squirrels, mice, pikas and other small
mammals and birds occur.[348]

Monte Creek Ranch was owned by the Bostock ranching family, with whom
Cowan continued a long relationship, as they sent specimens to him when he was
at the provincial museum and later at the university. While at Monte Creek, he observes an unusual behaviour of the Red Squirrels during a particular "scorcher" of
a day:

> They lie flat on a branch, chin to tail, touching the branch all the way
> along. The front legs are allowed to hang down on each side and a
> grip of the side of the branch is taken by the hind feet. The tail is held
> perpendicularly from the body and flat against the trunk. Four or
> five squirrels were seen in this pose on this particular day.[349]

Putting together the guide was his homework; his day job was to focus on the
ubiquitous groundhogs. He befriended a young one and observed it over a period
of time in an artificial burrow he devised:

> The young groundhog got to know me and would come out while I

was sitting on its cage, but if anyone else came near, it went in and stayed in. Today the groundhog brought all its bedding out and turned it over in intervals and towards evening it picked it up with its forelimbs and carried it back into its house.[351]

In his species descriptions for "Mammals of Kamloops," which would prove an early prototype for his *Mammals of BC* book 20 years later, he recorded another strange behaviour of a visiting male:

> On August 6th, a groundhog was seen to come down the eastern cliff of Peterson Creek Gully, crossed the creek without drinking and started up the western slope. To see if it was a stranger to the locality, the writer ran towards it; the animal immediately became very alarmed and ran around crouching close to the ground and finally flattened itself against the cliff face, where it stayed until shot. There was a long disused burrow within thirty yards of where this animal was surprised and he could easily have reached it. The only inference to be drawn is that this animal was travelling and was not familiar with his surroundings.[352]

Cowan was to have an unerring eye for the wandering young of all species, especially male, in unfamiliar territory. He came across a male shrew that gave him considerable difficulty in identifying it. It was a subspecies of the appropriately named Wandering Shrew a long way from his usual habitat of coastal swamp.[353]

Wandering Shrew [Vagrant Shrew]

Sorex vagrans obscurus
[Sorex vagrans vagrans]

Size small, about 4½ inches. Strikingly different summer and winter pelages ... Mating activity begins in January and February, with litters arriving from March throughout the summer. However, there is a rapid loss of the adult females and it is doubtful if most of them produce more than two litters before dying. The population born in the year is almost entirely eliminated by August of the following year.[354]

Cowan was intrigued by the puzzle of the shrews and went on to develop taxonomies and map distributions of shrew species all through the province, including the most remote islands off the coast, with several subspecies named after him. Shrews are also highly adaptable, as Cowan discovered with his wandering male.

One or more of the 12 native species occupy every inch of the province.

On August 16 he took up a vigil for pack rats in an old abandoned shack on Mount Dufferin. He entered with a flashlight and found the first one, which came close to him and didn't appear alarmed. He set a trap and waited. And waited.

> 8 o'clock shot a pack rat off the rafters. No ticks. 9 o'clock caught a white-footed deer mouse. 10 o'clock haven't heard a sound. 11 o'clock ditto. 12 o'clock hear a coyote. 1 am doesn't seem to be any more rats in this place so I'm going out into the open and turn in.[355]

By August 20 the marmots were holed up for the winter and by September the bears were down feeding on the berries along the river and grouse were abundant. Cowan was also noticing the differences in the pelage of some of the species, such as the Buff-bellied Chipmunk (another subspecies of the Yellow-pine Chipmunk), which "show more or less buff" depending on which side of the Thompson River he was on. This observation was to stand him in good stead through his second year of university as his curiosity about evolution flourished and even more importantly into his summer job the following year with the famous collector and writer Hamilton

Neotoma nest

Bushy-tailed Woodrat (Pack Rat)

Neotoma cinerea

This native rat of the western mountains is slightly larger than the common brown rat. Total length when full grown is about 16 inches, of which 3½ inches is the tail ... In adult animals there is a large scent gland in the middle of the abdomen that is particularly prominent in males and gives off an unpleasant smelling, yellowish, oily secretion. Whiskers very long, reaching to the shoulders.[356]

Mack Laing for the National Museum. Before that, though, he was to meet Mack Laing's famous friend and colleague Major Allan Cyril Brooks, an artist–naturalist.

At some time, perhaps en route to or from Kamloops, Cowan would have encountered Brooks, who lived at Okanagan Landing, at the northern end of Okanagan Lake near Vernon. Correspondence from December of 1929[357] suggests they met earlier that year, perhaps at Racey's house. Cowan's memory was that

> Major Allan Brooks was one of the figures of my childhood. He, as a child, grew up at Sumas Lake. He and his father [W.E. Brooks] lived there and he became a biologist. In fact he made some money as a child collecting fleas for Rothschild, who was studying the

systematics of fleas. From then he went overseas as a sniper I think and came back with the rank. He was a good artist. He was a meticulous artist. He studied one feather at a time.[358]

Laing wrote a biography of Brooks in 1979, documenting his many biological and artistic contributions, from the fleas to their small mammal hosts,[359] many of which ended up in the Museum of Natural History in London and the Museum of Comparative Zoology at Harvard.[360]

Brooks was already a well-known bird artist when Cowan first met him, a reputation that was only to grow as he started to be featured in *National Geographic* magazine in the early 1930s. Cowan had gazed for hours at his drawings in *Birds of Western Canada* and knew of his cachet in all the ornithological circles. Brooks and Harry Swarth from Berkeley (of Vancouver Island Marmot fame) had written the most up-to-date list of BC birds, which had been used as the basis for Taverner's book. The contemporary wildlife artists Robert Bateman and Fenwick Lansdowne considered Brooks one of the "foremost realistic bird painters of the early 20th century"[361] and both were highly influenced by him. Brooks's attention to detail stemmed from his observer's eye; he had held every animal in his hand, having shot it.

Brooks was never mentioned specifically as a mentor of Cowan's but he took on many roles throughout his life that Cowan

Young **Swainson's Hawk**

Buteo swainsoni

In the late 1800s and early 1900s, the Swainson's Hawk was far more abundant and widespread than it is today. R.A. Cannings et al. attribute the decline to scarcity of prey, namely grasshoppers and crickets, on the breeding grounds and locusts on their wintering grounds in Argentina. Persistent shooting was also a factor. Population declines were most evident in the Okanagan Valley ... The last large aggregation (75 birds) was reported by A. Brooks near Okanagan Landing in 1925.[363]

acknowledged. Brooks helped supply him with antlers for his thesis and offered important ornithological information garnered over a lifetime. He also provided a litmus test for an overly zealous attitude toward the elimination of predators. Brooks was dogmatic about killing predators, and even by 1929 he was garnering disfavour from many of the 'B' for his extreme views on the topic. He was never a member. Historian Richard Mackie writes, "In British Columbia, between the wars, several naturalists spoke up in protest against what they saw as the depredations of a trigger-happy permit-holding clique."[362] The tensions are clearly illustrated in the correspondence between Brooks and Joseph Grinnell, director of the MVZ at Berkeley, who was to become Cowan's graduate supervisor and another mentor in waiting.

Brooks was a supplier of specimens and art in equal volumes to the MVZ, and the professional relationship he had with the institution was founded on its high regard for his skill as an artist, ornithologist and preparator. Even today at that museum, the walls are lined with Brooks's meticulous and vibrant watercolours of birds, mammals, amphibians and reptiles of western North America. His first commission came in 1921 when Grinnell asked him to paint a California Golden Beaver. The museum bought many birds, and Brooks's own personal collection of 9,000 skins eventually went down to Berkeley. The relationship was not entirely smooth, however. Grinnell knew Brooks as a great artist and collector, but also as a hawk killer, which Grinnell didn't condone.

In a letter to Grinnell in 1926, Brooks writes glowingly about Jack Miner, who had become a major Canadian figure for setting up a waterfowl sanctuary in Ontario.[364]

> You must have heard of one Jack Miner, he is the whole thing in Canada – the great and only conservationist. Well, he has come out as an out and out enemy of the crow and that means a great deal to counteract the little bedtime stories of E.T. Seton etc. I am really hopeful of sane conservation in time. Here we are having the hardest time to keep the cougar down, no chance of ever being able to exterminate, worse luck. Fourteen were killed around Okanagan Landing ... To my mind the greatest curse nowadays is the number of writers who make a living or profit out of nature writing. Few of these find that it pays to write of anything but the accepted theories, that nature cares for all.[365]

Miner, whom Brooks was eulogizing, was a religious fundamentalist and one who ascribed to the literal interpretation of the Bible and the 6,000-year-old-earth theory[366] that Cowan's ancestor Hutton had challenged 300 years before. Miner had seized the public's imagination and had done much to reverse the small steps toward ecological understanding that Grinnell, Hoyes Lloyd, Taverner and the rest of the 'B' had worked to establish. In his autobiography, Miner states he had no time for evolutionary scientists. Grinnell wrote back to Brooks diplomatically and forebodingly, "Let us start something in the conservation line that we can all agree on – the control of the fuel oil menace or the saving of our marshes in the West!"[367]

Brooks was not content to let it lie, wishing to publish rebuttals on the growing scientific aversion to predator control in the journal Grinnell edited, *The Condor*. Grinnell responded:

> I am just taking up the job of assembling the manuscript for the January *Condor*, and again I encounter your article (which in essence is a rejoinder to McAtee and Stoddard). [H.L. Stoddard was

one of the 'B.'] Upon rereading the article, I come to the conclusion that as a friendly act I can do no less than to advise you to withdraw it from publication. In my opinion, it is polemically weak and would lay you open to further well-grounded criticism.[368]

Brooks's correspondence railed against the scientists of the time, from William Hornaday in New York to Stoddard in Florida, whom he had accused "all of them of extreme disservice in the cause of practical conservation."[369]

Finally on April 30, 1930, Grinnell wrote in exasperation:

> My dear Brooks,
> This hawk controversy is getting a bit heated and I think with you that it has reached also the limit of usefulness for the time being at any rate. In this present controversy, I tend to be rather strongly on the side of the hawks!… I long ago came to feel that carnivorous birds and animals were good for the health of vegetarious animals upon which they levy.[370]

Over the years, Brooks remained an important resource for both Grinnell and Cowan on ornithological details. The specimens he left to the MVZ became a key asset of the collection. Cowan collected his paintings and a folder full of Brooks's careful field notes, drawings and bird lists from a variety of times and locales. In these field notes and paintings, one sees the extraordinary attention to the details of the animals and his skill as both taxonomist and artist.

There is little to go on with regard to Cowan's relationship with Brooks. Brooks was never part of the 'B,' although he was a friend of Laing. The Brooks family ended up moving to Comox to live near the Laings. Brooks and James Munro were sworn enemies despite being neighbours at Okanagan Landing; likewise his friendship with Taverner faltered over the predator issue. Brooks was of the old world of hunter–naturalists who stayed true to his principles of defending smaller creatures from their predators. Cowan wrote in his 80s:

> In [the] 1920s and '30s British Columbia still behaved like a game-keeper on a Scottish grouse moor. Its fauna consisted of good and bad creatures. A species seen as a sporting target and eatable was "good"; all those that sometimes killed a "good" bird or ate its eggs were "bad"; all else was of little importance.[371]

Cowan spent a lifetime distancing himself from judgments of "good" or "bad" species in complex ecosystems, and so his relationship with Brooks remained guardedly respectful. He went on to teach and mentor Brooks's son Allan Cecil Brooks, himself a keen naturalist and well-respected scientist, whom Cowan outlived by a full decade. Brooks Jr. did his master's under Cowan, looking at breeding birds in the Chilcotin. For the younger Brooks's obituary, Cowan wrote, "He was a very thoughtful man. His influence was predominantly local, which is very right and effective because that is where the action is. He was a good citizen and a good naturalist."[372] To commemorate the work of three generations of naturalists in the Brooks family, the Allan Brooks Nature Centre was established at the Commonage, an important grassland area for wildlife near Vernon, BC.

During that summer of 1929, in addition to his job of documenting the ticks and their vectors, Cowan also found time to collect various spring migrant birds like the Townsend's Solitaire, a grey, long-tailed bird of the western mountains that descends to lower elevations to feed. Cowan investigated its stomach contents and found four large caterpillars, two beetle larvae, four crane flies, fir needles and wood pulp.

Townsend's Solitaire

Myadestes townsendi

During spring migration in the interior, Townsend's Solitaire is a bird of snow-free lower slopes and valley bottoms, where it forages in agricultural areas, open forests, burns, clear-cuts and logged areas.[373]

In his later years, Cowan would remark about the vividness of his first work experiences in the field and the impressions those summer explorations into new territory left with him:

> One of the things too that I learned is that as you move around the world, the things you see on your first exposure are going to be the most vivid, probably the most detailed. You can go back afterwards and fill in the blanks and increase your knowledge of an area, but the impressions you come back with from the first time in a new area are the most brilliant and they stay with you longer.[374]

CHAPTER 9

"I think that Cowan is the real thing."

Newgate, BC, 1930

Ian McTaggart Cowan, 19 years old, 6'2½", 153 pounds, third-year student of zoology and of "Scotch" nationality. I have studied and collected birds for the past seven years and can identify practically all BC birds. I have studied and collected the small mammals of BC for three years and have made a collection of over 200 mammals covering some 50 species. I have camped every summer for the past 15 years under conditions varying from 100 degrees in the shade on sagebrush plains to the edge of glaciers. I can make up first-class skins of mammals and birds. It might be pertinent to add that I am a fair marksman, an experienced trapper, can ride horseback and drive a car.[375]

Cowan's excitement is palpable in his application to the National Museum of Canada for a summer job in 1930 as field assistant to the famous "motorcycle naturalist," collector, writer and artist Hamilton Mack Laing. Laing, known to everyone as Mack, had been collecting for the museum since 1922 and was on contract for an exploration of the mammal fauna along the International Boundary region from the coast to the Rockies. The project was reaching its final stages in 1930 as the museum sorted out the Darwinian problem of isolated populations of small mammals, like Pocket Gophers, that inhabited the "islands" of prairie. The account of himself in his application is not unlike the format of "description, habitat and biology" he used in *Mammals of BC* for the gophers.

Cowan submitted two recommendations with the application, from his two professors, Hutchinson and Fraser. Wrote Fraser:

He is not merely a collector, since he becomes thoroughly familiar with the specimens he collects and takes an interest in their habits, ecology and life history in general. Furthermore, he keeps in touch with others who are collecting or have collected in the province. As he has had so much valuable experience in the field, he is especially competent to undertake work as an assistant in the field.[377]

Fraser had aptly captured the skills Cowan was to continue to hone over the next 80 years – including his flair for networking. Half a century later, a contemporary mammalogist of the National Museum of Nature, David Campbell, sent Cowan a copy of the original 1930 application with this note stapled to it: "Just thought you might be interested in this application, which is still on file.[378] Cowan's network was legendary in both its geographical and its chronological range.

The most important recommendation came indirectly, from the museum's chief mammalogist himself, Dr. Rudolph M. Anderson, in a letter to Laing:

> You are now about the only freelance collector in the West who is competent to do museum collecting and is familiar with the technique, and as an old apostle we want you to help pass on some of the tradition to a disciple. We have a young man in view who has been recommended to me from several different sources. His name is Ian McTaggart Cowan of North Vancouver, now a third-year student at University of BC. I met him at [J.W.] Winson's place in Huntingdon last fall, and Kenneth Racey and Allan Brooks spoke highly of him; also professors Spencer and McLean Fraser of the department of zoology at the university. Cowan was working for the Entomological Branch at Kamloops last summer. He was not specializing in entomology but was engaged in tick investigation and was collecting mammals all summer primarily to look for ticks, but incidentally made skins etc. They say his forebears were naturalists, and he has camped and hunted all his life. Spencer says he is one of the best shots in BC and is a go-getter in the field. I had only a short conversation with him last fall and was much taken by him. Fraser was in Ottawa recently and we arranged to have Cowan put in an application … I would not want to wish a student assistant on you such as we had last summer,

Pocket Gopher
[Northern Pocket Gopher]

Thomomys talpoides

About the size of a rat, tail about half-length of a body, slender, scantily haired. Head broad, eyes small; ears short, hardly projecting above fur; large fur-lined pouch extending back inside the cheek from an opening on each side of the mouth … The pocket gopher lives underground in long burrow systems; the excavated earth is thrown out in small mounds. In British Columbia, it avoids arid areas and soils with a dense brush or forest cover. Where suitable soils occur, it ranges from valley bottom to alpine meadows.[376]

but I think that Cowan is the real thing and used to bushing it in the West.[379] [emphasis added by present author]

Cowan's combination of field skills from the "old apostles" and newly acquired scientific training under the tutelage of his professors at UBC made him a suitable candidate for support from Anderson, whose zealous mission to bring scientific rigour to the expanding National Museum won him allies and enemies alike. The final feather in the cap for Cowan was the involvement of Taverner, still head ornithologist at the National and author of the now exceedingly popular *Birds of Western Canada*, which Cowan had received from Jim Munro.[380]

Laing had been collecting birds for Taverner in the boundary region of southeast BC and was going to continue through the 1930 season. Taverner had built up a friendship with Laing during the First World War when Laing had been stationed in Ontario. Although Taverner was viewed with hostility by his colleague Anderson for the twin follies of being popular and not a scientist, he had shaped the national ethos for birds through his bestselling books.[381] Cowan said "they fought like cats and dogs all the time."[382] Regardless, to be part of a project involving two influential curators of the National Museum and headed up by Laing, one of its most famous collectors, was a major achievement for Cowan.

Cowan described Laing to Richard Mackie (Laing's biographer) as "a dogged, tough, wiry little man with great determination."[383] A description not unlike the one he was to apply to the Yellow Badger – one of the other species they were seeking to collect that spring.

Photos of Laing show him cruising from the American desert to the glaciers of Mount Rainier in search of the fauna astride "Barking Betsy," his Harley-Davidson motorcycle. One photo captures him standing on his bike seat, clad in helmet and leather, looking through binoculars for Sandhill Cranes in Saskatchewan – looking like a crane himself while he peers over the tall grass prairie. The articles he published for magazines like *Outdoor Life*, *Field and Stream* and *Sunset*, out of San Francisco, had titles such as "Barking Betsy and the Chilled Volcano" and "Panthering with Smith." Born in 1883 and raised in Manitoba, he'd come from a frontier farming family, with some Scots ancestry like Cowan and a pragmatic duty

Yellow Badger [American Badger]

Taxidea taxus

A medium-sized carnivore, adult males about 30 inches in total length including the tail of 6 inches ... A narrow white stripe runs from muzzle to shoulder and white crescent-shaped markings are present below the eye and ahead of the ear.... The legs are short and powerful; the forefeet with very long claws developed for digging.[384]

to fill the pot with wild game. Powerfully built, with penetrating eyes tempered by an outdoor life, and a military moustache left over from his days as a gunnery instructor with the Royal Flying Corps, he was a man's man of that time, but with a sensitivity and emotional connection to the natural world.

Mackie attributes twin passions to Laing: love for nature and a love of hunting – a combination still possible in the early part of the 20th century, when a less-populated continent made the two compatible. There was a niche for the type of "frontiersman" that had grown up in the prairies hunting for food, killing "vermin," and developing the kind of bush skills necessary for finding specimens for museum collections. Laing, anxious to follow in the shoes of fellow Manitoban Ernest Thompson Seton, pursued training in both writing and drawing. He attended the Pratt Institute in New York for the latter. He was a disciplined writer of field notes, as well as his narrative tales, with an eye for accuracy that the new scientists were looking for. He constructed a career out of it, first as an adventuring naturalist and travel writer, with over 700 popular articles, and then, after his war stint, subsidizing his explorations through gathering specimens for museums and private collectors, with over two dozen scientific articles or notes. Laing wrote to Taverner in 1936, "I don't suppose anyone ever had more variety in living than I have. I've never made any money but I have had an awful lot of fun out of this old world."[385]

That spring, Laing had been finally coaxed into the 'B' by Taverner, Racey and Lloyd. Lloyd had also established a friendship with Laing while he was instructing gunners and writing about the birds he saw over the airfields. Laing accepted the invitation to join the 'B', thinking it a "fine idea" but he worried that the name (Brotherhood of Venery) was "reminiscent of a certain ward of military hospital, all too well patronized '14–'18."[386] (He was referring of course to soldiers being treated for venereal disease; and dictionaries do in fact define "venery" as an archaic term for the pursuit of sexual indulgence as well as for the hunting of game.) Laing never attended a meeting, but their emphasis on mentoring was a good fit for him, as he had originally trained as a schoolteacher. This talent was evident from the many students, such as Cowan, who remained friends of his. In one of his First World War training notebooks, Laing wrote teaching notes for his students in beautiful copperplate calligraphy about the care and maintenance of the trainee pilots' wartime-issue Lewis and Vickers machine guns, followed by an equally graphic description of the conception of human life when the sperm swims its way to the egg – the two topics are seamless in their treatment and would no doubt have appeared equally fascinating to his pilot students. Cowan also noted that Laing was able to make a living doing what he loved without the stress and interruptions of business life suffered by Racey.

Laing's versatility is evident in the journal account the day he arrives in Newgate just prior to Cowan's arrival:

> Half clear in a.m. Not a strike on trapline except 1 *peromyscus* and a fumbled #0 from platform. Pack and leave 10:50 a.m. for Newgate via Cranbrook, Wardner and Flagstone. The first yellow *Fritillarias*,

Dodecatheons in endless numbers and white cress on the prairie. All yellow-pine country southward – no tamarack – the ground squirrel, the ever-present animal even out in rain in a downpour, also a red squirrel. Only two large hawks seen; 1 sparrow hawk; many mountain bluebird pairs, 2 savannah sparrows and a few Vespers. As we stopped to look over Kootenay at first meeting near Wardner, heard sapsuckers tapping below and ruby-crown rejoicing. At Newgate the ruby-crown song filled the air – tremendous singers and entirely different from the coast song. Made camp in evening, met McDonald Customs and Mr. Joe Williams general storekeeper. Supper with Williams. Beaver splashing in dusk below camp. *Purshia tridentata* [antelope brush] the shrub here; horned owl hoots and killdeer shouting.[387]

Killdeer on nest

Charadrius vociferus

The Killdeer breeds in a wide range of habitats, a peculiar trait among shorebirds. However, all breeding habitat is characterized by open space and minimal vegetative ground cover, at least at the onset of egg laying. Nests were shallow scrapes in the ground, usually lined with vegetation or debris gathered from the immediate vicinity of the nest.[388]

The Latin name of the Killdeer (translated as "vociferous") is well deserved for this bird. Once the most widely recognized shorebird for its characteristic call and widespread occurrence in North America, the population has experienced a drastic drop and is now a candidate species for assessment by the Committee on the Status of Endangered Wildlife in Canada (COSEWIC).

There was other chatter going on than just the birds back in 1930. Cowan travelling up to Newgate was blissfully unaware of the correspondence flying back and forth across the country among the 'B' that had placed him on the Boundary, in the field and on the job of cataloguing the diversity of the nation's wildlife. He was later to become the grand master of this landscape, but that summer he was still a young man coming of age with a gun in his hands and an experienced naturalist–collector to guide him. He wrote of this month:

> I was instructed to join Laing in Newgate as soon as possible after my university term. It took two and a half days to travel from Victoria to the village of Newgate in the Kootenay valley near the Montana border. The journey included a day on the Kettle Valley Railroad, overnight on a paddle-wheel steamer down Kootenay

Lake, more train travel from Kootenay Landing to Fernie. There I slept, and caught a small gas-electric car that ran daily from Fernie to Rexford, Montana, with a stop at Newgate. Mack had driven up in his new 1930 Chevrolet van accompanied by his equally new wife, Ethel They had a comfortable field camp on the riverbank, by the bridge, so we had easy access to both sides of the river. It was an exciting month.[389]

The "comfortable field camp," sent out by Ottawa in two large boxes by train, consisted of 8 × 10 foot canvas tents with folding cots, a kerosene camp stove, lantern, maps and over 200 traps, including the lethal "nippers" and "blitzes," steel traps for pocket gophers, cotton batting, sawdust, oil of caraway, formalin, alum, twine and wire for specimen preparation. But the details of collecting were only part of Laing's mandate from Anderson in Ottawa. His contract, dated April 24, 1929, also took notice of the broader ecological picture:

> The region where you work is of particular biological interest because of the extraordinary and sharply defined variety of climate and topographical conditions that occur and because these differences are reflected in the fauna and flora. While the principal part of the work will be making collections of mammals and birds, other forms of life will be studied wherever practicable and full and careful notes kept on habits and range of species which come under your observation, their abundance and economic relations as pest to agricultural and stock-raising interests, food and fur value as well as any information which has authentic historical value or bearing upon the life history and conservation of these animals.[390]

Professionally, Cowan gets to develop his skill as a budding ecologist to read and describe the features of the landscape that shape evolution, whether it is vegetation, aspect, physiographic features or human uses. His first landscape entries read:

> Kootenay River flows north and south through the centre of the area covered. On each bank of this river is the usual thick growth of black poplar (*P. trichocarpa*) with some spruce and juniper on the non-flood areas ... On the west side of the river is a belt of jack pine and Douglas-fir, with the jack pine predominating. Directly west of our camp is an area of farmland, and back of that a short stretch, about a square mile, of more or less open plain where the chief vegetation is the shrub *Purshia*. In this area, the [Columbian] ground squirrel and pocket gophers are very abundant and consequently most of the badger work is confined to this area for a short distance into the surrounding woods ... On the east side of the river above the poplar belt is a nest of jack pine and Douglas-fir of perhaps two miles width and

then the true open Tobacco Plains. [Columbian] ground squirrels are common. Pocket gophers give evidence of having been very abundant, but are now very scarce; badgers absent, probably due to the proximity of an Indian Reserve.[391]

On their first day, April 29, Laing takes his new young assistant to the neighbouring Tomlinson ranch to "get local dope on region."[393] Starting a trip with local knowledge was standard practice for the 'B' and had already become a trademark approach in Cowan's research. Locals weren't thick on the ground at Newgate, however. The border crossing consisted of a general store, the adjacent ranchers like Tomlinson and Smith, and the Tobacco Plains Indian Reserve up the road. Tobacco Plains was one of the six reserves left to the Ktunaxa people. The only reference to the "Indians" by either Cowan or Laing, in both journals, is the mention of the absence of badgers close to the reserve. Apparently, getting the

Columbian Groundsquirrel [Columbian Ground Squirrel]

Spermophilus columbianus columbianus

Extremely variable; occurs on the alpine meadows and in the arid grasslands and brushy edges of the streamside meadows at low elevations ... Varies with the habitat. Generally colonial, living in burrows either in shelter or in the open.[392]

"local dope" didn't extend in this instance to any local trappers at Tobacco Plains, but this is not surprising for the time. Ktunaxa was still the first language spoken in most homes, and the community had been decimated by tuberculosis. Chinook Salmon coming up the Columbia to Canal Flats to the north, which had been a major part of the Ktunaxa diet, had disappeared from dams and overfishing. Hunters for the once plentiful game were restricted from even going off reserve without permits, so local game close to the reserve were all that people had to feed themselves. There is no evidence that either Laing or Cowan was aware of or sensitive to these difficulties faced by the Ktunaxa.

According to historian Elizabeth Vibert, the received wisdom about "the Indian" by the early British fur traders (who would constitute a similar class of men to the naturalist collectors) was largely "defined by an imagination that was white, male, middle class and British," but also "not intractable."[394] Cowan was to demonstrate a very necessary quality for a scientist: the ability to keep his mind open; and this extended to his own early prejudices and cultural norms around race and gender.

On the second day, the work began in earnest. Wrote Cowan in his field notes: "Pocket gophers very scarce though they have been common. Took five on flat of west side of river – north of the road. Chipmunks on the west side of the river small and very grey; those on the east side larger and redder."[395] Laing wrote on the same day:

> The Kootenay River here seemed a dividing line between mammalian forms. The chipmunks and pocket gophers seemed so divided. The larger, richer-coloured form of chipmunk [*E. a. luteiventris* inserted later, Yellow-pine Chipmunk] was taken east of the river, while the larger pocket gopher [*Thomomys talpoides saturatus* also inserted later] was obtained consistently from the flats of the valley west of the Kootenay."[396]

Nearly 70 years later David Nagorsen revisited the Yellow-pine Chipmunks and Pocket Gophers of the Kootenay region and confirmed the importance of the Kootenay River as an isolating barrier among subspecies of these species.[397] In another entry Laing wrote: "A sameness to life on the east side of the river. Lonely to the eye."[398] Having both Cowan's and Laing's field notes from that spring provides some insight into the skill of Laing as teacher and the speed at which his disciple learned. In 1946 Cowan would master the distribution of the chipmunks through southern BC, proposing two new subspecies and putting forward the theory that chipmunks repopulated the southern half of the province from origins on the West Coast, moving east through low passes and getting isolated by large rivers and mountain ranges.[399]

The task of trapping these animals was specialized to their nocturnal, underground or arboreal habits. Every species required a method of trapping that capitalized on the animal's behaviour and feeding characteristics. For example, gophers have extraordinary sensitivity to air quality, being underground dwellers. If the gopher detects, from an influx of fresh air, that a predator has been burrowing after it, it rushes to the tunnel section that has been exposed and starts pushing earth in front of it. Trappers triggered this behaviour by funnelling air into a tunnel through a ventilated box trap. The animal itself would trigger a bar, pinning it down as it rushed to push earth in front of the hole. The ingenuity of the Pocket Gopher in defending its home, and of the trapper in figuring out a capture system – along with the marked differences in colour of the animals in hand, depending on which side of the river they lived on – were all equally fascinating to the young Cowan:

> The plants, the [gopher] may get by furtive trips a few inches from a temporary opening in its burrow system, but more often they are pulled in from below. It is a quaint experience to watch a sturdy weed quiver before your eyes, then, in short jerks, disappear into the ground.[400]

Each night, the two men would write up their field journals, skin the day's specimens and transfer data on each to their specimen catalogues. The time needed for these tasks was one of the limitations on how much could be collected in a day. And the nights were already filled with hunting rabbits to eat, laying traps or watching for the Northern Flying Squirrel. Through that May, as they moved from trapping gophers and chipmunks, they headed a mile south of Horseshoe Lake to an area they called the Tamarack Swamp. "It is a fair-sized patch of timber, made up for the most part of western larch and Douglas-fir. In this the flying squirrels are found."[401] Northern Flying Squirrels presented another particularly diverse taxonomy, with their own unique challenges both to catch and identify.

In a 1936 published article, Cowan provided a more detailed narrative of the creatures and their nest:

> On May 23, while collecting for the National Museum of Canada at Newgate, British Columbia, latitude 49 degrees north, I examined a nest containing three very small flying squirrels with the eyes still closed and hairless, which were probably not more than three days old ... The breeding nest was built entirely of old man's beard lichen, *Usnea barbata* ... An axe notch in the base of a spruce tree about 3 feet from the ground had been filled with the lichen, and the nest cavity was hollowed out in the centre of this mass of lichen. In the vicinity were several stumps bearing holes, from one of which a male flying squirrel was taken ... The male, while occupying a separate nest from the female with young, nevertheless has his nest close to that of the female. The two animals are to be found feeding and playing together each night.[403]

Baby flying squirrels

Northern Flying Squirrel

Glaucomys sabrinus

The flying squirrel is one of the most distinctive of all the smaller mammals. The outstanding feature of its structure is the loosely fitting skin that is extended in a broad fold from each side between the foreleg at the wrist and the hind leg at the ankle ... The separation of many of the subspecies depends upon such subtle differences in colour that written descriptions are of little assistance without comparable specimens in hand.[402]

It is not hard to imagine him relating the courtship of flying squirrels to his own situation that summer with Joyce Racey. Although no correspondence from this time still exists, it is likely that some letters passed that summer between himself and Joyce, now an 18-year-old woman. Laing was meanwhile extending his foundational lessons to Cowan on the subject of women, having arrived in Newgate with his relatively recent bride, Ethel May Laing (Hart). Ethel was hired through Parks as a cook, despite being an accomplished markswoman and naturalist herself. She would only have been permitted to be there as a wife, since single women were not allowed into the field by agencies like Parks at that time unless there were separate facilities available.[404] Laing and Ethel had courted long distance for 12 years, and many of Laing's colleagues had assumed he was a confirmed bachelor from his comments on marriage, which he likened to "Leander stroking the Hellespont with a grindstone tied to his neck."[405] He wrote in his diary in 1918:

> Women have never been great naturalists, never will perhaps, but they can appreciate Nature on the surface of things. The emotional and imaginative faculty of the woman is adapted to appreciations; the systematist with his 5000-odd skins from Australia and the Far East – that is another kind of thing.[406]

The Horned Lark is a bird of open, treeless country and its distribution is closely linked to the presence of such habitat ... The nesting habitat of the "dusky" Horned Lark consists mainly of overgrazed grasslands. In the southern Interior Mountains, we have late May and early June specimens; these were collected on the Tobacco Plains near Newgate in 1919, 1931 and 1949. No recent nesting has been reported from the east Kootenay, however.[410]

....

Neither Ethel Laing nor Joyce Racey would have fit into Laing's 1918 characterization of women. By 1930 Laing has clearly had some sort of adjustment in his view. He is fresh into a marriage, and Ethel is working alongside the men. Cowan's summer with Ethel exposed him to another woman of exceptional independence with excellent naturalist and hunting skills and a love of the outdoors. Joyce, being raised in a taxonomist's family, was similarly accomplished. There is no mention of Ethel in either Cowan's field notes or Laing's (not surprising, given these were public documents and meant to inform curators of the collection details), so no record remains of Cowan's reaction to Ethel and vice versa. However, Cowan in his later years spoke very highly of the women who accompanied their partners in the bush. Contemporary ornithologist Susan Hannon and mammalogist Heather Bergerud, both of whom observed the changing role of women in what had been male-dominated worlds, have described the prevalence in those days of the "acolyte" or "helpmate" wives who were every bit as accomplished as their husbands but could only get into the field as assistants.[407]

The two men were trapping at the height of the breeding season at Newgate with the intention of determining breeding characteristics and phenology, for which there are graphic accounts. Cowan notes:

> May 2nd shot nursing female rabbit ... May 3rd pocket gopher taken on west side uterus much swollen ... May 4th took female red squirrel, 6 foeti ... May 10th took pair of breeding Cooper's hawks, female had double ovaries ... May 23rd found flying squirrel's nest, 3½ feet off ground in hollow burrow in a small fir. Female and three small young taken.[408]

Despite Cowan's claims of detachment from the specimens, there is plenty of evidence of an emotional attachment to them. The influence of Laing as a popular writer is evident in the emerging "measured" emotionality and enthusiasm for life in Cowan's own writing. The field journals of both men describe the measured tasks of their days. Cowan is staying on safe ground:

May 26th
Went due northeast on range to small lake north of Tamarack swamp. On the grassy uplands I took a pair of horned larks and saw 6 or 8 more. Took pygmy nuthatch and female squirrel that had completed moult except for tail. Badger abroad at 4:30. Set traps for voles in bearberry in timber. In the high areas of the Tobacco Plains, near Horseshoe Lake there is a large colony of horned larks, a pair of Bartram sandpipers [now Upland Sandpiper *Bartramia longicauda*] and 12 or 14 pairs of sharp-tailed grouse.[409]

Laing writes of the same day:

May 26th
Perfect day – clear; warmth after hoary frost. Off to badger line at 6:45 a.m. Cold; not a badger had moved anywhere. In forenoon I explored Big Spring up tracks. Followed both rills to sources. A cold, mossy green draw but not a sign of small mammal life. A water ouzel [American Dipper] flew downstream. A small colony of ten pairs of roughwings [Northern Rough-winged Swallow] making holes under high brow of slide bank above railroad. Heard wondrous MacGillivray [Warbler] song like mourning in valley. Fox sparrow in song and the first black-headed grosbeak in his usual warble. Two evening grosbeaks passed over spring. In late p.m. we went to badger sets. In bank by road, we could hear the badger digging. The trap with live ground squirrel had been pushed aside as had the pinioned dead victim. Probably he went in a hurry. I watched the hole 'til sundown. Ruffed grouse drumming and hooter hooting.

Pygmy Nuthatch

Sitta pygmaea

The Pygmy Nuthatch has a limited distribution and occurs regularly only in the Southern Interior ... During the winter, most of the Pygmy Nuthatch population remains associated with old-growth or mature ponderosa pine stands ... Pygmy Nuthatch is gregarious. Throughout much of the year, it often occurs in flocks of 15–24 birds...[412]

Ian discovered horned larks on the prairie of Tobacco Plains and took a pair; also a pygmy nuthatch.[411]

We know a lot about Laing, both from his official field notes, which were lodged with the institutions he was working for, and from what he called his "nature diaries," which he kept informally. Starting in 1918 and until a few weeks before he died in 1982, he made entries every day: about the weather, the landscape, the plants he noticed in bloom, the animals he encountered, but also his sensitivity to the place – the "wondrous" and "lonely-to-the-eye" type of entry. In the margins of his notebook are exquisite pen and ink renderings of his observations: a Bufflehead landing, a River Otter fishing, a grouse displaying, the measured footprint of a Cougar or the nest of a wren. His artistic eye was also put to the camera, which was not lost on Cowan, who was developing an aptitude of his own for photography.

....

Williamson Sapsucker
[Williamson's Sapsucker]

Sphyrapicus thyroideus nataliae

Summer visitant to open forests of Western larch, Douglas-fir and yellow pine in the southern section of the Dry Forest near the International Boundary.[418]

....

Laing was also a dedicated letter writer, corresponding with and about his young acolytes, so we have some insight into the student Cowan, whom Laing saw as "a born naturalist – not one of those biologists made in college and interested only in the cheque his PhD would pull in for him."[413] This would have come as high praise indeed for Cowan. The Henry David Thoreau tradition of learning from observation was well embedded in the 'B'. In his journal of 1930, Laing tucks away in a margin an excerpt from Thoreau's *Autumn*: "It is only when we forget all our learning that we begin to know … If you would make acquaintance with the ferns, you must forget your botany."[414] According to many of his students, Cowan took this to heart as well and insisted his students have bush skills beyond book learning.

In 1998, when he received the Society of Canadian Ornithologists' most prestigious award, Cowan singled out Laing as one of the four main influences in his life and described that summer with him: "I already knew a fair amount about collecting and preparing specimens, but Mack was a master of these arts and I learned a lot from him."[415] Laing was one of the last great amateur naturalists–conservationists of the late 19th century who were "captivated by diversity"[416] and poured their energies into documenting and cataloguing it. Laing was, to use the language of the trade, the "type specimen" of the progenitors of zoology who "preferred the gun and trap and the bedroll and campfire to virtually anything else."[417]

For a young biologist at the time, it was an adventurous lifestyle and British Columbia was the bonanza for exploring diversity – with virtually every small mammal having far more variation in British Columbia than in all the rest of the Canada. For example, the range of four of the subspecies of the flying squirrel along the boundary were confirmed by Cowan and Laing that summer. (In 1937 Cowan would add one more new subspecies at Lonesome Lake in the Chilcotin, which took the number of subspecies in the province to seven.) Birds were just as rich in variation too. One of the birds Cowan collected on May 22 was a Williamson Sapsucker, which in 1930 hadn't been found yet in the Boundary area. It was recognized as two subspecies in his and Munro's 1947 book on BC birds: the one he shot at Newgate (*S. t. nataliae*) and one found in the Okanagan (*S. t. thyroideus*). By the time Cowan was working on the 1990 version of *Birds of BC*, the Williamson Sapsucker had moved north and west and nesting birds had been observed.

The thrill of the chase and merit badges for describing variation had seized Cowan's scouting boyhood interest and never ceased. Eventually the chase matured into theorizing about evolution, biodiversity, island insularity and biogeography and the increasing importance of protecting these genetically distinct populations. The advent of a new decade in 1930, however, represented somewhat of a watershed in the direction of zoology. The Boundary Study (and the subsequent coastal work completed by Laing) comprised some of the last large federal collections for half a century, with the collectors tasked to confirm the range and biology of the many small mammals.[419] The old naturalists were slowly being pushed out of their habitat by various forces. The collections were nearing completion and biology itself was diversifying. Budgets had been drastically shrunk, first by the Depression, then by the war and ultimately by increased competition from other academic institutions for the same limited funds. The museums, such as the National, were coming under the direction of scientists like Anderson and colleagues and were adopting the codification of the discipline that was occurring all over North America whereby "the ground rules and style of research in natural history were gradually organized into a format resembling what was accepted as 'science' in biology."[420] Anderson illustrates the state of the art in one of his letters to the men in the field:

> I have been somewhat handicapped in forming any ideas about causes for some of the faunal complications in the vicinity of Newgate. Was the altitude of the places where you took the pocket gophers and chipmunks flying squirrels etc. much higher than east of Newgate? Was the soil and vegetation especially different? What would cause the separation of the species or subspecies on different sides of the river? The chipmunks are different, the pocket gophers are different? They might work up either side of the river and not travel after the river freezes over or the natural flood may be different?[421]

Cowan was mentored in this tradition but was already a year into his scientific training, which would culminate five years later in the first statistical analysis of a population of mammals, with his PhD thesis on deer. That summer of 1930, Laing and Cowan would have been crossing the watershed of change in scientific practices with the same frequency as they crossed the Kootenay watershed. Twenty years later, Cowan would embrace the potential of laboratory genetics for determining species when it arrived in his department. He was hiring geneticists like the young David Suzuki in 1963. Cowan was excited about the contribution genetics could make to science, but he always remained a keen advocate for observing the animals in the field as well.

David Nagorsen, who fifty years later was to oversee the updating of the original *Mammals of BC* in several volumes, describes the importance of Cowan's ability to view zoology through a variety of lenses:

> In the 50s the "biological species" concept came along and we lumped all the species together. Then came genetics, especially the use of DNA markers ... There has been a virtual abandonment of traditional taxonomy, as they have just applied the genetic analysis, but what this is showing is that traditional taxonomy stands the test of time. What is popping up with the mammals is that they "lumped" too many. Some mammal species show distinct genetic lineages that suggest diverging species. Some subspecies are turning out to be distinct enough to be put back as species again. A good example is, the flying squirrels in the Pacific Northwest to mainland BC are very distinct from the rest of the flying squirrels. They are a different species in the northwest and should be a higher priority for conservation.[422]

Nagorsen explains that although geneticists are interested in how patterns of geographic variation apply to the genetic variation, they generally aren't interested in putting names on the various species. "That is unfortunate; the genetics has sped ahead of naming, and to have no names means the conservation of the animal is difficult."[423]

Back in 1930, concern about killing specimens from populations that might be at risk was just starting to curb appetites for collections. Anderson, in a letter to Laing after the first delivery of specimens that summer, reveals the emerging sensitivity:

> I'm glad that you are having good success with the badgers. The way they are being killed for fur is making them scarce, which is a pity. Too bad to kill very many for museum purposes, but the museum collecting is only a drop in the bucket where fur mammals are concerned.[424]

Unfortunately, the curtailing of the activities of the collector was also a threat to their way of life and the schism between the collector–naturalists and the observer–naturalists widened. In December of 1930, Racey was writing Laing asking him to join yet another association. This time it was to be called the Canadian Ornithological Association and would include Taverner, Lloyd, Munro and others, besides himself. The organization's objectives were:

> to advance the cause of wild life conservation in Canada by means of biological research; to acquaint the public as to the past history and present aims of the scientific ornithologist; and to provide the

means by which collective action may be taken to protect the interests of the working ornithologist.[425]

In a confidential postscript, Racey reveals to Laing a greater sense of the old turf wars within the movement between the "two prongs of the calipers" that he had identified back in Burrard Field-Naturalist days:

> It is believed that the greatest danger to ornithology as a science comes from the misdirected zeal of the uninformed opera-glass specialist and his followers. Criticism of the scientific collector is increasing and the public are being misled as to his aims.[426]

Also being crossed back and forth in 1930 was the watershed that was emerging between securing statistical samples of population, and overzealous killing rationalized as scientific collection.[427] That May, according to Cowan's catalogue, over 93 specimens from 33 species were collected; Laing collected 99. Cowan said of this time:

> If you were collecting in the field, you didn't stop short of 20. If you had evidence that the two sexes were different in size and appearance, then you had to have 20 of each. So we started doing that with small mammals. You measured the skull. Then the skull had to be part of the specimen.[428]

Anderson was to write Laing that summer and suggest that their collection of 200 skins was not too bad "for two men in a month in a new country under rather difficult conditions."[429] However, later Cowan was to identify the habits of his mentors, like Mack Laing and Allan Brooks, as being on the "ardent killers" side:

> Mack Laing had a dead tree and he lived right on the shore on Comox Harbour. He had a .22 rifle with a telescope sight that was trained on that tree and anything that landed there got shot. I don't think he wasted them all; a lot of them he made into specimens, but he can't have made them all into specimens.[430]

The uneasy division between defending wildlife and defending a way of life was certainly a factor to Cowan's student Bob Weeden, who recounted how he drifted away from the 'B' over the years:

> As it was conceived as a profession, wildlife management served particular interests in society, mainly hunting and fishing, but this became too restrictive. Like Ian, I had a loyalty to it. You can't as a 20-year-old look up to a group of people and admire what they are doing and then suddenly abandon it; you still in your head remain loyal.[431]

Cowan was indeed loyal to his early mentors and their values but also to the broader interests in wildlife. His great skill in his administrative years was to create

a safe and legitimate forum for parties ne-
gotiating the shifting roles of the naturalist,
the hunter, the scientist, the wildlife manager and the environmentalist within the
highly politicized landscape of land use,
wildlife and the internal tensions of the
preservationists and conservationists. Like
the various subspecies of chipmunks he was
trapping in Newgate that spring, there were
subtle variations of stripes on the different players in the conservation movement.
Cowan also never ceased to keep an eye on
the greater threat to these small mammals,
greater than their own turf wars – their
predators. He had no illusions about the
greatest threats to biodiversity that come
from human industrial development.

In 1972, as part of the US and Canadian
implementation of the Columbia River
Treaty, the Libby Dam was completed,

McCown's Longspur

Calcarius mccownii
[now *Rhynchophanes mccownii*]

Three records ... The third record is
from the Tobacco Plains, across the
Kootenay River from Newgate, where
a female was collected on 29 May,
1930.[438]

flooding 145 kilometres of the Kootenay River, wiping out these low-lying grasslands on both sides of the border at Newgate. Some of the ecological communities described by Cowan and Laing are now under several dozen metres of
Koocanusa reservoir water. Twenty years later, in an emergency address to the
members of the legislature organized by fish and game clubs, Cowan held little back with regard to the impacts of dams. "Wildlife in British Columbia is
your business ... The three hazards that confront fish and game in BC are flooding, draining and chemical sprays."[432] Despite warnings of this sort, politicians
didn't pause in the building of hydroelectric dams. No biological inventory for
the Newgate area, other than the work done by Laing and Cowan, was ever carried out prior to the flooding. The Ktunaxa people were never consulted. In
2012 the Ktunaxa finally issued a statement that the dam had severely impacted
the Tobacco Plains Indian Band and that the Columbia River system, of which
Kootenay was a part, needed to be managed to protect ecosystems as well as provide power and flood control benefits.

Against this historical backdrop, Cowan's grassland experience with Laing was
to reinforce his grassland "track" for life. Forty years later, in his involvement with
the setting up and governance of The Nature Trust of British Columbia, Cowan was
a prime influence in guiding the protection of such grasslands and their rarer species. The Trust was started in 1971 as the Second Century Fund with a $4.5-million
grant from the federal government for BC's centennial. Cowan was active in the organization from 1971 until 2002 and then director emeritus for the final eight years
of his life. In 1993 he wrote to Bill Schwartz, at that time a trustee for the Nature

Conservancy of Canada, to ask for collaboration on protecting grasslands with the national organization:

> We have now turned our attention to the grassland areas of the prov-
> ince, several of which are magnificent landscapes of great impor-
> tance biologically and as renewable resources. Despite the generally
> mountainous geography of the province, there are a surprising num-
> ber of large grasslands with very different histories, biological com-
> ponents and resource use or misuse.[433]

One of the grassland mammals of highest concern in British Columbia today is the American Badger. The BC subspecies is listed federally by COSEWIC as endangered. Urbanization, highway mortality and continued trapping by landowners have left fewer than 200 breeding adults in BC. In 1930 they were widespread across the prairie, but Anderson was already anticipating declines. Cowan and Laing trapped three, and many of their field notes were devoted to discussions of the wily nature of the badger, its ability to make off with their other trapped ground squirrels, and its smell! Cowan's 1930 notes include the details of the badger burrow they discovered which sloped down ten feet to a chamber at the end. Another journal entry includes dissections of the three males they caught. "Stomach of one contained three young ground squirrels and one adult female. Young had been bitten once in back of head and eaten whole. Old one pulled in four or five pieces and bolted ... Do not roam on cold or wet nights in the spring."[434] The American Badger was an appropriate metaphor for naturalists like Laing in more ways than just temperament. They were a disappearing species, suffering from the impacts of urbanization and a declining public interest in the details of the natural world.

Nagorsen believes there have been few field zoologists the likes of Laing or Cowan since, to have contributed so much to BC's taxonomy. "Cowan dealt with just about everything from whales to shrews and rodents and ungulates and carnivores, which in this day and age is very unusual and is an outstanding feature of his work."[435] These scientific descriptions still stand the test of time. Cowan's memory of this time was so vivid at 90 that if asked, he could reel off the species he collected and dates and places he had visited that spring 70 years earlier, since many of them were firsts[436] – and as it now turns out are lasts – for the province:

> We added much new information on mammals of the region. Bird
> highlights were Williamson's Sapsucker and Pygmy Nuthatch nest-
> ing in open stands of western larch and ponderosa pine; Horned
> Larks, McCown's Longspurs and Sharp-tailed Grouse on the ex-
> tensive grasslands of the Tobacco Plains; I understand all are gone
> today.[437]

McCown's Longspurs have declined by 90 per cent.[439]

CHAPTER 10

*"I hope that you will curb the impetuosity of your assistant
if he dares to tackle grizzlies single-handed."*

The Rockies, 1930

On May 30, 1930, the weather turned bad in Newgate and a telegram arrived from Anderson in Ottawa instructing Laing to report immediately to Jasper, Alberta, where he was to serve as (the first) resident naturalist at the lodge in the newly created Jasper National Park[440] Cowan describes what happened next:

> He caught the next train, leaving me his new car, his bride and the field camp, with instructions to get the outfit to Jasper as soon as possible. Mack was a trusting soul, as was Ethel. She did not drive and had a fear of heights, and we had lots of both; but she was good company, and closed her eyes in the scary places. We all survived the adventure as good friends. On the roads of 1930 it took two days to drive to Edmonton and another two and a half days to negotiate the rain-slicked gumbo track 250 miles from Edmonton to Jasper – average speed about 7 miles per hour.[441]

Back in Ottawa, Lloyd and Harkin had finally negotiated this first educational position in the national parks, so they were able to hire Laing, one of "their own," for the first naturalist–guide program at Banff and Jasper. An educational program would have been totally consistent with the aims of the 'B' – and right up Laing's alley. Harkin wrote Laing with a description of the country's first nature guide:

> A nature guide is a hike leader, a schoolteacher, lecturer, scientist and game leader all in one; in fact he is a walking encyclopedia of outdoors information. His job is to tell you the names of the animals, birds, trees, flowers and to discover with you nature's secrets that lie hidden to the multitudes, but in plain view of one who has eyes to see.[442]

The secondment of Laing to Jasper park also enabled his young assistant, Cowan, to take on the collection duties in the mountains by himself for the rest of the summer. But first he and Ethel had to get to Jasper:

June 5th
Left Entwistle a.m. Arrived Edson 5:30 p.m. 72 miles, road terrible, got stuck three times, once pulled out by team.

June 6th
Arrived at Jasper on good road. Saw many mountain sheep and deer. A ram ran 30 miles per hour in front of the car for 100 yards.[443]

Cowan dropped off Ethel, who was on contract to cook for the Parks Branch and would join Laing, who had already started as a naturalist guide. Cowan was now the lead collector, and he would rely on the guidance of the wardens to help him complete a study of the park's small mammals. On June 9 he hiked in to warden Frank Bryant's cabin on the Snaring River and made his first camp 11 miles north of Jasper townsite, armed with his traps, guns, camping gear and collection kit. A map in his notebook shows his camp was located right where the current public campground is today. Frank Bryant hit it off with Cowan immediately and he and his family were to become lifelong friends. Joseph (Joe) Bryant, Frank's younger son, later became a student of Cowan's. Joe Bryant describes the relationship:

> Dad had been a very experienced trapper but stopped hunting and trapping once he was in the park. Dad's experience as a trapper really appealed to Ian, as, although Ian was a crack shot, he had no experience in trapping fur-bearers and he really appreciated my father's skills. It was a mutual admiration society. Right up to my father's death they were great friends.[444]

Bryant Sr. fit the mould of mentor. He had left England in 1912 as a barrow boy of 16. He didn't see a future in England, so he emigrated alone, finding work first as a farm labourer in Manitoba, then as a trapper. During the First World War, he went back to sign up in the British Army because the Canadian army had rejected him for poor eyesight. He survived the war with only minor physical injuries and returned to homestead in the Peace River country. Then an accident with a horse left him disabled for general farm work, although he could still ride horses.

> One day an outfit of 100 packhorses was going through the farm on its way to Jasper. Dad signed on as a wrangler and never returned. By fall the Park had hired him on as a warden and Mum and her two small eldest children packed up and moved to Jasper. I was born in Jasper a few years later, in 1927. I was a just a small boy when Ian first came to stay.[445]

Frank Bryant's experience trapping and, as a warden, combing the mountains for signs of poachers would have been attractive for Cowan in his youthful quest for field learning. Behind the scenes in Ottawa, the 'B' were attempting to rein in the overly exuberant killing of predators by the wardens themselves. After the 1928 Parks conference of superintendents, at which Grinnell addressed the audience about the value of predators, Harkin introduced a new policy: wardens were no longer allowed to keep the furs of any animals they killed or trapped, so there was no profit to be gained.[446] In 1929 Harkin characterized his new wildlife policy as one where "wildlife is given absolute protection, with the further exception that war is waged on predatory animals *to a reasonable extent* [emphasis added] in order that the safety of the remainder may be made more secure."[447] He and Lloyd had been struggling with the question of what a "reasonable extent" of predator killing in the national parks might be, versus the bigger ecological view to which they pledged as a scientific fraternity. The wardens trapped to supplement their income and told their superiors they needed traps to deal with the periodic influxes of coyote, wolf or cougar they were expected to control, for the bounty hunting going on outside the boundaries was making the parks even more a sanctuary for predators.

Meanwhile, the scientific approach to wildlife management was getting codified in documents by other members of the 'B'. Aldo Leopold was at work on his classic game management textbook, which brought together his field skills, science and art, but it was still three years away from being published.[448] Stoddard was pulling together his ideas in the grassland areas. In 1932 Parks were experimenting with limited control of predators with dogs instead of traps, and Bryant would lead that initiative. "Dad and another warden, Frank Wells, got equipped. Dad bought a pair of wolfhounds to hunt coyotes and Frank Wells got cougar hounds. That certainly generated stories."[449] It wasn't until 1943 when Cowan returned to do a scientific study of prey–predator relationships in the park that some of these thorny issues would be put in a bigger research framework. His formative experience in 1930, however, equipped him well with the anecdotal experiences of wardens that drove the early, ad hoc park policy. As Joe Bryant pointed out, "My dad was no naturalist. He was interested in mammals, their forage and how their environment was changed for and by mammals, with a keen interest in beaver."[450]

On that first day, Cowan had hardly paused for breath before heading off to scout the Athabasca River with Bryant, when they spotted a yearling beaver in one of the sloughs. He wanted a specimen, so he took out his .22 and shot it, except the beaver bolted for the river. Cowan stripped off, dove in and grabbed it, but the current took him and the beaver downstream to a bridge where a carload of tourists were watching:

> I was slowly freezing, hanging onto a bush with one hand and the dead beaver with the other. Fortunately Frank persuaded the tourists to move on and I extracted my lean and chilled frame from the muddy icewater. With the temperature of the water there would have been little evidence as to whether I was a male or a female anyway, but I didn't want them to see my dead beaver. It was #94 in that year's catalogue.[451]

Beaver populations in 1930 were low from overhunting.[453] Regulations for registering traplines and issuing licences were only four years old and the population was only just starting to recover. This early exposure to trappers was to give Cowan empathy for the trapper's life and livelihood, as well as a healthy distrust of overly anecdotal information. The June entries are full of information about fur-bearing mammals. His first mustelid (a member of the weasel family) in the park was a very old River Otter on which he proceeded to do a full dental inspection. It had already lost most of its teeth. For Cowan as a mammalogist, dentition was a major theme. His students said he would always preface his introductory lectures on mammals with "they only live as long as their teeth." This preoccupation with teeth was to come back at him for his 90th birthday celebration when the condition of his teeth was speculated upon by his many students there. In fact, his teeth were relatively fine then.

On June 16 Cowan joined Bryant, his daughter Kathleen and Bryant's brother-in-law Syd Williams on a trip over Jacques Pass and on to Swiftwater Creek on the east side of the Athabasca to check up on poaching activity that had been halted the previous year. Cowan later recollected the firsts of that trip: first time in the Rockies, first time tracking poachers and first time with packhorses. The pictures of the time show a happy expedition. Cowan is towering above everyone sporting a new Mack-Laing-type moustache. Kathleen, in her late teens with her big floppy cowboy hat, blazer and britches, impressed Cowan for being so "good-natured given the miserable weather we encountered."[455] She later became an ordained Anglican minister.

American Beaver

Castor canadensis

Large aquatic rodents, fur dark-reddish and consisting of coarse, reddish-brown guard hairs over a coat of soft, dark-brown underfur. Eyes and ears small; tail horizontally flattened, paddle shaped and scaly; hind feet large, naked, webbed ... [Habitat] The vicinity of freshwater bodies in forested vicinity. Streams and lakes of all sizes are equally favoured, but swift-flowing streams subject to flash flooding are unsuitable for permanent colonization by beavers.[452]

Fisher

Martes pennanti

A large marten, much like americana in proportion but larger, males often measuring more than 35 inches in length. Fur dark brown to nearly black, often with white tippings to some of the hairs of the upper parts, and with throat patch small and white, or absent ... Being a larger animal than the marten, larger prey is taken. Grouse, red squirrels, hares, porcupines as well as mice and shrews have been reported as food; insects, fruits and berries are sometimes eaten.[457]

Bryant looked every bit an Englishman in his pullover, britches, woolly socks and hiking boots. He was dealing with lots of poaching in the park at the time. As Cowan recalls, "It was during the depths of the Depression and people were desperate for meat and fur to make a few dollars."[456] Bryant and another warden had been shot at by a pair of poachers working a cave camp above the Snaring River the past winter, so the group's adrenalin was no doubt somewhat heightened.

When they got to the Swiftwater, they encountered the remains of a wolverine the poachers had taken the year before. Bryant had seized the hide earlier and sent it to the National Museum, so Cowan prepared the skull, which, he was proud to recount, was later reunited with the skin in Ottawa. Martens were scarce and Bryant reported the last Fisher he saw was in the Tonquin Valley in 1929.

The Swiftwater is a small tributary of the Rocky River that flows into the Athabasca. Commented Cowan: "The spot on which we were camping was in virgin spruce woods. Undergrowth was wanting and the smaller mammals very scarce."[458] This didn't seem to slow him down too much, though; during this trip he trapped mice, jumping mice, heather voles, chipmunks, squirrels and ground squirrels. On their way to Jacques Lake, they passed through the broad, grassy slopes between the aspen woods and the rocky peaks. He noted that Bighorn Sheep and Mountain Goats were common, and at the pass around 6,000 feet there were a number of Moose. He spent his 20th birthday in the mountains, and characteristically there is no mention of his birthday celebration in his field notes. He does mention preparing beaver specimen #10741, which weighed 68 pounds.

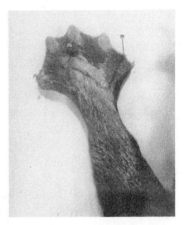

Canada River Otter paw
[North American River Otter]

Lutra canadensis
[now *Lontra canadensis*]

A long, lithe-bodied mustelid, adult males sometimes measuring over 4 feet in total length including a tapered, muscular tail of 16–20 inches. Weight up to 30 pounds. Female somewhat smaller. They are an abundant mammal along the coast and among the offshore archipelagos; inland they are very rare.[454]

Another picture of the group taken by Bryant shows Cowan atop the one enormous saddle horse and Kathleen and Williams scowling at the camera as they led the two pack horses through a log-strewn, fire-torched landscape around Jacques Creek. Cowan recalled very well his mount as being an "ex-racehorse as awkward as a man with three legs once you got him off the trail."[460] He describes the horse getting stuck astride logs when they encountered the brulé – blown-down trees after a fire. Bryant apparently had to dismount and physically lift the horse's front and get its legs on the same side of the log to get it to continue.

Cowan's labours through the brulé were to be pivotal in his subsequent understanding of landscape ecology as he revisited the park for research over the decades. Ironically, the burnt landscape had a role to play not only in the creation of the park in the first place but also in why Cowan had a job. In 1910, after a long summer drought, a combination of lightning storms and high winds led to a huge conflagration that swept through three million hectares of the US Pacific Northwest from Washington to Idaho and up into southern BC from the Cascades to the Rockies. Nearly one million hectares burned in the Canadian Rocky Mountain region, leading to the creation of Jasper Park and to a new appetite for conservation policy on public lands across North America.[461]

In his book *The Big Burn*[462] Timothy Egan argues that Roosevelt's forest rangers fought the fires against all odds, saved thousands of lives, and turned public opinion against pressures to privatize the forests. It led to the strengthening of the US Forest Service and its duty of stewardship and scientific enquiry and gave rise to budgets to support the work of wildlife managers and scientists. It was called the year of the Big Burn and out of its ashes came the birth of the newly-minted BC Forest Service which led to the retention of over 94 per cent of the province in public lands with a similar mission and structure for stewardship. Clyde Leavitt, chief forester to the North American Conservation Commission, developed the policy directive for Canada in his report *Forest Protection in Canada, 1912.*[463]

It directed the strengthening of the "game reserves of the Rockies" over nearly 15,000 hectares in both BC and Alberta and laid out the intention of the Dominion Forests Branch "to assist materially in the conservation of wild animal life in the Rocky Mountain Region." The Dominion Forest Reserves and Parks Act revision of 1911 "determined the future of Canada's national parks by placing them in a new administrative structure"[464] and led to the hiring of wardens who were tasked to patrol the lands for poachers, prevent additional fires and assist research into the wild animal life of the park.[465] This was the legacy that the 'B' stepped up to guard and strengthen.

Mountain Heather-vole [Western Heather Vole]

Phenacomys intermedius

This small, grey vole is most difficult to distinguish from several species of the genus *Microtus*. Tail short and more slender than in most other voles. In adults, the dorsal surface is predominantly grey-brown. The tooth pattern is completely diagnostic to genus … This mouse displays considerable variety in habitat. Typically it is found in dry forests of lodgepole pine, where it lives under decaying stumps and trunks and in patches of bearberry, *Arctostaphylos uva-ursi*.[459]

Golden-crowned Sparrow

Zonotrichia atricapilla

From spring through autumn, the Golden-crowned Sparrow has a widespread distribution throughout most mountainous regions of British Columbia, where it is a characteristic timberline species. In the mid-1940s, Munro and Cowan (1947) reported that a "few" Golden-crowned Sparrows wintered in the Puget Sound Lowlands … Since that time, the sparrow has become a regular wintering bird here, particularly on southeastern Vancouver Island.[467]

Throughout his life, Cowan watched this park mandate come constantly under attack from corporate and commercial interests, including trophy hunting, which prompted his 1943–1947 studies. He performed research, wrote articles, sat on committees and spoke publicly on the topic for the entire length of his career. The impacts of the 1910 fire on public awareness of the concept of stewardship would have been similar to the shift of consciousness that occurred around climate change with Hurricane Sandy. Events of such large magnitude leave a physical reminder of nature's forces that persists for years. The downside of creating an appetite for fire suppression led to the era of Smokey the Bear and new threats to the ecosystem. Without fire, trees encroached on grassland habitat, putting pressure on grassland species. The subsequent decline in those species was then often erroneously but publicly blamed on predators instead of on the suppression of fire. These were difficult messages to communicate, but the bandy-legged dudes and absent-minded professors like H.L. Stoddard would start drawing attention to fire ecology almost immediately. Cowan picked up the challenge and was involved in those early calls for caution during his seminal "saddlebag science" in the Rockies in the 1940s.

Meanwhile, that summer of 1930, Cowan continued his training in Rocky Mountain ecology and life:

> The rest of that summer was devoted to mammals of Jasper with some bird highlights. During three weeks alone in the Tonquin alplands my senses were sharpened by knowledge that I was the first person to occupy the cabin since the warden was killed the previous autumn by a sow grizzly with cubs. The bears were still in the valley! On the alpine slopes I flushed a Timberline Sparrow (*Spizella taverneri*) [now a subspecies of Brewer's Sparrow (*Spizella breweri taverneri*)] from her nest in a dwarfed spruce. This was many hundreds of miles south and east of its type locality and nearest known location, Atlin – a major range extension. Exciting stuff! Another surprise was nesting Willow Ptarmigan, also a southerly record. But it was the Golden-crowned Sparrows that were unforgettable.[466]

Cowan continues in his recollections of the Golden-crowned Sparrow:

> Their plaintive 3-note song greeted each dawn and closed each day. Just recalling, I can see the great sweep of alpine meadows to Amethyst Lake and the towering Ramparts beyond. A Columbian Ground-squirrel ate the chicks.[468]

That last sentence was typical of Cowan's dry humour; he was renowned for it. In his later lectures, popular writing and television shows he was to draw heavily upon observations from his days in the field to illustrate concepts. In his television series *The Web of Life*, he began one episode with: "Today we visit the roof of the world. I love alpine lands – I have had some of the most beautiful days of my life above timberline. Every plant is a different individual. If you surround yourself with beauty it changes your life. What else?"[469] His lectures inevitably kicked off with a personal anecdote, the summer of 1930 being no exception.

On July 4 he set out for the infamous Tonquin cabin where the warden had been killed by the grizzly the summer before. The Tonquin Valley in those days was the iconic valley of the park, before lodges and ski areas had started to erode the area south of the township. Cowan's notes describing Tonquin hint at the love he was to feel for this place in this coming-of-age summer. It is a classic U-shaped valley through which Maccarib Creek runs east to west from the summit of Maccarib Pass on the BC–Alberta boundary to where it angles northwest into Meadow Creek via Moat Creek, eventually reaching the Athabasca River. Along the Maccarib, Cowan describes the lush willows and sedges, a narrow belt of spruce and alpine fir, then lush, rolling uplands to the north side and an "abrupt wall of peaks" to the south with a complete array of prey and predators (including himself as the former). An invigorating place to be a biologist, alone and 20 years old. On his two-day journey to the warden's cabin, Cowan records tracks of coyote, fox, marten, bear, wolverine, porcupine, a large herd of caribou, goat and deer. He sees signs of bog lemmings and voles and observes moose, bear and rabbits. At the cabin, he finds a healthy population of Hoary Marmots (what were then called whistlers), more Horned Larks and very close signs of Grizzly Bear.

Grizzly Bear paw

Ursus arctos horribilis

An adult male from Jasper, Alberta, near the British Columbia border measured: Total length 73"; Tail 6¾"; hind foot 10"; and weighed 450 pounds. This is a good average specimen, although much larger individuals are on record.[470]

R.M. Anderson from the museum wrote to Laing on August 26, 1930, scolding him for having left Cowan underprotected in the Tonquin:

> I hope that you will curb the impetuosity of your assistant if he dares to tackle grizzlies single-handed. The grizzly might get peeved if shot at with an "aux" and eat the collector alive, incidentally swallowing some government equipment.[471]

Cowan never had problems with Grizzly Bears throughout all his fieldwork. Fourteen years later, he was to write recommendations about human–grizzly interactions for the Rocky Mountain national parks: "...do not pass sentence of death upon all members of the species as some most vocal individuals advise."[472] Instead, he quotes his old mentor Joseph Grinnell, who, in his address to the Canadian national parks superintendents in 1928, had said: "A world without any sort of hazard would be a tame and uninteresting place to live in, surely. Only a weak-spined, sap-headed, nerveless type of human being would find pleasure in a recreation place where there is not the faintest danger of bodily injury."[473] Cowan's student R. Yorke Edwards, who headed up the interpretation program for BC Parks, would give the same advice a generation later in his popular writings.[474] Cowan's skill at working with irascible grizzlies in both wild and political landscapes won him the honour of chairing a committee on the US Yellowstone Park grizzlies in 1973 on the recommendation of his student Bob Weeden, at the time a professor of wildlife management at the University of Alaska and a member of the 'B.'

The young Cowan, back in the Tonquin and oblivious to the concerns of his employer, got to work immediately, and by his second day in camp he had already killed, skinned and prepared the hide and skull of a crippled caribou. He shared the task and meat with warden John Curren, who had been transferred that summer from Banff to take over the Tonquin district. Cowan's small-mammal work over the next three weeks is prodigious – capturing and preparing specimens, leaving no population undinted: lemmings, voles, jumping mice, martens, weasels etc. He travelled miles each day, from the scree slopes at the foot of the ramparts for pikas down to the glacial lakes in search of voles, setting his traps at night and returning to them in the morning. For his 90th birthday celebration he received an accolade from a colleague for "his unrivalled proficiency of walking uphill," a skill that diminished only in his last couple of years, after his stroke.

In 1930 Cowan understood his role as being a collector–scientist committed to understanding the diversity of life, using the tools that were available to scientists at that time. The fact that collecting specimens was also consistent with a way of life that young hunters had been enjoying there for millennia, with freedom to roam the hills and test their skills, was also a factor in Cowan's exuberance and success. He was distinguishable from all other aspiring middle-class professionals not by his pelage, but by the fact that he was able to not merely survive, but thrive outdoors, alone, unsupervised, enjoying the extraordinary wealth of creatures around, with a heightened sense of adventure and imagination, and eating what he killed. Cowan

Western Jumping Mouse

Zapus princeps idahoensis

Confined to the Rocky Mountain Trench and adjacent mountain slopes ... These mice are easily distinguishable from all other small mammals by their yellowish-buff colour, with darker dorsal stripe; white underparts; long hind legs and short forelegs; and a very long, very slender tail that has no terminal tuft of hairs.[475]

Northern Pygmy-Owl

Glaucidium gnoma

This tiny diurnal owl prefers the edges of open coniferous forests or mixed woodlands ... Most records (64%) are from the late autumn and winter periods when pygmy-owls move from forested mountains to lower elevations where they are more visible.[477]

was learning that scientific rigour and the economic importance of livelihoods gained from wildlife (subsistence hunting, trapping and recreation) were the central (and few) arguments available against destructive, competing uses of the landscape. For the next 80 years of his life, he was to argue for the management of wildlife on the basis of scientific knowledge – not just to serve his own needs for venison but for legions of his students, for hunters, fishers and trappers, for First Nations and ultimately for the fauna themselves. Cowan had figured out his niche in the ecosystem and became highly successful within it.

For a swan song to that summer, Cowan took a weekend off from UBC classes to hunt venison with Laing on Constitution Hill near the Laing home in Comox on

Steller's Jay

Cyanocitta stelleri

Although the Steller's Jay is considered a resident throughout its range, it appears to be an altitudinal migrant.[479]

Vancouver Island. Laing's journal for November 8 and 9 records a heavy southeaster "raining pitchforks"[476] on the two men as they scoured the hill looking for coastal Black-tailed Deer. He comments that even the deer are stupid from the rain, as they have "no ears." On the second day, they kill a young male, which Cowan carries down the mountain on his back as Laing captures the moment on black and white film. They get back by nightfall, "rainwarm," but not before spotting a bear eating salmon in Wolf Creek; and not before catching some quail and dissecting their crops to determine what plants the birds had been eating; hearing a Western Tanager; and "calling up" some Pygmy Owls, which are easily lured by mimicking their call.

As the two men returned they had a welcome home committee: "Steller's Jay and Whiskey Jack were on the deck"[478]

All three species here, including the primates, were "altitudinal migrants" (returning in the summer to higher elevations).

CHAPTER 11

"I'm having a whale of a time."

Tofino, 1931

T he spring of 1931 was to start with a great disappointment for Cowan. He was poised to return to Jasper with Laing to collect for the National Museum and help out with the nature guiding, but the Depression was already straining federal finances. Correspondence between Anderson and Laing reveals deepening budget cuts in the Parks Branch. Laing's job was hanging in the balance, and Anderson wrote in March:

> [Commissioner J.B. Harkin] is still keen on getting enough data together for Parks bulletins on wild life, and I am sure that before long he will be able to show this feature to be an "economic necessity." It is essential to keep the custom or trade of the "customers," or tourists, in the park.[480]

But by April 21, Anderson is informing Laing that

> Our fieldwork is all shot to pieces this summer. Three temporary assistants –McTaggart Cowan and two botanical assistants who have worked for us in past years – were turned down. Taverner has given up any fieldwork. Racey wrote to me recently that he is taking the summer off and will spend the time collecting. He expected to collect in Vancouver Island during May. I am trying to arrange that if Cowan goes with him we can buy some of his specimens. We need Vancouver Island material.[481]

Racey had encountered his own downturns in the mining outfitting business and, as Anderson indicated, decided to pack up and take the spring and summer off. His instructions from Anderson were to look at nesting colonies on the west coast of Vancouver Island, sort out the rodents while he was there, check on the mysterious Vancouver Island Marmot in the Alberni mountains, which had last been recorded scientifically 20 years earlier, and then do some work up in the Chezacut region of the Chilcotin. For Cowan, going with his future father-in-law was a second choice not entirely without its attractions. Racey was intending to pick up daughter Joyce and family for the Chilcotin stage of the trip.

The two spent April preparing. One of the leads they were following was to reconstruct zoologist Annie Alexander's 1910 expedition for the MVZ at Berkeley. Cowan was no doubt being encouraged by Racey and others to explore grad school at Berkeley. Getting up to scratch about the Alexander expedition and its colourful characters so close to home was probably all part of his education. The 1912 report on that expedition describes the goals and personalities:

> In 1910 Miss Annie M. Alexander organized and financed an expedition for the purpose of collecting the higher vertebrates on Vancouver Island.... Miss Alexander, accompanied by Miss Louise Kellogg, left Berkeley on April 18, beginning the work of collecting at Parksville April 24. Here they secured the services of Mr. E. Despard, an expert hunter and trapper, who remained with the party throughout the summer and who secured nearly all of the larger mammals taken. The writer [Harry Swarth, curator of birds at Berkeley] left Berkeley on June 4, arriving at the expedition's camp at Beaver Creek [Port Alberni] on June 9. On July 1 Miss Alexander and Miss Kellogg returned home, while the writer, together with Despard, continued the work at various points until September 28.[482]

Alexander was certainly colourful. She was an American sugar heiress, raised in Hawaii, with a keen interest in natural history, travel and conservation, who seeded an intellectual dynasty for natural history on the west coast by funding expeditions and founding two natural history museums, including the MVZ beginning in 1909.[483]

> In an era when women in the sciences were either unheard of or (at best) considered unusual or even unnatural, [Alexander] became a premier scientific collector, spending months each year on field expeditions. When she financed a large expedition she usually accompanied it and, despite being treated as the camp housekeeper and cook by many of her male research associates, found time personally to discover and document a number of new species.[484]

As benefactor of the museum, and with the help of her partner, Louise Kellogg (whom she would remain with for 42 years), and their friend C. Hart Merriam of the US Biological Survey, Alexander selected the director, Joseph Grinnell, financed the expeditions and set the tone for who should come and study there, what they should be doing and why. Wrote scientist and historian Barbara Stein in her biography of Alexander:

> [Her] desire to establish a museum of vertebrate zoology on the Berkeley campus stemmed, in part, from her awareness of the rapidity with which the fauna in California was disappearing, succumbing to the state's spiraling growth, rampant agricultural development

and increasing urbanization ... She lived passionately and, perhaps most importantly, she dealt with the world on her own terms.[485]

Alexander believed that through knowledge came an awareness and desire to conserve the landscape, so she focused on what she saw was a pressing need to collect, catalogue, research and exhibit this diversity for public education. She insisted that her staff be "men with their accomplishments ahead of them, rather than behind them." She hired Grinnell because she was impressed with his "energy and enthusiasm and the neat and scholarly way in which his records were kept."[486] Grinnell for his part was a dedicated naturalist as well as a scientist and shared her philosophical values. In return, she supported him until he died in 1939.

A full biography of Grinnell and his contribution to evolutionary and conservation biology has yet to be properly written but there is no question that he and Alexander spawned an intellectual lineage in western North America. Many historians have credited him with being "the academic grandfather of mammalogy"[487] and vertebrate ecology, in addition to his ornithological contributions. Over 5,000 scientific papers and books have been published by Grinnell and his "academic descendants,"[488] and he is credited with a range of innovations in the way wildlife was studied, including bringing statistical rigour to evolutionary studies. The Grinnellian tradition was not just about conventional academic scholarship; it involved immersion in the natural world and a spirit of exploration. Students were to study wild animals in their habitat, not as specimens in laboratories. Cowan described Grinnell's contribution this way: "He pioneered the concept of the environment and avifauna as inseparable."[489] In trying to unravel the complex questions of evolution, Grinnell believed that the field researcher had to actively participate in the environment in which the animal lived, "because only that contact could bring from the field the detailed perception of each species of bird and its special niche."[490]

Grinnell's philosophy, which so closely paralleled Alexander's, wasn't surprising given his background. His family were Quakers, his father a physician who loved the prairie and worked for various Indian agencies of plains people as their doctor. Joseph spent his early childhood in the company of the Oglala Sioux with Chief Red Cloud's family. Chief Red Cloud had once successfully defended the Black Hills from colonization, but the gold rush had obliterated the treaties and ended with the Sioux wars. As a famous quote popularly attributed to Red Cloud put it: "They made us many promises, more than I can remember. But they never kept but one: they promised to take our land, and they took it."[491] The Oglala had been forced onto the Pine Ridge reservation in South Dakota, and it was the Pine Ridge Indian Agency that hired the senior Dr. Grinnell. Red Cloud continued to advocate for the Sioux lands but probably made more headway in the long run for ensuring some kind of future for his people's subsistence lifestyles by befriending the young doctor's son.

According to Grinnell's widow, Hilda, in the only biography of her husband, "he relied upon Indian companions for playmates. Undoubtedly, his senses were quickened by association with these alert comrades."[492] He developed a keen interest in natural history, took himself on long trips into the wild and had accumulated a large collection of specimens and ornithological knowledge by the time he was 18. He had joined one of his father's medical colleagues on a trip to Sitka, Alaska, which kicked off a return trip ironically to be financed by gold panning that had the same success as the forays for gold that Cowan was to make in 1932. For both men, gold was in the wildlife. Grinnell kept copious journals and met John Muir, who had heard about the "bird boy." Grinnell's expertise about coastal Alaska is what led Alexander to his door as adviser for her 1907 trip up there. His openness and desire to share information and enthusiasm for the region is what cemented their relationship of patron and scholar that would last until his death.

Grinnell and Alexander had developed a philosophy that resonated with Cowan's own intellectual inheritance. They were adamant about sharing information and making it publicly accessible. They also believed that all animals had intrinsic value. T.R. Dunlap, in his book *Saving America's Wildlife*, chronicles Grinnell's influence in changing the prevailing attitude towards wildlife in which some animals held greater value than others. The correspondence between Grinnell and Allan Brooks over the killing of hawks was typical of the copious advocacy he carried out in his lifetime and with which he inspired his students.[493]

Berkeley was the centre of action for ecology, with specialties in ornithology and mammalogy, and its influence was rubbing off on Racey. Racey had just visited Berkeley that year to attend a gathering of the American Ornithologists' Union, connecting with Taverner, Lloyd and other members of the 'B'. The 'B' were intertwined with the Alexander–Grinnell dynasty, including Grinnell's cousin George Bird Grinnell, a naturalist and anthropologist. For the young Cowan, the relationship of these two groups – a brotherhood and a sisterhood – provided an extraordinary exposure to liberal ideas and sensibilities. Alexander, a woman described by her biographer as "an articulate and keen observer of human nature ... a woman of vision who loved women and believed firmly in their capabilities"[494] (at a time when women didn't have the vote and weren't allowed in the field alone), was afforded the social freedom to be in the field with her long-time partner Louise Kellogg. This might have been considered another strike against field scientists, as at the time homosexuality was illegal.

So, in 1931 Cowan was about to trace his future benefactor's footsteps around Vancouver Island. Not surprisingly, he gave Alexander the first and most extensive acknowledgement in his subsequent doctoral dissertation. Publicly he always credited her when recounting early influences and the marmot story.[495] Cowan was also to be heavily influenced by Harry Swarth, another doctoral student of Grinnell's and later an ornithologist with the museum, who "relived for me his summers in the north and his concepts of the dynamics of bird and mammal distribution there."[496] One of those dynamics had been the interesting evolutionary story of the Vancouver Island Marmot – a species first described to science by Swarth and Alexander in 1910 and hardly seen since.

The Alexander expedition had visited the mountains and valleys around Port Alberni and various locales on the west and east coasts of the island. Racey planned to replicate at least part of the trip. To this end he had written Laing to ask him for advice on what to take for his five-month collecting trip:

> Would it be too much trouble to give me a list of necessary equipment etc. for a five months summer collecting trip for birds and mammals, such as tents, bedding, clothing, firearms, ammunition, cooking utensils. Strictly between you and me, I am figuring a trip of duration and need some advice. Most of the trip by car. Business has gone to blazes so why not go?[497]

After spring preparations, and finishing up the term at UBC, Cowan and Racey left Vancouver on the midnight CPR steamer to Victoria, driving up the next day to Port Alberni, where they left the car. Packing one month's camping supplies aboard ss *Maquinna*, they travelled up Barclay [Barkley] Sound to Clayoquot Sound. The steamer was a famous fixture on the coast at the time. As the enormous whistle announced her arrival in the Sound, the two men would have come on deck May 3 to witness much of Tofino's small population crowd the dock, anxious to pick up mail, groceries, perhaps have a meal aboard and load up with goods, candy and comic books. It was still a small fishing settlement at the time. Native fishermen, Chinese labourers, Irish priests, English shopkeepers and Swedish miners would all have been in the mix. The native village of Opitsaht lay across the Inlet from Tofino, on Meares Island.

Meeting them in his 16-foot flat-bottomed skiff was Dick Guppy, a young self-taught naturalist, to ferry their belongings down to a cabin on the Tofino Mudflats. Guppy was part of an extensive and famous naturalist–explorer British family that had members naturalizing all over the world. His grandfather was Robert John Lechmere Guppy (after whom the Guppy fish was named) who had been captured, then befriended for two years, by the Maori. During this time, he had chronicled much of the flora and fauna of New Zealand. Dick Guppy's father, a naturalist and soldier in the Indian army, had moved his family to Tofino to seek a more temperate climate for health reasons. They had dragged tiger skins, mynah birds and butterfly collections with them, but a pension from the Indian army failed to accompany their father, so he returned to India to sort it out. Dick as the eldest was supplementing the non-existent family income with sandpipers and sculpins for protein as well as guiding for a living. He was possibly the prototype "ecotourism" operator in Tofino, although a little trigger-happy by modern-day standards. His brother, author Anthony Guppy, wrote, "He had a great variety of birds' eggs, all placed carefully in cartons and labelled: bright blue robin's eggs, speckled eggs, large eggs and fragile little hummingbird eggs. He pinned his moth and butterfly specimens in neat rows in flat boxes."[498]

The Guppy family leased the original Chesterman farm–homestead, which spanned Esowista Peninsula between the open, sandy beach facing west,

Chesterman Beach, and the east-facing Tofino Mudflats, connected by four miles of rough trail through forest. One of the cabins on the mudflats at the property, still called Wit's End, was made available for guests, just outside the Tofino townsite. Cowan describes arriving at this thick forest of Western Redcedar and Sitka Spruce with the occasional green glade from the abandoned farm:

> The flora of the Long Beach vi region is remarkable not because of any conspicuous flowering plants but because it exhibits to an astounding degree the result of extremely high humidity and rainfall (up to 300 inches per year) and the result of continued strong winds from one direction ... The Cedars and Spruces also start to grow with abandon but after reaching a medium height their growing tips become exposed to ever increasing winds. In consequence the forest trees are characterized by great girth but little height and all soon die at the tip and are left with jagged brown spires – admirable perches for the numerous bald eagles and the occasional duck hunting falcon."[499]

Their small cabin, which is still there, looked over the extensive mudflats on the east side of the peninsula, through which shorebirds move in huge numbers during the spring and fall migrations. The area covers 32 square kilometres of mudflats and eelgrass beds intricately woven together with tidal channels and sloughs. It is an extraordinary place, sheltered from the open ocean by the narrow isthmus, enabling birds to easily move back and forth between quiet flats and open beaches, depending on weather. Greeting Cowan and Racey when they arrived were large flocks of waders feeding on the tide flats, including the first arrivals of Hudsonian Curlew.[500]

Long-billed Curlew (top)

Numenius americanus

On the coast it occurs rarely on Vancouver Island. Coastal migrants occur later in May, which suggests the birds are mainly non-breeders. Flocks of more than 50 birds may concentrate in good feeding areas at that time ... The breeding range is restricted to the dry grasslands of the southern interior.[504]

Whimbrel (bottom)

Numenius phaeopus

Flocks of up to several hundred Whimbrels have been recorded regularly in May and June near Tofino. Large numbers appear to forage on the mudflats of Tofino Inlet and Grice Bay and on the sandy beaches of Chesterman Beach. Records by several observers suggest that they forage by day and then fly to Cleland Island and other offshore rocks to spend the night.[502]

In those days, two birds that had the common name of curlew were known in BC: the Hudsonian Curlew and Long-billed Curlew. What Cowan called the Hudsonian, *Phaeopus hudsonicus*, was later determined to be a subspecies of the Whimbrel, *Numenius phaeopus*. In his first bird book with Munro, he notes his 1931 sighting.[501] In the later *Birds of BC*, the description of the Whimbrel is as follows:

Whimbrel numbers that spring were to swell to 150 at a time, staying a few days on the mudflats before heading north to breed. "Saw a flock of curlew feeding peacefully when all of a sudden they flew off giving frightened cries and an adult black merlin came along in full chase after a flock of sandpipers. He missed his birds and lit on top of a tall stump."[503]

Very occasionally the other BC curlew also appears along the coast, and Cowan would have been looking out for this larger cousin that he was to see nesting at White Lake in the interior grasslands.

Both species of curlews are spectacular birds. Both have long wader legs with even longer curved beaks that probe the mudflats for invertebrates. The Long-billed Curlew has a longer bill – not surprisingly. Their mottled brown plumage provides camouflage in the treeless areas where they nest. In Scottish culture, the curlews, or "whaups," figure prominently in folk songs and lore with their evocative *curlew* call and association with both the sea and the wilder parts of Scotland. Cowan was quite familiar with the respect the Scots had for these birds and notes his enjoyment of flocks of them on their way to the Arctic. When Cowan returned to Scotland in 1952, the *Scotsman* newspaper reported on a lecture he gave reconstructing the shifting migration patterns of the curlew as the glaciers melted and these ancient birds penetrated back into their northern habitats.

Over his lifetime, Cowan was to witness increasing numbers of Whimbrel moving along the coast, a conservation success story. The Long-billed Curlews, interior grassland nesters, were less fortunate. As their numbers declined, conservation of them became an important focus for Cowan. For many of his projects, they became the icons of the threatened grasslands that he was to spearhead. The Grasslands Conservation Council of BC adopted the Long-billed Curlew as part of its logo, and Cowan was a supporter of grassland habitat for them to the end of his life.

Western Sandpiper seeking food in the shallows of a slough

Calidris mauri

The Western Sandpiper is the most abundant shorebird in the province. Nearly the entire world population migrates along the British Columbia coast during the spring and autumn movements ... On the west coast of Vancouver Island, the extensive sand beaches of Long Beach, Chesterman Beach and the mudflats of Tofino Inlet are important stopping points.[506]

As well as Whimbrels there were large numbers of other shorebirds as they flew in for their two- to three-day stopovers: Least, Semipalmated and Western Sandpipers, Dowitcher, Dunlin, Sanderlings and Golden and Black-bellied Plovers. The Tofino region is now recognized as second only to the Fraser Delta in importance for sandpipers and other migrating shorebirds on the west coast of Canada. For the Western Sandpipers, over 8 per cent of the global population stages at the Tofino Mudflats alone on their way north or south.[505] The area has been designated an international Important Bird Area, a provincial Wildlife Management Area and part of the Western Hemisphere Shorebird Reserve Network to help conserve migratory shorebirds. During the migration, there is a constant stream of peeping and chattering as these shorebirds fly in. The flocks bank and turn in unison, causing a constant flashing of light as the sun hits their wings.

Over the next two weeks, the men crisscrossed the Esowista Peninsula on foot, visiting the mudflats, documenting birds and trapping small mammals on Chesterman, Garrod's (now Mackenzie) and Long beaches and taking a rowboat over to islands like Meares across from their cabin in Tofino Inlet. On May 12, with a clearing in the weather, they headed out with Guppy for a visit to Cleland Island, called Bare Island, a low, treeless island exposed to the open ocean. At the time, it was well known only to locals, who had fished and collected birds' eggs there for millennia. But the trip was the first scientific collecting foray to determine species on the island and eventually led to Cleland becoming a nationally recognized wildlife area. Cowan writes a particularly vivid (as well as lethal) account of this first visit in his field journal:

Rhinoceros Auklet

Cerorhinca monocerata

At the time of J.A. Munro and Cowan (1947) the Rhinoceros Auklet was considered a resident species and was known to breed at only 3 sites along the coast ... Colonies in British Columbia are situated on vegetated islands of 2–130 ha in size.[508]

> We cruised down the coast past the lighthouse, taking a Baird, [Pelagic] and 2 Brandt Cormorants, a Rhinocerous [sic] Auklet, 2 Marbled Murrelets and 2 California Murres [Common Murres] in breeding plumage and one in winter plumage. Turning about we cruised east to Bare [Cleland] Island about 6 miles distant and anchored off the southeast side. We then went ashore in a small boat, pulling it up on the rocks. The island is about 8–10 acres in extent and about 60' in elevation in the middle. The shore very rugged but

on the inner slopes there are dense growths of grasses, sedges and other weeds. Among these the puffins and other birds burrow. Our puffin was captured by hand in one of these places. We found about 15 pairs of oystercatchers preparing to nest. A few Glaucous-winged Gulls were making their nests but no eggs yet. Pigeon Guillemots, Baird's and Brandt's Cormorants were very common and could be seen sitting on all the rocks or swimming in the water. Song Sparrows and sooty Fox Sparrows were nesting in a few clumps of salal and numerous Winter Wren [now Pacific Wren] fledglings were seen. A Wandering Tattler was secured. And two Fox Sparrows. On the way home we saw Harlequin Ducks, Old Squaws [now Long-tailed Duck], Pacific Loon and several Rhinocerous Auklets. The scenery was wonderful. Rugged rocks with the surf breaking over them, backed by green slopes and the whole set off by the towering snowcapped peaks in the background."[507]

Black Oystercatcher

Haematopus bachmani

The Black Oystercatcher nests singly or in loose colonies on suitable islands. Cleland Island, with an area of 7.7 ha, supported 57 breeding pairs in 1971. Nests, usually well camouflaged, were situated on bare, exposed rock, shell, gravel and sand beaches, among drift-logs, on areas of short grass on rocky headlands ...[511]

The Rhinoceros Auklets, the only slightly less attractive cousins of the puffins, turned out to be a new colony for the ornithologists.

In a follow-up trip 10 days later in calmer weather, he writes about the courtship of the Pigeon Guillemots, which "showed signs of sexual excitement pursuing one another with their wings upraised over the backs, tails spread out parallel to the ground, all the time emitting their particular hissing squeal"[509] and the black oystercatchers, which he particularly liked:

The male stretches himself to his full height and bends the head sharply downward so that the bill almost touches the lower neck, which is straight upright. In this position the bird bows up and down chattering loudly all the while."[510]

A large nesting population of oystercatchers was also documented.

In a rare moment of pause during that trip, Cowan wrote to Joyce Racey about his time on Bare Island. "We had a whale of a time!"[512] The letter is the only surviving early correspondence from Cowan to Joyce. It was not your typical love letter, but rather an intimate communication filled with companionable exuberances of sightings of birds, their courtship antics and his disappointments. He breaks the news to Joyce that he had failed his chemistry exam and will have to sit some supplementals. "The whole trouble is that there are only 24 hours in a day and unfortunately one must sleep occasionally."[513] He also decried the lack of local sportsmanship. "It seems to be an unknown art to shoot a flying bird in this country. Here the inhabitants hunt by sneaking down to the shore and letting off a broadside into a flock of feeding birds and then picking up the dead and dying to the number of ten or a dozen..."[514] It isn't clear whether Dick Guppy was one of the "inhabitants" and if it was his shooting habits that Cowan was objecting to. Certainly Tony Guppy had something to say about his brother's shooting:

> Dick had a BSA air rifle he had brought from England. It shot cup-shaped pellets and was quite powerful and accurate. With this, while walking along Chesterman's Beach, he managed to bag enough so-called snipe to make a good-sized meat pie. These were not snipe at all ... but sandpipers ... it seemed such a shame to kill such pretty little birds. Perhaps because of this, snipe pie was never very popular in our family...[515]

Double-crested Cormorants

on nests

Phalacrocorax auritus

Bones of the Double-crested Cormorant are abundant in archaeological sites throughout the Strait of Georgia, which indicates occupancy of the area for the past 5,000 years. Their recent arrival as a breeding species may have been a reinvasion after a decline for some unspecified reason.[520]

Dick Guppy, however, appears to have eaten everything he shot, and Cowan's criticism was generally reserved for wasteful hunting methods, borne out of his adherence to the popular sportsman's creed of the famous American zoologist William Hornaday and icons of the 'B': "No man can be a good citizen and a slaughterer of game."[516] This creed never wavered for Cowan through the years, nor does his sharing of his observations and disappointments with Joyce – one of which wasn't cooking. "I'm chief chef today and needs must go and cook our asparagus for dinner. Bye-bye for the present and don't work too hard, but make a better job of it than yours truly. Yours, Ian."[517]

Twenty years later his student Charles Guiguet would conduct a seabird colony survey at Cleland Island, and in 1967 two more of Cowan's students, Wayne Campbell and David Stirling, were to write up a fuller report on its natural history for consideration as an ecological reserve. Forty years almost to the day after Cowan's trip, Cleland Island was named the very first ecological reserve in British Columbia. It remains one of the most important seabird colonies on the coast, supporting globally significant numbers of nesting Tufted Puffins, Rhinoceros Auklets and Black Oystercatchers, as well as other important seabird nesting populations and a roosting area for Whimbrels during their migration. Cowan's enthusiasms for the island carried through from his first rough landing to his on-going support of the Ecological Reserves system, headed up by Bristol Foster, who was to follow in Cowan's many-faceted footsteps.

"Bare Island" had a footnote. Besides Cleland, there were at least a dozen other Bare Islands on the coast in the 1930s. One was Mandarte Island, to the east of Saanich Peninsula, in Haro Strait, where Jim Munro had been working to document the first return of a colony of Double-crested Cormorants to nest in Canadian waters. The Brandt's and the Baird's, or Pelagic, Cormorants that Cowan was seeing in Tofino were relatively common, but the Double-crested, the largest of the cormorants on the coast, had not been seen for quite awhile. These prehistoric-looking birds, with their characteristic drying-wing pose, build huge, scruffy nests of mud and sticks at the top of the cliffs – very distinctive as you approach their colonies. Although they had nested in BC for thousands of years, they had disappeared, probably from overhunting. Munro observed their return in 1927 and it was a great cause

Pacific Loon

Gavia pacifica

Spring migration is coastal and may begin as early as February and March in southern areas, but it is difficult to separate foraging movements into Pacific herring spawning areas from general northward movement. Concentrations of up to several thousand loons may be found in spring in areas where Pacific herring spawn and other small fish concentrate in shallow waters along the coast.[522]

Pacific Coast Newt
[Rough-skinned Newt]

Triturus torosus [*Taricha granulosa*]

Canadian zone of the Pacific Coast region throughout the length of the province, east in the south at least to the watershed divide in the Cascade Mountains, west to include Vancouver Island and certain of the smaller coastal islands.[530]

for celebration to see these large birds return to their traditional nesting sites, a pleasure he had shared with Racey and Cowan. Cowan later recounted, "I said to Jim [Munro], you should write that up. He wouldn't, so I wrote it, but I refused to have my name on it. So there is a paper by Munro [written by Cowan] on the cormorant colony on Bare Island."[518] Bare–Mandarte went on to become an important research site that grew in prominence for its 30-year study of evolutionary adaptation, on par with the study of the Galápagos finches.[519] Mandarte work begun by Frank S. Tompa in 1959 was continued by Jamie Smith of UBC, both of whom had studied ornithology with Cowan. Peter Arcese, who now works with the Cowan Tetrapod Collection, is also a Mandarte researcher and sits on the board of The Nature Trust of BC doing work on the design of protected areas.

On May 17, while walking round a rocky headland to Garrod's Beach, Cowan and Racey come across one of the great natural wonders of the coast – a bait-ball feeding frenzy. On this particular day, a mixed flock of over 800 Pacific and

Common Loons, gulls, cormorants and murres were diving into, hovering around and feeding on a ball of surf fish which Cowan thought were viviparous perch close to shore. Bait balls can be any number of forage fish, such as herring, smelt, sandlance, sardines or various types of perch. The sea literally boils with the small fish as they get driven into a tight ball by the murres, cormorants and loons corralling them from below and the gulls grabbing them from above. Typically with bait balls, there are seals, sea lions and other marine mammals also getting a piece of the action. Bald Eagles will fly straight into the bait balls with talons extended and grab whole clusters of fish. Cowan wrote "This was a wonderful sight!"[521]

Cowan recounted details of trips offshore during their stay, to watch migrating phalaropes, "flock after flock at 10–15 minute intervals"[523] He, Racey and Guppy also travelled north past Cat Face Mountain to Ahousat to pick up a set of unusual deer antlers from the Gibson family, who owned the shingle mill near there. The Gibsons had five sons, all of whom came to dominate some element of the forest industry, including Gordie Gibson, "the Bull of the Woods," who as a Liberal MLA in 1978 became one of the most ardent critics of attempts to privatize Crown forests.[524] At the head of Kennedy Lake, Cowan visited Ed Armstrong, a trapper, to check out his marten skins. Armstrong was another eccentric character of the Sound who later moved to one of the islets in Tofino Inlet, called Dream Island, with his three "wild daughters who needed an island to contain them."[525] Cowan and Racey made a trip to the Long Beach Indian Reserve, where they measured a raven's nest and counted sea-lions off Sitkum Point: "One old bull had a bunch of [approximately] 25 cows grouped apart from the rest of the herd, and he was having a terrible time chasing off a couple of aspiring youngsters."[526]

On a trip back from Tofino, they visited Death Island, also known as Deadman's Islet, where they stumbled across a canoe, "8' × 4' × 4' hidden by salmonberry bushes,"[527] inside of which were four burial boxes, which Cowan measured as being five feet long. He inscribed beside the entry: "Opitsat Indians. Took one skull." Collecting skulls was common in the 1930s, as the infusion of cultural sensitivity advanced at a geological pace. Cowan and Racey note conversations with native hunters at Mitchell's store about the size and antlers of deer. Although little detail is recorded except numbers of antler tips, this might have constituted a more than average interaction with Opitsat people. As one historian of the region, Margaret Horsfield, notes of Tofino, "The Indians lived in their nearby villages, a continual background presence, almost entirely separate from the growing community."[528] Twelve years earlier the Spanish flu had swept through the community, killing over a dozen people, including children at the Kakawis (Christie) residential school, operated by Catholic priests across the water from them on Meares Island, just north of the Tla-o-qui-aht village of Opitsaht. Native deaths weren't recorded until 1917 and prior to that the smallpox had left a huge proportion of the population dead.[529] Cowan notes that this burial didn't appear to be the typical type of burial.

One of their last expeditions with Guppy was to Meares Island to look for amphibians in the lakes. Meares Island forest, then as now, is a statuesque climax forest with some of the largest trees in Canada and is one of the few large islands to have remained relatively unmodified by clear-cut industrial logging. In 1984 the very first successful native challenge was made to the plans to log the island by timber company MacMillan Bloedel. Initiated by the Opitsaht, a tribal park was proposed and today the famous Big Tree Trail is one of the best-known attractions for Tofino visitors. That trail of trees would have been not far from the route Cowan followed in 1931 when they hiked to an unnamed lake to collect Stickleback fish, Red-legged Frogs and the neurotoxic Rough-skinned Newts (what were then called Pacific Coast Newts), which Cowan wrote up for his review of amphibians of BC.

On the return from that trip, Guppy pointed out that he had seen voles on some of the tiny, isolated islets. The presence of a Townsend's Vole on an islet with not much more than a tree and clumps of salal alerted Cowan's nose for evolution. Small mammals on small, isolated islands were his version of Darwin's finches and perhaps even more interesting, as they can't fly. He immediately set to trapping some, burrowing into the thick salal to find the small runways. Colleague Charles Guiguet, during his later seabird colony survey, collected and named another distinct subspecies of this vole after Cowan: *Microtus townsendii cowani* – the largest and most isolated of them all – which he collected from the remote seabird colony of Triangle Island and is now on the provincial red list for species at risk.

Cowan's Vole subspecies (top); Female and male (bottom)

Townsend's Vole [Cowani subspecies]

Microtus townsendii cowani

Largest of the Townsend voles; distinguished by the woolly texture of the fur; chin and tail-tip white and a white mark often present on the forehead... Confined to Triangle Island in the Scott island group off the north end of Vancouver Island.[531]

Guppy appears to have been greatly inspired by meeting a young man like Cowan, who had such a keen eye for everything. As Tony Guppy writes, "From the beginning, Dick developed a meticulous, professional approach to collecting and cataloguing, and over the years, as his collection grew, he became a respected amateur entomologist. His articles and photographs were published in scientific journals and some of his collections are now housed at the Provincial Museum at Victoria."[532] The youngest brother, Arthur Guppy, also developed an interest in entomology, and Arthur's son Crispin Guppy went on to co-write the definitive tome on butterflies of British Columbia, published in 2001.[533] Ken Gibson, the son of the only Guppy daughter, also kept in contact with Cowan over the years, "keeping him clued in on things going on here,"[534] from rare beetles to fur-seal observations.

Fur-seals, whose pelts supported a major sealing fleet in Tofino in the 19th century, were decimated by the time the North Pacific Fur Seal Convention was signed in 1911, the first international treaty to address wildlife preservation issues. Cowan retained a keen interest in seeing this population recover and passed on his enthusiasm to H. Dean Fisher, who was one of his early grad students in 1944. Fisher went on become an international expert on seals in both Pacific and Atlantic oceans and was a colleague of Cowan's for 20 years at UBC.

Clayoquot was to remain another favourite place for Cowan. In 1952 he addressed a large provincial audience of hunting associations and game wardens about the failure of the provincial government to address the rights and needs of wildlife outside of a few wildlife reserves. He used the Tofino Mudflats as an example. An application was made by the Game Commissioner (Frank Butler, a member of the 'B') to preserve the mudflats as part wildlife reserve and part public hunting ground. The application was rejected by government on the basis of the flats being a potential log booming area or oyster lease.[536] Cowan said to the audience:

> … if any other form of land use expresses an interest in a given region, our interests usually take a back seat. I urge most strongly that the necessary Acts be amended in such a way that the wildlife resource be given a consideration in all decisions involving Crown lands …[537]

That call would continue unabated for another 40 years. Cowan kept a burgeoning issues file until the day he died, called Forestry BC, in which he collected the literature on forest ecology that coalesced partly in response to public protests against clear-cut logging. Cowan's student Fred Bunnell, who later became a professor of forest wildlife biology at UBC and headed up the Centre for Applied Conservation Biology, was named the chief scientist in charge of the Clayoquot Scientific Panel in 1993.

The panel was established to come up with principles for forestry management

Northern Fur-seal

Callorhinus ursinus cynocephalus

Females and young leave the Pribilof Islands rookeries in October, migrating southwards through pelagic waters as far as the coast of California and Japan … In British Columbia, these animals occur in pelagic waters off the west coast of Vancouver Island, the Queen Charlotte Islands … during migratory periods.[535]

designed to end the famous "War in the Woods" that saw over 850 people arrested trying to stop clear-cut logging of old growth there.[538] It was the largest single incident of civil disobedience in Canadian history and focused research and policy development into the protection of biodiversity in old-growth temperate forests in a way unprecedented in Canada. Cowan's contributions came not only from his legendary knowledge about small mammal and forest bird biology but also the influence he had on scientists like Bunnell, forest ecologist Ken Lertzman, biodiversity geneticist Chris Pielou, evolutionary biologist Tom Reimchen and forest canopy ecologist Neville Winchester, all of whom worked in Clayoquot. Cowan's PhD student C.S. (Buzz) Holling became the first director of the Institute of Animal Resource Ecology at UBC, established to study ecological interactions, for example, between fisheries and forestry. Holling, now a professor emeritus at the University of Florida, is internationally known for his work in resilience theory and how ecosystems recover from disturbance.

Bunnell himself was hugely appreciative of Cowan's knowledge and inspiration:

> It wasn't just Ian's enthusiasm as a teacher but the enormous amount of experience, so his lectures were full of anecdotes to connect it. I remember one day the Cackling Goose race of the Canada Goose flew overhead and he started talking about the subspecies and what he knew about them – where they were going and where they were coming from. It made things a lot more real.[539]

Bunnell had walked a familiar path to Cowan's door. Like Cowan, the North Shore Mountains of Vancouver had been his childhood training ground:

> I didn't fit in. I was an angry kid. My old man bought a ski cabin at Hollyburn and the deal was that as long as the grades were good I didn't have to go to school, and I didn't. I had to write every bloody

Cackling Goose

Branta canadensis minima **[now considered a separate species,** *Branta hutchinsii***]**

Breeds mainly on the Yukon–Kuskokwim Delta in Alaska and winters in the Central Valley of California. *B. c. minima* is the smallest subspecies of the Canada Goose ... Cackling Canada Geese occur regularly as spring and autumn migrants in the province, but usually in small numbers and often associated with other Canada Geese, Brant and or Greater White-fronted Geese. Infrequently, large, pure flocks are reported from both coastal and interior locations ... Early migrants may appear along the coast in March, but most pass through between mid-April and mid-May.[540]

exam every year. So when it came to university I was really good at it. I spent a lot of time on that mountain. I would walk up even in the fire season and be alone a lot. I just really loved the outdoors. The "angry young man" thing sent me to the forests, and the vision of my career was as a fire spotter so I wouldn't have to deal with people. Ian certainly made my goals reputable and visible.[541]

Cowan taught Bunnell an undergraduate course at UBC in 1964. Bunnell then went on to win successive scholarships to Berkeley, Yale and Switzerland. Subsequently, both the forestry and the zoology departments at UBC became interested in him and tried to get him back. Having been politicized at Berkeley, teaching ecology and joining in the protests of the '60s, he agreed to return on the basis of a flexible and joint appointment to both departments. UBC agreed and Bunnell set up in the early 1970s, co-teaching a graduate seminar course with Cowan in 1974. "I really liked the guy. He looked after you." Bunnell tells of a case where a grad student who had a stutter had gotten very tense in a comprehensive exam and wasn't doing too well. "So Ian shut it down (which no one else could do) and we reconvened the exam sitting in his house and the kid did fine."[542]

Bunnell felt his edge came from the field experience supported by Cowan:

You were a lot closer to the animal; you sure as hell weren't watching a satellite picture. That gives you a different way of understanding and appreciating an animal when you'd walked the same ground as they did. One of the things you are trying to do is how to figure out how they fit into the environment that is being managed and changed. It isn't anthropomorphism. These animals think and you start to see that and each animal doesn't act the same. They are trying to solve these problems too.[543]

According to Bunnell, Cowan supported activists behind the scenes. "He was a mentor and a statesman. He was too kindly to be an activist; it was the way he was raised." As he was heading into his ninth decade during the Clayoquot arrests, Cowan contributed a chapter for a book sponsored by the World Wildlife Fund laying out his thoughts about minimum viable population sizes for various species and the implications of that for parks and reserves.[544] There was no doubt in his mind that it was the large scale, intact, interconnected ecosystems of sea, rivers, estuaries and forests that sustained the diversity of the natural world. Places like Clayoquot Sound that he first experienced as a young man had cemented this understanding firmly in his mind and heart for life. Clayoquot was only the beginning of that summer, though, as Racey and he boarded the *Maquinna* and returned to Port Alberni.

CHAPTER 12

"What the heck are those brown things that I see up in the mountains?"

Vancouver Island, 1931

After catching the *Maquinna* back to Port Alberni, Cowan and Racey retraced some of the Berkeley expedition to Beaver Creek, just north of Alberni, where Annie Alexander and Louise Kellogg had explored for birds and mammals 20 years earlier. This is the description from the Berkeley article on Beaver Creek.

> This is a broad, level valley containing one large stream and innumerable small ones draining into the head of Alberni Canal. It is heavily timbered, mostly with Douglas-fir and cedar, both of which attain a great size, while the creek beds and swamps are thickly grown up with willow and alder, with a dense undergrowth of devil's club, skunk cabbage and other vegetation and with many thickets of salmonberry. A large part of the region has been burned over in years past and there are innumerable tall, dead stumps standing everywhere, while the ground is strewn with logs and fallen trees.[545]

Grinnell had written to Alexander while she was up there, commenting that "the more I try to find out anything in the literature about Vancouver birds and mammals, the more apparent it becomes that mighty little is known of the region. You are right in the middle of about the least worked locality you could pick out in all of western North America."[546] By 1932 the burned areas were recovering and Cowan and Racey trapped and prepared specimens of small mammals in the rain for a few days around the Beaver, Stamp and Somass rivers. Before heading back to Nanaimo, they passed through Cathedral Grove, which even back in 1910 was worthy of note for various reasons.

> The road between Alberni and the east coast, traversed by stage, lies mostly through forest, and a part of the distance ... through stands of prodigiously large trees. Even on a bright sunny day it is dark and gloomy in these woods, and the stillness is impressive. The ground is remarkably free from underbrush, and bird life is almost totally lacking.[547]

One of Cowan's jokes on himself was that they all missed the fact that much of the bird life in the old-growth forest was going on above the canopy. Just a couple of years later, in California, he would observe Marbled Murrelets circling high above the huge redwoods in their characteristic mating flight, and note it in his journal. He suspected their nests were somewhere in the canopy, but not until 1945 would he obtain verbal confirmation of this, from Ronald Stewart, a biologist friend of Laing's who had seen murrelets nesting in the ancient Sitka spruce near Masset, Queen Charlotte Islands (QCI –Haida Gwaii). Gathering something more than anecdotal evidence was still confounding ornithologists even in 1990, when the second volume of *Birds of British Columbia* was published.[548] Climbing up several hundred feet and exploring the canopy was one remote corner of the province Cowan had failed to explore in his youth but marvelled at in his later years. The work of biologist Neville Winchester in the canopy of the rainforest, and the hundreds of arthropod species he found there that were new to science, excited Cowan greatly in his declining years.[549]

Marbled Murrelet

Brachyramphus marmoratus

The unique preference (amongst alcids) of the Marbled Murrelet, for nesting in old-growth forests south of Alaska has been noted by numerous authors ... the principal factor affecting continued existence of the species over the southern portion of its range is the destruction of old-growth forest.[550]

Another species that seemed to have disappeared was the marmot. The populations of them found by the 1910 Berkeley expedition at Golden Eagle Basin, King Solomon Basin and Mount Douglas, all around Alberni, hadn't been seen there for years. All of two sightings had been recorded since then: a young male way down at the mouth of the Jordan River on the west coast, far from his subalpine habitat, and a tipoff from locals about a population at Coombs, near Parksville. Cowan recounts that they were sitting in a café in Nanaimo, drying out, when they met a young man who asked them, "What the heck are those brown things that I see up in the mountains?" Cowan said, "We perked our ears up and asked if he could show us."[551] The journal describes them picking up Racey's son Alan at the boat from Vancouver, collecting their young guide, Ed Torkko, and heading up Nanaimo Falls Road on a midsummer's day for what they had been told was "an easy day's round trip" to find the elusive animals.[552]

The journal account of the "discovery" and Cowan's memory of it 70 years later vary only in the dramatic detail. There is no drama in the journal; it reads like a typical Cowan scientific collecting expedition. But at age 90, Cowan recalled vividly the human misadventure that is only barely discernible between the lines of the journal entry. Torkko had told the group it was just a day's hike, so they set off with just a "light outfit," which in those days was a gun, a snack and a pack frame to carry out the specimens. The Nanaimo River–Green Mountain country through which the trapper's trail passed in those days was not easy to follow. There were constant blowdowns in the lower-elevation forests of Western Redcedar, Douglas-fir and Western Hemlock, with thick, prickly Salmonberry giving rise to thorny Devil's Club along the river. As they gained elevation to the snow zone, they encountered the shorter thickets of the Yellow-cedar and Mountain Hemlock. The weather in these mountains moves in quickly, and that day was no exception.

Vancouver Marmot
[Vancouver Island Marmot]

Marmota vancouverensis

In fresh pelage dark chocolate brown all over without white marking on face or feet except from some white clouding around the nose and occasionally some white spotting on the abdomen. In early summer fades to a rusty brown. Incisors pale to a yellowish-white ... Found only on Vancouver Island, where it is known from Jordan River north to the Forbidden Plateau.[553]

> [Torkko] said we could be in and out before dark. Then we walked, and we walked and we walked until finally it got dark. Torkko said, "There is an old trapper's cabin with some food in it. I think we better stay the night, there should be some food there. It's not far." So we stayed the night there, but we had nothing, no bedding, no food, nothing. We had gone out for an afternoon walk; we didn't even have any warm clothing, as it had been a hot day. I think there was some flour and oatmeal there.[554]

Leaving camp at 5 the next morning, they headed up Jump Creek for an hour and then struck to the right, following Jubilee Creek up to its headwaters at Jubilee Lake, then on up to Green Mountain–Haley Lake subalpine meadows at 4,000 feet. It had been raining hard all morning. They spotted a single doe at Jubilee, which Cowan notes in his journal was in winter pelage, whereas the two they had seen lower down at Boulder Creek had been in summer pelage. It appears that his father-in-law was not taking such careful note of changing pelages with the rising elevation:

> My father-in-law was a businessman. He was physically in reasonably good shape, but he was just played out. He hadn't had anything to eat. He sat at a desk all day. We took it pretty slowly going up. About the time we got to the lake the rain came down. Pouring with rain. There we were with no warm clothing, soaking wet. Kenneth Racy said: "I can't go down. I can't go anymore."[555]

Cowan had at least come equipped with a small hatchet and a chocolate bar. The party tucked themselves under an overhang for shelter, built a fire and dried out. As they came out into the rockslide, five buck deer and six does were standing within a radius of a hundred yards and "did not seem to be the least bit alarmed."[556] Cowan sized up the different bucks' antlers while Torkko "jumps" a doe with two very small fawns, when two marmots are spotted. In his journal, Cowan writes discreetly: "We decided to spend the night up the mountain on the chance of its stopping raining the next morning, so sent Torkko down for some more grub and spent the night in front of the fire in the rain."[557]

His later recollection had somewhat less of the bravado of youth to it:

> We were trying to get a fire going but we were all so cold that we couldn't hold a match in our hands; we had hypothermia. Fortunately I had my little hatchet that I never went anywhere without. I still have it. I beavered down this little dead tree, so we had lots of firewood. By the time I beavered that down I was warm. It wasn't long before we had some venison over that fire. So we sat there in the pouring rain all night long. Occasionally the smoke would blow into our faces and our eyes were just burning. We wondered if we would be able to see again. We were warm on one side, and the cliff was reflecting on the back. We were reasonably comfortable, sitting in the rain all night. We cut off the bits of venison that were cooking over the fire. It started to get light about 4 o'clock in the morning. The rain had stopped, the marmots came out, little thickets of marmots. Then we went home. End of story.[558]

According to the 1931 journal, that wasn't really the end of the story:

> At 7 am, we went along the mountainside to the grass slide and shot 6 whistlers. The whistlers taken consisted of 2 adult females, 1 adult male, 1 juvenile female and 2 juvenile males. All were very dark, especially the adult animals, which were almost black on the neck. The whistlers seemed to be living on the roots of lupin[e], the leaves and roots of an alpine dandelion and the leaves of the big, white-flowered parsnip. All three of us observed three Clarke's Crows [Nutcrackers] at close range flying overhead. No possible doubt as to their identity. We skinned the whistlers and hustled down the mountain, arriving at the cabin at 5:30 pm.[559]

When interviewed in 2006 by Rick Searle, author and park historian for the Elders Council for Parks in BC, Cowan described the nutcracker alongside the marmots as one of his favourites:

> The Clark's Nutcracker, strange little bird, member of the jay family, is one of the characteristic birds of the alpine. And funnily enough there is a similar bird in the alpine parts of Europe and Asia. They are free-flying with slow wing strokes as if they're never in a hurry. They have one of the most prodigious memories of all birds. They spend all summer burying the seeds of alpine trees above timberline

on ridges. They'll land, take a mouthful, dig a hole, bury it. They obviously intend to come back, but how in heaven's name can they ever find it again? They are all over these mountains from here to there and they spend all summer doing it, all day, getting another mouthful of seeds and then burying them, large like pinyon [white bark] pine. Boy, do you think you are going to find that again? They must do, if they are going to survive the winter.[561]

Clark's Nutcracker

Nucifraga columbiana

Much of the nutcracker population frequents subalpine areas from early spring to autumn. There, in the autumn months, they harvest the pine seeds, sometimes flying long distances to cache the seed in the ground on open slopes such as subalpine meadows ridges, rocky outcrops...[560]

When asked what his favourite bird was, Cowan replied: "... well I would be hard pressed to find a more interesting one than the Clark's Nutcracker. It lives where I like to be, high up in the mountains, and has an amazing capacity to survive."[562]

Cowan was fond of telling the Green Mountain story as a prelude to some of his other favourite topics: marmots for one, his father-in-law for another. (Marmots and his father-in-law were already linked because Racey had a BC subspecies of Hoary Marmot named after him by R.M. Anderson in 1932: *M. caligata raceyi* Anderson.) Cowan's early encounters with the marmots gained him some early scientific notoriety, and he delighted in his involvement with "rediscovering" them in 1931. He also had a deep affection for Racey. During the Green Mountain trip, Cowan may have had the best opportunity to show now only his prowess under pressure but also his likely reliability as a future son-in-law. He was also intellectually engaged in the mystery of the marmots and their upland occupation of a changing glaciated landscape. During his museum years in the late '30s, he was to prowl up and down the islands of the coast testing out his theories of glaciation and refugia as deduced from the distribution of the different mammals, which had started with the marmots.[563]

> My take on the history of the marmots is that there was a small colony of them surviving on the Brooks Peninsula [on the west side of Vancouver Island], and when the ice started to retreat, they moved right up to the edge of it and they followed it and the trees came in behind them. The poor things found themselves on top of some rather inhospitable stuff where they made a living up to this point in time. I suggested this back in the '30s and I was told that I was out to lunch.[564]

Interestingly, just months before Cowan died, David Nagorsen published an article with Andrea Cardini on the evolutionary divergence of the Vancouver Island Marmot using the same specimens collected that day in 1931. Cardini and Nagorsen theorized that the divergence of this species occurred when the landscape was rapidly changing, when the island marmots became cut off from mainland populations by ice and water in the late Pleistocene. The population declined, the habitat was fragmented and the marmot population ran into an evolutionary bottleneck.[565] The two authors also concluded that because most of the evolutionary change occurred rapidly in response to the changing environment after the last glaciation, the species would be very susceptible to climate change, which Cowan had also correctly predicted.

Even more interesting in the larger picture is that globally the Vancouver Island Marmot and the Mountain Pygmy Possum – for which Cowan and Joyce, did the very first live scientific documentation, in Kosciuszko National Park, New South Wales, in 1970[566] – have become two of the "poster children" for animals under siege from climate change. Both species hibernate. Both are found at the tops of mountains, rely on alpine habitat and were pushed there by earlier climatic events. Both now find themselves marooned on alpine tops with nowhere to go as temperatures rise: there is no more "up," and "down" is a death trap. Coincidentally, on the very day I wrote this particular section, the *Sydney Morning Herald* published an article headlined "Rising Heat to Endanger Many Species," and the Mountain Pygmy Possum was the lead photograph.[567]

Cowan reported additional sightings of the Haley Lake population in 1938. After that, not much is heard about the marmots until a tipoff in 1972 from the Nanaimo and District Fish and Game Club, who "rediscovered" (again) the Green Mountain–Haley Lake colony. They were raising the alarm when timber company plans showed logging activities coming right up to the colony. R.M. Humphreys wrote to Cowan that "the area in question is very beautiful, with Haley Lake at the bottom of the bowl, and logging would destroy the aesthetic value of the whole area … We ask your support in preserving this natural beauty spot and the unique colony of marmots."[568]

Cowan immediately contacted his former student Glen Smith, who had become chief of wildlife management for the BC Fish and Game Branch, and proposed the idea of a reserve:

> Both colonies are on the timberline, but close to areas that are to be logged, in one case by MacMillan Bloedel Company and in the other case by Crown Zellerbach. I am anxious to persuade both companies to refrain from logging in the area, and I would like to raise with you the possibility of exploring with your Minister the merits of establishing a reserve of some kind to cover the lands along the ridge to protect the essential ecosystem occupied by these mammals. You will be aware of course that they are one of the few Canadian species

included in the Red Book of Endangered Species on the world scene, so we have more than a local responsibility for their survival.[569]

Smith agreed, in a confidential letter, recommending a legal designation of an ecological reserve on the basis that "the major purpose of timber companies is to make money, not preserve common property resources, especially when they are so rare."[570] True to his word, Cowan immediately wrote to the presidents of the two companies to halt the logging. Within two weeks, MacMillan's assistant chief forester had responded and confirmed they had halted any further logging in the area, and the company later donated the land. There is no record of Crown Zellerbach's response.

The next spring when the marmots came out of their hibernation, Cowan headed into the field to do a pre-survey and started the search to find a master's student to take on a two-year behavioural study. The new student, Doug Heard, was found and spent two seasons in the Haley Bowl, completing his thesis in 1977. Also that year, another student, Bill Merilees, with David Routledge of the Federation of BC Naturalists (now Nature BC), who set up the Vancouver Island Marmot Preservation Committee, surveyed the population and prepared a status report. Cowan was ever present on these various committees, including the federal–provincial COSEWIC, which started reviewing the status of the marmot in 1978. By 1980 Cowan's student Bristol Foster, who had become the director of ecological reserves, had put forward a proposal for a Haley Lake Ecological Reserve, and the marmot's status as Canada's most endangered mammal had become official.[571]

The '80s generated lots of interest in the marmots, including proposals for research into their behaviour, distribution and genetics from BC and elsewhere. In the case of one research proposal Cowan had been asked to evaluate, he wrote, "I have problems with this study. It demonstrates no thought for the impacts of the research activity upon the marmot itself."[572] There were also heated debates about population dispersals and declines. Were these animals naturally petering out as a consequence of post-glacial climatic changes influencing vegetation, as Cowan had first hypothesized? Today we know from prehistoric (8,000–8,500 years ago) marmot bones found at 12 caves across the island that the range of the marmots has long been in collapse, supporting Cowan's ideas.

More controversial were the questions implicating humans. Were marmots being hunted to extinction with the opening up of the area through logging roads? Were surrounding clear-cuts drawing animals down to these "fake" subalpine areas and creating population sinks? The irony was that the marmots were colonizing clear-cuts, but researchers quickly discovered they didn't survive their winters there. Were clear-cuts becoming deathtraps because winter conditions were less ideal for the animals at lower elevations? Was the subsequent regrowth of the clear-cuts preventing natural dispersal? Finally, was the decline due to predators, whose access to the marmots had been opened up with roads? Had predators' tastes shifted to marmot, once a secondary preference, after elk and deer populations plummeted due to logging of their winter habitat?

Logging interests of course favoured the "natural causes" argument, while naturalists such as Routledge wanted to explore their hunches about the impacts of increasing logging in the area. Cowan continued to support "good science" to answer the questions, and in typical fashion he looked for independent funding for the survey work headed up by Routledge. He also kept up to date reviewing status reports by government scientists. Ministry of Environment and the Federation of BC Naturalists crossed swords many times.

Cowan was firmly convinced of the combination of all causes, or "cumulative impacts." In his time he called them "incremental impact." In a 1980 interview with the Ministry of Forests magazine *ForesTalk*, he was asked about the greatest threats to conservation. "[E]ach little change has its own impact," he replied. "The total consequence is destruction of the environment, although each separate act appeared insignificant."[573] Citing various case studies, he identified the incremental impacts of logging on winter range and on old-growth forests due to clear-cutting methods, as well as the consequences of access being opened to motorized vehicles. He finished with the problems of being a conservationist: "You can win over and over again, but you only have to lose once and the ball game is over. Extinction is forever."[574] The necessity for assessing cumulative impacts was one of Cowan's key messages throughout his career. His long-term observations in the field, his historical imagination for landscape change and his ability to synthesize multiple disciplines made cumulative impacts an obvious framework, but the concept faltered politically nearly every time he raised it.

Despite MacMillan Bloedel's donations of land for the marmots, it wasn't until 1987 that Haley Lake Ecological Reserve was finally designated. The '90s were disastrous for the marmots and by 1997 the population had shrunk so small that 55 animals, mostly from the reserve, were captured and brought into a captive breeding program. In 2004 the first captive-born pair released at Haley Lake bred in the wild. Haley Lake once again had marmots. At the age of 90, when questioned about his stance on the marmot reintroductions, Cowan answered: "Everything has changed and changes all the time. Animals have always gone extinct. In fact there are more animals extinct than there are alive. You have to be prepared to lose some animals. But you have to give it a try. If you are trying to reverse the actions that resulted from the introduction of man, I think that's worthwhile."[575]

An intriguing footnote to the marmot story came from Andrew MacDonald, the biologist who worked with Cowan latterly on establishing the professorship in his name at the University of Victoria. Cowan had confided to MacDonald during a lunch meeting one day that he knew what Vancouver Island Marmots tasted like – presumably as consumed on that hungry morning of the 1931 trip back from Green Mountain–Haley Lake.

CHAPTER 13

"... scenes from that summer guide my hand."[576]

Chilcotin, 1931

A fter coming off Green Mountain, Racey, Cowan and Alan headed back by boat to Vancouver to pick up the rest of the Racey family – Eileen, Joyce and Stewart – for the final leg of the 1931 collecting expedition. The destination was Chezacut Lake (now called Chilcotin Lake) up the Chilcotin River – four days drive from Vancouver at the time. There are no journal entries for the trip up but from his reminiscences we know that en route they "camped and collected in the pocket desert of the southern Okanagan where White-tailed Jack Rabbits, Burrowing Owls and Sage Thrashers provided fascination..."[577]

These beautiful long-eared animals that could clock up to 55 kilometres an hour had the unfortunate habit of eating young fruit trees and were shot on sight by orchardists. The last sighting of a White-tailed Jackrabbit in BC was in 1981 and it is now considered extirpated.[579] Cowan's unpublished journal sightings and earlier accounts of his mentors Racey and Hamilton Mack Laing are the only data available for this species.[580] Given Cowan's century-long association with rabbits and hares, it isn't a surprise that he would be the British Columbian to scientifically document both their appearance and their disappearance.

Around July 17 the Raceys and Cowan went south to explore the Vaseux Lake area. They got as far as Boulder Creek, five kilometres north of Oliver. In a stone pile they found an individual Pallid Bat roosting. This specimen, attributed to Cowan, was to remain the only example of the Pallid Bat in the province for the next 60 years until Dr. Brock Fenton captured four others in Vaseux Creek Canyon. Of the 16 bat species in BC, the Pallid is the only one that has made it on to the federal species at risk list as "threatened."

Leaving the Okanagan behind, they headed north for the long drive to the Chilcotin via Kamloops, Cache Creek, Williams Lake and Alexis Creek, reaching the Chezacut turnoff on July 23, a long and very bad road. The village of Chezacut, which consisted of not much more than a post office cum general store servicing ranchers and trappers, was farther up. They had come here to fill in some gaps in the small mammal distributions for this region of BC. The lake formed a transition zone from the many grassland species (Bluebunch wheatgrass) of the bunchgrass zone just to the south, to the Jack pine and the northern spruce forests. Bunchgrass follows the dry interior lowland banks of the Fraser, Thompson, Similkameen and lower Chilcotin rivers. Racey had been asked by Anderson at the National Museum to see what lived at the northern tips of the fingers of grasslands. Cowan had been surveying these types of habitats for the last two summers, but far to the south at Kamloops. They were there to tease out the subspecies of hares, rabbits, chipmunks, red squirrels, flying squirrels, pack rats and the various shrews, voles and mice, some of which hovered at low numbers.

Darwin was the first to detect the tension between those "splitting" the world into increasing numbers of species and those "lumping" them back together again. From the public's perspective it looked like a baffling activity. From the inside, it was a kind of love affair where the beloved is rendered in the most intimate detail. Around 1958–59, Cowan would deliver a lecture called "Extinct and Vanishing Mammals" partly based on a report of that name by zoologist Glover M. Allen.[582] Allen identified species at risk from human activities and in many of them several subspecies were included. In Cowan's talk, he laid down his ideas about the value of describing uniqueness. He began by distinguishing Rare populations (which always have existed in small numbers) from Threatened (where numbers are declining in a trend towards extinction). Cowan asks:

> We are plagued by a problem of criteria. Are we interested in the survival of all subspecies? Here we run into the current argument concerning the validity of the subspecies concept. There can be no objectivity here; my criteria can more easily be seen in retrospect than defined here.[583]

Some of the examples Cowan used were the localized forms of voles (*Microtus* species) and grizzly drawn from studies by members of the 'B'. The Mexican Grizzly was still around at that time; Aldo Leopold had rediscovered it in the Sierra del Nido a year earlier. It was a smaller, silver-coloured bear that lived almost exclusively on plants and insects. It only fed occasionally on carrion of small mammals and was not a cattle killer. A rancher had laid down the poison 1080 (which causes a slow, lingering death) that summer in the Sierra del Nido. Forty-two grizzlies

White-tailed Jackrabbit

Lepus townsendi townsendi
[now *L. townsendii townsendii*]

Large size; upper parts in summer pale grey tinged with black and brown; tail pure white. In winter entire pelage white. The Okanagan Valley from Osoyoos to White Lake. Formerly abundant but cultivation has reduced its numbers.[578]

Pallid Bat

Antrozous pallidus cantwelli
[now *pacificus*]

A large pale-coloured bat with very large ears ... Dorsal colour dull buffy drab washed with smoky brown, underparts creamy buff ... The single specimen was taken in a stone pile by the roadside 3 miles north of Oliver.[581]

were poisoned, wiping out half the population. Cowan asked the question: Do we care about them as a subspecies enough to protect them? Apparently we didn't: the Mexican Grizzly is now extinct.

In 1931 the Raceys and Cowan were also in Chezacut to collect birds and figure out one of the mysteries of the province: the habits of the White Pelicans that appeared every summer on Chezacut Lake but whose nesting sites hadn't yet been recorded for science.

Cowan's journal records the arrival of the Racey family on the grassy south-facing edge of the lake at 6 p.m. on July 23, 1931. It is the height of the summer in the Chilcotin. Swallows and swifts with their fledged young are swooping overhead eating up the ample insect life around the lake and meadows. Bluebird chicks have fledged and the brilliant flashes of blue dart over the meadows. Dusk brings the nighthawks, with their high-pitched nasal *peent* and booming sounds as the birds pull out of dives during courtship display. The Sharp-tailed Grouse with maturing chicks are venturing out into the meadows to feed in the declining light. Marsh Hawks [Northern Harriers] are still skirting the margins looking for prey. The Buffleheads are back in their tree nests and other ducks with young are well tucked in to the marshes. After setting up his tent on the grassy shores of the lake, and before retiring for the first night, Cowan suddenly spotted two pelicans feeding and courting in unison on the lake with much bowing and swaying of heads.[585]

That same night, Racey Sr. trapped a Navigator Shrew.

Pictures of the Racey family camping at Chezacut Lake show a happy crew. One picture, obviously taken by Kenneth, shows them all posing in black one-piece bathing suits – with little sexual dimorphism, at least in style. The younger boys are looking away and Eileen is looking at Ian and Joyce, who are beaming at the camera with their good fortune at having the rest of the summer together. A set of photographs captures Alan and Kenneth Racey sitting with Cowan, skinning specimens in their open bush "lab," peering into cameras on tripods photographing mice in the forest and looking under stumps and logs for runways. Another series of pictures shows various combinations of paddlers in their dugout canoe on the

American White Pelican

Pelecanus erythrorhynchos

The only known breeding location for the American White Pelican in British Columbia is at Stum Lake, 70 km northwest of Williams Lake ... In summer, pelicans forage primarily in the Chilcotin Plateau areas between 3 km ... and 142 km ... from the breeding colony. They do not forage at the colony itself ... use of lakes for foraging depends on distance from the colony, abundance and availability of food, and presence of loafing sites. The lake most consistently used for feeding is Chilcotin Lake, 71 km west of the colony.[584]

lake – Joyce's album has a picture of Cowan paddling with her father.

Each afternoon, Cowan laid his traps in the north-facing spruce forest, the south-facing grasslands or the low-lying marshes, returning at dawn to check them. A frequent journal entry was "Joyce + I went over to the spruce woods before breakfast on the way over seeing 2 herons."[587] While laying the traps, they searched for other signs of wildlife. Some of the highlights Cowan noted were finding two grebe nests, one of a Red-necked (then called Holboell's Grebe) and one of a Pied-billed. "On the way back we found a grebe's nest of some sort, built of water lily leaves + about 2 ft. in [diameter] contained 6 eggs. The bird had covered these when she left the nest."[588]

During the hottest part of the day, in the shade of their bush lab, they skinned. In the evenings, Cowan fished for trout with Eileen and Joyce – a tradition well-established since Alta Lake. There is more detail of pelican courtship than human courtship recorded from those extensive paddles round the lake, but this was the summer when and the place where they got engaged. (The official notice in the paper didn't appear until spring of 1936, prior to their wedding in April.) In 2002 (just before Joyce died) Cowan told Neil Dawe, who had written on the Chilcotin area and was soliciting some feedback, "I spent a month at that lake with the Racey family. In fact it was there that Joyce and I began our close friendship that built into now 66 years together. You will understand that we have a special fondness for the area."[589]

The official line was that they were engaged for five years and that it took Cowan that long because "I had to get enough money. We had seven hundred dollars between us to get married … those were the days when you didn't shack up, you know."[590] Cowan was always quick to enlist courtship behaviour as a way to engage his students. Past student Iola Knight wrote of this style, for his 90th birthday tribute:

> We had completed most of the internal anatomy and were studying the reproductive systems, male and female. My partner (a girl) and I had completed the sex of our cat, as had the two guys who sat in front of us. Since we had opposite-sexed cats, we switched partners. Ian entered the room, saw that we had switched partners and promptly remarked in a voice for all to hear, "Hmm, spring must be in the air, mating season." Me being prone to blushing, turned 40 shades of red, which my classmates and Ian took full advantage of. He has probably forgotten the event, but not me! A wonderful role model for men and women – small wonder I refer to him as my mentor.[591]

Navigator Shrew
[American Water Shrew]

Sorex palustris

Underparts silvery white.… Feeds very actively underwater upon insects, invertebrates and small fish. Ranges over the entire province from the alplands at 6,500 feet in the Rocky Mountains to sea level at Powell River and from the alpine arctic regions to the Okanagan Valley at Vernon.[586]

During the five weeks at Chezacut, they also made weekly excursions up the dirt track – which became an impenetrable mud trap after summer downpours – to the general store and post office. The rewards for getting there weren't just to stock up but a chance to talk to the proprietor, Frank Shillaker. Shillaker was an English First World War veteran who had bought the store at Chezacut in 1927 and according to local historians "fell in love with this place for the rest of his life."[592] Besides stocking his store, he was the postmaster and traded with the Chilcotin native trappers for furs, mostly muskrat and weasel. The added attraction for the Racey clan was that Shillaker was a keen naturalist and kept good notes of the comings and goings of the wildlife as well as having extensive knowledge of the area. He had tipped off the trappers whose territory the Raceys had moved into, and two of them, Laciese Cha and Moses Ronsin, reported to the Raceys the presence of Meadow Voles in the region. Shillaker presented Cowan with a specimen of one given him by Cha. Cowan's journal records these tips gleaned from Shillaker during their visits:

Mountain Caribou bull with fractured radius and ulna

Rangifer tarandus montanus
[now *R. t. caribou*]

Body colour deep blackish-brown; greyish-white on belly, buttocks and underside of tail and on neck of male. Antlers comparatively shorter than *osborni*.... The race is found also on the eastern slopes and outlying ranges of the Coast Range from the Bulkley Mountains south to the Rainbow Mountains, Itcha Mountains and Cariboo Mountains.[594]

> Lame Billy, the medicine man of the Chilcotin Indians, paid us a visit. He states that moose first came into this country 15 to 17 years ago. There used to be a great many elk in this country years ago and caribou. Still a small herd of caribou on the Itcha Mountains.[593]

Racey set off on horseback with Lame Billy into the Itcha Mountains, to track down the caribou. The Itchas are isolated volcanoes that rise above the Jack pine forests, with open alpine grasslands on their slopes that attract ungulates and provide refuge from wolves in the deep snow. Although Cowan didn't join him, he reported on Racey's findings in his journal:

> Mr. Racey returned back after a hard trip into the Itchas three days ride west of here. Beaver not much farther up than the falls. Moose very abundant but only the bulls living at the higher altitudes. Deer fairly common. Caribou getting very scarce owing to frequent depredations of the Blackwater Indians.[595]

This story is fairly consistent with the American writer–cowboy Rich Hobson's accounts of his first ventures into the Itchas with his partner Panhandle Phillips at about the same time Racey was in that country. Hobson wrote in his BC classic *Grass Beyond the Mountains* of the "legend of the Ulkatchos" who lived at the headwaters of the Blackwater. The Ulkatchos were rumoured to be a band of lost Sioux warriors who, in the aftermath of a Chilcotin invasion, had happened upon a group of Carrier widows with their children, married them and became hunters of caribou in the Itchas.[596]

The legends appear to have been passed on by locals like Shillaker to visitors to the region. Ulkatcho, or "people of the fat of the land," were indeed Southern Carrier people who occupied the upper Blackwater River that Cowan mentioned. The smallpox epidemic of 1862 had left the Southern Carriers decimated, and the movement of the fur trade westward into "the fat of the land" in the early part of the 19th century had put enormous pressure on game. The trade was supplying the forts with food as well, pushing species like caribou into remoter areas, and the disappearance of the caribou in turn pushed the Carriers into starvation.[597]

The Itcha Ilgachuz herd was eventually surveyed by a Cowan student, caribou specialist Tom Bergerud, in 1978 as part of a larger study on the status of caribou in BC.[598] Classified as the arboreal or Mountain Caribou, the animal was part of the larger population of the Woodland Caribou species. This ecotype was to draw increasing attention as numbers of isolated populations in different mountain ranges continued to dwindle and flicker out over the century. The Iltcha herd, counted at about 300 animals in 1978, had increased to 1,500 by 1998. Some protection had been provided in 1994 with the Itcha Ilgachuz Provincial Park designation, but the park fell badly short of what was needed for the herd. The protected area didn't capture sufficient old-growth winter habitat, and surrounding clear-cuts were seriously impacting the herd. In 1998 Cowan advised activists about the historic needs of the herd. Today, southern and northern mountain populations, or ecotypes, are now recognized. The southern population, including the Itcha, "the largest stable herd in southern BC"[599] is listed as Threatened under the federal Species at Risk Act and the northern population in the Chilcotin is of Special Concern.

Shillaker had obviously struck an enduring relationship with the young Cowan, as he left him his field notes. Cowan later used the notes for his 1947 book with Munro on bird fauna of the province, in which he acknowledged Shillaker's contributions.[600] One of Shillaker's entries shed some light on the elk die-off, which the local native trappers attributed to severe winter storms in the mid-19th century. Shillaker's interest was piqued in the wake of an accident when two cowboys got caught outdoors in a freak storm and drowned in the nearby lake a year after the Racey family visit:

> When the police were dragging for Alec Marshall's and Hutton's bodies in September 1933 in Puntze Lake, a very good complete set of elk horns were brought to the surface but unfortunately disintegrated rapidly ... How old was it or how long it is since these animals

roamed the Chilcotin, I cannot say. On Bayliff's Range south of the Bull Canyon a small opening is called Elkhorn Flat from the remains of antlers found there years ago. I have carefully questioned the older Indians such as Granbush, Lame Billy and others but they have no idea when the animals were to be found here. Charley Boy says his father knew of them as a boy. Lame Billy's age is probably between 75 and 80 years. Assuming his father to marry between 15 and 20 years of age, that would allow very roughly 85 years since they were here.[601]

Cowan's interest in the elk was also piqued by this story. A highly adaptable species and also highly prized by hunters, elk in the early 1800s were the most plentiful game species on the continent, divided into six subspecies, two of which, the Rocky Mountain Elk and Roosevelt's Elk, were in British Columbia. By 1931, however, the Rocky Mountain Elk's range had shrunk to small populations in the east of the province and the Roosevelt's had diminished to a small number in the mountains of Vancouver Island. The Roosevelt's had been extirpated from the southern mainland, and other than a few reintroductions into some areas, elk were not the ubiquitous animal we see today. Cowan's career spanned the re-expansion of the elk, and he witnessed the impacts of the reintroductions which, coupled with predator controls, had led to exploding populations in places like the Rocky Mountain national parks.

Both elk and caribou were to increasingly feature in Cowan's research and advocacy as he was brought in to assess populations. Whether it was impacts of introduced elk to the Rocky Mountain parks or impacts on boreal caribou from pipeline construction, northern developments focused research and expert testimony on the issue. The place was important too. Chezacut–Chilcotin Lake, where the Raceys were camping that summer, was identified by The Nature Trust of BC in 1987 as a site of scientific interest while Cowan was on the board. Six hundred acres of wetland habitat in private ownership were acquired and protected.

There is little evidence that the 22-year-old Cowan was challenging the assumptions of the day regarding native hunting pressures on wildlife – but he was open to hearing the stories of the local trappers and hunters. The seeds of understanding the bigger contextual story of changing industrial land uses, colonization and wildlife consumption were certainly being sown that summer, with exposure to people like Shillaker and the trappers. Over his lifetime, Cowan was to develop an increasingly broader critique of the impacts of industrial land uses on indigenous populations. In 1969, at the height of his career, he wrote:

> Population in an ecological sense is a relative concept and even in parts of the Arctic death from starvation has overtaken a distressingly large number of people in the last decade...; this has been a direct consequence of dramatic man-induced changes in the environment.
>
> While the crisis of numbers haunts the unindustrialized sectors of the human species, advanced peoples are pursuing a course

equally at odds with ecological prudence, a course that can only lead to impoverishment and misery to man and catastrophe to a large part of the world's living organisms.[602]

In correspondence with his close friend Tom Beck, Cowan discussed the role of human hunting pressures on wildlife populations over the millennia. The two veteran hunter–scientists had spent a lifetime providing data on wildlife populations to guide government land-use decisions and wildlife management. Beck's experience was in the North amongst the Inuit. He had written to Cowan about his understanding of traditional practices and conservation philosophies. Cowan, then 84, had responded:

> In general I think there has been too much generalizing by the archaeologists. North America presented a great diversity of ecological regions. Some of them present[ed] opportunities for hunting and some did not. The strong nations no doubt appropriated the easy living areas in which they became adept at putting together the seasonally available resources into a successful lifestyle. The not so successful groups were relegated to the regions of difficult living and led a hand to mouth existence ... I think your suggestion that a feeling of kinship and mutual responsibility between the hunter and his prey can have effects similar to our mathematically based calculations of sustainable yield, and so forth, is well put. I had not thought of it that way. So I am struggling on with what, for me, is a new field of thought and am learning things. Your help is much appreciated.[603]

Cowan then spent the autumn of his 84th year putting together a bibliography on the archaeological data, looking for correlations of changing wildlife and human populations in North America in pre- and post-Columbian times, against the backdrop of European colonization pressures and disease. His conclusion: "If wildlife is present in excess of need one can make choices as to what and when you kill. But if wildlife is scarce your very survival depends on taking at each opportunity. Conservation decisions are likely to be a luxury you cannot afford."[604] Having been hungry himself as a child and hunted all his life, he claimed this to be true in his case. By age 90 Cowan had boiled his ideas down to the species level:

> The Indians were keen observers. They knew that if they put a weir across a river and left it there, there were no salmon ... If you are out in the woods with your family you are in general hungry, and if you found an animal you killed it if you could. You didn't ask yourself if that was the last [caribou] cow around ... Not even our government in Ottawa can calculate that.[605]

That summer on 1931 in the Chilcotin was a seminal one for Cowan and he referred to it fondly. "To this day, as I write about Canyon Wrens, Black Swifts, White Pelicans or Waterthrushes, scenes from that summer guide my hand."[606]

CHAPTER 14

*"Sunk several [gold] pits with negligible results ...
Took female peromyscus in pit."*

Cariboo, 1932

T he 1931–1932 academic year, Cowan's fifth and final one, was full on. He was soaring with honours in zoology, had passed organic chemistry finally, and had a green light to go to Berkeley. He was now curator of the Biological Discussion Club, which had students, faculty and visiting scientists gathering at professors' homes for edifying lectures on Darwinism, genetics and evolution, entomophagous insects [insects that eat other insects] and oysters, among other topics. The objective of the club was to "stimulate interest in the biological sciences within the university by the reading of papers or addresses of general interest."[607] Cowan had presented various papers over the years from "Fauna of the Whistler Region" to his last paper on "Big Game in BC."

Big game was also the subject of his honours thesis, "The Ecology and Life History of the Columbian Black-tailed Deer in British Columbia." In a letter to Francis Kermode at the Provincial Museum, he set out his modest goal:

Dear Mr. Kermode,
In connection with my work at the university I am writing up the deer of the province. This necessitates the gathering together of authentic information from all possible sources and I wondered if I could enlist your aid on some points ... Have you any deer skulls in the museum collection that would be available for study? Hoping that you will be able to help me on these few points.
I remain yours very sincerely,
Ian McTaggart Cowan.[608]

Using his field notes "accumulated by myself during the past eight years," the thesis is attributed in his introduction to "a combination of circumstances [that] has enabled me to study rather fully the habits and ecology of the various species of the *Cervidae* found in British Columbia."[609] Those circumstances he lays out as the methodology proposed by Ernest Thompson Seton in his *Lives of Game Animals*;[610] the professorial direction of McLean Fraser; and the scholarly insight of Spencer (parasites) and Dickson (fungi). Laing is acknowledged for his notes on deer and

Racey for "wholehearted assistance whenever and wherever needed." It is in this paper that he raises the taxonomic question of British Columbia's deer, which he states is "entirely neglected"[611] and which subsequently becomes the proposed topic of his PhD dissertation.

This early thesis already holds all the ingredients of Cowan: the supremely confident researcher and enthusiastic educator. Like Seton, the natural history of the deer is narrated with a round-the-campfire flair spiced with some sensational chapters on Freak Antlers, Enemies, Parasites and Polygamy. His first page on Fawns is worth quoting in full, as it provides a real sense of what is to come with his later television shows, lectures and publications:

His fondness for the sociability of the male deer is captured in the chapter of that name:

> The Coast Blacktail is entirely lacking in gregarious instincts ... However, two and sometimes three bucks often form a very close friendship during their summer sojourn in the mountaintops. These blood brothers stick together at all times until the "mad moon" awakens the old unrest once more.[613]

And from the chapter on polygamy:

> During the period of the rut, the buck remains with a doe or even with a pair of does for two or three days before seeking further conquests. Thus during the period of sexual activity a buck may mate with upwards of ten does. The male coast deer never attempts to gather together a harem, as do some of our game animals, but throughout his brief wedded life with each spouse

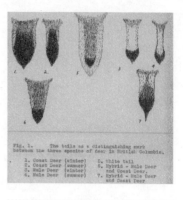

Illustration of tails of black- and white-tailed deer for Cowan BA thesis, UBC, 1932

Columbian Blacktailed Deer
[Columbian Black-tailed Deer]

Odocoileus columbianus
columbianus (Richardson)
[Odocoileus hemionus columbianus]

At birth the Coast Blacktail fawn is covered with a short, slightly woolly coat of fine dark-chestnut-coloured hair with several rows of yellowish white spots down the back and sides. These spots are due to the presence of small bunches of yellow-tipped hairs. When seen standing in some forest glade, the little fawn presents a striking and pleasing picture but seems to be unnecessarily conspicuous. However, let him lie down on the dead leaves of some thicket where the rays of the sun, filtering through the foliage, make yellow splashes on the fallen leaves, and in such a setting the fawn is almost invisible so perfectly do his colours blend with the background. As soon as the little fellows start following their mother about, their colours start to fade from exposure to the sun, so that by the middle of July the fawns are very little darker than their parents and the yellow spots are but indistinct smudges.[612]

Cowan with Black tailed Deer at Constitution Hill, near Comox, November 10, 1930

he is the exemplification of faithfulness and looks at no other. The rutting season over, he quickly loses all interest in the opposite sex and leads a life of aloofness and complete celibacy until the return of the autumn again sends him on the rampage.[614]

The document holds up today as a readable guide to the coastal deer, illustrated with Cowan's own ink drawings and black and white photographs. It also includes a lengthy discussion on the food of the blacktail (which troubled most gardeners and farmers then as much as it does today), which was to develop into a full-blown five-year research program while he was with the BC Provincial Museum. In the section on Moults, he writes about his observations of deer from the marmot expedition and their changing pelages as they climbed the mountain.

His final paragraph ends:

> When the crisp, cold nights of the late summer announce the approach of winter snows, the return migration takes place. The does and fawns first, followed by the young bucks, the old bucks generally braving it out on the mountain tops until the first flurry of snow gives them the ultimatum, and imbued with the spirit of the "mad moon" the lords of the herd hasten downwards to keep their tryst with the does among the towering firs and cedars.[615]

There are no personal letters to indicate that his Setonesque view of the world drifted into his relationship with Joyce, but there is no shortage of evidence that he had a romantic bent. Joyce was reportedly the more pragmatic of the two, although she didn't pursue a post-secondary education. She stayed at home, helping both her parents in their pursuits. As her daughter Ann observed, "She illustrated the benefits of homeschooling."[616] She honed her naturalist skills, improved her botany and fishing skills, diversified into gardening and food preserving and shaped herself into a staunch colleague, helpmate and companion for her future husband, a situation that didn't waver for the rest of their lives. Cowan was spending every spare weekend on the mountaintops with her and her father as well as Laing and occasionally dragging his brother Patrick Cowan along to hunt for venison on the side.

On one of his trips with Patrick up Black Mountain in the North Shore range in October, they observed two hardy Silver-haired Bats flying around the plateau each night, even as a snowstorm moved in and drove the brothers down off the mountain. Cowan had been presented with two living specimens of these bats in a torpid state, once in 1929 and again in the winter of 1931 from the same location at UBC: the loose bark of a giant Western Redcedar on campus. His notes on the hibernation of *Lasionycteris noctivagans*[617] were promptly written up for *The Canadian Field-Naturalist* and this is still today the only early citation for this little-known bat and one of few observations of its hibernation in BC.[618] Its hardiness and reliance on old-growth trees for hibernating, first noted by Cowan, raised the possibility in his mind of its being dependent on old-growth forests.

The place where they were climbing on Black Mountain is now a ski area in Cypress Provincial Park. Cowan and Joyce returned to Black Mountain countless times throughout their life but never saw the bats again. Joyce was an avid hiker until very late in life. She wrote to her daughter in 1977, "We climbed Black Mountain last Wednesday. We were in brilliant sunshine all day and we could look down on the fog-shrouded city with the odd tall building showing though."[620] A research opportunity lies in determining whether the bats are still scouring the slopes of Black Mountain for the last of the autumn's moths.

In Cowan's final year at UBC, his mother, Laura Cowan, received a small family inheritance and used the money to buy a car, which her two sons used for a trip to the Cariboo, to be financed themselves by panning for gold. It was the height of the Depression and there was little other work, the national park work having disappeared. Cowan had put out the idea to Racey that the museum might need some additional collections, including "the little-known interior marmot, or woodchuck".[621]

The two brothers left on May 9, headed for the Cariboo – first stop, 100 Mile House, where they did a bit of birding while fixing a leaky valve after a tricky summiting of Mount Begbie in snow. On day two they made it to Soda Creek, where they did their first six pans of gravel. They spotted a pair of Pygmy Nuthatches there but didn't secure enough "colour" to pay for lunch. There is one photograph of the two tall young men standing beside their dashing 1925 Dodge Brothers convertible at Quesnel, each with a foot on the running board. They cut quite the figures in their moustaches, broad-rimmed hats and dusty jeans and boots, with camping, panning and collecting gear piled high in the trunk.

Racey had connected Cowan with the Boyds at Cottonwood Ranch, their destination. The Boyds were well known in the naturalist community. Racey knew them through T.T. (Tom) McCabe, another one of the 'B' who lived just north of Cottonwood at Indianpoint Lake. Tom and Elinor McCabe figured strongly in Cowan's life. Although they weren't there that spring to greet the two brothers, they were orchestrating things from behind the scenes. The McCabes made sure the two young brothers were greeted by the matriarch of Cottonwood, Janet Boyd, of whom Tom McCabe had this to say to Grinnell down in Berkeley:

> The wonderful old lady in question (who arrived in these parts if you please from San Mateo County California in 1861) should have these for her two elderly sons, keen naturalists and the best natural observers I've ever met, who have just added to a very long list of favours by sending me lots of material. Cottonwood is our most westerly station, still in the timber but not far from the mountains.[624]

Marmot, or Woodchuck

Marmota monax petrensis

Central and southeastern districts from the Stikine River south to the Chilcotin River and through the mountains east of the Fraser River to Revelstoke and Creston.[622] *M. m. petrensis* is probably without exception the quietest and most unobtrusive member of the genus in British Columbia.[623]

Cowan was to bring Joyce to Indianpoint Lake four years later for their honeymoon. Tom and Elinor modelled the kind of partnership Ian and Joyce aspired to and were to have a lasting influence on both of them. McCabe was one of the four named mentors in Cowan's small memoir. "Tom McCabe, tall, athletic, impulsive, quick of mind as of temper (more often directed at malfunctioning equipment than at people) will forever stride through my memory."[625] Cowan described him as "badly beaten up" by his years as an artillery officer in the trenches of the First World War. He was eligible for a war veteran land grant, so Elinor had brought him to the "quiet but demanding environment of the wilderness"[626] at Indianpoint Lake to recover. She had a strong interest in the natural world and nursed her husband back to "physical and philosophical stamina"[627] by encouraging him in her interests. Elinor and he had built a two-storey log house seven miles into the bush. From there they made their observations, wrote articles and collected specimens for the museum for income, including northern deer that Cowan used later in his research.

For this first trip, though, Cottonwood Ranch was to be the brothers' base. It lay just outside Quesnel on the road to Barkerville, the Boyd family having supplied meat and a general store to prospectors during the gold rush. Besides being good naturalists, the Boyds also had good local knowledge of gold around their lands. Cowan writes that "[Boyd] advised us to try the Cottonwood, Lightning and

Swift rivers ... but there was no gold to speak of on the rivers, which were in high flood. One fellow out of 50 was making 75 cents a day, the rest nothing. Rabbits and moose plentiful."[628]

On the way into Quesnel, they stopped at Four Mile Creek and managed to get "16–20 colour" out of four pans – not enough for groceries – but the effort gave time to spot four species of warblers, the appropriately named Golden-crowned Sparrow and other treasures: the first being a sunny camp on a grassy bench overlooking a picturesque gorge of Four Mile Creek. In between panning they set out traps, and caught their next treasure, Caribou Slim, a trapper of few words who told them he'd trapped four Fishers last winter, one of which fetched $269 – far more lucrative than the gold dust they were sifting. Then came their ultimate prize, the silent interior Woodchuck, a male specimen coming in at 18¼" × 4⅜" × 3" which they found sharing their campsite in a burrow under the roots of the trees along the steep banks.[629]

In the introduction to an article for *The Canadian Field-Naturalist*, Cowan wrote:

> The species was first encountered on May 10th at Four Mile Creek, about four miles north and east of Quesnel, BC. On this date a single specimen, an immature male, No. 428 in the writer's collection, was secured. During the succeeding weeks five more marmot burrows were located and two more specimens taken ... The accompanying notes are presented as a slight addition to our knowledge concerning the habits of this rarest of British Columbia marmots ... Not a sound was heard from them throughout the month that we lived in sight of their burrows; even when thoroughly alarmed no warning cry was given to inform others of the presence of danger...[630]

The virtue of silence was one of the teachings of the 'B'. In 1935, Ernest Thompson Seton's "The Message of the Indian" (from *The Book of Woodcraft*) was delivered at their ninth annual meeting.[631] Seton quotes the Sioux author Ohiyesa (Charles Eastman), who wrote: "If you ask him 'What is silence?' he will answer, 'It is the Great Mystery! The holy silence is His voice!' If you ask 'What are the fruits of silence?' he will say, 'They are self-control, true courage or endurance, patience, dignity and reverence. Silence is the cornerstone of character.'"[632] Cowan was steeped in Seton's *Book of Woodcraft* and one detects a solidarity with those they encountered that summer who demonstrated these traits. Meanwhile the 'B' were silently ensuring that Cowan's path was cleared for his entry to Berkeley.

During their month at Four Mile Creek, the brothers had plenty to keep them busy. The first flush of success encouraged them to construct a makeshift rocking box, "the Rocker," to speed up the process. Alas, after eight hours on the Cottonwood banks with the Rocker on May 11, they had only garnered 10 cents worth of gold. They had, however, time to study the Woodchuck habits of feeding exclusively on grass, clover and dandelions. The next day, they hiked up the old Pacific Great Eastern railway grade to Ten Mile Lake, where they came upon a breeding frenzy of ducks, gulls, terns and loons. They investigated a Merlin pair (then known as the Pigeon Hawk) and their nest 25 feet up a white spruce tree, of which few nests had ever been described, Cowan climbed up, measured it (12 inches deep by 18 inches in diameter), noted the materials, took the two eggs, killed the pair, skinned them, then hiked the six miles back to camp.

The North American Merlin was one of the species most heavily hit by DDT. Spencer and Buckell had drawn attention to the problems for bees in 1946, but Cowan didn't observe the impact on birds until 1955 in his paper on fluorocarbons. The little falcon sat on the threatened list throughout the 1970s, but with the banning of DDT, populations started to inch back. Today their characteristic alarm call is familiar in many parts of BC. In 1931, the issues at the time were gold-mine tailings. The two brothers spent one more day working with the Rocker, sinking pits, working the banks and some "nice gravels," then abandoned gold mining for

Adult male black **Merlin**

Falco columbarius

Of 14 nests, 11 were found in conifers, including Douglas-fir, spruces and pines ... Thirteen nests were actually old nests of other species of birds ... Heights of 12 nests ranged from 6.1 to 45.7 metres....[633]

the more lucrative pursuits of fishing and hunting for food and specimens and observing the Woodchucks. Cowan had discovered that the prospecting pits they dug conjured up more mice than gold – which he promptly turned into specimens.[634]

They attempted to dig out a burrow of the Woodchucks but "it proved to be a Herculean task due to this habit of digging horizontally into the face of a steep bank."[635] Just as memorable were the mosquitoes, which Cowan notes as "particularly bad," which means they must have been vicious. One morning, he caught a Long-tailed Weasel prowling around the camp at 5:30 a.m. "while I was sitting by the fire cursing the mosquitoes."[636]

The brothers returned to Ten Mile Lake frequently and nearby Ahbau River, restocking at the ranch with the Boyds. It was a good choice. Ten Mile Lake lies in a basin that catches whatever is moving between the dry Chilcotin plateau grasslands and the wetter highlands to the east. The White Spruce in which they found the Merlin nest was on the other side of the lake to the drier-loving Saskatoon berry, dogwood and Douglas-fir browsed down by moose and deer. The Cowan boys were moving through a lot of country in the Quesnel–Cottonwood region, following along the old railway grade, and they quickly homed in on the biodiversity gold, if not the real stuff. When they wanted to cross the Cottonwood, they chopped down trees to make bridges between bars and built rafts where the crossing was wide. They lived on deer and trout, and at least two afternoons were spent lazily lying by the river investigating the nasal passages of their prey for botfly larvae and the intestines for worms. They stumbled onto a bear eating a deer, which they scared away so Cowan could do a postmortem and measure the size of the two embryos. Hiking up the Ahbau River, they tracked mule deer, bear, porcupine, moose, coyote, fox and wolf all in one day.

As spring caressed the Cariboo, Cowan noted the arrival of each of the songbirds, including his first Magnolia Warbler, which he struggled to identify – not surprisingly, it turns out.

Cowan was to return to Ten Mile Lake four years later with Joyce in their honeymoon year, 1936. The couple stopped by twice, taking in Ten Mile Lake – which he had such sweet memories of – and Indianpoint Lake to visit the McCabes, on their way to and from a museum expedition farther north. Ten Mile Lake, at the time of their honeymoon was not the warm, fecund place he remembered from his earlier visit. It "rained torrents" and was "cold and miserable"[638] and they spent a week trudging around soaked, crouching under canvas to skin specimens and diving for their tent when the mosquitoes got bad. Cowan noted that the Magnolia Warbler, despite the inclement weather, was still there singing his sweet song, "which consists of five syllables *swee-swee-swee-whitl-swee.*"[639] A sighting that was underlined in red was another appropriately named bird, the Northern Waterthrush. They had failed to find its nest. These birds are notoriously good concealers

Magnolia Warbler

Dendroica magnolia
[now in genus *Setophaga*]

The Magnolia Warbler entered the known avifauna of British Columbia relatively late. Prior to ornithological explorations in the Peace River area in 1938 (Cowan, 1939), the species had been known only from Revelstoke in 1890, Field in 1892 and the Quesnel area in 1932 and 1936. By the mid-1940s it was known to be widely distributed in the Sub-Boreal interior and the northern regions of the Southern Interior Mountains ecoprovinces and to be less common, or transient, in the Peace Lowland (Munro and Cowan 1947).[637]

Northern Waterthrush

Seiurus noveboracensis

Typically it establishes and defends by song about 1.0 ha [hectare] of breeding territory in a wooded swamp or along a willow-bordered stream.[641]

Red Crossbill

Loxia curvirostra

McCabe and McCabe (1933) conducted research on Red Crossbills at Indianpoint Lake north of Bowron Lake Park in British Columbia and contributed a thoughtful paper on the breeding ecology of this enigmatic species. Their thoughts on timing of nesting, age of first breeding, and moult patterns stimulated early discussion that helped focus future worldwide research.[643]

of nests in habitat which, like the Cowan's camps, were "damp situations among debris and fallen trees"[640]

The honeymooners' breeding territory in the wooded swamp was subsequently abandoned, but their return to the Cariboo at the beginning of August to stay with McCabes was far more successful. They tramped the seven miles of boggy trail to Indianpoint Lake and spent ten happy days there. The journal notes:

Hermit Thrush nest

Hylocichla guttata
[now *Catharus guttatus*]

In arriving at the conclusion that four races of hermit thrushes should be recognized in British Columbia, our judgment has been influenced by an important ecological factor, viz. that each of the four subspecies occupies in summer a distinct habitat.[645]

> The McCabes' house is situated in a clearing in a section forested with spruce and aspen in mixed association with the north side of Indianpoint River. This river has a muskegy border supporting in places clumps of green alder and willow. About a mile downstream is a shallow marsh lake locally known as One Mile Lake. Indianpoint Lake on its south and west sides is bordered by dense forests of spruce and balsam with a few large Douglas-firs; on the east is a large burn and a river delta, both supporting considerable deciduous growth. Along the lake edge are scattered alders, birch, willows and poplar. At the north end is a very large beaver meadow containing one lodge and many canals.[642]

The two couples spent the week exploring the beaver dams and observing breeding and migrating birds. They recorded nests from 20 species: Pine and Evening Grosbeaks; White-winged and Red Crossbills; Song, Chipping and Gambel's [White-crowned] Sparrow; Blackpoll; Magnolia, Audubon, Myrtle, Townsend and Yellow Warbler; Northern Waterthrush; Redstart; Common Loon; American [Common] Merganser; Red-eyed, Warbling and Cassin's Vireo. The most mysterious among all these were the crossbills.

This bird was an elusive nomad of great curiosity to the McCabes as it swarmed areas in large numbers depending on where the bumper crops of cones were that year. Cowan referred to them as "violently" cyclic in nature. They start laying eggs as early as mid-February and keep nesting until mid-August. The McCabes themselves were somewhat nomadic, though non-breeders. They migrated down to Berkeley in the winter for work and warmth and were keeping Joseph Grinnell in touch with the BC scene, including Racey and his young acolyte. They were also committed activists. During the early 1920s, they had lobbied the provincial government (along with locals John Babcock and Joe Wendle) for a no-hunting conservation area on the circle of lakes in the Bowron Lake area. By 1925, a 240-square-mile reserve was established which started the concept of the Bowron Lake Provincial Park. The boundaries were enlarged several times, culminating in 1961 with the provincial park being officially designated.

....

Calliope Hummingbird

Stellula calliope

The Calliope Hummingbird is widely distributed throughout the southern interior, north through the Cariboo–Chilcotin ... to Charlie Lake in the Peace River parklands.[647]

....

Neither the Cowans nor the McCabes could have anticipated the significance of this legacy in the context of what was to come. The sanctuary stands in stark contrast to the "Bowron clear-cut" that surrounds it – the largest clear-cut in the world at more than 300 square kilometres – in the Bowron River valley. This huge area of forest was levelled in the 1980s to "salvage" trees that had succumbed to a widespread outbreak of the spruce bark beetle. The bark beetle infestation in this region, coupled with the mountain pine beetle, which affected the pine in the western side of the park, are regarded as one of the most visible and poignant indicators of climate change as vast areas of forests turned red with needle die-off. Poor forestry practices that created huge stands of young trees provided unlimited opportunities for beetles to expand during the warmer winters. More devastating still was the industrial response – one of the few man-made features visible from space.[644] Bowron Lake Provincial Park still stands out like a slender silver necklace of lakes and emerald forests in the slowly regrowing industrial clear-cut. The park provides an ecological benchmark of nature's ability to withstand "violent" cycles, compared to the experiment of industrial mitigation just outside the borders.

Cowan had noted on that trip another type of outbreak around Vanderhoof, where the aspen were badly eaten by a brown moth on which the Hermit Thrush were feasting. This was probably the Large Aspen Tortrix Moth (*Choristoneura conflictana*), which are also "violently cyclic" every 10 years.

Cowan observed cycles of infestations, bird predation and particularities of habitats over 80 years of field observations around British Columbia. There have been few naturalists before him or after with that spatial and temporal range and breadth of knowledge in fauna and flora. His reaction to the folly of the Bowron clear-cuts was stated eloquently in the final chapter of volume 4 of *Birds of British Columbia*, which he contributed to at age 90 with lead author Neil Dawe:

> Clear-cutting, because it removes all living and dead trees older than the cutting cycle, takes away habitat of all those species of birds dependent on older trees and snags for their survival ... even with tree and snag retention, unless all the habitat components required by birds remain, there will still be likely be declines in bird numbers, for it is the ecosystem – of which trees are only a part – that matters.[646]

One of the birds reliant on a standing forest was the hummingbird. Cowan had described Ten Mile Lake as being alive in May with tiny Calliope Hummingbirds, at the northernmost edge of their range. The nests made of lichen, moss and spider webs were duly measured – the smallest nests for the smallest birds in the province. They feed on sap that pools in little wells of birch trees drilled by sapsuckers.

The larger Rufous Hummingbirds were also there, and Cowan had recorded a curious but furious battle between a territorial male and a wasp.

In both these species, the males have iridescent red throats, the Calliope more purple-red, the Rufous more ruby-red. Nothing heralds spring like the first flash of the gorget. Joyce too loved hummingbirds and for the rest of her life she kept careful notes of the March arrival of this feisty, rufous-coloured visitor to her feeder. After she died in 2002, daughter Ann Schau read her father a poem about hummingbirds by Ontario poet Rae Crossman called "One Ruby-throated Moment," which begins: "If only / for one / ruby-throated moment / your life could hover / rapid / radiant / rare you would never let the quiver / out of your bloodstream..."[649] The poem "galvanized" Cowan. Ann remarked, "Dad wasn't a religious man in the formal sense; however, he had an intense spiritual side, perfectly represented by this poem."[650]

Rufous Hummingbird
at sapsucker wells

Selasphorus rufus

The Rufous Hummingbird is distributed throughout most of British Columbia, becoming sporadic in the northeastern corner of the province. The first male Rufous Hummingbirds arrive on the south coast in early March ... The main movement occurs in April on the coast and in May in the interior.[648]

The Ruby-throated had another important significance to Cowan. When he first met his future father-in-law, Racey showed him the first bird he ever collected in Quebec – it was a Ruby-throated Hummingbird. Its range stretches from the Rockies east, though it occasionally turns up in northeastern BC. Crossman's poem was read out at Cowan's memorial on April 21, 2010, just at the time the male hummingbirds all across Canada were in full ruby-throated moments.

June 9, 1932, is the last entry in the Cariboo for the Cowan brothers. They finish up by measuring more flying squirrel nests and botfly. Although the gold panning seems to have been a washout, the collections from the Cariboo certainly weren't. Cowan spent most of July at Alta Lake collecting small mammals with Joyce, including his last Canadian specimen for a while – a shrew. It was a subspecies of the Wandering Shrew, which today is a distinct species, the Montane Shrew. Cowan then wandered south via Vancouver to Berkeley to start his new life as a

PhD student at the University of California. It would be four years before Joyce and he would travel again in the Cariboo, by then together as a couple.

His first step after returning to the Vancouver area was to travel to the Provincial Museum in Victoria to meet up with Kermode. Cowan had sent him a letter earlier in the winter asking for a list of all the specimens, to which Kermode had responded:

> I would like to assist you all I can in this matter but at present we are so short handed, having had to cut down to minimum, I have personally not the time to go into this matter as I would like to do for you. However, if you come to Victoria this summer as you are planning to, I will be only too pleased to assist you as much as possible.[651]

Cowan went for his orientation to the collection (which he noted as "small") and made the diplomatic comment that he was "cordially received." Armed with his limited data, he was ready for Berkeley.

Cowan's mother, Laura McTaggart Cowan (Mackenzie)

IMAGE #COWAN_PP_071 [CLOSE-UP FROM PP_069] COURTESY OF UVIC LIBRARY SPECIAL COLLECTIONS.

Cowan's father, McTaggart Cowan (b. 1883), about 1930.

IMAGE #COWAN_PP_070 COURTESY OF UVIC LIBRARY SPECIAL COLLECTIONS.

Opposite top left **Back row left to right: Donald Mackenzie (d. at about age 15), nurse, Cowan's grandmother Laura Augusta Mackenzie, his mother, Laura A. (Mackenzie) Cowan and Alice (Mackenzie) McWilliam. In front are Cowan's uncles Archie and Daniel Mackenzie (father of Brian).**
IMAGE #COWAN_PP_334 COURTESY OF UVIC LIBRARY SPECIAL COLLECTIONS.

Opposite top right **Cowan's maternal grandfather, Danald Mackenzie, father of Donald, Laura, Alice and Daniel (n.d.).**
IMAGE #COWAN_PP_103 COURTESY OF UVIC LIBRARY SPECIAL COLLECTIONS.

Opposite bottom left **John Holden, grandfather of Eileen Racey and great-grandfather of Joyce McTaggart Cowan (Racey).**
IMAGE #COWAN_PP_343 COURTESY OF UVIC LIBRARY SPECIAL COLLECTIONS.

Opposite bottom right **Cowan Coat of Arms by Valerius Geist.**
IMAGE #COWAN_PP_066 COURTESY OF UVIC LIBRARY SPECIAL COLLECTIONS.

This page top **Kenneth Racey's parents: John Racey, MD, and Martha Sofia (Richie).**
IMAGE #COWAN_PP_340 COURTESY OF UVIC LIBRARY SPECIAL COLLECTIONS.

This page bottom **Jimmy Simpson sitting on a "Rocky Mountain Chippendale Bench" outside Num-Ti-Jah Lodge, 1970.**
IMAGE #COWAN_PP_213 IMAGE COURTESY OF ALPINE FILMS. PHOTOGRAPH BY BRUNO ENGLER.

Baby Ian McTaggart Cowan and his grandfather Peter McTaggart Cowan, Edinburgh, 1911.

IMAGE #COWAN_PP_001 COURTESY OF UVIC LIBRARY SPECIAL COLLECTIONS.

Kenneth Racey with Eileen Racey and one of the sisters, Alta Lake, ca. 1912.

IMAGE #COWAN_PP_248 COURTESY OF UVIC LIBRARY SPECIAL COLLECTIONS.

Above **Hamilton Mack Laing, Mount Hood, Oregon, September 1916**

IMAGE #J-0026 COURTESY OF ROYAL BC MUSEUM, BC ARCHIVES. PHOTOGRAPH BY HAMILTON MACK LAING.

Left **Cowan in Vancouver, 1914.**

IMAGE #COWAN_PP_003 COURTESY OF UVIC LIBRARY SPECIAL COLLECTIONS.

Below **Eileen Racey on the beach with Alan and Joyce, Vancouver, 1915.**

IMAGE #COWAN_PP_176 COURTESY OF UVIC LIBRARY SPECIAL COLLECTIONS.

Joyce and Eileen Racey at Alta Lake, ca. 1918–1920.

Cowan as a Boy Scout, North Vancouver, ca. 1919.

Alan Racey at Nita Lake, next to Alta Lake, BC.

IMAGE #COWAN_PP_161 COURTESY OF UVIC LIBRARY SPECIAL COLLECTIONS.

Hoyes Lloyd, ornithologist, 1921.

IMAGE #J-00259 COURTESY OF ROYAL BC MUSEUM, BC ARCHIVES. PHOTOGRAPH BY HAMILTON MACK LAING.

Christmas Greetings 1921 from Hoyes Lloyd

Collecting camp, Comox, BC, 1921.

P.A. Taverner, A.C. Brooks and T.L. Thacker, Vale of Inkaneep, Osoyoos, BC, 1922.

Patrick, Joan and Ian McTaggart Cowan at Mount Gardiner, BC, 1923.

IMAGE #COWAN_PP_214 COURTESY OF UVIC LIBRARY SPECIAL COLLECTIONS.

Ron Stewart, Blue Grouse, September 13, 1924, Comox, BC.

IMAGE #J-00277 COURTESY OF ROYAL BC MUSEUM, BC ARCHIVES. PHOTOGRAPH BY HAMILTON MACK LAING.

Above **Alan, Stewart and Joyce Racey with Rika Wright sitting on roof of house at Alta Lake, 1925.**

IMAGE #COWAN_PP_158 COURTESY OF UVIC LIBRARY SPECIAL COLLECTIONS.

Left **Kenneth Racey bringing down a porcupine at Mount Whistler, August 1927.**

IMAGE #COWAN_PP_297 COURTESY OF UVIC LIBRARY SPECIAL COLLECTIONS.

Opposite **Cowan's North Vancouver High School graduation photo, 1927.**

IMAGE #COWAN_PP_125 COURTESY OF UVIC LIBRARY SPECIAL COLLECTIONS.

Joyce with Hoary
Marmots and
Blue Grouse, 1927.
Standing compan-
ion is either Alan
Racey or Cowan.

IMAGE #COWAN_
PP_300 COURTESY OF
UVIC LIBRARY SPECIAL
COLLECTIONS.

Ashnola camp,
1928.

IMAGE #J-00268 COUR-
TESY OF ROYAL BC
MUSEUM, BC ARCHIVES.
PHOTOGRAPH BY
HAMILTON MACK LAING.

Cabin, looking north on Mount Whistler showing Red Mountain slope, August 24, 1928.

IMAGE #COWAN_PP_351 COURTESY OF UVIC LIBRARY SPECIAL COLLECTIONS.

J.A. Munro with grouse, October 18, 1928, Okanagan Landing, BC.

IMAGE #J-00269 COURTESY OF ROYAL BC MUSEUM, BC ARCHIVES. PHOTOGRAPH BY HAMILTON MACK LAING.

Black death oiled White-winged Scoter and California murre, Comox, BC, 1928.

IMAGE #00306 COURTESY OF ROYAL BC MUSEUM, BC ARCHIVES. PHOTOGRAPH BY HAMILTON MACK LAING.

Cowan at lake on Black Mountain, November 11, 1929.

The Racey gang at large: [left to right] Eileen Racey, Cowan, Alan, Joyce and Stewart Racey and Daphne Winson, Huntingdon, BC, March 30, 1930.

Cowan with Hamilton Mack Laing and his bride, Ethel May Hart, Jasper, Alberta, 1930.

Cowan on horseback with Kathleen Bryant and Syd Williams at Jacques Creek near Jacques Pass, Jasper, Alberta, 1930.

Cowan with deer on his back and rifle at Constitution Hill near Comox, BC, November 10, 1930.

Above **Cowan with horses at summit of Maccarib Pass, Jasper National Park, packing in to Tonquin Valley, June 30 to July 1, 1930.**

IMAGE #COWAN_PP_023 COURTESY OF UVIC LIBRARY SPECIAL COLLECTIONS.

Below left **R.M. Anderson, National Museum, White-tailed Deer, Yahk, BC, 1929.**

IMAGE #G-03661 COURTESY OF ROYAL BC MUSEUM, BC ARCHIVES. PHOTOGRAPH BY HAMILTON MACK LAING.

Below Right **Frank Bryant, Syd Williams, Kathleen Bryant and Cowan at Snaring River, Jasper, 1930.**

IMAGE #COWAN_PP_114 COURTESY OF UVIC LIBRARY SPECIAL COLLECTIONS.

Cowan with Kenneth,
Eileen, Alan and
Stewart Racey
car-camping at
Aldergrove, ca. 1930.

Cowan's father,
McTaggart Cowan,
with Kenneth Racey at
Huntingdon, probably
early 1930s.

Above **Ian McTaggart Cowan with badger, Newgate, BC, May 25, 1930.**

IMAGE #J-00271 COURTESY OF ROYAL BC MUSEUM, BC ARCHIVES. PHOTOGRAPH BY HAMILTON MACK LAING.

Above **Winter camping, ca. 1930. Eileen, Joyce, Alan and Stewart Racey, with Cowan in the middle.**

IMAGE #COWAN_PP_305 COURTESY OF UVIC LIBRARY SPECIAL COLLECTIONS.

Opposite top **Cowan [standing] with Kenneth Racey in the field photographing small mammals, Chezacut Lake, Chilcotin, BC, August 1931.**

IMAGE #COWAN_PP_007 COURTESY OF UVIC LIBRARY SPECIAL COLLECTIONS.

Opposite middle **[Left to right] Alan and Kenneth Racey and Cowan preparing specimens at Chezacut Lake, August 1931.**

IMAGE #COWAN_PP_008 COURTESY OF UVIC LIBRARY SPECIAL COLLECTIONS.

Opposite bottom **Cowan with Kenneth Racey, photographing in the field at Chezacut Lake, August 1931.**

IMAGE #COWAN_PP_009 COURTESY OF UVIC LIBRARY SPECIAL COLLECTIONS.

Cowan with Kenneth Racey canoeing at Chezacut Lake, August 1931.

Cowan with [anticlockwise] Joyce, Eileen, Alan and Stewart Racey, dressed in "Canadian" outfits, Spences Bridge, BC, August 1931.

Top **Camping with the Raceys at Osoyoos Lake, July 1931. Left to right are Cowan, Joyce, Eileen, Alan and Stewart Racey.**

Middle **UBC zoology class 5, 1931. Cowan is in the back row at right.**

Bottom **Anarchist Mountain, BC, July 1931.**

Ian and Patrick McTaggart Cowan, Clinton, BC, June 1932.

Top left **Cowan photographing, California, 1932.**

IMAGE #COWAN_PP_155 COURTESY OF UVIC LIBRARY SPECIAL COLLECTIONS.

Top right **Cowan grad photo at University of British Columbia, 1932.**

IMAGE #COWAN_PP_130 COURTESY OF UVIC LIBRARY SPECIAL COLLECTIONS.

Bottom **Ian and Patrick McTaggart Cowan on gold-panning trip near Barkerville, BC, 1932.**

IMAGE #COWAN_PP_143 COURTESY OF UVIC LIBRARY SPECIAL COLLECTIONS.

Top left **Cowan with pinecone, California, 1932.**

IMAGE #COWAN_PP_156 COURTESY OF UVIC LIBRARY SPECIAL COLLECTIONS.

Top right **"Our house" cabin at Alta Lake, 1932.**

IMAGE #COWAN_PP_362 COURTESY OF UVIC LIBRARY SPECIAL COLLECTIONS.

Bottom **Pictured at a meeting of the American Ornithologists' Union are Hoyes Lloyd, Joseph Grinnell, Kenneth Racey, J.H. Fleming, Percy Taverner, Allan Cyril Brooks, Harry S. Swarth and V.C. Wynne-Edwards, Quebec City, October 1932.**

IMAGE #COWAN_PP_281 COURTESY OF UVIC LIBRARY SPECIAL COLLECTIONS.

UBC zoology class with Dr. C. McLean Fraser, ca. 1932–1934.

IMAGE #COWAN_PP_310 COURTESY OF UVIC LIBRARY SPECIAL COLLECTIONS.

McTaggart Cowan family in bathing suits: Joan, Pam, Ian, Laura and Patrick, ca. 1933/34.

IMAGE #COWAN_PP_357 COURTESY OF UVIC LIBRARY SPECIAL COLLECTIONS.

Investigating a hawk's nest, ca. 1934.

IMAGE #J-00246 COURTESY OF ROYAL BC MUSEUM, BC ARCHIVES. PHOTOGRAPH BY HAMILTON MACK LAING.

Cowan with deer skulls in his office at Berkeley, 1935.

IMAGE #COWAN_PP_044 COURTESY OF UVIC LIBRARY SPECIAL COLLECTIONS.

Cowan with Eileen and Joyce Racey at Joshua Tree in Mojave Desert, Calif., May 1935.

IMAGE #COWAN_PP_301 COURTESY OF UVIC LIBRARY SPECIAL COLLECTIONS.

Opposite **Cowan graduates with a PhD from the University of California, Berkeley, May 17, 1935.**

Top left **Cowan graduating at Berkeley, Calif., May 17, 1935, pictured with his mother, Laura.**

Top right **Ian and Joyce McTaggart Cowan wedding picture, Vancouver, April 21, 1936.**

Below **Ian and Joyce McTaggart Cowan camping with Provincial Museum truck, 1936.**

Left **Cowan pushing the train-car on Whitesail/Eutsuk portage, July 17, 1936, during his and Joyce's honeymoon in Tweedsmuir Park.**

IMAGE #COWAN_PP_370 COURTESY OF UVIC LIBRARY SPECIAL COLLECTIONS.

Below **Teddy Stanwell-Fletcher, Driftwood Valley, ca. 1937.**

IMAGE #COWAN_PH_302 COURTESY OF UNIVERSITY OF VICTORIA SPECIAL COLLECTIONS. PHOTOGRAPH PROBABLY BY JACK STANWELL-FLETCHER.

Opposite **Newly marrried Ian and Joyce McTaggart Cowan at their house in Victoria, 1936.**

IMAGE #COWAN_PP_194 COURTESY OF UVIC LIBRARY SPECIAL COLLECTIONS.

Above **Charles J. Guiguet, Mt. Brilliant, Tweedsmuir, 6500 feet, September 9, 1938.**

IMAGE #J-00278 COURTESY OF ROYAL BC MUSEUM, BC ARCHIVES. PHOTOGRAPH BY HAMILTON MACK LAING.

Left **Alan Brooks painting in his studio, 1938.**

IMAGE #J-00264 COURTESY OF ROYAL BC MUSEUM, BC ARCHIVES. PHOTOGRAPH BY HAMILTON MACK LAING.

Opposite top left **Cowan rowing, 1940s.**

IMAGE #COWAN_PP_014 COURTESY OF UVIC LIBRARY SPECIAL COLLECTIONS.

Opposite top right **Joan McTaggart Cowan on her motorcycle, ca. 1940s.**

IMAGE #COWAN_PP_315 COURTESY OF UVIC LIBRARY SPECIAL COLLECTIONS.

Opposite bottom **Kenneth Racey with Garry McTaggart Cowan, 1940.**

IMAGE #COWAN_PP_198 COURTESY OF UVIC LIBRARY SPECIAL COLLECTIONS.

Left **Ian with Garry McTaggart Cowan in backpack in spring of 1941.**

IMAGE #COWAN_PP_372 COURTESY OF UVIC LIBRARY SPECIAL COLLECTIONS.

Below **Jimmy Simpson on horseback overlooking Mount Southesk, Jasper Park, Alberta, August 1943.**

IMAGE #COWAN_PP_091 COURTESY OF UVIC LIBRARY SPECIAL COLLECTIONS.

Opposite top **Joyce and Garry McTaggart Cowan and Eileen Racey at Huntingdon, ca. 1942/43.**

IMAGE #COWAN_PP_255 COURTESY OF UVIC LIBRARY SPECIAL COLLECTIONS.

Opposite bottom **Warden Charles Phillips at Head of the Southesk, Jasper, Alberta, August 1943.**

IMAGE #COWAN_PH_277 COURTESY OF UNIVERSITY OF VICTORIA SPECIAL COLLECTIONS. PHOTOGRAPH BY IAN MCTAGGART COWAN.

Jim Hatter with bighorn sheep at Cairn Pass, 1944.

IMAGE #COWAN_PP_232 COURTESY OF UVIC LIBRARY SPECIAL COLLECTIONS.

Garry and Ann McTaggart Cowan, Edith Lake, Jasper, Alberta, June 1946.

IMAGE #COWAN_PP_146 COURTESY OF UVIC LIBRARY SPECIAL COLLECTIONS.

Above **Jim Hatter at Indian Pass looking east, July 4, 1944.**

IMAGE #COWAN_PP_252 COURTESY OF UVIC LIBRARY SPECIAL COLLECTIONS.

Left **Cowan at Thompson Pass, July 26, 1945.**

IMAGE #COWAN_PP_119 COURTESY OF UVIC LIBRARY SPECIAL COLLECTIONS.

Below **Garry, Ann and Ian McTaggart Cowan, Jasper, Alberta, 1946.**

IMAGE #COWAN_PP_239 COURTESY OF UVIC LIBRARY SPECIAL COLLECTIONS.

Laura Alice Mackenzie Cowan (1909), Joan (Zink), Pam (Charlesworth) and Patrick McTaggart Cowan, July 1947.

Ward Stevens and muskrat, Aklavik, NWT, 1947.

Cowan examines Elephant Seal skull in the "bone room" at UBC, ca. 1950s.

Cowan, with Joyce dressed up as a Spotted Skate, Kerrisdale Figure Skating Club, ca. 1950s.

Garry McTaggart Cowan and Daniel Mackenzie doing archery in Scotland, 1952/53.

Vero and Janet Wynne-Edwards, Lochnagar, Scotland, November 11, 1952.

Laura and McTaggart Cowan
Sr. with their four children: Ian,
Patrick, Joan and Pamela, ca.
late 1950s.

IMAGE #COWAN_PP_313 COURTESY OF
UVIC LIBRARY SPECIAL COLLECTIONS.

Cowan off to coronation reception at Holyrood Palace,
Edinburgh, 1953.

IMAGE #COWAN_PP_005 COURTESY OF
UVIC LIBRARY SPECIAL COLLECTIONS.

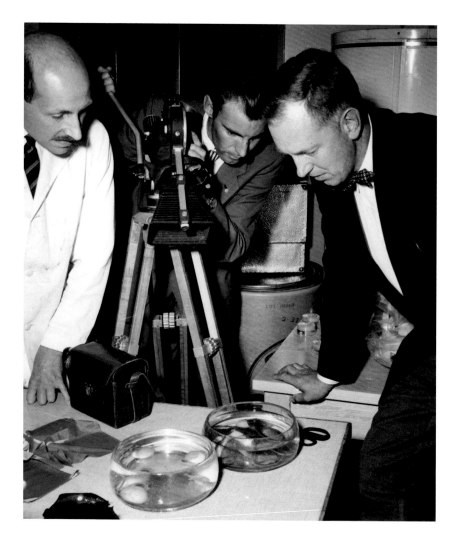

Cowan filming fish for a CBC episode with V. Udvardi and cameraman Robert Reid, ca. 1955/56.

Ian and Garry McTaggart Cowan with M.F.M. Meiklejohn, Scotland, 1953.

IMAGE #COWAN_PP_142 COURTESY OF UVIC LIBRARY SPECIAL COLLECTIONS.

Cowan on the beach at East Point, Saturna Island, with students and family dredging, ca. 1955–1959.

IMAGE #COWAN_PP_118 COURTESY OF UVIC LIBRARY SPECIAL COLLECTIONS.

Cowan with Joe Bryant and Robin Leech at Aklavik, NWT, during National Research Council visit to the Arctic, June 1956.

Cowan in the middle with two colleagues at Vaseux Lake.

Cowan and Bristol Foster at Rose Spit, Haida Gwaii (Queen Charlotte Islands), 1960.

Cowan eating breakfast with Keen's Mouse specimens at Bristol Foster's research site at Rose Spit, Haida Gwaii (Queen Charlotte Islands), 1960.

Cowan leading the procession at a UBC event, May 25, 1961.

Cowan with Bill and Jim Gibson and his brother Patrick McTaggart Cowan, 1961.

Four generations:
Cowan's father,
McTaggart Cowan,
with Cowan and
his son, Garry
McTaggart
Cowan, hold-
ing great-grand-
daughter Mariana,
Vancouver, 1962.

Cowan with
Norman
Mackenzie on
H.R. MacMillan's
boat, the
Marijean,
San Juanita,
Mexico, 1962.

Above **Ian and Joyce McTaggart Cowan with Denny family and Genge family, July 1964.**

IMAGE #COWAN_PP_149 COURTESY OF UVIC LIBRARY SPECIAL COLLECTIONS.

Opposite top **Cowan at 11,000 feet on Mount Kenya at freezing dawn, July 3, 1967.**

IMAGE #COWAN_PP_095 COURTESY OF BRISTOL FOSTER.

Opposite bottom **Speakers at the scholarly sessions for the Smithsonian's bicentennial celebration, September 1965: (left to right) Ian M. Cowan; Fred L. Whipple, director of the Smithsonian Astrophysical Observatory; Stephen E. Toulmin, Arthur Koestler, Claude Lévi-Strauss, Sir Kenneth Clark, Jerome S. Bruner and Herbert Butterfield.**

IMAGE #COWAN_PP_025 COURTESY OF SMITHSONIAN INSTITUTION ARCHIVE.

Left **Cowan in a log on the Central Coast, ca. 1964?**

IMAGE #COWAN_
PP_264 COURTESY OF
UVIC LIBRARY SPECIAL
COLLECTIONS.

Left **Cowan officiating as UBC dean of science at PhD ceremony for his son Garry and son-in-law Mikkel Schau, 1969.**

IMAGE #COWAN_
PP_291 COURTESY OF
UVIC LIBRARY SPECIAL
COLLECTIONS.

Opposite top **Cowan on beach with son Garry, daughter-in-law Ana and two grandchildren, Robert and Mariana, Mayne Island, 1967.**

IMAGE #COWAN_PP_292 COURTESY OF UVIC LIBRARY SPECIAL COLLECTIONS.

Opposite bottom **Cowan at Vaseux Lake, 1968.**

IMAGE #COWAN_PP_035 COURTESY OF UVIC LIBRARY SPECIAL COLLECTIONS.

Below **Vancouver Island Marmot release with Doug Herd and Jack Evans, Green Mountain, 1974**

IMAGE #COWAN_PH_197 COURTESY OF UNIVERSITY OF VICTORIA SPECIAL COLLECTIONS. PHOTOGRAPH BY IAN MCTAGGART COWAN.

**Cowan as Chancellor
of UVic with
HRH Elizabeth II, 1983.**

IMAGE #COWAN_PP_159 COURTESY OF UVIC LIBRARY SPECIAL COLLECTIONS.

**Cowan and Joyce with
Special Expeditions at
San Pedro Martin, Baja
California, January 1983.**

IMAGE #COWAN_PP_224 COURTESY OF UVIC LIBRARY SPECIAL COLLECTIONS.

Top **Prince Philip presenting Cowan with the World Wildlife Fund Golden Panda award, Empress Hotel, Victoria, 1992.**

IMAGE #COWAN_PP_284 COURTESY OF UVIC LIBRARY SPECIAL COLLECTIONS.

Middle **George Sirk, Ian McTaggart Cowan and Bristol Foster.**

IMAGE #COWAN_PP_097 COURTESY OF BRISTOL FOSTER.

Bottom **Cowan and Muriel Guiguet.**

IMAGE #COWAN_PP_099 COURTESY OF BRISTOL FOSTER.

Yorke Edwards, Ian McTaggart Cowan, Robert Bateman, Bristol Foster, John Livingston, Joan Edwards and Joyce McTaggart Cowan, at Foster's house on Saltspring Island, 2001.

Cowan's study at home on Woodhaven Road, Victoria, 2002.

Cowan's address at the inauguration of the Ian McTaggart Cowan Professorship in Biodiversity Conservation and Ecological Restoration, University of Victoria, 2005.

IMAGE #COWAN_PP_219 COURTESY OF UVIC LIBRARY SPECIAL COLLECTIONS.

Renata Geist, Cowan and Val Geist at the announcement of the Professorship in Environmental Studies, University of Victoria, 2005.

IMAGE #COWAN_PP_374 COURTESY OF UVIC LIBRARY SPECIAL COLLECTIONS.

Above left **Racey and Cowan specimen preparation kit.**

IMAGE #COWAN_PA_002 COURTESY OF ANN SCHAU COLLECTION. PHOTOGRAPH BY MICHAEL WALL.

Above right **The Cowan family house in North Vancouver in 2014.**

IMAGE #COWAN_PP_324 COURTESY OF UVIC LIBRARY SPECIAL COLLECTIONS.

Below **Cowan at the Victoria warehouse where the blue whale skeleton was being reconstructed before transfer to the Beaty Biodiversity Museum at UBC, March 2010.**

IMAGE #COWAN_PP_280 COURTESY OF UVIC LIBRARY SPECIAL COLLECTIONS. PHOTOGRAPHER/ARTIST JOANNE THOMSON.

PART 4
THE BERKELEY YEARS:
1932–1935

CHAPTER 15

"If you were studying them [deer], they took you everywhere."

Berkeley, 1932–1933

Upon arriving at Berkeley, Cowan was met by the new, gleaming-white classical Life Sciences building rising above the treetops of the campus arboretum of oaks, madronas (arbutus) and exotic eucalyptus. Still imposing today, Athenian columns rise up from bases with bas-reliefs of birds, snakes, shells, bighorn sheep and other native fauna of northern California; the Trajan inscription "Zoology" spans the elegant stairs up to the Museum of Vertebrate Zoology. For a 22-year-old fresh from a small Canadian campus, there would have been no doubt that the life sciences and museum were a going concern at Berkeley.

Characteristically, Cowan makes no comments on the built landscape in his journal. His first entry is made up the hill behind the campus where the city limits end, not surprisingly featuring a rabbit:

> Left the museum at 2 p.m., proceeded up Strawberry Canyon road – taking the first fire trail on the right leading up behind the tobacco fields of the horticultural department. Here in association with Artemisia and poison oak I set some eight traps for Perognathus [pocket mice]... While setting these traps I noticed large deposits of rabbit droppings in and around the sage brushes and in several places well marked runways from dense thickets out into open areas of grass and sage. I jumped one adult Brush Rabbit.[652]

Brush Rabbits are part of the cottontail, or Sylvilagus, family, related to both the Eastern Cottontail and Mountain Cottontail, the latter of which is British Columbia's smallest and rarest rabbit, confined to the arid grasslands of the south Okanagan and Similkameen river valleys.

Cowan's discoveries didn't end there that day: "Returning through the eucalyptus groves to the north of the botanical gardens, I ran into a pair of [Great] Horned Owls by their nest. They were making the peculiar screams characteristic of the species at this time of year."[654] His first reference to owls was fitting, being symbols of wisdom, but he wasn't one for metaphor – at least not publicly. He was always careful to keep even a whiff of anthropomorphism away, wanting no fuel for detractors.

He had landed on his feet with the "wisdom" awaiting him at Berkeley. In addition to the wildlife he found all around campus, Cowan was delighted with Grinnell.

> I was lucky because the head of the big museum of vertebrate zoology said when I arrived: "I'd like you to work for me. You'll be the only mammal student I've got, all my other students are bird students and all the other mammal students work for a guy that I don't particularly like." So I got to work with Joseph Grinnell, who was one of the two first quantitative ecologists in North America.[656]

Luck wasn't really part of it. The brotherhood and sisterhood had worked hard behind the scenes to get him there. Annie Alexander, patron of the museum, who had long funded Grinnell's salary, the collecting expeditions and the teaching–research fellowships associated with the museum, had run into some limits to her philanthropy that summer: the Depression and the new construction of the Life Sciences Building and Museum had drained her annual bequests. In correspondence with Alexander, Grinnell voluntarily opted to take a 25 per cent cut in his salary that year, together with a staff readjustment, to free up $1,200 for several fellowships.[657] Cowan squeaked in on one of those.

Grinnell, meanwhile, was in Quebec for the meeting of the American Ornithologists' Union to stimulate discussion about conservation issues on both sides of the border. Canadians and the 'B' figured strongly in the elections. Hoyes Lloyd was promoted to the Fellows. In a letter to Alexander on October 24, 1932, Grinnell writes about the connections:

> These were happy choices ... Our union is American and that surely includes Canada! The Canadians are truly fine people; also lots of good naturalists among them, mammalogists as well as ornithologists. During the meetings I had pleasant personal visits with Kenneth Racey of Vancouver, Frank Farley of Camrose, Alberta, R.M. Anderson, P.G. Taverner and others of Ottawa ... I was especially glad to meet for the first time Kenneth Racey, a freelance mammal collector, who is working chiefly in British Columbia north of the Territory being worked by the McCabes. From Quebec, Racey was going off to collect in the Gaspé and elsewhere until the weather gets bad. It would certainly have been beautiful weather for collecting during the past week in Quebec. Racey voluntarily proposed to

send MVZ things needed to fill in our representation of northwestern mammals."[658]

Grinnell was to meet Racey many more times with Cowan now at Berkeley, and the McCabes were due on their annual winter migration to the campus. Grinnell was also writing Annie Alexander about the young graduates:

> I think further of the group of younger people entering here now – eager, enthusiastic – and each one with opportunity provided to aid him to develop along the line of his prime interest. There was practically no such opportunity 25 years ago; and I don't believe there would have been such opportunity today except for the existence of MVZ ... It is a deep satisfaction to me that we are thus reaching with our natural history ideas so many people who within a few years will be widely scattered and many of them leaders of thought and action in their own communities.[659]

As a graduate student in vertebrate zoology, Cowan was given an office in the museum. With fall enrolment leaping up, Grinnell's assistant, E. Raymond Hall, wrote to Alexander as term started:

> As a whole the students are an exceptionally fine lot this fall and that makes the added work less burdensome, at least to me ... A new graduate student, Mr. Ian McTaggart Cowan, has elected to study the morphologic characters of deer from the Pacific Coast and his preliminary work thereto is now bringing many skulls of deer to the museum. These he acquires in devious ways. Since the deer season is on, he can get numerous skulls from taxidermists hereabout.[660]

Cowan had come to Berkeley with the thesis that he had started on as an undergraduate – that the complex evolutionary story of deer had yet to be properly told.

> I did my work on the deer of western North America. Mine was the first published document using statistical treatment of a big mammal. The US Bureau of Biological Survey had realized that long

Great Horned Owl baby

Bubo virginianus

The Great Horned Owl is found in all types of timbered areas. It also frequents river valleys, lakeshores, agricultural and residential areas, swamps, fresh, brackish and marine marshes, and estuaries. Occasionally it is found in cities, especially near golf courses or parks with adjacent woodlots.[655]

before, because of one or two men [Joseph Grinnell and Edwin Van Dyke] who started the idea of thinking statistically.[661]

What better task for an acolyte of the venery than to describe the distribution of deer (venison). Asked at age 95 why he chose deer as a topic, Cowan replied: "They were a medium-sized mammal, grow antlers seasonally and are adaptable to a wide number of habitats from wide open plain to deep forests like our coastal Black-tailed. If you were studying them they took you everywhere. I found them fascinating and there isn't any better reason for studying anything."[662]

One of Cowan's later colleagues, Dr. William Lidicker, curator emeritus of mammals at MVZ in 2013, worked with him in various capacities, sharing committee work for the American Society of Mammalogists, for which they both served as vice-president. Lidicker wrote that mammalogists had unique perspectives on ecology:

> Mammals are among the more complex inhabitants of this planet; so if we can understand them, we can provide guidelines for the rest. Also, being larger and cleverer than most creatures, they often represent keystone species (strong interactors) in their communities. As such, they often can serve as indicator species for the status and stability of intractably complex chunks of the biosphere.[663]

Cowan was always up for a challenge and wanted to statistically test and map the distribution of the "races" of Mule/Black-tailed Deer and the White-tailed Deer (at that time they were also referred to as blacktails and whitetails, all within the genus *Odocoileus*) that made it to the west side of the mountains from Baja to Alaska. It came from his experience with small mammals where variation between valley and islands revealed their evolutionary history. In his introduction he writes, "The present study was undertaken in an endeavor to subject a large mammal to the same critical analysis as had been afforded some of the smaller forms."[664]

Evolutionary biology was surging as eager young scientists, such as Cowan, sought to explain the complex history of a species in the landscape. The pursuit inevitably raised questions: Why did some species vary over geographic areas and others remain the same? When did one species stop and the next start as you moved north–south or up a mountain? What were the implications for evolution? Growing up in such a biologically diverse and geologically complex landscape naturally made him receptive to some of the new ideas coming from evolutionary biologists like Bernhard Rensch, who was formulating his ideas around what he called "variable" species.

In 1929 Rensch had coined the term *Rassenkreis* – literally "circle of races"[665] – to describe what happens when a species diverges into a series of races creating a pattern of replacing one another geographically. His famous photographic images show the same beetle changing form as it moves up a mountain until it has turned into a completely different species. *Rassenkreis* was a hot new idea and Cowan seized on it immediately, citing Rensch's influence in the introduction to his graduate thesis. His fieldwork had taken him up and down mountains and north and south, finding variation due to geography among small mammals. His observations bore out this concept of a circle.

Rensch was a natural fit for Cowan, as the German scientist had had his training as a field collector–curator in the Natural History Museum in Berlin and was experienced with animals in hand, being an expert not only in birds but also in molluscs, which Cowan was to master in his middle years. Rensch was an interesting early influence, later working with the British scientist Julian Huxley after having been banished to Prague during the war. He finished his long career with his magnum opus, *Das universale Weltbild: Evolution und Naturphilosophie* (*The Universal Worldview: Evolution and Natural Philosophy*), exploring the philosophy of evolution. As an elderly man who had weathered extraordinary times, Rensch came to see the evolutionary process as one of infinite complication and differentiation accompanied by the "spiritualization" of matter.

In 1932 the new science was quantitative ecology, which required statistical samples to test assumptions of uniqueness. Cowan had to get hold of hundreds of specimens from a large geographic area. His training with Racey and Laing in the art of citizen science was put to immediate use upon arriving in Berkeley. He wrote far and wide to local naturalists, hunters, trappers, taxidermists, game wardens and curators for deer skulls and hides from Baja to BC. Amongst his earliest collaborators was Gus Nordquist, an "enthusiastic" taxidermist from Oakland, California. Nordquist sent him his first specimen seemingly hours after Cowan arrived in Berkeley on August 15: a freak three-antlered buck that had died in the Yosemite Valley. Nordquist would send more than 100 skulls over the next two years. Cowan's journals contain a detailed log of all the people he travelled with and received specimens from, including their observations on the races of deer.

In the days before DNA, teasing out the subtle differences between species and subspecies very much relied on what is referred to as the "taxonomic eye." The best taxonomists had an uncanny ability to detect distinguishing traits (obscure pelage, skull or dental traits) from visual inspection. These were often later confirmed from measurements and statistical analysis. Field biologists had to be able to distinguish uniqueness of similar populations that might already vary internally depending on age, sex or nutrition. Ernest Thompson Seton had established a framework for describing animals based on physical features, behaviours and geographic range, which Cowan used in his undergraduate papers. The great skill of the early taxonomists was to have such an intimate understanding of a population that they could select a type specimen to typify the race, taking into account the natural variations of the population, so that, for example, a malnourished young female would not be mistaken to represent a smaller race. Grinnell had built on that foundation by taking the bush arts and quantifying them into a science.[666]

Grinnell was also establishing the framework for conservation biology. The key to detecting a decline in any given population was to know what had been there to start with – a baseline. To this end he handed out a small typewritten note at the start of each year that was to be attached to his graduate students' field journals:

> The objects of our field work are: to ascertain everything possible in regard to the natural history of the vertebrate life of the regions traversed, and to make careful record of the facts gathered in the form of specimen and notes, to be preserved for all time. All this is for *the information of others*; strive to make your records in all respects clearly intelligible. Remember that the value of our manuscripts increases as the years go by and faunal changes take place. Some of our earlier notebooks describe conditions now vanished in the localities they dealt with.[667]

In a sense, the Grinnellian training was the first attempt to legitimize traditional ecological knowledge garnered from "outdoorsmen" whether native trappers or non-native hunters. Merriam, with whom Grinnell and Alexander developed the principles of the MVZ, was as much a scholar of North American indigenous cultures as he was a naturalist; likewise Grinnell's cousin, George Bird Grinnell, a member of the 'B'. Joseph Grinnell himself was not a member although he shared their values. Leopold was also arguing at this time for a greater synthesis of two disciplines.

> One of the anomalies of modern ecology is that it is the creation of two groups, each of which seems barely aware of the existence of the other. The one studies the human community almost as if it were a separate entity, and calls its findings sociology, economics and history. The other studies the plant and animal community [and] comfortably relegates the hodgepodge of politics to "the liberal arts." The inevitable fusion of these two lines of thought will, perhaps, constitute the outstanding advance of the present century.[668]

Cowan's approach was that anyone who had good observational field skills (often measured by their success as a hunter) was a legitimate and important source of information. This was totally in keeping with the style of his mentors. McCabe up in the Cariboo, for example, had no training, yet Grinnell had corresponded with him assuring him of his value to the discipline and the quality of his data. Replied McCabe:

> I expect the vocabulary of an old-time mule skinner couldn't do more than give a vague and colourless outline of the sentiments you and Hall entertain towards me. In spite of the overloads you both carry, you have taken time to write me from two to three letters each, from which I have derived both pleasure and profit in large quantities...[669]

Membership in the 'B' relied on the fine balance of knowledge, experience and discretion. There was a constant threat of being discredited. McCabe would write to Grinnell for reassurance: "Anyone who has seen an animal once and listened to a little half-witted old-timer's talk can, and usually does, reel off paragraphs that sound like storehouses of wisdom and information."[670] Grinnell's comment was:

> Yes, the only possible way to counteract that sort of thing is to plug away gathering *facts* of as many sorts and in as great multitude as possible; and then to *publish* them, together with inferences explicitly and exclusively derived from those facts. Let us do that very thing![671]

As zoologist Carleton Phillips notes, these mammalogists were "heavily influenced by factors other than traditional academic scholarship. In particular, hunting and trapping, exploration, collecting and general 'outdoorsmanship' underlie the origins of museum-based mammalogy."[672] Michael Mares, another zoologist, characterizes the older breed like McCabe as being "accustomed to the hardships ... including disrupted home lives, unsympathetic administrators and frequent health problems [and therefore do] not suffer fools gladly."[673] Grinnell and McCabe had great respect for one another and corresponded for years about the things that were on their minds: trying to ban strychnine and arsenic, or the contents of the stomachs of northern mice (75 per cent grubs!).[674] They both loved being out in the field and found a profession to put them there.

Cowan collected anecdotal accounts and then measured and analyzed his specimens to map the ranges of what he proposed as a circle of nine coastal "races" of black-tailed deer, between which there is limited gene flow. The deer he was most familiar with was the Columbian Black-tailed Deer (*columbianus*), coinciding with the range between his own summer and winter habitats of Vancouver and Berkeley. The notion of a wandering buck ranging over this low-lying oak woodland ecosystem backed by the Coast Mountains would have been a credible scenario to Cowan, given the travelling back and forth over the same landscape to see Joyce. There were only a few minor barriers like rivers to cross (deer are adept swimmers). The other races included the geographically isolated Sitka Black-tailed Deer (*sitkensis*) of the northern islands and coastal mainland of BC; Rocky Mountain Mule Deer (*hemionus*) of the eastern mountain ranges; the California Mule Deer of the Sierra Nevada (*californicus*); the Peninsula Deer of the southern Baja (*peninsulae*); the

Mule Deer bucks fighting

Odocoileus hemionus hemionus

Differs from the Coast deer in larger size. Winter pelage grey rather than brown, under chest blackish, ears much larger (8¾ instead of 7½ inches from notch), tail white with black tip and surrounded by a white rump patch. Metatarsal gland 3½ to 5½ inches. Summer pelage paler buff than that of the Coast deer.[675]

Desert Mule Deer (*eremicus*) of the Mexican mainland; Cedros Island Mule Deer from the islands of that name off Baja (*cerrosensis*); and two new races that he proposed, the Southern Mule Deer of northern Baja (*fuliginatus*) and the Inyo Mule Deer on the eastern slopes of the Sierra Nevada (*inyoensis*).

Cowan was interested in statistically testing his hunches about which of the many external features "were of the greatest significance in the discussion of geographic variation."[676] He started with the characteristic most obvious to the hunter (and maybe to the deer themselves), their tails. Deer use their tails to raise the alarm of danger, and tail colour varies with the landscape. Much of the thesis and the journals are taken up with descriptions and detailed pen and inks showing the subtle and not so subtle variations of their black and white tails. Cowan also marvelled at and measured, as hunters do, the variation in antlers. Two other external features he measured were the colour of the winter coats and the specialized skin glands that differ between the races. The metatarsal gland, which lines the outside of the hind leg, plays a role in laying scent and breeding. Seton was particularly interested in skin glands, since they had important roles in mammalian communication, breeding and defining territory. Cowan's dissertation remarks have all the loving detail of an artist's eye masked in scientific language. The story of the Inyo Mule Deer, as Cowan recounts it, is a good example.

Popular stories about this unique race of deer started appearing in 1922, when a local newspaperman and conservationist named Bill Chalfant published his first collection of stories about the Inyo Valley. He and his father, who owned the local newspaper, used the local stories to raise public awareness in the community's epic fight against development interests and the City of Los Angeles for the water of the region. One of the stories involved a long-time resident, E.H. Ober, a specialist in the sheep and deer, who described the Inyo Mule Deer's unique history and their adaptation to a marginal land. At some time in history, a small herd of mule deer, forced off the peaks as the winter snows hit, made a decision to go, not west into the lush, ocean-facing valleys like their California cousins, but over to the barren east side. The herd made their way down the valley through the desert to the winter range of the Inyo Mountains, but not before passing through a canyon keyhole, which forms a major bottleneck and predator trap. "A long, sandy hill projects into the valley, and down this they come, crossing the marshes in the valley and the ford at the river." Ober's report led to one of the museum collectors, H.A. Carr, following up the lead in 1911 and collecting a specimen at 11,000 feet on Kid Mountain.

Cowan came across the specimen in the museum and read the Chalfant stories. He decided to gather a statistically viable sample of this population and determined that they were indeed unique, with much lighter colouring than their western California cousins and different jaw structure. The bottleneck of their migration and the limited winter range led Cowan to infer that the bucks at some stage had chosen a route down the mountainside into a totally different environment and thereby started the herd down a new evolutionary path. The specimen at Berkeley became the type specimen of the new subspecies.

The first published article from his research on the proposed race of *inyoensis* came out within six months of arriving at Berkeley; Cowan was well on his way to establishing himself as a hot new rising star in the Grinnell tradition. Berkeley in turn was keen to maintain its international status in ornithology and mammalogy – at a pace even Cowan described as "a zoo." As Phillips describes, Grinnell was blazing a trail that had begun with the deep philosophical schism in the late 19th century between the "laboratory" men and the "outdoorsmen" connected to museums who were "captivated by diversity and focused their energy on collecting, cataloging, housing and describing specimens."[677] The laboratory scientists were going after the college curricula and regarded the natural historians as "non-scientific amateurs."[678] As Phillips notes, "To appreciate fully the significance of this schism, one need only examine an example of the academic pathways that ultimately led to the ... development of the Museum of Vertebrate Zoology..."[679]

Cowan also recognized a conservation issue when he saw one. Like Chalfant, he was witnessing some of the intense pressures these animals were under. In his thesis, Cowan's discussion of the mule deer demonstrates his ethic:

> The colouration and behaviour of the living representatives of the race "hemionus" are those of an animal pre-eminently suited for life in the broken country of the foothills of the great mountain chains of western North America. In many parts of its range, the mule deer has as its wintering grounds country that is easily accessible and forms good grazing for domestic sheep and cattle; consequently this deer has suffered heavily in the general overgrazing that has been condoned in the last few years. In such areas, starvation in the winter has reduced the numbers of deer to a fraction of the former population, or eliminated them completely.[680]

Olof C. Wallmo later argued against the distinction of the Inyo, lumping them back into the broader population of California Mule Deer.[681] Now called Round Valley Deer, they have become recognized again as a distinct population of special concern,[682] with only 3,000 individuals left. Their very limited migration corridor – less than a mile wide between the cliffs and canyon of the Lower Rock Creek gorge – is now under threat by vehicular traffic. Their winter range at only 30 square miles has shrunk from urbanization. The Eastern Sierra Land Trust has been trying to buy up their winter range and protect their migration corridor.

The schism between the laboratory men and the outdoorsmen with a conservation ethic was to continue all of Cowan's career. He always advocated for erring on the side of caution in maintaining genetic diversity. Giving special consideration to a race with the ability to withstand drought in an increasingly warming and hostile world would have been a prudent Cowan observation.

Deer specimens dominate his journals but his enquiry into small mammals also continued. On August 27, 1932, before classes started, he was back up in Strawberry Canyon near Berkeley, trapping pocket mice, *Perognathus* [now *Chaetodopus*] *californicus.* These mice had yet to be distinguished into subspecies but Cowan was already ruminating on their geographic variability.

Living with scant resources was also top of mind for Cowan himself. He supplemented his small income with the venison and wild food he could glean from his fieldwork.

Great Basin Pocket Mouse

Perognathus parvus

About the size of a white-footed mouse, ears small and clothed with short fur, long tail covered with short hairs, grey above and white below. An easily visible, external, fur-lined pocket on either side of the mouth ... These are nocturnal mice, spending the day in burrows excavated in the sandy soil at the base of some small shrub. Food consists of a wide variety of plant material ... They are capable of existing without access to water.[683]

I had a teaching assistantship, not a scholarship, which I was always glad of because my career was going to be teaching as well as research. I was attached to the teaching of the first-year class, which at that time was 2,000 students. They were divided up into groups of 32 for labs. There were four laboratories, so we took 120 of them at a time. I was put on the registration desk for my first task. I was instructed by the professor, Frank Daniels (of elasmobranch fish fame, who wrote the first major books on sharks and rays). He said: "When these students come in, they will be from varied backgrounds. I want you to size them up, I want you to use your judgment." ... I was surprised how well you could sort these people out. If they were bright and talked to you, they were definitely interested. And they gave me one of the first-class student rooms every year. It was fabulous. When you study the cat and take it all apart and stuff, I didn't get [house] cats, I went to the game warden and I got lynx, I got bobcats, I got mountain lions. We studied comparative anatomy ...

And another thing the professor said: "Now look, you have 32 students here." (I had three successive classes, 96 students.) "I want you to know their names and something about them within a month." You had all the names on a list at the front desk and he'd come around and say, "How is she doing?" and I'd say, "Oh, she's not doing too badly," and he'd say, "Well, she probably needs a little extra help. Her father's been very ill for some time and her mother's not doing too well. She's got a difficult road at home." We were expected to know this and we were supposed to recognize those young people. They weren't just numbers on the registration card. So you became friends with your students. The relationship was quite different.[684]

Cowan's alignment with Grinnell on the importance of teaching stemmed right back to his Scottish roots. "Berkeley was good because it produced a lot of good teachers as well as good scientists. It imbued you with a standard of what was acceptable in teaching."[685]

During Cowan's winter break, Joyce and her parents came down for a visit. It was a touring trip, prowling the winter ranges of the various deer. Cowan was trying to determine where exactly the mule and black-tail overlap in the Cascade Mountain divide – what he described as the intergradation zone. They travelled through San Mateo county and the western foothills of the Sierra Nevada near San Francisco, where Cowan excitedly notes a Columbian Black-tailed Deer in a narrow foothills corridor between the developed Sacramento Valley and the mule deer range to the east. The quality of the insight that comes from this exercise of figuring out history through species and landscape is described by lichenologist–naturalist Trevor Goward:

Whitetail Deer fawn
[Northwestern White-tailed Deer]

Odocoileus virginianus ochrourus

Colour in winter greyish-brown; underparts, including chest, insides of hind legs, backs of lower forelegs, patch on throat chin, and underside of tail, white ... Tail very long and bushy, in alarm carried elevated and moving, thus exposing white underside. No white rump patch. Inhabits the Kootenay-Columbia system north to Tête Jaune Cache and west to Oliver, Penticton and Armstrong.[687]

The specimen, as open window into the past, brings forward not merely the moment but also the context. Worked at long enough, you eventually get a feel for not just the parts of the puzzle you've assembled, but also the parts still to be found: what they probably look like, how they likely fit together. At length the field naturalist begins to place the objects of his study into a broader ecosystem and finally evolutionary context – an opportunity simply not given to those who do their work largely indoors ... something changes when you move from field-based science to science indoors, segregated from the living green world.[686]

All four of them were naturalists, so Cowan's sizable imagination was bolstered with the addition of the Raceys, who offered their own insight into the evolutionary history. Cowan carried a topographic map of North America around in his head, populated with the movement of deer and how they would react to their varied geographies: terrain, climate, elevation and physical obstacles. The older Raceys would have been sharing their experiences of the decline of the White-tailed Deer across much of its traditional range.

In his dissertation, published in the journal *California Fish and Game*, Cowan attributes the decline of these populations "to the choice of habitat, for the one preferred by it was the first to be pre-empted by the white men. Their routes of travel lay along streams and the fertile bottom lands and were the first to be used as places of permanent residence."[688] The White-tailed Deer had virtually disappeared in BC except for a small population in the southern valleys. Cowan and Racey overlooked one tiny population of whitetails, though, which had long been known to fishermen as the "tideland" deer at the mouth of the Columbia River. They finally got written up for science in 1940.[689] Named the Pacific White-tailed Deer, *Odocoileus virginianus leucurus*, they were the only population still surviving on the Pacific Coast. In his later lectures

Nests of **Cliff Swallow**

Hirundo pyrrhonota
[now *Petrochelidon pyrrhonota*]

The Cliff Swallow has been reported from near sea level to 2200 metres in elevation. It is a bird of open valleys, rangeland and parkland. During spring migration it makes extensive use of lakes, ponds, sloughs and their associated marshes, which are important sources of flying insects.[691]

at UBC, Cowan would use them as another example of the importance of protecting subspecies. Their survival at that time depended on the whim of the owner of the private island where most of them lived. They have since recovered enough to be taken off the endangered species list as a distinct subspecies.

For Cowan, the pressure was still on in the classroom, despite the school's field bias. While at Berkeley, graduates had to take three courses and achieve "first class" in order to stay on at grad school. One course had to be their specialty, vertebrate zoology, and the other two could be accessories, which in Cowan's case were vertebrate paleontology and vertebrate physiology. The latter was taught in the medical school, so he got what he called "the full treatment" that the MDs were getting, with five top experts in their fields. For vertebrate paleontology, he was taught by a well-known expert who brought in four trays of bone fragments from a dig in Texas and made students reconstruct the animal – which they did. As Cowan notes, "It was smart of him, because we learned and he got his job done. It was a new reptile. I like independence in study."[690]

His field journal entries pick up again at the end of term, when the deer are also leaving their wintering range. Cowan headed off, this time by Greyhound, to check out the overlap zone farther north around the Mount Shasta region where Merriam applied his life zone concept. His journal describes birding-by-Stagecoach on an all-nighter, during which he managed to spot his first Yellow-billed Magpies south of Red Bluff, Mourning Doves sitting on the railway tracks and Cliff Swallows near Arbuckle.

Once at Shasta, he was met by Fred Johnston, a local hunter Cowan provides few details about. In the US Census records, he is described as a labourer born in 1888. He was obviously an experienced outdoorsman and well known to a variety of local game wardens, foresters, trappers and ranchers to whom he introduced Cowan. They headed out on a week-long expedition skirting mountains and snowstorms in the Klamath and Siskiyou mountains to pinpoint the deer range overlaps:

> We passed through several miles of open pine and broad, open expanses where the vegetation was made up of bitterbrush, white thorn and manzanita. At an elevation of 4500 feet the road skirted the south base of Black Fox and Buck mountains. Here the timber stands were much more dense – the yellow pine being replaced by knobcone and lodgepole pine, incense cedar and a large amount of white fir. This type of country is the favourite summer range for deer in this sector.[692]

At Black Fox, by the local game warden's cabin, they collected mule skulls and skins and followed the well formed trails of the blacktails making their way there from Mount McCloud. They ascended the 7,000-foot slopes of Mount Miller in a snowstorm and descended "into the jungle of mountain mahogany"[693] which are favoured by the Mule Deer. By day four on Mount Hebron the weather is "still positively foul – snowing and hailing all day to the accompaniment of intermittent thunderstorms. A high wind whips the hailstones against your face with the sting of a whiplash."[694] Still Cowan was clearly happy with the landscape and writes lyrically despite the cold conditions: "We entered the national forest, passing up over one of the lava escarpments that radiate out from the heads of the valleys like the rays of the sun coming through the cloud."[695]

On a foray up Garner Butte, he stumbled across the largest Wood Rat nest he had ever seen (six feet across and four feet high up a tree), which he excavated and drew. He also made note of the paradoxical jumping habits of Pronghorn Antelope and jackrabbits; the larger mammal, the antelope, doesn't appear to jump fences and jackrabbits appear to want to. "In running they take 2 or 3 short hops and then a long one that is much higher than the short one and carries them 18 inches off the ground."[696] They visited the Klamath River in a windstorm and hiked into Garry [Oregon] oak country with associated small mammals and birds, including a "depressed" California Jumping Rat [Kangaroo Rat] a pair of crested jays [Steller's Jay] "perturbed by their presence" and several shrikes not perturbed by either the visitors or the wind in pursuing their "butcher" behaviour.[697]

The trip was clearly a success on three counts: for his dissertation, his small mammal collection and supplementing his diet. He came back with ample specimens of mule and blacktails as well as hybrids of the two. His journal notes that "the Sacramento River forms the boundary between the ranges of mule and blacktail."[699] He left Johnston behind at Shasta and boarded the night coach again to Portland to map out the Oregon dividing line. He wasted no time on the night trip, spotting blacktails at 3 a.m. on the Pacific Highway, despite new-moon darkness. The driver stopped the bus for him "to enable me to observe them better."[700] One has the impression that few could resist Cowan's enthusiasm for his research.

In Portland he met with Stanley G. Jewett of the US Biological Survey, who had assembled specimens from the Willamette River region for the young graduate, including two sets of 11-tined antlers locked in mighty combat. Another pivotal source of local knowledge, Jewett was originally a Canadian from New Brunswick and one of the classic naturalists of the ilk of Laing and Taverner. An obituary in 1955 described him as "one of the rare broad naturalists in this age of increasing specialization."[701] Grinnell wrote to Miss Margaret Wythe about Jewett's collection of 10,000 skins, saying it was the "best collection in the northwest, public or private – unless Brooks's equals it, which I have yet to know."[702] Cowan spoke admiringly of him in both his journals and his acknowledgements. Jewett's work with the Survey gave him extensive field experience, and Cowan recorded many pages of his accounts of mule, blacktail and whitetail occurrences in the region, the latter having formerly had a much wider range.

Jewett had also spent time on the islands of the Columbia River as a young ranch hand. These islands, from a biologist's point of view, were of special interest because they provided staging spots or geographical limits for species distribution across the huge river. It was a formidable boundary to many species such as the California Jackrabbit. Cowan records that Jewett found one jackrabbit on a sand bar in the Columbia, making it the northern limit of the southern subspecies. Cowan's own observations of the northern White-tailed Jackrabbits in BC showed them only just making it over the border and they were a species of concern even back then. Strangely, Jewett too missed the Pacific White-tailed Deer.

On May 15 Cowan wrote that Jewett had confirmed the Cascades as being the dividing line between the mule and blacktail. It was his last entry before stepping back on the bus and doing another all-nighter to Vancouver.

The journals paused for a month as he caught up with family and Joyce. A month later, he was back in the field, but in North Vancouver with game warden G.C. Stevenson comparing notes and accompanying him on his beat to investigate wildlife concerns. The two headed up to Horseshoe Bay to check out deer that had been causing problems for market gardeners. It was a subject close to home, since Cowan's father was one such gardener on the North Shore. Cowan spent two nights waiting in a hide with little success but managed to record the midsummer early-morning bird chorus, including Marbled Murrelets passing overhead to and from the mountains. Their presence around Vancouver was much more common then.

He also mentioned two other wildlife sightings that are unheard of in these regions today: Mountain Goats on Mount Seymour and Grizzlies just north of Whistler. On July 12 the journal entries were in a different handwriting – Joyce's. They were up at Alta Lake and she was meticulously recording their first week's trapping together around the cabin and at Cheakamus Lake. It is on this trip that Cowan writes lyrically about the Varied Thrush song.

CHAPTER 16

"Each of those boys is now free to bear down hard on his thesis – Orr on the rabbits, Cowan on the deer."

Berkeley, 1933–1935

Just three days before Cowan's departure back to Berkeley for the 1933 fall term, bad luck befell him in a boating accident on the coast. His foot got caught between rock and rowboat in surf, breaking both bones and crushing the ligaments. He was ten days late getting down to Berkeley, where a challenging situation faced him:

> When I got there they said, "We may have a problem between now and the winter because somebody else has your job until Christmas. We just had to have someone and there was a fellow available." I had a little money but not very much. I was hobbling around there in the hot weather in September. I got ground down to the point where I was disgusted. I said [to Grinnell], "I don't think I can hang in there. It's just too much. I don't have any money." He said, "You don't mean to tell me you would sacrifice the brilliant career that I know you're going to have. How much money do you need?" I had done my homework and $75 would see me through to Christmas. He pulled out his chequebook and wrote me a cheque for $75. He said, "Now don't be such a damned fool. I don't want the money back, give it to some worthy student down the road, because I know you're going to have plenty of them." You can't but love a teacher like that. Seventy-five dollars didn't mean much to him but it meant a hell of a lot to me.[703]

Cowan would never forget the kindness of Grinnell and he repaid the debt innumerable times to his own students. For his 100th birthday tribute (which he would not see) past students prepared a tribute to Cowan which included the various financial "rescues" that spanned three decades of students. It was consistent with the code of ethics of his mentors and Cowan felt privileged to be in a position to do it. There would be another benefit to that boat accident, too: it would bolster Cowan's case against military service, though that was several years away yet.

Cowan obviously recuperated well and in his second year he was made head teaching fellow, in charge of 12 teaching assistants for the princely sum of $600. "They doubled my stipend, which, believe me, saved me from death by starvation."[704] One of his tasks was to assist his professor, Frank Daniels, with lecturing in the big classroom, which held 400 people. From Daniels he learned both lecturing and media technology skills. "He was absolutely meticulous in his teaching preparation. As head teaching fellow I was also responsible for choirmastering his lecture theatre, and that included arranging for an overhead projector, which was on a translucent screen above him projected from another room. It was a great big projector, a carbon-arc; this is dark ages stuff now."[705]

The carbon-arc projector required constant adjustments of its electrical rods,

North American Opossum [Virginia Opossum]

Didelphis marsupialis virginiana [Didelphis virginiana]

Cat size, with long, naked tail, large, naked ears; hind feet with 5 toes, first large without nail and opposable; head long with slender, pointed face. Fur-lined pouch on lower abdomen of female. It was first taken in British Columbia at Crescent Beach in 1949. Since then it has increased greatly in numbers and has extended its range up the Fraser Valley ... as far as Spuzzum.[709]

while the slides had to be perfectly synchronized with Daniels's unusual lecturing style. He never looked at his slides while referring to them. This demanded a whole new skill set in timing and telepathy.[706] Cowan's administration skills had already been spotted, so he was inducted into the seemingly squalid interrelations among faculty members "and the games they were playing ... It's not all friendly."[707] Cowan described one incident with Daniels as an example:

> He was pacing up and down in his room and he was mad as hops: "That silly old buzzard down the hall" (this was the head of the department he was talking about). "Ian, will you go down and tell him so and so and so and so." Like hell I would. So I dutifully go down there and say, "Professor Daniels seems to be upset about something. He's particularly ..." – this sort of thing. I gave him the message in very quiet, diplomatic words. Then the head, Colford, said, "Yes, he is a silly old buzzard, but he sure knows his stuff. Would you tell him ..." As a messenger, I was a filter. Anyway, that was good training.[708]

He made two field trips to Mendocino County and the Coast Range with zoologist James Moffitt and his wife, Elizabeth. Cowan mentions that Moffitt was a fish and game commissioner but not that he was from a well-known family of university patrons with affiliations to John Muir and the early Sierra Club. The family had a library and medical departments eventually named after them – Moffitt's father was the dean of the college. Grinnell had a decade-long correspondence on natural history topics with the older members of the family, initiated through the unlikely subject of opossums – a specimen of which was sent to Grinnell by the couple.

Opossums are an introduced species of marsupial on the west coast of the continent. They arrived (according to Grinnell in his letter to the Moffitts) in 1910 at San Jose with

> … a Negro caterer [who] essayed to fatten a batch of opossums for some special occasion. These he had obtained live from Tennessee. A part of the consignment got away. Within two years opossums were reported from several suburban neighborhoods in Santa Clara County and they are now being reported more and more widely and frequently throughout west central California and even in Southern California. I personally feel it will become a nuisance.[710]

Which indeed they did as a predatorless predator. Cowan's student Charlie Guiguet would collect the first specimen for BC at Cloverdale in 1946 for the UBC museum. Although the opossum was native to North America ("the ancestral stock of the marsupials" goes back 20 million years)[711] they had died out and re-entered North America two million years ago over the Panama bridge. Cowan subsequently watched them cross into British Columbia, but not without problems. Their ancestral predators had been gone a while too, especially on small islands like Hornby off Vancouver Island, where they were introduced. Songbirds were some of the first casualties. Cowan's relationship with opossums continued with his live capture of the first Mountain Pygmy Possum for science in Australia a few years later.

Accompanying the Moffitts on extended camping trips would have been a high honour for the young graduate student and provided him free transport and access to some of the large ranches, like the 20,000-acre tract of rolling grasslands and live oaks owned by the Ogles and Mailliards in Mendocino County. John Mailliard was an amateur ornithologist and chair of the California Academy of Sciences in San Francisco, for which his brother Joseph Mailliard and later Moffitt were curators of ornithology. Cowan describes the landscape in his journal:

> The general type of the area is rolling, the higher reaches being covered with Scrub oak, Tan oak and Live oak, with the northern exposures covered with chapparal in places. In the deeper ravines the timber is mainly of the Redwood and Pseudotsuga association, with the underbrush made up of Tan oak, Madrone, Alder and Elm.[712]

During the day Cowan roamed the ranch with the Moffitts. The evenings were spent by the fire sharing ideas on deer characteristics, skulls and antlers and the utilization of acorns and oak leaves by the deer. One night he narrowly sidestepped a rattlesnake and during another was awakened in his tent by the unforgettable calls of Pygmy and Spotted owls.[713]

Spotted Owl numbers drastically declined with the accelerated post-war logging and it became a poster bird for conservation. Cowan sat on the board of the US National Audubon Society in the mid-1980s and one of the last things he did in that capacity was commission a special report on the Spotted Owl, which gave the Society "substantial leverage in its efforts to protect the old growth forests in the northwest."[715] The scientific report was part of the rationale for inclusion under the US Endangered Species Act, which led to a protracted battle between industry and environmentalists that culminated in 1990 with the owl being officially listed as threatened.[716] Meanwhile, Cowan's student R. Wayne Campbell wrote the status report for Canada for 1986, when the owl was designated endangered.[717] Less than a dozen owls remain in the wild in BC today.

Cowan's friendship with the Moffitts was short-lived. After a brief stint as director of the national Audubon Society and curator at the California Academy of Sciences, Moffitt was killed in a wartime airplane crash. In his obituary he was described as combining the

Spotted Owl

Strix occidentalis

It is a non-migratory, secretive, nocturnal species that inhabits dense, coniferous, old-growth forests (over 200 years old) in mountainous areas ... The Spotted Owl has become a species of concern throughout its range in the Pacific Northwest and in California.[714]

> ... best qualities implicit in the words "amateur" and "professional." His love of the outdoors, his eagerness to share its pleasures with his friends, his warm sense of fair play, made him the ideal sportsman. As a zoologist, his capacity for careful

observation and painstaking study gave him high rank, and made him, among other things, a recognized authority on the wild geese of North America.[718]

Moffitt's specialty was the ecology of the Brant, the charismatic small goose that migrates along the Pacific flyway and became an important focus for Cowan and his colleague Neil Dawe. The Englishman River estuary on the east side of Vancouver Island was protected by The Nature Trust of BC and Dawe started the Brant Festival to raise awareness of the bird locally. The festival brought naturalists to the beaches to explain why it was important not to disturb the animals as they fed in the intertidal zones, building up their fat reserves and resting along these staging points of their flyway. These actions led to the establishment of the Parksville–Qualicum Beach Wildlife Management Area, 17 kilometres of protected foreshore habitat for the Brant and myriad other waterbirds.

The postscript to the Mailliard ranch – inland from the Brant bays – was that before his death in 1954 the eldest son of John Mailliard, John Ward Mailliard Jr., helped ensure much of it was protected as a state natural reserve, the Mailliard Redwoods.[720]

Over the winter of 1933-34, Cowan did two more trips. The first was to a veterinary laboratory to meet William H. Boynton. Boynton was keeping deer in captivity to look into the disease anaplasmosis carried by wild deer. Another project McCabe helped Cowan on was recording the effects of captivity and hybridization of mule and blacktails in Ukiah Park, where captives of both species had been allowed to interbreed. The results weren't pleasing. "These deer had the disgusting habit that I have only seen before in goats, viz., drinking of urine."[721] After these experiences, there was no question where his preference for wild venison over captive ungulates came from. It also informed him of the potential of research on captive deer to understand the role of nutrition, disease and broader ecosystem factors in health, in which he would do experimental work during the 1950s. The nine-acre Ukiah Park was donated in 1945 to the Save the Redwoods League by Robert Orr, Cowan's colleague at Berkeley with whom he graduated. It was added to over the years and is now the Montgomery Woods State Natural Reserve and houses one of the world's tallest trees.[722]

Brant

Branta bernicla

Circumpolar. Breeds in arctic North America and Eurasia.... winters along the Pacific coast from southern Alaska and the Queen Charlotte Islands to Baja California. During the past 100 years, the Brant has declined drastically as a wintering species in British Columbia ... Spring populations build in California bays in early January and peak in mid-March (Moffitt 1939). Spring migration occurs from late February through mid-May and peaks in late March and early April in extreme southern British Columbia.[719]

The oak grasslands of Mendocino imprinted themselves on Cowan. He forever had a great affinity for this coastal grassland–oak woodland ecosystem that started around Berkeley and stretched up a narrow coastal strip to its northern limit in the rain shadow of southern Vancouver Island.[723] His first job at the museum and his last job as the chancellor of the University of Victoria were in this northern limit of the coastal grasslands, where he eventually retired. The Garry oak ecosystem is among the most endangered in Canada (his father had written about their cultural significance half a century earlier) and is under enormous pressure from development. Cowan's modest retirement bungalow on Woodhaven Terrace was one of the many homes built in this endangered ecosystem. Cowan protected many of the native trees and wildflowers in his garden and let the Columbian Blacktail Deer browse through. It was there that he oversaw the writing and editing of *Birds of BC*.

The summer of 1934 was spent studying and bouncing between Vancouver,

Victoria, Huntingdon and Alta Lake. There are no journal entries, and only two specimens were catalogued: a mole at Huntingdon and a Little Brown Bat at Alta Lake, recorded in Joyce's handwriting.

The family albums from this summer record a joint expedition of the whole Cowan and Racey families up to Alta Lake. The only picture that exists of the two fathers-in-law together was taken at the dock at Alta Lake. McTaggart Cowan is towering above Racey, the two men apparently in amiable conversation. Another photo shows the younger siblings peering through the docks at the life underneath.

Cowan's third and final year at Berkeley was flat-out busy. He wrote and passed his final qualifying exam. He later told the story of how his examiners had said to him, "We've had our fun grilling you – how would you like to ask us a few questions?" And Cowan's response was: "I certainly would, but I'd be a damned fool if I did."[725]

Grinnell immediately told Annie Alexander of the success:

Little Brown Myotis [Bat]

Myotis lucifugus

This species frequently gathers in very large colonies in the attics of buildings and similar locations. Such colonies, sometimes several thousand strong, are made up of females and young. The males live a more solitary life.[724]

Sitka Mouse [Keen's Mouse]

Peromyscus sitkensis prevostensis [now *P. keeni*]

Very large size and short tail, along with several cranial characters ... Throughout all habitats on certain outer islands of the Alaskan Archipelago and Queen Charlotte Islands.[727]

> Mr. [Robert Thomas] Orr as well as Mr. Cowan passed their qualifying examinations in good shape. This noon I talked with Prof. [Samuel Jackson] Holmes, who was on both committees, and he expressed himself well pleased. His field, genetics, is the one that stumps most zoology candidates. So each of those boys is now free to bear down hard on his thesis – Orr on the rabbits, Cowan on the deer.[726]

Alexander was delighted and wrote back too. Now Cowan was free to write up his thesis, but he was still teaching, and wanted to access the collection at Berkeley to write up the distribution of the different races of Sitka White-footed Mouse (now officially a separate species called Keen's Mouse).

Alexander, Swarth and McCabe had been collecting on many of the islands to the southeast of Alaska and Cowan compared those specimens to Racey's and his own collections from isolated islands in BC to propose a series of new races.[728] That study precipitated the major research project into island insularity a decade later.

In the spring of 1935, with his doctorate in sight, Cowan was also looking for a job. He had to secure a reliable income before he could marry Joyce, and the job prospects were poor:

This was the Depression. There weren't a lot of jobs. One came up in New York City at the American Museum and I applied and my roommate applied. Two of us shared an office. Grinnell came in and said, "Ian, I have to break it to you: you didn't get that job, your classmate did." He said, "Don't feel too bad about it; you wouldn't have liked that job. You don't know this, but Eric Hill has a heart condition. He can't work in the field. This job he has in New York is to sit inside and measure skulls for the rest of his natural life, and live in New York City. You don't want to do that. Don't worry, another job will come up." And about the next day I got a letter from McLean Fraser, who said: "Well, I guess you're just about through, Ian; what are the job prospects?" So I wrote back and said: "As far as I'm concerned, there aren't any." He said, "Well, the government's changed in British Columbia."[729]

It had changed, radically. Under the former Conservative government, the operating grant in 1932 had been cut in half, decimating UBC. The faculty rebelled and five professors joined Thomas Dufferin (Duff) Pattullo's Liberal party on a "socialized capitalism" platform, running for office in the next election. One of them was George Weir, a professor of education at UBC who became Minister of Education and provincial secretary. Bent on social reform of education, Weir had a pivotal role in selecting and placing the brightest and keenest from UBC ranks in "the upper-levels of those professional hierarchies"[730] where they would be able to provide the schools and institutions with the quality of teaching and guidance that was needed. (Weir was also responsible for bringing in one of the early forms of public health insurance.) University budgets were quickly restored, and McLean Fraser at UBC was scouting for talent to restaff the institutions that had been cut. Cowan was one of the prospects he contacted:

> "There's a job in the Provincial Museum, and if you want it, write to the head of the Department of Education." He [George Weir] wrote back and said, "I understand from McLean Fraser that you are interested." I said I was interested and [asked] how did I apply. He said, "I got your application and come and see me on the 31st of May or as soon as you get back."[731] [When Cowan got to Victoria he was told:] "All we've got in the budget for that position is $1,250 a year. If you want it, it's yours." I said, "Sure I want it." So I was hired as the biologist for the Provincial Museum.[732]

For his commencement exercises on May 17, 1935, his mother, Joyce and the Racey family all travelled down the coast via Mount Shasta. The ceremony was held outdoors in the University's Greek Theatre. The pictures show a delighted young couple standing in front of the columns of the Vertebrate Museum and Laura Cowan and son in front of one of the cedars – close to where he had spotted the Great Horned Owl nest. They spent a few days in Berkeley with celebrations and packing up, then headed into the Mojave Desert to look for the White-tailed Antelope Squirrel and Mohave Ground Squirrel for Racey's and Cowan's collections.

Interestingly, the Mohave Ground Squirrel they captured that day (and other ground squirrel specimens prepared by the two men) were used in 2012 by two Czech researchers looking at the drivers of sexual dimorphism, or the difference in size or colouration between the sexes. Ground squirrels don't exhibit much sexual dimorphism, despite having a wide range of behaviours that might cause it.[734] What Cowan had observed in grasslands from Chezacut to the Mojave was that despite this family of animals sharing qualities (liking open country, using burrows, being diurnal and omnivorous and reproducing once a year) they vary greatly between species as to body size, behaviour and social systems. For example, some ground squirrels demonstrate quite conservative mating behaviours, while others are highly promiscuous. Bernhard Rensch, who had developed the *Rassenkreis* concept, later posited Rensch's Rule, which predicted that the greater the demand for male aggression against other males to hold females, the greater the male body size. But the rule doesn't hold up with ground squirrels. In fact they are an exception. It is fitting that just as Joyce and the families came to fetch Cowan home for job and marriage, he was laying the foundation for future research into a greater understanding of the battle of the sexes with some of his favourite mammals.

The Cowans displayed more sexual dimorphism than the Raceys, but behaviourally Joyce was just as much a specimen hunter as her father, brothers and fiancé. She wrote to her brother Stewart on May 23 from the Mojave Desert:

> Daddy and Ian put out some traps yesterday and got quite a good haul, also we have been getting a lot of good stuff off the road – a rabbit and three birds this morning.
> Love,
> Joyce."[735]

Her photographs of the desert show her father in his pith helmet, hunched over a portable dissecting box, no doubt wishing to prepare his specimen before the hot sun renders it unusable. Relaxing on the coast at Half Moon Bay, Joyce and her mother are captured in black and white collecting shells on the beach, while Cowan is pictured in a pensive moment gazing out to sea from a rock – much like the pre-breeding California Sea-lions he observed moving back into BC waters for the spring.

Mohave Ground Squirrel

Spermophilus mohavensis

The Mohave Ground Squirrel is a brown-coloured ground squirrel, without stripes or conspicuous markings on the body, but with a short, broadly haired tail.[733]

PART 5
THE MUSEUM YEARS:
1935–1940

CHAPTER 17

"I stretched what a museum was all about."

Victoria, 1935–1936

In July of 1935, Cowan received his notice of temporary appointment to the Provincial Museum at a salary of $125/month – which he annotated in red ink: wow! His youthful enthusiasm to get working was spawned by more than professional interest. He was getting closer to a reliable income in order to marry Joyce. He had one year to get himself scrutinized, a permanent position secured and $700 in savings banked. It was probably this motivation that cushioned his entrance into an institution that had accumulated more than dust: rumours about dodgy accounts, a controversial firing of his predecessor, a public exposé of fraudulent specimens, poor science and a general malaise due to what many pointed to as the increasingly lacklustre direction of Francis Kermode, the ill-chosen namesake of the cream-coloured race of the American Black Bear of the central and northern coast of British Columbia, also called, more fittingly, the Spirit Bear.

Cowan was leaving behind "one of the great institutions of the world in terms of systematic collections,"[736] MVZ at Berkeley, and returning to a smaller museum that had become stalled in the era of preserved specimens and artifacts in drawers and glass cases. Until Cowan was hired, the museum had never had a staff member with any formal training in either museology or natural history. However, Cowan would have been stoked with enthusiasm for its tremendous potential, given the start made by its well-loved first curator, John Fannin.

Fannin had been from the old amateur-naturalist cohort – a familiar breed to Cowan – with an excellent reputation as a naturalist, collector and educator, setting a high bar for the museum at the time. This modest man, who had come from Upper Canada during the gold rush, survived an eventful career in the gold fields and developed a great love for the natural history of the province, with curatorial skills to match his interest in education. Photographs of the time portray a wiry, curious man sitting amongst a menagerie of stuffed animals in the new east wing of the provincial legislature, where he had encouraged the political specimens over in the west wing to house the collection.

Under his watch, Fannin started an organization that encouraged scientists and members of the public to do active research, the Natural History Society of BC, which met monthly in the museum. The society attracted the rising star of Charles F.

Newcombe, a naturalist–anthropologist who, according to Cowan, was "looked upon as a god."[737] He travelled the coast in a dugout canoe and administered medical services to the remote communities as well as buying up their artifacts, which earned him a mixed legacy amongst those coastal first nations.[738] With his British compatriots, he created a strong public following for the museum and the province's natural and cultural history.[739] He had also forged affiliations with individuals and institutions all over the world, including with Harry Swarth, the curator of birds at MVZ, whom Cowan knew. Both Newcombe and his son William (Billy) worked with Swarth on his various expeditions on Vancouver Island, starting in 1904.[740] Swarth even gave a lecture for Newcombe in Victoria. During these early years, the museum grew in stature as well as attendance. But in 1904 everything changed. Cowan told his version of the story:

Dawson's Caribou

Rangifer dawsoni [now considered an extinct subspecies, *Rangifer tarandus dawsoni*, of the Caribou from the BC mainland]

This species is distinguished by its small size and dull, mouse-grey colour without dark-brown, black or white marks ... This species was confined to the area of Graham Island, Queen Charlotte Islands, west of Naden Harbour. Only three specimens have been taken and these were from close to Naden Harbour ... This species may be extinct, as nothing definite has been seen of it since about 1920.[744]

> ... then Fanning died unexpectedly and [Francis] Kermode was made the director. Kermode had absolutely no education; he was an office boy. But because he was on site, he was made director ... The Honourable H.E. Young was the provincial secretary at the time. What I heard was the natural history group wanted Newcombe appointed director. Newcombe would have been a first-rate person to get it. He was an MD, to begin with, he was well known up and down the coast, was a passionate anthropologist. He knew a lot of people....[741] Anyway, the group slowly died ... When Kermode was appointed, he immediately ousted these people from the museum.[742]

Museum historian Lorne Hammond conjectures that Kermode may well have made a pitch against Newcombe on fiscal grounds to a revenue-hungry provincial secretary, casting himself as an alternative to what might have appeared as an overly demanding "bunch of provincial naturalists going on Sunday picnics."[743] The truth is impossible to know, since most of the documents of that time were thrown away by Kermode. The slender annual reports of the museum, which provide virtually all we have of Kermode's 36-year reign, indicate that his beginnings were competent. He reports that he travelled around the world to other institutions, engaged in correspondence with curators like William Hornaday at the New York Zoological Society, who was to name the white bear after him, and continued to build a substantive collection in both natural and cultural history using volunteer and paid collectors, including J.A. Munro and Charles F. Newcombe. His early achievements included securing specimens of the last Dawson's caribou, a species endemic to the Queen Charlotte Islands (now called Haida Gwaii).

Kermode also saw the museum formally recognized under the new Provincial Museum Act in 1913 with the objectives:

(a) To secure and preserve specimens illustrating the natural history of the Province;

(b) To collect anthropological material relating to the aboriginal races of the Province;

(c) To obtain information respecting the natural sciences relating particularly to the natural history of the Province, and to increase and diffuse knowledge regarding the same.[745]

The absence of any reference to the Natural History Society, however, put Kermode "firmly in the saddle" of directing the museum, and any official affiliations with the original scientific community were lost.[746] Visitors continued to come though and in his annual reports he was quick to note auspicious ones, such as US President Theodore Roosevelt and the Duke and Duchess of Connaught with Princess Patricia.[747]

Historians describe him as "an embattled dinosaur,"[748] with little to draw an opinion because of so little historical documentation. Cowan suggested that, "Considering his background and upbringing, he didn't do badly ... He started out well. He put together some museum exhibitions. He hired J.A. Munro early on as a biologist to do some slave field work in the Okanagan."[749] Cowan had several Kermode stories he loved to repeat in his later years. One of them was about the origin of the naming of the Kermode bear, as he heard it from Kermode himself:

> The specimens came from a fur trader who was working up and down the coast and he got them from the Indians up there on Gribbell Island. Kermode got the idea that all the bears up there were white. He sent the specimens to Hornaday at the New York Zoological Society. He said, "This is fascinating and I suggest that I write up the description and we'll call it *Ursus alba*." Kermode wrote back and said, "No, I think it would be much better if you name it after me."[750]

Kermode's dubious science caught up with him. It wasn't just that he had messed up on the bear, but ornithologist Major Allan Brooks accused him in the ornithological journal *Ibis* (a 1923 volume) of taking an imported Japanese Plumed Egret and passing it off as a BC specimen. By 1935 Kermode was three decades into his reign and the blush was long off the museum's early promise, both internally and externally. Funding was barely trickling in during the Depression years, his energies appear to have been on a similar stale trajectory and the youthful Cowan was coming in as assistant curator after a very controversial firing of William (Billy) Newcombe from that position. Cowan was appointed not by Kermode but by George Weir, the new Minister of Education, as one of four bright PhD grads from BC to enliven the province's flagging institutions. After Weir had called Cowan to his office to appoint him, Weir's assistant had called Kermode to announce that the new biologist, Dr. Cowan, would be over to see him in a few minutes. Recounted Cowan years later:

> By the time I got there he was gone. He [Kermode] hadn't any idea that it was in the mill that they would appoint me. Not any idea. The previous biologist, Billy Newcombe, was the son of the former Dr. C.F. Newcombe and he had been fired after an altercation with Kermode. Kermode insisted that nobody was to sign a letter under his or her own name; everything had to be signed by him. Billy Newcombe knew a lot of people that he wrote to all the time. So there was a row and he was let out, and one of the ostensible reasons was that Newcombe had stolen some specimens [fossils]. Newcombe maintained that it was not so and he was let out.[752]

Kermode Bear

Ursus americanus kermodei

The occurrence of a white colour phase in this population of bears led to its description. At present not sufficient material is available to present a comprehensive diagnosis, and the two adult skulls available here show great individual variation ... Bears of black pelage are far more common than the white colour phase in the area where the latter occurs, but if the name *kermodei* is valid it is applicable to both black and white bears of the region.[751]

A full account of this period – the disarray at the museum, the controversial Newcombe firing – is given by historian Peter Corley-Smith.[753] An interview he did with Cowan about those five years was embargoed until the death of Kermode's second wife in 2010. In it, Cowan revealed some evidence for the disarray. Soon after he started, while looking for a book in Kermode's office, he had found the allegedly "stolen" fossil behind a book.[754] Later, Kermode had asked Cowan to sign vouchers for travel expenses Kermode himself had incurred while visiting a mistress, who later became his wife. Cowan refused and sought legal advice. Thereafter, he kept a notebook of voucher numbers and dates because "I was afraid that he was trying to do for me what had been done for Newcombe."[755] When he arrived at the museum he had also documented the condition of the collection, which was, according to Cowan, "in pathetic shape. There was no catalogue of any of the material; most of it had not been kept fumigated, so the specimens were in poor physical shape, except for the anthropology section, which was well-maintained."[756]

In earlier interviews, Cowan characteristically focused on the relationships that were productive. For example, he describes the welcoming reception he received from Nancy Stark, the stenographer:

> She showed me around the museum and told me various things about it. There was a very nice general factotum there who swept the floors and polished the glass cases, a fellow by the name of Ed Cook, who was a likeable senior fellow that had knocked about the world a lot. He had two sons, both of which became provincial police. He and I got along very well. I got along well with everyone there. I even got along with Kermode...[757]

With no other jobs on the horizon, the prize of his bride attainable only with a permanent position and the opportunity for making a real name for himself, it's not hard to imagine Cowan going to extraordinary efforts to get along with Kermode.

He was also not alone. Another of his colleagues was W. Kaye Lamb, one of the other PhD grads hand-picked by Weir. In Lamb's obituary, he is described as one of the most under-celebrated figures of British Columbia's literary history. As well as a competent administrator, he was a prolific historian, having famously said: "Any country worthy of a future should be interested in its past."[758] Lamb and Cowan both stayed that year at a well-known old Victoria boarding house called Rockabella, close to the Empress Hotel, run by the formidable Mrs. Tuck and her daughter. According to Lamb,

> It had no central heating and there was only one bathroom on each floor. But it was a very comfortable place and most people came to stay forever. When Ian arrived, he came there. Ian stayed there only for the year before his marriage ... while he was there, we were in and out of one another's rooms.[759]

Lamb too was a born-and-raised Vancouver boy and had known Cowan at UBC, though he had been in history and two years ahead of Cowan. He had gone on to do post-graduate work at the Sorbonne and at the London School of Economics, which according to Cowan, was "a real radical place at the time."[760] After teaching at UBC, Lamb had accepted the position of provincial librarian (now chief archivist) the year before Cowan was hired, and they worked in the same building. Lamb's official function was of course to organize and preserve the province's historical documents, but since no policy existed for the collection of historical objects as well, he extended his job to artifacts. Part of his unofficial collection was an Emily Carr painting – an inspired acquisition given the valuations placed on her work today. A strange footnote was that Billy Newcombe, for whom Cowan had respect as a naturalist, had retreated to Carr's "House of All Sorts." Wounded by his museum experience, Newcombe formed a strong friendship with Carr and eventually became her executor. One can only guess at the cross-fertilization of ideas between two generations of Cowans and Newcombes, Lamb and Carr, the myriad topics of art, place, natural history, anthropology and history, and the long-lasting effects these conversations undoubtedly had on BC's major institutions and cultural identity.

> **[Western] Small-footed Myotis**
>
> *Myotis subulatus melanorhinus*
> [*Myotis ciliolabrum*]
>
> Very small size, small foot (6 mm or less) and pale colouration identify this species ... Known only from Vaseux Lake, Oyama and Osoyoos Lake, in the most arid part of the Okanagan Valley.[763]

The collection Lamb started back in the 1930s wasn't officially brought into the museum until 1967, but his foresight ensured that a vital part of recent Canadian history was collected and preserved. His sophisticated scholarship in cultural history also rubbed off on Cowan:

> He was a good colleague. We saw a lot of each other. When my hair was getting a little thick, he kept it smoothed down. He was a very wise individual and he worked very close to the seats of power in the government, so he was a good counsel.[761]

Lamb's obituary describes him as having had an innate understanding of organizational behaviour and human nature, and no doubt some of his understanding came from his friend the acute observer of animal behaviour. Lamb's approach to all positions of authority throughout his long career in administration was to trust his staff and delegate responsibility. The support one imagines the two men provided one another – out of hearing, back at Rockabella – was on the appropriate course of action with difficult bosses and on how to run prestigious provincial institutions on a shoestring.

What Kermode did provide as boss, when managed sensitively by his employee, was a relatively free rein for Cowan to do his job. Much of his first year was spent rescuing the poorly conserved collection, cataloguing it and finding out what he could about the specimens – 1,560 mammals and 5,247 birds. He started a Saturday morning children's lecture series under a Carnegie Corporation grant, using specimens and lantern slides. He prepared a special study, *Bats of British Columbia*, which led to the discovery of bat specimens in the collection that hadn't been documented in Canada before.[762]

He was also free to pursue fieldwork, not only to increase the collection for taxonomic purposes but to do the first provincial park baselines "with a view to recording the flora and fauna peculiar to the regions and to publish the results in the annual reports so as to be available for tourists and others visiting the parks"[764] This took Cowan all over the region. It also involved a daily walk to the museum via Beacon Hill Park, an inner city park with extensive but rare Garry oak wildflower meadows and a duck pond, where he conducted the Beacon Hill Park duck census. Another ornithologist and acolyte of the 'B', Patrick W. (Pat) Martin, with whom Cowan would have a long friendship, joined him for the census. Martin recalled Cowan spotting a mallard–pintail cross on the pond and deciding he needed it for the museum collection. Early next morning, Cowan took his collecting rifle with him and shot the bird, only to have it fly into the middle of the pond and die.

Mallard nest with eggs

Anas platyrhynchos

The Mallard is the most abundant and widely distributed duck in British Columbia and has been recorded from sea level to 3000 metres elevation. It occurs virtually everywhere open water is present ... In urban environments, ponds, puddles and other damp areas attract Mallards.[766]

Nothing daunted Cowan: he waded out into the pond up to his armpits and retrieved his prize. A soggy Ian changed his clothes, ate his breakfast and proceeded to work. The bird is still in the collection, catalogue #5650.[765]

In that first autumn Cowan managed to persuade Kermode to allow him two field trips to the lower Fraser Valley and Alta Lake, "where considerable collecting is done."[767] Probably, considerable visiting of his fiancée was done too. His first official field trips, accompanied by Joyce and his future father-in-law, were to the islands of the Fraser Delta, including Iona, Lulu and Westham, where the massive Pacific flyway migration comes through and large populations of birds overwinter. Here is his description of Lulu Island – now the busy metropolis of Richmond – in the winter of 1935:

> We drove to the muskeg in the north-central part of the island. This is a barren sphagnum muskeg, with no open water. Stunted willows and Jack [shore] pine, bog laurel and Labrador tea are the dominant features of the vegetation.[768]

Some of the birds they saw no longer occur, their habitat long gone.

> We drove down to the dike south of Steveston + hunted the marshes at the end of the Island. Dunlin were numerous, 500+ Dunlin, 2 Dowitcher, 2 Snipe, 5 Heron, 1 Short-eared Owl, 1 Cormorant

(Double crested), 5 Blackbirds (Redwinged), 10 Song sparrows, 20 Meadowlark, 1 Western Sandpiper, 1 Green-winged Teal, 2 Killdeer.[769]

Seven hundred acres of the Fraser Delta that was not lost to urbanization was an area on Westham Island owned by the George C. Reifel family, which the BC Waterfowl Society leased in 1963 from the son (also named George) as a migratory bird sanctuary. Two of the 'B' were signators of the lease: Cowan and Frank Butler.[771] Today, it is federally owned, designated as the Alaksen National Wildlife Area and still managed by the BC Waterfowl Society as the George C. Reifel Migratory Bird Sanctuary, after Reifel's father.

Cowan also started his study on the ecology of deer, which met the third objective of the museum – the encouragement of the natural sciences. In December he was up at Alta Lake with the Racey family doing his research. His first entry in his deer study journals begins: "Tracked a large deer along the hill behind the Racey cottage. In one place it had pawed through the snow down to the Labrador tea."[772] He fitted the deer study in around the weekends for the next five years, which took him into the major forestry and agricultural regions of southern Vancouver Island and the Gulf Islands. Influenced by his experiences in the agricultural valleys of California where large prey–predator systems had been extirpated by loss of habitat, Cowan was interested in how farmers and foresters might coexist with wildlife. He was looking closely at the diets of deer and the timing of pressures on certain plants and trees, with an eye to reducing damage. He made friends with wardens and landowners, who allowed him access to observe deer on all the islands, big and small.

In a letter to biologist Rodger Hunter, he talks about one such friendship with Suzanne and George Buchanan Simpson of the Cowichan Valley:

> The study of the Columbian Black-tailed Deer led me to this beautiful spot on the lake. I was looking for a study area where deer were numerous, where the vegetation was open enough to permit long-distance observation and the animals not too wild from harassment. The local game warden told me of the oasis the Buchanan Simpsons had created and of the band of deer they entertained, even inside their house. It was a bonus to find in this talented and interesting couple a shared interest in gardening. He was a lover of special plants and grew many of them well. For the following three years, I parked my car on Buchanan Simpson's property about every second week. My biological mission was to study ways in which the deer used the native vegetation on a year-round basis – the interaction between the deer and the forests. On each visit after my day's studies were over, I enjoyed many a cup of tea at their table and many a long chat about plants and the other living things that surrounded them. Their friendly deer were a self-made problem.[773]

Suzanne Buchanan Simpson would leave the property to the University of

Victoria in 1966, to "be used ... for scientific research, or study, in related fields," with the express wish "to preserve the virgin forest and other undisturbed natural habitats."[774] Cowan had maintained a friendship with the couple for years afterwards and no doubt had some influence in their decision.

The deer study was also fulfilling his ongoing fascination with the effects of islands on evolution. In his first year at the museum, he was preparing his doctoral research for publication, and musing on what factors made island deer smaller – teasing out the effects of genetics and environment. Cowan was particularly interested in how islands might cause malnutrition in deer due to limited availability of winter browse, or the different nutritional quality of island plants, or the inability of the deer to migrate. Not being able to move led to increased incidence of disease. Small islands are often associated with the absence of predators to provide checks on the population and limit overgrazing. His ideas of diminishing health as a factor of diminishing size of island were clearly building on island biogeography concepts that he first mused upon as an undergraduate. His idea of the UBC campus forest as an "island" within a sea of urbanization had developed through witnessing the transformation of the entire state of California into small, fragile islands of native habitat.

Other "island" studies he was pursuing while at the museum included mice distribution on islands and the island-like effect of a place called Rocky Point, a grassy and forested knoll jutting into the Strait of Juan de Fuca near Metchosin, forming the narrowest stretch of water for migrating birds to cross, a kind of Gibraltar. It had a relatively undisturbed old-growth Douglas-fir forest with a rich bird population, both overwintering and resident, as well as being a prime staging point for migrations of species such as Western Bluebirds.[775]

Bluebirds nested on sparsely vegetated slopes, also prime habitat for armies in training, which is one of the reasons why Rocky Point was expropriated after the

Western Meadowlark

Sturnella neglecta

In the south coastal areas of the province, including southeastern Vancouver Island, the Gulf Islands and the lower Fraser Valley, the Western Meadowlark was a regular breeding species in the early 1900s, but by the early 1940s it was becoming less common and more restricted as habitat was being lost to urbanization ... on the Lower Mainland, the meadowlark has not been reported breeding since 1986.[770]

Western Bluebird

Sialia mexicana

The decrease in numbers of Western Bluebirds on the coastal mainland of British Columbia parallels changes in numbers in Washington state, where in the regions west of the Cascade Mountains there were only two records of the species between 1948 and 1974. This period of decline of Western Bluebird numbers west of the Cascades in both Washington and British Columbia coincides with the arrival of the European Starling and its rapid increase in numbers.[776]

Second World War. Ironically, these federal military lands have become some of the most important areas for wildlife in the region. Cowan had a role to play in this location being identified nationally as one of the 25 observatories in the Canadian Migration Monitoring Network. In his correspondence file for 1998 was a letter supporting the research of ornithologist Rhonda Millikin, who was working at Rocky Point. Millikin conducted an innovative survey on migratory birds, using radar techniques. Cowan felt she was "providing an objective picture of the timing of migration of the many passerines that follow some of the major geographic features of the province."[777] His earlier work provides baseline data for these types of projects, and he was still writing supportive letters for young researchers at the age of 88.

Meanwhile, in 1935, he had some other serious work to do: get the Provincial Museum collection into shape, get married and establish his own nesting habitat on a sparsely forested slope of Victoria. Little documentation exists for these modest activities, for various reasons. On the question of museum work, Kermode had thrown out most of the correspondence. As for personal correspondence, only the wedding announcement exists, perhaps due to the constraints of the Depression. The wedding was a very simple affair held on a Tuesday night, April 21, 1936, in the middle of a work week, with a small family reception at the Racey home in Vancouver. The ceremony was at the Fairview Presbyterian Church. Joan Cowan, Ian's sister, was a bridesmaid and Joyce's brother Alan Racey was best man.

In the three wedding pictures that exist, they are both in their full breeding plumage. Joyce is dressed in her mother's simple bridal dress and veil, while Ian is looking enthusiastic, minus his moustache. The two other pictures in Joyce's photo album are of a bouquet of spring garden flowers – tulips, daffodils and iris – with some native Oregon Grape and Swordferns, and a wedding cake. The only other document saved is a telegram from Olive and Jim Munro – of the 'B' – wishing the couple "happiness and good fortune."

They did have happiness. Both were shy, private people with the foundation of their friendship built up as teenagers. They were to remain close companions with shared interests for the next 66 years. As a naturalist in her own right, Joyce pursued an outdoors life both with and separate from Cowan. When she was able to, she would join his research and collecting expeditions, though generally unpaid. Alone, she would join a hiking and snowshoeing club with her women friends and faculty wives. It was a traditional marriage in many other ways. At home, she ruled the domestic roost and was a talented seamstress, smocker, knitter, gardener, food conserver and cook. One close friend of the couple noted that both were close observers, but Joyce especially in her quiet way. "She wasn't missing a thing. At a personal level Ian might misplace something and she would know where it was. She was watching over him but she was unobtrusive about it."[778] She provided the emotional stability that enabled Cowan to shine.

The photographs that were collected of Joyce throughout her life captured her on hikes in the mountains, out in the garden, on beaches in her bare feet, outside watching children play. She kept bird lists all her life, including a daily journal of bird feeder and garden visitors wherever they lived, and cultivated the wild community around her. In a tribute to Joyce, she was described as a combination of "grace and grit," eminently practical and capable of turning her hand to anything: equally at home with a chainsaw, "shooting a rat off a deck with a .22 rifle," shingling a cedar roof, butchering an animal or deadheading a rose.[779] She was thrifty and financially astute and the wedding simplicity spoke to both the times and her own practical nature.

They postponed a honeymoon until June, when the couple would be heading out on a two-month field trip, and they spent May moving into their new home in Victoria, searching for a museum vehicle (a Dodge humpback panel truck was eventually secured). Cowan gave lectures around Vancouver and finished his scientific papers, keeping in regular touch with Kermode:

> So far the lectures have gone splendidly. Yesterday morning I had 2 sessions at the High School in the afternoon one at North Star. Today I lectured 4 times in West Vancouver to about 600 students. All the teachers are most enthusiastic and the youngsters are most attentive and eager. All in all, things are just as they should be."[780]

On June 17 the preparations for their field season–honeymoon were finished. Cowan jots a quick note to Kermode: "I have been slightly delayed getting out of here. Reading the galley proofs for my deer paper. PS: You should see the back of our car; it looks like the bargain basement at Spencer's on the 95 cents day sale!"[781] Their itinerary is the Okanagan, the Cariboo and Ootsa Lake in the Chilcotin, for a long summer of adventure and freedom together and alone (at last) in some of the most beautiful regions of British Columbia.

CHAPTER 18

"Up at 5 a.m. as usual."

Okanagan Honeymoon, 1936

N ow in possession of the light-delivery Dodge panel truck converted into an expedition vehicle, the newlyweds planned a full summer honeymoon expedition in the interior, starting in the Okanagan grasslands. They drove up via Merritt and Princeton to Anarchist Mountain, near Osoyoos, as their first stop. Anarchist rises 1500 metres out of the pocket desert that straddles the US border and was a favourite birding site of local naturalists such as Allan Brooks, whom they had visited in the summer of 1931. At Anarchist they camped for four days in the shade and orange scent of Ponderosa Pine at 17 Mile Creek. Water is a natural draw for birds and mammals in dry landscapes and Joyce and Ian observed and collected ample specimens of both. At dawn the breeding Red Crossbills and ill-named Evening Grosbeaks would sing them awake with their high *kip kip* or *burry* chipping calls as they came in to drink.

In an interview with the *Vancouver Sun* in 1952, Cowan spoke about his love of the early morning. "It is the liveliest period of the day; the birds are all in song. Chipmunks and squirrels are swearing in the pine trees. Even the trout put on a show in the early morning."[782] *Vancouver Sun* reporter E.G. Perrault described Cowan as a '

> … conductor in the midst of a symphony of bird calls and animal sounds. When a new note rings out he is alert immediately. This is discord that brings joy to his heart. It may be a new species of bird or a mammal ranging far out of its usual environment. On more than one occasion his sharp ears and expert stalking tactics have rewarded him with a "first" – the naturalist's brief term for a major discovery.[783]

Dusk brought its own symphony, although a more poignant one from the mourning doves, swifts, nighthawks and poorwills that filled the evening air. And there were a few "firsts" for the young couple there too.

The still of their evenings was also interrupted by the antics of the deer mice and ground squirrels that invaded the campsite while they prepared specimens in the cool air. They shared all the prep work, including entries in the catalogue, so the museum was getting two for the price of one. It was not a conventional honeymoon, but the adventures were undoubtedly happy for the pair – exploring exquisite wild country together, unchaperoned at last.

They hiked through most of the south Okanagan from Okanagan Falls to White Lake, an alkali lake, where they watched Sage Thrashers and Brewer's Sparrows making second nests under "the broiling sun" and hunted around in alfalfa fields "where all the rattlesnakes in the country were there, there must have been 500 if there were 10 – nice country to find birds in!!"[785] Then they followed the Okanagan River to their favourite spot at Vaseux Lake."[786] Huge cliffs tower above the west side of the lake, and it was in these cliffs that they had previously observed the elusive Canyon Wren, first spotted by Brooks in 1909. "Did a prodigious amount of climbing at 100 degrees but no luck."

Common Poorwill

Phalaenoptilus nuttallii

Uncommon to fairly common local summer visitant to the southern interior ... The Common Poorwill's breeding distribution includes the Okanagan valley from Osoyoos north to Coldstream. It frequents semi-arid, open habitats, including ponderosa pine forests, lower-level Douglas-fir forests with parkland character, dry pastureland and rocky sagebrush–bunchgrass hillsides. Breeding has been reported from 330 to 580 m elevation, though birds are regularly found singing at 1000 m elevation in the south Okanagan.[784]

The Canyon Wren's song is a cascading waterfall of sound: *tee-you, tee-you, tee-you, tee, tee, tee, tee*. It is the sound of the bunchgrass canyons and cliffs, landscapes to which the small wrens have unwavering loyalty. Cowan had heard the Canyon Wrens in his California wanders and was anxious to locate them for both science and his bride but he felt he'd left it a little late in the season. They went back one more time but with no luck. That evening he visited Mr. Perem at the south end of Vaseux, who told him:

> "Munro has shot all the canyon wrens, most of the chats and bobolinks in the country" – everyone very bitter as regards said official. It is certain I could not find any wrens no matter how hard I hunted. Saw one chat in the sanctuary but did not attempt to get it.[788]

This journal note about Munro's over-zealous collection of wrens marks the start of Cowan's philosophical shift away from his mentors on the question of collections. His decision to leave the chat was a new Cowan, with an adjusting set of conservation principles emerging. Nesting in the rose thickets in the northern margins of the lake below the cliffs was the aptly named Yellow-breasted Chat, BC's largest wood warbler, with its distinctive whistling call.

The Cowans' sighting and protection of nesting chats at Vaseux Lake was repeated over the years by many ornithologists, including Neil Dawe, whose 1996 photograph of the rose thicket where "a pair of chats nest ... most years"[790] was taken roughly in the same spot where the Cowans observed their pair. The continuity of the site had many implications for Cowan. As Trevor Goward notes, collections are biographies. Vaseux held a particularly important place in Cowan's own biogeography at the start of his married life and throughout his career. The presence of the chats also symbolized an indicator for him of continuing habitat health over the decades. Not just on the grounds of adequate food, shelter or security for an animal but on the basis of disturbance through noise. Chats, despite their name, have no tolerance for noise when nesting, especially traffic noise. The account of chats in *Birds of BC* goes on to state "The valley bottom habitats that it prefers occur mainly on lands in demand for human exploitation. These circumstances have led to the designation of the chat as a species of conservation concern in the province."[791]

The requirement of continuity of site was also a characteristic of the White-throated Swifts that were "chattering away from dawn to dusk"[792] as they swooped high up on the cliff faces at Vaseux into nests tucked into crevices.

Continuity didn't just represent health of the ecosystem. Cowan drew enormous strength from the continuous support of Joyce over their 66-year marriage. According to Ann Schau, their daughter, "I would guess she always was dad's sounding post. She was a very good naturalist, as she came from a naturalist's family. It was a world that was entirely familiar to her."[794] They would return to Vaseux Lake all their married lives. In 1966 Cowan supported the Okanagan Similkameen Parks Society's purchase of 500 acres of Vaseux Lake for a wildlife reserve. In various articles, he notes:

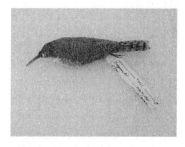

Canyon Wren

Catherpes mexicanus

The Canyon Wren reaches the northern limit of its range in southern British Columbia. It was first reported in the province at Vaseux Creek in March 1909 (Brooks, 1909).[787]

Yellow-breasted Chat
male and female

Icteria virens

All nests were placed in thick shrubbery, including rose bushes, snowberry and a small willow. Nest materials were mainly grasses, along with plant fibres, twigs, leaves and bark strips. The nest cup was lined with fine grasses.[789]

In establishing a badly needed reserve to provide winter food and refuge for the rare California Bighorn, the Parks Society is taking the first step in a plan to provide for the survival of all those living forms that, since the departure of the ice age, have clustered close to the bighorn on this unique bit of Canada.[795]

He undoubtedly included his own family in the living forms that clustered close to the bighorns in this unique bit of Canada.

After the blistering heat of the Okanagan, the couple headed up into the "cold, miserable rain" of the Cariboo, where they tromped around Ten Mile Lake in the rain at the old gold-panning haunt from his summer with his brother Patrick.[796] The couple abandoned this breeding territory for new territory to the northwest, trading the rain of Ten Mile for the winds of Ootsa Lake.

White-throated Swift

Aeronautes saxatalis

The White-throated Swift is known to breed only in the Similkameen valley ... and in the Okanagan valley from Vaseux Lake north to the Naramata area. The breeding centre of abundance appears to be the 20 km stretch from Vaseux Lake to Penticton.... In the Okanagan, the breeding colony at Vaseux Lake was estimated at 7 pairs in 1917 and the site is still in use some 70 years later.[793]

"We started collecting the creatures that would document the biology of Tweedsmuir Park."

Ootsa Lake – "The Way Down," 1936

T he Cowans left the Cariboo and headed north and west through long stretches of Jack pine and aspen to the open, rolling foothills called Grassy Plains. The backdrop to Grassy Plains are the Quanchus, a mountain range around which once snaked an extraordinarily rich network of rivers, ribbon lakes and sloughs that the Cheslatta T'en had been navigating and portaging between for millennia, an area they called Ootsa, or "the way down towards the water." Three and a half million acres of this region, stretching from Ootsa Lake in the north to Monarch Mountain to the south, had just been declared Tweedsmuir Provincial Park, named after Canada's then Governor General, Lord Tweedsmuir (author and Scotsman John Buchan). The Tweedsmuirs were coming to the region the following summer to explore 'their' namesake park and officially open it. The Cowans had the happy job of doing the reconnaissance in the northern part, where they were to "find out what lived there,"[797] collect specimens (Joyce was the 'honorary botanist') and vet the area and guides for the Tweedsmuirs' visit.

They were the first biologists to do any kind of floral and faunal inventory work in this area. Tragically it will be the only work ever done there, since 16 years later 92,000 hectares of the rich valley bottomlands, which the Cowans travelled through in the newly formed park, were flooded for the largest hydro-electric project of its time in North America – the Kemano project. The Kenney dam turned the Quanchus Mountains into virtual islands surrounded by reservoirs that had once been an intricate watershed of the Nechako River, draining seven lakes: the Ootsa, Tahtsa, Whitesail, Eutsuk, Euchu, Natalkuz and Tetachuck.[798]

But in 1936 the dam was nowhere on the horizon and there seemed little risk of this possibility. The region's future as a conservation area seemed secure as the provincial government had officially designated the park. The Tweedsmuirs, both avid naturalists and hunters, were to follow the Cowans' route a year later, a trip which Lady Tweedsmuir wrote up in *National Geographic* magazine: "The ranges of western Canada can provide many scenes of savage grandeur, but none of them, I think, comparable to Tweedsmuir Park for grace and beauty."[799] Pronounced Lord Tweedsmuir at the opening ceremony: "I have now travelled over most of Canada and have seen many wonderful things, but I have seen nothing more beautiful and more wonderful than the great park which British Columbia has done me the honour to call by my name."[800]

The Cowans' dry run around the lakes was to be an exciting highlight to their honeymoon. The survey records they created during this experience also provide a sobering baseline of what has been lost through the flooding of this highly productive area for wildlife. This was another landscape for which the Cowans' journal remains the only scientific record of birds, mammals and plant communities now underwater.

They arrived July 10 at Ootsa village, which is right on the lake, and rented a cabin. The Bennetts, who ran the hostel, had a son-in-law, George Kempple (married to their daughter Mary), who had a 24-foot, flat-bottomed Chipewyan skiff powered by a 10-horsepower motor. "He was delighted to help. I had enough money to take him on staff for three weeks. They were outdoors people and enjoyed the project. So we started collecting the creatures that would document the biology of Tweedsmuir park area."[801] In the first few days of planning their expedition, they spotted 45 species of birds. One of the birds Cowan noted, and placed a question mark beside to remind him to check its range, was a Rusty Blackbird.

Rusty Blackbird

Euphagus carolinus

The paucity of breeding records from large areas of northern British Columbia is mostly a reflection of poor access and a scarcity of observers. The highly secretive nature of this blackbird during the breeding season and the inhospitable nature of its wetland habitats also contribute to the general lack of summer records ... The winter status and known breeding distribution of the Rusty Blackbird in British Columbia have changed considerably since Munro and Cowan (1947). In the mid-1940s this blackbird was considered to be a summer visitant in the northern interior ... There was only a single breeding record ... and a single winter record. Today the Rusty Blackbird nests in all ecoprovinces of the Interior ... The modest increases in winter records, however, is almost certainly the result of more birds wintering in British Columbia.[802]

Early in the morning of July 16 the Cowans and Kempples set out, loaded with gear covered with tarps. They planned to travel the entire river system, going counterclockwise. First they headed 24 miles west to the junction of the Tahtsa and Whitesail rivers, a low-lying delta land with dense growth of willow, Red-osier Dogwoods and giant Black Cottonwoods interspersed with meadows of swamp sedges. Cowan spotted both Sora and Virginia Rails and remarked ... "All along the Tahtsa is a wonderful place for birds."[803]

Breeding waterbirds such as loons, scoters, harlequins, grebes, goldeneye and mergansers were plentiful in the delta. Warblers, crossbills, thrushes, waxwings and woodpeckers were abundant along the riversides. Eagles were frequent companions as were moose and, less frequently, beaver foraging in the wetland sloughs. Kempple was pointing out Herring Gull breeding colonies on river islands, muskrat sloughs and weasel country. They ran down the Whitesail River to the Eutsuk portage, which consisted of a narrow-gauge rail line and a flatbed railcar that they hauled the boat and gear onto and then pulled along the kilometre to Eutsuk. Once in Eutsuk, they headed to Surel Creek, where they trapped for small mammals, scaled a mountain and stopped by a trapper's cabin to pick up some skulls. Those two days in Eutsuk are written here in Cowan's spare account:

Sora Rail nesting habitat

Sora

Porzana carolina

July 18th, 1936
Traps held 4 *Peromyscus* [White-footed deer mice], 1 *Clethrionomys* [Boreal red-backed vole], 1 *Phenacomys* [Heather vole], 12 *Zapus* [Meadow jumping mouse] 1 *Sorex* [Dusky shrew] observed. Saw two chipmunks – very wild, a squirrel and shot a *Myotis alascensis* [Little brown bat northern race]. Climbed slope of Mount Musclow for 700–800 feet. From the lake, the going looks fair but the vegetation consists of a jungle of green alder, devil's club, hellebore, wild parsnip, salmonberry and willow about 6–8 feet high. There were many bear trails through this and the dog found a porcupine. Musclow Lake, just to west and south of Eutsuk and emptying into it from west, is a gem, with mountains falling into it all around. There are small patches of *Abies grandis*, *amabilis* and *Tsuga mertensiana*, also some *Thuja*.

The Sora breeds from near sea level to 1220 metres elevation in a variety of freshwater and brackish wetland habitats, including marshes, sloughs, lakes, ponds and wet meadows, that usually contain cattail, bullrushes and sedges.[804]

July 19th, 1936
Left Surel Creek this morning and ran down Eutsuk Lake to mouth of Pondosy Bay. On the way we stopped at Fred Knowles's trapping cabin in Grell Cove. We made camp on the north shore looking up Pondosy Bay. The timber opposite mouth of Pondosy Bay is mostly spruce with some *Abies amabilis* and some Jack [lodgepole] pine. Quite a bit of old beaver works in a slough just back of beach. Many of the points on Eutsuk have their sloughs behind them and they all showed past beaver work.[805]

Some days were so windy, they couldn't travel. Movement was also slowed to the pace of hand poling as the rivers widened into the shallow sloughs and they had ample time to observe birds. They recorded wildlife encounters at Pondosy Lake from another trapper, Tom McKinley, including his face to face with an all-black wolf pack. A large amount of local information was being exchanged about the animals, the land and the tightly knit but scattered community of natives and settlers. The inter-ethnic relationships were many and tight, shaped by trading and shared ways of life – bonds which later strengthened with the threat of hydro to that way of life.[806] Cowan found the community very open. "We found all sorts of people up there interested. They got behind you and helped you."[807]

The Kempples also introduced the Cowans to Jack Shelford and his family, including his son John, who "was very interested in the birds and mammals and does some amateur taxidermy"[808] and led John to a friendship with R.M. Anderson at the National Museum.[809] Jack Shelford's life was written up by another son, Cyril Shelford, who eventually became a member of the provincial legislature and cabinet and fought the dam in the 1950s. In the biography *From War to Wilderness*,[810] Cyril describes how his father and uncle, British soldiers traumatized by the Boer war, came to Ootsa to "get away into the wilderness, where he could get himself together – and where for months on end, he wouldn't see anything except wild animals and birds that he thought were more civilized than humans during wars."[811]

Shelford's book describes the region in 1910 when Jack first arrived there to homestead. He had made connections with a Cheslatta family, the Andrewses, at the head of Ootsa Lake. There the big meadows in the delta land were hunted for duck and geese in the spring "when thousands of them came in for a stay before migrating north or south in the spring and fall. Most of these meadows were over 100 acres with old river channels winding between them."[812] The family were raised as keen naturalists, lived off the land and had strong relationships with the Andrewses and other families. Cyril Shelford helped form a joint aboriginal–white protest group in the 1950s which strengthened the community against the larger industrial interests. Although they failed to stop the first dam, the second one, proposed in the 1990s, was defeated. When Shelford, as Minister of Agriculture, was pressured by trophy-hunting interests to bring in a wolf control program in 1979, he wrote Cowan to ask him to explain the scientific evidence on wolves and prey.[813]

Cowan was to encounter veterans of the Boer conflict and the First World War all over the wilder parts of British Columbia, where they had retreated. Later his students would return as veterans of the Second World War. Cowan never experienced war but had great empathy with those who had. Tipped off by John Shelford, Cowan set up a trap of wild gooseberries in an old brush pile and caught the shy and elusive Least Weasel, the smallest of all the carnivores, which he noted as a new provincial record.

The Cowans also sought out and talked to Norman Schreiber, the storekeeper who was buying pelts. Trappers did well in this watershed and Cowan noted local skunk, weasels, marten, fishers, lynx, fox, coyote, muskrats, beaver, wolverine and wolves being traded – not to mention all the smaller fur-bearing mammals. Cowan was a big advocate for many trappers and supported trapping if done sustainably and humanely; it was one of the few economic rationales for wild-land preservation that could stand up against the political forces. Eric Collier, another Chilcotin trapper, of *Three Against the Wilderness*[815] fame and founding head of the BC Registered Trappers Association, said this of Cowan's advocacy and support of citizen science: "Here is a mind which isn't frozen like some prehistoric fossil beneath a polar ice cap."[816] Cowan, along with Frank Butler of the BC Game Commission, had advised Collier on his studies of the Meldrum Creek watershed in the Chilcotin after the famous re-introduction of the beaver documented in Collier's book.

Cowan, on the other hand, was also the first to speak out against bad management or inhumane practices. In 1982 he appeared in a documentary film called *The Truth about Trapping*, made by Vancouver freelance producer Shane Lunny for the Association for the Protection of Fur-Bearing Animals. Alongside David Suzuki and two other television stars, Loretta Swit and Bruno Gerussi, Cowan argued the leg-hold trap was inhumane.[817] He wrote several papers on the humane collection or capture of animals.[818]

Least Weasel

Mustela rixosa [now *M. nivalis*]

A diminutive weasel, smallest of its kind, conforming in general features to the other species but with much shorter tail in ratio to body length. Tail usually without black tip or with a few scattered black hairs. Pelage in summer is a rich brown; completely white in winter ... The animal is not plentiful anywhere in its range.[814]

Pygmy Shrew

Microsorex hoyi intervectus [*Sorex hoyi*]

The smallest of all North American mammals. Total length about 3¼ inches ... Nothing is known of the life history of this shrew.[820]

Back at Ootsa, Cowan wrote to his boss, Kermode: "I have been extremely busy hereabouts and have taken some very nice things, including a fine specimen of *Microsorex hoyi intervectus*, one of the rarest of North American animals and the smallest mammal in the world."[819]

Cowan loved to write and lecture about the Pygmy Shrew and shrews in general:

> The insect-eating shrews and moles deserve mention ... Not only do the shrews include the smallest living mammals, but the most tremendous appetites of any. The pigmy shrew, four grams or so in weight, may eat three times that in insects every day and quickly dies if it cannot obtain food in such quantities. The shrews have other

claims to fame, as they are among the shortest-lived of all animals. Few of the small species reach the age of ten months and none see the calendar round.[821]

Cowan's mammal list is long for this region, supplemented by information from trappers. Casualties from trapping were relatively small compared to the future casualties from the flooding by dams, which was an unprecedented killer at a scale difficult to assess. The wider tragedy of the destruction of wildlife, their habitat and a cultural way of life to the Cheslatta still remains largely unknown to many Canadians,[822] despite its being the biggest industrial project of its kind in North America at the time. In a 1951 article in *Popular Science* magazine reaching millions of readers, the project for exporting electricity to the coast for Aluminum Company of Canada's Kitimat plant was described with characteristic 1950s boosterism:

> It's like the old gold-rush days again. Boom towns. Adventurous men carving civilization out of the wilderness. But not for gold this time. Now they are after commoner yet more valuable things – electricity, wood, minerals and oil … engineers now plan to reverse the flow of a chain of huge wilderness lakes in the uplands of British Columbia and thus produce more water power than the Bonneville, Shasta and Muscle Shoals projects combined.[823]

In the face of this kind of expansive industry of the post-war era, when energy boosters were in power – literally and figuratively – it is hard to imagine any kind of opposing voice having any weight. Beginning March 17, 1949, the Minister of Lands and Forests, Edward Kenney, and the coalition government of Conservatives and Liberals rammed Bill 66, "An Act to Promote the Industrial Development of the Province," through all three legislative readings and Royal Assent in just seven days.[824] During a five-day adjournment before the Bill was scheduled for Second Reading, Opposition MLAs Ernest and Harold Winch (father and son), of the Cooperative Commonwealth Federation, sought public opinions. Cowan, as adviser to the BC Game Commission, had prepared "a preliminary brief covering some of the possible influences of this project upon the wildlife values of Tweedsmuir Park."[825] Pointing out the tight timeline and the need for a comprehensive review, he tried to appeal to policy-makers as a moderate, taking the line that there were substantial revenues in furs and sport fishing, as well as indigenous subsistence, that would be lost in the flooding of these valleys.

In the morning session of the legislature on March 24 Harold Winch moved for a six-month adjournment of Third Reading, but the motion was defeated 34 to 10. Third Reading proceeded and the bill was passed. Soon after noon that same day, the 1949 Industrial Development Act received Royal Assent and became law without further discussion,[826] effectively green-lighting the $300-million Aluminum Company of Canada Kenney Dam (although the project itself was not named in the legislation). The Act was said to give "blanket powers" that "would enable the government to override any other statutes if it is necessary to reach an agreement for establishing the industry."[827]

The policy submission from the Game Commission had been an important challenge to the project, headed up by two members of the 'B', James G. (Jim) Cunningham and Frank Butler. Cowan considered them a formidable team: "Jim was the field runabout man – outgoing, brilliant personality, sportsmen liked him. And Frank was the indoor man, the policy man. And he was an intelligent individual; he saw what he could gain from the application of science."[828] Cunningham died of a heart attack in 1954, but Butler, who had started service as a provincial game and forest warden in 1914 stayed on as sole commissioner and then director of a newly minted Fish and Game Branch until 1962. He was nearly a half century in service.

At the urging of Butler and Cunningham, Cowan also made his appeal at an "emergency meeting" of MLAs in 1950 on further repercussions of the Industrial Development Act.[829] The Opposition likely took some comfort from the fact that the Act contained a clause stipulating that "any agreement entered into pursuant to … this Act shall provide for such protection as may be considered advisable by the Lieutenant-Governor in Council of any fisheries that would be injuriously affected."[830] The 'B' brought forward Peter Larkin, a Cowan colleague who was chief fisheries biologist for the Game Commission, to investigate sport fisheries, though construction of the dam had already been started. As Larkin wrote, "By the spring of 1950 the industrial boom was moving into high gear … Between April of 1950 and April of 1951 came many major industrial projects that posed problems to sport fisheries and which demanded attention – the Alcan project in Tweedsmuir Park was mooted…"[831] Apparently, nothing would be allowed to stand in the way of Alcan.

In 1952 there was no public recognition that the dam and reservoirs would have profound impacts on the wildlife and local people, not just in the Ootsa region but downstream to the Henaksiala and Haisla people on the coast. There, populations of oolichan and salmon were severely harmed by the changes to the Nechako River. The legal story of the Cheslatta surrender and final court case 30 years later is told by the Cheslatta themselves.[832] A concise summary of the damage done appears in the five-volume report of the Royal Commission on Aboriginal Peoples (the "Erasmus–Dusseault Commission," 1991–1996):

> … the Cheslatta were treated as an afterthought, with completely inadequate regard for their rights. The government initiated the surrender negotiations just as the dam was completed and flooding was about to begin. The flooding began before the surrender. The families were told to start moving without assistance the day after the surrender was signed. Because of the spring thaw they had to leave most of their belongings behind. The homes and many belongings of the Cheslatta were destroyed before most families could move their effects to the new location. There was no housing or land

provided for families or livestock at Grassy Plains for the entire summer. When land was finally purchased for the Cheslatta, moneys were taken from individual compensation allotments to pay for it – contrary to the Cheslatta understanding of the surrender agreement. The new lands were not established as reserve lands, and the rights the Cheslatta had enjoyed as a result of living on reserves were lost for many years. Graveyards above the planned flood level were washed away. Adequate compensation was not given until the settlement of a specific claim in 1993."[833]

In coming years, the flooding of the Ootsa, as with the Kootenay, Columbia and other major river systems, would add to Cowan's unease with the impacts of northern development on wildlife and the lives of people who depended on wildlife for their subsistence – both native and non-native (a distinction Cowan didn't refer to). In 1955, representing the Canadian Conservation Association, he delivered a report to the Royal Commission on Canada's Economic Prospects (Gordon Commission). In it he argued that wildlife was a renewable resource with major economic benefits. He had scoured the literature to quantify this claim and document what he identified as the highest priority: "The wildlife resource is the primary source of food and wealth for the Indians and Eskimos of Arctic and Subarctic Canada, but with increasing exploitation of these areas it will progressively lose this position."[834] The Canadian Conservation Association had been started in 1941 by concerned scientists wanting to publish scientific reports on game species, headed up by biologist John Detwiler from the University of Western Ontario. But the organization stumbled along through the war and post-war years and Cowan's report to the Gordon Commission may well have been its last submission.[835]

By 1979, when Cowan was named International Conservationist of the Year by the US National Wildlife Federation,[836] he had identified that the most important direction of the environmental movement for the future would be to rein in these massive developments and enable aboriginal people to access "life-supporting wildlife" in the face of diminishing populations of animals.[837]

For the Ootsa region, that one month's inventory by the Cowans, together with some archaeological work done under the direction of Dr. Charles Borden and Larkin's emergency work on sport fish in the Nechako, is all the inventory work that was ever done on this huge system and the Cheslatta people prior to the flooding.[838] There was also Lady Tweedsmuir's *National Geographic* article, reaching a wide North American audience, which began

> At Ootsa Lake, we reached the beginning of the park. There we embarked in boats on our journey to our base camp. Our boat was of the type of the old Hudson's Bay York boat plus a "kicker." All afternoon we chugged along in a stately procession. X [Lord Buchan] and I in the first boat feeling like Antony and Cleopatra ... It is a paradise for northern fauna...[839]

In Cowan's letter to Kermode about his trip, he had some rave reviews and strong recommendations for the future visitors:

> We covered about 200 miles in the six days and saw a lot of truly magnificent country as well as taking some highly interesting specimens. Moose were abundant but other game scarce. For another time I have everything lined up as to where to go and, better still, who to employ to take you there; there are one or two first-class skin-game artists here, good men to avoid. I may say that I have entirely changed my idea as to the most desirable and profitable of places to visit another time.[840]

Cowan finally met Buchan – Lord Tweedsmuir – in 1939, when the Governor General visited the museum. The two men would obviously have had a great deal to talk about. In Kermode's annual report, he states that "His Excellency was greatly interested in the exhibits of the fauna and flora of this Province, especially those found in the area confined to Tweedsmuir Park."[841] Tweedsmuir's views on conservation were probably also a hot topic, as Ootsa was a subject close to his heart. In November of 1936, Tweedsmuir had issued a national "Message to Sportsmen," which made his passions very clear:

> There is no question in Canada which interests me more than the conservation of Canadian wild life. Canada should be the playground of North America, but in order to make this playground attractive it is most necessary to safeguard the assets which nature has given us, both in flora and fauna and scenic beauty. At present these assets are enormous; but it is only too true that the richest resources in the modern world will, unless they are safeguarded, disappear with tragic rapidity. I have seen in other countries carelessness in one generation destroy the wild life. I want to see facilities for sport open to every sportsman, to whatever class he belongs. To make that possible we must preserve the wild game. We must have wise game laws, and they must be strictly enforced, and this is not in the interests of any coterie, but of the nation at large. I cordially welcome the excellent work which *Rod and Gun* is doing in this most vital matter.[842]

In the *Rod and Gun in Canada* issue in which the "Message" appeared, the magazine's editor commented on the sea change towards conservation amongst the clubs and the importance of having a high-profile conservationist leading the cause:

> Those who have read Lord Tweedsmuir's thrilling novels, certain of which contain some of the finest descriptive writing of deer stalking and fishing, and who read in our last issue of his masterly fly-fishing, will easily appreciate his interest in the ancient and noble pastimes

with rod and gun. His message to the sportsmen of Canada should prove a great inspiration to those who have taken upon themselves what still is very largely a sportsman's burden.[843]

The Buchan encounter was an interesting one, as various threads of Cowan's life were intertwined with this major literary and political figure who had considerable influence in both Scotland and Canada. They were both cut from the same cloth of Scottish sportsman sensibilities. Buchan had a romantic temperament and affinity for the wilderness which Cowan shared in many regards. This soulful streak was captured in an anecdote by Lady Tweedsmuir in her *National Geographic* story:

> He [Lord Tweedsmuir] is always looking for sanctuaries as if someday he might be forced to be a fugitive from justice, and now he discovered the perfect one. We looked into a cup on the top of a mountain perhaps 6,000 feet high. There was a lake, a half moon of wild meadow and behind it another half moon of forest.[844]

Buchan was actually given a sanctuary of sorts by Premier Duff Pattullo during that visit, which became a de facto ecological reserve while he was alive – a Gulf Island called Sphinx Island – which was coincidentally close to Cowan's eventual summer home on Mayne Island. In other respects, Cowan was of a different generation and sensibility, moving away from Buchan's more privileged European notion of a "playground" of the wild, since the wild no longer existed there. Cowan was clearly positioned to lead the new scientific management of wildlife and this may well have been part of his growing interest to move back into university life.

One poignant recollection of Ootsa for Cowan came to him many years later when Mikkel Schau, a young geologist, had started courting his daughter, Ann. Schau had been invited to dinner at his prospective in-laws and described his geological research on the remote shores of Tahtsa where he had come across an ancient campsite. Cowan knew the site well, having visited it on their honeymoon and finished the description. "I went on to marry his daughter."[845]

After the Ootsa, the Cowans did their stopover with Tom and Elinor McCabe and planned their joint trip up the west coast. The McCabes had befriended naturalist–fisherman Patrick Martin, whom they had joined for three summers in a row travelling up and down the coast aboard his fishboat, MV *Seabird*. The Cowans didn't actually team up again properly with the McCabes until 1939 and by then the Second World War was casting its shadows on the coast. Cowan was back up in the interior again before then, with Martin in the Peace country.

The winter of 1937–38 was spent cataloguing and restoring the Provincial Museum's amphibian and reptile collections and preparing a review of species from published accounts. Only three reviews had ever been attempted: one in 1866 by John Keast Lord, who found 16 species and subspecies of snakes, lizards, turtles, newts, salamanders, frogs and toads. John Fannin, 30 years later, listed 15, and E.B.S. Logier brought the list up to 29 in 1932. Cowan had never been a specialist of amphibians and reptiles. He had, however, helped Laing and Racey with some collecting for the National Museum in the 1930s and was always noting the odd rattlesnake, toad or northern alligator lizard, the latter found sunning itself atop Mount Newton near the museum. Characteristically, it started him down yet another specialty track, this one focusing on updating a museum handbook about BC's reptiles and amphibians.

Northern Alligator Lizard

Gerrhonotus principis
[*Elgaria coerulea principis*]

Widely distributed over the southern parts of the province from the East Kootenay west to include Vancouver Island; north of the coast at least to Stewart Island; but northern limits unknown.[846]

That spring, Cowan got a leave of absence to go visit all the big museums of Canada and the US, with the aid of a grant from the Canadian Museums Committee of the Carnegie Corporation. His objective was to research the most effective and economical displays in the museums. He also was going to use his time to check out the mammal specimens for papers he was working on and meet some of the men behind the scenes in Ottawa and New York.[847]

Cowan's report still stands as an excellent observation of the public's museum-going behaviour and preferences. He set himself up at an observation station in each of the museums and scientifically observed how long people looked at different exhibits.

> ... with my limited experience, the visitors are confronted by so much in so short a time that definite impressions on any one subject are probably few ... Oftentimes, to take a visitor behind the scenes into the laboratories is sound psychology, as it develops in that person a more genuine interest in the work of the museum.[848]

He recommended that crowding be avoided and that artifacts or specimens be placed as though in situ or in their habitat. Of exhibits he saw, "the poorest type – one with almost no educational value – is the rows of glass bottles containing as many bleached specimens in discoloured preservative with no labelling beyond name and date of capture."[849] He also suggested modelling the small animals in celluloid, after Chicago's Field Museum, and reconstruction of their habitat with dioramas.

He proposed a travelling extension of the museum to go to schools, in the manner of the American Museum of Natural History, with slide shows, movies and mini-exhibits. In a newspaper article reporting on his Carnegie tour, Cowan is quoted as saying:

> In the educational field, the museum is trying to develop methods to

take itself outside its own walls, to bring it closer to teachers and pupils in out-of-the-way places … The museum is a vital part of our educational system. We have 65,000 visitors to our Provincial Museum here each year, and I think it is sufficient reason for its existence.[850]

Cowan would start implementing all of these changes over the next few years. His complete vision for the museum, as sketched out in the report, would eventually be completed some 30 years later, under the leadership of his student Bristol Foster.

The message of funding for education was a tough sell in the depths of the Depression. It was a familiar cry for all the 'B' across the country. The footnote for 1936 was the retirement of the grandfather of conservation, and Master of Venery, J.B. Harkin, back in Ottawa. After a long struggle to balance the ideals of managing national parks on scientific and educational principles, as against the weight of political expectations, Harkin voluntarily or perhaps involuntarily took early retirement.[851] His interest and legacy lived on, however, and that was to influence the direction Cowan would ultimately take in 1943 when he was asked to do the first scientific study of prey–predator relationships in the national parks. In Harkin's farewell letter to the Banff Advisory Council in 1936, he set out that blueprint: "I am passing the torch on and my earnest prayer is that the work will continue to be based on idealism. If that is ever lost, Parks will lose their soul, will become like the tens of thousands of ordinary resorts throughout the world."[852]

CHAPTER 20

"At last I believe I have found a colony of these elusive mice."

Mount Revelstoke, 1937

The field season planned for 1937 was Mount Revelstoke in the southeastern part of the province, via Monashee Pass and the town of Merritt. Cowan invited Joyce and his father-in-law, Kenneth Racey, as honorary assistant biologists. They plotted their route to do inventories in some new parks and sort out a few of the more ticklish subspecies. Despite two tire blowouts and an overheating radiator they made it to the top of Monashee Pass and camped for a few days to sort out the races of Pika, or Rock Rabbit. Cowan typically overcame many odds to study pikas because of their interesting evolutionary history. They featured heavily in his popular writing, television shows and scientific work, but their small, teddy bear appearance belied their more epic history. "Pikas are somewhat less than guinea-pig size, short legged, have no external tail and almost circular, quite prominent external ears. The soles of the feet are furred, except for the small black plantar pads."[853]

On either side of the pass are the Monashee Mountains, which rise above 3000 metres. The area was of special ecological interest because it is a relatively high mountain range rising out of the arid grasslands right at the southern edge of the glaciated area. The mountains served as nunataks and refugia where certain species may well have gone upslope and persisted despite the thick layers of ice passing around them.

Between them, team Racey–Cowan would eventually describe three of the nine subspecies of Rocky Mountain Pika that existed at that time: one on the coast, one in Wells Gray Provincial Park and the third in the Itcha range. When Cowan wrote up his analysis of the pika subspecies in 1954, he had pieced together an intriguing evolutionary story that tracked the movement of this small, sedentary rodent through the glacial cycles between these widely dispersed mountain ranges. His theory worked on the assumption that pika camouflage was critical to survival and that the little rodent was less vulnerable to predation when its fur colour matched the colour of the rock it sat on. "Rain-drenched, moss-clothed talus slopes" produced darker pikas. More than any other mammal, the pika demonstrated a "variation that results in dark races inhabiting humid areas, pallid races the adjacent dry regions."[854] The finding was consistent with what European evolutionary zoologists had been writing for over a century: that warm-blooded animals tended to be more heavily pigmented in more humid environments. The phenomenon even had a name: Gloger's Rule, after the German zoologist Constantin Gloger, who described it in 1833 (though it had also been noted by Peter Simon Pallas as early as 1811). But though Cowan's observations about the pika followed Gloger's Rule, the evolution- ary puzzle of how these small animals evolved, dispersed and disappeared in the complex geography and glacial history of British Columbia was a mystery. Cowan was adept at finding patterns and clues as to how and why it happened.

The type specimens of the pika were at Mount Monashee, so the threesome watched and recorded their habits, making a careful study of their diet, their hab- itat and breeding behaviour. The latter they observed as sedentary, i.e., they didn't roam far for their sex, which was a departure from the species' industrious pursuit of making hay while the sun shone:

> In every mountain range in British Columbia, the rock falls are in- habited by the pika, or rock rabbit. Its strident nasal squeal is bet- ter known to travellers in the hills than is the animal itself. Perched upon a large boulder in the midst of so many, it resembles one more stone and escapes detection, rather aided by the somewhat ventri- loquial effect of its calls. Through the long days and short nights of July and August the pika toils indefatigably. Day after day it scuttles to and from the meadows, almost hidden by its loads of leafage. This is all carefully dried and stored beneath large boulders. I have taken as many as 50 plant species from the hay piles of one pika. When the snows come its food supply is assured.[855]

In 2010, assumptions about the Monashees pikas being a sedentary subspecies were substantially revised. Using genetic markers, call dialects and traditional in- dicators of skull measurements, pika researchers David Hafner and Andrew Smith discovered that there was actually less isolation and more intermingling than Cowan and Racey had first suspected.[856] They reduced the number of subspecies in North America to five, with only two in BC, with the inference that pikas could travel greater distances for sex than early researchers gave them credit for. Still, al- though not all the Racey and Cowan classification and theories stood the test of time, much of their natural history and observations of the pika did.

Once finished at Mount Monashee, the Cowan–Racey outfit continued west and north to Mount Revelstoke in the next range of the Columbia Mountains to the east, the Selkirks. More specifically, this peak lies in a subrange of the Selkirks called the Clachnacudainns and is backed to the north by the glacier of that name rising out of the junction of the Columbia and Illecillewaet rivers. The mountain had been made a national park at the start of the First World War and a road to the summit was finished in 1927 for tourists seeking ski jumping and mountain scen- ery. The Racey–Cowan truck was still chronically boiling over, so they stopped ev- ery mile or so during their ascent to add water from the creeks, climbing slowly through zones of Yellow-cedar, Mountain Hemlock, spruce and balsam to the sub-alpine. Once they reached the top on July 1, Cowan wrote to Kermode, "We are finally encamped on top of the alpine meadows, surrounded on all sides by acres of avalanche lilies dotted here and there with patches of anemone. Fox sparrows and hermit thrush are abundant and in full song. It is quite a treat to hear them again after a lapse of 2 or 3 years."[857]

They were stationed at the ranger's cabin, basing their various expeditions from there. The park ranger, W.K. Moore, left them with some clues of what wildlife was around, including his recent sightings of Mountain Caribou and Grizzly. One of their first sightings was an unusual flock of Black Swifts flying overhead far from their known breeding grounds.

Black Swift

Cypseloides niger

Despite the large flocks of Black Swifts observed throughout the species' summer range, only 2 breeding sites have been confirmed for the province. Undoubtedly, this is due to a number of factors, including its precipitous breeding habitat and its movement far from the breeding area during cyclone passages, at which time it may be away from the nest for days. The breeding distribution and biology of the Black Swift in British Columbia remain for determined and careful observers to reveal.[858]

During the next two weeks, in between thunderstorms, they prowled the rugged rockslides and summits of the region. Rockslides were "hives of activity" for small mammals. Here is Cowan's explanation of why:

> Above the forest altitudes, where the trees give up the losing battle with the elements, the sun's life-giving rays again reach the soil and it erupts in a welter of vegetation: meadows of dwarf willow, heliotrope, saxifrage, lupines and asters, drier uplands of heath, crowberry, lousewort, avalanche lilies, the hardy rock lovers the fleabanes, moss campions, saxifrages and hosts of others produce nutritious leaf, stem, bulb and seed. Here a populous mammal community has developed to fill all the ecologic niches. All have faced the common problem of the alplands – summer abundance followed by the freezing famine of winter. The ways in which the common problem has been mastered make an interesting story.[859]

On July 3, 1937, the entries of both Cowan and Racey recount some of these "interesting stories" as the first real warmth of the summer brings the small mammals out of their burrows en masse. Marmots that sleep for eight months of the year are out eating wildflowers and basking on the rocks, keeping an eye out for coyotes or golden eagles – one of which flies by that day with a mobbing falcon.

The Golden Eagle was a target of ranchers in those years. Certainly they caused some damage to domestic livestock, but like many predators they also became the scapegoat for poor ranching practices. Twenty thousand eagles would be killed as part of an eradication program in the south-western US from 1940 to the 1960s when it was finally stopped. In 1990 Cowan and his colleagues wrote that "public attitudes have changed and laws aimed at preventing the destruction of the species are now in place, although the illegal killing of the birds still continues."[861]

That May spring day in 1937, Cowan describes Columbian Groundsquirrels browsing lazily in the meadows while their solitary cousin the Mantled Groundsquirrel, "the handsomest of the province's mammals,"[862] is stocking up on seeds.

Meanwhile the various species of chipmunks are storing seeds in their cheek pouches before depositing them in their underground storage chambers. The Pack Rats are gathering up heaps of debris for the winter. They don't hibernate, so they pack in everything that will keep them amused and fed in their rocky tunnels beneath the blankets of snow. The Red-backed Voles are in the mossier rockslides nosing out insects, and the Pikas continue to toil away on their hay piles. In the open meadows and glades the trio were finding Northern Bog-lemmings and the "graceful, long-legged jumping mice" building up their stashes of neatly cut grasses in the runways. They came across the old diggings of grizzlies after ground squirrels, coyote scat on rotting logs at timberline, and their first sign of caribou. Then, on July 5, Cowan wrote – with great excitement in his journal, which was not common – about a puzzle that had eluded him for years: where does the large rodent referred to as the Richardson Vole (mouse or Water Rat) breed?

Golden Eagle

Aquila chrysaetos

Rare to uncommon resident in mountainous and hilly country across southern British Columbia. Most nests were situated on cliff ledges. Other nests were found in trees among overhanging rock faces, on top of rock bluffs and pinnacles and in caves.[860]

Mantled Groundsquirrel [Golden-mantled Ground Squirrel] in his first autumn

Citellus lateralis tescorum [Spermophilus lateralis tescorum]

In summer pelage the head and shoulders bear a "mantle" of rich hazel. Conspicuous white line above and below the eye ... The richly coloured mantle, strongly marked inner black stripe and pale yellowish-white sides separate this species from C. saturatus.[863]

At last I believe I have found a colony of these elusive mice. I have set several traps in large runways along a rapid mountain stream. Took a female last night in a trap set between a little waterfall in a mountain stream ... In one place under a log I found a cup-shaped nest made of dried grass. From this a well-worked runway led 6' to the stream, across it, through a clump of willow and into another stream 12' away.[864]

Richardson Vole (Water Rat) [Water Vole]

Microtus richardsoni richardsoni

A giant among the voles and the largest member of the genus. Body colour dark grizzled reddish brown; underparts grey, sometimes with white spotting. Tail long and thick.[865]

The "water rat" was the common name given this vole by British expats used to their own similar European Water Vole (*Arvicola amphibius*), a creature immortalized as Ratty by Kenneth Grahame in his classic children's book *The Wind in the Willows*. Ratty was a slightly different creature from the North American "water rat," but Cowan would have been struck by the similarities and delighted that he had cracked the secret of this creature from his early childhood books. His descriptions of the Richardson Vole remain one of the most important references today for that species account.[866] The resemblances between the two voles were more than whim. Later geneticists suggest that *M. richardsoni* is "a primitive vole that originated from an ancestral form in Siberia about 1.5 million years before the European Water Vole formed in Europe."[867]

Coincidentally, while Cowan was documenting this vole that had found its way to North America, the North American Mink was finding its way to Britain. Fur farms introduced the mink, which, when it escaped, had a catastrophic impact on the mild European Water Vole. Today this vole is one of the most endangered mammals in Britain and the place people are more likely to see old Ratty – or at least a reasonable facsimile of him – is in the isolated colonies of BC and the Pacific Northwest where they still remain.

A further question that challenged Racey and Cowan was why these colonies were discontinuous. Large expanses of forest and valleys between colonies proved "insurmountable barriers to overland movement."[868] Pre-forested, recently glaciated landscapes seemed to be the habitat of preference for these animals, and the remnant populations may have shrunk first with the advancement of forests, then with climate change and the shrinking of glaciers. Today there is evidence that during population peaks, this vole disperses into forest habitats and to lower elevations.[869] This might maintain some connectivity between these normally discontinuous populations. Like the possum and marmot, the vole provided yet another clue for Cowan on adaptability to climate change.

In an interview when Cowan was 96, he was asked to recollect a memorable research moment in the parks. "Colonies of alpine field mice," he replied, alluding to Revelstoke. "Meadows might be swarming with rare creatures … right there, dozens or hundreds of them, while over there none or very few. Behaving like small muskrats swimming in the little alpine rills or chopping off the sedges for their food. You could go over the country using the talents of a detective."[870]

On July 7, 1937, the weather held and they headed out over rough terrain towards the Eva Lake ranger's cabin. Scrambling over huge boulders and up rock outcrops, the threesome ranged from 5,500 to 8,000 feet of elevation gain. They commented on the hard going as they dead-ended on pinnacles and cliffs:

> We made a backpack trip into the arctic alpine zone of the higher peaks in search of ptarmigan and Rosy Finch. After much hard work we found both these and took specimens. These peaks are, if anything, more jagged and straight up and down than the coastal mountains. I'm sure I wore an inch off the bottom of my legs as well as completely finishing a pair of boots in 4 days.[871]

En route, they also ran smack into a Black Bear. Cowan wrote, "The unexpected suddenness of the old lady's assault startled me out of a week's growth."[872] They also witnessed a Coyote catching a marmot, then flushed a Porcupine on arrival at the cabin. The Porcupine escaped into their outhouse and tried to make a bid for freedom by chewing its way out. It failed and is now immortalized in the Beaty Biodiversity Museum.

Porcupine

Erethizon dorsatum nigrescens

A large, blackish rodent, often with long, yellow-tipped guard hairs; upper surfaces of the body covered with quills, which, except on rump and tail, are hidden beneath the fur. [Habitat is] the forested areas in all parts of the province but infrequent in coast forest; most abundant where broken rock, cliffs and open pine forests occur together.[873]

The Cowans' return to Victoria in August 1937 coincided with a chance encounter with a much larger mammal, a Minke Whale that had got tangled up in the salmon traps at Sooke, an easy day's visit from Victoria. At the time, minkes were not well known. There were a few skulls knocking around in the museums in Washington, DC, and San Diego and no one knew for sure if this was the same as the Atlantic species or was a new Pacific species that an earlier biologist had called the Sharp-headed Finner Whale. This brand new specimen, following hot on the tail fluke of another partial skeleton that had washed up the year before on Vancouver Island, meant Cowan had two specimens to measure and provide a little more weight to that question of new species or not. He writes, "The paucity of material relative to this whale seems to warrant the preparation of a more extended description of our specimens…"[874] He lived to eat his words: the preparation of the specimen was epic and as Cowan says, "When I think back to what I did, it was just absolutely ridiculous!"[875]

Ian and Joyce took receipt of the whale on a Saturday, delivered by barge to the Inner Harbour, and spent the weekend measuring, dissecting, flensing and taking the meat off. They put the bones in the museum truck and carted them to the museum storeroom on Superior Street. As Cowan recalled, there were only two ways to get the grease off a whale's skeleton in those days: bury it in sand for three years or boil it in gasoline. Eager to win some rapid taxonomic laurels for the museum, and desperate to rid the storeroom of the stench of the rotting whale, they opted for the gasoline. "So I got a barrel out in the yard at our house on Superior Street, filled it with gasoline, ran a hot-water coil through the bottom of the barrel. Gasoline boils at a lower temperature than water does. It boiled away all day."[876]

Eventually, the bones were degreased enough to measure for comparison with the US specimens, and Cowan and Ed Cooke assembled the first whale for exhibit in the museum. It turned out that the two specimens didn't provide enough evidence to definitively say whether they were or weren't a distinct species. Cowan found a few slight differences, but those, he felt, could be attributed to age. It was an ordeal by fire, but the minke skeleton remains in the research collections of the Royal BC Museum to this day. Undoubtedly that early experience of dissecting the whale with Joyce was to have a lasting impact on all his later work on whale conservation, culminating as chairman of the Canadian Committee

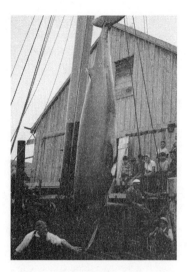

Sharp-nosed Finner, Minke or Pike Whale [Common Minke Whale]

Balaenoptera acutorostrata

A slender, torpedo-shaped small whale reaching a length of 26 feet. This is the smallest of the baleen whales. Colour blackish, dorsally white beneath. A distinctive mark is the white band across each foreflipper ... This is a common whale in the shallower coastal waters. Here it follows the schools of sandlance, herring, anchovy and other small fish upon which it feeds ... Inhabits the entire coastline but does not enter the deep inlets nor the eastern parts of Georgia Strait.[878]

on Whales and Whaling at a heady time for whale conservation – 1978. Cowan was advising Ottawa on the scientific rationale behind a moratorium on whaling, as Canada was still a member of the International Whaling Commission (IWC) then. Interestingly, it was the minke that became the main target of the countries not in support of the moratorium. The pro-whaling countries argued in favour of killing them for "scientific purposes."[877]

Cowan's correspondence, notes and committee reports from those years contain a wealth of insight into the politicization of the issue and the role of the scientific committees and NGOs like Greenpeace, which he believed had brought forward some of the more credible arguments and/or data. He laboured over the difficulties of making decisions in the absence of good data, but in his capacity as chair of the Committee for Canada, he came out in 1980 with a scientific recommendation to the IWC for Canada that "all whaling should cease"[879] on the basis of the precautionary principle. Significantly, that recommendation preceded by two years the first adoption of the precautionary principle in an international treaty – the World Charter for Nature – adopted by the UN in 1982. Cowan's report to the committee ended with:

> I would not even exempt the Antarctic stocks of minke whales, even though they are apparently increasing. This is a pragmatic decision unrelated to the matter of changing human attitudes towards whales or to the questions arising from the ethics of whaling or to the human killing issue.[880]

He acknowledged that the greatest dilemma Canada faced, in his view, was how to fairly address the local subsistence use of Arctic whales, including the endangered bowhead whales by the Inuit. "It is important that Canada think through all aspects of the general topic of subsistence and aboriginal use of cetaceans and arrive at a well-thought-out position relative to other peoples that use whales predominantly as food and not for sale as manufactured products outside their national boundaries."[881]

In 1981 Cowan attended the 33rd annual meeting of the IWC, where Canada was lining up to reject his recommendation for a moratorium. Canada's political decision makers decided to pull out altogether from the IWC and any obligation to adhere to the Convention, and thus avoid a difficult political position. Cowan concluded that Canada's withdrawal actually gave the pro-moratorium nations a better chance of winning the vote, which they did the following year. Cowan notes in his committee report that the NGOs recognized the useful role Canada played in pushing for a scientific basis for decision making and with regard to support for conservation initiatives.[882]

During his 25 years in whale conservation, he got to know Paul Watson, one of the co-founders of Greenpeace in 1972 and founder of the Sea Shepherd Conservation Society set up to do research, investigate and monitor adherence to international whaling regulations. Watson was one of the representatives from the non-profit organizations Cowan had made reference to in his 1981 report. In 1998, Rideau Hall wrote to Cowan asking him to comment on the nomination of Watson for an Order of Canada. His two-page response is worth reproducing in full, for it provides a comprehensive description of Cowan's philosophy and gives considerable insight into his importance as an arbiter of a certain national ethos, still at the age of 88:

> Paul Watson is a unique individual; in my mind there is no doubt that his concern for and dedication to conservation of the whales of

the world is genuine. Furthermore, I believe his concerns are well founded. My experience, over some 60 years of involvement in various aspects of wildlife research and conservation, is that the organization of our society makes it most difficult to achieve truly sustainable relationships between men and wildlife within the usual procedures of parliamentary democracy. It would require more space than we have here to explain some of the details leading to that conclusion. This said, to achieve the urgently needed action, not only must you have good science and sound reasoning, but you must be able to get public attention and effectively use the selling techniques that our market-oriented society is tuned to. And sometimes you must be unorthodox.

This is where people like Watson come in. While those of us on the science end of the equation spend years of our lives gaining the knowledge to a level that it will stand up to political challenges, he can accept the preliminary evidence, and unfettered by the constraints imposed on many of us by our upbringing, can take action that gets more results than we can achieve in a lifetime of struggle through the morass of ignorance, obfuscation and dishonesty that clogs the "normal procedures." Unfortunately, the way the cards are stacked, we need a few of those who will protest and take direct action, as well as those who will steadfastly pursue the expansion of knowledge and its application to human affairs.

So I understand what drives him and his colleagues and I admit to some admiration of his steadfast and unorthodox pursuit of his objectives, often in the face of considerable personal discomfort. I have no doubt that organizations such as Greenpeace, the Sea Shepherd Society and the Sierra Legal Defence Fund have contributed greatly to conservation achievements of the last 30 years. In fact, it has sometimes been necessary to exchange information with, and provide support for, those that seek change by ways that we more orthodox citizens cannot bring ourselves to use.

This said, has Paul Watson become one of those who "exemplified the highest qualities of citizenship" and have his activities "enriched the lives of his contemporaries"? I know a number who would say yes, and many others that would think we had taken leave of our senses to suggest such recognition. Does "good citizenship" at the world level include the willingness to drive changes in the behaviour of those who operate outside the boundaries that existing political arrangements can control? For the most part, this is what Watson has done. No lives have been lost through his actions, and many whales are now alive that would not have been.

If Robin Hood were nominated, the Sheriff of Nottingham

would be scandalized but many of the local community would celebrate an unexpected wisdom. So I probably have not been helpful. But the quandary delights me. I don't know what my decision would be if I had to make it. I would like to think that our system of honours is mature enough to recognize some of the mavericks in our society. But I am not sure that it is. We all recognize the difficulty of putting acceptable limits on maverick behaviour, and perhaps one of the considerations should be, Would the suggested recognition give encouragement to those who see violence, or the threat of it, as an acceptable way of enforcing their views?
Yours sincerely,
Ian McTaggart Cowan[883]

Watson never did receive the Order of Canada. A petition was started in 2012 to reinvigorate the application, but Cowan had first-hand knowledge of what such whale advocates were up against. When he was named international conservationist of the year in 1979, he told BC interviewer Donald Stainsby the story of attending a banquet and being seated next to the head of a major whaling company. Wrote Stainsby:

Predictably, McTaggart Cowan began chiding his neighbour about the effect the whaling industry was having on the world's largest mammals. "Whalers," he suggested, "were driving the whales to extinction."

"I suppose so," the whaler responded, "but they're going to last long enough for me to get my money out."

"That," says Ian McTaggart Cowan today, "was the ultimate expression of an attitude that I found abhorrent."[884]

It was an attitude that was already well in place back in 1937. To combat it, Cowan was already arguing for more budget and time to deliver school programs. Despite having neither, he still managed to give 20 lectures to classes and groups during that year. On Cowan's recommendation, after his North American museum tour, an artist named Lillian Sweeney was hired to do the painted dioramas and models for the museum exhibits. One of their first projects at the museum was a subject of great public interest that was to be replicated in every museum remodelling thereafter – the Columbian Mammoth.

Cowan encouraged Sweeney to start modelling the ancient mammoths and dioramas from remains that had been dug out of the sandy cliffs around Victoria. The ancient teeth and portions of tusks were just ripe for an interpretive exhibit to illustrate the scale of the animals that were roaming the region less than 10,000 years ago. The exhibit was a great hit and was written up in the local paper with Cowan quoted as saying: "The exhibit must arouse the curiosity of the visitor and at once put a question in his mind of the habits and characteristics of the animal displayed."[886]

Another exhibit they collaborated on was a tide pool section, which Cowan animated with prepared specimens of intertidal animals. He retired many of Fannin's stuffed animals and worked on improving the quality of the unique ones like the Dawson Caribou from the Queen Charlotte Islands for which there were no other specimens anywhere else in the world. "The old stuff that Fannin had done, were done to the order of the day. They were quality stuff in the 1890s but this was the 1930s; times had changed."[887]

In the spring of 1938, Cowan figured out how to deal with the floorspace issue in the museum. With the growing number of exhibits and the scientific collection, the museum was beginning to run out of room to house everything. Cowan, poking around his new territory of the museum one day, clambered up a ladder into the rafters of the domed roof of the legislature and found a large space just sitting empty. He enlisted the support of the building's head carpenter and, choosing a time when the Assembly was not in session, they built a stairway, strengthened the floor and constructed a third floor under the domes. In these spaces

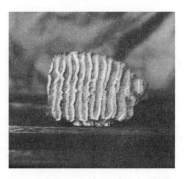

Mammoth fossil

Columbian Mammoth

Parelephas columbi
[*Mammuthus columbi*]

Remains of this elephant are the most abundant of all Pleistocene species and are represented in our collection from the following localities: James Island; Island View Beach, Saanich; Cadboro Bay ... The Vancouver Island occurrences have all been from the superficial Pleistocene gravels on James Island or on the adjacent west coast of Saanich Peninsula.[885]

Cowan started to store his growing collection of specimens. They finished in three weeks.

Part of the reason the collection was expanding rapidly was Cowan's interest in extending the collecting network around the province so that there could be representation of mammals and birds from all the regions. One of his most colourful and enduring contacts was Dr. Theodora "Teddy" Stanwell-Fletcher, who, with her first husband, John (Jack), did an extensive 18-month biological inventory of the Driftwood Valley in north-central BC starting in 1937 and a follow-up study of the Omineca Mountains in 1941. She wrote a book about their experiences, *Driftwood Valley*, which she dedicated to Cowan.

Stanwell-Fletcher was part of the famous naturalist–paleontologist Cope family, Quakers from Pennsylvania. Her parents had set up the Dimock Nature Study Camp in Woodbourne, Pennsylvania, which promoted nature education for local children. She herself was an accomplished naturalist by the time she was 8. She got her masters, then her PhD at Cornell in vertebrate ecology in 1936. Her dissertation was an ecological study of her parents' old-growth forest that they had protected at Woodbourne. Stanwell-Fletcher's biographer, Marcia Bonta, describes her twin themes as conservation of old-growth forest and reforestation of marginal farmland, which in the 1930s were relatively new concepts. In personality, Stanwell-Fletcher sought a quiet life in nature. Her idea of studying the remote parts of British Columbia was to leave a record of what forests contained "before [they] had been ruthlessly changed by the hand of man."[888] After completing her doctorate she was doing fieldwork at Churchill, Manitoba, when she met her first husband, a British Arctic adventurer who had spent years up north, first with the RCMP and later as a trapper–explorer. Through correspondence over permits to collect migratory birds with members of the 'B' – Taverner and Munro – the couple were led to Cowan as a contact.

Striped Skunk

Mephitis mephitis hudsonica

Very similar to the next subspecies, with narrower white stripes and certain distinctive cranial features ... The entire province east of the Coast Range and north at least to the Liard River. Specimens examined from Tetana Lake, Bear Lake, Chezacut Lake, Lonesome Lake, Indianpoint Lake and vicinity...[890]

Cowan struck up a correspondence and friendship with them when they first approached the museum for permits, and continued with Teddy until the day she died at 94. In the summer of 1937, the Stanwell-Fletchers travelled 200 miles to Tetana Lake on foot and horseback and built a log cabin as a base, with the help of the Bear Lake Indians 20 miles down the trail. When the occasional mail was collected from Bear Lake, Cowan's letters were always welcome. The correspondence has all gone but Fletcher's accounts in her book reveal a growing friendship:

> Letters from Dr. Cowan of the Museum are enthusiastic over the mammal skulls and bird and small mammal specimens that we've sent. The skunk skull apparently extends the range of this species considerably and there are some unusual subspecies of birds, which they cannot yet place, and so on. They seem anxious for more material. Dr. Cowan, that delightful and versatile person, has been especially nice about writing us letters of information and just the kind of advice we need about everything, from the kinds of wildlife which might occur here to the best methods of preserving any kind of specimen.[889]

Teddy Stanwell-Fletcher's book provides a graphic narrative of life as a collector. Much of their work was preparing specimens to be sent back to the museum. Her accounts of skinning birds at subzero temperatures in difficult conditions provide more insight into the hardships of the field preparator than Cowan's sparse and seemingly effortless journal entries convey:

> The skin is peeled off the body so that only the skull, wing and leg bones remain and then turned right side out again. The feathers of a bird lie in certain tracts along the body, and they and the wings must be arranged exactly right when you wrap up the prepared skin. Once the skin has dried the feathers can't be changed, and if they are set wrong, the result is wretched-looking. To prepare a skin it is powdered inside with a preservative like borax or arsenic, and then stuffed with cotton to take the place of the body. It takes me an hour to do even a small bird, which an expert might do in twenty minutes.[891]

She also graphically describes an essential quality of collecting, which was eating what you collected:

> Until we can get a skin identified by the museum, we are not sure whether the grouse, which are common and very tame, are a species of spruce or Franklin's, as the two are closely related and almost alike. We've eaten quite a number of them as well as some wild ducks, for we're badly in need of meat.[892]

Likewise, she provides some insight into moving through difficult country with the amount of equipment the collector needs:

> If only we could forget that we are scientists, our packs might be reasonably comfortable! In addition to the absolute necessities, we have camera, field glasses, notebooks and skinning kit. J. carries the heavy movie [camera], I the Leica. The chief weights are cameras and guns.[893]

The Stanwell-Fletchers were also important to Cowan for their detailed behavioural study of wolves around Tetana Lake, greatly assisted by the native trappers at Bear Lake: Chief Charlie, Michelle and Sapolio. Their work, which was published as an article by John Stanwell-Fletcher, was used by Cowan as a model for his wolf studies in the Rockies.[894] They also supplied all the large-mammal skins and skulls for the museum and guided the couple through the country. Having a direct conduit of the experiences of native trappers alongside each of the couple's observations of wolf behaviour greatly benefited Cowan, offering a range of different insights:

> February 15, 1938
> Last night we heard the love song of the wolf! There had been fresh snow followed by clear sky and a full brilliant moon. Our thermometer stood at 24 below. I proposed a snowshoe hike to Wolf Hill on the chance that we might be able to observe wolves down on the lake.

J. scouted the notion of actually seeing them, but the night was so beautiful that he couldn't resist the idea any more than I could. We stepped out in a dazzling world.[895]

Returning home by snowshoe at night another time, she had been accompanied to the door by two wolves whose tracks paralleled hers. This experience raised her credibility even amongst the trappers. Stanwell-Fletcher got pregnant shortly after writing this, leaving Tetana Lake to have her child and rejoining her husband 18 months later. They tracked the animals through the seasons, looking at behaviour, diet and reproduction. As Stanwell-Fletcher wrote, "Wolves do not, like sportsmen, kill for the sake of killing, but for food. Unlike man, they never waste meat or kill unless necessary. So far we have not found any instances or heard of any kills which have been made and then neglected."[896]

Red-winged Blackbird female

Agelaius phoeniceus

By the mid-1940s there had been only 2 occurrences of the Red-winged Blackbird north of the Boreal Plains ... The appearance of this species in the northern one-third of British Columbia west of the Rocky Mountains seems to have occurred recently.[899]

In 1942 Jack Stanwell-Fletcher left the North to enlist in the US army as an Arctic expert. Teddy returned to her home in Pennsylvania to raise their daughter, and the couple eventually parted company. Their monograph for the museum was published in 1943.[897] Teddy Gray (she took her second husband's name) went on to write several more books and set in place the protection of her family's forest at Woodbourne through the Nature Conservancy of the US starting in 1956. The letters to Cowan reveal that the two of them appeared to share many things: a love of nature; a deep reverence for predators and the conservation of forests; a desire for a simple life; a scientific worldview; a love of books, especially Ernest Thompson Seton, John Buchan and Kipling; a realistic appreciation of wilderness and a respect for anyone that lived off the land. In 1999, three weeks before she died at Woodbourne, Teddy Gray wrote her last letter to Cowan:

> Dear Ian,
> Do so wish my stiff old fingers were adequate to answer your wonderful letter of Oct. 10th. It is a joy to have it and hear your news and all you do, and Joyce too! I'm pretty useless but I do manage to stagger out [to Woodbourne forest] twice daily on someone's arm with help of a folding chair. ... Enclosing copy of new paperback of *Driftwood Valley*, which you contributed so much to and made possible.[898]

On the letterhead from her daughter informing Cowan of her death was a picture of the ubiquitous Red-winged Blackbird, the unmistakable breeding song Teddy Stanwell-Fletcher heard in the Driftwood Valley as well as her home in Woodbourne.

Teddy Gray would have been heartbroken to have known that her community, Dimock, Pennsylvania, was to be ripped apart a decade later by industrial fracking. Featured as the first stop in the Oscar-nominated documentary *Gasland*, Dimock is now "famous for being the township where gas drilling went wrong."[900] When a Fletcher biographer, Rhoda Love, wrote Cowan thanking him for his assistance with an essay on the couple and asking for advice on visiting the region, Cowan replied:

> When you make your trip to Tetana Lake, be prepared for many changes ... This province has been engaged in very destructive logging practices for many years. These have led to noticeable alteration of the birds and mammals. No serious losses of species have occurred, but the mix has changed with an increase of the generalist and decrease of the specialist species. Transportation is much easier but the wilderness has shrunk in proportion. Go prepared for mosquitoes.[901]

The Driftwood Valley now has a highway and BC Rail corridor running through it and it is further striped with clear-cuts and logging roads. The mosquitoes, generalists, are still there. A 1999 Integrated Resource Management Plan (now functionally ignored) for the region stated:

> Tetana Lake is featured in the book *Driftwood Valley*, an account of life along the river from 1937 to 1941 ... *Some Accounts of Flora and Fauna of the Driftwood Valley Region of North Central British Columbia* (1943) is still considered a good historical biodiversity reference for the area.[902]

It is, in fact, the only such reference.

CHAPTER 21

"With pathetic frequency our groping hands have left irreparable scars on the beauty we sought to serve."

Peace River, 1938

October 25, 1937, was the 50th anniversary of the official opening of the Provincial Museum and the institution celebrated throughout the ensuing year. In three years, Cowan had helped boost the natural history collection to over 92,000 specimens, modernized how they were preserved and reinvigorated the exhibits. As he noted,

> There was a lot to be done because we had to catalogue all the collections. Every specimen has a label on it and a catalogue number on it which matches your catalogue so you can trace where it came from and all the details that you know about this specimen. It isn't just a lot of drawers with things in them.[903]

A living seasonal wildflower exhibit was established in front of the building, showcasing the native flora of the region, such as the spring flowering Easter Lilies (*Erythronium*) and Shooting Stars (*Dodecatheon*). Spring flowerings coincided with a big gathering of the Pacific Northwest Bird and Mammal Society[904] (started by the Washington State Museum in 1920) to commemorate this sister museum's anniversary. The society included many of the scientists and naturalists in Cowan's circle, including those westerners from the 'B'. The event celebrated his promotion to assistant director.

In his spare time Cowan had been reading the various early travel accounts for the region he knew little about: the northeast of the province, in Peace River country. This is the only area of BC that lies east of the Rocky Mountains and is the western portion of the relatively flat Alberta Plateau. In his files were notes on the accounts by Simon Fraser in 1805, Sir George Simpson in 1828, George M. Dawson in 1879–80, D.W. Harmon in 1904 and botanist Mary Gibson Henry in 1931.[905] Most of these expeditions headed into the northern Rockies but none lingered in the Peace district. Cowan decided to focus his fieldwork there that season, where "to the best of our knowledge no zoological collecting has been done..."[906] He wanted to check out reports of the fabled spring bird migration through this area, so the plans were to do two months of fieldwork on birds, mammals, fish, amphibians and plants around the Peace region for May and June. The biological inventory of what he called "the climax aspen woodlands" would become the first of the museum's *Occasional Papers*.[907] This series started by Cowan would run for another 50 years, with 26 papers appearing, before technical publications were eventually abandoned by the museum.

Cowan did not know at the time that there would be little zoological collecting done thereafter. Like Kootenay and Ootsa before, these watersheds were to be the focus of massive energy and resource projects, from hydroelectric dams to natural gas extraction, with plans starting in the late '50s. Construction for the W.A.C. Bennett Dam – a result of Premier Bennett's Columbia River policy spat with Ottawa – began in 1961. No environmental impact assessment was ever done for the project. Prior to 2005, "Cowan's 1939 monograph was still the best reference on the vertebrates of the Peace River. When we are doing small-mammals work, it is still Cowan's publication that we refer to," said biologist David Nagorsen.[908] An update on birds of the North Peace was done by ornithologist Chris Siddle in 2010 – nearly 70 years after Cowan's paper.[909]

The proposed Site C dam has generated new studies to estimate populations for some species, using modern techniques unavailable to Cowan – for example, radar for bird migration, bat detectors, radio-telemetry for ungulates and carnivores etc., but the surveys have focused on specific sites for hydro, coal mines, gas extraction and wind energy projects. Nagorsen notes, "With staff and budget cuts, government agencies such as the RBCM and the Ministry of Environment have abandoned general biodiversity survey work."[910] Cowan's report today is an historic benchmark and still remains a vivid record of a vital part of BC's biodiversity.

The 1938 season was an exciting proposition, but personal challenges were facing the young couple. According to Ann Schau, Joyce had three pregnancies during these years, two of which came to full term but the babies died. Their first child, a boy, was stillborn at some point during 1938–1939. He was described to relatives as a hydrocephalus baby. Cowan confided to a grandson that it was the only time but one that he saw Joyce cry. The second child, Garry, was born in July of 1940 and was a healthy baby – he was Rh negative, luckily. Then came the third child, who was stillborn or miscarried, again due to Rh complications sometime around 1942. It was after this stillbirth that they opted for adoption in light of the Rh blood issue, and Ann joined the family in 1944. The young couple would have been struggling with the emerging understanding of Rh couples (Joyce was Rh negative), since the importance of rhesus blood type was only discovered in 1937. The first stillbirth to be written up in medical journals was in 1939. Testing and treatments were not available until the late '40s and even then were risky. Not until the early '60s would anti-Rh immunoglobins become available. As Ann stated, "Dad was always in dismay that the medical understanding and technology for Rh couples arose too late for our family."[911] Rhesus complications were particularly mystifying and ravaging to couples in those days, with little to explain the deaths of their babies. Cowan with his medical background and physiological interests may have had greater access to information, but even if they were aware of the risks, there was nothing to be done at the time.

Joyce, dealing with either pregnancy, post-partum or grieving, didn't join her husband in the field that year. There are no letters from this time, but Ann describes the recognition by the family that field biologists were going to be away for several months of the year. Of her mother's acceptance of this, Ann said, "She had married a biologist and this was part of the package."[912]

Cowan needed a field assistant and Pat Martin was a natural choice. Like Cowan, he was born in the UK and raised in Canada, although on the east coast. They had both been mentored by gentle men of the 'B' but at opposite ends of the country. Martin's early interest in birds had been cultivated by Robie Tufts, the migratory bird officer for the east coast, Munro's colleague, friend and ornithological counterpart in Wolfville, Nova Scotia.

Tufts, like Munro, was a modest man who loved his birds. In a handwritten, illustrated manuscript for his guide *Some Common Birds of Nova Scotia*, he wrote:

> One of the most pleasant duties in connection with my work as Chief Migratory Bird Officer for the maritime provinces during the past 15 years has been that of lecturing to schools, clubs and other societies. The rapidly increasing interest in all phases of bird study cannot be but gratifying for someone who has made ornithology a lifetime hobby."[913]

Today when visitors come into Wolfville they see the Robie Tufts Nature Centre, which includes a restored chimney habitat for Chimney Swifts. Interestingly, the western equivalent of the Chimney Swift, Vaux's Swift, hadn't been documented in British Columbia at the time Martin arrived on the west coast. It wasn't until 1955 when Leo Jobin, another colleague, naturalist, subsistence hunter and game warden and a contemporary of Mack Laing, spotted the first one up in the Chilcotin.

Tufts mentored Martin as a boy and when Martin migrated west, he moved easily into the network of western ornithologists. His interests in exploring the coast and the distribution of seabirds were sustained by cobbling together a living as a fisherman to enable him to be on the water while collecting for the Provincial Museum. He was BC's first seabird specialist, and with his easygoing nature and enthusiasm for evolutionary taxonomy, he was a natural fit for assistant to Cowan.

The two men left Victoria on April 28 in the museum van, travelling in a big counter-clockwise arc through Washington up to Alberta and then north and west again to the Peace country. They drove for three days straight, without stopping, staying just ahead of an incoming storm: "The locals say it is a record for the distance."[915] Their first stop was Swan Lake on the Alberta–BC boundary just south of Dawson Creek. They made camp at Tupper Creek, which flows into Swan Lake, landscape that appealed to Cowan. "The lake shore is bordered with willows, a few aspen and cottonwood but there is much open country – the hills around are largely covered with aspen but in the lower areas some spruce and Jack [lodgepole] pine occurs. Along the creek, red osier dogwood is abundant."[916]

Cowan was well pleased with their choice of a base camp to start their research and wrote an ecstatic letter back to Kermode that night. "We have a perfect campsite on Swan Lake – yes it had 2 swans on it when we arrived – believe it or not – at a point where Tupper Creek enters the lake."[917] His journal notation is "Swan (Trumpeters?)," although he later amends it with Whistling (now Tundra) Swan. Cowan's excitement and confusion were understandable – both species of swans were rarities. Records of observations and sightings were very spotty. His father-in-law's field notes on Whistlers coming through Ladner in the 1920s recorded only four sightings of individuals or small flocks between 1924 and '34. Presumably Racey took Cowan to see the 1929 sighting of a flock of ten swans, which spent three days in a bay between Ladner and Woodward Island in mid-April.[918] Racey notes that many people went to see the swans and even the purser on the ferry plying the river was keeping an eye on them.

It is unlikely Cowan had seen a Trumpeter Swan; they were still hovering on extinction in 1938. In Racey's notes stretching back to the 1910s, the only reference to trumpeters is to one that had been found dead, stuffed with hay, in a shack

Trumpeter Swan

Cygnus buccinator

Formerly a winter visitant to Vaseux Lake Bird Sanctuary, this band was destroyed by lead poisoning. For obvious reasons the precise location of winter bands is not made public. The population, estimated to be at 400–600, is at least maintaining its numbers under a vigorous policy of protection by the Canadian Government.[919]

Whistling [Tundra] Swan
nest and babies

Cygnus columbianus

Transient both on coast and in interior. A flock of swans of this species, wintering on the South Thompson River 12 miles east of Kamloops, constitutes our only winter record of healthy birds.[920]

near Alpha Lake in 1922. His notes appeared to be the basis of an investigation for a game warden, with all the suspected parties mentioned. Both swan populations had been decimated from overhunting prior to the enactment of the Migratory Birds Convention Act in 1917 and their fate was still precarious in 1938. When Munro and Cowan wrote *Bird Fauna of BC*, no nests had been documented for either species in the province. Taverner's *Birds of Canada* the same year described them as "approaching extinction."

Cowan's infectious enthusiasm for these birds was caught by one of his students, R.H. (Ron) Mackay, who went on to pioneer the work of bringing species at risk back from the brink. A veteran of the Second World War, Mackay was another gentle lover of the wild, anxious to distance himself from the confines of naval boats. He got his degree in wildlife biology under Cowan, who also found him summer employment on migratory birds with Jim Munro. Mackay eventually took over from Munro as dominion wildlife officer for the West, and his first assignment was to find out how many trumpeter swans there were and where they occurred. His work took him along the migratory route, which included Tetana Lake, where Teddy Stanwell-Fletcher had reported them flying over one spring,[921] and Lonesome Lake, where Mackay provided Ralph Edwards, known as the "Crusoe of Lonesome Lake,"[922] with supplementary feed to boost the flock as they gained in numbers. Today they are a common sight along their flyways, overwintering in many parts of BC, but it is not hard to imagine how the vision of these large, ethereal white birds circling down out of the grey, stormy skies hoarsely bugling or "whistling" to each other as they land would have filled the hearts of even the most seasoned of ornithologists.

Back at Swan Lake, Cowan continued his letter to Kermode:

> It is still very early spring. When we arrived the lake was still frozen but today the ice went out. No leaves at all yet, just pussy willows. The migration is in full swing, ducks, geese and gulls and many species pass hourly and as we are beside the only mudflat on the lake all the shorebirds "check in" at our camp as they enter. Some of them do not check out again! Yesterday afternoon a small but noisy company of Hudsonian Godwit pitched suddenly out of the snowstorm onto our mudpatch. Two minutes later I was gloating over the second BC record for this magnificent, almost extinct species.[923]

The little-known godwit, characterized by its long, upturned bill, is a shorebird that has "incredible non-stop, transcontinental migratory movements"[925] travelling thousands of kilometres between South America and remote Arctic breeding ranges with no break except for a few staging grounds, Swan Lake being one of them. Its status was unknown in the 1930s, other than being rarely seen. Even today the exact number of birds is not known, as they are so elusive, hardly touching down on their long migration. The single nesting record for BC is on top of Chilkat Pass.

The diversity of the migrants was spectacular for Cowan. He noted the following birds arriving in waves just over the first three days: Franklin, Herring, Bonaparte and California gulls; Western, Holboell's [Red-necked] and Horned Grebes; Mallard, Pintail, Shoveller, Old Squaw [Long-tailed], Ring-necked, Canvasback and Scaup ducks; Marsh Hawk [Northern Harrier]; Savannah, Vesper, Chipping and White-crowned Sparrows; [Tundra] Swans; Snipe; Greater and Lesser Yellowlegs; Semipalmated Plovers; Phoebes; Fox, White-throated and Lincoln Sparrows; Purple Finches; Tree Swallows; Lapland Longspurs; Pipits; Yellow-bellied Sapsucker; White-winged Scoters; Buffleheads; Canada and Snow Geese; Bohemian Waxwings; American and Barrow's Goldeneye; Least, Baird's, Pectoral and Solitary Sandpipers, Killdeer; Green- and Blue-winged Teal; Brown-headed Cowbirds; Rusty and Red-winged Blackbirds; Hudsonian Godwits and Sandhill Cranes. On May 8 he wrote, "Today the hardy Myrtle Warbler appears in small numbers – the vanguard of the warbler hordes to follow.[926]

Hudsonian Godwit

Limosa haemastica

In the interior, the Hudsonian Godwit uses thawing areas at outflow streams and muddy shorelines of lakes. Early spring migrants are seen occasionally resting on ice ... Spring migrants arrive at the Peace Lowlands in late April or early May...[924]

Their days began at 5 a.m. and ended at 10 p.m. In daylight they were observing and collecting birds and plants; each evening was spent setting traps, pressing plants, frog and toad hunting, bat watching and preparing between 10 and 20 specimens. Refrigeration of specimens (including themselves) was not necessary, as Cowan explains to Kermode:

> Our birds freeze solid every night in the back of the car. The first night we were here we woke to find an inch of ice on the water bucket and though I could not see it I am sure there was a quarter of an inch of the same material on my back. Now by dint of dressing up rather than undressing for bed and piling everything movable in camp on top of us including the extra tent, rug from the car and Mackintosh coats we manage to arrive at the next dawn tolerably mobile. No mosquitoes yet, praises be.[928]

They worked between storms, but on May 10 the winds came up again:

> We have had three days of terrific winds, blew the grommets out of the heavy fly and at one a.m. one of our tent poles – more fun at dead of night, however we managed to keep the tent from becoming an

observation balloon. After 2 days of touch-and-go we finally had to take the tent down or have it ripped to shreds. We are now very snugly ensconced in an abandoned houseboat. The floors are at rather a rakish angle but it cannot blow away. The collecting goes on apace. The vanguard of the main warbler migration is coming in force – have taken a lot of what should be first-class pictures. The new camera is first rate. I only hope the telescopic lens arrives soon – I have a groundhog all set up for a sitting as soon as it does ... P.S. Pat is working like a slave!!![929]

Myrtle Warbler
[Yellow-rumped Warbler]

Dendroica coronata
[now considered a subspecies of the Yellow-rumped Warbler, *Setophaga coronata coronata*]

Although the trees were without a vestige of foliage when we reached Tupper Creek on May 6th, Myrtle Warblers, in small numbers, were already passing through. Later these birds were found to be a characteristic element in the avifauna of the black spruce and white spruce habitats.[927]

Rose-breasted Grosbeaks

Pheucticus ludovicianus

The Rose-breasted Grosbeak reaches its highest numbers in the Boreal Plains.... The 1938 I. McTaggart-Cowan and P.W. Martin expedition to the Peace River region obtained the first specimen records for the province and elaborated on the migration pattern and habitat use of the Rose-breasted Grosbeak there.[936]

With winds abating, the migration continued. One day a flock of over 100 Red-winged Blackbirds arrived, all singing at once: "The din was terrific."[930] Then the first bittern of the year "cruised in while I was setting traps and landed within 60 feet of me."[931] Blue-winged Teal are "becoming abundant and evidently going to nest here."[932] New flycatchers, vireos and warblers were arriving every day, each with their distinctive songs. "Sora Rails are abundant and noisy now."[933] On May 19 "The toads came out of hibernation yesterday – the first really warm day and night we have had."[934] On May 23 they saw their first bat and a Semipalmated Sandpiper (a "peeps"). On May 24 the American Redstarts had arrived, the Black Terns had returned in numbers to nest, and the American Bitterns had started their "pumping" display call. The Tree Swallows and Yellow-bellied Sapsuckers were starting to lay eggs. On May 25 a Short-billed Dowitcher performed a display flight, the flying squirrels had emerged and the first Western Tanagers and Rose-breasted Grosbeaks were singing.[935] (The former is described as a robin with a sore throat, the latter as one that's had voice lessons.)

Cowan wrote home:

> Our collecting continues apace, little short of phenomenal – to date we have obtained about 17 new records for the province; 2 or 4 amphibians, 3 mammals, and 12 birds as well we have taken things

known from but one or two previous records. So far we have put up a few over 350 specimens – by the time the month is out it will be over the 400 mark and the biggest month I have had in 12 years of field work. Pat is working like a Trojan and doing very creditably indeed; in fact all goes swimmingly. The plants are not being neglected: I have taken so far everything that has come into bloom.[937]

Drummond's Meadow Mouse [Vole]

Microtus pennsylvanicus drummondii

A female and three young, one and three-quarter inches in length, were captured on May 22 and kept in confinement for a week. At this age the young were already feeding exclusively on green vegetation. They ate green grass avidly, commencing on the succulent bases and eating toward the tip. The thin blade of the leaf was usually discarded.[938]

Few species had an opportunity to be neglected by Cowan; he had even packaged up a live frog, a frozen grayling and a pickled pike and sent them back to Lillian Sweeney to be modelled and cast for exhibits. They worked the country north to Dawson Creek and south to Peavine Lake. In the midst of all this, Cowan also went to the Tupper Creek School and gave a lecture on "Local Birds," at which time he discovered a small colony of Northern Lemming Mouse [Northern Bog Lemming] inhabiting a 50-square-foot patch of moss outside the school house on the muskeg honeycombed with tunnels. Small mammals were coming out of hibernation and filling up his traps: the Hudson Bay Jumping Mouse [Meadow Jumping Mouse], which he found in the mud of the riverside at the base of eroded banks; Mackenzie Heather Voles under logs at the outer edge of the willow fringe surrounding the ancient aspen groves; the Athabasca Red-backed Mouse [Vole] that he found in an old crow's nest 11 feet above the ground; and Drummond's Meadow Mouse [Vole], which was the most abundant small mammal of the Peace and was living in chambers within large tussocks of grass at the edge of the lake. Cowan's observation of these small creatures was augmented by capturing them live and observing them in captivity.

The winds didn't abate much until June, making their collecting activities difficult. "However, some phenomenal takes have come our way, for instance Sabine's Gull and Wandering Tattler – two species unknown far from salt water, and also a Red-backed Sandpiper – common enough on the coast but never recorded in Alberta or Interior."[939]

The cacophony of a bird migration was more than music to the ears of the two scientists. As Cowan explained to a Vancouver audience in 1961:

Most birds sing not because they're happy, but because their adrenal glands are … kicking them around and their pituitaries are active and they can't do anything else about it. They sing to establish a territory. If they cannot establish a territory, they will not make a nest and they will not bring off young. This territory is absolutely a sine qua non of essential reproduction. Now a great many creatures are this way: no territory, no breeding. This territory is the area upon which they will make their nest and raise their young, and apparently it has about the right area through the history and experience of the population to provide the food that is necessary to feed

Wandering Tattler

Heteroscelus incanus
[*Tringa incana*]

Transient, chiefly observed along the outer coast and the islands in Queen Charlotte Sound; nests near the British Columbia–Yukon boundary; casual in Peace River Parklands.[940]

the young. It also permits the animal to become thoroughly familiar with every possibility of escape…, so that on this area, it knows all the nooks and crannies and can get away from its enemies. This, then – this business of conflict for territory – is avoiding the issue before it happens. They don't have to fight for food, because they've established it when they established their territory. This has advantages; it also has disadvantages; and here again you can draw human parallels…[941]

Human parallels were never far from Cowan's mind. It was at Charlie Lake, their next camp, where he would experience his first refugees from human "conflict for territory." Lying just on the northwestern outskirts of Fort Saint John, this small farm community had recently swollen in numbers with the arrival of Polish-Russian-German immigrants fleeing Europe in the wake of persecutions during and between the two world wars.[942] The post-war independence of Poland had triggered a wave of emigrants from overpopulated areas where minority groups and the very poor had been pushed. Large families had ended up near Charlie Lake, where Cowan and Martin moved their camp to on June 9.

The lake itself was mostly rocky shoreline with only a few marshy areas. To the east was open country "rolling with aspen and willow in the depressions."[943] The first thing Cowan did was to hike west through aspen and spruce forests and climb a low ridge heavy with saskatoon berries, stunted aspen and wild roses. Along the ridge there were several large outcroppings of sandstone, which would yield many surprises. They found packrat colonies, woodchuck burrows and fox dens. Late in the evening of June 13 they saw Little Brown Bats, which Cowan tracked to the sandstone cliffs. Modern bat surveys for the proposed Site C dam some 70 years later would confirm the importance of these cliffs for bat summer roosts and winter hibernation. The Large Brown Bats came out a little later and he tracked them to a hollow poplar in a large grove.

The men met up with Ted Morton, a local trapper, who filled in more local knowledge of the area. Morton reported that weasels were common, mostly Short-tailed but some Long-tailed and Least Weasels. Wolves, deer and moose were abundant to the north, especially in the willow and aspen strips along the streams. Morton brought Cowan a living Pygmy Shrew on June 14 to add to his live small-mammal collection. They also set up observation areas in the climax aspen forests and it is in these woods that Cowan noticed the ecological importance of one of the keystone species of the region – the Yellow-bellied Sapsucker.

The concept of a keystone species was certainly emerging at this time but Cowan was also looking at it through his population lens. He used the sapsucker–bluebird relationship to illustrate what are called "special requirements," factors other than food that limit population:

> [In the Peace River region in 1938] we found that there were very large areas that were well populated with bluebirds and tree swallows and house wrens and things of this sort

Large Brown Bat

Eptesicus fuscus

The high, steady flight and slow wing-beat rendered field identification of the species easy. The three males and four females seem to represent the northernmost record for the genus in North America.[944]

Yellow-bellied Sapsucker

Sphyrapicus varius varius

This is the most abundant woodpecker in the district and is either resident or a very early migrant, as it was a present in full breeding numbers on May 6. The population density of this bird seemed to be dependent on the cover type. Highest concentrations, averaging about one pair to the acre and reaching as high as five pairs to the acre, were found in climax-type aspen forests in which aspen trees six inches and over in basal diameter formed a dominant element in the flora. Trees of this size were found in the majority of cases to have a decayed core, thus providing easily excavated nesting sites. In second-growth aspen and aspen–spruce stands, the sapsucker population was not more than one pair per quarter section (160 acres).[945]

and there were apparently equally suitable areas that had none of them. Something was limiting these animals to certain particular areas. And there were also quite large numbers of these birds that weren't breeding at all, they were just hanging around: if you shot one of a pair from a nest, there was immediate replacement, as a clear indication that there were all kinds of spare parts lying around, waiting to take up the slack in any family vacancies.

A closer look revealed an interesting situation. All these birds were what the birdwatchers know as hole nesters: they nest in holes in tree trunks. And their main source of holes was a small woodpecker known as a Yellow-bellied Sapsucker and [those] were only nesting in aspen trees that were greater in basal diameter than 4 inches, because at this diameter the aspen becomes rotten in the centre and it's easy digging. Just drill a little hole in, you get a lot of pulpwood, you throw it out and you're in business with a nest. So then, wherever you've got aspens 4 inches or over, you've got sapsuckers, tree swallows, bluebirds, house wrens and all this rest of the gang that follow along behind. Aspens less than this and you've got none. This is just an example of "special requirements." I could cite all sorts of other examples...[946]

Eastern Sucker

Catostomus commersonii commersonii

They were the only large fish present in Charlie Lake, where together with minnows and sticklebacks they comprised the entire fish fauna. At this locality they were extensively utilized as human food. Here also they were being subjected to wanton destruction that according to local report has already reduced their numbers to a small fraction of the original condition.[948]

It also became an example he used to critique forest policy that failed to recognize critical habitat features provided by different aged stands of trees.

On June 27 Cowan wrote Kermode again with good and bad news:

We returned from Charlie Lake in the Fort St. John district about a week ago after a most successful two weeks' collecting. The only trouble with the place was the water supply. The creek there was full of suckers [fish] in various stages of decomposition and though we took such precautions as boiling all drinking water became quite ill after 10 days of it. In fact we have not recovered our accustomed pep though we are feeling fit again. Apart from the collecting, the country thereabouts was most unpleasant. It is populated almost entirely by indigent Germans, Russians and Poles, all with terrific families. The smallest family in the district had 9 children – the mother was 31 – the largest family had 16 – all of a light-fingered disposition ... This combination made it necessary for one of us to be in camp the whole time. The entire district lived on relief and suckers – washed down with triple-infused essence of sucker.[947]

The impact of the refugee settlement had lasting impressions on Cowan. Their situation was to prompt the question that preoccupied many biologists at this time: What are the lessons of population ecology for human societies? Few scientists had studied over such a long period, first-hand, so intimately and in so many different species, the variation of reproductive strategies. Just the variation in nesting birds in the Peace alone is notable for different brood sizes, survival rates, number of clutches and maternal care, which Cowan documented in his journal. The Canvasbacks regularly sat on clutches of 9–11 eggs, while Northern Shovellers typically had 7. Horned Grebes had 2–4, while Buffleheads had from 1–20. Cowan asked the simple question Why that particular number? And why were some selective and others prolific in egg production?

Cowan was captivated by the Buffleheads. They are abundant breeders, quite long-lived and very faithful to the specific trees in which they make their cavity nests. They are also tasty to eat – their folk name is "butterball." Large broods experience high predation and this is not surprising: these little ducks conveniently transport the rich nutrients of the coast to the interior for the summer, along much the same migration route as Cowan himself took. He wrote about them in 1952[949] and supervised a student, Anthony Erskine, who became a leading authority on the species.

On the topic of maternal care, Cowan documented a number of approaches. He watched a mallard take her brood away from the polluted stream and walk them to Charlie Lake, a distance of half a mile, a strategy that was somewhat less developed in the Canvasbacks, which fell back on survival through sheer numbers of offspring. He observed two grebe nests concealed in thick horsetails, while another two nests were floating with no cover, suggesting a strategy of not "putting all your eggs in one basket." Cowan's immersion in the natural variation of breeding success and recruitment of the young gave him the naturalist's pragmatic framework in which to think about human populations and overpopulation.

Decades ahead of his colleague Edward O. Wilson at Harvard, who would attempt to formalize the methodology in the 1970s, Cowan briefly ventured into the uneasy terrain of sociobiology – the bringing together of biology with the social sciences. It was an interdisciplinary leap that would prove to be "an intellectual and doctrinal minefield" as Wilson would later put it, paraphrasing "Nobel-laureate economist turned public philosopher" Paul Samuelson's reaction to the idea.[951] Like Wilson, Cowan quickly found that it was indeed a minefield, or rather a wilderness which he (for once) had little training to navigate. Scholarly historical work on the ideological abuse of biology would not take place for another 40 years, but Cowan, as a population ecologist, evolutionary biologist and taxonomist, would be swept along in the turbulent public reaction to these ideas by the very nature of what he studied. The field biologists studying Buffleheads or Rock Rabbits were thrust onto an international stage at the brink of a world war when genocide and eugenics on unimaginable scales would be perpetrated on the basis of

Bufflehead

Bucephala albeola

Adult males leave their breeding territories once incubation has begun, and flocks consisting entirely of males can be found from the end of May to mid-June ... The main autumn movement to the coast occurs from late October to November.[950]

biological ideas of race, fitness and natural selection attributed to Darwin. As historians Denis Alexander and Ronald Numbers indicate, biological ideas promoted in good faith found applications "in ways remote from the original goals of the scientific investigator."[952]

Cowan's vulnerability was exacerbated by association with British scientist and naturalist Julian Huxley, whom he would later meet in Britain and work with on major international conservation campaigns. Huxley became vice-president of the British Eugenics Society in 1937. Many of the left-leaning intelligentsia in the UK and the US at this time, from George Bernard Shaw to John Maynard Keynes, were also "social Darwinists" exploring ideas on how to apply the scientific understanding of controlling populations to avoid human suffering.[953] Social scientists such as ethnographer Napoleon Chagnon, economist Paul Samuelson and sociologist Pierre van den Berghe were looking for biological explanations for human behavior.[954] Historians today comment that "the assumed linkage between a reclusive Victorian naturalist and twentieth century demagogues and Nazi perpetrators of genocide is curious, strained and – when historically scrutinized – tenuous."[955] It is a connection no less tenuous than the political and religious right continue to try to make today in denouncing conservation biologists (and their stance against resource development).

For Cowan it became increasingly risky over the next decades to be an interdisciplinary thinker. Social scientists studiously developed theoretical frameworks separated from any reference to biology or the rest of the animal kingdom and vice versa. He would only have had to look to his colleague Ed Wilson to see a sociobiologist under fire. Wilson had argued that "history did not begin 10,000 years ago in the villages of Anatolia and Jordan. It spans the two million years of the life of the genus *Homo*"[956] but was summarily dismissed by the academic community for these positions.[957]

Meanwhile, the new era of molecular specialization presumed that you could peer through the microscope to understand the animal.[958] The old naturalist–macrobiologists crawling through the bush – with their finely honed skill for field observation and teasing out diversity as a myriad of complex relationships with each other, their prey, other species, the weather, the plants, the soil and the rocks – became has-beens. Evolutionary field biologists were being replaced by the molecular biologists, who were "focused more on the search for general principles at one or two organizational levels."[959] Wrote Cowan in 1955 (using moles as quite a telling metaphor):

> The problems that confront us in maintaining or developing our resource potential are so many and so varied that the tendency towards increased specialization in the training, activity and viewpoint of each one of us is almost irresistible. However, this trend leads inexorably to the end that each specialist, burrowing ever deeper and mole-like, throwing up detritus on his back trail, becomes isolated

in thought from his fellows, who are often paralleling him out of sight.[960]

Cowan ducked the crossfire of both the sociobiology controversy and micro vs. macro debate raging on in institutions like Harvard and Cambridge, not to mention his own university, for various reasons. He had come to an important realization as to where his energies were best placed. He believed in education and scientific objectivity and he was practical. In 1961 he concluded his "Of Mice and Men" lecture with:

> The principles that can be learned from the study of animal numbers have not been transcended. The principles still operate. But the means of application are unique. In spite of what has been said about human populations, I contend that all we can do today is to point out the problem, and that we really don't know the answers but we must strive hard to find them. Thank you, ladies and gentlemen.[961]

His belief that education was the key to eradicating human misery may explain in part his sidestepping from the zoology department at UBC to dean of graduate studies in 1964, and then becoming a strong advocate of open learning as first chair of the Academic Council of BC. In 1981, at the end of Cowan's long service to the council, Ron Jeffels of the Open Learning Institute wrote:

> Ian knows many things, knows them brilliantly: number work, the habits of wolves, the migratory paths of crows, the language of the newt, the whale's way and the plans of the porpoises. But I'm not sure how he had the courage and boldness to sit through some of the dissertations that came his way, to wit: Shakespeare's use of silence ... I have known Ian Cowan for thirty years. I never knew him, even under provocation of the worst kind, to demean or belittle another human being. I never saw him lose temper or courtesy. He has abiding respect and affection for others and his life is based in deep humanistic conviction. He is – in that remote but accurate sense of the word – a gentleman: savant, wise, understanding, sympathetic. He knows brotherhood. He understands camaraderie.[962]

Back in 1938, brotherhood and camaraderie were much in evidence in the field. Cowan and Martin had intended to travel southwest from Charlie Lake to the East Pine River but they were halted by big forest fires and their upset stomachs, both considerable deterrents. Cowan wrote in his journal of the "reckless homesteaders"[963] and their "short-sighted practices" of setting older aspen forests alight.[964] Cowan appeared to have been less sick than Martin from the bad lake water, so he was the one who drove them back to Fort St. John to recuperate. Cowan didn't waste much time in bed, though. He went to meet a game warden named Williams [not BC's first game warden, Bryan Williams], who shared his insight on a topic that interested Cowan: the history of the buffalo, or bison. Williams gave them two skulls and told the story of the last bison being shot in the district 50 years earlier by "Indian hunters."

Unbeknownst to Cowan and Martin at the time, they had been exploring very near what would one day be revealed as one of the most important archaeological sites in Canada – Charlie Lake cave, containing the earliest evidence of bison hunting 12,000 years ago.[965] In fact this cave is the most significant site for all post-glacial vertebrate remains in BC. Its stratigraphic layers tell the story of seasonal visits by hunters and gatherers from the ice age all the way to 1940. Successive generations of hunters dropped waste bones and blunted tools in the pit by the cave. The oldest of the bones had striations – the cut marks of fluted stone tools found with the bison remains. This made Charlie Lake unique as the oldest site where both butchered bones and tools apparently used for that task were found in close association. The theory is that Charlie Lake lay within a narrow, ice-free corridor through which humans had driven game up from the south. Charlie Lake cave was discovered 50 years after Cowan had explored the sandstone bluffs looking for packrats, marmots, foxes and bats. Like all the hunters before him (12,000 years of them), it seems that Cowan knew a good site when he saw one.

Today Charlie Lake and Swan Lake are provincial parks surrounded by a landscape ripped to shreds by urban and industrial energy tenures and development. Logging, mining, oil and gas development (both conventional and unconventional such as fracking), water withdrawals, stream crossings, the existing large-scale hydro developments (the W.A.C. Bennett and Peace Canyon dams – Site A and Site B, respectively) and urban and agricultural conversion occupy one-fifth of the landscape. "When the zone of influence of these changes on wildlife populations is calculated, over two-thirds of the region is what Dane-zaa elder May Apsassin calls "broken" country for wildlife and the communities that rely on them. In two of the five watersheds of this region, the percentage of broken country is over 90 per cent."[966] Swan and Charlie lakes are already among the worst-impacted areas. What's more, the proposed Site C dam, which would flood 83 kilometres more of the Peace River watershed, would lie within a few kilometres of Charlie Lake. The impacts to the surrounding countryside are predictable, since the impacts of the W.A.C. Bennett dam are now well documented.

The surviving members of Fort Ware and Ingenika Point (now known as the Tsay Keh Dene of the Kwadacha First Nation) endured irreparable damage from the flooding. The lives of the 125 families, their traplines and the caribou herd on which they had subsisted were completely disrupted and destroyed. Art Napoleon of the Saulteux First Nation, who interviewed Betty Wilson and her sister about the Ingenika trapline, related what happened when the waters started to rise: "No one told them that they were flooding the valley; there was nothing on the radio. Suddenly the waters started to rise and they had to grab their belongings and evacuate their cabins. Their trails, campsites and burial grounds were flooded out. Coffins were floating around when the water uprooted the graves."[967] Hugh Brody, who corresponded with Cowan and used Cowan's Peace River work and mammal references for his classic book on the Dane-zaa (also known as the Dunne-za and Beaver) called *Maps and Dreams*, opened with the poignant statement that "the hunting societies of the world have been sentenced to death."[968]

The downstream interviewees all described the devastating impacts on the once large Woodland Caribou herd that used to cover the hills during their migration. The population had been decimated by the dam and dwindled into small remnant herds that dispersed from the region. How they and other wildlife died was captured in horrifying accounts:

> The water was full of floating trees, debris and turbidity. Whole trees would suddenly shoot up from the bottom. With the migration route cut off, the caribou and moose tried to swim across but they couldn't make it to the bank because the log jams and debris on the shores prevented them. They slipped and drowned because they couldn't get out. The water was full of bloated corpses.[969]

The Tsay Keh people, few of whom spoke English, had previously subsisted largely on caribou. They were hurriedly provided with a "reserve" several hundred kilometres south near the coal boomtown of Mackenzie with $35,000 to cover all damages to property. None stayed. Some returned to the banks of the Williston near the old Fort Ware and Ingenika, but many ended up destitute in the cities.

In 1966 when the Bennett Dam was three years into construction, Cowan made an address at the Smithsonian Institution in Washington, DC, as one of the featured great thinkers of the 20th century alongside Claude Lévi-Strauss, Lewis Mumford, Sir Kenneth Clark, Arthur Koestler and S. Dillon Ripley.

> With pathetic frequency our groping hands have left irreparable scars on the beauty we sought to serve. Superhighways, garbage dumps, golf courses, hydroelectric impoundments, cattle grazing, mining and deforesting are only a few of the incongruous and destructive activities we have condoned...[970]

In 1973 Cowan attended a national conference on "environmental impact assessment," a new concept in Canada at the time, where a case study of the Bennett dam was showcased as an example of a project for which little thought was given prior to construction. The few voices challenging the dam were the people most affected. For example, one of the biggest measurable impacts to a way of life (food and trapping for the Beaver/Cree) was the change in muskrat populations, which dropped from 250,000 before the dam was built to 17,000 afterward.[971] Even with a new federal environmental impact assessment process beginning, Cowan had this warning about what he felt was already an inadequate procedure:

> The major criticism of our current modes of planning and environmental impact prediction ... is that they are piecemeal. They usually consider only one project within a region, or even one aspect

of a project ... With this approach, it is impossible to do a thorough job of assessing the combined effects of projects, and generally one concludes that the environmental effects of a single project are not very "significant." ...The result is not the ecological "disasters" which make headlines, but a process of slow attrition in which, year after year, project by project, we haphazardly approach subtopia.[972]

Cowan didn't live to see the greenlighting of the Site C dam downstream of the Bennett, which will drive one of the final nails into the coffin of this region. The Joint Review Panel of the BC and federal governments concluded that BC Hydro had not fully demonstrated the need for the project, that there would be damage to the environment and First Nations rights and that the damage could not be mitigated.[973] The BC government (ironically another Minister Bill Bennett, not to be confused with the Bill Bennetts of the Bennett dynasty) approved the dam in December 2014.

CHAPTER 22

*"Our observations tend to support the theory that colonization
was by means of huge rafts of logs and debris..."*

Coastal Islands, 1939

I n 1939 the onset of war brought restrictions to Cowan's productivity, but not many. He didn't enlist. When asked about this he said: "I was of an age that I could have been drafted, but I wasn't in the draftable category."[974] He told his family he was exempt because he was instructing medical students in anatomy and was "on patrol." Other circumstances suggest this was indeed the case – the government ascribed value to a pair of observant eyes with extensive knowledge of the province that could be mustered if needed, and Cowan was connected with just about every warden and naturalist in the province. His fellow 'B' member Frank Butler, the chief game commissioner, issued a directive that game wardens

> ... were not to enlist in the non-permanent or overseas forces un-
> less they first received permission from headquarters. Given their
> intimate knowledge of the districts they patrolled, the BC Game
> Commission and the BC Attorney General felt game wardens could
> be of more service to their country at home than overseas. If "trou-
> ble" should arise in any of these districts, or hostilities ever reach
> BC's shores, the expertise of Game Department staff would prove
> invaluable.[975]

There was some speculation that Cowan had health issues from his early lung condition or broken ankle. Neither affliction seemed to slow him down for his fieldwork, though other ailments were starting to manifest. It was a stressful time for the family. Joyce would have been pregnant in the late autumn of 1939. Both her brothers enlisted and went to war. Budgets were restricted domestically and at work, but Cowan adopted his usual "can-do" attitude. "It doesn't cost much more to get out of the office and do some work in the field than sit in the office reading books."[976]

It was during this time that Jim and Dorothy Genge and Tom and Margo Denny entered the Cowan circle. They all had met as young nearly- and newlyweds: the two men were friends; the two women, sisters. Both couples were sailors and in-troduced the Cowans to exploring the local waters of the Gulf Islands, in return for the trademark Cowan–Racey enthusiasm for natural history. Cowan liked to tell the story that he and Joyce were the official chaperones of the affianced Jim and Dorothy. Over the years, they shared their love of adventuring on the sea together in various boats and these enduring friendships were one of the factors in the Cowans' move back to Victoria to take on the chancellorship of UVic before retiring. The introduction to the sea was a critical one at a time when Cowan was grappling with evolutionary puzzles like the colonization of islands by animals.

Over the winter, he was writing up the Peace River report, preparing the collection of birds, mammals, fish and reptiles and studying the ethnobotany of the Bella Coola Indians,[977] sharing his desk with a young Norwegian ethnographic researcher named Thor Heyerdahl, who came to Victoria to study the movement of early people across the Pacific.[978] Heyerdahl had been in Fatu Hiva in 1937 and the two men no doubt talked about the role of rafts in transporting humans, plants and animals across the oceans. The raft idea was to influence Cowan's own theories about mammal distribution.

Bighorn Sheep

Ovis canadensis

A large sheep, brown in colour, with belly, insides of legs, large rump patch, and usually part of muzzle white. Small preorbital glands; ears small, pointed, hairy; tail short, chin without a beard; horns distinctive; front hooves longer than hind....The horns of large males constitute one of the most sought-after of the big-game trophies. The largest heads come from the Rocky Mountain area adjacent to Fernie.[980]

That winter, Cowan also managed to fit in a paper to sort out the taxonomy of Bighorn Sheep of North America. He was never one to shy away from a head-butting challenge.[979]

Bighorns had always fascinated Cowan, as they were a mountain species overlapping in many places the range of deer. They had also been decimated by trophy hunters and competition with cattle and domestic sheep. Two subspecies were recognized then, the California Bighorn and the Rocky Mountain Bighorn. Many small populations of both had been extirpated. Cowan set about the task in the same way he had with the deer – collecting skulls and hides and gathering accounts from hunters, naturalists and scientists. One of the scientists he worked with was Richard Bond, who wore two hats: as a scientist for the Soil Conservation Service in California and as a volunteer director of the Hawk and Owl Society, set up to stop the persecution of birds of prey. Bond and Cowan had communicated over the persecution of Peregrine Falcons by Allan Brooks in the Okanagan, and Bond had shared his information about an extinct population of Desert Bighorns from Lava

Beds National Park in California. This population formed another piece of the puzzle of how these sheep had dispersed around the continent after migrating here during the Pleistocene.[981] Cowan was to really take up the conservation of the bighorns later in the 40s.

Right at the end of May, his mentor Joseph Grinnell died suddenly of a heart attack at 63. The timing was right to pay his respects to the family in California, visit his alma mater, measure up the sheep skulls in the Berkeley collection and attend the annual meeting of the American Ornithologists' Union at Berkeley, where many of the 'B' were gathering, including Starker Leopold. Earlier that spring the 'B' had met in Washington, DC, and Aldo Leopold had delivered his address called "The Song of the Gavilan," about the Rio Gavilan in Mexico's northern Sierra Madre, where Leopold found a benchmark for a "healthy watershed." It is a lyrical essay about the oak- and pine-lined watercourse where "there once were men capable of inhabiting a river without disrupting the harmony of its life."[982] The four-page essay ends with Leopold's warning to his own profession about the vulnerability of scientists in becoming the agents of progress:

> Professors serve science and science serves progress. It serves progress so well that many of the more intricate instruments are stepped upon and broken in the rush to spread progress to all backward lands. One by one the parts are thus stricken from the song of songs. If the professor is able to classify each instrument before it is broken, he is well content ... That the good life on any river may likewise depend on the perception of its music, and the preservation of some music to perceive, is a form of doubt not yet entertained by science.[983]

Cowan was given permission to take the museum's van for the journey down. He and Joyce left on June 7 and arrived three days later at Berkeley. No correspondence exists from this visit except for the confirmation of arrival, having coasted down the hills to keep the bill for oil and gas to $11.60[984] [$194.30 today, based on the Consumer Price Index]. They returned June 24 and then the Cowans headed directly up the coast to meet Tom and Elinor McCabe and Pat Martin for a proposed two-month biological survey of British Columbia's coastal islands north of Queen Charlotte Sound. Ian and Joyce had grown close to the McCabes during their honeymoon at Indianpoint Lake and time with them in Berkeley. Cowan was keen to implement their plans to figure out the distribution of birds and mammals along the central BC coast. "[F]ive of us squeezed into MV *Seabird*, owned and skippered by Pat Martin, the first marine bird specialist on our coast. Tom died too young, of a heart attack, not surprisingly, but his contributions were many, well beyond the evidence of his bibliography."[985]

Cowan's full journal notes for the 1939 trip have yet to be located in the museum archives and there are no photographs. There are some field notes from Pat Martin[986] and a specimen index of Cowan's to help piece together the trip.[987] It is not clear from the journals that Joyce was up there with them. Possibly the Cowans boarded one of the CPR *Princesses* from Vancouver to Namu to meet the boat tied up at the dock. Namu, some 150 kilometres north of Port Hardy, opposite Hunter Island, was a big cannery at that time. We know the party headed out from Namu on July 3. We also know that Cowan was back in Vancouver by July 18[988] due to an illness that at first was suspected to be heart trouble.

In the museum report, Cowan notes that their survey included Calvert, Hecate, Goose, Spider, Hunter, Ruth, Smythe, Townsend, Campbell, Dufferin, Horsfall, Yeo, McCauley, Chatfield, Campania, Banks, Pitt and Porcher islands and the mainland at Koeye and Neckis rivers.[989] Princess Royal, Swindle, Reginald and Estevan Islands had also been visited by the McCabes for the museum in the preceding two years.[990] Unlike today, these islands off BC's central and north coast were relatively well known in the 1930s. There was far more fishing activity in those days. There were all the coastal First Nations fishermen from the Heiltsuk, Kitasoo, Oweekeno, Gitga'at and Tsimshian communities fishing in their territories. Non-native hand loggers, miners and fishermen like the McCabes were pushing in everywhere.

Canneries, mining and logging camps dotted the coast, serviced by the CPR steamship division. It took intrepid visitors, though, to confidently navigate the treacherous waters and weather, even in the summer. The less hardy visitors aboard old CPR steamships en route to Prince Rupert would have gazed out from the decks over this blur of islands and inlets up the Inside Passage, much as they do from cruise ships today, hardly experiencing the extraordinary richness and biodiversity of this region. For example, the Koeye Valley is one of the few places in the world where, with five species of salmon, herring and other forage fish in the estuary, you can see a Humpback Whale and a Grizzly Bear at the same time. Today the names of these islands are mostly unknown until oil spills – or the threat of them – raises them in the public's awareness.

Cowan was intrigued by this convoluted archipelago and coastline from an evolutionary point of view. He described the mainland areas where they collected as "separated by many miles of tortuous, precipitous coast in which several rivers and many extensive inlets penetrate from the humid outer coast climate to a less humid inland climate."[991] Lining the narrow, deep fjords are steep, granite, ice-capped mountains to which conifers and mountain goats cling. At the mouths of the inlets, spectacular, highly productive estuaries, packed into a tiny area of flat land, draw large seasonal concentrations of wildlife, mostly centred on salmon runs, from shrews to grizzlies – hence its modern-day name, the Great Bear Rainforest. The inner, forested islands are separated from the mainland by narrow straits sometimes less than a stone's throw across. The outer islands lie farther out and resemble the tonsured heads of monks rising out of Queen Charlotte Sound – treeless, domed bogs rimmed with forests. The islands at the outer edge of the continent are isolated, rocky crags, many with white sandy beaches which take a good bashing from the open ocean. Landings by boat are limited to calm days or in lee-shore lagoons.

There were two objectives for the study by Cowan and company. One was to undertake a survey of pelagic, or ocean-going, birds, which required being on the outside coast and finding safe anchorages. The other goal was to determine the evolutionary effects of isolated islands on small mammal populations. The features small mammals need to survive on these islands are not dissimilar from what humans need – a place that is not saturated, rocky, vertical and/or exposed to the elements. That leaves protected beaches and estuaries, which is where the Cowan outfit sampled on their first stop – Spider Island.[992]

Spider was an interesting choice. It was selected by the RCAF soon thereafter as one of several sites for Pacific early-warning radar installations and communications stations. By 1942 work had started on this tiny, two-mile-wide rock on a 30-man unit to watch for low-flying aircraft from Japan. The air force no doubt picked Spider Island because it presented a spectacular bastion to the sea, with a massive granite cliff on which the radar station was built. The rest of the island was a bog, over which a log road was floated, eventually dropping down to a lagoon with a perfect anchorage, not common on the coast. A lake had plenty of fresh water, and a population of Sitka Black-tailed Deer provided a change from canned goods. Interestingly, the lack of information in the museum files about these expeditions may have had some strategic reason, although there is no hard evidence for this. If some secret military reconnaissance work needed a scientific-research cover story, pelagic birds and island evolution were an excellent choice. However, in July of 1939, few could have anticipated Pearl Harbor and the events that followed.

On Spider, Cowan and the McCabes spent three days setting out hundreds of traps along the lakeshore, mossy logs and rock crevices along the seashore. They caught no mice at all but found two species of shrews on the beach. They had set out to sample the differences in mice but found that the shrews posed even more interesting evolutionary questions. Being far less adept (or so they thought) at being stowaways with humans, one obvious question was: How did they get to these islands? These tiny mammals with high metabolic rates and poor insulation with short fur can barely survive an afternoon rainstorm without eating, let alone swimming 20 miles in a hostile ocean on an empty stomach or floating on a log with no protection from the elements, yet they appeared on almost every island. And what happened to these animals when the islands were subjected to periodic tsunamis and major storms? Waves washing over their habitat were a predictable characteristic of this environment. Was there a time when there were ancient land bridges to these remote islands?

The final enigma was over the difference between the two species of shrew they found. One (the coastal variety of the Common Shrew) displayed "remarkable uniformity."[993] This suggested either a "recent arrival" given the preponderance of wandering males or that they were "a stable species producing little material for selection influences to segregate."[994] Meanwhile the other species, the Dusky Shrew, *Sorex obscurus*, had large and often confusing variations even between neighbouring islands, which suggested evolution through speciation was well underway.[995]

Darwin had his finches but Cowan was fascinated by his non-flying shrews!

One of the first things the Cowan team discovered was that the Spider Island shrews had the darkest summer coats and were the amongst the largest on any of the islands sampled, although Spider was one of the smallest islands they visited. When they moved over to Hunter, a large mountainous island, shrews were lighter in colour and slightly smaller. As Cowan wrote, "Besides these well differentiated races our collections indicate a race in the nascent state on Spider Island and possibly others on one or two islands from which the material is too scant to be informative."[997] The shrews of the very remote islands of the Goose group looked much like the mainland ones at Koeye, which caused Cowan to think they were recent imports. Then, on Calvert Island, which is another larger one with high mountains, they found much shorter, smaller and paler shrews, which they declared an actual subspecies. When the McCabes went to Banks Island later that summer, a shrew identical to those on Calvert Island turned up again but the two islands were separated by a hundred miles. How did they become disjunct populations?

The MV *Seabird* had anchored in Kwakshua Channel off the north end of Calvert Island, making use of a traditional fish camp cabin at Pruth Bay. Kwakshua is a choice location on the coast. At the north end of Calvert is a tombolo connecting a small proto-island to it with a flat and habitable, forested sandy spit. The result is a huge beach with pounding waves facing the open ocean to the west and the quiet lagoon/bay Pruth facing east. Just round the corner from Pruth Bay, facing Kwakshua Channel, is one of the oldest continuously occupied village sites on the coast, with nearly 12,000

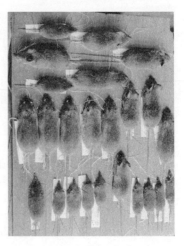

Small mammals, including Common and Dusky Shrews

Cinereus Shrew [now Common]

Sorex cinereus streatori

One of the smallest of the shrews, with a total length of about five inches, of which one-third is tail. Fur short and velvety ... Occupies the immediate vicinity of the coastline through the length of the province, except the lowlands of the Fraser Delta region ... Eats all kinds of small invertebrates, such as insects and their larvae, earthworms, isopods, snails, millipedes and centipedes. Breeds first in mid-May, with up to three litters per year.[996]

Dusky Shrew

Sorex obscurus longicauda
[now *Sorex monticolus longicaudus*]

Largest race of the species, with a length of about 5 inches. Much larger and darker, with hind foot and tail longer ... Skull larger in all dimensions. Winter pelage black. [995 bis]

years of archaeological remains embedded in the stratigraphic layers of the shore-line.[998] There are two reasons for Kwakshua's human popularity: there is lots to eat there, and it has the distinction of never having had a fluctuating shoreline throughout those 12 millennia, unlike all the rest of the coast. Amid the seesawing of the land caused by the terrain rebounding after the glaciers' weight had melted away, the region around Kwakshua was the fulcrum and didn't move.

Cowan again seemed to have an uncanny ability to home in on interesting bio-diversity and evolutionary hotspots. In 1939 these major archaeological and pa-leoecological discoveries were still 70 years away, so all he had to go on was local knowledge and the puzzle of the shrews. To that end he spent a lot of time watch-ing where they foraged, what they ate and how they interacted with the sea. One ac-count of July 13 was from Kwakshua:

> Captured an immature shrew as it ran from a pile of seaweed 12' be-low high tide mark. Captured a second juvenile in a rock pit behind the cabin and saw a third escape into a burrow under a log. All these seen at mid-day and not later than 3 o'clock on a bright day without rain. One individual kept captive ate a small beetle, 3 earthworms, about a cubic centimetre of squirrel liver and yellow salmonberry in 12 hours. It died during the night.[999]

Cowan's time with Thor Heyerdahl may have led him to theorize:

> It is possible that certain of the islands were populated by gla-cier-transported debris containing small mammals ... our observa-tions tend to support the theory that colonization was by means of the huge rafts of logs and debris that annually slip from the precipi-tous and water-sodden hillsides and float out to sea.[1000]

Cowan was on to something again. Insectivores have recently taken the lime-light in their role in surviving another major global event – the mass extinction from the Chicxulub asteroid impact circa 66 million years ago, which wiped out the dinosaurs and everything else that wasn't under a foot of soil or water. Humans have a lot to be grateful to shrews for – specifically our existence – because these early insectivores are the common ancestor from which all mammals repopulated the earth.[1001] They are one of the most ancient mammal groups, their fossils dating back 130 million years. Paleoecologists speculate that the ancestral shrew survived the temporary scorching of the asteroid impact by virtue of their shrewish dispo-sition – preferring wet, marginal, subterranean, insect-rich environments. What is it about this group that enables them to disperse in hostile environments and through catastrophic events, whether fire or ice? Wrote David Nagorsen: "The col-onization of the numerous Pacific coastal islands by shrews remains one of the un-explained mysteries of island biogeography."[1002]

Small rodents as well as insectivores continued to pose a great puzzle for Cowan and McCabe. Throughout the war, McCabe, who also kept a presence in strategic areas at the request of the BC government, continued to collect specimens. At the end of the war, Cowan and McCabe published their seminal work on the island races of Keen's Mouse,[1003] which really brought together all their ideas about evolution on the islands and set the scene for later graduate work by Charles Guiguet and Bristol Foster. Nagorsen notes that there have been few mammalogists after Cowan to follow up on these questions:

> Basic surveys of small mammals haven't been done in ensuing years and have not received any attention. My favourite one is the work they [Cowan, Martin and McCabe] did with birds and small mammals off the central and north coast, and much of that now falls into the Great Bear Rainforest. I have always had an interest in these mammals. And I get a bit frustrated because all the focus is on the great charismatic mammals but no one is looking at the small mammals. Not too many people were having these thoughts. He was ahead of his time. For many of these islands the only information we have for the species of shrews and small rodents found on the islands is based on the specimens collected by Cowan & McCabe.[1004]

By the middle of July, Cowan was beginning to suffer an acute medical condition that put him/them back on the steamship from Namu to Vancouver. In a letter to his boss from his in-laws' house once home, he writes:

> Dear Mr. Kermode,
> Just to let you know that I visited the doctor today and he has advised me to do no strenuous work for a couple of weeks at least. The heart condition that I have been noticing for the past two weeks turns out to be nothing serious, thank heaven; just the result of overdoing it when I was running a temperature with the mild attack of flu I had when I left here. The doctor assures me that everything should be perfectly all right in two or three weeks. This being the case, I will take life easy for perhaps two or three days + then home to Victoria, where I shall busy myself with some of the many less strenuous tasks waiting to be done down at the museum. I have with me about two hundred very interesting animal and bird specimens, the product of the last two weeks collecting; included are two albatross, a Chilean Skua (northern record) and a Flesh-footed Shearwater (new BC record).[1005]

According to his daughter, Ann, Cowan suffered chronically throughout his life from gastrointestinal problems, probably hereditary and possibly exacerbated by the ailment he picked up from the contaminated water in Charlie Lake (giardia or other bacterial gut infection). He had also been working hard. His entries and recollections include many hours standing on a rolling deck spotting pelagic birds through field glasses, crawling through a bog to see the skittish Red-throated

Loons nesting on Spider Lake, and following Sandhill Cranes "running like rabbits" up forest trails to their nesting sites in the bogs.[1006]

We know now that there are three subspecies of Sandhill Cranes: the Greater, the Lesser and the Canadian. The Canadian were so named because early American ornithologists knew only that these birds disappeared somewhere in Canada to breed. Cowan suspected that these island cranes he saw might be a distinct population. It was difficult to do any kind of taxonomy, though, as the cranes were scarce and nervous. They had been one of the species heavily targeted by milliners at the turn of the century, for their showy feathers, causing their populations to drop perilously low. The cranes were only just beginning to recover at the time Cowan spotted them. They probably were aided in reviving by the remoteness of their breeding habitat. The *Lesson* of the 'B' two years earlier had been a tribute to the crane:

Canadian Sandhill Crane

Grus canadensis rowani

Virtually nothing is known about populations of Canadian Sandhill Cranes, *G. c. rowani*, in the province.[1007]

> Thus always does history, whether of marsh or marketplace, mice or men, end in paradox. The ultimate value in these marshes is wildness, and the crane is wildness incarnate. But all conservation of wildness is self-defeating, for to cherish we must see and fondle, and when enough have seen and fondled, there is nothing left to cherish.[1008]

Leopold's crane was the Greater Sandhill, subspecies *Grus canadensis tabida*, which are more commonly interior birds. They are a fascinating species to ornithologists for their antiquity. Fossil remains of cranes nine million years old are relatively indistinguishable from the modern species, making this one of the world's oldest bird genera, dating back at least to the Miocene. It also makes them a haunting animal to come across, as they have an almost prehistoric call and gait that evokes the wild so vividly – about which Leopold wrote. The distinctive behaviour of the coastal cranes running up to breeding bogs led Cowan to suspect that the birds were well adapted to the specific geography of coastal islands. By the time he was involved in writing *Birds of BC* in the late 1980s, work still had not been done on this population. Keen to encourage investigation into the question, he acted as an adviser (at age 96) to the Raincoast Conservation Foundation to promote fieldwork on the islands into this unique population of cranes as well as other species.[1009]

Researcher Chris Darimont, who worked on the wolves of the coast wrote in 2005:

[Cowan] blazed a path of discovery in an incredibly interesting ecosystem but one so remote and challenging in which to work that almost nobody has had the tenacity to follow for a full 60 years. As we embarked on similar studies six decades later, armed with little more than quixotic ambitions, he very kindly contributed by carefully reviewing our study design and proposals as well as penning a letter of strong support to deliver to potential funders. And all of this plus having me over for a cup of tea![1010]

The MV *Seabird* crew went twice to the Goose Island group, a birding hot spot where deep ocean currents hit the continental shelf, setting the whole food web off. "Vast numbers of shearwaters were observed at the Goose Island Banks today; they were feeding on needle fish and later in the day could be seen resting upon the water in large, loosely knit flocks."[1011] Shearwaters, aptly named, as they "shear" the waves with their wings, glide opportunistically for thousands of miles along the surface of the ocean looking for food. Mostly the crew were seeing Sooty Shearwaters, but a separate population of Pale-footed Shearwaters [now called the Flesh-footed Shearwater] turned up, much to their delight. Martin had spotted one there two years earlier, and on this trip he had his friends there for confirmation.

Flesh-footed Shearwater

Puffinus carneipes

Breeds on islands off Australia and New Zealand; part of population winters in north Pacific Ocean ... The Flesh-footed Shearwater was first recorded near the British Columbia coast in 1937 (Martin 1942), and has remained an uncommon but regular visitor in offshore waters.[1012]

Fork-tailed Storm-Petrel

Oceanodroma furcata

Large numbers historically foraged on offal from the coastal fish canneries but the canneries are now closer to mainland industrial centres and farther from the storm-petrels' preferred natural foraging areas ... Storm-petrels have a well-developed sense of smell and may be seen in strings following the scent of fish oil on the water. Very little is known about where the Fork-tailed Storm-Petrel forages off British Columbia, its feeding habits or foods. It is well known, however, that food resources are important on influencing reproductive success.[1019]

The Chilean Skua, mentioned in Cowan's letter to Kermode, was way off course — "almost three hundred miles north of the previous northern record and is on the north-flowing branch of the Japan Current, whereas in other records have been on the south-flowing California Current ..."[1013] These pirate birds typically feast on what terns and gulls cough up when the skuas harass them. The skuas Cowan dissected had been eating Gooseneck Barnacles from floating debris. Albatross, which hang in the air like huge 2 × 10s circling the fish boat, were feeding on squid, cuttlefish and needlefish scooped from the surface of the ocean.

Floating debris has turned out to be as deadly to albatross as longline fishing lures. The other killer was damage to their remote island nesting colonies. One of the breeding colonies of Black-footed Albatross was Wake Island, in the middle of the Pacific, which had been taken over first by the US in 1899 and then by Japanese military during the war. Cowan visited the island with a film crew in December of 1957 during a trans-Pacific trip.[1015] While there, he noted that the nesting colony had been destroyed.[1016] One of the episodes of Cowan's *The Living Sea* television series, called "Bird Island," captured the rich natural history of the place. Today, Wake Island is part of the US Fish & Wildlife Service's Pacific Remote Islands Marine National Monument, one of the largest protected areas on the planet for coral reef and seabirds. The Black-footed Albatross has been reintroduced there.

Cowan returned home July 21 and Germany invaded Poland five weeks later. It was an end of an era for Cowan on many fronts, personally with the death of his mentor Joseph Grinnell. Fittingly, Grinnell's last research article was on the geographic variation of Fork-tailed Petrels, posthumously published on July 15, 1939, in his journal *The Condor*.[1017] Petrels, now called storm-petrels, are another common offshore bird observed on the outer coast. In Cowan's specimen index for July 18 at Goose Island Banks (possibly in Joyce's handwriting) there is this entry:

Black-footed Albatross

Diomedea nigripes
[now *Phoebastria nigripes*]

Breeds on western Hawaiian Islands and on Torishima, off Japan. Ranges throughout the north Pacific Ocean ... The Black-footed Albatross is the only albatross seen regularly off the coast. It is widely scattered in offshore waters and is only occasionally seen inshore. The Black-footed Albatross, being essentially a surface feeder, is usually attracted to any floating object. Plastic and aluminum objects discarded at sea are cause for concern, as they are picked up by the birds as food. Two birds washed ashore at Long Beach in autumn 1971 were grossly underweight and contained 17 man-made objects in their stomachs.[1014]

> Petrels, Fork-tailed. Saw large numbers of Fork-tailed Petrels but did not bother to collect any. We saw small flocks on the water. Upon approaching the spot there was no sign of feeding of any sort except a light, almost imperceptible oil slick. This we observed several times and wonder if the birds were feeding on the oil slick or what caused the oil slick.[1018]

For Ian and Joyce Cowan, reproductive success was shortly to come. That first winter of the war saw a slowing down of everyone's activities. They completed the third floor of the museum to house the large-mammal collection and moved the materials up. Joyce helped Sweeney set up intertidal exhibits and Cowan went out to lecture, including giving an illustrated talk on the ducks of British Columbia, which went down well at the annual gathering of all the fish and game clubs around the province. He was finishing up his sheep study and shifting his focus to an update on the amphibians and reptiles of BC. This allowed him one short field trip up-island

....

Northwestern Salamander

Ambystoma gracile

Southwestern British Columbia, including Vancouver Island. Occurs from sea level to timberline in Canadian and Hudsonian zones.[1020]

....

to the alpine meadows of Mount Arrowsmith to obtain a living specimen of the Northwestern Salamander. This large, brown, secretive coastal dweller is unique for its ability to breed in ponds in both its adult and larval forms. He observed that they live primarily on a diet of slugs.

To keep costs down at the museum, requests went out to Cowan's contacts far and wide for live and pickled specimens. The museum reported the donation of one rattlesnake by his old professor George Spencer. Spencer's rattlesnakes had been featured publicly before in the book *Lone Cone*,[1021] all about Tofino in the early 1920s. The writer, Dorothy Abraham, had put up Dr. Spencer for the summer while he was doing insect and marine invertebrate studies. He had brought along his pet rattlesnake, which intrigued the locals, rattlesnakes being confined to the interior grasslands. Their enthusiasm diminished when the snake escaped. History doesn't record whether the snake that came to the museum in 1939 was the same one and had been retrieved (rattlers live up to 30 years) nor even whether it was alive or dead.

The museum had had good success with keeping amphibians alive in their vivariums. Cowan wrote up, for a herpetological journal, the story of the final demise of a Red-legged Frog that had been in the museum for almost as long as some of the staff:

> On May 4, 1940, the frog was weakening noticeably and could no longer elevate itself or its legs and moved very little. In June it became necessary to place food in its mouth before it would feed. The frog died July 9, 1940, at the venerable age of approximately fifteen years, thirteen of which were passed in captivity.[1022]

In the spirit of the indomitable cycles of life, the Cowans' son, Garry McTaggart Cowan, was born the very same day. Garry was Rh negative, like Joyce, and so this baby, at just over 6 pounds, was happily going to survive. The newspaper birth announcement stated: "Both doing well."[1023]

The spring 1939 trip to Berkeley had set some ideas in motion for Cowan. He missed the stimulation of a local academic community. The only other group of biologists anywhere on the island was at the federal Pacific Biological Station at Nanaimo. The marine scientists there offered him intellectual discourse and friendship. The ethos of the station had been established by his old professor Charles McLean Fraser at UBC, who had been the director prior to going to UBC to head up the zoology department. Fraser's successor at the station, Wilbert A. Clemens, and the other scientists, Andy Pritchard, Earl Foerster, G. Clifford Carl and John Hart, were a big attraction for Cowan:

Red-legged Frog
[Northern Red-legged Frog]

Rana aurora aurora

The south coastal region, including Vancouver Island; northern limit unknown.[1024]

> Whenever I had work to do [up island] I tried to schedule it for a Friday because every Friday afternoon they had a scientific seminar at the biological station and I was given a very warm welcome to go and participate; and I used to do that maybe two or three times a year.[1025]

Cowan had heard from Clemens that McLean Fraser was retiring at UBC and that there may be some openings alongside the other two professors in the department, George Spencer (another former teacher of Cowan's, of rattlesnake fame) and Gertrude Smith.

> I heard there were changes being contemplated at UBC and I'm interested in universities – I like teaching; I liked students; so I went up [to the Station] to talk to Clemens about, How did you let it be known that you were interested in being considered for any positions that were at my level of expertise? I wasn't pretending I would be a substitute for McLean Fraser, head of department. Clemens said that he was going over to Vancouver tomorrow to talk to its president, Dr. [Leonard S.] Klink, and "I'll tell him that you're interested in being considered, that you're a British Columbian; you're here; you've got a good degree. I know you and so on." So I thanked him very much and drove home.[1026]

Cowan had hardly got home when Clemens called him on the phone and said, "'You won't believe this but you'd hardly got out of the office before Klink came in to see me and asked me to take McLean Fraser's position as head of the department. I said I would, providing he took you too."[1027] In a later interview in 2001, Cowan told the next part of the story, which was a surprise visit:

> A week later, I had a knock at the door and there was Klink, the president of the university, who was on a recruiting campaign. He sat

opposite me in my office and we yarned for half an hour, then he said, "Well I like what I see. If you want to join me you are invited."[1028]

When Cowan submitted his resignation, the provincial secretary, George Weir, who had appointed him to the museum, appealed to him to change his mind. Kermode's retirement was imminent and he was first choice for replacement.[1029] Cowan was firm in his decision. He had also picked up some other news from a colleague at the Friday seminars at the Pacific Biological Station that made the decision easier. He had a replacement in mind: G. Clifford Carl, a top marine biologist who had been at UBC with Cowan under McLean Fraser and later got his PhD at the University of Toronto, had moved to Cowichan to work for Fisheries at the hatchery. Cowan had been stopping by the hatchery during his research into deer ecology around Cowichan over the years and the two had built on their friendship and mutual scientific interests. Carl was one of the acolytes of the 'B,' but was underemployed at the hatchery and looking for a more stimulating job.

Cowan recommended Carl to Weir for the museum director post. This was someone he could collaborate with and thus maintain strong ties to the institution he'd worked so hard to restore. There were three further considerations: Cowan's friend and old roommate William Kaye Lamb, the provincial archivist, had also accepted a position at UBC, as librarian, and was leaving the same month; Cowan's salary at the university was likely to improve over time; and finally, Joyce would be close to her family and have help with the new baby.

On August 30, 1940, Cowan submitted his final "List of all Property Returned to the Museum" for signature by Kermode. It included his cameras, all his camping gear, microscopes, tools, dissecting equipment, a cedar dinghy and the Dodge truck![1030] By September the young family was back in Vancouver. And by the end of the month, Kermode was gone too. Cowan sent notes back to the staff that were left. Mrs. G.A. Hardy, the director of botany, received this note:

> Dear Mrs. Hardy,
> I have no doubt that you are finding things a little difficult at the moment, but I have every confidence that you will very soon readjust yourself to the new situation.[1031]

Mrs. Crummy, the secretary, received similar good wishes, with a request to borrow a museum book on the life history of the porcupine. He finished with: "In the meantime, my best to yourself, Mrs. Sweeney and Mrs. Hardy. I think of you all frequently and can honestly confess that I miss you."[1032]

Kermode sent Cowan a letter that same month, saying, "As no doubt you are aware, I received notification to retire the end of this month. I expect to be in Vancouver for a few days next week and may see you then. With best regards."[1033]

When Corley-Smith interviewed Cowan in 1985, he asked him why he decided to leave the museum. Cowan replied:

> I was uncomfortable in the situation I was in here. I was enjoying

my job but there wasn't a big future here and I knew it, or at least I guessed that there wasn't at the time, and university was my first love. No, I didn't have a falling-out with Kermode. We got along. He was not a well man: he had terrible bad sinuses and he had a lot of pain. He wasn't sleeping well at night. He was over 60 and he was sort of an unhappy chap. His wife died somewhere about that period and he married his girlfriend, and she is still around; she is a nice person.[1034]

Clifford Carl later approached Cowan about giving a lecture at the museum, and Cowan's letter in response would reveal some of the frustrations he had had with Kermode. "There were constant requests for running a lecture series during the last four years I was in Victoria, but Kermode ran them so lavishly and inefficiently that they would have been a major financial burden that we were unable to shoulder."[1035] Cowan's later contribution to the museum was not just to be a guest lecturer; his collaborations would continue for the rest of his life. The lineage of curators and directors he influenced was biblical. He assisted not only the new director, Clifford Carl, but also the next vertebrate curator, Charles Guiguet, and Guiguet's successor, Alton Harestad and Carl's successor, Bristol Foster, and Foster's successor, Yorke Edwards, and Edwards's successor, William (Bill) Barkley. All six had been students of Cowan's and he supported them in whatever way he could. He variously would join them in their fieldwork, give public lectures or co-write or advise on their papers and on various museum guides to animals of British Columbia. In fact, he was to hand over his half-finished manuscripts on amphibians and reptiles that year to Carl, who finished them as separate guides under his own name, with Cowan's blessing. It was a watershed year for Cowan, 1940. He was starting a family and a long-intended new career as a teacher, and he had moved imperceptibly over a threshold from being "the mentored" into becoming "the mentor." And he was still only 30.

Cowan felt his legacy to the museum was "getting out into the province and studying the great diversity of living animals and plants to be found there." He also revitalized the place as a public and teaching institution. Corley-Smith, the historian of the museum, wrote, "In short, he did a great deal to revive what had been, a few short years before, a dying institution." Cycles in and out of political favour were nothing new to Cowan. At the end of his life, he was saddened by the latest political cycle that saw another starving of that institution as a place of research, inventory and education. He was appalled at the axing of budgets for curatorial staff, fieldwork, school-outreach programs, public information lectures on the natural history of BC and the shift towards generic entertainment. He also mourned the loss of the museum as a research institution. "The museum now has got a sort of a basic pittance from the government, and is trying to run on what they earn. They have those American Imax movies, which are dramatic for twenty minutes and they don't tell you anything."[1036]

Cowan knew the Provincial Museum was not alone in this regard. While researching *The Birds of British Columbia*, he and his co-authors found it difficult to obtain specimens or even get responses from such institutions as the Museum of Comparative Zoology at Harvard, one of the leading museums in the world. Institutions worldwide have not been receiving sufficient support for maintaining collections or replacing curators, ornithologists and mammalogists, preventing the passing down of knowledge about what was where.[1037] Biological collections have long played a critical role for human public health and epidemiology, in everything from detecting dangerous levels of toxicity by using early specimens as baselines, to tracking epidemics like hantavirus and avian influenza. But public understanding of the usefulness of such knowledge fluctuates with the political landscape.

Cowan was no stranger to political cycles. He told one interviewer in 1979 that you could tell the level of support for ecology by where the government situated the Wildlife Service. "Whenever the Tories were in power, wildlife was part of the old BC Provincial Police. Under the Liberals, it became a separate branch."[1038] By that point, Cowan had experienced an up-cycle of three and a half years for wildlife under the New Democrat government led by Dave Barrett. The NDP had come to power in 1972 after 20 years of the conservative Social Credit party. That year, the *Vancouver Sun* ran a full-page opinion piece called "Land, Wildlife and People: It's Time to Put Life Back into the Wilds of BC" after such long "governmental indifference to wildlife."[1039] Two guest editorials of half a page each were by Cowan and Roderick Haig-Brown, also a renowned conservationist, essayist and angler of the time from Campbell River.[1040] Haig-Brown was the marine equivalent of Cowan. The newspaper positioned the two men as the key scholars to summarize what they thought were the most pressing needs to revitalize the wilds of the province. Cowan opened up with both barrels: "It matters little whether ignorance, avarice, political chicanery or short-sighted judgment are at the root. The immediate result is unnecessary environmental damage and a poorer place to live."[1041] He then turned the gun on himself and wrote that the "advent of the organized naturalist group, to parallel the organized sportsman who used to be almost the only voice for conservation, has changed the scene more than most hunters realize.... it seems to me that a change in the general ethic of hunting is imperative."[1042]

Cowan argued, as he had been doing in 1939, that if the public didn't know what was out there, they couldn't be expected to miss it when it was gone – a convenient situation for those supporting increasingly aggressive industrial development of Canada's natural areas. The central coast he had fallen so deeply in love with that year was one region he was going to make sure people knew about. Although his time there had been cut short by illness, Cowan returned many times and it became a focus both for his fieldwork and for summer holidays with Joyce later on in their lives. In the Denny and Genge sailboats, the couples spent weeks exploring this region every year from 1963 onwards, poking into inlets, collecting, fishing, cooking dinner on remote beaches and photographing the beauty of the territory they were exploring for public lectures. The journals from these trips record the birds, plants, molluscs and of course the small mammals they observed.[1043]

In 1990, MacMillan Bloedel was making plans to log the Koeye Valley that Cowan had surveyed back in 1938. Peter McAllister, a director of the Sierra Club of western Canada, organized a reconnaissance voyage to take biologists and other environmentalists, including his son, up to the watershed. The week-long trip in the region led to the creation of the Raincoast Conservation Society (later Foundation) by two generations of McAllisters and other founders. Raincoast established a mandate to use science to inform advocacy on the coast with regard to industrial threats to this region, and Cowan was interviewed to provide his knowledge and baseline data of the area. It was Raincoast that coined the term the Great Bear Rainforest. Prior to this, the coastal region was referred to by government as the mid-coast timber supply area.

Cowan remained in contact with wolf and bird biologists of the Raincoast Foundation, such as Chris Darimont, up until 2005. Darimont completed his PhD on wolves, using Cowan as one of his early advisers on wolf behaviour. Darimont's work on the wolves of the Great Bear Rainforest was featured in a 2004 National Geographic documentary called *Last Stand of the Great Bear* as well as in the narrative and photographs in Ian McAllister's *The Last Wild Wolves*.[1044] The mouth of the Koeye Valley was purchased through the efforts of the Heiltsuk First Nation, the Raincoast Conservation Foundation, Ecotrust and The Land Conservancy of BC and handed back to the children for a science and culture camp. Across the channel from the Koeye, on Calvert Island, is one of the many parks and conservancy areas co-managed by the province and coastal First Nations. The Kwakshua camp where the crew of the MV *Seabird* stayed in 1939 is now the location of the Hakai Institute, dedicated to scientific research and traditional ecological knowledge, where Brian Starzomski, the Ian McTaggart Cowan Chair at the University of Victoria, brings his students for studies of biodiversity in the landscape.

CHAPTER 23

*"They seem to spend their time playing
and every sand dune bears their tracks."*

UBC *and Okanagan, 1940–1942*

Cowan skimmed into academic life at the University of British Columbia like a Bufflehead to water. He told the faculty head, Wilbert Clemens, that he wanted to set up the first wildlife program in Canada, in fact at any university. As Cowan recounted, "Clemens said 'Fine, go ahead'; that was the way he did things ... I started by teaching two courses: the biology of vertebrates and then another on the applied side."[1045] Cowan modelled his approach on the parallel department of fisheries set up by Clemens's colleague J.R. Dymond at the University of Toronto, to provide training with a strong conservation bent for professional fisheries positions. Both Clemens and Dymond were friends with members of the 'B' – they had their own informal aquatic brotherhood. Clemens had been educated at the University of Toronto and Cornell (which had its own school of conservation biologists), starting in 1908. He was a member of the executive of the Toronto Field-Naturalists, which was affiliated with the Ottawa Field-Naturalists, while Hoyes Lloyd was leading it. When Clemens headed west to take on the directorship of the Pacific Biological Station at Nanaimo in 1924, he worked extensively with Jim Munro on natural history articles about bird and herring associations[1046] and fish-eating birds such as mergansers.

Dymond had also spent a year on behalf of the Royal Ontario Museum collecting marine specimens on the east coast of Vancouver Island. Dymond and Clemens were coastal counterparts of one another and their interests overlapped. Between them, they were educating a whole new generation of Canadian fisheries biologists to have conservation awareness. Dymond shared Cowan's desire to end the bounty system in Canada, and the two men orchestrated a lecture campaign across the country that officially started in the spring of 1942. The campaign to end the bounty was promoted through the structure of the Canadian Conservation Association headed up by another Cornell-educated scientist who had landed in the east, John Detwiler.

In his very first year on the UBC faculty, Cowan was as busy as he had ever been. There were the two courses to develop and teach (having had less than a month of preparation), while Joyce had the task of dealing with a new baby and moving house to West Fourth Avenue on the outskirts of the campus. Cowan, as the only instructor, had to cover a lot of new ground and work within a nearly non-existent budget, including doing his own embalming of cats and dogfish for student dissections in the vertebrate course. On the applied side, he was feeling his way in the entirely new discipline of wildlife management. "Techniques were pretty primitive then. Your eyes were still the best instruments you could get, maybe aided by a pair of [field] glasses, which weren't anywhere near as good as they are now. Keen observation."[1048] The first intake of students provided him with all the reassurance he sought that the move had been the right one. "These people, you know, were a wonderful group of men and women. There were a few women, you know. The first was a lady by the name of Margaret Merry [later Arsenault], one of my first students, she liked working on the Creeping Vole.[1049] That was a break, before that there was nothing but men."[1050]

Cowan was also intent on pulling together various specimens in the university and starting a departmental vertebrate museum, still closely connected as he was to the goings-on at the museum in Victoria. In the course of the first year, his correspondence with G. Clifford Carl explored the expansion of pilchards up the coast, Bighorn Sheep distribution, the preparation of plant specimens, details of Harlequin skins, the stranded Killer Whales at Masset, Lynx skulls and various fossils and subfossils of mammals for a paper. He also managed to hunt down the background on a fossil horse tooth.

He also substantiates, through a photograph, the sighting of a "Squarehead" off the coast, which added another species to the list for his lectures series "Whales: Great and Small" that he would deliver to museum audiences in 1942.

Carl sent him three commonly asked questions from the museum public, for which he wanted definitive "Cowan answers":[1054]

> Do hummingbirds ride on the backs of geese?
> The main difficulty would be that hummingbirds migrate between

Red-breasted Merganser

Mergus serrator

Largest numbers occur in bays, estuaries and inlets; coastal lakes, rivers and large sloughs are visited infrequently. In winter the centre of abundance appears to be the Strait of Georgia on the coast and the southern Okanagan valley in the interior. In some years, over 1,700 Red-breasted Mergansers have been reported to winter in the province, which is about 28 per cent of the 6,000 reported to winter in the Pacific Flyway.[1047]

Creeping Vole

Microtus oregoni serpens

Size small, legs and tail short, ears almost concealed in the fur, fur texture plush-like with guard hairs projecting little beyond the underfur ... Confined to the deciduous forest region of the Puget Sound Lowlands Biotic Area, where it lives largely underground, burrowing in the loose soil and making elaborate runways under fallen logs half buried in the soil.[1051]

a month and two months before the birds on which they are supposed to ride, an embarrassing fact that the authors of such delightful tales have lost sight of.[1055]

Have eagles carried off children?
There are no authentic instances of this occurrence in North America, but I am not prepared to say that throughout the world somewhere or other this has not occurred. In fact, it would be most extraordinary if it had not occurred at one time or another. The golden eagle is a bird powerful enough to carry off young sheep or deer weighing upwards of 10 or 11 pounds and I should say it was quite in the cards that the un-tended young of certain human primitive races or even of more civ-ilized races had occasionally been taken by these birds.[1056]

Where did the tale of groundhog day and seeing their shadows come from?
I do not know where this peculiar American fable arose. Possibly some of Seton's writings might throw some light on the matter.[1057]

Giant Pacific Horse

Equus pacificus [*Equus* sp.]
tooth found at Horsefly, BC

The discovery in 1922 of the 2nd lower premolar of a horse in the gold-bear-ing gravels 6 miles from Horse Fly Post Office in the Quesnel Lake region pro-vided the first evidence of this genus in the Pleistocene of British Columbia.[1052]

Carl also came to Cowan for some as-sistance with replying to some letters on cryptozoology from a fisheries researcher from the Cowichan days. The letter began:

"You know, you won't believe this, Dr. Carl, but I have a sasquatch living with me. I was going up Pitt River, and just at the entrance to Pitt Lake I heard an awful noise and I went ashore and here was a sasquatch who had had a fight with another sasquatch and it was badly beaten up so I took him on board my boat and took him up to my camp at Pitt Lake, and since then I've been feeding him back to health and learning a lot about sasquatches."

So Carl brought these letters over to me and said, "Ian, we have to follow these up, we've gotta see that sasquatch." And I told him that I had a perfectly good $10 bill that said he was being taken. I had a friend in the provincial police and he came back to me a few months later and said, "We've found research station X and he's the assistant there and is as mad as a hatter. He was a biology teacher at school so he knew the right lingo."[1058]

The 1941 correspondence was also full of their collaborations on amphibians and reptiles. Carl wrote to Cowan: "Dear Ian, The salamander arrived Tuesday afternoon but apparently it did not survive the trip. However, [Frank] Beebe made a sketch of it while it was still fresh."[1059] Cowan sends Carl the name of the "young chap who sent you frogs and salamanders from Stanley Park"[1060] and checks up on the delivery of a new red-legged frog for the vivarium to replace the one that died that summer of his son's birth, "Hope the *Rana aurora* arrived OK and all goes well."[1061]

Scammon Blackfish – "Squarehead" [Short-finned Pilot Whale]

Globicephala scammoni [G. macrorynchus]

Length to 20 feet. Black body frequently with white stripe on undersurface, expanding into heart-shaped figure on throat ... Head with prominent, bulging forehead and short, rim-like beak ... Known in British Columbia from one authentic sight record in Barclay [now Barkley] Sound and from unsubstantiated early reports from the Queen Charlotte area.[1053]

Most importantly, they started organizing their fieldwork for the spring to the Okanagan to look for amphibians, reptiles, fish and mammals (especially bats) to fill some gaps in the knowledge about Canada's only pocket "desert" (technically a semi-arid shrub-steppe). Two of the animals they were both very interested in were the Spadefoot Toad – an amphibian that had adapted to life in the desert – and the fabled and "ferocious" Pygmy Horned Lizard, which had only been documented twice in BC, though was relatively common in California deserts. At the time, the only known specimens of the latter were two taken at Osoyoos by the late Commander Charles de Blois Green at the turn of the century. They are now extirpated in BC.

Once all the planning was done, they left on May 18, 1941, in the museum truck, heading into the rain-shadow region east of the Coast Mountains. Carl describes May 20th in his journal:

> Up at 5:30, Ian finished skins of birds taken day before. Collected two Kingbirds before leaving about 8 am. Past Keremeos 1 mile collected 5 Hawk Sparrows [American Kestrel *Falco sparverius*] in open range brush land. Birds were calling *heech! heech! toodle ... oo!* And mating. Meadowlarks also present. Further along road collected Clark's Crow [Nutcracker] and caught downy young of Kildeers on road. Took photographs (colour) before killing bird. Saw Orioles, Red Wings, Quail (natural immigrant). Heard pheasant, Tanagers, Pee Wee, warblers, Ravens, Lewis Woodpecker, Magpie, King Birds, Mourning Dove. In pond on top of Richter Pass (4800') collected

Ambystoma larvae [salamander] and *Hyla* tadpoles [treefrogs]. Stopped at Spotted Lake on way down and collected *Phyllopods*. Water level much higher than when seen in May 1936. Fairy shrimps quite numerous along edge ... Brown string of eggs above ledge of water. Took colour pictures close up and also of lake ... Ian got 2 Northern Phalarope in lake. Set up camp in Cottonwood copse across lake from Osoyoos. Swim and supper. Set out 24 mousetraps at nightfall. Heard Spadefoots and *Hyla* along lake edge. Collected 5 Spadefoots.[1063]

·····························

Pygmy Horned Lizard
[Pygmy Short-horned Lizard]

Phrynosoma douglasii douglassii

General body form short and squat. Total length about 4¾ inches. Ears small, naked or covered with scales. Spines on head very short. Spines on upper and lower lips small but prominent. The Pygmy Horned Lizard is easily distinguished from all other reptiles by its flattened body and spiny appearance.[1062]

·····························

The description of the Spadefoots, as they appeared in the first museum guide to amphibians, captured the spirit of those moonlit evenings traipsing across the sand dunes and along the shorelines of the alkali lakes in search of the toads.[1064]

Cowan loved these animals and wrote about them rapturously. He talked about their ability to conserve moisture in the arid desert lands and the rapid transformation from egg to toadlet in a matter of days to take advantage of the brief appearance of pools of rainwater. The two men eventually tracked the Spadefoots half a mile from Spotted Lake – named after its circular alkali crust formations, hence the "spotted" – to their foraging grounds in the sand dunes. They measured the toads digging half a foot down for moisture under the sand. On the dunes, Cowan also found tracks of the White-tailed Jackrabbit. "They seem to spend their time playing and every sand dune bears their tracks."[1066] In various rain ponds, they found the breeding toad congregations in mid-amplexus. Amplexus is the mating clasp of the male where he grasps the female from behind to squeeze out the eggs and then fertilize them. One unfortunate Pacific Treefrog was mistakenly clasped in lust by a male Spadefoot, which Cowan reported was a fatal attraction. In the larger lakes, Cowan and Carl were seining for the various fish species of carp, perch, catfish, bass and suckers but also caught Western Painted Turtles in their various sizes and colours.

They were successful in collecting other reptiles for the museum such as Rattlesnakes, Wandering Garter Snakes and Western Blue Racers, but alas no horned lizards.

After a week of collecting around Osoyoos, they moved to White Lake, where they confirmed two pairs of breeding Long-billed Curlews, a species that hadn't been seen there since 1893, according to the same Commander Charles de Blois Green who had spotted the lizards. They picked up naturalist Sid Darcus and Adam Monk, a game warden and noted cougar hunter, to check out Penticton for rare birds and non-native problem rodents. Then they moved northward to look at ponds around Westbank

> … to collect frogs (*Rana pretiosa*) turtles, snakes (*Thamnophis sirtalis*) and a few leeches. Stopped at village to see Harold Menzies, the schoolteacher, who gave us a scorpion collected in the village. Drove on to ferry Kelowna and finally OK Landing, where we set up camp at J.A. Munro's garage. Visited Mr. Mackie at Vernon Prep. School, Coldstream, who kills rattlesnakes.[1069]

The visit to the Vernon Preparatory School would have provided a nice diversion for the dusty camping duo. Rev. Augustine ("Austin") Clark Mackie, an Anglican priest, was one of the Okanagan fraternity of naturalists that included Jim Munro, Mack Laing, Allan Brooks, Theed Pearse, George Spencer and Pat Martin. This collection of "men's men" had a regular migration back and forth between the coast and the Okanagan with the same regularity and timing as the Bufflehead ducks Munro had written about. Mackie was known as an avid naturalist, ornithologist (his bird collection was bequeathed to the Provincial Museum) and rattlesnake hunter. Rattlesnakes, great predators of rodents, were a consuming theme for many of them, for many reasons. As biologists, they ran into rattlers in the grasslands where, despite the species' intense shyness, the snakes were one of the few occupational hazards. All wise field scientists carried a "snake kit."

The Mackie family is another dynasty of naturalist–academics whose lives have intersected with Cowan's over the decades. Austin Mackie's youngest son, Patrick, was a well-known naturalist and local historian. George Mackie, a nephew of Rev. Mackie, who spent his childhood years hunting snakes in Vernon with his uncle, was a well-known BC marine evolutionary biologist at the University of Victoria focused on glass sponges and tunicates.[1071] George's son Richard Mackie is Mack

**Western Spadefoot Toad
[Great Basin Spadefoot Toad]**

*Scaphiopus hammondi
[Spea intermontana]*

The Western Spadefoot toad may be distinguished from the Northwestern toad [Western Toad, *Anxyrus boreas*] by the vertical pupil, black spur on the hind foot and lack of the median strip down the back … The Spadefoot toad is one of the least commonly seen of our tailless amphibians, since it spends a great deal of its time underground, emerging only at night [1065]

Laing's biographer. Mackie Lake House, a large Arts & Crafts-style residence that sheltered many a naturalist coming to the Okanagan, is now a heritage site.

Rattlesnakes from Osoyoos provide another story concerning Cowan. As a little girl, Trisha Guiguet, Charles Guiguet's daughter, was staying with the Pat Martin family for a summer holiday in Kamloops. Cowan had been charged with bringing her back to the coast in the mid-50s:

> When Ian came to the Martins' house, he'd been down in Osoyoos. He had rattlesnakes in his boots and we drove all the way back to UBC with rattlesnakes in them. He had lace-up boots, and the rattlesnakes would be down inside. He wanted them alive for some reason, and that's where they were. I was about 12. Awful trip.[1072]

Trisha Guiguet wasn't completely daunted by her experience and went on to work at the museum and the provincial Fish and Wildlife Branch. In 1993, when rattlesnake populations were last evaluated,[1073] no one knew how many were left. They were placed on a provincial species at risk list, where they remain.

On June 4, 1941, Cowan and Carl moved camp to Kamloops, Cowan's old stomping grounds from his first job with the Dominion Entomological Lab, to meet up with George Spencer and Ron Buckell. The two entomologists were keen to team up with the vertebrate zoologist to get access to the lice and ticks that inhabited the birds and mammals Cowan was collecting. They all headed up the dirt track in a downpour to the old schoolhouse–cabin owned by Spencer at Lac du Bois, located smack in the middle of the rolling hill country north of Kamloops. Over the course of the week, they visited McQueen Lake, Pass Lake and Bachelor Lake to sample water quality, determine amphibian populations and the timing of breeding cycles, do an extensive bird survey and trap

Western Painted Turtle

Chrysemys picta belli

The Western Painted Turtle can be distinguished readily from the Pacific terrapin by the brilliant colour pattern on the underparts and by the longitudinal stripes on head, neck and limbs ... The Western Painted Turtle is nearly always found in or near water. Its favourite habitat is a permanent pond or small lake, but occasionally it is also found along the margins of large lakes, such as Osoyoos Lake and Okanagan Lake in the interior of the province. In these places turtles are commonly seen resting on floating logs or other objects near the water where they bask in the sun for many hours a day.[1067]

Western Blue Racer
[Western Yellow-bellied Racer]

Coluber constrictor mormon

General form long and slender. Total length up to 48 inches. Head distinct from the neck: large, long with flattened top and rounded snout. Eye large and regular ... Little is known regarding the breeding habits of this snake ... A female collected and sent to the Museum on July 2, 1941, by Mr. H.C. Dalziel of Okanagan Landing laid a batch of five eggs on July 18.[1068]

for small mammals. During this time, they encountered a mother black bear, which Cowan shot.

Bear taxonomy was part of the Darwinian evolutionary puzzle for BC. Getting data on large carnivores that had wider geographic ranges presented the kind of intellectual challenge Cowan relished. He had been researching black bears while in Victoria at the museum, where he had had easy access to the provincial archive rooms next door, run by his friend W.K. Lamb.

In the archives were the notebooks of Hudson's Bay Company chief factor James Douglas, who had kept careful records of every pelt that had passed through the ten or so fur-trading forts under his watch in the company's territory, stretching north to Bella Bella (Fort McLoughlin), east to Kamloops and south to Washington. Douglas noted not only the type of pelts but their colour phases, since these represented different prices. When sorted out as to region, each fort's skins presented graphic evidence of the geographical distribution of the different colours of the bears.[1075] It was another case of Gloger's Rule. The bears in the dry grassland Kamloops region were categorized as the light Cinnamon bear subspecies, getting blacker as they moved to the wetter (more colour-saturated) coast.

Pacific Rattlesnake [Northern Pacific Rattlesnake]

Crotalus viridis oreganus
[Crotalus oreganus oreganus]

The Pacific Rattlesnake is easily recognized by the presence of a button, or rattle, on the end of the tail and by the distinctive colour pattern of the back ... The rattlesnake is perhaps the most interesting reptile to some persons because it is the only venomous species occurring within the province. It is usually found in dry areas where there is some shelter from the sun, such as at the base of rockslides, and in sagebrush country containing boulders and other places of retreat ... In BC rattlesnakes congregate in "dens" partway up a bluff to spend the winter. Sometimes a hundred or more snakes are found in these hibernating places, and while still sluggish are easily killed. According to Rev. Austin C. Mackie, of Vernon, BC, who has kept records for over twenty years, rattlesnakes are seldom seen in the fall later than September 15...[1070]

Coastal varieties were known as Black Bears, with the occasional chocolate-brown overlaps and vice versa. The types from Vancouver Island and QCI (Haida Gwaii) were very black but fell into their own subspecies, again based on their greater size and massive skulls, the theory being that they were essentially filling a niche left vacant by the absence of Grizzlies on these particular islands. There was also the Kermode subspecies, which had been defined on some skull traits, not the white phase which occurs in about 10 per cent of the population due to a recessive gene.

On that 1941 day in the field, what grabbed Cowan's imagination was that the female was black in traditionally "cinnamon" country. After he had shot her, three cubs appeared: two black and one cinnamon, which he also shot. Cowan was building the vertebrate museum at UBC, so the need to capture "uniqueness" to test dispersal theories was strong. He was also hot on his mission to provide data about predators and their diet. With the entomologists on hand to identify invertebrates in the stomachs, Cowan dissected all four bears. He recorded the stomach contents of the female as three quarts of vegetation, a pint of ants and some larvae, with similar proportions for the young, then notes the female "was still milking slightly." No evidence of domestic cattle, losses of which ranchers were keen to attribute to bears. He traced the mother bear's back trail to an aspen tree, which she had climbed, as he did, to "open a sapsucker nest, in which there were young."[1076]

American Black Bear

Ursus americanus

Large, bulky, carnivorous mammals with highly variable weights ranging in adults from 125 to over 600 pounds. Colour varies from jet black through brown, bluish to white, depending upon geographic location.[1074]

Black Bear ecology continued to interest Cowan during his research in the Rockies. Finally, in 1959, he and his graduate student Charles Jonkel embarked on a seven-year field study of the Big Creek Black Bears outside of Glacier National Park. Looking deeply into the bears' ecology,[1077] the study examined how they interacted with their environment and what forces came into play to affect their numbers. The hypothesis was that food and climate accounted for the biggest changes in population, but Jonkel and Cowan also wanted to look at the role of predators, parasites, diseases and evolution and even test out the genetic theory of their colleague Dennis Chitty:

> This was pretty hands-on stuff. We set live traps for the bears – padded traps so they didn't hurt their feet. We had about 140 bears marked. One of the things that [Jonkel] was particularly interested in showing was that the death rate in the second year was about 60%, about 5% in the first year. The bear's a very good mother but that first year after graduation was tough. And very few of them survived it, and that's got to be so, or we'd be knee deep in bears.[1078]

In 1970 Cowan presented on the status and conservation of bears of the world[1079] at a conference sponsored by the International Union for Conservation of Nature and Natural Resources. The basic recommendation: manage people, not the bears.

During the trip in the Kamloops region in 1941, bird predators were also of great interest to Cowan for their role in controlling rodent populations. He was equally keen to determine bird predator diets. He spotted a goshawk nest, so climbed up the twenty feet from the ground into a fir tree to see what was in the nest, and shot the entire family to examine the contents of their stomachs. Goshawks were normally thought of as preying on birds, but Cowan found Columbian Ground Squirrels in all their stomachs.

The other outcome of the fieldwork was a realization that there were many questions regarding the bats, an animal that was far from understood in 1941. Although we now know that the Okanagan has the greatest diversity of bats in Canada, with 14 summer-resident species, there were notable gaps in knowledge about these mammals then. Cowan was to briefly revisit the bats and the Okanagan the following summer to get a better understanding of species in mid-season. He believed then that most of BC's bats were migratory and suspected he and Carl had started their research too early in the spring. The Silver Haired Bat was present, but it was the only one Cowan knew overwintered. Today we know that most of them do overwinter. All the rest of the bats caught that spring he simply lists under the genus *Myotis*, to be identified and analyzed back in the lab later that summer.[1081] There was one exception, the Fringed Myotis, which was found in the attic of a house in Vernon occupied by a Mr. Chapman, whom Carl and Cowan visited.

Whether Cowan was watching for bats or listening to the chorus of the mating toads, these sensory images of the

Juvenile **Northern Goshawk**

Accipiter gentilis

Rare to uncommon resident throughout the province, including Vancouver
Island and the Queen Charlotte
Islands ... Dense mature stands of coniferous forest are the most often reported breeding habitats; mixed woodlands and pure deciduous stands,
which vary in size from small groves
to large forests, are also used ... Nests
were positioned in main crotches, in
forks of branches, against the trunk or
on the broken tops of trees. One nest
was built on top of an old Red Squirrel
nest. Nests were fairly large structures
of coarse sticks and twigs....[1080]

grasslands and in particular the sand dunes resonated with him. They certainly animated his lectures. One of his popular talks, called "The Frigid Desert" (also "Desert Lecture"), described Canada's unique ecosystem and the animals that have adapted to its harsh conditions. His lecture notes started out with the Spadefoot Toads and their extraordinary ability to sense rainfall, which triggers their migration to temporary rain ponds for a brief courtship and hatchings.[1083] He also wove in stories of the White-tailed Jackrabbit playing in the dunes, with its long legs and ears evolved to disperse heat; the Great Basin Pocket Mouse, with its cheeks stuffed full of seeds from redgrass; the Fairy Shrimp, ancient crustaceans, surviving in the alkali lakes as if in vestigial seas; the elusive Pygmy Horned Lizard burying itself to sit motionless waiting for ants; and the chemical-producing cacti that "deter creatures that would seek their stored water."[1084]

Cowan's lectures were electrifying for his students and moved several generations of biologists to point their lenses at the area, both to better understand it and to protect it. Human activities in the Okanagan have had a profound impact on all these grassland and semi-arid species, and no biologist or wildlife manager could avoid the evidence that agriculture and urbanization were some of the greatest threats. Cowan found his greatest ally in this regard at UBC, in his friend and guru of the grasslands Bert Brink. Cowan described him as "an agronomist by training and a geneticist by trade, keenly involved in environment from the very beginning ... He was ahead of the game in his concern for the environment."[1085]

This was hardly a surprise, as Brink was another acolyte of the 'B.' Bert Brink was a Cub Scout when the Burrard Field-Naturalists, under Kenneth Racey, had taken yet another young Scout under their wing. Wrote Brink:

> They were not scientists, but were skillful, dedicated naturalists from very different walks of life. They were always courteous and informative to both the curious and interested; they appreciated the fact that curiosity and wonder often precede interest, that *curiositas* precedes *studiositas*.[1086]

Mr. Racey's rodent collection was the biggest attraction to the young Brink, but he was also captivated by Frank Muskett (of the Muskett naturalist family), who taught him "to appreciate the beauty of an individual flower."[1087] Cowan's zoological interests together with Brink's botanical bent made a dynamic duo, and they were doing fieldwork and publishing papers together within two years of Cowan joining the faculty. Cowan thrived on the collaboration. Both men would go on to receive the highest civilian awards of their country and their province – the Order of Canada and the Order of British Columbia.

> You see to the extent that you know, and you can put two people from different backgrounds into the same environment and they won't see the same things at all. It's a little hard to explain. When I go through an area with people like Bert, Bert will see the grasses, the forbs, and the way they are put together. He'll know them in detail. He may see some wildlife, but he may not count them.[1088]

Cowan was also benefiting from Carl's unique background in fish and reptiles. The two returned home in the middle of June to clean up their "skulls and skeletons." They continued to correspond frequently on their results, discussing the bats, their analysis of toad reproduction and Cowan makes a rare mention of his own progeny:

> About the Scaphiopus, the abundant tracks on the big sand dune half a mile from the lake. There it was obvious that the toads were merely foraging nightly and not undertaking a mating migration.... In my last letter I had meant to ask you if you have any objections to my including the Osoyoos bats in a note recording the discovery of another species new to Canada at Vancouver. I am off to Alta Lake on Monday and don't look forward to the seven-hour boat and train ride with our young dynamo. I hope to get some writing done up there...[1089]

The summer fieldwork in the Okanagan was over but the conservation work all over the province never stopped. For the rest of their long lives, Cowan and Brink became tireless advocates for a protected area in the south Okanagan. They both sat on the boards of the organizations that spearheaded conservation efforts: The Nature Trust of BC (established in 1971) and the Habitat Conservation Trust Foundation (a quasi-governmental funding organization, supported by hunting and fishing licence revenue, which Cowan and Brink helped establish in 1981). Frustrated by government inaction, the two led the South Okanagan Conservation Strategy initiative in 1990,[1090] which laid down a five-year plan to protect the critical habitats of the south Okanagan over a large enough area that species would survive. The objective was for all levels of government and non-profits to carve out their roles in an integrated plan, with a national park to be part of the mix. White Lake Biodiversity Ranch was bought by The Nature Trust of BC while Cowan and Brink were on the Trust's board, and the organization has since acquired well over a dozen properties in the south Okanagan. At the time of both their deaths, a national park still had not been created, which was a huge sadness to them both.

In 2013 the provincial government designated the McTaggart-Cowan/nsək'łniw't Wildlife Management Area on the east side of Skaha Lake in the south Okanagan, protecting 6491 hectares of habitat for species at risk, most notably Bighorn Sheep, which use the area for lambing and foraging. The Penticton Indian Band co-manage the area. The name nsək'łniw't – "a gash on the side" – is in Nsyilxcen, the oral language of the Syilx people. The site is contiguous with the Okanagan Falls Biodiversity Ranch, another of the conservation projects led by The Nature Trust of BC under the guidance of Cowan and Brink.

There is a footnote to story of the Pygmy Horned Lizard, which manoeuvred itself back into Cowan's life. Helen Stewart, a naturalist, author and illustrator who had grown up around (and later worked in) the zoology department at Berkeley, moved into the Cowans' Victoria neighbourhood. She had kept these lizards in her Berkeley bedroom as a girl, having been introduced to the desert by the renowned herpetologist Robert Stebbins and his family. While she was doing some illustrations of Canadian reptiles, she wrote to Stebbins (also an accomplished artist, who created his own illustrations for his famous guides to California reptiles) for information. He replied that the obvious person to start with was Ian McTaggart Cowan. She tracked him down only to discover he lived 50 metres up the street, and they became friends. Stebbins died at age 98, having played a major role in establishing the Mohave National Preserve, among myriad other conservation projects.

The bats of BC continued to interest Cowan throughout his life. Bat researchers Brock Fenton, Gregory Woodsworth and G.P. Bell from Carlton University and Stan van Zyll de Jong of the Canadian Museum of Nature came out to the Okanagan in 1979 to detect bats using echolocation sonograph machines. In the course of recording bats, they not only reconfirmed the presence of the Pallid Bats that Cowan had collected there 60 years earlier, but found the first Spotted Bat for Canada. Cowan wrote Woodsworth in 1981 to congratulate the team and get information on the bat so he could update his *Mammals of BC* list. At the time, he was also sitting on the World Wildlife Fund selection committee for grants and supported the group's applications to establish the status of both bats.

Spotted Bat

Euderma maculatum

This is a large bat with a striking colour pattern. Overall colour black with large white patches at the base of the ears, base of the shoulders and on the lower back ... Only a few specimens of this bat [only 1 from BC] are known, but recent studies in British Columbia using sonographic techniques and line capture...[1091]

Woodsworth wrote back to Cowan: "It may be of interest that since the discovery of *Euderma*, it has been afforded protection ... I hope this information has been of some use to you in the revision of your handbook."[1092] In 2005 the federal government listed the Spotted Bat as a species of special concern. Cowan never did revise the handbook, leaving that task to David Nagorsen, who completed it in 1993. Unfortunately, little work has been done since that time on the protection of the Spotted Bat. It remains a species at risk on both sides of the border.

The summer of '41 was a significant moment in the evolution of mammalogy. There were various undercurrents at work. It was wartime, and according to US historian Gary Gray, "War years are wasted years, years when respect for any form of life – wild or human – is diminished ... The years from 1941–1945 were no exception."[1093] Many of Cowan's contemporaries were heading off to war. Budgets were also redirected to the war effort. Opportunists were looking to unlock the bounty of the parks and refuges, whether for big-game hunting, hydro development or forestry. Pressure was on the mammalogists to justify their existence. Cowan was at the front of the cohort moving away from what William Lidicker, a younger colleague from Berkeley, characterized as the earlier "preoccupation" with "documenting the occurrences and distribution of species and subspecies of animals"[1094] and toward quantification and applied wildlife management. To accurately determine numbers, they were now using methods that recognized that "populations are not collections of identical individuals, and that these assemblages of individuals also have features beyond those of the individuals that make them up."[1095] In the background, though, they were working against the ever-present threat that if they wanted wildlife at all, they had better come up with an economic rationalization for it.

After 1941 Cowan was venturing down all these paths with even less time in his day. His next foray into the field would find him counting populations and describing individuals, an idea that was to take zoology up another notch in understanding. First, though, he had to launch what he called his first biopolitical campaign!

CHAPTER 24

*"Our dilemma may become that of the mole in the mating
season – with relatively well-formed immediate objectives
but no sure idea of which way to go to achieve them."*

Fraser Valley, 1941–1942

The next academic year was full for Cowan getting his fledgling wildlife management course off the ground. "The teaching week was five and a half days, classes were crowded, life was busy and interesting."[1096] He writes to Carl in September of 1941, now that the amphibian book is underway, with his modest proposal:

> Do you want me to go ahead with a similar handbook of the mammals? The unbroken ground will make it quite a long job – one that can hardly be adequately covered before this time next year – at least. However, inasmuch as there is virtually no other publication covering the mammals of our region, I feel that the job would be well worth doing. I already have the literature well in hand and several groups worked up fairly well.
> Sincerely,
> Ian.[1097]

He underestimated the "long job" and couldn't have anticipated Joyce's third, and again unsuccessful, pregnancy, nor the national war rationing to conserve gasoline that limited his mobility. Over the next 18 months, he stayed close to home, making only short forays with the family to sort out a variety of mammalian mysteries in the Fraser River valley. His parents-in-law had bought a farm at Huntingdon near J.W. Winson's place and close to the US border. There were many pairs of Racey and Cowan eyes now watching to record new species moving into Canada from the south, from the cottontail rabbit to opossums. The region was also the epicentre of moles, mountain beavers and other species whose northern boundary was the Fraser. This included five different insectivores that weren't found anywhere else in Canada: all three of BC's moles, including Canada's largest and rarest one, Townsend's Mole, the smaller Coast Mole and the fossil-like Shrew-mole; and two specialist shrews, Trowbridge's Shrew and the Pacific Water Shrew. This made nine insectivores in all collected on the farm, once he added in his old friends the generalist shrews, Common, Dusky and Vagrant, which managed to find their way everywhere. Huntingdon farm to this day figures disproportionately as a biodiversity hot spot in the museum collections of Canada. With such biodiversity in just this group alone, Cowan had plenty to keep him busy, and close to home.

For the next 50 years, the only information and breeding populations known for Townsend's Mole in Canada were the Huntingdon moles documented by Racey and the Cowans.[1099] During later years, Joyce Cowan was to continue the mole research while Cowan was away in the field. Cowan writes to Joyce in 1944 while away in the Rockies: "Your mole episode sounds most amusing, they are tough beggars to skin even at the best of times so I can imagine your troubles."[1100]

Unfortunately, there was far more interest in the economic development of the Fraser Valley and eradication of moles than in the study of their evolutionary history or well-being – even if they were our evolutionary ancestors. It wasn't until 1995 that other populations of moles were even found – just northwest of the farm. This precipitated the listing of Townsend's Mole as endangered. Being such a specialist species, unlike the widely distributed Coast Mole, this mole is restricted to a particular soil type that occurs in a small area around Huntingdon. The soil is also prime agricultural land, hence the conflict. These somewhat doomed moles earned a place in Cowan's heart during those years and led to his famous 1955 mole metaphor on the perils of specialization (see page 259).

Townsend Mole [Townsend's Mole]

Scapanus townsendi [townsendii]

The Townsend Mole occurs in the same region of British Columbia as is occupied by the Coast Mole, but the two are easily separable on size alone. Adult *S. townsendi* always measure more than 190 mm total length, while *S. o. orarius* adults measure less than that figure. The Townsend Mole has a very limited distribution in Canada, where it crosses the international boundary only for a mile or two in the vicinity of Huntingdon in the lower Fraser Valley.[1098]

Trowbridge Shrew

(also in photo above)

Sorex trowbridgii trowbridgii

A medium-sized shrew, total length about 4½ inches.... twenty–six specimens from Huntingdon and Cultus Lake measured.[1108]

Fittingly, later in this speech, Cowan used another vivid wildlife metaphor, this time of the Sharp-tailed Grouse, to demonstrate a concept that was also close to his heart:

> One caution I would make to future planners, authors and editors of our conferences: In the spring, as the prairie chickens [Sharp-tailed

Grouse] converge on their booming grounds and the wildlife men follow suit, let us not lose sight of the fundamental point that while noise may be the obvious feature of the booming ground activity, fertility is the most important one...[1101]

Much like the Sharp-tailed Grouse, the specialist small-mammal insectivores have not fared well. Their habitat has been encroached upon by the rapidly expanding suburbs of Vancouver. One of the last technical review committees Cowan served on was for a survey of Burns Bog, which lies on the southern side of the Fraser Valley, not too far from Huntingdon. The biologists, including Cowan's student Mark Fraker,[1102] found Trowbridge's Shrew (*Sorex trowbridgii*), Pacific Water-shrew (*Sorex bendirii*) and Southern Red-backed Vole (*Myodes gapperi occidentalis*) in the unique lowland bog.[1103]

Cowan had found this rare vole 50 years earlier, as described in *Mammals of BC*. It was thought to have been extirpated until found again at Burns Bog by the 1999 study. The vole and Pacific Water-shrew are listed by the province as threatened and the latter is a federal species at risk.[1105] Trowbridge's Shrew is listed provincially as vulnerable.[1106] Similar to the mole in its limited distribution, this shrew species seemed to have its entire population centred in this area where the Racey–Cowan cohort collected. Cowan even took the Vancouver naturalists to see them in 1945: "...Dr. Cowan set a trapline the day before and as the party proceeded along the lakeshore, various specimens were collected, including white-footed [deer] mouse, wandering [vagrant] shrew and dusky shrew. Other species observed in the marsh were muskrats, ...the blue [Trowbridge's] shrew and the two shrews of which we saw [trapped] specimens."[1107]

Ultimately the presence of so many rare mammals led to a large chunk of the bog being bought and protected by the federal government. The federal Minister of Environment of the day, David Anderson, from Victoria and a supporter of Cowan, had a large role to play in securing the federal money. The Burns Bog reports also altered the proposed route of the South Fraser Highway to avoid the most critical habitat of the vole. One of the report authors, Royal BC Museum paleoecologist Richard Hebda, described Cowan this way:

> Don't be deceived by Ian, he is a fighter all the way. During the legal debate over the protection of Burns Bog recently, there was Ian arguing that it is the only place in Canada that you'll find the Western Red-backed Vole. He found the first one for science back

Western Red-backed Vole [Southern Red-backed Vole]

Clethrionomys occidentalis occidentalis [Myodes gapperi occidentalis]

The dull-brownish *microtus*-like colour pattern, with the red dorsal stripe barely distinguishable, makes this species easily separable from *gapperi* ... Known only from the extreme south coast, south of Burrard Inlet.[1104]

in the 1930s and he's damned if he's going to see them wiped out by a highway.[1109]

Cowan's extensive knowledge of the lower mainland mammals had been honed during those war years around the Raceys' Huntingdon farm. Cultus Lake, just east of Huntingdon, was another interesting place from the perspective of island biogeography, as the watershed of the lake forms a natural barrier for southern lowland species that could work their way north up the valley. At Cultus, Cowan tried to figure out the migratory nature and distinguishing features of the small bats that flitted across the border with no regard for political boundaries.

Another southern finger of lowland habitat pushing up into the mountains close to Vancouver is Indian Arm. Cowan and Brink travelled up the Arm by ferry for a few days in the winter to hunt venison and check out the flora and fauna. Cowan wrote Carl about their adventures.

> During the last weekend Bert Brink and I were up Indian River some five or six miles and while up there found an adult *Ascaphus* [Tailed Frog] sitting in the middle of the trail. The precise locality was close to a small creek tributary to the Indian River about four miles from the head of Indian Arm. We can add this to our present notes.[1111]

The only other museum notes for tailed frogs were from Hatzic Lake, near Mission, BC, supplied by Kenneth Graham of the Dominion Department of Agriculture. The specimen was collected early in September of 1941 while Graham was travelling along Cascade Creek. Carl wrote Cowan about the amazing resilience of their first live Coastal Tailed Frog. "The specimen was carried in the pocket [of Graham] until camp was made, after which it was transferred to an empty can, where it remained until Sept 15 when it was delivered to the Provincial Museum at Victoria. The toad was then placed in a small vivarium, where it is still living at the time of writing."[1113]

Another animal that Cowan had "spotty" information about made its presence felt up Indian Arm. "A *Spilogale* woke me several times as he investigated ourselves and belongings and stamped his disapproval."[1114]

Yuma Myotis

Myotis yumanensis saturatus

A small brown bat with large hind feet, distinguishable only with difficulty from *Myotis lucifugus* … One characteristic of this species is the lustreless hair tips and almost woolly hair texture … Critical identification depends upon the skull. Migrates except possibly on the extreme southern coast. Little else is known of the habits of this species in British Columbia.[1110]

Tailed Toad [Coastal Tailed Frog]

Ascaphus truei

The male Tailed Toad may be easily recognized by the conspicuous "tail" a structure found in no other toad or frog … This rarely seen toad is most often found in the vicinity of cold mountain streams at altitudes ranging from near sea level to about 6,000 feet.[1112]

Cowan also took the family by train up to Alta Lake where they could all help fine-tune the subspecies of jumping mice while never missing an opportunity to record birds. His journal entry for September 9, 1942, at Alta Lake recorded a large list of residents, such as Spotted Owls, as well as some late migrants. The most stunning of the latter were the handsome Hooded Mergansers amongst the loons and grebes on the lake.[1116]

The Cowan family joined the mergansers on their migration back to the coast for the school year. Despite his best efforts, there was no way Cowan was going to pull together the mammal guide within the year. He was also launching his public lecture campaign against Canada's bounty system, not a lightweight issue. There was virtually no public awareness of the problem then, even on the campus of a higher-learning institution such as UBC. It was a situation about which he had a clear opinion:

> Oh, this province was pathetic. Every creature that ate anything with meat in it had a bounty on its head. We had bounties on crows and ravens and eagles. I remember one of the game wardens boasting to me that he had shot 50 eagles on the UBC campus in the previous five years. That was criminal! He couldn't understand why I wasn't enthusiastic.[1118]

Cowan's first radio address, "In Defence of Predators," was broadcast in the spring of 1942,[1119] as part of a series sponsored by the Vancouver Society for the Prevention of Cruelty to Animals. Other academic colleagues were roped into delivering talks, such as George Spencer, who spoke on "The Balance of Nature." Cowan developed three strong arguments for the campaign in defence of predators: predators prevent unnatural abundances of prey species; they keep the prey populations healthy; and they keep rodent populations down, which is essential in the fight to prevent diseases and adverse agricultural impacts. He argued that without predators, prey populations tend to increase dramatically and individual animals get sick and die from disease or starvation. And because predators naturally target the sick and ailing ones, the prey population that remains is healthier. These points particularly interested members of the SPCA.[1120]

With Clemens's blessing, Cowan and his Fisheries colleague J.R. Dymond in

---

[Western] Spotted Skunk

Spilogale gracilis latifrons

This small skunk is black in colour with a pattern of white lines, spots and irregular markings along the back from the head to the tail ... The anal glands produce a strong-smelling oil that can be ejected to a distance of several feet.[1115]

Hooded Merganser

Lophodytes cucullatus

On the south coast, autumn migration is evident in late October and may carry into early December. The centre of winter distribution on the coast appears to be the Strait of Georgia ... At least 1,000 birds winter there.[1117]

Toronto were the main instigators of the campaign, and the radio series kicked off what would become a very long struggle to eradicate the bounty system in Canada. Cowan described it as a talking campaign.

> Remember, there was no television, and very little radio (the radio was invented when I was a child)… so it was personal talking … anybody that could be talked to was talked to. We gave hundreds of lectures. We went to all the sportsmen, because in most cases the administrator wasn't thinking about these things; he got pressure from the sportsmen.[1121]

Working hard with them were Cowan's stalwart 'B' vanguard, BC Game Commissioners Jim Cunningham and Frank Butler. Butler established a small group of advisers, which included Cowan, and that group led the policy charge from behind the scenes while Cunningham orchestrated the public lecture series for Cowan at the various clubs and societies.

Dymond was doing the same thing back east and the 'B' network provided the venues in between. Cowan felt in hindsight that what ultimately swung public sentiment against the bounty was something he hadn't reckoned on – the level of corruption their investigations exposed:

> For instance, the year that the Yukon stopped giving a bounty, there was something like 600 or 700 wolves bountied in Telegraph Creek. Now, there had never been more than just a few before that … The local office was being run by a woman who had grown up in that area and she thought, "Oh, there aren't any wolves up in that country and never have been," so she found it to be straight fraud. There were two people up there just working the system. About the same time there were coyote pelts coming in the front door and going out the back window and coming round 'til they were almost threadbare they'd been round so many times. It took us 10 years, but we beat the system. In ten years there was not a bounty paid on anything anywhere in BC, in Canada, except seals, hair seals.[1122]

It took more than 10 years. The bounty for coyote wasn't removed until 1954, for wolf in 1955 and for cougar in 1957. Bounties paid out by the provincial government in 1953 overall were $45,645 and by 1956 they were down to $7,420.[1123] Lyn Hancock, in her historical analysis of the ending of the bounty in BC, states that Cowan was "directly responsible for improving attitudes to predators in British Columbia."[1124] Asked in an interview why he chose the lecture campaign over other, more direct forms of political protest, he replied:

> I've always believed in quiet diplomacy. I have never stood on the line with a placard. That's all right, you need the ultra campaigners … they stand for the club and if you're talking to a mule, you have to

get his attention. Once you've got his attention, then you can start educating.[1125]

To prove the value of predators, the 'B' needed not just a lecture campaign but a high-profile research project. On May 22, 1997, a spry, 87-year-old Cowan strode onto the stage of the University of Northern British Columbia[1126] and began telling the story, to a packed auditorium of students, teachers and parents, about the project that was to turn the tide in favour of big predators:

> In the 1930s, when I was into my graduate studies, [predators] were outcast, all of them – with a price on their heads. The BC and US governments were embarked upon a campaign to eliminate the last wolf in the nation – by any means conceivable – and they were almost successful. In the 1940s our western national parks were under siege by a group of wolf haters among the Alberta sportsman associations who claimed that Banff and Jasper were breeding grounds for multitudes of wolves and mountain lion that flowed out into Alberta, ravaging the big game and livestock of the province.[1127]

The national parks became the scientific battleground to prove or disprove those claims. J.B. Harkin, the commissioner of Canada's national parks and co-founder of the 'B', had made gallant attempts to bring in the scientific approach to wildlife management. He had faltered and stumbled without a sufficiently high-profile researcher. The 'B' knew they had to provide the evidence in favour of predators and they knew the Rocky Mountain national parks were the place to do it. Cowan described how the study was triggered by the infamous letter from Bill Fisher of the Calgary Fish and Game Association, published in *Rod and Gun in Canada* magazine.[1128] Historian E.J. Hart documents that the elite Calgary association's motivation was to have "the park thrown open for big-game hunting, on the premise that game populations were being wiped out by predators anyway."[1129]

William "Bill" Chauncey Fisher was a perfect foil for the 'B' in every way. A prominent Calgary lawyer and big-game hunter, his land, according to the *Ottawa Citizen* newspaper in 1955, "gushed oil."[1130] He was loud and brash, and his biggest boast was a legal decision in his favour concerning natural gas rights flowing with his oil. The article on Fisher's African safari to "bag a lion" provides some indication of the moneyed interests that were marshalled against the campaign:

> The two-month safari itself cost $9,000. What with the cost of mounting his massive trophies ("I'll have to build a new wing on my home when they arrive from London") and a week in Paris plus a more restful week in London, realization of the boyhood dream cost him $13,000 [just under $115,000 today, based on the Consumer Price Index]. But he gets that repaid in thrill dividends just telling about his lion. "My safari consisted of a white hunter, Geoff Lawrence-Brown, 13 negro natives, one Land Rover ... and a five-ton truck

on which was included a refrigerator for making my own drinks."[1131]

Fisher and his push for mountain lion and bighorn sheep trophies was not the only threat to the national parks. Calgary Power had been lobbying for years for a dam on Lake Minnewanka, and suddenly, in December 1940, the Mackenzie King government made an Order in Council under the War Measures Act, executively amending the 1930 National Parks Act to allow the dam.[1132] The few concessions Harkin had won against industrial development in the parks during the Depression were rapidly being eroded for "war purposes." With the gathering storm in Europe, the 'B's rearguard defence of predators was in jeopardy. In 1939 Harkin had asked mammalogist C.H.D. Clarke (another member of the 'B') to do an early reconnaissance of the wildlife of Banff National Park. Clarke, who had moved from the National Museum to the Canadian Wildlife Service, spent July and August of that year in the park counting animals. He prepared a 25-page report on numbers of game and the status of various predators and recommended that Canada adopt the policy articulated in a November 17, 1938, speech by Colonel James Stevenson-Hamilton, superintendent of Kruger National Park, where "complete protection is given to all animals and plants without distinctions between predators and others."[1133]

Behind the scenes, members of the 'B' were fighting for predators and even for their jobs. Bill Fisher, nicknamed Cougar Bill, was lobbying Ottawa hard on all fronts with his colleagues from the Calgary faction of the Alberta Fish and Game Association, dentist R.A. Rooney and lawyer Austin de B. Winter, to increase the cougar bounty. His approach was to canvass all the guides, outfitters and hunters, bring them over to his side, and deliver the report to Ottawa. At an executive meeting in Mr. Fisher's Calgary law office on May 11, 1940,

> It was urged by this executive present that the provincial bounty be raised to $25. Mr. Wallace explained that he was already in touch with Ottawa for the review of the situation, urging Dominion authorities to assist the province in a reduction of these pests, as well as a grant to increase the bounty in a reasonable manner. Dr. R.A. Rooney, VP, will visit Ottawa and take this matter up this week (May 14th) and it is hoped some action will result from his visit.[1136]

A month later Rooney mused with Winter:

From the big-game standpoint, our mountain national parks are the

Rocky Mountain Bighorn Sheep

Ovis canadensis canadensis

The western slope of the Rocky Mountains from the Crowsnest Pass and Bull River north to just south of Golden and at the head of Sheep Creek north of Mount Robson.[1134] The horns of large males constitute one of the most sought-after of the big-game trophies. The largest heads come from the Rocky Mountain area adjacent to Fernie.[1135]

greatest potential menace to big game in the country, and while men may laugh at Fisher and call him Cougar Bill, there is no question at all but what he says is absolutely true, and what he says about it doesn't begin to give a quarter of the picture. Just today a letter came in from one of the guides in Jasper, probably as well acquainted with the whole of the northern half of the mountain areas as any man, and he says that, on reliable authorship, he is informed that Ottawa has again forbidden the destruction of any predators. He also says that there are more coyotes and they are doing more damage than he has ever known in any one year, all of which doesn't make very pleasant reading.[1137]

Harkin officially "retired" immediately after this letter was sent, although there is no evidence that this was directly attributable to Fisher and his lobby.[1138] A new controller of the National Parks Bureau, James Smart, was appointed in Ottawa. Smart was quietly sympathetic to Harkin and managed to keep the pressure on for a scientific assessment of the wildlife. Clarke repeated the study in both Jasper and Banff in the winter and spring of 1941. He cited the conclusions of the symposium on predator control at the 1941 North American Wild Life Conference (the conference the 'B' dovetailed with their meetings), which "indicates clearly that even in managing areas where the game is harvested by hunting, a great deal of predator control has been wasted effort, and before the problem can be intelligently appreciated *careful investigations have to made on each area*"[1139] [emphasis by present author]. He cautioned that "the question of predators still remains a contentious one with certain individuals and organizations outside the parks."[1140]

The certain individuals were Fisher, by then president of the Alberta Fish and Game Association, and his Calgary colleagues, who continued to strike back, both within their group and at park officials. At their 14th annual convention in 1942 (the slogan "Game is a crop" graced all the literature), Fisher gave his presidential address, which included "the need to stress why the government should support this parent association financially and otherwise; …that all game and fish both in the national parks and outside in the province should come under a competent independent fish and game commission; …and the need for the control of predators in the national parks and the province."[1141] Interestingly, two of the guest speakers were William Rowan, on the science of bird migration, and Frank Butler, who demonstrated the economic inefficiency of the bounty system. Fisher didn't have the unanimous support he needed; the association was undergoing internal strife on this matter; and the tide was beginning to turn.

Meanwhile, on the other side of the mountains, Cowan's star was rising with his new wildlife management course and his quiet-diplomacy campaign. He was also well known for establishing good relationships with the same wardens being lobbied by Cougar Bill. Cougar Bill was promising them substantial increases to their salaries through higher coyote bounties. Somebody who could feel their way around the science of predator–prey relationships, uncover the underlying motivations for opponents of the parks and gain the respect of the wardens was needed to continue the fight for the parks – not a job for the faint of heart. It was a major coup that funding for the survey was secured to get Cowan to Banff the following spring. His task was to start a "careful investigation on each area."

PART 6

THE EARLY UNIVERSITY YEARS:
1941–1950

CHAPTER 25

"I was asked by Parks Canada to seek out the facts."

The Rockies, 1943

The last meeting of the 'B' during the war was held in February of 1943. Aldo Leopold read the lesson called "The Geese Return," an anti-war address in which he wrote: "Geese are a semi-annual reminder of the community of the earth; if nations could share ideas as they share the wind, sun and geese, there would be less need of war, and a different concept of peace."[1142] Those close to the corridors of power would have had few illusions about who was benefiting during the war. Lobbying from industry for access to park lands and resources was constant,[1143] yet on the other hand, Harkin had worked hard to maintain a national parks ethic – the parks were part of what Canadians were fighting for. The address he wrote in 1916, in the midst of the First World War, still had resonance for this new conflict:

> National parks are maintained for all the people – for the ill that they may be restored, for the well that they may be fortified and inspired by the sunshine, the fresh air, the beauty and all the other healing, ennobling and inspiring agencies of nature … [The parks] exist in order that every citizen of Canada may satisfy his craving for Nature and Nature's beauty; that he may absorb the poise and restfulness of the forests; that he may steep his soul in the brilliance of the wild flowers and the sublimity of the mountain peaks; that he may develop in himself the buoyancy, the joy and the activity he sees in wild animals; that he may stock his mind with the material of intelligent optimism, great thoughts, noble ideals; that he may be made better, happier and healthier.[1144]

Those were still powerful ideas for a nation decades later and justification enough for a scientific study of the flora and fauna led by an experienced field biologist. There was another reason to have experienced men doing reconnaissance of the mountains. The British army was secretly sending 600 Lovat Scouts, special unit officers, to train in the Rockies over the winter of 1943–44 under the leadership of Victoria climber and Alpine Club member Rex Gibson. Cowan was well acquainted with members of the Alpine Club of Canada, Bert Brink being an active member. Since the war was spreading out onto the glaciers of Norway or the high passes of the Alps, the military wanted to test out new equipment, build skills and practise winter manoeuvres. It is likely that Cowan's presence, his annual reports on predator activity and his good relations with wardens in the field provided some level of information for the war effort. In any event, he was able to secure funding to embark on the most comprehensive inventory of wildlife in Canadian national parks that has ever been undertaken, even to this day. It stretched into a four-year project that lasted until the end of the war.

When Cowan gave his address to the University of Northern British Columbia in 1997, he summed up his research questions in a short paragraph:

> I was asked by Parks Canada to seek out the facts. Through a fascinating five years, I rode horseback, hiked and climbed throughout the length and breadth of Jasper and Banff ... There were wolves in the park. What Parks wanted to know was: How many? Where? What were they feeding on? What influence was this having? What evidence was there of increasing numbers and migration from the parks?[1145]

The central questions of where the wolves (and other predators) were and what they were eating meant he had to identify all the prey animals and where they were throughout the seasons, the condition and number of the herds, and their ranges. He also had to begin to decipher the complex relationship between the carnivores and their prey. In that first year, Cowan had four months to cover 7,000 square miles. He didn't waste a minute or a penny. He finished classes and headed east, timing his arrival in Jasper to be just ahead of the budding-out of plants for spring. This would allow him to see the condition of the animals after a winter and measure the intensity of their winter foraging. He planned to stay until the autumn die-off of plants, enabling seasonal observation of the movement of the big prey and predator animals. The day he arrived, April 17, 1943, he collected chief warden Charlie Phillips and went to Devona, a lookout over the Athabasca River, to count the animals on one of their most critical winter ranges. Cowan had done the exact same trip his first day in Jasper back in 1930 with warden Frank Bryant when he had skinny-dipped for the lost beaver. Looking out over the landscape 13 years later, he knew that something had gone terribly wrong.

"Along Talbot Lake all deciduous trees or rather aspen and willow dead or removed,"[1146] he wrote. And the next day: "There is much evidence of pawing out of grass roots ... Fine-leaved grass 95–98% last year's growth removed, 75% of the new growth has been eaten at least once ... All willows in dry areas have been killed but in some moist draws there is some life near the bases of the tree clumps. These living twigs have been browsed 100% of cases to a length of about 300 mm."[1147] "Higher on the ridge there are some aspens, all bear "chew" marks and there are no seedlings anywhere. Aspen seedlings and sprouts 100% browsed. Ditto for willows. Considerable wind erosion on top of ridge." [1148] The winter range was in bad condition from overgrazing and many of the animals he saw were in as poor a state. Most significantly, most of the animals he was seeing were Rocky Mountain Elk – an ungulate which he hadn't even seen there in 1930, as it wasn't reintroduced to the Rocky Mountain Parks until 1931.

Elk are highly adaptable. Mostly grazers of grass, they prefer parkland with shelter trees interspersed, but can survive on a browse diet of trees. Lots of predators love elk meat, but the main cause of death was winter starvation and ticks. When Cowan had been in the Chilcotin and the Cariboo, he had collected the stories of regional elk populations dying off in bad winters. In the absence of bad winters, maintenance of healthy elk numbers was reliant on preda-

....

Rocky Mountain Elk calf

Cervus canadensis nelsoni

This subspecies occurs along the western side of the Rockies from the International Boundary north to the Kicking Horse River valley ...[1149]

....

tors. In 1943, Cowan noted, "Indications were that in the aggregate, predator losses were light. Coyote predation upon elk is unusual and wolves are not in sufficient numbers on the elk winter ranges to keep the animals removed."[1150]

Cowan spent the next five weeks reconnoitering by foot and vehicle in the easily accessible winter ranges around Jasper and Banff – the Bow, Brazeau and Saskatchewan valleys – checking out conditions and numbers of animals. He met up with wardens like Frank Wells (who had spent time with him 13 years ago) to collect local information. He did his first short pack-horse trip of the season with warden Ernest Stenton, battling the elements up Carrot Creek to get to Minnewanka:

> Weather fine when we left Banff, clouding and beginning to rain at about 9 p.m. During the night snowed about 6 inches. Snowed heavily until noon on the 5th and lightly off and on during the afternoon. On way in saw 8 elk in the Bow Valley, noted tracks coming up Carrot Creek and in emerging saw 2 large bulls feeding on the sidehills near camp. ±6-year-old ram feeding north of camp. An old billy goat and yearling seen on hoodoos beside trail coming in. Found an 8-year-old ram near the two lower kills previously killed. Indications are that it was a lion kill but I could not be positive...[1151]

Warden Stenton had been in the area earlier that winter and noted a large herd of 50 sheep overwintering on a snow-free, south-facing hillslope. He'd also seen tracks of three or four Cougar, "including positive evidence that a single animal moving up the creek had killed at least the two sheep [Stenton] found on the trail and probably also the one I found today."[1152]

Cowan was studying a number of predators: wolf, coyote, black and grizzly bears, wolverine and cougar, all of which were said to have "aptitudes" for killing things. Critics like "Cougar Bill" Fisher claimed cougars were big killers of sheep, yet not much had been written scientifically about cougar behaviour as of 1943. Cowan did know they could be prolific breeders, with no fixed breeding season and a gestation period of only 90 days. He addressed important questions for these dynamic prey–predator relationships, such as whether cougar were a primary factor of shrinking Bighorn Sheep herds. The full picture he was to uncover over the next three years was of a community of animals under siege from much larger forces.

The parks were too small and didn't include the full seasonal round of habitat for these big prey–predator systems. Big-game trophy hunting was occurring outside every boundary, killing any sheep that stepped outside the parks. Most importantly, low-lying, prime winter range inside the parks was being carved up by roads, railways, town and resort development and hydroelectric projects. What remained was being shared with other domestic or introduced animals, from horses to elk. The populations of Bighorn Sheep and Mountain Goats were outcompeted, persecuted and vulnerable. Cougar predation was a problem, but to what extent? And was it significant relative to the impacts of industrial interests? A lot was riding on the answers to those questions.

Cougar or Mountain Lion cub

Felis concolor
[Puma concolor concolor]

A large unspotted cat; adult males measure up to 9 feet in length including the tail of 30 inches. The weight is up to 180 pounds in the interior parts of the province. Females are smaller ... The animal frequents the ranges of large ungulates, principally those of deer. It remains in the cover, usually lying up by day and hunting during the hours of twilight and darkness...[1153]

At that time, one or two Cougars were being shot every day in BC, for the bounty alone. Even when the bounty for cougars ended in 1956, the legal killing – either by hunters with trophy licences or by wardens dealing with nuisance cats – continued at the same rate. The range of the cougar was also shrinking all over North America, to a few localities such as the Rocky Mountain parks. Wrote Cowan of the predators that summer:

> We find that the few direct studies conducted do not indicate that direct predation of one species upon another is so drastic as to threaten the existence or seriously limit any species, <u>as long as environmental conditions are favourable for that species</u>.[1154] [underlined in original]

And therein lay the rub, as Cowan proceeded to systematically document the deterioration of the range. The day after their Carrot Creek visit, Cowan and warden Stenton headed for Minnewanka Cabin, which now looked down on the new lake raised 30 metres by the building of Calgary Power's dam the year before, not on the grassy low-lying valley of winter range that had been there in 1931:

> June 6th
> Left camp on Carrot Creek this morning at 9:20 and climbed to the pass in a snowstorm. On way down found going bad with 2–3 feet of winter snow lying beneath new snow. Spent a hard 3 hours cutting out windfall on the trail along the south side of the lake and finally reached the cabin – in the rain – at about 4:30. Most of the south side of the lake is heavily timbered with spruce, pine and fir and is devoid of game food. The north side of the lake is open grass and rubble hills below the crags above … Game count today: 2 sheep, 7 deer.[1155]

Cowan's 1940s work on cougars in the Rockies only just touched the subject. In a letter to Frank Butler in 1947, he wrote that the hunters in the Game Division "are in a position to contribute much basic information to our knowledge of the life histories of the various predatory animals…"[1156] Citizen scientists and his students would follow up and begin to flesh out the biology of this elusive animal which had survived a long history of demonization, being literally "hounded" all over the continent. Cowan attracted some of the hottest young biologists in North America to the topic. In 1964, one of his PhD students, Maurice Hornocker, began a comprehensive study of the cougar. Hornocker's work built on what Cowan had started, and continued to alter public perception of cougars. Hornocker went on to become the world's authority on the animal, and like Cowan, managed to get his research featured in popular magazines, books and television documentaries. Cowan followed and supported Hornocker's work throughout his life. Beginning in 1986 he sat on the board of the Hornocker Wildlife Institute,[1157] which continued some of the most extensive field research ever done on cougars and their prey.[1158]

Another student of Cowan's who looked at prey–predator relationships was Daryll Hebert. Hebert over the years worked on bighorn sheep, their forage and the relationship of their nutritional health with cougar predation.[1159] Hebert's interest in prey and predators had come at an early age. As he recounted:

> When I was in Grade 8 in Cranbrook, I came home from school one day, turned on the TV and there was this marine biology program with Ian McTaggart Cowan and I thought that was really neat, so I would come home every week on a Wednesday afternoon to watch it … When I was in Grade 11, I wrote to Ian McTaggart Cowan and asked him what courses I should take to become a biologist. I get this personal handwritten letter back telling me all the courses I should take … I went through first, second, third year classes in biology and in fourth year went into Ian's office to see about a master's. We talked and he said, "Before we go ahead you should talk

to other people – Mary Taylor, Jim Bendell, Dennis Chitty." I went to talk to them, but then I came back and said, "Nope, I want to work in the Kootenays, I want to work in big game and I want to work with you." So he said okay.[1160]

Hebert's most poignant memory of Cowan was in the 1960s, coincidentally on a bluff not too far from Banff:

Least Chipmunk

Eutamias minimus selkirki
[*Neotamias minimus selkirki*]

Found only in the southeastern parts of the Selkirk Range, known only from the type locality, Paradise Mine, Toby Creek, timberline environment.[1163]

> Ian and I are up on Paradise Mountain working on mountain goats and we start climbing about 7 o'clock on a beautiful July morning, and we get up above the treeline in the alpine, south slope sun shining on us, and we sit down. We are chatting away about a variety of things when he points down below us and says: "Daryll, see that rock ledge down there? I collected a Least Chipmunk there in 1943." I said, "That was before I was born, for god's sake." He was the only guy that would have done that or remembered that. It was a neat experience to know that that history just became that much broader when he started talking about those things. He could probably recount those stories all over British Columbia from the time he started writing *The Mammals of British Columbia* to the time he finished.[1161]

Cowan or Hebert recollected the wrong year, but the species was correct – the smallest of the chipmunks. It was August 29, 1945: "Paradise Mine. Took 1 [adult] [*Microtus*] *longicaudus*, 1 [*Eutamias*] *minimus*, saw some [*M.*] *richardsoni* sign, 3 or 4 squirrels *Citellus* abundant + still active. Saw 11 mule deer."[1162]

Cowan was very good on his chipmunks and their distribution.[1164] They are endearing, especially when they form an informal welcoming committee as you arrive after a long climb up a mountain. Hebert's experience as a grad student was typical for the dozens of students Cowan supervised over the years:

> I started to do my fieldwork up here in 1964. In June my mum got a phone call from Gladys, the secretary – she was the general, she did everything. She said: "Is Daryll home?" And my mum said, "No, he's in the field." Gladys says, "Can I leave a message for him? Can you tell him that Dr. Cowan likes to hear from his students at least once in the summer." He always had time for me ... except once when she said: "Dr. Cowan's got an appointment with the president and he can't meet with you until 1 o'clock." We never talked about the weather ... We did 15 or 20 minutes about what I was doing, what he was doing, and then I'd come back in another three months ... What I learned from Ian was ... find the best people, give

them the most responsibility, and let them do what they want to do. And that was why he was able to take on so many grad students all the time, because he had good, independent people and they were responsible.[1165]

Hebert went on to develop research methods that tracked Bighorn Sheep kills in the Chilcotin by radio-collaring individual cougars. He concluded in his 1986–88 study that most of the kills were attributed to two individual females killing sheep that were in poor condition.

Cowan's style of mentorship had yet another model. After coming down from Minnewanka on June 8, 1943, Cowan was to meet a master of the mentoring arts, Jimmy Simpson – guide, naturalist, artist and raconteur. Even in the '40s he was already a "legend of the Rockies."[1166] He had been guiding parties of hunters, scientists, artists and tourists, from English nobility to American movie stars, for 45 years before being assigned to Cowan. Of all the skills and knowledge Cowan attributed to Simpson, the one he referred to first was not one normally celebrated by the scientific community:

> Jimmy was a poacher. He'd been trapping there since 1902. His headquarters cabin was Bow Lake and that little shanty there was his cabin. He took me to all his cabins in the woods. He felt it was his right to indulge himself a little bit. Sort of like that story about John McNab by John Buchan, which I enjoyed thoroughly.[1167]

The weather during the first few days wasn't auspicious and there appears to have been little exchange between the two men:

> June 10th
> Left Banff this morning at 10 a.m. with 10 horses – 2 of them without loads. At 10:30 it began to rain and continued in a downpour until about 4:30 p.m. We became soaked and very cold but thawed out in the Spray River cabin. En route we saw Elk: 3 bull, 5 cows, 1 calf, 3 Goats. June 11 Altitude 5400' held up here by incessant rain.[1168]

Cowan loved to tell the story that would cement their relationship:

> We started out going up the Spray River, which they have now converted into a reservoir. We went up to Healy Creek and camped there using the warden cabins, as a lot of them were empty then, being the war years. The first morning old Jimmy got up and we went outside and he said, "What are you going to do today?" I said, "There is a pretty sick goat on the ridge up there and I want to find out what is the matter with them so I am going to go get him." He said, "You are, eh? Humph. I'm going to go get the horses." So he came back at lunchtime and I had the whole goat down there, guts and all. He said, "You got it?" I said, "You didn't expect anything else

did you?" But the point was, I did find out what was the matter with him. He had ear ticks attached to his eardrum, first record from Canada. He also had lungworm pneumonia. And I went through this with Jimmy, who got closer and closer, because here was something he understood. After that we were friends.[1169]

The two men were following the Spray Valley, which was a broad river valley with wetlands and rich valley grasslands prior to its flooding in 1950. En route from Bryant Creek (named after warden Frank Bryant) they crossed Whiteman Pass to the summer meadows of Mount Assiniboine on the BC–Alberta boundary. Assiniboine rises nearly 12,000 feet out of an upland plateau, spectacular in its pyramidal form and setting by Lake Magog.

Mountain Goat and kid

Oreamnos americanus

This is an antelope with little resemblance to, or kinship with, the goats. The colour is white throughout, though kids frequently show a strong intermixture of brown hair along the back. Shoulders high, and along midline of neck and shoulders hair is long and stiff, producing an abrupt ridge ... The goat inhabits the roughest possible terrain, generally at altitudes at or above timberline.[1170]

> Worked benchland + riverbottom on [west] side of river + find willows + lonicera [honeysuckle] browsed to capacity. Some aspen reproduction but very little. Even poplars are just holding their own. I should judge that this valley for this distance is fully stocked. Elk 16, Moose 3, Mule deer 2, Goat 13, Grizzly 1. This country is definitely a summer range in which a few moose and goat winter. The critical situation here is winter range, particularly for deer and elk. These animals almost all pull down to the Spray Lakes area.[1171]

Flooding the Spray Valley by Calgary Power, as Cowan knew, would erode populations even further in the southern parks. The lack of winter range put greater stress on the goats and sheep in the higher country, as they had to compete with larger ungulates in the winter which invariably out-ate them.

Cowan and Simpson repeated their observations in the Healy, Brewster and Redearth creek watersheds working their way north. Cowan described their daily routine with Jimmy leading the pack train:

> Old Jimmy did a lot of walking; he was the head lead horse and his little legs almost stuck straight out, so he walked a lot ... We

climbed as high up the mountain as we could get, we worked around the mountain over one ridge and then stop and use your field glasses. You'd lie down and count everything you could see in the bottom there and age and sex them the best that you could. Sheep were reasonably easy. Then you go [to] the next ridge. And you never disturbed those animals, because if you did, they'd get all mixed up, and forget it, your study is over.[1172]

Wolverine

Gulo luscus [*Gulo gulo*]

A powerful, long-haired mustelid somewhat resembling a small, short-legged bear ... Food mainly flesh of birds and mammals. Known to attack smaller mammals such as ground squirrels, marmots and beaver. There are also authentic records of attacks upon mountain goat, moose, deer and caribou. On the big-game ranges it subsists upon winter kills and the kills of other predators.[1173]

At Shadow Lake, in the open muskeg meadows between the clumps of Engelmann Spruce they found Grizzly, Coyote, Marten and Wolverine tracks on the trail. Wolverine had been virtually eradicated around North America and the Rocky Mountains remained one of the last strongholds for these large mustelids. Simpson's nickname was "wolverine-go-quick," or "Nashan-esen" in the Stoney Indian language, for his prowess on snowshoes.

Simpson wasn't a natural born wolverine-like character or mountain man. Like Cowan, he was born in the UK to an upper-middle-class family. Raised in an English market town, thirty-three years before Cowan, they shared an early childhood love of nature. His father had been a scholar and historian while his mother had died early. Growing up adjacent to the Marquis of Exeter's estate he filled his "rascally youth"[1174] prowling around the estate and poaching the odd pheasant and rabbit for food. His father died when he was 18, and he was dispatched to Canada by relatives. Simpson ended up at Lake Louise station after being chucked off a CPR train as a stowaway and became enchanted by the mountains and the lifestyle of the man who was ultimately to lure him back to Banff, Bill Peyto, a trapper and prospector.

After hanging out with Jack London in California, crewing on a sealing schooner off Vancouver Island and getting into some misadventures in New York, Simpson returned to Banff to guide expeditions into the mountains. That was 1898. Forty-five years later, Simpson was happy to share a lifetime of observations with Cowan, who was equally happy to bring him up to date on the science. Not surprisingly, the two had mutual respect for one another. "All the things he had been seeing of his life, which he told me as he went along, and it started to come together for him in

a pattern as we talked. He was a bright, intelligent man and I loved him dearly."[1175]
The teaching went both ways:

> When I came out of Berkeley, I was about as good as I was going to
> get on the actual detailed facts of zoology. But putting them together
> in a field situation was quite a different art … That's why my experi-
> ence with Jim Simpson was so important. In the months I went out
> with him, I learned how to translate my book learning into field situ-
> ations: I learned what the difference was between the range that ewe
> sheep use versus ram sheep; I learned where the earth [salt] licks
> were and when they came to them.[1176]

Salt licks were poorly studied at that time and remained one of Cowan's research interests. Knowledge of licks was critical in determining animal migration
routes of the sheep and goats, since they visited licks at least once a year during the
spring. He conscripted students like Daryll Hebert to work on the licks. They discovered the chemical content of licks, the frequency and style of the animals' use of
them and what purpose they served from a dietary perspective.[1177]

Another insight from that trip, perhaps an outcome of his conversations with
Simpson, was the importance of long-term knowledge of the individual animals.
This was to be the secret to accurately determine the numbers of wolves. The prevailing attitude in 1943 was that wolves were one of the causes of the decline of
sheep and goats. Clarke, who had written the earlier studies in the parks, had found
that the declines in the sheep and goat populations at Banff persisted despite the
wolves being eradicated there. Jasper appeared to still have its legendary packs of
black wolves, so why were the populations of sheep and caribou the healthiest in
that region of the park? Cowan decided to collect wolf scat to find out. "I had two
saddle bags, this one had my lunch in it and the other was full of wolf scats, both in
paper bags. So every time there was a wolf scat I had to get off the horse and put it
in."[1178] Simpson, walking ahead, quickly inducted Cowan into a more efficient process. "I started to find the wolf scats hung up on the trees, so I could pick them off
without getting off the saddle. You had to be careful eating your lunch after picking
up scats all morning, because they did have echinococcosis [hydatid] disease."[1179]

Cowan and Simpson didn't see any living wolves that summer, but that wasn't a
huge surprise. Wardens had been shooting wolves and coyotes for years; it was their
job and they made good money from it. One of the wardens Cowan worked with,
Frank Camp, wrote a memoir about growing up in a warden's family (his father
also had worked with Cowan in 1930). Camp eventually became a warden himself
in 1946. "All wardens were encouraged to shoot, snare or poison all the wolves they
could,"[1181] he wrote. Fur-bearers were also susceptible to poaching. As Camp recounted, "It was always suspected that some of the old-time wardens in outlying areas travelled a fine line of honesty. It was easy enough to make a deal with a neighbouring trapper to overlook his activities for a cut of the action."[1182] Though Camp
started working with Cowan at the time recommendations for policy changes

were being made, old traditions died hard. Wardens got more and more sophisticated in their techniques, such as killing with cyanide guns set off by trigger devices.[1183] Cowan noted, "It went on quite a while afterwards, too ... particularly with the bears, the big bears. Several of the wardens were scared of them. They shot everything in sight ... So the bounty was the signal, the trademark of that mentality."[1184]

Cowan's mission that year included getting an accurate snapshot of the seasonal diets of the wolves, and he needed a way to count them. While on the trail, he and Simpson hatched the idea of getting an accurate census by having wardens keep track of individual wolves over the winters, when heavy snows confined their travel to the valley bottoms.

> Nobody had done this before ... The wardens reported to me that the colours [of the wolves] were very mixed: they went all the way from almost white to black ... So I set up a network; they were all interconnected by telephone. I asked [the wardens]: "When [wolves] pass through ... count them, the number of greys, the number of blacks and so on. And then phone your colleague down the hill and tell him they are coming through." Exactly the same way, years later, that they did the killer whales. I knew there was a pack of five – two greys and three blacks – here, and there was another pack of seven brindles [streaks of colour are irregular] here. And so on. So the packs were all

identifiable, and then you know how many there are. To study individuals, you've got to have markers on them. And that hadn't happened then. Nobody had put a marker on a wolf. In fact, I must have been in my forties before a radio was built that was reliable enough

[Gray] Wolf den

Canis lupus

Wolves are the largest of the dog-like carnivores, more heavily built than the coyote, with shorter ears, broader muzzle and shorter tail. The pelage is long, heavy and varies greatly in colour and texture with individuals and geographic location. Black colour phases occur in many populations ... In British Columbia, wolves feed largely upon deer, moose, caribou and mountain sheep and are usually found where these ungulates occur. All kinds of domestic stock are utilized, while most species of smaller mammals and birds, including rodents, foxes, coyotes, grouse and waterfowl, are also taken as a food ... The effect of wolf predation upon game-animal population has been questioned in recent years and evidence has been presented (Cowan, 1947) contradicting the widespread belief that wherever wolves occur, big-game species are greatly reduced in numbers.[1180]

to be useful or small enough to be carried by something other than an elephant.[1185]

This was one of the first times a zoologist had collected data on the basis of identification of individual animals. "The biggest advances in my lifetime in the field aspect of biology," Cowan said, "is the knowledge that you could identify individuals and they are just as different as you and I are. I'm not quite sure where it started, but I'm pretty close to where it started."[1186] The next Canadian to adopt and run with this idea was Cowan's student Bristol Foster, who used the technique for a giraffe study:

> We used to think that all giraffes were the same, but every one of them was different. It's like so many other things: once the idea gets in there, the idea spreads. It wasn't long until Mike Bigg … got the idea to identify [killer whales]. At the same time, the students of the humpback whale realized that every humpback had a different underside of the tail. Little by little it has permeated; it's just a question of time until we recognize that we can probably identify almost everything as an individual.[1187]

The understanding of how packs of wolves, pods of whales or a tower of giraffes interacted with one another was to completely change the public's perception of animals. In the public's eye, Bigg's work turned killer whales from being roving bands of thugs to complex kinship groups where matriarchs passed on knowledge and the offspring were raised by uncles and aunts. Cowan's excitement about the study of individuals stemmed from his first interest in evolution and variation. "We changed biology when we started to work with individual animals rather than populations, because individual animals indicate variation; they give you the stuff of which evolution is built."[1188] This was an idea that was to permeate the world of naturalists. One of his colleagues, the artist and naturalist Sir Peter Scott, who ran the Wildfowl and Wetlands Trust at Slimbridge, England, had become familiar with a flock of swans. "When I was there [in 1952], I think there were a couple hundred of them, and he could identify every one of them. He made sketches of the colour of the yellow on the beaks on every one of them."[1189]

Once Cowan and Simpson had finished the valleys of Banff, Cowan took a break from the horses. He did a vehicle reconnaissance of Kootenay National Park – a long, narrow park that follows the Vermilion River, then jumps to the Kootenay River and the Columbia over two passes. The road had been put through in 1914 and the national park was designated in 1920. As Cowan drove the road, he described the condition of these three narrow valleys, burnt and scoured since the building of the road. He ended up in Invermere, at the bottom of the trench, where he found another Rocky Mountain legend, Walter Nixon. Nixon had started trapping in the Kootenays at the same time as Simpson. He had also received his share of romantic characterizations at the hands of travel writers and had a few geographic features named after him. American writer Lewis R. Freeman described Nixon in 1921 as:

> ... a fine up-standing fellow of six feet or more, black-haired, black-eyed, broad-shouldered and a swell of biceps and thigh that even his loose-fitting mackinaws could not entirely conceal. I liked particularly his simple rig-out, in its pleasing contrast to the cross-be-tween-a-movie-cowboy-and-a-Tyrolean-yodeller garb that has come to be so much affected by the so-called guides at Banff and Lake Louise.[1190]

Nixon had witnessed the arrival of elk in 1904, of moose in 1906, and the explosion of both populations in the region thereafter. The confirmed scarcity of wolf, cougar and even coyote was indicative of a major trapping program. "Nixon may be the author of the oft-repeated assertion that the wolverine is the chief predator of goat," wrote Cowan,[1191] with uncharacteristic irony, since wolverines were the least of the goats' worries with Mr. Nixon around. In 1919, he had also trapped 29 lynx, which then became, not surprisingly, scarce.

Cowan then met the two provincial game wardens at Radium Hot Springs: "Both are of the opinion that the parks are a breeding ground for predators."[1193] He describes how he spent much of his time instructing the wardens how to look for signs of the real killers – parasites. Tracking cause of death or illness and educating wardens on the relationships of health of the grasslands, health of the ungulates and health of the predators was a big part of his job. Cowan's entries in his journal typically look like this: "*Ovis canadensis* [Bighorn Sheep] [adult] Cairn Pass, Aug. 4, 1943. *Cysticercus tenuicollis* [parasitic tapeworm], *Protostrongylus stilesi* [lungworm]."[1194]

In July he rejoined Simpson and they headed off by pack-horse again to search the large wilderness region north of Banff. They started by going up the Cascade Valley, which was "burned clear to timberline,"[1195] and climbed the mountains that provided a view into the Bone and the Panther valleys, ending up at Ya Ha Tinda Ranch on the eastern boundary. The park owned the ranch and operated it for the park's horses; it was looked after by warden Cliff Murphy and his wife, Nellie.

> July 6, 1943
> Rode here today from Sulphur Springs, a distance of about 22 miles. Got a late start thanks to the horses leaving us but arrived about 6 p.m. Trail in poor condition – 14 river crossings on the Panther – need for a lot of slashing along the riverbank. Several trees on the trail. Sheet erosion beginning on the hills.[1196]

There was a pack of black and grey wolves at Ya Ha Tinda, and the Murphys were enlisted to watch with the network that winter. Cowan's next destination was northwest up Red Deer Creek to a rare "beautiful stand of mature pine, 2000' to the alpine meadows"[1197] at Snow Creek Pass. They skirted Mount Tyrrell looking for game but got snowed in for several days at Indianhead cabin, so he watched deer dietary choices in bad weather. An opening in the weather allowed them to descend into the Clearwater River valley, only to be buffeted by another windstorm. They found shelter in the heavy spruce forest filled with moose. At Clearwater Lake the horses escaped towards Pipestone and home, and the men didn't catch up with them for 18 miles. En route Cowan "interviewed a goat – a billy – backtracked it and studied the food plants in meadows."[1198]

They crossed Clearwater Pass in another snowstorm at 8100 feet, but Cowan paused there, remarking that "this is a most interesting spot."[1199] There were many signs of game traffic and an abundance of his childhood bird friend the pipit, which nests on the ground in mountainous country. He found a nest with six eggs, which he packed up for specimens, and they rode the horses home.

The final leg of the summer took Cowan and Simpson into the country east of Jasper. The trip became one of the most vivid times of both men's lives. The bad weather of early July had passed and they were in more remote country.

> July 18/43…
> A long, tiring day through some of the finest alplands I have ever seen. Distance 35± miles. Game seen: Caribou 5, Mule deer 5, Moose 9, Goat 3, Elk 2, Coyote 1.[1201]

They saw coyotes regularly, but Cowan doubted the claims that they were serious killers:

> Devona warden Frank Borstrom tells me that the coyotes killed 5 or 6 sheep to his knowledge last winter between Devona and Miette Ranges. In the same distance the train killed 8. Borstrom is skeptical that the coyotes get many sheep.[1202]

Cowan had been told that when a Coyote quota had been assigned to each warden, at least two of the Kootenay wardens had bought hides from native trappers outside the park and then turned them in as park-taken. He wrote in his field journal: "Criticize bounty system." Then he jotted down a recommendation for the park that they create an instruction manual giving details of where the game

American Pipit [bis]

Anthus rubescens

Nests were small cups placed in shallow depressions under tufts of vegetation. Nests were composed mainly of grasses, sedges, mosses, plant stems, rootlets, lichens and animal hair and were lined with finer grass … Dates for 47 clutches ranged from 5 June to 27 July.[1200]

were throughout the seasons. Cowan followed up with a more detailed Coyote study in the summer of 1946 by tagging the animals and tracking them. It involved live trapping, which proved problematic. In the first weeks of experimentation, they managed to temporarily entangle a Black Bear, a horse and a Golden Eagle (whose numbers had increased in response to a "plague" of Meadow Voles and Northern Bog-lemmings) but altogether failed to catch Coyotes.

Cowan maintained a keen interest in Coyotes and went on to sponsor a student, Dan Bowen, who did a radiotelemetric study of the Jasper packs in the late 1970s. The study demonstrated that the Coyotes had similar pack behaviour to Grey Wolves, with a quarter of them being solitary individuals. They had territories of up to 20 square kilometres, well defined through an intricate network of scent marks which Bowen found and recorded.

On July 29, 1943, Cowan and Simpson encountered a ram of record size. Simpson described that day to his own biographer:

Coyote

Canis latrans

The coyote is a medium-sized dog-like carnivore with a sharp-pointed face, sharp, prominent ears and a long, bushy tail. Males are noticeably larger than females, measuring up to 52 inches in total length, including the tail of 15 inches. The pelage is long, heavy and variable in colour; generally it is grey with buffy tints on the upper parts; light buffy to white in colour below. Some individuals heavily washed with black.[1203]

> I took Professor Cowan up to the gap in the range, passed two big bunches of sheep as I went up, saw a lone ram on the top of a hill, above timberline of course, sneaked up on him with Dr. Cowan behind me and jumped on his back. He went out from under me like a cablegram going out to the old country for more money.[1204]

Cowan's account appears to be of the same day but for a different audience:

> In two long, sunlit August days I worked the mountain slopes from the Pass to the farthest ridge, my companion that dean of mountain men, James Simpson of Banff. We worked long and carefully to complete our count of the sheep before a change in the weather or some other unpredictable disturbance should move the bands, mix them up and nullify our efforts. The area was perfect for stalking: long, knife-like ridges ran from the mountain like rays from a star, while

high, bare corries [cirques] to 8,000 or more feet offered unseen passage from one ridge to the next. Our first sheep – 14 ewes and young rams – were seen scarcely 200 yards from camp, and hour by hour the total grew as we crawled to within working distance of flock after flock, made out counts, tallied sex and age and as carefully withdrew.

Never will I forget the largest ram band, 83 of them, almost all mature animals with majestic full-curled horns. They lay in a green swale, surrounded by the lush fodder of alpine grasses and dwarf willows they seek with such relish. They ruminated, dozed in the sun or stretched full-length with horn-heavy heads resting on the turf, and slept secure in their solitude. Alone among his companions the finest ram of the lot remained alert. He stood on the summit of a small knoll, head erect, eyes gazing into the blue distance. We could see his massive horn point full six inches above his eyes. He was the most majestic ram I have ever seen before or since among the 5,000 or more bighorn I have studied. It was with difficulty that we drew ourselves from that spectacle to continue the urgent job. As so frequently happens, the next ridge provided the sharpest contrast. Our first cautious survey of the new slope revealed two old rams close at hand. Tired and battered by years of wresting a living from the hills, they lay in the sun chewing their cud with teeth worn to gum-line. One old fellow, in some battle for supremacy or fall from treacherous footing, had broken off a horn close to the skull. As we watched he gently lowered his head and slept, unaware of two men within 20 feet of him.

Very slowly we moved closer, sound and scent whipped away by the rising wind, until we finally touched him, actually grasped the shedding fleece in our hands before he awoke and in a few bounds reached the protection of a low cliff. In all my years in the hills this remains the only time I have been so close to a wild bighorn ram.[1205]

On August 4, Cowan was to end up at Southesk's Cairn – the namesake of the Scottish Earl of Southesk. It was Simpson's 67th birthday. It was one of the high points of both men's lives. This is Cowan's account:

We climbed a cairn that evening, it was a beautiful evening, on top of Cairn Pass, and we sat there and we could look out down the hill and we could see a small group of elk, mostly bulls, a few dry cows and a 143 sheep. I can remember them to this day. And then we saw, coming over the pass, two bull elk running as if their lives depended on it, big fellows, antlers still in development. We speculated what was the problem. A little later we heard something rattling below us. We were sitting on top of a cliff and we looked down and the bull elk were coming up the cliff and they came out right in front of us..., both of them totally exhausted, heads hanging down and tongues hanging out. They stood there for maybe five minutes and we were sitting on stones. Full view. Then they looked out, saw the cows and were off. It was a marvellous experience, just sitting quietly. People don't understand wilderness unless they experience it.[1206]

This story of the two bulls that he told on himself at 90 was only wrong by one ewe and four nights off Simpson's real birthday, but Simpson at 67 (and far away from a calendar) was just as likely to have lost track of the days. It was the summer Cowan would most recall and it was captured in his popular account of the bighorns, published a few years later:

Of all the mountain game, the sheep is my first love. It has a dash and bravado, a sureness of foot and physical self-confidence found in no other. Goats climb a cliff, sheep tear up it; even the wobbliest newborn lamb only just dried off in the June sun will bounce from knob to insignificant knob on cliff faces that send cold shivers down the human back.

In the early spring, the winter flocks break up, the rams travelling to the highest pastures, there to graze on the tender grasses, sedges and two-inch willows that clothe the last bits of soil. The ewes with their young favour more precipitous summer range, where a few quick bounds will take them to places impossible for a prowling coyote to reach. By October the downward movement begins and by the beginning of the breeding season in late November the flocks are together again on the exposed grass slopes. Here the rams engage in combat to establish supremacy or merely for the sensation. Horn-heavy heads crack together with pistol-shot sounds that echo from the surrounding hills and chips of horn fly at the impact. January finds the excitement over and the flocks settled down to the grim business of keeping alive until the warming sun brings new life to the grasses and the strength to the sheep that eat them.[1207]

August was spent in the northern area of Jasper at places like Willow Creek, where they spotted 18 moose and 47 goats. At Sirius Peak, Cowan painstakingly mapped the transition of grass communities above timberline: the downy rye and wild oat thinning out to a tall tussock grass, replaced by a sedge and then a dwarf hair grass – all blond summer grasses shot through with the dark purples and blues of the monkshood, delphinium and aster wildflowers. Byng Pass became another favourite, not least for the dramatic geology of the area and its population of caribou:

Rode here from Hoodoo Cabin about 7 miles. Made camp about a mile west of the summit of the pass close to three licks used by moose + caribou. The pass is a wide + open one. Scrub timber extends to about 6800 [feet] but above that is only rolling grass + forb-covered uplands with lakelets here + here. On the north these lead back to crags of grey + red quartzite. On the south the [mountains] are mixed quartz-volcanic rock + shale + shale slides are the most prominent feature. Game seen: 15 caribou.[1208]

The federal mammalogist C.H.D. Clarke had reported in 1939 on the genera *Cladonia* and *Cetraria*, life-essential lichens for caribou, whose diet was "eked out through necessity with other vegetation..."[1209] Cowan was intent on defining the winter range that supplied that food:

> ... they descend before the deep, soft snows of the early winter and take up temporary residence in the spruce forests. Here they feed on the abundant tree lichens that go by the name of "old man's beard" and supplement their diet with willow tips and other tasty twigs.[1210]

He had also recorded the heavy infestations of parasites: warbles and bots, the parasitic flies that plague the animals, and stomach worms. These were clearly animals under stress. "Wolves undoubtedly account for numbers of caribou, during the winter months at least. Grizzly occasionally attack them ... [but] not until after detailed study of the species can any evaluation be made of present numbers in relation to carrying capacity..."[1211]

Cowan's last entry was September 11 as he was leaving the park. "To Columbia Icefields. Beautiful day. Game: 1 goat, 2 moose, 3 elk, 2 deer, 1 coyote."[1212] He said goodbye to Simpson, pledging to work with him the next year. Simpson couldn't make his schedule work, however, and the two men wouldn't see each other again for another two years, and then only briefly. Nothing ever touched the perfection of that summer for Cowan, though, and it seems that was true for Simpson as well: "His wife told me that it was the most interesting summer that he ever had."[1213] Cowan's report that year contained the following acknowledgement:

> Above all, it is the writer's wish to express his sincere appreciation of the efforts of James Simpson, guide and outfitter for the expedition. His knowledge of the terrain, his interest in the game, enthusiasm for the study and unfailing good humour contributed immeasurably in ways that will be understood only by those who have spent like periods in similar endeavours under the vicissitudes of montane conditions.[1214]

In 1994, Cowan wanted to revisit the study and inventory the same places half a century later, but Parks Canada declined his offer. In 2000 he voiced his regrets:

> The one thing they should do as a Millennium project is to make an inventory of what they've got. They hadn't done an inventory before I did this one, and they haven't done one since. Now they've worked at certain things to get more detail but I realized that we couldn't do

it [now]. None of those fellows know how to travel except by helicopter. And when you float over sheep with a helicopter, forget it.[1215]

Cowan regretted the disappearance of field observations on foot because he felt
it broke the bond with the animal, the place and a commitment to protect those.
"The field is the only place you can do that. They [contemporary biologists] have got
two purposes. Their primary purpose is to try and get that bear protected. Their
primary purpose is not to find out about those animals. Those animals are just a
unit that will help them get that area protected."[1216]

Doing an annual inventory was just one of Cowan's 24 recommendations in his
report that winter, recommendations that stand the test of time. Many of them have
not been implemented, even today. Besides a census of game, he suggested an annual assessment of the condition of the grasses on the winter range. With this information, the park could determine the carrying capacity for the ungulates. He recommended several interim measures to improve winter range: move horses out of
the park during the winter, erect exclosures as benchmarks and cull the elk population in the three main valleys until natural predation caught up. Long-term policy
included a provision that "predators be left to live their lives without further interference from man."[1217] It also urged administrators to get rid of all garbage in the
park to protect bears and visitors; hire wildlife technicians; and get public information out to correct the predation fallacy propagated by the Calgary faction of the
Alberta Fish and Game Association.

The political battles over the park, however, continued. In fact, they have never
ceased. Cowan was invited many times over the years to wade in on park issues.
During the tenure of R.M Anderson, who obviously had some sway as director of
the Museum of Nature, Cowan was frequently consulted:

> Jasper and Banff were the main issues. The whole question of what
> was going to be done in parks and how it was going to be done was
> quite naturally acrimonious. A lot of effort had gone into informing
> people about the parks: what they had, what it could mean and how
> it could be destroyed. The only way if there are differences of opin-
> ion is to talk it out. By the time the talking is over, everyone is better
> informed ... I never had a particular problem with acrimony. People
> feel strongly and people voice opinions. You have to be true to your
> beliefs even if they are not as accurate as they might be.[1218]

One of the most controversial issues for Cowan was the proposed $30-mil-
lion Village Lake Louise development in 1971. Cowan was hired by the developers
(Imperial Oil and Lake Louise Lifts each held a one-half interest). His hiring was assumed to signal his support of the proposal.[1219] He denied his support:

> They [some of the opposition] appeared to have the impression that
> this [plan for the] area (that was going to be clear-cut to make a
> huge hotel site) was being done with the support of biologists. It

wasn't ... At one point someone suggested that I proposed that, but it wasn't true. It got straightened out when people started to listen to one another.[1220]

A newspaper article said of Cowan's involvement: "Once it became clear the project would probably go ahead, he said he agreed to become consultant to keep it as ecologically sound as possible."[1221] It was a difficult time for someone who had a reputation of impeccable scientific integrity. One of the activists he credited with leading the eventual rejection of the proposal was Gavin Henderson, a long-time naturalist and activist who became a major driver for many watchdog organizations, from the Conservation Council to the National and Provincial Parks Association. Henderson received a medal from the Canadian Parks and Wilderness Society named after J.B. Harkin of the 'B'.

As a result of the Lake Louise issue, Cowan leapt into the more comfortable role of preparing a set of recommendations for research in the national parks. The 20 recommendations were not too different from those he had made 30 years earlier: inventories, sample plots, population data, visitor use data, impacts of development and, most importantly, independent science in conjunction with universities. He was also adamant that Parks not forget "the small creatures like insect fauna."[1222] As this chapter was being written, Parks Canada, pressured by the Conservative government to increase use in the park, allowed construction of a commercial, glass–floored, covered observation walkway, called the Glacier Skywalk, reaching 30 metres out over the Sunwapta Valley floor some 300 metres below. The objective was to increase use of the national park by urban dwellers, providing sheltered and expansive, not to mention expensive, views of the Columbia Icefield. The controversial development raised a national debate on the role of the parks.[1223] One can anticipate Cowan's response, as funding for Parks Canada scientists was slashed during the same period.

On the last day of 1943, a major chapter in the fight for the protection of wildlife was to end in Canada. Hoyes Lloyd, the Grand Master of Venery, was to retire from the federal government after 25 years. That winter also brought the war directly into Jasper and Banff National Park when 600 special unit troops from the Scottish Lovat Scouts arrived to do their own "glacier skywalk," testing armaments and driving the precursors of snowmobiles all through the winter range of an already stressed wildlife population.

CHAPTER 26

"It would really take some tall imaginings to keep
track of your wandering husband!"

The Rockies Again, 1944

Back on the coast, Joyce was raising their growing first-born on her own during the summer while Cowan was away doing fieldwork. Their photo album, like that of most young families, was full of pictures of Garry in a backpack, Garry on a sled, up trees, down mountain trails, on glaciers, by lakes, at picnics – around Alta Lake, the family farm in Huntingdon, the Columbia Icefield and home on Fourth Avenue in Vancouver. In the absence of correspondence from this time, Cowan's natural history accounts of Mountain Goats probably provide the best indication of his take on family life. "From an early age, they accompany their mother, staying close, and when danger threatens take refuge beneath her shaggy body. By October the little fellows of both sexes have sharp black spikes of horns protruding from their heads."[1224]

The extended Cowan and Racey clans were always on hand for the young family. "Nannies and younger billies gather in small flocks."[1225] Cowan was still on a very small salary of $2,500 per annum and was having to carve out territory in the increasingly competitive male domain of the university. He was sure to have drawn some parallels between academia and the alpha-male battle scenes he watched with the elk. "The elk, or wapiti, has had a checkered career. It is a spectacular animal. The majestic bulls, yellowish buff with almost black necks, pinkish buff rump patch and sweeping five-foot antlers, each tip gleaming ivory ... They live in noisy unconcern for the rest of the world..."[1226]

Sometime between 1942 and 1944, after Joyce's last stillbirth, the couple had decided to adopt. Being wartime, it was a period of unprecedented numbers of babies being put up for adoption. Ann was born "on or around January 21, 1944" and adopted by the Cowans in March.

> [The caribou's] newborn young are unspotted and are on their feet almost as soon as born. From two or three days old they are constantly at their mother's side running tirelessly on gangling legs, frolicking on the snowdrifts and sampling the growing assortment of tender greenery that springs to life in the summer sunshine."[1227]

Ann spoke about the supporting role of her mother:

> Mum did a lot for our family. She had two kids to raise. She sewed our clothes; she knit; she grew food and preserved it; she was involved in parent care as her parents died in their 70s ... She was a busy woman ... I think it was a good relationship. They presented a fairly united front as far as family life and rules, and I don't remember any discussions about it.[1228]

Young **American Robin**

Turdus migratorius

The American Robin is widely distributed throughout the province from spring through autumn, but is absent from most of the northern and central interior during winter. It reaches its highest numbers in winter in the Georgia Depression. It is the most widely distributed breeding songbird in British Columbia.[1231]

Letters to Ann from her father when Joyce's health was deteriorating close to the end of her life, show Cowan's great respect for his wife's stoicism: "I hate to see her having one problem after another – but she never complains – she is a really spunky soul and takes the view that what she has to put up with is a hell of a lot better than the alternative."[1229]

Meanwhile, registering at UBC that September of 1944 was third-year student Jim Hatter. Cowan had first met Hatter as a boy in 1937 at Cowichan. Cowan would stop off at Clifford Carl's house at the fish hatchery, where the teenaged Hatter hung around. Hatter had lost his father and had found friendly encouragement in the Carl family for his naturalist interests. Cowan too looked out for the boy and had taken him up Bald Mountain on day trips as a research assistant to measure deer browse. Hatter was to eventually become the province's first professional game biologist, and in his self-published autobiography he attributes his success to those early mentors. "[Cowan] became aware of my interest in collecting specimens of birds and mammals and recommended me for a migratory bird collecting permit when I was only 16."[1230] Permits were very difficult to come by, even for seasoned scientist–naturalists, but Cowan convinced his own mentor Jim Munro to issue one, and Hatter became the youngest person in Canada ever to hold a migratory bird permit. Hatter later donated his specimens to the Provincial Museum. They included some unusual ones such as an albino junco. Cowan was confident in Hatter's skills as a preparator, having seen his technique demonstrated with a robin specimen Cowan provided.

Hatter finished school in 1940 and got a job at the Dominion Entomological Laboratory in Kamloops just as Cowan had done ten years before. Spencer and

Buckell were still pulling strings, although not directly. Hatter was joining neighbour naturalist and artist Frank Beebe to look at the possible spread of bubonic plague through fleas and rodents by looking for lesions on Columbian Ground Squirrels.

Hatter was encouraged to get his foundational courses at Victoria College. Then, after a season as a whistle punk on a logging operation, he moved to Vancouver for his third year, entering UBC, where he did vertebrate zoology and wildlife management courses with Cowan. He was in a good position to be chosen as an assistant by Cowan for the next spring's fieldwork: they shared the dubious distinction of having flunked Chemistry 300. For obvious reasons, Cowan was always sensitive to chemistry-challenged students and gave Hatter the opportunity to redeem himself by doing a BA honours thesis on the food habits of coyotes during his summer in the Rockies. The two of them planned for their trip to Jasper in May.

Jim Hatter was one of the first students Cowan had mentored from boy naturalist to professional. It was a role Cowan drew immense satisfaction from. In a letter to his daughter Ann in 1988 he ruminated on the topic (while preserving some peaches that triggered a "philosophical ramble"[1232]) about what constituted "a sense of achievement." He notes that the pleasure of gathering or catching one's own food was paralleled only by teaching – a vocation which he, Garry and Ann all pursued:

> A well-done publication, a graduate student who leaves with a warm feeling to embark on his independent career, students who thank you at the end of a series of lectures, are all matters of personal satisfaction. But where do you get it from punching a computer, or typing all day, or cataloguing books in a library, or slaughtering beasts in a slaughter line, or endlessly waiting in a passing line of cars? Perhaps one of the most useful things we can do as teachers is develop in people the ability to achieve a sense of satisfaction from a task well done.[1233]

He mentored the public too, giving accessible talks and walks in the Vancouver area on weekends, bringing Garry along. Starting in 1943 Cowan would lead naturalist groups for the newly formed Vancouver Natural History Society. He and Bert Brink were popular leaders of these jaunts, taking members on bird, mammal and botanizing expeditions. One member enthusiastically wrote:

> On Saturday, April 24th, Dr. Cowan, accompanied by his small son, conducted a party of five through part of the University area. Quite a number of small mammals were found in the traps that he had set the day before … using walnut meat for bait; the mammals caught were a Creeping Vole, …a Scheffer … mole and three shrews – Wandering, Dusky and Bendire's Pacific water shrew. Shrews are carnivorous and one will prey upon its own kind when found in a trap…[1234]

On another spring expedition he led a group to Burnaby Lake, where they looked for amphibians, including a new invasive one. A participant wrote, "A Bullfrog was heard croaking and both a Northern Toad and a [Pacific] Tree frog were studied. Their breathing was noted; they have no diaphragm but pump air by lower jaw action that gives them a panting effect..."[1235]

Another time, he led 60 members on a bird walk. "Dr. Cowan explained that the warblers, especially the Orange-crowned, come through with the first appearance of leaves.[1237]

Sometime during the height of the warbler migration in 1944, Cowan and Jim Hatter packed up their camping gear and collecting kits and headed for Jasper. They arrived May 2 and Cowan replicated his reconnaissance survey from the previous year, even less happy with what he saw:

> Range conditions have deteriorated even since last year. Jack Hargreaves + Nelles [warden Alex Nelles] both remark on the absence of wild flowers on the valley floor. They are quite right. Except for scattered *Anemone patens*, some gillardia and aster there is nothing. They speak of the profusion of wildflowers 20 years ago.[1239]

The park had reached a critical stage of overgrazing by the combination of horses and incoming elk and moose. Then weeks of driving snow and rain hit the two. May 23 Cowan wrote from Willow Creek:

> After 36 hours snow + 14 hours rain the country was a mess this morning. Rain stopped in mid morning + remained off until after dinner, then sleet began again. This morning the pond near the cabin was

[American] Bullfrog

Rana catesbeiana
[Lithobates catesbeianus]

General form stout. Length 3 to 8 inches. Head about as broad as long. Eyes moderate with horizontal pupil. In British Columbia it is known only from a few localities such as Burnaby Lake and tributary streams, where it is now established, having escaped from artificial ponds or from "frog farms"...[1236]

Orange-crowned Warbler

Vermivora celata
[Oreothlypis celata]

On the south coast, spring migration begins with the arrival of a small number of warblers in late March. This species and the Yellow-rumped Warbler are consistently the earliest migrant warblers. The spring movement increases rapidly and reaches its height in mid to late April ...[1238]

swarming with birds. Among them I noted Robins, Thrush, Water thrush, Pipit, Rosy Finch, Lincoln Sparrow, Savannah Sparrow, Golden-crowned Sparrow, Yellowlegs, Solitary Sandpiper, Kildeer [Killdeer], Redwing, Redstart, Myrtle Warbler, Yellowthroat. They seemed to be getting insects from the snow-covered surface.[1240]

It turned out to be one of the worst summers for weather in decades. Instead of accompanying a seasoned guide like Jimmy Simpson, Cowan was in turn teacher and adviser to a younger Jim. The only letter that still exists between Ian and Joyce Cowan during this decade contains some of the story of that summer. His comment to Joyce was it would "really take some tall imaginings to keep track of your wandering husband!"[1242] The long letter started on July 4, 1944, which he posted upon arriving back in Jasper at the end of the summer, offers an intimate view of his fieldwork, their relationship and their family life:

Poboktan Pass, July 4, 1944

My darling, two days out of Jasper now and certainly glad to be away from the place. It was getting me down. Yesterday morning the remaining 6 horses and ourselves were driven out to Poboktan cabin at Mile 45 on the Highway and we finally were packed up and on the trail by 2 p.m. The horses behaved well and we made a quick trip of the 10 miles to Waterfalls cabin.

Not much to be seen on the way, as the trail lay through pine forest. The Waterfalls cabin is, however, on the edge of a small meadow with a beautiful view across a narrow valley to the jagged peaks beyond. Had some fun trying to keep the horses with us and finally just made them eat "post hay" for the night and turned them loose in the morning to feed before we moved on. The night was very cold – I was chilled even in my sleeping bag with an extra blanket and tarp over me. Tonight I am sleeping in my long woollens. Our present camp is just at timberline on Poboktan Pass. A good spot and comfortable camp. It is only 6 miles above last night's camp but I want to stay here a couple of days to hunt for caribou. Jim [Hatter] and I went out after lunch today. First we climbed to see whether Indian Pass was where Jim [Simpson] and I left it – it was and looked just as interesting as last year. We then made a big circle at about 8000' and in so going saw 15 moose and 6 caribou. One of the latter, a good big bull, had a bad front leg, so after a fairly easy, if long, stalk we bagged him. Suppertime was heading our way fast. By the time the beast was skinned and gutted it was seven o'clock and still two miles or more from camp. Tomorrow we head up the hill with horses to bring in the steaks; pretty nice-looking steaks they are, too!

I am now spread out full length in the old snoozing sack and quite glad to be there, too. We were up at 5:30 and it is now 10 and there have been many inches passed under my feet in the meantime. I got your letter, darling, just before I left Jasper. My, but I was glad to get it. Our little fellow must have been pretty sick for a couple of days. I wonder where in the world he picked up the infection? You must have been very worried. I hope it is all safely over with now, poor little beggar. At least he will have a grand chance to pick up again out at the farm. I'm getting pretty sleepy now, dear, so I think I will call it a day. It has been a grand day but wish you were here too.[1243]

July 6, 1944

Today I have been glad you weren't here. It has been one of those ultra-miserable days that only the alpine region can produce at this time of year. The change started shortly after noon yesterday when a big cloud bank came up in the northwest. By suppertime it was raining hard and by dawn it was snowing a blizzard. That continued all day and you can imagine the results – about 10 inches of soggy wet snow all over everything. On days like this one wonders how anything ever persuaded us to leave a nice comfortable home and come up into a stormbound wilderness like this. Despite the weather, we haven't been too uncomfortable, though. Nothing to do but sit around the fire in the snow – it is a good fire, liberally supplied with huge roots and stumps dragged from surrounding woods. It is getting to the point now where we have to go a couple of hundred yards for our wood. At the moment there are a few small parcels of blue sky showing – about big enough for rompers for Ann – and for the moment the snow has stopped. The barometer is rising, so let's hope that tomorrow will show a vast improvement in the general appearance of things. Thank goodness we have lots of good meat in camp. Yesterday morning before the storm broke we took a horse up on the hill and brought in the hide, head, one haunch – about 40 lbs. – both back strips and four large sirloin steaks off the other side – the latter for immediate consumption. The old bull was fat as butter – fat about one and a half inches thick on his rump and the meat is so tender it can be cut with a fork. We had our steaks for lunch yesterday – heaped with multitudes of onions. Liver and bacon for supper. Chops and bacon for breakfast and sirloin again for supper tonight. Jim swears he has never tasted steaks like them.

Before we left Jasper we both resolved we wouldn't shave our upper lips until we came in. Jim has been taking quite a ribbing as his product is decidedly skimpy – just a hair here and there – within hailing distance of one another but not much more than that.[1244]

Jim Hatter wrote his own story of that summer in his autobiography. He filled up an entire chapter with anecdotes far more colourful than Cowan's journal. Collecting coyote scat for his study, he earned the nickname "Hatter the Scatter." Cowan made him prepare a moose skeleton in the field, weigh the animal on a tiny scale and do an autopsy, which took him all day. "I will never forget how much that moose weighed … exactly 519 kilograms." Hatter was watching coyote and reported one memorable incident:

> Cowan and I saw a coyote in close pursuit of a bighorn lamb. The coyote gained as they raced downhill towards a creek in the gully below. We sat on our horses and watched. The lamb increased its distance from the coyote as they swam the fifteen metres across the stream. When they reached the far bank, the lamb was well in the lead but then suddenly turned back across the creek towards us, with the coyote gaining in hot pursuit. By then we were off our horses and, as the coyote pulled itself out of the water just behind the exhausted lamb, I fired. Then I felt badly and apologized to Cowan, saying I had made a mistake by shooting, as it would have been interesting to witness the final outcome. We walked over to the dead coyote and Cowan smiled as he pointed to two bullet holes only 2.5 cm apart. There had been an emotional reaction when the soggy little lamb barely pulled itself out of the water. We had fired simultaneously and did not hear each other's shot.[1245]

From Hatter we learn that they both got diarrhea and had problems with ornery horses. The bonding experience of that summer cemented Hatter's resolve to follow in Cowan's footsteps and he enrolled in the new course on wildlife management. His textbook was Aldo Leopold's recent *Game Management.*

One of the other young hands helping Cowan was 12-year-old Al Brady, whose father was James Brady, the park mechanic in charge of the Dodge 4×4 Cowan used for getting around. Brady Senior told his son, "You'd better go with that fellow and see that he looks after the truck."[1246] Al obliged and Cowan, characteristically, involved the young boy in the research. Brady recounted:

> We went down to one of the sheep ranges right across from Jasper Lake and went up on the bench. [He'd say] "You can dig a hole here," and then he would explain to me the different times, you know, a fire had gone through … and you could see it. It was a very windy place, and a lot of glacial silt. The lake filters some of it out, but then it's quite windy and that stuff just flies everywhere.[1247]

Cowan's journal pointed to the cause of the dust storm:

Below Windy Point there was as bad a sandstorm as I have seen in a long time. Visibility was reduced to about 200 yards on many occasions. Much of the sand was coming off Jasper Lake [shores] but I think at least as much was coming from the overgrazed bluffs along the valley.[1248]

For a young kid it was a novelty to meet a scientist. Brady notes that "he was a strange person coming to Jasper at the time. People asked what he was doing [and I'd say] 'Oh, he's a turd inspector.' He was picking up scat! Bears and wolves and coyotes and such."[1249] Brady also recalls how the wolf network phone line worked:

[In the] early days they had the old crank-up phone, and they used to string and make their own phone line. And they'd just hang it from tree to tree, just a single line, and sometimes it would join four or five cabins. Everybody was knowing what was going on up and down the line for miles and miles.[1250]

Brady had a lifelong interest in wildlife and raised his family on the edge of Jasper Park in BC with his wife, Mavis. The Bradys visited the Cowans in Victoria just before Ian's stroke; Cowan remembered Brady well, though he had last seen him as a boy of 12. They remained in contact for the remaining eight years of Cowan's life.

Meanwhile, back at Brazeau Lake, Cowan continued his daily account to Joyce:

July 8, 1944
We finally got started with yours truly on "All Day" breaking trail. It was quite a grind up to the pass, with the snow going to about 18 inches deep in spots. The sun was brilliant – even with my polaroid glasses my eyes were quite bloodshot by the time we got to camp. Going was slow – much of the way I had to hike and lead the horse. The wet snow balls under their feet until they have difficulty navigating. We didn't see much wildlife, only a few fresh caribou tracks, a couple of moose, an elk and a deer working their way back out the alplands from the timber where they had taken shelter. On my way down through the timber a beautiful marten crossed the trail and scampered up a tree. I bagged him with "the old 44" and skinned him last night. It took just over 5 hours to get here, which made it rather a late lunch. However, with a bit of fruitcake, an orange and a chocolate bar in the saddle bags I had not fared badly.[1251]

The letter resumes:

Cairn Cabin, July 11, 1944
Well, my darling, you will see that our location has changed by some 38 miles since I wrote the last instalment. We have had three passable days – a few scattered showers, but mostly nice. On the first of these

we dried out our outfit and all took the opportunity doing some washing. I had 4 pairs of dirty sox, some underwear and 2 shirts, I gave the "longs" the works ... Let's hope that any stretching has been in the right segment and I don't find the storm door flapping around my knees!

Yesterday we rode 18 miles from Brazeau Lake to Isaac Creek in just 6 hours. We ride about an hour ahead of the luggage convoy where there are likely to be many coyote and wolf scats. In this way we do not hold up the entire outfit. Then, too, I carry an axe on my saddle and cut a hole through or round any windfall so that the pack train can come right along. I meant to write to you last night, but after supper we all went fishing in the Brazeau River. We had a lot of fun and ended with about 8 Dollys, of which the largest and smallest were my contribution – smallest 8 inches – largest 25 inches = 5 lbs. And quite a fish. We ate them all today and thoroughly enjoyed the change of diet. The mosquitoes in Isaac Creek were terrible – about what they were like in the spruce swamps of Ootsa Lake. They kept after us all night and as a result our rest was disturbed. We have ridden 20 miles today, which adds to the fatigue. The horses are all comfortably fed and are asleep in the alpine meadow across the creek. I have a very comfortable pile of spruce boughs in the corner, and as the light fails I think bed is indicated. Tomorrow we hit those wonderful ram pastures behind the cabin here. Already we have counted 61 ewes and young on the nursery slopes opposite us – this from the cabin window.

Marten

Martes americana

A small carnivore of weasel-like shape similar to the mink in size but with longer, fluffier pelage, longer legs, a longer, more bushy tail and with more prominent ears ... Habitat ... coniferous forests throughout the province ... It occurs from sea level to timberline at all times of the year, but is more abundant at higher elevations during the summer months.[1252]

July 13, 1944

Yesterday was quite a day – weather not too bad. We spent about 10 hours on the ram range. We found the sheep just where Jim [Simpson] and I left them last year – and looked them over at great length – 165 of them. About 5 o'clock we picked out a couple of likely looking rams in a bunch of 40 and made our stalk to a range of about 200 yards. I let Jim shoot one and you never saw such excitement. He made a clean kill with a heart shot – a very nice animal and as it turned out a most interesting heart from my standpoint. By the time the echoes had died away and we had removed their viscera it was 6:30 and time to head for camp. We left our rams in the basin to be worked on today. As luck would have it, the weather today was a sweet-scented son of a gun – one blistering snowstorm after another. We went up at about 10 this morning and didn't finish until 3 this afternoon – rather a late brunch – but it was so cold that one just couldn't work fast. Coming home through the willows we got simply soaked from the waist down – more fun. Bob and George are busy swapping yarns, so don't be surprised if there is a little lack of continuity in this letter. Our last snow flurry passed about 2 hours ago and just now the sky is clear and the mountains sharply silhouetted. I certainly hope it stays that way until morning. I'm getting a bit fed up with snowstorms …

Brewer's Sparrow *taverneri* subspecies (Timberline Sparrow) nest with eggs

Spizella breweri taverneri

Abundant summer visitant to the alp-land areas of the species' range.[1254]

July 14…
I stumbled onto a timberline sparrow's nest – the first I have seen. It contained only 2 eggs, a partial set but I took it anyway.[1253]

The Timberline Sparrow proved to be an enigmatic bird in Cowan's life, turning up usually wherever he looked: Newgate, the Rockies, and then up in the far north. In the 2001 volume of *Birds of BC*, Cowan et al. ask the question, "Has it somehow been overlooked because of its secretive nature?"[1255] Cowan was ever cautious that some birds were deemed rarer than they really were because people just hadn't looked enough. His letter to Joyce resumes with a long discussion of looking for horses that kept disappearing to find better gazing, until they at last they move into the valley that had captured Cowan's imagination since he had first heard of the travels of the Earl of Southesk.

Tomorrow will be our last day in this camp. From here we go over the top of the elusive Southesk River valley. I have heard so much about it, I'm now most anxious to see the region. Well, my darling, the lamp is without oil and I know what you would say if you would see the writing under present light conditions, so I guess I had better give up. By the look of the above writing you might almost guess that the light was non-existent. It is now just before lunchtime and I have been having a "domestic" morning washing clothes. Thought I would get my outfit cleaned up before we start tenting it again tomorrow.

Jim has been having trouble with boils. Already he has had two small ones on his neck and seems now to be getting one on the back of his right hand. I don't know what the trouble can be, because our diet has been just as good as it can possibly be where fresh fruit and vegetables cannot be had. I've noticed one thing – just like Pat Martin in the Peace River, he cannot leave sweet stuff alone and I think that has something to do with it. The rest of us are in fine fettle. I twisted my knee a few days ago and had to go easy for a couple of days. Bob had a bottle of Absorbine horse liniment for massaging horses' legs, so I borrowed it and used it on my sprained shank – it certainly had no ill effects and may have helped. It is practically all right again now. I'll just have to watch it a bit on the steep downhill so as not to twist it again. Well the month is half over now – another two weeks and I'll be in Jasper again and three weeks until I'll be home. It will certainly be great to be back with you again, my dearest, my but I miss you. The lunch call sounds, so here goes – all my love, darling – next instalment weather permitting will be from the Southesk.[1256]

Rocky Forks, July 21, 1944

Darling, I don't know where the time has gone to since the last chapter was added to this epistle, but it would seem that five days have vanished into the great beyond. Believe it or not they have been five fine days in succession – certainly a record for this country. Thank goodness they were fine, too, for we have come through some of the toughest country imaginable – so tough that in wet or snowy weather it would be virtually impassable. When we arrived here yesterday, I announced that so far as I was concerned today was a holiday and all hands promptly agreed. I'm still sore all over and I know the others are too, but the worst part of the trip is over – we are in a cabin here and back on the main trail and just two days ride from Jasper. Of course, we will be more than two days getting there, because there is still work to do en route.

To begin at the beginning, our first day out of Cairn was grand – one steep pitch with no trail over into the Southesk Valley, but once there the going was first class. We followed a small beaten elk trail up the valley for about ten miles through scattered patches of open spruce forest, groves of Jack pines and acres of our peculiar riverside meadows of the Rockies with their stunted willows, clumps of tall delphinium and dark-blue monkshood and scattered bushes of cinquefoil just now covered with large yellow flowers. There was not much bird life en route, but every turn brought groups of elk into view, with here and there a moose.

We made camp just below Southesk Lake in a very comfortable spot with the 3 essential elements: wood, water and horsefeed present in abundance. We made camp there on the evening of the 17th, and on the 18th Jim and I made a climb. We followed up a stream that enters the Southesk from the northwest just below the lake and found that about five miles up it reached timberline in a beautiful alpine basin that was crawling with marmots and whistlers. There were 49 elk in the basin when we came out of the timber and their shiny red summer coasts made a most pleasing contrast with the brilliant green of the basin, the cold grey rock and pink shale of the higher levels. We continued the length of the basin, gaining altitude steadily, hunched at the limit of vegetation and then toiled up a steep sheep trail in the footprints of a large grizzly. At 8400' we kicked footholes into the face of a snow cornice and 8' higher came over the skyline. From the summit we could look right down the Restless River to the Rocky about 3 miles up from where I now sit. The day was very warm and by the time we got back to the lake I was quite ready to soak my legs in the lake, while Jim folded up on a moss bank and went to sleep. After an hour's rest we pushed along the last mile to camp. Bed felt pretty good that night I can tell you.

Next day, we paddled out at about 10 o'clock, heading for Southesk Pass. The trail was just an old Indian pack trail – narrow, rough, almost without blazes and it really kept me on the go to follow it at all, but we made it and were pretty near the summit of the pass when we stopped for lunch. It is the most rugged, awe-inspiring pass I think I have ever seen and very difficult to travel. Right on the summit, with the great icefields of Mount Maligne on the west and a precipitous wall of clear grey limestone on the east, lies a completely blind lake – great quantities of water of the soupiest consistency comes in from the glacier but there is no outlet. Beside this lake we waited for the pack train to catch up. They had lost the trail and had lots of fun and were almost two hours behind us, tired and hungry. So we piled down off the pass and about 600 feet below the summit level came to half a dozen large springs of beautiful, clear, cold water – apparently the runoff from the lake above. It was most interesting to see a stream 10 or 12' wide appear suddenly from the side of a hill. There was good horse feed there, so we set up a camp. I gathered several armloads of nice soft moss under a spruce tree, spread my old snoozing sack and next thing I knew it was morning.

Yesterday the trail was worse than ever. First about 3 miles through an old burn with a lot of exposed rock where two of the horses went down, a pack came off and much fun was had. Later in the day, following the Rocky River, we ran into some terribly swampy going. My saddle horse got into some mud right up to his over-upholstered midriff and was all for quitting. But I gave him a couple of hard ones with the quirt and he gave a tremendous plunge and broke clear. I think, going like that, if a horse once steps and lets the mud settle in around his legs he is really in a bad way. Our youngest horse is always getting into mischief. He is a bit of a dope and has lots still to learn. The pack-horses are all strung together and of course have to follow one another – but sure as fact, he will start to get on the wrong side of a tree and will get his nose skinned for his trouble. Yesterday he had a fine time. First he got himself caught in some roots and nearly broke a leg, and then, when a horsefly got him where he couldn't scratch, he decided to roll – pack and all. As a result, he had to be re-packed. Another pack rope broke when we were right in the middle of the Rocky River. However, we eventually got here and all feel that a day of rest is in order. We saw very little

Two female Harlequin Ducks

Harlequin Duck

Histrionicus histrionicus

The Harlequin Duck frequents both marine and freshwater habitats throughout the province. On the coast, birds usually frequent the often turbulent waters adjacent to rocky islets and rocky shores and bays, feeding amongst kelp beds and moving to the islets and exposed rocks or reefs to loaf and preen ... In the interior, birds are most often found on rivers, lakes and creeks, the rivers and creeks often with fast and turbulent waters.[1258]

wild life yesterday, probably because we were so busy looking for the trail and keeping out of other difficulties. However, just about a mile above us here I saw a female harlequin with 3 downies. I'm going to take a walk that way this afternoon to see if can locate them again.[1257]

In a letter written once back in Jasper, Cowan has received news of the children:

I was so glad to hear that Garry is quite himself again – he certainly lost weight quickly, didn't he? But what a grand time he must be having out there. Ann sounds like a most unusually well behaved young one – poor little mite must find the weather most trying. Your dad will be interested to hear that we took an adult Pacific Loon on Maligne Lake – a first record for the park. We had quite a lot of fun getting it. It was feeding in shallow water, close to the beach, and I stalked it by crawling along behind the low bushes. The trouble was that is was about as fast as I could crawl and I must have wriggled nearly half a mile before I caught up with it, by which time I was puffing so hard I missed it – however, it didn't see me and I got another shot a few minutes later.[1259]

The loon and Cowan were heading for the coast:

I wired you yesterday as soon as I got in … I hope it got there before you left for the farm so that you got word of my safe arrival back in the burgh. Guess I'll get dressed now, my darling, and get the day's work started. First item in the list is a haircut. Last one was in Vancouver, so you may imagine that the camouflage is excellent – no wonder the loon couldn't see me. Bye bye for now, my sweetheart. Next letter will probably be from Field. Heaps and heaps of love and kisses, dearest.

Please tell Garry that his daddy will be home very soon now.

Ever your own,
Ian[1260]

That winter (1944–45), Cowan and Hatter were to return to Jasper with Joyce and the children. The family stationed themselves in a cabin at the Athabasca Lodge and Jimmy Simpson joined them on various days to check out the various winter ranges. After another full but brief spring term and the announcement of the German surrender, Cowan and Hatter were back in the field again. On May 5, 1945, they were ready to start another full season of research, which was to focus primarily on wolves as well as the third-year census of the other populations. After the reconnaissance, Cowan taught warden school at the park, reporting his findings about wildlife populations and an update on the network that was collecting wolf data during the winter. Hatter covered the entire month of June down the Snake Indian River area. Cowan then returned in July with Simpson and crew through the northern Banff area and the Tonquin region of Jasper. It would be Cowan's last trip with Simpson, but they would correspond with cards over the years.

The venerable old poacher died in the autumn of 1972. In his will he left an envelope labelled "for Ian Cowan's eyes only." In it he had written:

Dear Ian,
I have been grossly negligent in the reporting of the world-record Rocky Mountain Bighorn Ram. That animal was actually shot on the front lawn of the ranger station at Saskatchewan Crossing in Banff National Park. But now that I'm dead, nobody will be coming after me.[1261]

Cowan's earlier mentor Hamilton Mack Laing received an update from Cowan about the Tonquin Valley, where the two of them had worked together in 1930:

The last three summers have proven about the most interesting imaginable. I have been steadily engaged from early may to mid-September hiking, riding, climbing and driving up over and through the Rockies. Stalwart and often footsore nags have carried my elongate carcass draped about with a rifle, pistol, 2 cameras, dissecting instruments, weighing scales, field glasses, packets of vials and jars of fixing fluid, pockets of shells, assorted small eatables and a waterproof coat and pants over some 2,500 miles of trail reaching from the Smoky River to the 49th parallel. Another couple of thousand leagues have gone under my hobnails. During the course of this work it has been my lot to devour some very fine steaks removed for the purpose from a wide assortment of horned and antlered game. In September this year, we were camped on the BC–Alta border in the Tonquin Valley – my first time back there since our Jasper summer. I took the opportunity of combining larder filling and museum collecting by collecting a bull caribou. In the same area, we found willow ptarmigan tolerably common and between times took the odd specimen. This was the first time in the three years that my tracks had crossed those of the willow ptarmigan. Even the white tails have been quite scarce, but there was a marked upswing this last year.[1262]

White-tailed Ptarmigan

Lagopus leucurus

The White-tailed Ptarmigan breeds throughout its range in British Columbia in alpine areas characterized by dynamic physiography and poorly developed vegetation ... The two subspecies of White-tailed Ptarmigan occur in the province...[1263]

White-tails were another specialty of Cowan's. He had spent many weeks in the mountains above Comox with Pat Martin scoping out the Vancouver Island alpine subspecies (*saxatilis*) to determine their status and distribution. As with the Timberline Sparrow, the scarcity of white-tail observations may well have been due more to their remote habitat and cryptic coloration than to low numbers. Cowan was always up for a challenge; his predatory instincts were refined when it came to game birds. That summer, he also managed to fit in work on the elk in Waterton Lakes Park, a survey of threatened wildflowers and another on beavers, and while wandering on Castleguard icefield at Banff, he and Hatter found a fossilized wolf tooth:

> Watchman Lake, Thompson Pass, Alta., July 27/45
> Left camp at 9:30 + climbed the shoulder north of camp to timberline,
> then proceeded around to the glacier (Castleguard)… On the sur-
> face of the glacier found a dead *Microtus longicaudus* [Long-tailed
> Vole] + a large canine tooth, apparently of a long-dead carnivore.[1264]

The tooth was identified by a paleontologist at Berkeley as *Canis dirus*, the Dire
Wolf, believed to be the northernmost record of this Pleistocene wolf. The tooth
was 71 mm long. (Interestingly, another taxonomist from LA had a look at it nearly
30 years later and declared it a modern day grizzly.)[1265] That wasn't the only opportunity for Hatter to get close up to large teeth that summer. He was on his own at
the winter sheep range across the river from Jasper when he came face to face with
a nine-member wolf pack. He wrote: "My lack of knowledge about wolves left me
in doubt about the motives of those animals near me. They knew I wasn't a sheep …
Most likely these unhunted Jasper wolves were just curious."[1266]

With tips from warden Frank Wells, they found two wolf dens of the big pack
that approached Hatter. By Athabasca Falls, "We hiked straight east to the wolf den
on the lower slopes of Mt. Signal. It is within ½ mile of the beaver lodge den."[1267]
Descending a short slope they approached the entrance to the den, concealed between two large rocks. "A tunnel measuring 16 inches high by 18 inches wide had
been excavated under the largest of the two boulders. It led back about 7 feet into
a dry, slightly enlarged chamber that apparently served as the nest."[1268] The Buffalo
Prairie den and pack became familiar images in Cowan's slide shows that he took
round to game clubs in his "end the bounty" talks. Cowan had pieced together
the movements of the pack, from the wardens' reports and his own observations
over the three-year research period. He did the same with the other packs: Willow
Creek, Brazeau Valley, Smoky River and Blue Creek.

Back on the podium a half century later, addressing students at the University
of Northern British Columbia, Cowan summed up his research of 1945:

> In five years we had the basic answer to our five questions: There were
> between 35 and 50 wolves in the 7,000-square-mile area. They were
> in 5–6 packs, each with a finite range. Food was primarily elk, and
> their impact on the large animals (bighorn sheep, goats and deer)
> was inconsequential. I wish I had time to give you the details.[1269]

The details were to unfold through five years of reports and articles.[1270] Never
before had a zoologist described a population of animals as sums of individuals
with emerging personalities and relationships; the patterns of their seasonal movements around the territory; the diversity of their feeding habits; their diseases; and
the interconnected play among predators, prey, habitat, diseases and the condition
of the grasses, wildflowers and soil.

Cowan referred to another important relationship, an early form of citizen
science:

There was a change in attitude towards wolves in the Park Warden Service. They now knew their wolves – had helped me work out the details of their lives – they became protectors of "their" packs and could answer questions with facts. A small fire had been ignited.[1271]

One of the small fires he later ignited was under Gordon Haber, a park warden at Denali National Park in Alaska, who approached Cowan with an idea of studying the Denali wolves for his doctorate. As Cowan recounted:

> The next five years were for him an extraordinary adventure in one of the most superb wilderness areas in the world. As he gained the confidence of two wolf packs living at the base of Denali, he slowly built up a picture of how wolf packs work and how they use the resources of their territory to live out their lives. For me they were years of fascination and frustration as I strove for the dollars to keep the project going, moved the rocks from his path, helped him unravel and reorganize the tangled web of data...[1272]

Haber went on to study the wolves for four decades until his accidental death in a research plane in 2009. The book on his life and work, *Among Wolves*,[1273] describes the day-to-day lives of the two wolf packs over the four decades. Cowan highlighted what he had shared with Haber:

> ... watching the pups make their first appearance above ground; the primal drama surrounding and testing the courage of a cow moose as she faced them down in defence of her calf; ...the time when the big black alpha male left the den and came straight to within easy eye contact and for several minutes these two, the young scientist and the leader of the pack, locked eyes.[1274]

Cowan was not long to remain the alpha male of the wolf scientist pack. Interest in the opportunities he opened up brought a steady stream of bright, enthusiastic students to his door – and they took over. Cowan was still assisting young wolf biologists at the age of 90. He had correspondence with most of the wolf researchers in the 20th century: L.N. Carbyn, R.M. Petersen, J.M. Scheidler, J.E. Bryant, John P. Kelsall and David Mech, right up to Chris Darimont, and his work on the wolves of the central coast.

Cowan's wolf file remained the largest of all the animal files he had kept over the years. In it is a range of correspondence that paints the "wild west" attitude of the times: an account by a game warden in 1948 about how predators were getting scapegoated for poor ranching methods to extract illegal compensation claims; correspondence from a constable in the Chilcotin who was insisting native trappers kill wolves; a 1980 letter to a US Republican senator critiquing her advocacy of wolf eradication programs and misrepresentation of his research;[1275] a 1979 letter to BC Minister of Agriculture Cyril Shelford (from Ootsa Lake) outlining the science that wolf control would not result in an increase of prey, while protection of habitat would; a letter from the Sierra Club in 1981 inviting him to talk about wolf populations on Vancouver Island; a letter in 1984 asking him to review a position paper on wolves for a very unpredatory Rosemary Fox of the Canadian Nature Federation.

One particularly interesting file is a 1947 questionnaire survey of 32 trappers on wolf sightings and kills. Half the trappers had never seen a wolf kill; the other half had seen kills totalling 44 animals (deer, moose and elk) but also described 25 railway kills. One trapper, O.E. French, wrote, "Disappearance of caribou, once plentiful, not due to wolves. I can't account for it, they just dwindle away to nothing. Had all the appearance of some disease or lack of virility, often saw cows without calves. Their decimation is not due to hunters. Very good subject for investigation."[1276]

The other event that brought students to Cowan's door was the end of the Second World War and a new generation of veterans anxious to find legitimate careers that would bring them freedom in the wild after the savagery of war.

One of the fires that Cowan damped was a poaching ring run by some wardens. Valerius Geist, one of Cowan's post-war students, recounted Cowan's story of how he had broken the operation:

> He discovered that one man by the name of Johnny Musco[1277] was organizing these wardens ... in such a fashion that they would put the fur in a certain place in the park and he would pick it up and bring it either to Vancouver for sale or to Winnipeg ... Musco would arrive in Jasper and feign drunkenness, holing up in a hotel. Then, in the middle of the night, he would stow away aboard a train, jump from the train before it got into Banff in a snowstorm when his tracks couldn't be followed, pick up the stash of furs, deliver them and be back before his three-day "drunken" stupor had worn off.[1278]

Cowan's tip-off was some strange behaviour by one of the wardens. While working systematically through each valley, this warden made a point of "slipping past" a certain area and directing Cowan away.

> That was getting a little bit too interesting for Ian ... and so he went alone ... once he got off the trail ... [to] the first trap set. He continued up the trail and ... there was a little cabin standing there ... there was also a set of long johns hanging there. Johnny Musco was a little man. And so Ian said, "Well, if he catches his martens here and skins them, he will keep the skin here and he's going to take the carcass and chuck it, and most of the time it'll fly 5 or 6 paces," and he picked up 37 skulls.[1279]

Cowan gathered the evidence, took the warden back there and confronted him with it, whereupon he broke down and confessed.[1280] Johnny Musco fled to the Yukon, where Geist later ran into him having a coffee at the research station of the Arctic Institute:

I walked in and said, "Johnny, you know what, I'm from Banff, and I know all about you." And he said, "What?! You do?" He had not been forgotten … When he had [J.B.] Fitzgerald, the [game] commissioner for the Yukon Territory, visit him, he served him some great roast. Only, Fitzgerald never realized this was from the protected swan, Trumpeter swan. That was typical, typical Johnny. He just loved the fact that he was remembered. He died a very short time after that. Ian told me this because he detested dishonesty. Which is so wonderful about him, because I detest dishonesty too, especially in science.[1281]

Thinhorn Sheep fighting

Ovis dalli

A medium-sized sheep with slender horns. The usual form of horns in the male is a much more open and spreading spiral than in the Bighorn Sheep. Horns in life are paler than those of the Bighorn … In general habits the Thinhorn and Bighorn sheep are closely alike. The rut is from mid-November to mid-December and the gestation period about six months.[1282]

Val Geist was familiar with dishonesty and betrayal, having fled from the Wehrmacht and the SS during the war. He was a young German–Russian refugee who was smuggled out of Russia by his single mother in the winter of 1943. He went on to become one of Cowan's star students in ungulate research. After finishing his undergraduate work at UBC with Cowan, he studied both Bighorn and Thinhorn Sheep, including the Stone's (*stonei*) subspecies of the Thinhorn in the Spatsizi Plateau starting in 1961.

Geist's work ultimately contributed to a collaboration with Cowan and forest ecologist Vladimir Krajina in the 1975 establishment of the largest ecological reserve in BC, around Gladys Lake in the Spatsizi, in a new provincial park, spearheaded by the advocacy work of Tommy and Marion Walker. The couple, who in 1948 had set up the licensed hunting camps in Spatsizi before turning into passionate advocates for protection of the area, asked Cowan to write the foreword to their book:

> The Walkers' love for the Spatsizi grew into a full-blown campaign to save it and the magnificent ecosystem it represented from total destruction … Tommy and Marion have had a dream for their country and for the small group of Indian friends who lived there with hardship before they arrived … It was the Walkers who provided the steady pressure, by films, by photographic presentations, by letters and personal exhortation. As a road moved up one boundary and a railroad up another, the Stone's sheep, caribou, goats and grizzlies

decreased in numbers, and it seemed for a time that there was little hope.[1283]

Cowan's winning combination of supporting the activists who were "getting the mule's attention" and the scientists "pushing from behind" was admira-
bly demonstrated with Spatsizi. And he chose his scientific acolytes well too. Geist
had grown up learning about the natural world from his German grandmother.
When the Germans invaded Russia, he and his mother, a Russian-trained engineer,
fled by cattle wagon to Austria and then on to Canada, where they ended up in
Saskatchewan. As a 15-year-old, Geist first heard of Cowan from the wildlife artist
he met painting the mural of the grasslands for the Regina Museum, R.D. Symons.
When he graduated from high school, he headed for UBC and signed up in zoology.
Geist points to the first instance he experienced of mentoring by Cowan when, as
an undergraduate, he was pulled into Cowan's office from the hallway. "He showed
me his wonderful collection that he had acquired in the national parks. And I mean
a large number of the bighorn collection came out of that. He spoke about his relationship there with old Jimmy Simpson, who I met."[1284]

Geist did his PhD on the parallel evolution of antlers and horns from ruminants
to rhinos. He argued that aggression was modulated by natural selection at the individual level, an idea that built on Cowan's early wolf work. Geist wrote the first
scientific paper ever to discuss this notion.[1285] Another first for Geist was the use
of the word "homosexual" in a zoological journal.[1286] His work on the social structure of Thinhorn and Bighorn Sheep identified never before described homosexual
behaviour of some young male sheep:

> The young male tries to associate himself with the big male, and tries
> to make sure he doesn't lose him. And he does that by playing fe-
> male. And his behaviour is that of a female in heat, and it is exactly
> the same – qualitatively and quantitatively … So there's this bonding
> between the two. I had quite a struggle with that. With Ian we man-
> aged to get, in 1968, the word "homosexuality" into the *Canadian
> Journal of Zoology* – the very, very first.[1287]

Geist ended up a professor emeritus of environmental science at the University
of Calgary. During his academic career, he was as much a maverick in pushing
back the conservative boundaries of political attitudes as well as scientific para-
digms. His advocacy came from straight out of the pages of the 'B.' He has published 17 popular books and seven documentary films on wildlife and ecology. He
and Cowan co-edited an anthology on wildlife conservation policy in 1995. Its introduction read:

> This book focuses on an ongoing, but ancient, struggle between pub-
> lic and private ownership of wildlife. Historically, wildlife has been
> a pawn in the eternal battle between the rich and powerful and the
> not-so-wealthy of modest political power. Today's tensions arise not

only from private interests gaining on public ones in the area of wild-life conservation and the negative consequences that entails, but also from the inadequate application of available knowledge to decisions on this matter. Beware: these pages are not free of controversy.[1288]

Geist is also a fine artist, and his pen and inks of the different horned animals accompanied his work. He drew a personal bookplate, or "coat of arms," for Cowan that he placed in all his books: an illustration of a bighorn sheep.

Another student who started his career looking at Mountain Goat populations[1289] in 1970 was Wayne McCrory, from a mining family in the Kootenays. He and Cowan had sparred over the academic standing of his research,[1290] but McCrory lost little time in proving himself as one of the top experts in bear ecology and went on to become a high-profile conservation biologist and co-founder of the Valhalla Wilderness Society, an organization that has helped protect thousands of hectares of habitat in BC.[1291] Wayne's sister Colleen McCrory was also a leading activist in BC, working with her brother before her premature death. The lineage of researchers for Rocky Mountain species burgeoned from this time on, and Cowan's role increasingly became one of finding them the resources they needed to do their work.

CHAPTER 27

*"I have had the saddening experience of revisiting, after the
clear-cutter, some areas that formerly supported gigantic
spruce trees, clear, fish-rich streams and an assemblage of
the birds and mammals found only on these islands."*

Queen Charlotte Islands, 1945–1946

The university had been on a tight rein through the war, but with the return of the veterans from overseas the campus population surged from just over 3,000 to 11,500. Cowan had great respect for the mature men coming into the program; most of them were not much younger than he was.

> They [the veterans] were in a hurry – understandably – so they got every benefit. We had courses twelve months a year; there were no TAs, because we hadn't been training any ... We had one lab that held 32 people and there were 200 people in each of two courses that had to go through that in one year, every week. It was a killer.[1292]

Cowan started embryology and comparative anatomy courses in addition to his vertebrate zoology and wildlife management courses and had hired on two new professors for the job. The first was physiologist William (Bill) Hoar, on the basis that he was a "first-rate researcher, teacher and good proctor of students."[1293] Then Peter Ford, an embryologist, was hired. Bill Hoar wrote, "It was an exciting period when much depended on the stamina and drive of people like Ian Cowan, unfettered by committees, ready to experiment and open to change."[1294] Cowan's lectures were legendary, often standing room only. It wasn't unheard of that students would desert their assigned lecturer and sit on the stairs to attend Cowan's class.

The first cohort of veterans arriving at the university was an exceptional one. They were to shape and guide the various institutions – old and new – that were expanding or popping up across Canada: the Canadian Wildlife Service, wildlife and parks departments, universities, museums, conservation organizations. Cowan related that "at one time every province, as far as I know, that had a biology division was headed by one of my students; and at one time so was the head of parks and head of the wildlife service. The information flow was great – there wasn't much we didn't hear about."[1295] In particular, the western cohort of Charlie Guiguet, Pat Martin, Don Robinson, Tom Sterling, Jim Hatter, Bob Harris, Glen Smith, Dave

Munro and Ward Stevens formed lifelong friendships and a strong connection to Cowan. Yorke Edwards wasn't a veteran but he too joined this group. As Guiguet's wife Muriel characterized them, "They were the early 'environmentalists,' though they didn't call themselves that."[1296]

Tom Sterling was a typical Cowan student of the time. He loved being outdoors, had been raised in the prairies and was both a naturalist and a hunter, used to hunting for the pot. "I had come from a farm, where no one intentionally taught us anything; everybody just got on with it. No one-upmanship and putting people down."[1297] As a teenager, Sterling had been attracted to a career outdoors through the mentorship of Bertram (Bert) Cartwright, the chief naturalist with the fledgling conservation organization Ducks Unlimited Canada. Before the war, DU consisted of only a handful of waterfowl enthusiasts, and Cartwright ran the show in Canada, providing keen students with odd jobs counting ducks. When the war hit, Sterling enlisted at 17, a move which lost its allure very quickly. "Don't believe the story that we are heroes. War is insane."[1298] When he returned, having been grounded from his air combat assignment due to airsickness, Sterling joined the line of veterans looking for work. "We were all desperate … When I saw Bert (he must have had thousands of people asking him), he said: 'We only hired a couple of students but this is what you should do – go get an education.'"[1299]

Sterling was directed to UBC:

> I found the university and went in to sign up for courses. There was a big room with tables all over the place and when there was an empty table we would walk over to it … and an empty table came up. I walked over and a gentleman was there. I told him I wanted to be in the sciences. I wanted the outdoors, nature, the woods and birds. "Well," he said, "there is a new course just underway." And he explained it to me. I couldn't believe it. You see, I wasn't university material.[1300]

Sterling was not unusual in not having senior matriculation. He was the beneficiary of UBC president Norman Mackenzie's "no man left behind" policy. His existing grade level and veteran status got him in. "I still didn't know who this chap was behind the table but he was just like Bert Cartwright. Well I turned up for my first day of classes and it was this same guy! McTaggart Cowan. So he has been my godfather, along with Bert Brink, ever since."[1301]

Sterling did undergraduate work on scoters (large seaducks), somewhat challenging for a prairie boy prone to motion sickness. Cowan found him a boat and instructed him to collect three age groups of the three different species, which meant sitting for long hours in a boat in the Strait of Georgia in the middle of winter when the big flocks come in for the early spring herring roe.

Sterling managed to survive both seasickness and some epic winter squalls. He shared quarters with the fisheries students, who, he observed, "were serious scientists. They were a good bunch and we [the wildlife students] were sort of different."

The difference he noted was from their naturalist roots:

> Scientists want to do quick things, do an experiment and get the truth of whatever they are looking for. But I'll take a naturalist anytime. I'm more in awe of them than the science. Ian knew that we had enough science right from the beginning, even from the hunters and gatherers ... they had science although they didn't call it that. They knew the habits of the animals, what trails they used, what food they ate, and when they were born and when they bred ... That is why I always said volunteers did it because they loved it, not because they were getting paid. Too many have the book learning and want the job and be a scientist, but they'll do it and not be advocates. Ian was very much the naturalist and advocate.[1304]

The unmarried veterans had accommodation in the wartime Nissen huts at "Fort Camp" overlooking the water on the UBC campus. They lived in one hut and cooked their meals in another. The herds of young, single men on the campus at the time would occasionally turn up hung-over for classes. Cowan would stop in the middle of his lecture, if he was getting no response, and say, "You know, you'd be far better off if, instead of spending your money on a bottle, you'd buy a good book and spend the evening reading that." Sterling never forgot that advice, and when he used to set up his tent on the outskirts of the small towns he visited in the course of his work, he would go to a second-hand bookstore and buy a book. "When I retired I had 3,000 books, all in natural history."[1305] Sterling spent the rest of his career with Bert Cartwright and Ducks Unlimited, moving from the prairies to the coast and finishing his professional career in the Yukon. A large number of

Surf Scoter

Melanitta perspicillata

In late winter or spring, spectacular numbers of Surf Scoters are often seen where Pacific herring are spawning. An unusually large concentration was noted by Martin (1978),[1302] who reported a flock of 300,000 scoters, almost exclusively Surf Scoters, from Big Bay ... a sizable proportion of the North American population depends on British Columbia's coastal habitats for their survival.[1303]

Ring-necked Duck

Aythya collaris

It breeds on freshwater lakes, marshes, ponds and sloughs, often in wooded situations, mainly from 300 m to 1200 m elevation. J.A. Munro notes that nesting birds in the Cariboo parklands seem restricted to slightly acid lakes when yellow water lily covers much of the water surface.[1306]

critical wetlands throughout western Canada were protected by Sterling's negotiations with landowners. He maintained, "The ducks were doing fine before man was there. You just provide the right habitat. We still have to measure and weigh. You look for plants that they are eating. Ducks know best."

One of the married veterans of the cohort was Charlie Guiguet.[1307] Cowan had known Guiguet for many years and they had shared the same mentors from the 'B'. Both Jim Munro and Hamilton Mack Laing had encouraged the young Guiguet and guided him through many of the same landscapes that Cowan had traipsed. Guiguet had been born in the prairies to French immigrant parents and was another "butterfly boy." He started his own natural history museum in Grade 8. When Munro heard about it, he arranged a visit to the school under the auspices of the National Museum of Canada. Munro taught Guiguet how to properly prepare a specimen: a local Black-footed Ferret the schoolkids had shot[1308] (now an endangered species of the grasslands). In 1934 the Guiguet family moved to Vancouver. After the young Charles graduated, he, like Cowan before him, joined a National Museum expedition with Laing up north and on the coast. They worked for four summers together, 1936–39. During one of the trips, exploring the Rainbow Range of Tweedsmuir Park, they used Phyllis and Don Munday as outfitters. These were the mountaineers who had befriended Cowan as a teenager on Grouse Mountain in Vancouver.

While collecting specimens in the Cariboo for the Provincial Museum, Guiguet had met and married Muriel Waller from Wells, BC. That was 1941, and a year later he was overseas with the RCAF. By the end of the war, he had flown 48 missions over Germany and eastern Europe. He was due to fly from southern Italy to Warsaw when Churchill interceded and stopped all further missions because of the number of casualties. Guiguet had told his wife, "[Churchill] saved our life. If we'd gone out again, we would have been shot."[1309] According to Muriel Guiguet, Charles declared: "'I'll never leave you again.' Next May, he was gone to the Queen Charlottes [with Cowan.]"[1310]

Cowan had managed to persuade him to go by promising that his family could join him up there for the summer. The Rocky Mountain research was wrapping up that spring and a whole new research project was opening up – a survey of the birds and mammals of the Queen Charlotte Islands (Haida Gwaii) with a special look at the endemic species. In lecture notes on the isolated archipelago, Cowan described his interest:

> Islands have long intrigued me. Earlier studies made on other insular forms led me to survey the known facts about QCI [Haida Gwaii] critically. There were features that it seemed to me could be explained on the basis of the islands as an unglaciated faunal reservoir from pre-ice-age days. This was one large question mark before me. Other questions: small mammals; the caribou; the great unknown areas of the west coast and alplands; the seabird colonies; the behaviour of ungulate populations in a predator-less environment.[1311]

He also had a practical need to build up a set of specimens for the UBC collection and complete his mammal work on the islands for his book. All he needed was a self-sufficient student who could cope in an unforgiving environment. He found these qualities in Charlie Guiguet. Guiguet was given a list of species to collect and instructions to go on ahead to Masset to work in the northern region including Langara Island, an important seabird colony. Cowan planned to join the Guiguet family in the field in August. Guiguet arrived in the middle of the nesting season in May and connected with local naturalist–ornithologist Ronald Stewart and his wife, who had the essential boat and local knowledge.

Cowan had met Stewart through Laing, Brooks and the other Comox naturalists. Stewart was a very close friend of Laing's, affectionately known as "Martukoo." Laing referred to him as "the fastest man with a gun I ever knew." Professionally, he had worked as a game warden all over the province before retiring to Masset after his last posting there. He was another larger-than-life personality – unofficially the discoverer of the Marbled Murrelet nesting site – and provided invaluable information to the two men, including the best crabbing spots.

Before heading up the coast, Cowan had to wind up the Rockies' final year of range surveys and get student Bert Pfeiffer started on a coyote study. The whole Cowan family travelled up, basing themselves at Lake Edith rental cabins near Jasper. Ann recalls an apocryphal family legend that she, as a 2-year-old, helped her older brother to scare a bear away from visiting their cabin. Also visiting from his next-door cabin, where he was working on a manuscript, was Dr. William (Bill) Rowan. Cowan and Rowan share more than their rhyming last names. Rowan started the department of zoology at the University of Alberta and was internationally renowned for his work on avian migration. He had devised a famous field experiment with crows which concluded that lengthening days triggered migration and reproduction. Cowan described Rowan's famous experiment to his young audience in an episode of his *Web of Life* television series called 'Migration':

> Migration is a dramatic event, but far more than just drama, migration holds some fascinating biological questions … Dr. Rowan from the University of Alberta asked the question, what starts migration? He placed some juncos and crows outside in a cage in a northern Albertan winter. The first cage was normal and the second cage had lights, creating a longer day like in the spring. He found he had produced birds that were in full breeding condition, ready to lay eggs and when released most moved north.[1312]

At the time, Rowan had a fine reputation as one of Canada's most admired and colourful scientists and conservationists, being a great popularizer of natural history and science on radio.[1314] He was a young naturalist, a lover of Ernest Thompson Seton, and honed his skills in natural history illustration and photography. He was friends with many of the 'B', including Taverner and the Grinnells. He had also resisted the pressures of industry boosters within the university – even his own president, Henry Marshall Tory, who had commanded him to abandon fieldwork and go back to the laboratory to do "real" zoology.[1315] According to Rowan's biographer, Rowan had to fight a president who only favoured "utilitarian projects with huge financial returns."[1316] Rowan ignored him. As an early proponent of 'citizen science,' Rowan had public goodwill on his side, having mobilized local people all over Alberta to observe and report on the early migrating crows. That spring he was up in the mountains at a Lake Edith cabin (which he had been visiting since 1935) to revise his manuscript of *As the Crow Flies*. Rowan never found a publisher for his crow manuscript, which may or may not have had to do with his being a pacifist and an outspoken critic of the suppression of scientists after the war.

The secret to his success was captured in his obituary, written by colleague F.M. Salter:

Young **American Crow**

Corvus brachyrhynchos

The American Crow is migratory over most of British Columbia. The American Crow migrates in flocks rather than as single birds, but flocks are smaller in the spring migration than the autumn ... It is normal behaviour for this crow, once the young are on the wing, to gather into large flocks to roost ... It is easy to confuse evening flights to roost with migration flights.[1313]

> Many-sided, many-gifted, Dr. Rowan was a man of the keenest, boyish enthusiasms. No one who had spent five minutes in his company would ever forget him. He made the science that was not a science meaningful to a whole province; and as an artist, lecturer and man he served his time and his generation well.[1317]

Rowan and Cowan were two birds of the same feather and would have had plenty to talk about in their spring sojourn in the mountains. Rowan retired in 1956 and died the following year. Cowan was to deliver his own memorable lecture of putting ecology before commerce to the graduating class of Rowan's old alma mater in 1971[1318]. History doesn't reveal how the speech was received. Today, Rowan is virtually unknown and uncelebrated on the University of Alberta campus, despite his earlier international stature.

Cowan spent two months in Jasper, taking the family out on his surveys when he could – Ann strapped into a wooden frame, Garry being a sturdy hiker and Joyce an experienced volunteer research assistant. The final entry in the journal for the Rockies was somewhat anticlimactic after wrapping up four years of research.

July 16

Rode the 10 miles to here [Wolverine Pass] with Bert [Pfeiffer], George Nesatyk + a Shuswap Indian named Joe? Thunderstorms + snow made travelling most unpleasant. Today, however, has been good: high-driven cumulus clouds + generally sunshine. Hiked over to head of Helmet Creek, also to head of Dainard Creek + Bert [Pfeiffer] crossed to head of Numa Creek this afternoon. Lots of *Larix lyallii* [Alpine larch] here – in fact it is dominant at timberline. Alplands here do not feature the great willow beds of those on the east slope + are still heavily snow-covered. Took 4 [*Microtus*] *richardsoni*. Not much point in spending longer here so decided to leave. Found wardens had run out of alcohol + gone to town.

July 18

In a.m. had Joe bring in the horses + I packed them + we set out. Met the wardens just before we got to the highway – an embarrassed pass. Joyce, the children + I packed up + returned to Vancouver on July 20.[1319]

The report he prepares is short that year. It pointed to the 1942 epidemic in the bighorn population as the main cause of their decline, as well as the "deplorable range conditions," which hadn't improved even with elk culls, due to too many horses and elk still remaining in the winter ranges. He proposed continuing involvement of the wardens in monitoring the winter range. Meanwhile, Austin de B. Winter of the Alberta Fish and Game Association received a letter from another Calgary colleague, C.P. Sissons, the publisher of *Game Trails Magazine*, about the results:

> You know, Austin, I have never taken for granted the answers on these questions; they are given by our learned university professors. I met Dr. McTaggart Cowan a short while back and I told him that I still thought he was all wet on the Wolf situation in our National Parks. I pointed out to him that had he spent a year making a survey of the parks, I would concede that he would have something definite on this controversial matter, BUT I was sorry to disagree with him when his opinion was expressed after spending 30 days in such a vast area.[1320]

The evidence, however, was out there after the four-year study, and the Calgary sportsmen were losing their hold on "the truth."

Cowan was already moving on to other work. Ten days after leaving Jasper, his journal opens up with the heading: "USS *Cassin*, Queen Charlotte Sound."[1321] In another rare moment of inaccuracy, Cowan refers to the wrong vessel. He wasn't on the USS *Cassin*; the *Cassin* was a famous naval destroyer that had recently been decommissioned and was nowhere near the Sound in 1946. He was on the more modest ss *Cassiar*[1322] near Pine Island lighthouse, watching the feeding frenzy of various coastal members of the puffin family (also known as alcids), which includes none other than Cassin's Auklet. It is tempting to think that perhaps Cowan was confusing his boats with his birds. The Cassin for whom the destroyer was named had nothing in common with the one that named the bird. The alcids Cowan saw from the rail of the *Cassiar* included Rhinoceros Auklets, Tufted Puffins, Pidgeon [Pigeon] Guillemots, Marbled Murrelets and Common Murres.

In a file entitled "Island Lecture," which contained notes from one of his classes, Cowan provides a rather cryptic list of talking points that appear to summarize his trip up to the Charlottes (Haida Gwaii) that spring of 1946:

- ss *Cassiar*
- the pulse of the Charlottes (seasonal birds)
- the chef
- the cabins and their bulky occupant
- the bridal suite[1324]

Given his predilection for engaging his students on the topic of reproduction, it is likely he was tracing the seasonal feeding frenzy at sea – and on board – through to its logical conclusion to the bridal suite. An alcid feeding frenzy is one of the wonders of the world. Large flocks gather around the silver, sandlance or herring coming into spawn. With their perfectly adapted swimming wings, these little seabirds herd the forage fish underwater into large balls, working the ball from all sides. The fish are pushed to the surface, which boils with activity, making it easy pickings for the marine mammals below and the gulls and eagles waiting to swoop down and collect them from above. The "bulky occupant" may have referred to the post-feeding state of the birds – or to Cowan himself and the quantity of his equipment.

As they approached the islands, the *Cassiar* called at the three big logging camps of Cumshewa, Sandspit and Skidegate. The islands were still reeling from the depredations of the war. The highly prized, fast-growing Sitka Spruce had been high-graded all through the islands for building the wooden Mosquito combat airplanes. The ports of call provided Cowan with an excellent opportunity to check out various bird colonies and the nesting sites of Peale's Falcon (an aerial-combat master itself) on cliffs close to colonies.

When they landed at Queen Charlotte City (more a hamlet than a city), he met Charlie and Muriel Guiguet and their daughter Jo Ann, as well as his other students Dean Fisher and Ed Barreclough, at the Queen Charlotte Hotel. Cowan writes:

[August] 3, 1946. [Queen Charlotte] City
Rowed over to the two small islets in the bay + found about 7 or 8 pairs of Glaucous-winged Gulls nesting on the easternmost + one pair on the other islet. Several pairs of [Pigeon] Guillemots were nesting on the eastern islet. They had deep burrows dug in the earth beneath tree roots or between rocks. Definite pathways led in under

the shore vegetation + to them. One contained a young bird that we dug out. This burrow had a mess of faeces at the entrance. The young bird was taken + is Guiguet's specimen #290.[1326]

The group started with one-day field trips from the village. They went to Tlell, the coastal hamlet beside the Tlell River, and recorded big flocks of Brant, shorebirds, loons, grebes and songbirds in the estuary. Another day, they penetrated "the climax forests north of the village."[1328] Cowan described a forest understorey that was showing impacts from over-browsing from the introduced Sitka subspecies of the Mule Deer. The Sitkas had been brought to Graham Island from Porcher and Pitt Islands between 1880 and 1925, and with no competitors or predators in their new home – perhaps an occasional Black Bear – their population exploded:

> It is evident that the Sitka Spruce is a pioneer tree. In the present forests it occurs as scattered very large trees. Hemlock + Red Cedar are the climax species. Over large areas there is no undergrowth but here and there sword fern, ostrich fern + two or three deer fern occur. The birds of the climax forest are: 1. In the summit stratum: Townsend Warbler, Red Crossbill, Golden-crowned Kinglet + Chestnut-backed Chickadee. 2. In the ground stratum: Varied Thrush, Winter Wren, Red-breasted Sapsucker and Tree Creeper [Brown Creeper].[1329]

Cassin's Auklet

Ptychoramphus aleuticus

The Cassin's Auklet occurs along most of the outer coast, with only scattered records on the inner coastal waters of the Strait of Georgia. It forages in offshore waters more frequently than the other alcids and is only rarely seen close to shore, even near breeding colonies.[1323]

Peale's Peregrine Falcon

Falco peregrinus pealei

Essentially resident on the islands and headlands of the Pacific coast from Oregon northwest through the Aleutian Islands to the Commander and Kurile islands of Asia. It is a marine peregrine and seldom occurs inland ...[1325]

Pigeon Guillemot

Cepphus columba

... It is the most conspicuous breeding seabird in the province. The Pigeon Guillemot is a colonial species only in the vicinity of large rocky islands and headlands that provide suitable nestsites. Otherwise it readily breeds as isolated pairs along the shoreline, provided sites are devoid of mammalian predators, and soft banks (for burrowing) crevices are available for nesting ... Over one-half of all birds sighted were in the Queen Charlotte Islands.[1327]

When Muriel Guiguet and Jo Ann headed home, Cowan and Guiguet hooked up with Howard Fairbairn, who was heading to Rose Harbour, on Kunghit Island at the south end of the archipelago. Cowan described Fairbairn as "a local fisheries guardian." Local historian Kathleen Dalzell had a more expansive description: "Few people knew the coastline of the Charlottes better than Mr. Fairbairn."[1331] He had arrived on the islands in 1911 as a hand logger and ended up running a tugboat business and working the west coast as a fishery protection officer. During the twelve and a half hour trip down the east coast, they no doubt exchanged some useful information as well as passing alcid hotspots at Cumshewa Inlet and Reef Island – large flocks of Common Murres with the odd Marbled and Ancient Murrelet mixed in.

The alcids were of particular interest to the two men, as so little was known of their life cycles. It was not yet documented that Common Murres nested on the rocky Kerouards off the southern tip of Cape Saint James. Nor was it yet documented that murres displayed interesting parenting techniques where the males exclusively raised the young fledglings once they were out at sea – the females are nowhere to be seen. Although parenting duties in the Cowan household were conventional for families at the time (un-murre-like), Cowan was quite open to the idea that there was a diversity of parenting behaviours and that they were a reflection of complex factors and dynamic environments. Both his sisters pursued professional careers while raising families.

The two murrelets were both nesters on the forested islands but at opposite ends of the forest – on its vertical axis. The Marbled Murrelets, according to Ron Stewart, were suspected to nest high up in the old-growth trees, while the Ancients were in burrows at their roots. Chicks of all the alcid species are born fat, fuzzy and ready to go. These animals have "precocial" young, meaning that as soon as they hatch, they can feed themselves and flee to the safety of the open ocean upon the urgings of their parent.

Brown Creeper (Tree Creeper)

Certhia americana

Farther north, the Brown Creeper has a scattered and sparse distribution except on the Queen Charlotte Islands, where it occurs regularly throughout the year ... On the coast it frequents mature and old-growth coniferous forests ...[1330]

Ancient Murrelet

Synthliboramphus antiquus

The Ancient Murrelet is primarily a plankton feeder and forages in areas of upwelling and mixing such as surge narrows, channels and other areas with strong eddies and tidal streams. At sea its distribution is patchy and poorly understood ... The Ancient Murrelet breeds mainly on the Queen Charlotte Islands. In most cases downy young found close to coastal islands away from the Queen Charlotte Islands do not indicate local breeding but illustrate the species' rapid post-breeding dispersal. Radio tracking studies indicate that Hecate Strait can be crossed by chicks in 24 hours.[1333]

Alexandrian Rat [Black Rat]

Rattus rattus alexandrinus

Scarce in Vancouver and North Vancouver; abundant in the wild on Queen Charlotte Islands, where it is in pure stock on Langara Island. Specimens also from Sandspit, Kunghit Island, Burnaby Islands, QCI.

Little else was known of the birds except these odd sightings as they were on their way back out to the open ocean.

Fairbairn dropped the two men at the abandoned whaling station at Rose Harbour, which had closed four years earlier. After processing hundreds of right, sperm, blue, fin, sei and humpback whales and housing hundreds of workers over its 31-year history, the station had accumulated considerable industrial debris. Old boiler sheds, ramps, flensing sheds, workers' housing and docks – all were starting to rot back into the rainforest, while the detritus of 40 years of bones, blood, ash and whale oil still littered the shore. Cowan and Guiguet found an old building in which to set up a camp and started immediately trapping for small mammals, searching for the endemic mice and shrews. Unfortunately, when the whalers pulled out, they had left an even more deadly invading predator, the Black Rat, *Rattus rattus alexandrinus* and *Rattus rattus rattus*, which filled Cowan's and Guiguet's traps.

Common Murre

Uria aalge

All nesting sites are on offshore islands. The small number of colonies in British Columbia may be due to the scarcity of suitable cliffs ... Habitat on the Kerouard Islands is bare rock ...[1332]

The full impact of rats on seabird populations was not to be fully understood for a few years yet. Cowan and Guiguet were just starting on the groundwork. Populations of seabirds weren't counted yet, and their colonies still needed to be located. Guiguet would follow Tom McCabe as the next foremost seabird specialist on the coast, conducting the first comprehensive catalogue of seabird colonies during his tenure at the Provincial Museum.[1334] Rats are predators of seabird eggs, but to what extent was unknown at that time. The Alexandrian rat (a subspecies of the Black Rat) was actually to be displaced by the more aggressive Norwegian Rat (*Rattus norvegicus*), which appeared in the 1980s. Collectively the rats were to become the single biggest threat to the ground-nesting alcids, and it wasn't until 1997 that the rats were eradicated from important seabird nesting islands like Langara.

Cowan had found an old whaling station boat but declared it "a wreck"[1335] after trying to use it and failing in his efforts to collect a Rhinoceros Auklet on the water. More successful was their ability to live off venison in their shanty-town encampment. The two men split up and covered the ground on foot for the next week. Guiguet battled the salal on a badly overgrown trail out to Moore's Point on the southeast tip of Kunghit Island while Cowan pushed his way west and up into the easier open country of the sphagnum muskeg, where he found the endemic race of the Dusky Shrew. Guiguet's travels led him to signs of an active seabird colony on a rocky headland covered in salal. The two returned there to investigate the inhabitants of the burrows in the night – armed with spades and flashlights. Cowan refers to Guiguet's notes at this stage.

They arrived at dusk around 9:15 and the adults had already started flying into the burrows from the sea. They set about digging up the burrows to learn more about them.

> Digging is difficult. First bird uncovered was a Rhinoceros Auklet (fledgling stage). This bird was about eight feet underground; that is, the burrow was about eight feet long and about three feet of soil and roots above it at the distal end.[1336]

The fact that the auklets are clumsy flyers was noted: "Two birds flew onto the rocks about three feet in front of me, striking very hard it seemed."[1337] Not surprising for an animal that lives virtually all its life either on top of or under the open ocean, except for brief forays to islands to breed. At 10 p.m. the activity ceased. "The assumption is that the adults were all in the nests with the young and were staying there."[1338] Then, at midnight, it started up again, with the adults leaving the burrows and flying out to sea, peaking at 2:30 in the morning and tapering to nothing by dawn. The men returned to their own "burrows" for a short nap after dawn, then were back out to the colony to photograph in sunshine the battleground they had left.

With specimens to prepare, Fairbairn turning up a day late posed no problem. The two just had more specimens to load onto his boat. Unlike the trip down, which was calm, they now had tide and wind in their face. They missed the slack high tide at Burnaby Narrows and so had the opportunity to go ashore and observe a famous low tide there. These islands have huge tidal

Common Raven

Corvus corax

Munro and Cowan (1947) summarized the evidence as to the status of the species in British Columbia, considering it a local resident most abundant on the coast … The Common Raven is more numerous and widespread today. It now breeds in areas where it was previously known only as a winter visitant, and populations have increased along with increasing human settlement.[1339]

Keen['s] Myotis

Myotis keeni keeni
[*Myotis keenii* no ssp. recognized]

This bat inhabits the dense timber tracts, where it flies high along the forest aisles and around ponds and other clear areas. The flight is usually direct and rather slow. It is apparently a solitary species, hanging up in tree cavities and crevices in cliff faces.[1342]

Northern Saw-whet Owl

Aegolius acadicus brooksi

The owl roosts in dense tangles of branches as well as natural cavities and man-made structures. Two subspecies are recognized in North America, both of which occur in British Columbia. *Aegolius acadicus brooksi* is endemic to the Queen Charlotte Islands; *A. a. acadicus* is found elsewhere throughout the province.[1343]

ranges and the volume of water that moves between the narrows of Moresby and Burnaby islands has created an area of such rich intertidal life that the only limiting factor for an organism is finding room to attach. That day, Cowan recorded 150 crows scrapping around over the narrows, an eagle flying over, two pairs of oystercatchers doing the rounds, Wandering Tattlers and Least Sandpipers working the rocky shores and cheerful flocks of chickadees, wrens, kinglets and one Western Flycatcher [now Pacific-slope Flycatcher] foraging in the shoreline shrubbery. They trapped another shrew, tracked a bear and watched the ubiquitous ravens checking them out.

Burnaby Narrows was to become the focus for pioneering research on ocean–forest interrelationships by Tom Reimchen, who was encouraged in his research by Cowan and Bristol Foster during the '80s and '90s.[1340] Reimchen stationed himself at Bag Harbour near Burnaby Narrows and measured the movement of oceanic nitrogens (nitrogen-15 with radioactive signatures) via salmon and intertidal life from the ocean into the forest. The movement of these 'fish fertilizers' was through the network of birds and mammals hauling their dinners up into the forest and excreting the undigested remains. When asked what excited him most in the field of biology in 2000, Cowan responded:

> … the role of the salmon in the environment in which we live. That was as exciting as anything that has been proposed in biology for a very long time. It started out with an idea in [Tom Reimchen's] head and he set a series of questions that wanted answering and he answered them. That is how all good ideas spread. It opens a new window. You have to keep being out there."[1341]

In the middle of their 1946 trip, Cowan and Guiguet restocked their supplies up in Queen Charlotte City, then spent the next week between Copper Bay and Sandspit interviewing trappers and looking for the endemic subspecies. Besides rats, they were also observing island bats and collected three species of myotis while they were there: Little Brown, California and Keen's.

They had had no luck in spotting either the endemic Queen Charlotte Marten or the Haida Weasel (Ermine), and Cowan met with various locals to find some skulls or skins. They were also beating the bushes to get specimens of the endemic subspecies of the Northern Saw-whet Owl.

On the morning of September 3 they were finally successful in trapping a saw-whet. Then the two men packed up their equipment and boarded the ss *Cassiar* after lunch. This was Cowan's last entry for the summer:

> Hecate Strait, Sept 3/46
> 9 miles off Reef Island saw a beautiful Pink-footed Shearwater at very close range; close to the same place saw a pale Gray Shearwater with black primaries + some black on the head + white underwings; another of the same kind seen just 5 or 6 miles off Aristazabal Island. Saw some 30 Sooty Shearwaters + 1 Slender-billed, 4 Fork-tailed Petrels,

2 rhinos [rhinoceros auklets], 4 murres + 3 Pigeon Guillemots, 3 Herring gull; 1 Thayer's gull (taken) + many Glaucous-wing [gulls]; 3 Humpback Whales + 10 or 12 Sea Lions.[1344]

The shearwaters starred in just one of the many spectacular natural history stories that originated from these images of the trip, and Cowan told them all in his CBC television series during the 1950s. In the "Migration" episode of the *Web of Life* series, he described the route of the fellow

Pink-footed Shearwater

Puffinus creatopus

Breeds on islands off Chile, migrating north offshore along the Pacific Coast of South and North America. It has been recorded from 26 April to 14 October, with 85% of all records occurring between July and September when birds gradually return to their southern breeding grounds.[1345]

Sooty Shearwaters who "leave their lush feeding grounds of the northern waters, head south along BC and California, loop across the Pacific to the Tasman Sea and complete their 11,000 mile round trip." Sooties are often found in flocks with the Pink-footed despite their different breeding grounds in different oceans.

The Web of Life followed *The Living Sea* series, in which Cowan narrated 26 documentaries on the oceans. That series also contained powerful images from his time in these islands. One of the episodes, called "Whales," featured Coal Harbour, a whaling station on northern Vancouver Island from which whaling was still being done in Hecate Strait the year he was filming, 1958. The cameras caught the whaling boats bringing in five animals – Orca, Sei and Humpback. He took the cameras to a tail and pointed out the muscles that drive the animal at 25 knots; he compared the ridges in the roof of his own mouth with the huge plates of baleen that strain out the water. The camera then zoomed in on the blow holes, where the whale takes "its heavily charged breath – and it *is* heavily charged too if you are downwind of its breath!"[1346] He moved on to a Humpback that had unborn twins and showed the viewers the umbilical cord, the hair on the fetuses (a remnant of their terrestrial origins), the mother's teats and ability to inject milk (an adaptation for underwater living), and the regulation of heat through the tail. "Isn't this a fascinating cooling idea! We couldn't have designed a better one if we'd tried." The show ended with a tribute: "These are simply fabulous creatures, tremendously large and powerful, tremendously speedy in their chosen environment. So, long may they stay there so you and I, when we're at sea, can look out and say: 'Spout off the starboard bow.'"[1347]

Coal Harbour, the last whaling station, closed in 1967 when whale populations dipped so low that there was little commercial viability. Even the humpbacks, which weren't a favoured species, were nearly hunted to extinction. Cowan had files full of "Whales" lectures spanning the decades. One, delivered sometime around 1969, tracked the humpback catches at a time when there were less than 4,000 left in the world. The talking points in a "Whales and Man" lecture earlier in 1963 revealed Cowan's condemnation of the whaling nations and their inability to regulate themselves: "It is commercial whaling of European and American stimulus that has spelled disaster to the large whales of the world. By the 1940s it was obvious that the great whales were declining everywhere."[1349] The International Whaling Commission had set up a scientific committee in 1955. Their recommendations for conservation, however, were defeated on many counts, such as with the humpback, through the "politics of whaling," so "whale catches continued."[1350] In one of his last lectures on whaling, Cowan described the frustrations of the scientific committee he had lately been a member of. The return of the humpback in numbers to North Pacific waters was one of the great joys of his later years. Very recently, the Humpback Whale was downgraded by the federal government from 'threatened' to 'species of special concern.' This was cause for both celebration and dismay. It signalled the trend upwards of the Humpback Whale population, true enough. But on the other hand, the downgrading meant that all types of protection for the whale and its habitat were effectively dropped, and proposed industrial projects like the Northern Gateway pipeline had one

Humpback Whale

Megaptera novaeangliae

This is a migratory species that frequently enters the partially enclosed straits and inlets. Breeds mainly during winter months. Sometimes humpbacks are found simultaneously pregnant and lactating ... Found mainly along open coastal waters; sometimes enters the Strait of Georgia, mainly during summer months. A few humpbacks winter along the coast of British Columbia, but most of the population return to low latitudes for giving birth and pairing.[1348]

of their major obstacles removed – the threatened status of the humpbacks.

The summer on QCI (Haida Gwaii) raised other interesting research questions for Cowan, which he found no shortage of students eager to solve. Guiguet, in addition to his seabirds expertise, picked up the baton on island insularity in mice. He became known as the Mouse Man and worked all over the coast collecting specimens. Cowan and Guiguet shared that love of evolutionary research. As Muriel Guiguet put it: "They enjoyed working together because their brains worked the same." Guiguet worked on films, lectures and popular books for the BC Provincial Museum, including co-authoring *Mammals of BC* with Cowan. In 1969 he established a research and educational program for birds and mammals in the new Provincial Museum. One of Guiguet's lasting contributions was to identify the critical nesting habitat for 80 per cent of all seabirds and provide protection under the provincial Ecological Reserve Act.

The next time Cowan came to the islands was the spring of 1951, to study the impacts of deer browse on forests.[1351] Successor to the "Mouse Man" title was Bristol Foster, whose links with Cowan and Guiguet were to become as intertwined as the kelp beds of Haida Gwaii. Foster took over as director of the museum while

Guiguet was there, then took on the task of setting up the provincial ecological reserves unit. The bonding of Cowan with Foster took place in QCI (Haida Gwaii) for five days in the spring of 1960 and a week in 1961 when Cowan came up to lend a hand to his new graduate student, whose journal entries record that time:

> May 21, 1960, QCI
>
> … Cowan arrived and we made off directly for the north. Camped for the night by Watun River and road about 8 miles south of Massett. Used small red and green hut by the road. Supper first. Cowan strangled a kingfisher on its nest. Set our traps. Weather clear. Found sapsucker nest about 70' up. At dusk 3–4 blue grouse hooting in scrub spruce forest. Shot one. Saw-whet owls hooting. Cool, clear night. Cowan turned in early, we went on to twelve.[1352]

Foster first heard about Cowan when he was doing his masters at the University of Toronto on a rare boreal rodent. According to Foster, "Ian Cowan was known as *the* mammalogist of Canada. He was the guy."[1353] Foster had just been travelling for a year and half in Africa with his friend the artist Robert Bateman and now wanted to do a PhD at UBC. Cowan told him his marks weren't good enough, but Foster persevered. He'd started with work on the Vancouver Island Marmot but had immediately run into problems: "I had trouble just trying to find them and they sleep for maybe 8–9 months of the year, so I went into his office. [Cowan responded:] 'Yes, well, I thought you might have a bit of a problem but I wanted you to have a go at it,' which is his way and much admired."[1354]

Foster was interested in the adaptation of species to local environments, so Cowan suggested looking at the uniqueness of deer mice on the coast with Charlie Guiguet. Foster jumped at the opportunity and expanded the study to look at all the distinct endemic Haida Gwaii mammals: caribou, marten, river otter, black bear, weasel, deer mouse and shrew. Cowan arranged a scholarship for $200/month from Canadian Industries Limited (an explosives and ammunition manufacturer which funded many of his graduate students), found money to hire an assistant and found an outboard motor and Zodiac boat.

For the 1960 trip, Cowan stayed five days at Rose Spit at the north end of Graham Island to trap for mice, shrews and other small mammals with Foster and his assistant, Paul Joslin (who would go on to study predators on several continents). Foster writes:

> About noon we had left for Rose Spit. Road had degenerated into strips of board thru the mossy forest. As we entered the beach drive we had to wait for the tide to drop. A glorious day. The mountains of Alaska and mainland BC clearly visible. Nearby the 400' head of Tow Hill looms dominantly. Supposedly a falcon nesting here. We had lunch on the beach, with Cowan chasing after molluscs and me trying my luck for a trout for supper.[1355]

They drove on the old corduroy road until they reached the end of the forest, where the huge sandspit continues on for many miles, depending on the tide.

> Here we found an ideal campsite under a windswept spruce forest. Set up tent and made ourselves comfortable. Cowan shot a deer and Paul was highly entertained by its copious parasites, especially nematodes in the cecum … Magnus fluke in liver, so must be appropriate snail in ponds. As twilight descended, Cowan and I went along the beach picking up agates, noting many otter tracks, flock of semi-palmated sandpipers, small flock of Brant. Brilliant sunset. Mouse skinning bee. Caught 50 last night so kept us going until midnight![1356]

Foster took photographs of the three men skinning mice at the breakfast table; porridge bowls, spoons, mice and skinning tools all intermingled. Cowan seemed to relish dipping in and out of a diversity of worlds – as comfortable around a camp stove as a television camera or a lectern. But as Foster also pointed out:

> He was so happy to be out of the office. He did part of the cooking and cleaning. I remember when we headed off one day and realized we had forgotten all the cutlery – he had a wry smile on his face – and I made a set of chopsticks – I like chopsticks – and he was quite happy with that.[1357]

Cowan prided himself on maintaining his pelage, though. During that trip they had stopped in at Paul Henson's, the Indian agent, who was also a keen mollusc collector. Foster notes: "We tidied up by puddle side, Cowan putting 'scruffy us' to shame with his blazer, *pressed trousers* and shave!"[1358] In another incident Foster noted, "He did his utmost to keep the standards of decorum up, but had his troubles when he found his sea razor blades missing – so used the [scalpel] in his [dissecting] blade holder."[1359]

The 1961 July trip was to include a revisit of Masset and a trip by Zodiac down to Hotspring Island in the south. Foster was assisted that year by another Cowan student, Mike Bigg. (Bigg would go on to chart the orca whale social structure and have the transient orca subspecies named after him.) Hotspring, so named for its natural hot springs, is a tiny island set amidst the other islands of Juan Perez Sound. It looks out over Moresby Island to the west, Ramsay Island to the south and a host of little islands scattered round. It was an ideal place to base themselves as they checked for endemic mammals and breeding birds.

> In the [afternoon], reached our Tar Islands and found nothing in traps. Some set off, definite Ancient Murrieta sign. Caught 7 mice and 2 shrews on Ramsay. Made up shrews and kept mice alive to send down with Dr. Cowan to start a colony of *sitkensis* for John Hayward's study. Found two eagle's nest – one very large (tall) on island just East of House Island, 45' up spruce and other with one large young on north side of Ramsay.[1360]

The last collaborative biological research Cowan was ever to publish was an article called "Sixteen Years with a Bald Eagle's, *Haliaeetus leucocephalus*, nest." It appeared in *The Canadian Field-Naturalist*, fittingly the journal edited earlier by the 'B' mentors Hoyes Lloyd and Percy Taverner.[1362] He was 88 years old when he co-wrote the article with naturalist Elizabeth (Betty) Kennedy about a pair of Bald Eagles on a nest that was observed on Galiano Island. The editor of that article, Francis Cook, who also worked at the Canadian National Museum of Nature, wrote to ask a favour of Cowan:

> Have you put down anywhere your recollection of working with the museum in the days of Taverner, Anderson and Patch? ...I have been starting to put together some history of the museum – the staff has changed so radically in the last few years that soon there will be no one left who remembers it had a past.[1363]

Having observed the relationship between eagles and alcids, mice and men, Foster, Cowan and Bigg finished up at Hotspring and returned to Graham Island. Cowan stopped in to go molluscing with Peter Henson before heading out with his students to the boggy tableland near MacIntosh Meadows to collect plants and cyclops (freshwater crustaceans) and look for more of the Canadian Sandhill Crane nest sites.

Until the day he died, Cowan was convinced of the possibility that a vertebrate species – whether bird or mammal – might be a relic from the ice-free refugia days. His theory was that the "big" mice found on the islands were such relics that they hadn't yet been invaded or displaced by newcomers. Foster's research established that, as a rule, rodents become larger on islands and ungulates become smaller, regardless of glacial history. While this was first evident in QCI (Haida Gwaii), Foster saw it in the Aleutians and on islands off California and Scotland. Foster's Rule, or the Island Rule, still stands today and has been broadened to other groups of vertebrates and other types of island worldwide.[1364] It has joined other ecological rules such as Bergmann's Rule (mammals' extremities get shorter as one goes north); Gloger's Rule (warm-blooded animals tend to be darker in humid environments, which the Pikas clearly showed); and Allen's Rule (warm-blooded animals with the same volume have different surface area, which will aid or impede their temperature regulation). Foster hypothesized that since islands always have fewer predators and competitors – in contrast to the nearby mainland – selection pressures are invariably different, especially on isolated islands. The more isolated the islands, the more differences, the fewer the species. Haida Gwaii is more isolated than any other island group in Canada, so it had more differences in its mammals, birds and plants than anywhere else in Canada.

Foster's Rule built on other attempts at unifying theories that were emerging at the same time. E.O. Wilson and Robert MacArthur first presented in 1963 the forerunner to their elegant island biogeography theory,[1365] which postulated that the number of species declined with the size of the island, suggesting that extinction

and colonization rates reached an equilibrium. This theory supported the arguments
put forward by conservation biologists in
favour of protecting large areas and not re-
lying on small sanctuaries of nature surrounded by industrial landscapes.

Other scientists like Ted Case and
Martin Cody from Berkeley, who researched the islands in the Sea of Cortez,
argued that there was still a role for thinking about relic populations, as Cowan
did – what they called the historical legacy model – and that the diversity of biological processes of immigration, extinction
and evolution made it unlikely that any one
unifying theory would account for all the
variation that one saw in islands.[1366] The
southern, unglaciated islands had much
older fauna than Haida Gwaii had. At the
first Queen Charlotte Islands International
Symposium, held at UBC in 1984, Cowan
was invited to present his final paper on
the subject, called *Birds and Mammals of
Queen Charlotte Islands*. He carefully re-

Bald Eagle

Haliaeetus leucocephalus

In summer, aggregations occur only
along the coast where "herring balls"
and surface-feeding fishes attract both
breeding and non-breeding eagles ...
The centre of abundance is along the
coast, where dense populations are
found in the Queen Charlotte Islands
and Gulf Islands.[1361]

viewed the recent research to see if he could determine whether any vertebrate species had been present over the last 100,000 years on the ice-free refugia. Whether
islands were inhabited by ancient relic populations of mammals or not, Cowan
was less interested in proving his theory than protecting the islands themselves.
In 1985 the BC government established the Wilderness Advisory Committee and
Cowan submitted two proposals, one on behalf of the Association of Professional
Biologists, the other as a personal submission.[1367] In both, he advocated the protection of the South Moresby Wilderness area. In 1987 he wrote to BC premier Bill
Vander Zalm, saying:

> It is nearly 30 years since I made my first biological studies on the
> Queen Charlotte Islands. Since then I have worked on all the major
> islands and many of the smaller ones. When I was a faculty member
> at the University of British Columbia, several graduate students of
> mine undertook detailed studies of the unique biology of the islands.
> I have had the saddening experience of revisiting, after the clear-cut-
> ter, some areas that formerly supported gigantic spruce trees, clear,
> fish-rich streams and an assemblage of the birds and mammals
> found only on these islands. The ecosystem was totally destroyed. I
> can appreciate your concern to maintain employment ... If the few

remaining areas are cut, never again will we, our children or our guests be able to experience forests of Douglas-fir, Redcedar or Sitka spruce 600–1,200 years old.[1368]

Cowan made one error in this letter: it had actually been over 40 years since he started his biological work there. He continued to do public slide shows about Haida Gwaii well into a fifth decade. His last slide show, still loaded in a projector carousel in his study when he died, contained glorious pictures he had taken of the village of Ninstints (Sgaan Gwaii) and the totems, the old-growth rainforest, the logging, the estuarine glades, the tidal streams, the endemic species of flora and fauna, sunsets, waves, clouds, Joyce silhouetted at sundown and a Varied Thrush, the bird of the forest with its characteristic boy scout whistle song.

Foster had been one of the key scientists and behind-the-scenes activists, providing the rationale for the conservation of the South Moresby area of the islands (which reverted to their original name, Gwaii Haanas). He was aware of growing concerns from the Haida, in particular the Skidegate Band, about renewed logging in their traditional territory, which ended in stand-offs by the elders on Lyell Island. In his role as director of the Ecological Reserves Unit, Foster proposed and created ecological reserves of the seabird collector colonies and the old-growth watershed of Windy Bay.

In 1977 Foster sent a report to Parks Canada that first coined the name for the islands "the Galápagos of the North."[1369] He also sat on the intergovernmental panel called the South Moresby Wilderness Proposal Committee to study the whole southern part of Moresby for a proposed protected area. He used the arguments of island biogeography to scientifically justify the large protected area. Foster supported Haida claims of ecological significance, and he was the first public servant to seriously address the proposal put forward by local activists called the Islands Protection Society. Foster became a friend of many of the key leaders of the movement: Miles Richardson, Guujaaw, Keith Moore and John Broadhead. He provided scientific reports and committee support, shot documentaries and wrote a chapter called "The Canadian Galápagos" for the local group's award-wining book *Islands at the Edge* (1984), which became a national bestseller. Another of Cowan's later students, Wayne Campbell, who became the chief ornithologist at the Provincial Museum, wrote the chapter on birds for the book. Campbell was already collaborating with Cowan at this time on the first two volumes of *Birds of BC*.

In a letter to his daughter July 8, 1987, Cowan wrote: "The best news this week was the agreement to establish a national park on South Moresby Island in the Queen Charlottes. Many of us have been pushing hard."[1370] The relationships with the islands and activists were not to end there. Cowan and Foster became some of the first naturalist guides involved with ecotourism boats bringing guests into the area starting in the 1980s. The two men were to remain friends all their lives, and Foster spoke at Cowan's memorial of the countless contributions Ian had made to his life. Humour was among Cowan's most memorable gifts, and it hadn't failed him even when Foster handed in his dissertation, a thesis that challenged – head-on – his supervisor's own island theory:

> Finally I type up my thesis … hand it in and don't hear anything for a month or two. And he calls me in to say, "You have trouble with existence, don't you." I think to myself that all graduate students have trouble with existence, so I just accepted it as a comment until I read his comments on my thesis: I had spelled "existence" wrong. That is his sense of humour, which is often left-field, quirky and sharp.[1371]

Cowan joined Foster in Africa in 1967. Foster had gone to Kenya to work on his PhD in 1963 and invited his old mentor and friend to join him to see his research on giraffes. Cowan kept a journal of the trip they took by Land Rover, camping in the national parks of both Kenya and Tanzania. Cowan's description of one night was emblematic of a trip of a lifetime for him:

> June 25, 1967
> What a night, one of the most memorable of my entire life. All night long, the gnu, zebra and hyena kept up their continuous noise, twice minor stampedes went by. Three times I woke to the roaring of lions. There was a ¾ moon rising about ten and setting well after sun up. By its light you could see the dark circle of animals some 100–200 yards away all round us. The sounds are difficult to describe. The hyenas had a variety of calls … in strife the laughing call was used. The zebra had a high-pitched barking sequence and the groaning grunts of gnu.[1372]

He and Foster were in the Serengeti Plains of Tanzania witnessing the wildebeest migration: "The rushing sound of thousands of wildebeest running through the long grass must be one of the world's most interesting noises."[1373] Cowan was entranced by the spectacle of life that the Serengeti prey–predator systems presented. He had first experienced Canada's own Serengeti in the Mackenzie Delta of the Northwest Territories, where life revolved around the big herds of barren-ground caribou. It was in this Serengeti north, his next project in 1947, that he was to deepen his understanding of the complex interplay of wildlife, traditional hunters and the intervention of imperialist policies.

CHAPTER 28

"We have led them into a pauper's mental state – a most degrading result."

Mackenzie Delta, 1947

In 1947 the Northwest Territories Administration asked Cowan to do some research in the Mackenzie Delta. Various concerns had triggered the study. People were hungry. There had been "violent fluctuations"[1374] in numbers of muskrat, fox and beaver, all of which provided food and furs for the people of the delta. Hunting of beaver and marten had been banned for a decade, and a cold winter had exacerbated an already low muskrat population. Duck numbers, such as the Pintail and American Wigeon (formerly Baldpates) had also declined drastically. A reindeer herd, complete with Lapland herders, had been imported by Ottawa with the objective of providing an alternative supply of food to the native caribou herds, which had collapsed. This well-intentioned but not well-thought-out project was proving problematic. Cowan was to come for the summer to try and provide some guidance to the Territory and make recommendations for a wildlife management plan that was critical to keeping indigenous populations from starving.

There were lots of prospects for Cowan to recruit an assistant for the work. The UBC zoology department was now offering graduate programs and Cowan was attracting bright, experienced master's students. Among them was Ward Stevens, only nine years his junior, and a seasoned veteran. Stevens had also been influenced by the 'B', albeit indirectly. He was raised on a southern Alberta farm, his father had died of pneumonia before he was 10 and he had retreated into nature.

> My mother raised me along with four other kids. The outdoors was a refuge. My mother had a whistle and would blow it to call us in for meals. It put you so much on your own resources. I didn't always agree with my mother and I blamed her for my father's death – that was another story. You are on your own and you never get over it. I was the eldest and my mother wasn't at all well, so I had the job of helping with the cooking and housecleaning and looking after the little kids inasmuch as she depended on me.[1376]

Stevens's love of the outdoors had been encouraged early by his father, who had given him Taverner's *Birds of Western Canada* and the promise of pocket money for trapping gophers at one cent a tail. "I got good at snaring, trapping gophers and ran around without any shoelaces to snare them."[1377] He got his first degree in forestry and range management from Utah State University, where Starker Leopold had also been training. Stevens was first qualified as a forester. "I used to belong to the Canadian Institute of Forestry, but when I got out to BC and saw what the Canadian Institute of Forestry had done to the forests I sent in my resignation."[1378] Then the war hit. With his bush experience, he had an aptitude for a style of navigation that relied on a sextant and the stars, so he was trained as a navigator to work in southeast Asia, where radar wasn't much use.

> I spent a lot of hours flying in that part of the world, putting agents behind Japanese lines, like *The Bridge on the River Kwai* ... The people they worked with were the Karen people, who were so brutalized by the Japanese that they'd do anything to help out. It was an organization called Force 136. Some of these flights sound unrealistic now because they were 22 hours in the air. When I came [to Burma] I was in damn good shape; when I left I was worn out – a wet rag.[1379]

The difficult task of navigating by the stars was exacerbated by the fact that a Liberator aircraft could only carry one navigator. They had room for replacements for pilots, copilots and radio operators but only one navigator. He had to stay awake to keep the other seven men alive; this was to serve him well for the kind of hours he had to put in during the research season in the North. After being chased and nearly shot down over Sri Lanka, Stevens was discharged; he was 25 years old. Through a veterans grant he pursued a master's degree in zoology and entomology at Iowa State. When he started looking around for a doctorate supervisor, Cowan was recommended.

> There was a fellow there at the university who said he was going to a conference, so I said, "I don't know anyone in Canada, as I'd gone straight to Iowa State from war service. Could you get in touch with them for me?" He said, "I'll do what I can," and he came back with this tip on Ian McTaggart Cowan. So I wrote to Dr. Cowan and we exchanged a bit of correspondence and he asked me to come on as his summer student in the Mackenzie Delta and spend the summer there, looking at the wildlife and fur resources. It was 1947.[1380]

The big event at the time was the Twelfth Annual North American Wildlife Conference, held in San Antonio, Texas, which Cowan and Aldo Leopold both attended. Cowan was giving a talk on his Rocky Mountain fieldwork.[1381] As was the tradition, the 'B' withdrew to a private room at the hotel where the conference was held, to have their annual meeting at the same time. It would have been an historic moment, as assembled 'B' members heard Aldo Leopold read, for probably the last time, "On a Monument to the Pigeon," about the extinction of the Passenger Pigeon. It was to become one of the most-cited essays from his classic book *A Sand County Almanac*:

> It is a century now since Darwin gave us the first glimpse of the origin of species. We know now what was unknown to all the preceding caravan of generations: that man is only a fellow voyager with other creatures in the odyssey of evolution … and that his captaincy of the adventuring ship conveys the power, but not necessarily the right, to discard at will among the crew.[1382]

It was Leopold's last *Lesson* to the 'B': he died April 21, 1948, while fighting a grassland fire on a neighbour's property. *A Sand County Almanac* was published posthumously the following year. Fittingly, a Leopold quote was used for the last chapter of Cowan's last major collaborative work, *The Birds of British Columbia*:

> We end, I think, at what might be called the standard paradox of the twentieth century: our tools are better than we are, and grow better faster than we do. They suffice to crack the atom, to command the tides. But they do not suffice for the oldest task in human history: to live on a piece of land without spoiling it.[1383]

Cowan left for Edmonton on June 4, 1947, then caught another plane to Fort Smith, where he met up with Stevens and the superintendent of Forest and Wildlife Services, E.G. Oldham, to sort out arrangements. They caught the milk run plane via Great Slave Lake to Norman Wells on the Mackenzie River. There they bought an outfit of skiff, outboard and canoe with other supplies that would follow them by riverboat at spring breakup, when Great Slave Lake and the Mackenzie River became navigable. Stevens describes their final leg together and arrival at the tiny settlement on the Peel channel of the Mackenzie Delta, 100 kilometres south of the Beaufort Sea:

> On the 7th of June, 1947, [Cowan] and I took a Norseman plane out of Norman Wells and landed in Aklavik, NWT. That was the first time I spent some time with Dr. Cowan. The plane was on floats and we pulled up to shore and the fellows on the shore said, "Just a minute while we get the plank up between you and the shore," and Ian said, "Oh I can jump that far." That was a mistake – he soon realized – after he jumped and landed in the mud up to his knees. That was something we learned about: the Mackenzie mud. In the delta, everything is mud.[1384]

Cowan described the delta from that initial plane ride in:

> The entire delta is a maze of waterways. Ponds, lakes, sloughs and channels are the dominant features of the landscape as viewed from

the air. One is left with the conviction that over the greater part of the delta, water area exceeds that of land."[1385]

Meeting them onshore were leaders of the small community that lived at Aklavik: archdeacon D.B. Marsh, inspector Kirk of the RCMP and game warden Lee Post, who, aside from hauling Cowan out of the mud, took him back for a cup of tea and briefed him on the situation. Chief among their concerns was the decline in muskrats, accompanied by a low price of 80 cents a pelt, so there was little cash or food in circulation in Aklavik. Cowan wrote in his journal after their meeting on the first day:

> General opinion is that the following are responsible for poor take: 1. Late breakup, 2. Shortened season, 3. High water flooded many sloughs and made rats hard to get, and 4. Overhunting during the last two years.[1386]

The muskrat was the main fur resource relied upon by the local population of some 600 Loucheux Indians (Ehdiitat Gwich'in) and about 500 Eskimo (Inuvialuit). Rev. Marsh told Cowan that "the Alaskan Eskimos came in here after the government took over trading posts and closed up a lot of them. The Alaskans came to Aklavik to trade and stayed to trap,"[1388] along with about 30 white trappers. Stevens described the situation:

Muskrat specimens

Ondatra zibethica [*zibethicus*]

A large, heavy-bodied, rat-like mammal; body colour rich brown, overhairs long and glossy, underparts paler, buff to greyish buff. Hind feet without fur, partially webbed and with the toes margined by short stiff bristles. Tail as long as head and body, round at base, becoming flattened sideways about 2 inches from body ... The muskrat prefers the marshy borders of lakes and rivers, where it feeds upon the sedges, pond weeds and other plants growing in and near the water. Dead fish, freshwater mussels and other animal matter are eaten when available ... The muskrat is polygamous or monogamous in its mating habits; it breeds from April to August or September, with two or sometimes three litters a year.[1387]

> They [trappers] turned the furs in to the Hudson Bay Company and got money for them or the Company (being good at such things) gave them credit. They kept their skins to pay off their credit from the spring before. By the time the spring was half over, two or three of the trappers who were good at cards or dice had all the muskrat money and the rest [of the trappers] went back to the company for more credit. They were all locals; a few people who had gotten on

the Mackenzie River and there was only one way to go – they ended up there.[1389]

Cowan and Stevens met with Bert Boxer, the president of the local trappers association, one of the few white trappers. They made arrangements to travel with him to his trapline, nine miles north of Aklavik. The first day out, the weather was in their favour.

> Came up here this afternoon in brilliant sunshine. After unloading the canoe, we went for a tour of the lakes near at hand. Some are ice-free, others still partially icebound. The flood is rapidly receding. It has been 3' higher than it now is…[1390]

The next day, they put out live-traps baited with apples near where muskrats had been seen feeding. The muskrats didn't like apples, so they tried potatoes. "Apparently potato is no more attractive than apples." They struggled during the week to experiment with live-trapping as flood waters continued to fluctuate.

Nests of **Pintail [Northern Pintail]** wrapped in down

Anas acuta

Pintail were uncommon in the forested parts of the delta, and a total of just 117 were counted. Two broods were seen, one of six small young at Reindeer Station on July 14 and another of two young 36 miles south of Aklavik on August 5.[1394]

The plan was to do reconnaissance for a more detailed population study the following year. The objective of the live-traps was to tag muskrats so that their territories could be determined. Stevens explained that "the locals had ideas that muskrats all swam down towards the ocean every year."[1391] Cowan and Stevens wanted to set up long-term field stations where they could live-trap and tag. When the trapping season was over, the trappers would provide them with the tags, which would list the age of the muskrats; whether they were young of the year or older; and where they eventually turned up. Stevens spent the next three and a half years working on this project for his PhD dissertation.

> We established the fact that they didn't move. During the floods, they all got flooded out of their bank heads and swam around during the breeding season hunting for mates; and then by the time the floods had gone down, they could look for a place to make their dens.[1392]

While trapping they also surveyed the ducks, geese and swans they encountered nesting along the riverbank, to compare with observations made 15 years earlier by ornithologist A.E. Porsild for the National Museum of Canada.[1393] On June 14 they saw the staple ducks of the region: Old Squaw, Lesser and Greater Scaup,

Surf and White-winged Scoter, Mallard, Red-breasted Merganser and a glimpse of a Pintail – a strikingly marked duck aptly named for its long, needle-pointed tail.

After a week, they paddled over rough water back to Aklavik and a meeting with the trappers association. Cowan's assessment of the meeting was included in his field notes:

> The difficulties of working in 3 languages becomes very apparent. The Eskimos were handled by Owen Allen, who strikes me as capable but big physically and a bit inclined to bulldoze certain of his compatriots. Some of the natives did not seem very happy about the decisions reached. Size of present family seemed to be taken into a lot of consideration. And a young man not married given a small line + a young man with one or two children also a small line – actually these men have just as much need of a big line now as the older men with large families. There is no provision made for expansion…[1395]

The meeting covered trespass, royalties and registration of traplines recently introduced. "I got the impression that the trappers association was led by whites more or less forcing the registration program and that only some of the natives got the idea."[1396] The criterion for registration was five years residence in one area, but Cowan noted that although the Loucheux (Ehdiitat Gwich'in) had lived in the delta forever, they had migrated within their territory. Traditionally, they didn't restrict themselves to one area, but moved as the wildlife moved. Cowan made a note at the end of his entry: "Send Co-op literature to Bert Boxer."[1397]

Cowan at 92 described the importance of his "first really close contact with the aboriginal people. I met and got along well with both the Loucheux Indians (the tribe nearest town) and the Inuit [Inuvialuit]. You got a new look at the world when you began to see even a little bit."[1398] On June 24, while they waited for their own boat, they traded their canoe for a sturdy Chipewyan skiff with a 10-horsepower Johnson motor. Stevens noted that it was "slow transportation but it got us there. They arranged for us to have a guide, Henry Firth. He was a local Metis. Henry Firth said: 'I am a Scot' and Dr. Cowan said: 'I am a Scot too.'"[1399] Firth's father was the original factor of Fort McPherson, the Hudson's Bay fort back in the 1880s, and he had married one of the local women, who was half Loucheux and half white. According to Stevens, Cowan and Firth enjoyed their shared heritage, especially since Firth looked far more native than his only one-quarter native blood suggested. Firth was in his mid-50s when he joined the two men and was also a man of few words:

> I remember going across the Mackenzie River and the wind was blowing to the north, so the waves were getting pretty steep, and it was getting late in the afternoon and Ian elected that we go on. So we did it and we slapped all the way across, bailing with the teapot, and [when we] got to the other side, Old Henry said: "We shouldn't have done that, it was too rough."[1400]

The enamel teapot was rarely far from hand for bailing or drinking tea. Cowan was a confirmed tea drinker. However, the two men only made the mistake of drinking Firth's tea once. "Firth said: 'I'll tell you how to make real tea' and threw a handful of tea leaves in the pot and boiled it 'til it was so full of tannin it would pucker your lips."[1401] The three travelled companionably throughout the region in the skiff, camping with canvas tents and bedrolls, towing the canoe for exploring the smaller sloughs.

> We used to go from one ratting camp to another. These were family camps who skinned the muskrats and put them on stretchers. There was always a tripod over the fire and a bucket hanging on that and over the edge of a bucket were muskrat tails. So it was 'help yourself.' I didn't like them because of the musky taste during the breeding season. We used to catch a few and fry them.[1402]

Stevens said he preferred to eat whitefish, which they caught by putting a net in the river at night. Cowan was also keen to do some collecting of plant specimens in the tundra. On June 27 they crossed the Canoe River and climbed their first mountain up to 2,000 feet:

> Sides are very steep + composed of dense vegetative cushions; higher there is dry ground vegetation such as saxifrage + slopes of pure vegetative lichen such as I have seen nowhere else. The knolls worked by ground squirrels had a vegetation peculiar to them. From the top we had a magnificent view all the way across to the Caribou Hills.[1403]

This landscape and the Arctic breeding birds would have been very reminiscent of the Scottish mountains of Cowan's early childhood, with Hudsonian Curlew, Horned Larks, Pipits, Wheatear, Long-tailed Jaeger and Willow Ptarmigan with their comical, characteristic call, *get back, get back, get back.* Cowan felt a certain proprietorial interest in Willow Ptarmigan, since he had collected BC's southernmost specimen in the Rockies in 1930.

Much of their time was spent interviewing local native trappers. One was Reverend J. Edward Sittichinli, who was married and had five children. Cowan noted the details of his livelihood: $95 monthly from the church plus heat, light and a house, with a small trapline to supplement his income that produced about 300 muskrats a year. Sittichinli emphasized the question that the trappers wanted answered: Where did the rats go during the floods and between litters in the midsummer? Cowan also interviewed the local doctor, Dr. J. Harvey. "[Harvey] agrees with me that the debt system of economy is the curse of the territories – During good times, the natives are encouraged to spend every cent they make + then when hard times come they have difficulty getting credit + have no financial backlog."[1405] Cowan suggested that a co-operative such as had been set up near Fort Yukon in Alaska might be useful. They visited another white trapper, Knud Lang, to see about setting up another field station. Lang, who had trapped for 30 years, attributed the decline to overtrapping and winter kill-off. At Lang's trapline, a drop in the wind brought out the mosquitoes and they got beaten back from research.

Insects are an ever-present consideration in the Northern summer. Stevens, who had trained in entomology, remarked, "You didn't have to go looking for them. That was the worst place in the world for mosquitoes."[1406] Both he and Cowan had adopted anoraks that had a hood and high collar so that only their noses were exposed. "That is what saved me. We wore them out the first season."[1407] On July 4 the first Mackenzie riverboats finally arrived with their outfit – all of which was in poor condition. Wrote Cowan:

> The skiff is an antique piece of junk; there are no oars + it needs caulking + painting. The canoe needs some patches scraped + painted before it is used + the outboard, though tested + found defective, was sent down in an unserviceable condition.[1408]

Willow Ptarmigan

Lagopus lagopus

Holarctic. Breeds in North America from Alaska east across the Arctic islands to Baffin Island and south through western British Columbia, Yukon, Mackenzie, northern Manitoba, northern Ontario, Quebec and Newfoundland. Winters mostly in the breeding range. Also occurs in Eurasia.[1404]

Glaucous Gull

Larus hyperboreus

Breeds in North America on Arctic coasts and islands of Alaska and Canada. Winters from the Bering Sea south along the Pacific Coast to California and on the Atlantic Coast from Labrador to Florida. Also occurs across northern Eurasia.[1412]

It took them five days to refurbish the gear. Then, when loading the boats with a jeep, they got mired in the mud. The archdeacon had more than clerical skills and pulled them out with a two-cylinder tractor. They eventually set off for Reindeer Station on July 9, battling a brisk headwind from the north. Reindeer Station was a research facility for farming European reindeer, which the Canadian government had tried to establish in the Mackenzie Delta in response to the decline of the native caribou. They had hired Laplanders (Sami) to drive the reindeer along the coast from Nome, Alaska, which took five years. The intention was to convert the Inuvialuit into herders; they asked Cowan to investigate.

Six hours into the boat trip to Reindeer, with rising winds, they put in at an experimental mink farm run by a man named Semler, an outfit that was causing administrative headaches and conflicts with traplines and hunting areas. Cowan took extensive notes, then set off again in late afternoon to finish the crossing. They got in at 1:40 in the morning, still light of course, but cold. Stevens remarked, "We were in this old skiff heading for the Reindeer Station and it was in July, but the wind was blowing off the ice cubes and there was Ian digging in his kit bag for his long johns. I remember thinking 'Maybe he was human after all.'"[1409]

Once they reached Reindeer Station, they had more bad weather and equipment that kept breaking down. They were continuing to do waterfowl surveys – found their first whistling-swan nest, with four downy chicks – interviewing and preparing for the annual reindeer roundup and harvest. In an uncharacteristic journal entry, Cowan wrote: "July 16th. We were exhausted today after several hard days with little sleep and took it easy."[1410] The exhaustion was partly driven by a sense of urgency to make the time useful. Dr. Harvey had arrived at Reindeer Station at the same time and reported that the majority of the Indian trapper families upriver (whom he had visited to deliver treaty money) were on the verge of starvation. He emphasized that the trapline registration concept was unworkable because the families must be free to travel to find food. Being forced to stay put was a hopeless strategy for a culture reliant on widely dispersed wildlife populations. Wrote Cowan: "It seems to me to be a poor reflection on our administration that in 150 years we have not given any idea of providing for the future to the natives. Instead we have led them into a pauper's mental state – a most degrading result."[1411]

The reindeer's summer pasture was Kidluit Bay on Richards Island, which is a large chunk of the delta before the Mackenzie River pours into the Beaufort Sea. The day they arrived they assisted in a Beluga Whale hunt with Owen Allen and other Tuktoyaktuk (Inuvialuit) families. The Beluga were corralled, butchered and skinned and the meat was put up for drying on racks. That day, Cowan also took detailed notes on the health of the twelve Tuktoyaktuk families who were suffering from tuberculosis, mumps, pneumonia, meningitis, measles and severe bacterial infections like thrush. Also on that trip, he examined a white-fox den, collected a King Eider, photographed a large pingo – a mound of earth-covered ice caused by frost upheaval – trapped two species of lemmings and found a breeding colony of the snowy, all-white Glaucous Gulls, whose eggs were traditionally an important bush food.

The next day, they corralled the reindeer, counted them, castrated the males and harvested 236 of them. As Cowan later described, the government numbers were badly off. "They asked me to count the reindeer because they had been told that there were 32,000 of them, but they were beginning to wonder if there were as many as that. So we counted the reindeer and there were 4,600 of them."[1413] More importantly, the basic premise of turning the Inuvialuit into domestic herders like the Sami was questioned. Cowan's student Joe Bryant, who later took over Stevens's job, said:

> Inuvialuit were hunters. Herding was a very foreign way of life. Not many of them enjoyed it. You had to stay with the herd 24 hours a day 365 days a year, but being stuck on the barren land winter and summer with not many days off and working to a schedule, it just was a foreign experience, and not many stuck with it. I certainly wouldn't want to do it.[1414]

For the final two weeks in August, they headed back to Lang's trapline to set up the research station. A big storm came in, with rising waters making the burrows impossible to find. They portaged the canoe around to different lakes where different water levels might increase their success with muskrats. "Looked over three lakes further downriver to find two that should be suitable for our work. Upon re-examination, these lakes proved to be duds. Very disappointing after a lot of hard paddling and portaging."[1415] Stevens was in agreement on the paddling. "We spent so much time paddling in a canoe. He paddled on the right side at the back and I had to paddle on the left side all summer."[1416] They finally found some lakes with visible burrows and managed to tag over 27 muskrats.

The rest of their days followed a typical schedule. "7:30 rising, run the traps, notes + lab work + some rest in afternoon, supper at 5:30 then into the field again until about 11 p.m."[1417] August brought advantages, in particular fewer mosquitoes. As Stevens noted, "Around about August, it gets to be a little more bearable, as the leaves have all fallen off the trees, and first thing you know along comes the 20th of August and it is snowing." Stevens was staying on but August 15 was Cowan's last day in the field. "At last a fine day ... Minimum temperature 36 degrees. Maximum 60 degrees. This morning we lifted our traps, collected some aquatic plants. This afternoon worked on dissections. Waterfowl, 42 widgeon ... The summer fieldwork is over for me and I shall be most happy to get back home."[1418]

Cowan was not to join Stevens in the field again, but he supervised his PhD from afar. In the report acknowledgements he writes, "The study upon which this report is based would have been a difficult and unpleasant undertaking except for the companionship and able support of W.E. Stevens..."[1419] Cowan was mentor and model to Stevens, especially with regard to the rigour of a field scientist. "Ian made you really think about what you were doing ... He instilled in his students the necessity to report. People were spending money on you, so you had to think."[1420]

Ward Stevens ended up being hired by the Dominion Wildlife Service while doing his PhD. He lived in Aklavik for three and a half years in a 16 × 16-foot shack and sent his reports down to UBC, spending just his last year in Vancouver to write up his dissertation. There, he was pleased to have accommodation in one of the slightly larger Nissen huts at the edge of campus. One night the cook, who had been in charge of Army supplies, told the men he had a treat for them – kippers. "We said, 'Oh boy, we haven't had those for a while.' And then the high school students asked why we had to eat rotten fish. With the veterans we weren't kids and couldn't be treated like that."[1421] Cowan and Bert Brink won the respect of that cohort. Most of their war-veteran graduates went straight into heading up new departments in wildlife, whether in government or in universities.

Stevens's own career spanned Canada and the globe. He was superintendent of game for the Mackenzie District in Fort Smith. In 1958 he took an administrative position as chief mammalogist of Canada before moving back to his first love – fieldwork – as chief research scientist in charge of the Western region. He also did contracts overseas in Kenya and Malaysia, helping those developing countries do biophysical inventories and design wildlife reserves. He hired or worked with the top Northern scientists, many of whom had passed through Cowan's classes: Don Flook, Stevens's first assistant the following year in Aklavik, who went on to become the chief wildlife adviser to the national parks, picking up where Cowan left off on the conservation of wolves and bears;[1422] Ian Stirling, who went on to become a world authority on Polar Bears and set up Polar Bears International; Richard Fyfe, who became one of the key scientists with the Canadian Wildlife Service, responsible for bringing back the Whooping Crane and Peregrine Falcon from near-extinction; Frank Miller and Tom Bergerud, who spent their lives on caribou; and Francis "Bud" Fay, who became a world expert on walruses.

Every one of the stories of these men has much the same qualities as Bud Fay's, as recorded in Fay's obituary:

> Ian McTaggart-Cowan ... sent Bud north to investigate the life history of the Pacific walrus. In the spring of 1952, Bud hitched a ride on a military ship to the village of Gambell on St. Lawrence Island. He had little money, but he possessed a wealth of interest in the natural environment and respect for the islanders' knowledge. The patience and skills he learned from the people of the island proved more valuable than money in feeding himself over the five months he spent there. His teachers on the island, especially Charles and Vernon Slwooko, taught him a great deal about walrus ecology, and they provided him with specimens he used to describe the reproduction, growth and anatomy of Pacific walruses ... On St. Lawrence Island Bud developed a reputation as a great walker, for he travelled many miles over the tundra on foot. Stories of his exploits in that era are still told today on the island. His efforts on St. Lawrence Island from 1952 to 1954 culminated in his doctoral thesis on the spatial ecology, life history and population biology of Pacific walruses.[1423]

Another student, Joe Bryant, who took over the Aklavik research position in 1955, tells a story that illustrates Cowan's interest in linking human health to wildlife health for indigenous people. Bryant was working in the bush with Charlie Peter Charlie, chief of the Old Crow band (another Gwich'in band, west of Aklavik), and Cowan's name came up. "Charlie and I had eaten supper and were just settled back, talking, when he asked if I knew anything about hydatid disease (echinococcosis)."[1424] Hydatid disease is a parasitic infection that requires dogs or wolves and caribou as vectors, with humans substituting for caribou if an opportunity presents itself. The disease causes dangerous cysts in the liver, lungs and brain. Bryant knew about the disease and told Charlie what he knew. "[Charlie] nodded and when I was done, he reached into his pack and pulled out a three-page typed manuscript on hydatid disease that Ian McTaggart Cowan had prepared for the warden service in northern British Columbia." Bryant speculates that the reduced incidence of the disease in Old Crow was due to Charlie's insistence on people following

Cowan's recommendations to improve sanitation and handwashing after handling the dogs.[1425]

Joe Bryant was familiar with the scope of Cowan's work. As a boy, he had been out in the Rockies with his father, Frank Bryant, and Cowan back in 1930. Bryant had maintained an interest in wildlife and wanted to be a park warden, but his father recommended he follow in Cowan's footsteps instead:

> [My father] had had the experience of making some wildlife management recommendations as a park warden, particularly [for] elk, and getting absolutely no response from Park headquarters. Ian would come along a few years later and make exactly the same recommendations and, bingo! So he said: "You get yourself a degree first."[1426]

Bryant came to UBC from an introductory year in Alberta and signed up for comparative anatomy and biology of BC in 1949, at the age of 17. He missed the war by five months, though his brother wasn't as lucky. Cowan played more than just a teaching role for Bryant:

> ... being in [Cowan's] class was just a joyous thing. He was such a tremendous lecturer, always happy and smiling; enthusiasm and absolute sound knowledge of his field; the ability to communicate with various audiences. He was very frequently on the radio and TV and in great demand because he was such a clearly spoken communicator.[1427]

Cowan was linked to Bryant through the Rockies and Aklavik, but they also had another important connection: Mary Harrington, whom Cowan had first met independently in Aklavik in the summer of 1947. She was the schoolteacher there and regularly took the children on exploring walks to observe birds and record their names in the three languages. She was also an artist and would draw the birds on the blackboard and the children would learn the names of them. On one of these bird walks one day, she and her students ran into Ward Stevens and Cowan along the banks of Peel Channel. Harrington (now Mary Bryant) describes that first meeting:

> I noticed a different figure coming up from the river boats. [Cowan] was tall, slim, with a pale-coloured jacket – evidently not a native to the delta. After four years living there I could, I thought, recognize the local individuals. With him was Mr. Ward Stevens, a student from UBC whom I knew well. They waited for us to approach, and I was introduced by Mr. Stevens to "Dr. Cowan – my boss." While Mr. Stevens disappeared into the Hudson's Bay store Dr. Cowan and I had a lively conversation – he was interested in, well, just about everything. In just a few minutes he had asked me many questions. This wasn't usual with visitors to Aklavik. Most wanted to take our

pictures or be shown the Mission or to meet someone.[1428]

In 1949 Harrington went down to UBC to complete a biology degree and she enrolled in Cowan's course. "As I walked into the first lecture in comparative vertebrate anatomy I was greeted by my name – 'It's Mary Harrington.' Then he saw Joe Bryant by my side."[1429] Bryant had signed up for the same course, and as he notes, "We were both early birds and got to the classroom before others. It was two or three weeks before we began to talk. The spark was there."[1430] Cowan spotted the budding romance and remarked to Harrington, "You've picked a good friend if he's like his dad." The romance flourished and Mary Bryant recalled: "That was 61 years ago – that inquiring mind has proved an amazing future teller as well [as] an amazing lecturer. I have profited greatly from his knowledge as well as his friendship."[1431]

Mary Harrington Bryant, who was also a botanist and a professional illustrator, provided the images for the handbook on ferns[1432] published by the Provincial Museum. She also continued her career as a teacher while raising children. Bryant went on to do his master's on Manitoba moose, returning with Mary and their daughter to Aklavik with the Canadian Wildlife Service in the '50s. Bryant worked with Ward Stevens up there. The two shared a harrowing experience of getting caught in a storm flying between Old Crow and Aklavik. Stevens's skills as a navigator saved their lives.

Cowan's interest in his students' lives was only matched by his interest in the lives of the animals. Bryant recalled a telling incident:

> As part of the course on the biology of BC he taught us a lot about fur-bearers, which involved us working in the museum. On one occasion, he had been telling us we should get to know these furs well enough that if we ran into a situation in the field, we could identify the species by touch. Mary Jackson, one of the grad students, came up behind Ian and asked him to put his hands behind his back, and put a fur in his hands and he instantly identified it. We were all impressed.[1433]

The fox was one of the icons of the North. Cowan's scientific defence of the North and indigenous rights to wildlife became one of his strongest campaigns towards the end of his academic career. The year 1968 was pivotal, as the recommendations of the UNESCO Biosphere Conference for preserving "the rich genetic resources that have evolved over millions of years"[1435] faced off against powerful commercial interests. It was the year of the Prudhoe Bay oil field discovery in Alaska. British American Oil Ltd. had increased their stake across eight million acres of the Yukon and Northwest Territories. It was the need to move Prudhoe Bay oil that was to prompt the proposal for a pipeline through the Mackenzie watershed.

Cowan wrote an article which appears like a small, lone voice in the context of the oil boosterism of the time. He begins with a description of a vast, diverse and beautiful landscape populated by people who have been living off the land for thousands of years. "The entry of European man into the Canadian North made dramatic changes in the environment which had impact on the native inhabitants."[1436]

He covers the decimation of caribou, beaver and bowhead whale populations from commercial overhunting, the airborne fallout of strontium 90 and DDT found in caribou bones and by far the biggest footprint – mineral exploration projects, with all their infrastructure that "crush the fragile vegetation" and leave "the tons of virtually indestructible litter defiling even the most remote areas of the North."[1437] Cowan attempts to argue an economic future based on tourism and improving yields of beaver, caribou, fox and muskrat for food and furs. He rejects other scientists' claims for the ecological viability of Arctic agriculture, timber production and genetically modified organisms, which he calls "novel, creature[s] 'tailor-made'" and concludes: "Our success will depend as much upon the sophistication of our ecological knowledge as upon our technological competence."[1438] In 1969 the industrial footprint was just a mere forewarning of the immense presence looming today.

In 1972 Cowan was asked to sit on an early prototype of an environmental assessment panel, paid for by the oil and gas companies that were proposing the Mackenzie Valley pipeline – the biggest private development in history. The panel's mandate was to predict the environmental impact. The $2-million project did highlight potential impacts, but was criticized on many grounds, which Cowan agreed with: "We have proposed to government that a larger interdisciplinary team be formed to consider the broad questions of energy, transportation and development in the western Arctic."[1439] He argued for an independent board that would take into account cumulative impacts and indigenous voices and would be "insulated politically and economically from the project developers."[1440]

Cowan's recommendations in 1973 were to resonate with Justice Thomas Berger when the jurist was appointed to conduct the government's own inquiry into the Mackenzie pipeline proposal in March of 1974. Berger took up many of the innovations proposed by Cowan, the most important of which was to provide funding for First Nations, environmental organizations and health authorities to bring in their own witnesses and to take a year to get ready for the hearings. Cowan was brought in as a witness, specifically for his expertise on caribou, but as Berger noted, "He was also an expert on the whole ecosystem."[1441] Having such hearings in a public place and broadcast in four languages over the CBC had never been done before.

> We held the formal hearing of the experts in the Explorer Hotel. Classes came from the Yellowknife schools every day to sit in. Engineering was hard to follow, but with someone like Ian McTaggart Cowan, who explained things so well, I still remember him saying, "The caribou herd tied the ecosystem together. The wolves, bears, predators…"[1442]

The Berger inquiry shook the nation: "Once the hearings got started Canadians were interested. No one had ever heard aboriginal people speak. The other thing they were interested in with the environment is that they knew very little about the North."[1443]

The inquiry also set a new international standard for energy hearings, for it considered not only the global energy context (the world's economies, struggling with widespread inflation yet stagnant growth during the 1970s, had already endured one OPEC oil-price shock, and more trouble was looming amid political turmoil in the second-largest producing nation, Iran), but also the local impacts to aboriginal subsistence and the expanded concept of an "energy corridor," complete with roads, platforms and infrastructure. Cowan's voice was a critical part of those hearings and Berger cited him throughout the report:

> What you should know is that [Cowan] was a very good witness. He was obviously an authority ... He was the granddaddy of environmentalism. If you look at the transcripts and look at my report, you'll see that I relied on Ian, and Ian supported my recommendations of no pipeline across the Arctic coast and Yukon and the idea of an international wilderness area on the northern Yukon–Alaska coast. And of course the best thing was all the research that got done.[1444]

Cowan's ability to secure funding for environmental groups and First Nations captured the interest of the international community. In 1975 while Cowan was in New Zealand, one of the leading newspapers reported on his talk:

> "Obviously both government and environmental groups will be strong-willed, so that there is no chance of the conservationists becoming dependent or subservient to the government," he said. "Men and women of stature are required in the government who will respect the environmentalists' objectives and not cut off funds if there is too much interference in the government's wishes," he said.[1445]

Today, the National Energy Board hearings on pipelines have regressed to a pre-1955 format. The ability of the board to adequately address issues has been hampered by restrictive timelines, reduced involvement of communities, refused access to media recording of witnesses, non-independent panels, reduced scientific expertise in government, and government interference generally. Even more egregious is that testimony is not allowed on the global energy context (all the more relevant today with climate change) nor on the impacts at either end of the pipelines. Any small gains made since Cowan's day in assessing cumulative impacts are being shaved back to nothing. In 2012 the Canadian Environmental Assessment Act was "eviscerated," according to Ecojustice, a watchdog group on public oversight. All the hard-won gains made by Cowan and Berger to establish a federal role, increase timelines for communities to respond and serve the "long-term interests of all Canadians and the environment we depend on"[1446] were eliminated.

Most important for Cowan was the need to continue to support the role of environmental and community groups. He wrote this of the environmental groups concerned with marine mammal protection, but he applied it to all the issues:

> I was most interested in the changing role of NGOs [non-governmental organizations]… It seemed to me that to an increasing extent they were not just there as protesters but had been doing a lot of hard work to bring to light situations which appeared to be escaping the attention of the [regulatory bodies] through regular channels.[1447]

One of the people of stature from the NGO movement that Cowan supported was Elizabeth May, a young environmentalist at the time, who would go on to become Canada's first Green Party MP. She had this to say about Cowan:

> I met him when he chaired the Canadian Environmental Advisory Committee. It was in 1978 and was my first trip to Ottawa. I was invited to present on budworm spraying. I wrote a 50-page paper with footnotes, "The Case Against Aerial Insecticide Spraying." At the time I had nothing beyond high school, and was waitressing and cooking. He took me aside, as did a few others, to ask what I was doing with my life and to encourage me to get back to school. They were so encouraging and praised my report in front of the NGOs … It was very kind of him and we stayed friends.[1448]

That same year, Cowan was called up again, to sit on an international panel of 13 caribou specialists to review the impacts of another northern project, the Dempster Highway, on the Porcupine Caribou herd that was critical to the Gwitch'in and other First Nations. Two of his grad students, Tom Bergerud and Val Geist, were on the panel with him. The highway, which was to be completed the following year, threatened to cut off one-third of the range of the barren-ground caribou. The panel's conclusion was that unless special management measures were put into effect, the road would cause the herd to decline due to collisions, to the road acting as an artificial barrier and to increased access for hunting. At the time, the herd was estimated to be 105,000 animals. The area was put under control of the Porcupine Caribou Management Board and the most recent census, taken in 2010, counted 169,000.[1449]

Round about this time, Cowan first met Tom Beck, who was to become one of his closest friends during the last quarter-century of his life. Beck too was a quiet activist, with the dual distinction of being founder of the Alberta Wilderness Association and spending his entire career in the oil and gas industry in the Arctic, trying to bring to it an environmental and cultural sensibility. A soft-spoken man, Beck shared Cowan's Scottish roots, though he came from poorer, working-class Glaswegian stock. His father had been a worker in a Glasgow steel mill that produced military armaments for both wars before being killed in an accident in 1943. There was no compensation for his wife and their 14-year-old boy still at home.[1451]

> I left high school and went to the mill because my mother, after my father died, went back to work ... for the London Midland and Scottish Railway. To go to school I had to go on a pedestrian overpass that looked down on the railroad where she was working loading freight. And this was a woman who then was 47 or so. She had worked through the First World War. When I saw her [that day loading freight] I think it made a mark on me, so I dropped out of school and went to work at the mill.[1452]

Tom's older sister had gone to Canada as a war bride and Beck and his mother emigrated there to be with them. Beck secured a job in a cement factory. In his spare time, he developed a real love for the foothills country and supplemented their diet with wild elk, mule and white-tailed deer. He moved on to what was then a fledgling oil industry and developed a reputation for being able to address the issues that fell into the realm of environmental and human rights. When the French national oil company ELF moved into Alberta, Beck went to work for them as their environmental coordinator in the Arctic. That's when he first heard about Cowan.

> I knew of him long before I met him because I started working in the Arctic in the '70s. They hired me to take care of a certain aspect of their operations involving environment and, unknown to them, the degree to which native people's rights were a considerable barrier to what they wanted to do ... Whoever I talked to in the government who really knew their stuff turned out to be students of Ian McTaggart Cowan and I thought, Who was this guy?[1453]

Beck's first region was the western Arctic (Banks Island, the mainland coast

Arctic Caribou [Barren-ground Caribou] migration, Yukon

Rangifer tarandus [groenlandicus]

Most of the caribou are creatures of the tundra community or its alpine counterparts ... Summer foods include grasses, sedges, horsetails, a variety of flowering plants, and the leaves of willow and dwarf birch. During the winter foliose lichens are a major food item; but weather-dried grass and some willow and birch tips are taken ... The breeding season is in October. The bulls are aggressively polygamous, and a master bull may hold a group of as many as 30 cows together.[1450]

and the Beaufort rim), where the main source of revenue for the Inuvialuit was the Arctic fox. The Inuvialuit naturally were worried about the oil and gas activities having an impact on the animals. Beck would get information on populations from both the wildlife service scientists (Cowan students) and the Inuvialuit, and the data meshed. "I began to think, this must be quite the fellow," he recounted. At the time, the Canadian government had failed to even tell the Inuvialuit that the land had been leased for exploration.

> Our company showed up and the people wondered what we were doing there. That was a very black mark against our government and the company I was with was caught in the middle of this. I was trying to understand what the concerns of the people were and obviously it related to wildlife because they really did rely totally on the wildlife for sustenance and income.[1454]

Both men were assigned to the Arctic Land Use Research Advisory Committee, which coordinated the research into land use mapping with a core group of scientists.

> [Cowan] and I quite quickly got together on some of the stuff that was going on. And neither one of us was particularly interested in the political aspects, so that's what I came to call Ian's "kindly, scientific-based mafia." He knew every step I had made and when I came to know him, if you asked him about something, some specific thing happening in the Arctic, he knew who was involved scientifically because they were all his students.[1455]

Beck and Cowan went on to share more committee positions on the Canadian Environmental Advisory Council and the Arctic Institute. Over the years, the two of them helped keep the oilmen out of the Arctic in the sensitive times and the sensitive areas, whether it was arctic fox den nesting areas, snow geese breeding places or caribou grounds. Beck supported the Inuvialuit land claim; he chaired the committee at their request. Out of the settlements came the creation of Aulavik National Park.

Like Cowan, Beck decided to fight from within. He was once asked to give a talk at the Audubon Society in New York while he was chairing the Canadian Environmental Advisory Council, and he had initially refused, but then the Mulroney Conservatives got elected:

> [Mulroney] proceeded to take a carving knife to Parks Canada and the Canadian Wildlife Service ... to people with scientific expertise, so I said, "Yes, I'll be there." I told Ian and he said, "Well, good for you." I quite frankly thought I was going to be banned from coming back to Canada. But in fact it didn't work out that way.[1456]

Cowan had alerted John Fraser, a Conservative minister who was very sympathetic to wildlife, and Beck was welcomed back to the Advisory Council.

> Cowan may have said that his most significant contribution was through education, but I think his significant contribution was through the "Cowan mafia," which a lot of people don't know about. I found out that as time went by there wasn't a damn thing that went on in this country that was going to affect the environment in any serious way that he didn't know about, and he knew who was responsible. He had his finger on so much.[1457]

Consulting on the Arctic was to continue throughout Cowan's career. He went back many times in various capacities. Even at 92 he still had his finger on the Northern pulse. He also had faith that a subsistence reliance on wildlife could be maintained:

> Our concept of conservation in North America can only be based on a pretty luxurious lifestyle. You can't afford it if you're a developing nation. So if we want to help the developing nations develop a conservation effort, build a stable life base. It doesn't mean they've got to eat everything in sight. So few people remember that.[1458]

His next destination upon leaving the Mackenzie would be back to BC's grasslands to set up research stations a little closer to home for his burgeoning grad students.

CHAPTER 29

"The function of the university is to help our students ... It has been a
marvellous place for them. I think Dr. Cowan will agree with me on that."

Chilcotin and the Ashnola, 1947–1948

S ometime during 1947, Cowan and J.A. Munro sat down long enough to complete a 285-page manuscript of *A Review of the Bird Fauna of British Columbia.*
Munro was two years away from retirement and was still passionately advocating conservation. Not as spry as he once was, he had turned to collecting the
more inanimate plants for the Provincial Museum. It had been 30 years since the
two had first corresponded as scientist and scout over Purple Finches and Bewick's
Wrens, whose ranges had changed dramatically during that time.

Since 1926 when Cowan first recorded Bewick's Wren, its range had rapidly
expanded as the old-growth forests were cleared and the forest edge and second
growth the species preferred increased. The Munro and Cowan bird book opens
with an appeal to conservation, the authors having noted the changes since the last
list had been prepared 20 years earlier. "Since that time, modifications in the physical character of the province have been brought about by agricultural expansion, by
logging and by other activities, all of which affected the distribution of birds ..."[1460]
The biggest changes had taken place "along the mainland coast and Vancouver
Island until, by 1940, more than two million acres had been thus divested of forest
cover, and the denuded area now extends northward 190 miles in an almost unbro-
ken coastal strip to the vicinity of Seymour Narrows."[1461] The section of the book
called "Modifications in Environment" takes up most of the introduction. Munro
had been the spokesperson all this time for birds of western Canada and the book
represented a culmination of his life's work. For Cowan this was a prototype for the
much larger, four-volume tome that he was to co-author 40 years later. The book
with Munro came out in December 1947 and the two men turned their sights on
a summer field season for their families and students in the Chilcotin, doing what
they loved best.

Cowan had done a field survey on Chilcotin Lake (Chezacut) with the Racey
family in 1931, but Munro wanted to show Cowan some of the other lakes farther
to the south where he had worked on nesting birds. The Chilcotin Parklands that
lie west of the Fraser are flat to rolling grasslands, and the lakes form wherever
there are depressions, varying in size and depth. Most of them are very shallow

over a thick, rich layer of black mud, ripe for shoreline vegetation, hence their popularity with so many species. As Munro and Cowan's book stated earlier that year, the region supported "the largest nesting population of ducks anywhere in British Columbia, including the only known population of the Canvasback."[1462] It was also cattle country, home to some of Canada's largest private spreads, such as the Gang Ranch and Riske Creek. The former was over a million acres, much of it native grassland.

Cowan and the whole family – Joyce, Garry, now 8, and Ann, 4 – met up with Munro and American ornithologist W.H. Ransom at Lac la Hache in the summer of 1948. Although not a member of the 'B', Ransom was definitely 'B' material. He worked as a game commissioner in Washington state and his naturalist–scientist leanings are evident in his submissions to *The Murrelet* journal. "Red-shafted Flickers (*Collaptes cafer collaris*) were seen to be entering holes (probably nesting holes of kingfishers) in late afternoon with evident intent of roosting there. They certainly evaded the cold December winds and spent their nights in cozy comfort."[1464]

They were also joined through the summer by various students. John Tener and Dave Colls were first to join them. Tener was a veteran air force pilot and had taken Cowan up flying over Lulu Island in Vancouver to do aerial surveys of water birds. Later he was to head to Britain for his PhD. Already in the area were R. Yorke Edwards and Allan Cecil Brooks (son of Major Allan Cyril Brooks), who had been surveying breeding populations of ducks in the western Chilcotin Lakes since May for their master's theses. Jim Hatter was to join them with his research into moose.

Cowan had done a quick reconnaissance alone earlier that May. He met with farmer Sam Sorenson and checked in with local naturalist Leo Jobin, who had found him some specimens of the elusive Mountain Beaver farther to the south

Bewick Wren [Bewick's Wren]

Thryomanes bewickii

Resident in forest edge and second-growth woodland habitats of the Puget Sound Lowlands and Gulf Islands biotic areas. The population has shown marked fluctuations in numbers during the past 20 years.[1459]

Canvasback nest with eggs

Aythya valisineria

The [breeding] centre of abundance is the Chilcotin-Cariboo region from about 100 Mile House north to Williams Lake and west to Riske Creek ... The migrant and wintering populations of the Canvasback have been in a 30–year decline. As Tate (1986) notes, we must reverse the loss of quantity and quality of wetlands for the sake of the Canvasback and, indeed, all wetland species.[1463]

around Merritt. The first stop was Westwick Lake, where Munro had spent some time studying the various grebes during the war.[1466]

May was also the month when the grebes arrived – a spectacular event. The grebes are famous as a family for their elaborate courtship dances during which they preen, posture, shake and perform "the penguin dance." Julian Huxley had made "the courtship habits of the Great Crested Grebe" in Europe famous in his 1914 book of that name. Cowan was later acknowledged by his grad student Nancy McAllister (Mahoney) for his "enthusiastic support"[1468] of her research on the courtship rituals of the Eared Grebe.

Cowan spent a few days establishing where to put base camp, planning to return with the family once school was out for Garry and the birds had built their nests in the dense sedges, bulrushes and cattails. The egg-laying season began at the end of June. The "outfit" of the Cowans, Munro, Ransom, Tener and Colls arrived July 3. The day they arrived they did a census by canoe and foot and counted well over 150 nesting pairs of Eared Grebes around the mile-long Westwick Lake and its sister, Sorenson Lake. The two lakes, separated only by a man-made causeway, are no deeper than 12 feet and teeming with freshwater invertebrates, providing unlimited food for both the herbivores and insectivores. It wasn't just the Canvasbacks and Eared Grebes taking advantage of the lush conditions: Buffleheads, Shovellers, Blue-winged Teals, Lesser Scaups, Ruddies, Mallards, Barrow's Goldeneyes, Redheads, Coots and American Wigeons inhabited the lake. And that was just the ducks. Their objectives were to count and band nesting waterfowl in the region to get a sense of their migration and life histories. It was a great adventure for the children. Ann remembers as a very little girl duck banding from canoes – with one capsizing![1469]

Red-shafted Flicker [Northern Flicker] and nest

Colaptes cafer [Colaptes auratus]

Resident in, or summer visitor to, the southern half of the province, including Vancouver Island and, less commonly, the Queen Charlotte Islands Biotic Area.[1465]

Eared Grebe

Podiceps nigricollis

Centre of [breeding] abundance is the Chilcotin–Cariboo Basin. The Eared Grebe usually nests colonially, often in tight, compact colonies. Habitat includes shallow, often sheltered, freshwater marshes, lakes, ponds and sewage lagoons with moderate to heavy growth of emergent vegetation.[1467]

For the next month, they surveyed and banded, on foot and horseback and in canoes and boats: Meldrum Lake, Chimney Lake, Fish Lake, Hourglass Lake, Watson Lake, Cummings Lake, Dragon Lake (where they found a rookery of 2,000 crows), 130 Mile Lake, Murphy Lake, Caribou Bill Lake, 150 Mile Pond, Lewis Lake (they found a colony of Townsend's Big-eared Bats in a nearby miner's prospecting shaft), Soda Lake, Jones Lake, 149 Mile Lake, 105 Mile Lake, Boitano Lake, 103 Mile Lake, unnamed lakes around Springhouse, Anahim Lake, Rush Lake, Alkali Lake, Upper and Lower Dam lakes, Third Lake, Felker Lake, Epsom Salt Lake and Williams Lake – the only known nesting colony of Western Grebes at the time.

Western Grebes, with their long, elegant, two-tone necks, have their own distinctive courtship on the lakes, running over the water together with outstretched necks. During the herring season on the south coast, Cowan would watch them gathering in numbers. The critical requirements for grebes are enriched herring oil with which to fatten up for breeding, peace from predators and stable water level at their interior breeding lakes. Two of these were at risk through the great herring fishery bonanzas and agricultural irrigation projects.

Western Grebe nest

Aechmophorus occidentalis

Historically the Western Grebe has nested at 7 sites in British Columbia, of which only 4 remain active: Shuswap Lake, north arm Okanagan Lake, south end Kootenay Lake, and Duck Lake (Creston). The others have disappeared, due mainly to industrial development, recreational activities and unstable water levels ... The colony at Williams Lake was active for at least 30 years. It was discovered in 1935 (J.A. Munro, 1939), reached peak numbers in 1941 and was last used in 1964.[1470]

Halfway through the field season, on July 25, Cowan wrote: "Sunday + we took the day off. Drove down to Watson Lake to the abandoned mansion in search of bats. Found that the colony was deserted except for a single individual. The big colonies apparently break up as soon as the young can fly."[1471]

On another day off, when they were heading into Williams Lake, the hub of the ranching community, Cowan and Colls ducked behind the stampede stands while they waited for some car repairs.

> We set a trap below the cattle pens + attempted to capture the several broods of Baldpate [American Wigeon] + Canvasback there. We were not very successful, because the birds all took to the reeds. Dave Colls + I, however, got a great infestation of cercarial [swimmer's itch] for our trouble.[1473]

The itch story made it into his introductory biology lectures about mammalian vectors, and one of his students, Betty Copeland, recalled his telling the story of the itch up at Williams Lake, which had resulted in the timely removal of Dave Colls's underwear because of the intensity of the itch. Copeland recalled:

> In the front row were two lovely women academics from Saint Paul's Hospital – one was Sister Mary Scholastica, who was my colleague, and the other, Sister Mary Celestine. After Dr. Cowan had recounted the story, the two women in their full garments and wimples gathered up their notes and started to walk up the aisle of the Biomed amphitheatre of 400 students. Dr. Cowan said, without missing a beat: "Ladies, you are out of luck; the [research] site has stopped and you won't find them there." Everyone exploded … Nobody had the love of academia more in his eyes than Dr. Cowan.[1474]

Most of the time they were camping, with students and colleagues coming and going. Brooks and Edwards arrived at Westwick at the beginning of August. Edwards followed in Cowan's steps in many respects. After his master's degree he worked for the BC Parks Branch and the Canadian Wildlife Service and set up internationally recognized naturalist and interpretation programs, introducing the natural world to British Columbians and visitors. During his time at Wells Gray Provincial Park he followed the mountain caribou herd and documented the parallel decline of the old-growth forest and the caribou.[1475] Cowan joined Edwards in Wells Gray for a few days in the spring of 1956.[1476] Characteristically they didn't waste any time and climbed three mountains in three days, checking out the winter range for ungulates.

> Climbed Pyramid. The south face is extremely arid, a lava cone covered on the south with an open growth of *Ceanothus velutinus + sanguineus*. *Acer glabrum + Shepherdia*. Lots of fresh deer tracks, tracks of 2 wolves + one bear (grizzly) along the 3 miles of trail to the pyramid. The [north] face of the lot is dense Jack pine with deep snow patches lying.[1477]

Edwards eventually succeeded Bristol Foster as director of the Provincial Museum and published extensive papers and books on birds and environmental topics, such as the *Illustrated Natural History of Canada* series, for which he wrote *Mountain Barrier* in 1970. Edwards, like Cowan and Grinnell before him, became an ardent advocate for not sanitizing the wild:

> Our generation is witnessing a worldwide disaster to overtake the thin film of life that paints our planet green ... When all the dangerous cliffs are fenced off, all the trees that might fall on people are cut down, all of the insects that bite are poisoned ... and all of the grizzlies are dead because they are occasionally dangerous, the wilderness will not be made safe. Rather, the safety will have destroyed the wilderness.[1478]

....

White-crowned Sparrow [Gambel's]

Zonotrichia leucophrys

In the interior, the White-crowned Sparrow spring migration occurs very quickly, and although it is rather abrupt in some areas, large numbers of birds move through ... In the Southern Interior Mountains, numbers build in the third week of April and peak in the first week of May.[1481]

....

Westwick Lake as a long-term research base continued to be a favourite hub of Cowan's in ensuing years, and he would send many of his students and colleagues up there on research projects. Having established a key baseline for the region, the later research projects could document changes in populations and the impacts of encroachment, such as the Western Grebes that had suffered continual declines as recreational and motorized use of the lakes increased and herring stocks on the coast declined.

In 1952 Cowan visited Westwick for a day to check up on students Mary Jackson and Nancy Harris "hard at work"[1479] finding nests. He later attended a meeting with trappers to discuss moose. Few could move as fluidly between the ecosystems, genders and species as Cowan. In 1955, at the beginning of May, he drove his grad students Nancy Mahoney [later McAllister], Nancy Anderson, Mary Jackson and Timothy Myers up to Westwick Lake. He had two days to help them get the camp set up and get started on their research. His journal entries record those days before handing over the research and journal writing job to Mahoney. They are essentially the last entries by Cowan in his old style of journal format:

> May 2, 1955
> Drove from Vancouver yesterday in 9 hours; good weather. Not much of note along the way but large flocks of Gambel's [White-crowned] Sparrows seen at intervals along the road north of Ashcroft. Saw a yellow-bellied marmot near Cache Creek + another near 10 Mile House. Westwick + Sorenson lakes still have some ice on them but plenty of open water.[1480]

He counts the different waterfowl with a question mark for numbers of Eared Grebes, orders 200 feet of lumber from the mill at Springhouse for their camp, notes Horned Larks, Pipits and some "magnificent" Mongolian [Ring-necked] pheasants on the range of Alkali Lake Ranch, then finishes with this entry:

> May 4, 1955, Westwick Lake
> Dawned clear + sunny after a calm moonlit night with heavy ground frost. Some light ice on water buckets. In a.m. walked around Westwick Lake down east side + up west side watching courtship of Goldeneye + Bufflehead, looking for nest sites + generally prospecting the area ... Erected a fallen Goldeneye nest at the [south] end of the lake.[1482]

Barrow's Goldeneye

Bucephala islandica

Natural sites included cavities in deciduous trees ... and coniferous trees ... Only cavities excavated by the Pileated Woodpecker are large enough for Barrow's Goldeneye; other woodpecker-created cavities are suitable only after they have been enlarged by decay, but by that time they are fragile and subject to blowdown.[1483]

The handwriting in the journal then shifts to Nancy Mahoney's on the afternoon of May 5, 1955: "Dr. Cowan left at 9:30 a.m."[1484] It wasn't just the handwriting that was shifting; Cowan was handing over the field research to his students, and it was fitting that it was to women.

Cowan continued this tradition by hiring Mary Taylor, a taxonomist and mammalogist, to take over his teaching load in 1965 – an almost unheard-of appointment then for the male-dominated discipline of zoology. Taylor went on to become the first president of the American Society of Mammalogists (ASM) and the first woman mammalogist in North America to hold both a professorial appointment in a department of zoology and a curatorial one as director of the Cowan Vertebrate Museum at UBC. In the published history of the ASM,[1485] to which Taylor is a contributor, the role of women is discussed:

> Although women have increased significantly in a society that was essentially male (with active support from wives) at the beginning, in 1991 they still constituted only 20–30% of the membership and were first authors on about the same percentage of papers. This increase in the number of women has occurred principally since the early 1970s and largely as a result of an influx of female graduate students ...[1486]

Even in 1955, Cowan was way ahead of the national average in terms of female graduate student intake, albeit the benchmark was low to begin with.

Winifred Kessler, a zoologist and the second woman (in 75 years) to take on the presidency of the Wildlife Society described the openness that Cowan offered to women like herself breaking into the male-oriented discipline: "If you were interested in biology, zoology, conservation or nature, he made you feel welcome at the table." Kessler had ample opportunity to observe Cowan in action. A zoology major at Berkeley, she had taken classes with Bill Lidicker and was first aware of Cowan for his "groundbreaking work" on wildlife management. "What I later found out was how broad his interests were and how modern he was in his inclusiveness."[1487] Kessler succeeded Cowan as chair of the Habitat Conservation Trust Foundation, to which he insisted on getting representation of women on the Public Advisory Board. Cowan brought to his colleagues a "walking encyclopedia" that could recall so much of the natural history of the province, whether it was Ground Squirrels, Fishers, Tailed Frogs or Bighorn Sheep. The accuracy with which he could recall the animals, their habitat, the dates, the weather, the researchers and even their literature on the topic ensured that their decision-making was rooted in deep knowledge. "He was thrilled with everything, from butterflies to frogs. That was what most impressed me – the scope of his knowledge."[1488]

His professional approach to women in other disciplines of academia was similarly welcomed, according to Margaret Fulton, a colleague of his at UBC. Fulton, who was one of Canada's leading advocates of women's rights and received the Order of Canada for her work, had arrived at UBC in 1974 to take on the unenviable position of dean of women. Cowan was just winding up as dean of graduate studies at the time. Fulton said of him:

> Cowan encouraged me to participate in activities with the women that weren't encouraged by the administration, by getting a women's centre ... He was at the leading edge of the feminist movement that was avant-garde. I would give him credit for opening more free-thinking of the whole role of women on campus and breaking down the old guard.[1489]

Cowan brought the backing of other deans with him, but breaking down the old guard was no easy matter. According to Robert Scagel, a botanist appointed to UBC in 1952 and a friend and colleague of Cowan's, the university was steeped in a patriarchal culture. "There was no appointment of a woman in the faculty of arts and science until 1962. [Garnett] Sedgewick [a professor of English who retired in 1948] would have nothing to do with women and only taught men."[1490]

Scagel, a specialist in marine algae, spoke of Cowan's very great interest in establishing research opportunities for men and women students. He and Cowan were responsible for selecting the pioneering co-educational marine research station at Bamfield on the west coast of Vancouver Island for the five western universities. Prior to this there had been only the Minnesota Seaside Station, located down the coast, for women researchers. The established federal Pacific Biological Station was traditionally a male bastion.[1491]

The two of them had set off in the summer of 1968 to review various sites on Vancouver Island, trailering Cowan's old rowboat for the marine part of the survey. They ended up selecting the abandoned Pacific Cable Board Station near Pachena Creek at Bamfield, at the end of a very long, rough dirt road toward the sea. Cowan, in his capacity as co-instigator of the National Research Council (now NSERC, the

Natural Sciences and Engineering Research Council), had helped bring money to the project. By 1972 the doors were open and Bamfield became one of the pre-eminent marine research education stations on the North Pacific coast.

Cowan's interest in marine research stations was matched by his interest in freshwater bases as well, like Westwick Lake. He would keep a constant research presence there, through his students and collaborations, for the rest of his career. His next journal entries at Westwick are from 1956, when he was up there again to check on students (and also noted 300–400 Horned Larks)[1492] and again in 1959. For the latter trip, he also brought along a full television crew from the CBC to tape an episode of the *Web of Life*.

The TV crew themselves were captured on film by Geoff Scudder, whom Cowan had just hired as an entomologist at UBC. Introduced to the Cariboo–Chilcotin lakes, the UK immigrant immediately began what would become a 15-year study of the invertebrates of the place.[1493] Scudder was fresh from the domesticated confines of the Oxford countryside, having studied there under the famous population ecologist Charles Elton, whom he had followed around in the field, "sampling bugs in decaying logs."[1494] The Chilcotin was a bonanza for a young entomologist used to the over-studied, over-groomed English countryside in which native biodiversity had been modified by millennia of agriculture. However, Scudder was also fresh from the heady intellectual atmosphere of Oxford under Elton, and Cowan greatly enjoyed the stimulation of having a hot new, young ecologist on the faculty. Scudder was appointed in 1958 to replace George Spencer when the latter retired from the zoology department, and eventually Scudder became Cowan's successor as head.

Scudder, like Cowan, inspired thousands of undergraduates, helped mentor over a hundred graduate students and had an annual lecture series that built on his predecessor Spencer's Memorial Lecture Series. Scudder's ecological insight into the relationships of insects, hydrology and climate and how that meshed with wildlife patterns was invaluable. Cowan used his collaboration with his students and colleagues to inform himself for consulting around the world on waterfowl ecology and conservation. He became a research member of the Select Committee on National Parks for the US, evaluating wildlife refuges in the late '60s. In 1970 he was invited down by the Australians to make policy recommendations for their wetlands and waterfowl.[1495] The Freckled Duck and the White Pygmy Goose, two of the many colourful species, like the other Australian flora and fauna, evolved separately on the island continent during millions of years of isolation. Cowan was fascinated by their adaptations to the "boom and bust" of water supply. As he put it in a letter to the Australian policy-makers who had invited him: "On no other continent does a single political jurisdiction hold responsibility for the survival of so large an assemblage of living creatures of the world. The responsibility is a grave one ..."[1496]

The responsibility for the survival of a large assemblage of living creatures in North America in 1949 was falling on a new set of shoulders. The 'B' were losing their foundational members. T. Gilbert Pearson had died four years earlier. Aldo Leopold, E. Lee LeCompte (who had just written his book on soil, forest and wild-life restoration of farms) and Tom McCabe all died that year. McCabe's death from a heart attack had a direct impact on the Cowans. Both of the McCabes, like the Munros, were important friends and role models for the young couple in how to embrace the wild in their married lives. When Cowan wrote his own short memoir he opened again with a Leopold quote: "There are some who can live without wild things and some who cannot" and stressed to his audience that though nationwide organizations were essential, "knowledgeable, dedicated individuals drive conservation and identify its directions."[1497] Four 'B' flames may have flickered out but many more were igniting.

The UBC zoology department that year started to offer one of the first PhD programs in the whole university, just behind physics. Cowan's administrative work just kept growing, since he was also a very successful fundraiser for his students. In 1949 there were no field journal entries for Cowan at all. From then on he would be snatching small blocks of time to check up on students and do small forays close to home with Jim Munro and Pat Martin and other colleagues, but the demands for his time were starting to shift. Cowan's long summer field seasons had already come to an end with the Chilcotin duck survey. After 1949 he was looking for close to home research opportunities to bring his family, as well as his students, into the field.

One such chance presented itself with the Ashnola Mountains, a 36,000-acre grassland region south of Keremeos. The Ashnola River is a tributary of the Similkameen, which, after rising in Washington state and crossing the US border, flows west to east through the mountains that divide the BC coast from the interior. This unique area, less than a day's drive from Vancouver, provided the perfect wildlife field school at which Joyce and the children could join Ian. It was also perfect for his colleague Bert Brink and his students learning about grassland ecology. The Ashnola is unique for many reasons: it is one of the few areas of the province where grasslands are more or less continuous from the valley floor to the alpine; it was a refugium during the last glaciation. But most importantly for Cowan, it was North America's last stronghold – then – of what was known as the California Bighorn, a population on the verge of extinction.

In the opening frames of a television episode about the Ashnola, part of a series called *Klahanie: The Great Outdoors*, Cowan and Bert Brink discuss what brought the two of them together to this place. Brink had been introduced to the area while working for the Kamloops Range Station back in the '30s. He was also a keen mountaineer and was as curious about the weird, wind-eroded rock formations called "Stone City" as he was about the grasslands. Cowan had heard about the Ashnola from Hamilton Mack Laing, who had explored the area during the Boundary Survey in the early '30s for the National Museum. Laing had brought back three sheep skulls for the museum's collection. At that time, the Ashnola herd was one of the last ones left in the world. As Cowan points out, "It was a famous sheep ground for all the big, roving sportsman hunters ... Every pub in the country had a ram head above the bar; misshapen, miserable old rams' heads glowering down at you from the wall ... every ancient and honourable Order of the Elk [sic] had to have one."[1499]

In the TV episode, while black and white images of the sheep and rolling grasslands unfold, the voices of the two men discuss how overhunting, overgrazing by domesticated sheep, cattle and horses and imported diseases all had their impact on the wild sheep. Cowan states: "So I thought we should take a serious view of this population ... Dr. Brink, and his keen range interest, and my interest in wildlife got together on this operation." Between the 1930s and '40s lots had happened with changes in the ownership and land use. Things were actually getting better, but there were still lots of puzzles for the two scientists and their students.

On his first trip back to the Ashnola, in May of 1950, Cowan established a base at the cabins relatively close to the Flatiron herd range. On his first day he climbed up north of Juniper Creek, away from the areas the cattle had damaged, up into the Flatiron, which was still flourishing with bluebunch wheatgrass and the pink-flowering bitterroot that are real indicators of a healthy grassland. He found 18 rams, 45 ewes, 15 yearlings and 15 lambs that day, some of them only a day old. Over the next week, he went up Crater Creek to the mountain and investigated other ranges, all of which were damaged by cattle, with sidehills chewed up, gullies eroded and in some cases sheet erosion over the whole slope. There were also signs of poaching.

Cowan had read up on early accounts of wildlife in the region, in *Camp-Fires of a Naturalist*, by Clarence Edwords (for that is how he spelled his name), who described the adventures of Professor Lewis Dyche in the 1880s. He was amongst the first European hunters into the traditional upland summer hunting territory of the Syilx First Nation. Another account by the Richter family, who grazed cattle there,[1500] described the size of the sheep herds on both sides of the Similkameen at the turn of the 19th century. Francis Richter's widow had married an Englishman named Haliburton Tweddle and it was a junior Tweddle who was now running cattle all over the mountain. Cowan investigated the mortalities of wildlife from starvation and disease due to the winter range being so eroded. He could find only one example of a cougar kill.

The following summer, Cowan returned with students and family. They climbed up to the Flatiron and counted the sheep. The Flatiron range was in better shape and the lower ranges were recovering; Tweddle had sold out to an American hunting

California Bighorn [Sheep]

Ovis canadensis californiana

Differs from [*O. c.*] *canadensis* [Rocky Mountain Bighorn Sheep] in slightly darker colour, less white on face, horns with more open curl and usually with tips complete or nearly so ... About 200 head in the Ashnola Mountains ...[1498]

syndicate and the cattle and most of the horses were gone. Cowan did an overnight hike 14 miles straight up to see the condition of the range around Cathedral Lakes.

> July 8/51
>
> Hiked out from the Lake today, passing the Natural History Society on its way in to its summer camp. A doe + twins had been on the trail ahead of me, also a [mountain] lion. Saw, in Spruce + parkland: Franklin Grouse, Golden [Crowned] Kinglet, Fox Sparrow, Canada [Gray] Jay, Hudsonian [Boreal] Chickadee, [American] 3-toed [Woodpecker], Clarke's Crow [Clark's Nutcracker], [Mountain Chickadee], Hermit Thrush, Pine Siskin, Red Crossbill, 2 [Golden-crowned] Sparrow, Ruby [crowned] Kinglet, [Common] Raven.[1501]

Cowan and Joyce brought their brood of two to the Ashnola. Ann was 6 when she started going there and has vivid memories of the place:

> ... The whole family would go. At the Ashnola camp, [Joyce] was the food producer and of course looking after two kids. In the Ashnola we set up camp and I remember that as a collecting expedition, as I remember my brother learning how to make specimens. He used Dad's tools. The camp at Ashnola was a lot of cabins. I don't remember where we slept but I remember the kitchen counters, the table, the wood stove, very basic. I remember another little story from that period – we were probably there for a month – at which I remember some disturbances in the kitchen and there were maggots dropping on to the kitchen table. It turned out they were from the skulls that had been put on the sod roof to bleach and the maggots had burrowed and gone through the sod. ... There were graduate students there and I remember a song one of them used to sing to me: "She has a dark and roving eye and her hair hung down in ringlets, She was a nice girl, a proper girl but one of the roving kind." I can't remember who the grad student was, but having a musical head, I remember that song. Dad played the harmonica all his life. When we were out, singing around the campfire with the harmonica, that was part of my remembrances.[1503]

The Cowans returned in most of the next five years with various grad students. Don Blood did some of the first work on the life history of the bighorn and how they were using the range. He charted the movements of the rams and the ewes in the summer and the winter, studied growth rates and escape trails and made the first attempt at a census – 150. Ray Demarchi looked at quality of the range. Fred Harper and Jeff Barr looked at the rodent populations and Doug Morrison did a study on the impact of deer on the young regrowth of Douglas-fir.

The Ashnola episode of the *Klahanie* series was shot in 1971, and the cameraman was Rick Maynard, who was also another student looking at the link between grasshopper epidemics and overgrazing. This was an observation that Ron Buckell had made doing experiments with exclosures back at Kamloops in the 1920s. As Cowan explained, "Good quality range is not damaged by grasshoppers; they are a secondary user. They come in when the range has been mishandled by us."[1504] Cowan explained on camera that wild sheep don't eat the mature seed heads of grasses; domesticated horses, cattle and sheep do. They strip everything, including the seedheads. Grasshoppers only eat the tender shoots, so they proliferate in damaged grasslands where there are no mature plants. Once the grasses are stripped, Cowan continued, "the soil is exposed, the rivers start to erode their banks and the whole thing starts to go to pieces, and you see these poor, miserable animals are dying around you." Bert joins in at that point to say that what they are seeking to do is to take an "ecosystem approach to management "and "the implications are very, very many." Ecosystem management was a new term but an old concept for the 'B'. Brink and Cowan were probably some of the first scientists in Canada to talk about it on television.

American Three-toed Woodpecker

Picoides tridactylus
[*Picoides dorsalis*]

The Three-toed Woodpecker frequents sub-alpine, sub-boreal and boreal forests, and the higher elevations of the interior Douglas-fir and western hemlock forests from 450 to 2100 m elevation, often near openings made by ponds, lakes, bogs, muskegs, clearcuts and burns. It occasionally wanders to lower elevations. Sizes for 17 broods ranged from 2 to 4 young, with 10 broods having 2 young.[1502]

The other great threat to the sheep and the region was the emergence of snowmobiles and all-terrain vehicles. At the close of the program, Cowan gives an impassioned plea about the threats of motorized vehicles in the precious winter range of the herd: 2 per cent of the country holding 90 per cent of the game. "If you start getting mechanical devices into this area, then they'll crawl up into a corner and die."[1505] The two of them talked about the value of the protected areas for recreation and conservation, and then Brink finished with this closing thought: "One of the biggest dividends is the impact on our students. The function of the university is to help our students … It has been a marvellous place for them. I think Dr. Cowan will agree with me on that."[1506]

Bob Weeden describes his first foray into the Ashnola as a graduate student with Cowan:

> That trip was in the fall and there was snow in the high elevations. We tried hard to get to the point where we could see sheep, and climbed high enough to see where the sheep were shortly going to

be, when the winter snows got even deeper, …in the winter ranges. It was really obvious that this guy was used to being in the woods. You meet someone often enough on the campus and half their day is spent talking to bureaucrats in academic officialese and the other half interacting with grad students, but not much of that tells you what will happen when their boots freeze overnight … it was fun … it helped my growing admiration for the guy that he was a very, very seasoned field person.[1507]

Cowan and Brink were well aware that the "function" of a university and the priority assigned to students cycled with the same periodicity as snowshoe hare populations and political interest in wildlife. The freedom to write curriculum on conservation that Cowan enjoyed in the 1940s had all but disappeared by the 1950s. According to Bill Lidicker at Berkeley, conservation in the curriculum popped up briefly in the 1970s but it wasn't until the early '90s that applied conservation biology regained some of its former footing. "It became a fringe political thing until the early '90s. It was something you taught in your spare time. In the late 1980s it was not easy to get conservation biology through the curriculum committees; it took me a couple of tries."[1508]

Back in the territory in June of 1955, Cowan's notes drew attention to something very wrong with the sheep despite good range conditions and an absence of cattle. While counting the herd he noted, "My estimation [is that] grass on South Slope has improved about 20% over the last 5 years + I can see no reason to suspect shortage of winter range as the factor limiting the increase of this herd of bighorn … Something is killing a fairly large part of the young group before it is a year old."[1509] At his 1961 Vancouver Institute public lecture, "Of Mice and Men," Cowan uses the Ashnola herd as an example of a population that is controlled by what he called "environmental resistance":

Why is it that over 50 years we have had virtually no increase of bighorn sheep in the Ashnola River valley when there's apparently lots of food and the young ones are born and they look healthy and they get through their first summer in fine shape and they come back to their winter range in fine shape and they don't seem to die in the wintertime but by the end of next summer there aren't any? Something has put the lid on them and it's difficult often to find out. Now, there have been some very interesting questions asked about these things and some very interesting answers discovered. Many things obviously can influence the rate at which a population increases: the number of young per litter or brood, the frequency of litters or broods, the age of the animals before they have their first young, the survival, both prenatal and postnatal, of the young that are conceived, their breeding habits – are they monogamous or are they polygamous – the proportion of the population at any one age that's actually breeding. Now this may involve a lot of things. If a large proportion of your population is over breeding age or under breeding age, then you're not dealing with the real population when you're talking about the whole number that you can count.[1510]

Population puzzles like the Ashnola were to lead him in the 1950s to a long-term study with animal physiologist Alec Wood of the adaptation of wild ungulates to differing environmental circumstances. Through the '50s they used deer born in captivity as controls for deer kept in optimum conditions. This was the era in which Ann recalls "fawns coming through the house that had to be fed with bottles."[1511] However, the beauty of the Ashnola continued to call to him back to conservation. According to Scudder, "Cowan's knowledge of vertebrate zoology was tremendous, but he was also very involved with conservation."[1512] In 1960 the provincial government had purchased Crater Mountain from the previous owners, on the urging of Cowan and a Richter descendant, also named Francis, who had become a member of the Legislative Assembly and helped to designate the area as a game reserve.[1513] The adjacent Cathedral Lakes Provincial Park was created in 1968 (expanded in 1975) through the advocacy of the newly created Okanagan Similkameen Parks Society, whom Cowan advised. In 2001 Crater Mountain became the Snowy Mountain Protected Area, which, together with Cathedral and four other contiguous parks, comprise the largest protected wilderness area anywhere along the Canada–US border: 1.2 million hectares.[1514] In 2005 the Habitat Conservation Trust Foundation, which Cowan chaired for 19 years and Brink vice-chaired for almost as long, funded the transfer of 23 bighorn sheep from the Ashnola to Okanagan Mountain Provincial Park to restore a population that had become extirpated.

Cowan spoke of the work he and Brink did in that organization:

> We went through 13 ministers in 19 years. Now that is quite remarkable, because they trusted us, no matter what their political orientation. It's exhausting to have to re-educate them, but there were some pretty darn good people there that went by as ministers. There were some that just did it as a job, you know, they were appointed and they just did it as best as they could. There is no training of politicians and no measurement of intelligence either. The one thing is, Can I get elected? But anyway that is another story.[1515]

At the end of his life, Cowan foresaw the increasing political attacks on research and research stations, though he didn't live to see the worst excesses. The budget for the Bamfield Biological Station, for example, was slashed in 2013.[1516]It was the same year that the federal Experimental Lakes Area freshwater research facility was also shut down by government. A survey at the time commissioned by the Professional Institute of the Public Service of Canada reported that 90 per cent of some 4,000 federal scientists who responded said they were being muzzled.[1517]

Scudder was still working at UBC 56 years later, despite trying to retire in 1999.

He says he is witnessing the dismantling of much of what his generation set up, both in terms of research opportunities for ecologists and in resources for systematists like himself who provide the evidence for disappearing or changing populations of species. Visiting Scudder's office in 2014, the author saw boxes of insects from all over the world, piled high waiting to be identified. The reason he is still there, Scudder explains, is because there is no one else to do the job:

> Systematists are not hired now. No one can identify anything anymore. They do the DNA but don't know what they are looking at. So I get sent boxes of specimens like this one from University of Alaska. I identify them and send them back. But I'm the last one standing ... Teaching systematics is virtually all gone in North America now. They got rid of the library in Fisheries and Oceans. It's a tough push, especially with this government.[1518]

In 2004 Geoff Scudder had helped organize a visit for the two nonagenarians Cowan and Brink up into the grasslands of the Flatiron Range to assess the population of bighorns. The photograph shows the two men on a lovely spring afternoon in a meadow of *Lewisia*. Neither of them would make it up into the mountains again. Brink died in 2007 at 95. The tributes that poured in following his death spoke repeatedly of "a pure sense of kindness and humanity; a genuine and fundamental curiosity about our natural world."[1519] Cowan, at 96, was not able to make the memorial service, but he had this to say about the exquisitely trained eye of his old friend and collaborator in the grasslands, who knew the value of getting students into the field:

> If you're a scientist, you start with where you are. My familiarity is with vertebrates and I'll be looking at the vertebrates. I'll only get down to this little quill grass when I start looking at what deer eat, but Bert Brink will be standing there looking at that ... a trained eye is a trained mind.[1520]

PART 7
TRAVEL, TELEVISION
AND ADVOCACY
1952–2010

CHAPTER 30

"Climatic changes in northern Continental Europe are real."

Scotland and Europe, 1952–1953

C owan had not been back to Scotland since he was 3. With the opportunity of a sabbatical year and a Nuffield Travelling Fellowship, it was an obvious choice to return to Scotland with Joyce and the children, now 8 and 12. He had plans to finish *Mammals of BC,* look at museum collections and catch up with European researchers and his Scottish clan. He was sailing into an inner circle of naturalist–scientist–conservationists who were changing world views in the same way their Scottish forebears had done 300 years earlier. It was a heady brew, and as usual Cowan wasted no time getting to know the landscape and its inhabitants in all their diversity. His time in Scotland also plunged him more deeply into the marine realm and into the air – with broadcasting.

On July 8, 1952, the family boarded the Olympia Hiawatha train eastbound for Montreal. Cowan now had the freedom to record his impressions in a journal that didn't have to be shared with an institution. It captured more candid observations and daily goings on and provided the first real glimpse of their family life with anecdotes like "Ann has a swelling in the right submaxillar region. The poor little tyke is keeping smiling but feels punk."[1521] The journal still has the familiar references to who they met (like Pat Martin in Toronto and the Racey aunts and cousins in Montreal), what they did (but with more domestic details like "Joyce did laundry as usual"[1522]) and of course what they saw. They boarded the ship on July 11 and steamed down the St. Lawrence past the seabird colonies established by Percy Taverner and Gordon Hewitt, although Cowan was disappointed to miss most of them because of fog banks. In between the fog, they were out on the deck watching gannets and towering icebergs encircled by raucous flocks of Herring Gulls, Kittiwakes, Puffins and Fulmars – the latter following them all the way to Scotland. The Fulmar became a recurring theme through the trip, most memorable to naturalists because of the young bird's projectile vomiting as a defence strategy, shared somewhat by one of Cowan's own progeny recovering from the mumps.

"Where the action is" was not how Cowan described Britain when they first arrived in Edinburgh via Liverpool. He remarked on the general down-at-heel atmosphere of post-war Britain, from the archaic fittings in the kitchens to the spartan university lecture seats on which "sleep, as an escape from intellectual effort, would be elusive."[1524] The people appeared to him beaten down and one of the shared lodgers at an accommodation reminded him of "a hybrid Pekinese x tawny owl [who] does little but walk from a barrel of Perry cider to his easy chair. His sister calls him 'barrel'; most appropriate. He has a good wit + is quite entertaining."[1525]

The Mackenzie and Cowan cousins seemed to have weathered the war more kindly and helped the family settle into a flat. Ann remembers a stream of "elevenses" and high teas with great aunts and uncles. Cowan immediately hooked up with the ornithologists. In the first week, he joined a "ringing" ["banding"] expedition to the Isle of May observatory and field station that monitored a famous bird-breeding colony in the Firth of Forth close to Edinburgh. The Isle of May is a small, grassy islet that lies in the shadow of the huge cantilevered railway bridge crossing the Forth. Spring and summer, the isle pulses with bird life, and the men had gone to band the chicks of the three species of terns – Sandwich,

Fulmars and Albatross off Prince Rupert

Northern Fulmar

Fulmarus glacialis

The Northern Fulmar occurs regularly throughout the year in offshore waters. It is occasionally seen from shore. It prefers cold waters ... with high salinity. Large flocks occur locally in areas of upwelling ..., along lines of convergence, and other areas of turbulence ...[1523]

Roseate and Common – that nested there. Cowan was familiar with the Common Terns because they also occur in BC. The chicks "were easily distinguished by their very black chins when new hatched + their flesh-pallid legs + feet."[1526]

The Cowan children, fresh from the Strait of Georgia, were adapting quickly to their new surroundings, and accompanying their father on expeditions before they started school. Garry was developing an interest in all things marine and he and Cowan would return to the Isle of May a month later to help on another banding expedition. The whole family also travelled to the Aberdeenshire coast to visit the seabird colonies. These colonies are overwhelming sensory experiences. Birds are packed on every square inch of rock or whirling around the colony. The smell of guano is pungent and cries can be deafening. Each species occupies a different niche: puffins burrowing in the grassy tops of cliffs, murres and fulmars nesting on ledges of the cliffs and certain types of guillemots in crevices low on the cliffs. The family visited Saint Cyrus, a national nature reserve, and Fowlsheugh (an old Scots name for "birds cliff"), where over 200,000 kittiwakes nested in the geological formations that had so intrigued Cowan's ancestor Hutton. Wrote Cowan:

> They are of boulder conglomerate with oblique dykes of sandstone. Huge caves have been eroded in them + the face is studded with

projecting boulders + with the cavities from which they have fallen. These provide the nest sites.[1528]

Kittiwakes nest all around the northern hemisphere but didn't nest in BC until the 1990s, an event that warranted a Change in Status addition in *Birds of BC*.

In 1952 the Scottish kittiwake population was just starting to recover in the Atlantic after centuries of persecution and the collapse of their main source of spring food, the herring. Accompanying them at Fowlsheugh was ecologist–ornithologist Vero Copner Wynne-Edwards from the University of Aberdeen, in whose company Cowan delighted. Wynne-Edwards was a born naturalist "butterfly boy" and spent the pre-war and war years as a zoologist in Canada at McGill. Travelling back and forth across the Atlantic watching seabirds, he had developed the terms "inshore," "offshore" and "pelagic" to describe the zones that different seabird species occupied. His reputation at the time largely came from this work on zonation. Similarly in his work on seabird colonies, Wynne-Edwards had mapped out how the different colony nesting species not only arrange themselves on the cliffs and offshore islands for protection from predators, but pace themselves throughout the breeding season to maximize their use of food supplies.

Common Tern

Sterna hirundo

Breeds in North America from Alberta east to Newfoundland ... Also found in the Old World ... The Common Tern is a transient in the Strait of Georgia...[1527]

**Black-legged Kittiwake
[simply Kittiwake in Europe]**

Rissa tridactyla

On 23 June 1997, 3 nests were discovered on Holland Rock in Chatham Sound, south of Prince Rupert on the Northern Mainland Coast.[1529]

Wynne-Edwards gained his highest honours for his theory of group selection – how groups of animals like the seabirds used mechanisms like hormones and territoriality to regulate populations and avoid overuse of their food.[1530] For example, if there isn't enough food, the whole colony simply won't breed. Wynne-Edwards argued that the groups that were best able to self-regulate had an evolutionary advantage. The two men with their common interests were wandering under Fowlsheugh, shouting above the din and looking at another population regulator – geology and geography itself and what Cowan called the "limitation of security." In other words, the number of birds able to successfully breed can be influenced by the type and availability of rock for secure nesting sites. In his "Of Mice and Men" lecture he told the story of another Scottish seabird colony they visited at Bass Rock, famous for its large white gannets:

... you'll find that the earliest comers to the colony nest in the middle of the most inaccessible cliffs. Then little by little the late comers fill up to the bottom of the cliff, to the top of the cliff and out towards the edges and then out onto the grasslands. The ones in the centre of the cliff have a far better history of raising their young than the ones at the edge of the cliff because they are not molested by the other creatures of the environment that come along and eat up the eggs and destroy the young of those that are nesting in the insecure localities around the edge, so here, then, secure nesting sites is what is contributing.[1531]

The key factor in determining the size of the population was the number of secure sites. Geology and ornithology were once again inextricably bound to evolution, including human evolution. Cowan considered himself lucky later on to have acquired a son-in-law, Mikkel Schau, who was a geologist and with whom he could share his deep interests. In a letter to Schau he recollects:

I would find great interest in being able to look at a landscape and glean from it some understanding of the forces that sculpted it and how these have interacted with the living world to give rise to what we see today. As a biologist, [I know that] eskers are where groundsquirrels can find ice-free terrain to burrow in. The great silt cliffs on some of the island shores were the only places I could find Arctic fox dens. The landscapes that guided caribou migrations, that gave rise to certain vegetation complexes that in turn governed the seasonal whereabouts of muskox, caribou, hares and therefore people. Sea bird cliffs were another focal point for biota and man.[1532]

Back on the cliffs of Fowlsheugh, conversations with Wynne-Edwards roamed to their shared interest in supporting naturalist clubs. Wynne-Edwards had revitalized the Scottish Ornithological Society (soc), on par with Cowan's involvement in the Vancouver Natural History Society. Cowan had given a public lecture on "Wildlife in the Canadian Rockies" to the soc to raise funds for Wynne-Edwards's causes. They also shared an interest in deer. Wynne-Edwards had been researching the current management of private deer estates, the same ones that had tried to exclude Cowan's ancestor Balfour a century before. Overstocking of deer was continuing to destroy any hope of regenerating Scotland's forests. The strategy that Wynne-Edwards adopted was to position himself on scientific committees to review and guide government policy, on everything from forests to whales. Tedious but effective. Cowan also attended his friend's lecture on what in those days was called "climatic change":

Wynne-Edwards paper was most informative + I have noted the following:
Climatic changes in northern Continental Europe are real.

Mean increase in north 3–5 degrees, winter increase in Finland
2–3 degrees. East Greenland winters are 5–7 degrees warmer.

Utah Salt Lake has lost 50% of its volume in 50 yrs.

Caspian Sea + other Steppe lakes are drying up. Pack ice of northern Asia has receded until almost 100 ships ply the NE passage annually.

Britain has not shared this warmup. Only about 0.7 degree mean annual increase + coldest winter temperatures are now lower.

The mildest climate in N Europe + Britain since the ice age was about 5000 BC[1533]

Unfortunately, neither of the two scientists would be able to convince any political party of the true severity of the problems of climate change over the course of their equally long lives, despite raising the alarm as early as 1952. Wynne-Edwards died in 1997, decorated but largely ignored. Prime Minister Margaret Thatcher in 1990 was the first world leader to champion climate science. Naturally, her enthusiasm waned as she began to see the economic impacts of any policy that would curb appetites for North Sea oil.

After Aberdeenshire, the Cowans headed by bus to Tynron, Dumfries, where they were greeted by Ian's aunt Alice (Mackenzie) and her husband, Rev. Jack McWilliams, and his uncle Daniel Mackenzie. Tynron is an ancient hamlet with a church built in 700 CE. The Cowans were amused but unfazed that the manse had no running cold (let alone hot) water, was cold and damp "like an igloo," that the floor was tamped earth and the housekeeping was rough, the kitchen sink being shared by chickens, three cats and a dismantled hive of bees. Daniel had retired from a life of military service around the world, after surviving the First World War, so primitive conditions didn't trouble the widowed soldier. Ann remembers the tea trolley rumbling over the uneven dirt floor laden with rattling teacups. Cowan was speaking one night to a group of scouts in the village and Garry made some friends among the troop, erecting a tent in the garden, which appeared to be warmer than the manse. Garry subsequently joined the wolf pack of the local scouts. In the margin of his journals, Cowan recorded a joke inspired by the church attendance: "A Sunday school teacher asked a class, What would Noah be doing on the ark? Small voice: I guess he'd be fishing. Another small voice: 'e'd na' be fishin' long wi' only two wurrums."[1534]

The family group joined Arthur Duncan, a researcher of the newly created national research council, the Nature Conservancy, and made it out to the Solway flats – famous for shorebirds – a sojourn which did not disappoint Cowan. Duncan became another rich source of expeditions and information, with the added attraction of also having a family eager to accompany their father. They covered large areas of Dumfriesshire, finding species new to the Cowans such as Water Ouzels and Stonechats, "an exquisite bird resembling a diminutive black wren-tit except that it is not a skulker."[1535] They did meet a few skulkers, as not all their contacts were as stimulating as the Duncans. They were obliged to attend various social events with local dignitaries, for some of whom they had little fondness: "Joyce and I are agreed that we have heard more intelligent adults use more verbiage saying less than in any week of our lives ... a common fault hereabouts [is] affectation and banal garrulousness ..."[1536] Cowan's tolerance for a certain class of discourse was limited. A decade later at a meeting in Switzerland for the International Union for the Conservation of Nature, he had a similar reaction to the well-heeled acolytes of the conservation movement. Cowan wrote: "In the evening we were entertained by Mr. Nicola at his beautiful estate outside Morges. The most interesting item of the evening was the finding of a slow worm or legless lizard crawling on the lawn."[1537]

They were back in Edinburgh in time to catch a ballet and a Royal Tattoo at the Edinburgh Festival. Cowan's detailed reviews were as enthusiastic as his descriptions of the alpine species at the Edinburgh Botanical Gardens, of which his ancestor Balfour had been the Royal Keeper. As Cowan had been trotted down to the zoological and botanical gardens as a child, so did he trot his own children there. Ann had somewhat more eclectic memories of Edinburgh than her father did, though:

> Garry and I were both day students at a boarding school. We had the upper floor of a house with a common front that belonged to the major. An ex-military guy owned the house and it was all red carpets and huge wide staircases and we had the top floor and there was another floor where Garry and I had little pokey rooms. The school was just over the fence. We were there from 8 'til 5, Saturdays as well. I remember visiting old castles and being locked into dungeons by my brother, a bit of bird watching, but as an 8-year-old you have a limited understanding. I remember the Queen because that was the year she was crowned. It was also post-war, so we were on rations.[1538]

Cowan described a host of ailments the children and Joyce succumbed to during the winter, including lumbago from having to stoop over low sinks and more serious problems requiring surgery. After a visit to the Edinburgh zoo, he discovered from the Keeper that the beavers were not much better at resisting English germs and had all died from enteritis.

Over the next month, Cowan had investigated a domesticated British vole colony, written up the BC voles chapter for his book, researched specific domestic sheep parasites and had a meeting with oceanographer Maxwell John Dunbar, internationally renowned for his work on the Arctic, climate change, paleoecology and zoogeography.[1539] Dunbar and Cowan shared Edinburgh as their birthplace (born four years apart), both had emigrated to Canada and both shared a wide range of interests, including conservation. Dunbar, like Wynne-Edwards, had also ended up at McGill but had spent much of his time in the Arctic doing research. He was on sabbatical in Copenhagen, so encouraged Cowan to "pop over" and take advantage of the researchers and museums. Popping over included crossing a stormy North Sea in a "barrel" which provided security only to some storm-bound Wheatears who caught a ride. Wheatears were one of the distinctive circumpolar birds that winter in the Old World and breed in the New, a fact which Cowan was to deliver at an Edinburgh Royal Society lecture upon his return from Scandinavia.

The lecture was billed "The Origin of the Vertebrate Fauna of Western North America." Cowan was at the top of his game that night and took his audience on an entertaining tour back in time to the glacial era, ranging across the northwest corner of the continent and around all his favourite places and species. Tidbits of his lecture were reported in the press: "Far to the north of the ice sheet the Yukon Valley, central and northern Alaska and large parts of the Aleutian chain also remained ice free. Here a more limited subarctic fauna waited out the refrigeration."[1540] He saved his island insulation theories of the Queen Charlotte Islands (Haida Gwaii) for the end and concluded that new species might be "accomplished in less than 50,000 years" and that "the parts of the puzzle were beginning to fit together."[1541] The talk had attracted a full house and received rave reviews in *The Scotsman*.

Cowan had his own view of the evening:

> The whole performance was most interesting and almost comic opera in its seriousness. The doorman in morning trousers, cutaway dewlaps, drooping black moustache, bags under his eyes + top hat set the style. The incongruous touch was a red + gold band around the topper...[1542]

The formality of the occasion wasn't entirely unappreciated by Cowan. He was winding down the field aspect of his research into mammal taxonomy and paleoecology and the event represented a swan song to that active part of his career. It was also a celebration of the intellectual legacy into which he had been welcomed with open arms. He further described the event: "Some 40 of the inner circle gathered in the dining room beneath the quizzical stare of Rayburn's beautiful portrait of John Robison, the first president of the ERS [Edinburgh Royal Society]. The dinner was excellent + the conversation even better."[1543]

The founder John Robison had been professor of natural philosophy at Edinburgh in the last quarter of the 18th century and was very much part of the old inner circle of the Scottish Enlightenment. Ironically, at the end of his life, Robison was much obsessed with secret societies taking over religions and governments, being a Freemason himself. The paradox of Robison was not, however, the subject of the evening's conversations. It appears that professor James Kendall's account, "in glowing details,"[1544] of how he met his future wife while crossing the Atlantic was of more interest. Kendall was a chemist, much attracted by electrolytes and the young, beautiful Alice Tyldesley from British Columbia, whom he met before the First World War. No doubt he was keen to share with the other British Columbian in the inner sanctum the wonder of those days. Cowan's final comment on the evening was his delight at reminiscing with William Wright Smith, Keeper of the Royal Botanic Gardens, who had known his dad, McTaggart Cowan, during their student days as botanists. Cowan had lost no time developing his contacts for his own passion that consumed his final decades – the flora of the northern temperate zone.[1545]

Once the boat landed in Copenhagen, he was off on various missions. The first was to visit museums and hunt down more Pleistocene fossils and North American specimens from early hunter–collectors to help "complete the puzzle." He was fascinated by the fact that the larger mammals on the island of Zealand, which separated from the mainland 6,000 years ago, were smaller than their Pleistocene counterparts, an idea he had raised in his lecture and which was to occupy graduate students like Foster and Guiguet. Cowan liked Copenhagen: its tidier appearance, the robust health of its inhabitants and their reliance on bicycles. "Some of the designs of bicycles are most ingenious,"[1546] he wrote. There were other things he was less impressed with: the whaling ships lined up in the harbour (he discussed with Dunbar a moratorium that prevented Danes from killing walrus in the Canadian Arctic); and Danish deer estates, like Scotland's, reserved for the hunting elite. "Few farmers shoot; they cannot afford to."[1547]

He moved on to Sweden and was more impressed with their national forests, which had both public hunting areas and permanent nature reserves, governed by more equitable, democratic game management boards and scientific staff. He attended their game warden school and became an honorary member. "The Swedes have a very sophisticated management. So much of the land is owned by the forest companies, [which] use the game as a blandishment to keep their workers."[1548] In these journals, Cowan has rare moments of candid observations, like a particular fondness for a Swedish professor, "a white-haired, arty type of man in an office cluttered with budgerigars, a pet starling and a rabbit."[1549]

Starlings had wreaked havoc in North American in Cowan's lifetime. As a cavity nester highly adapted to holes in everything from telephone poles to offices of Swedish professors, they had usurped other native cavity nesters such as bluebirds, swallows, martins, wrens, owls, ducks and woodpeckers, with devastating results. Invasive species emanating from Europe were a big concern to Cowan and he was ever on the lookout for the next invasive species. He counted himself among those invasive species, taking a particular interest in old Uppsala, as it had been a Viking town, evoking images of his own Viking Cowan roots before they too "invaded" the world.

Uppsala was also an ancient university town and he was delighted to chance upon the surgical theatre of the early anatomist Olaus Rudbeck, who both discovered the lymphatic system and laid out the royal botanical gardens; the house of the pioneer botanist Carl Linnaeus; and next door the home of Anders Celsius of thermometer fame. Cowan spent the rest of the day with the head of the Zoology Institute, Sven Horstadius, an expert on sea urchins. Cowan describes him as "a gentle, kindly little man and a brilliant scholar."[1551] Horstadius discovered a key anatomical feature, the neural crest, or limb bud, which he identified as the common foundation from which the evolution of vertebrates sprang.

Cowan continued by boat to Helsinki and met various researchers at the Finnish Zoological Institute. They took him round the countryside (somewhat tamer than British Columbia's), reviewing the management of their wildlife. Cowan told the newspapers that "he found that when it came to climbing, he outstayed most of the Finns."[1552] On private lands, management consisted of bounties on predators and conventional approaches by local hunting clubs, which he noted without enthusiasm. He was, however, very enthusiastic about their saunas, woodstoves and breakfast spreads. An elderly wildlife artist, Matti Karppanen, whom he called a Finnish Audubon, captivated him for an afternoon. In the national forests, he noted, to his delight, that there was more ecological emphasis on management. He wryly mentioned the Finnish preoccupation with hunting large male game birds, and how researchers were trying to demonstrate the unfortunate consequences of unnatural selection on the populations. One researcher was looking at the impact of storms on the survival rate of yearling White-winged Scoters. Scoters he was well familiar with from their breeding lakes in the Chilcotin and wintering grounds in the Strait of Georgia.

Cowan admired one Finnish student who sat in a tree all summer observing a hawk's nest. The conclusions of the student were that what is left in the nest bears little resemblance to what was consumed, a fact Cowan was quick to note. He also met Erkki Kalela, who charted the changes in the distribution of birds in Finland from 1850 to 1950 in response to changes in winter and spring temperatures. Cowan wrote, "His maps show clearly that the winter birds and those arriving in the early spring have advanced."[1554] Climate change was a hot topic for the European ornithologists, finely tuned to bird arrivals, and appears in Cowan's journals frequently.

He returned to Scottish shores brimming with ideas and sightings of pelagic Razorbills which beat the boat there. Razorbills are cousins to the Thick-billed Murres in BC. These murres had special significance for the Cowans because Kenneth Racey had found what he thought was one of the first specimens in BC. One had washed up dead at Boundary Bay in 1941, although it later proved to be

European Starling

Sturnus vulgaris

The European Starling was first reported in British Columbia in 1945 (Munro, 1947) and the first specimen was taken in 1947 (Munro and Cowan, 1947) ... The European Starling is widely recognized as a problem species.[1550]

White-winged Scoter

Melanitta fusca

Many adult females migrate to salt water in early autumn and may head farther south than the other groups. The young of the year follow before freeze-up in the first weeks of November.[1553]

Thick-billed Murre

Uria lomvia

The colony is situated on the southwest peninsula [of Triangle Island] from 76 to 91 m above sea level.... No nests were built; eggs were laid on bare ground on exposed, narrow ledges of steep, rocky cliffs, or on level, open areas near cliff top.[1555]

a Common Murre. A Thick-billed Murre breeding colony did establish itself on Triangle Island off Vancouver Island in 1980.

Cowan, like the murres, came back to assume some of the parental duties, especially with Garry, who was rapidly fledging at sea. Garry eventually ended up on the Atlantic side of Canada as professor of fisheries sciences at Memorial University, his Atlantic exposure having begun on Scottish expeditions during his father's sabbatical year. Cowan returned to Saint Andrew's University in Perthshire in time for the annual conference of ornithologists. There he also had his first meeting with Peter Scott, which was to influence the course of the next decade of his life. As the only son of the Antarctic explorer Robert Scott (who died on his way back from the South Pole when Peter was a toddler), Peter Scott was already well known to the British public. It helped that he was also a bird artist, popular writer and lecturer on natural history. He was emerging on the scene in 1952, having founded the Severn Wildfowl Trust at Slimbridge in England six years earlier. Slimbridge was already becoming a popular destination where the public watched and learned about birds and wetlands. (Cowan stopped in there with the family on their way back to London.) That same year, Scott had started a children's radio show on the BBC called *Nature Parliament*, and in 1955 he would launch a television career that would make him a household name. His experiences were ripe for adaptation in Canada by Cowan.

In the spring of 1953 Cowan toured the Highlands in a 1928 Rolls Royce with Frank Fraser Darling, camping as they went. Darling at the time was senior lecturer in zoology at the University of Edinburgh. He was a renowned naturalist, ecologist and writer, later knighted, who captivated audiences with his natural history books that popularized science and ecology. They were intimate accounts of the years he spent with his wife, Marian "Bobbie" Fraser, and young son Alasdair on the remote islands of Scotland. Darling had received a small research fellowship between 1936 and 1939 to do an ecological survey of the west coast seabird colonies, grey seals, red deer and the interactions with the fishing and farming communities. The concept of the ecological survey, using a combination of biological observation, traditional knowledge and social, political and economic methodologies, was attributed to him.

The family lived in tents and travelled around in kayaks (new to the UK then and somewhat less comfortable than the Rolls) from which they made their observations. The trilogy *A Herd of Red Deer*, *Island Years* and *A Naturalist on Rona* became international bestsellers, and although his methods were questioned by some, few questioned his ability to engage the public's imagination. Darling had collaborated with Starker Leopold on the deer work and Cowan had an instant entrée through the 'B.' Recalled Cowan:

> I learned a lot from Frank Darling. That work opened my eyes to
> something I'd been struggling with out here (we were pretty much
> alone here then): I became convinced of the importance of animal

behaviour in opening our eyes to the potential impact between man and animals and to understanding animal populations.[1556]

Their first stop in the Highlands was at one of Darling's new ecology research projects on red deer at Glen Strathfarrar, known as the "last of the great unspoiled glens,"[1557] west of Inverness. It was 300,000 acres of the last ancient Caledonian pine forest still with vestiges of prey–predator systems of deer, fox, wildcat and raptors. The wolves, beaver and bears had long gone but Cowan remarks on the unusual lush understorey of the forest and the life starting to creep back in the glen after centuries of overgrazing by the landowning sheep and deer syndicates. Researchers through the Nature Conservancy had been looking at the ecology of the soil, the trout and now Darling's work on the deer. Darling was adamant that the economic, cultural and ecological restoration of the land had to be linked together. Ironically, everything was washed away in 1962 when the valley was flooded with the construction of Britain's largest hydroelectric arch dam. It sparked outrage in Scotland, and the story (as well as the narrator) were brought back to the New World by the 'B.'

In the early 1960s Darling joined Leopold and Cowan as scientific advisers to an American non-profit called the Conservation Foundation. The foundation was the brainchild of George Brewer, Henry Fairfield Osborn Jr. and Samuel Ordway, set up in 1948 with some help from Laurance Rockefeller "to promote knowledge of the earth's resources." It had a mandate for research, education and "to encourage human conduct to sustain and enrich life on earth."[1558] Some of the colourful trustees included James Cagney, the Hollywood actor with an early passion for soil conservation, Gifford Pinchot, S. Dillon Ripley of the Smithsonian and Lucius D. Clay, a war hero. The foundation was instrumental in laying down the scientific groundwork for most of the 1960s environmental campaigns, such as the fight against DDT and for soil conservation.

One of the projects they initiated was a conference on "Future Environments of North America," chaired by Darling and Cowan, who also edited the conference papers. It made sense to have Darling. What the scientific community was trying to avoid was a bleak future environment – that is, one that might look like Scotland. During one of the sessions, on future energy, a debate was recorded in which Darling and Cowan tackled an economist on the true environmental costs of energy (Scottish hydroelectricity and Kentucky coal were referenced). They were arguing for placing a value on these external costs, a view developed by British economist Arthur Pigou earlier in the century. In one heated exchange about these costs, American economist Joseph Fisher asked: "Frank, why do you lay this – or blame this – on the economists?" Darling replied, "Because this is called the economic price of coal"[1559] Darling was adamant about the failure of economists to properly account for the external costs of environmental damage caused by the energy sector, whether coal, oil or hydro.

Cowan and Darling had also toured a dam at Pitlochry, where they had observed the smolts of brown trout hungry and marooned behind the barrier. His detailed notes of how to remedy the situation were typical of Cowan, ever mindful of the delicate interplay of prevention and restoration within the complex problem of energy provision. Nothing was as stark a reminder of the cost of energy as Scotland, with its inhabitants resorting to the last energy source before you hit bedrock: the burning of the soil – peat.

After Strathfarrar, Cowan headed north and got a good dose of the peat-burning communities. "Thence to Lairg + along Loch Shin, where the real character of this part of the Highlands shows. A small island in the Loch is treed but all else is barren and overgrazed by sheep."[1560] His discomfort at the bleak landscape was only surpassed by the bleak quality of life for the people. It was a Sunday and deserted when they arrived at the village of Scourie. Sabbath observance was strictly kept in the far north. After a discussion with the parish doctor, he wrote:

> There is no light, love or comfort in this religious interpretation, only fear + resignation. We camped by the roadside 10 miles below Scourie + went to sleep with a cuckoo's notes in our ears.[1561]

It was Cowan's first cuckoo, but Darling was well acquainted with them, as he was with the stigma of being a cuckoo himself. He was an illegitimate child and had struggled with the "crippling social disadvantages"[1563] in a class-ridden Scotland during the early part of his life. It was zoologist Julian Huxley who recognized the young Darling's talent in integrating science with social economics and took him on as a student in London.

Huxley's mentoring talents and intellectual landscape were familiar and fertile for Cowan, but Huxley had waded into swampy terrain again. The British intelligentsia of social activists and humanist scientists at the time, including Julian Huxley, were still involved with eugenics. Huxley remained with the British Eugenics Society from 1937 off and on until 1962. Huxley was an enigmatic personality, and much has been written on his life and his criticism of "the unscientific and inhumane appropriation of its [Darwinian] theories" by the Nazis.[1564] As a population ecologist Cowan was vulnerable through his association – albeit fairly distant – with Huxley, but Cowan's eye as a conservationist was always on what he observed as the real threat. In a letter to Neil Dawe, congratulating him on the writing of the last chapter of *Birds of BC*, he reiterated the old position of the 'B' that the important

Cuckoo [Common Cuckoo]

Cuculus canorus

About the size of a collared dove, cuckoos are a scarce summer visitor to most of Britain, arriving in April; their familiar *cuck-oo* call heralds the start of spring. The adults leave for Africa by June or July, almost as soon as they have laid their eggs, while the young birds follow them in the autumn. Adults are "brood-parasites," famous for laying their eggs in other birds' nests and fooling them into raising their young for them.[1562]

questions to be addressed in North America were greed, over-consumption, inequity and lack of education:

> It appears to tackle the much-neglected topic of the demands different societies make on the living world in economic terms. We often point to the areas of Africa, Asia and South America with high rates of population – but the worst effect certainly involves the northern societies with modest growth in population but with a soaring appetite for products and an equally exploding capacity to pollute.[1565]

Genetics in its other guises was also exploding onto the academic scene at the time. On May 14, 1953, after a Royal Society lecture, Cowan reports Crick and Watson's first explanation of DNA:

> Attended lecture by Critch [Francis Crick] of Cavendish Laboratory on the structure of nucleic acid + the influence upon the theory of the reproduction of chromosomes. He did a most interesting job of interpreting the data known about the dextral form + concluded that it is a double spiral with the two "strands" in reversed direction, the bases adenine, guanine, Tyrpine [tyrosine] + one other are in balanced pairs. His paper in collaboration with D.S. [James Dewey] Watson should be a most interesting piece of work.[1566]

Much of his time in Scotland was spent sizing up young researchers he could sign up, and genetics was one of the areas in which he was recruiting. He didn't lure Watson and Crick but ended up attracting a hot new population geneticist from Oxford, Dennis Chitty. He later also recruited a young unknown who had grown up in a Japanese Canadian internment camp in Kaslo, BC, David Suzuki.

For the final week in Britain, Cowan travelled down to London with the children to rejoin Joyce, who had been staying with friends. He described a full day in the zoology department of the University of Southampton with John Raymont, who gained international distinction for his work on plankton and the productivity of oceans. Raymont was part of the Edinburgh group originally and had worked with Huxley and Nicholson on ocean issues for UNESCO. On July 20, 1953, Raymont was in full sail describing to Cowan his experiments on the harmful impacts of chemical fertilizers on plankton and their seasonal blooms, research that was to figure strongly in the understanding of oceanic chemistry and carbon sequestration as well as biodiversity such as sea bird research. Just before the end of the day, Cowan excused himself. His journal entry read: "5 pm embarked on Queen Mary." His year in Scotland exploring regions of upwelling and lines of convergence had come to an end. Joyce had carried the lion's share of the organizing, to allow him to take advantage of every opportunity until the very last minute. There is little that Europe had to offer that didn't catch Cowan's eye.

"... between the Scylla of commercialism and Charybdis of stuffiness."

Saturna Island, 1954–1960

Within two years of returning from Scotland, Cowan was presenting the idea of television shows to the 'B' and other wildlife scientists at the 20th North American Wildlife Conference. It is worth presenting his talk in its entirety:

> Gentlemen, there is no more sterile human emotion than pessimism ... It is easy to train technicians; it is very difficult to produce socially conscious, well-educated men and women who are also competent in the technical field. May I also commend public speaking as a worthwhile art in our calling. The inarticulate are not followed ... turning to the larger field of public education, Cottam has pointed out forcefully that we spend too much of our time preaching to the saved. Evangelism is best directed towards the damned. Wildlife and fisheries conservation is a natural for this medium [television]. With some concept of the new medium and with a keen imagination, the opportunities for programs of the greatest human interest are unlimited, and by skillful preparation each can do more than interest; it can educate, it can spread the gospel of wildlife conservation ... I must refer here to the well-known fact that the printed word will only educate the already sympathetic and that visual materials as by television and motion pictures or the demonstration of a personal approach are the only ones likely to make inroads on the very large group of apathetic or unsympathetic in the populace. These then should be our tools of evangelism, while the written word keeps the interested informed. Educational effort is also best directed to the leaders in the human community, as whether we delude ourselves or not, they are the people who influence the decision and actions of our fellows.[1567]

He launched immediately into television after the conference, starting with a single program, *Exploring Minds*, that involved the dean of medicine and two UBC academics. It was the first of the CBC University television series.[1568] According to Cowan, the CBC producers liked it and asked him to come back and do something else. "The TV adventure was really fun … The first one was done live, and that's hair-raising."[1569] That first series was called *Fur and Feathers*, for which they did 52 quarter-hour programs for children.

For *Fur and Feathers*, Cowan went down to the CBC studio once a week.

American Moose swimming

Alces alces

The largest of the American deer. Its large size (about horse size); generally blackish-brown colour; long legs; high shoulders; long, pendulous, slightly inflated muzzle; and throat appendage are found in no other species.

> I had a very bright youngster, an 8-year-old boy [David Maxwell], a son of a single parent who taught English at the university. If you confront a bright child with something they had never seen before, you get fascinating reactions. I once brought in a baby moose to the television station. This kid was fascinated: "What is this nose?" Then you called attention to its hooves and how they spread out so the animal could run on soft ground and the 15 minutes was over before you knew it.[1570]

The second child he invited was the daughter of a colleague, Tommy Taylor, who "was a natural for the television show and we just continued. We did a Christmas program and went through the animals of the Bible. It was a fun series, so many children loved it."[1571]

The Living Sea series was next, first airing in May 1957. It was longer, at half an hour each week on Thursday nights. CBC assigned a producer, Ken Bray, and a cameraman and they spent part of each summer with Cowan getting live material photographed on film.

> I designed every program in advance. They'd say, "Sure, that's great," so then I'd put the detail out for what I needed and scattering it over the world and getting the stuff in … It took about 1,200 feet of film well taken to make a half-hour program. When the film came in you went through it and made the first cut – "I'll take that bit and that bit and this bit," and this is how we'll put it together.[1572]

CBC advertised it as "the fabulous seven seas of the world come into focus as indoor oceans on your television."[1573] The first episode opened with Cowan showing a model of a volcanic island and how it formed the "Cradle of Life." As he admits, "Looking back, some of it was pretty corny. We had to start with the mountain-building process and we had [to capture] it all in a model. When you photographed it you didn't know if that mountain was going to let off steam or not."[1574] Each subsequent episode developed the theme of life in different marine environments: "Bird Island," "Salmon Story," "Whales," "Shellfish Story," "Life under the Sand," "Life above the Sand," "City Shores," "Among the Waves," "The Ancient Mariners," and so on.

The first series was done on a shoestring, and for his efforts Cowan received the princely sum of $300 a month.[1575] He used whatever free sources he could find. "I was chairman of the [Vancouver] Aquarium committee for a while, and I had free run of the aquarium at night, so we could do anything we liked ... so long as you didn't end up with dead animals."[1576] His 1953 grad student Murray Newman had started as the head of the new Aquarium and was happy to hand him the keys to promote the educational services of the institution. Cowan also used the aquaria at Friday Harbour Marine Station through the University of Washington exchange with grad students and family. He collaborated with marine biologist Dixie Lee Ray. "And she had all sorts of neat things that she had found out. She later became a governor for the state of Washington."[1577] For the "Fish Swimming" episode he wanted to capture the diversity of fish movement. "They don't just swim, some go forward, backward, and in all directions and I had access to the Aquarium, and a friend in charge of the big aquarium in San Diego said, 'Come on down.' It was very international in scope."[1578]

Cowan also developed his own outdoor aquaria at Jim Campbell's farm on Saturna Island overlooking Plumper Sound at East Point (in what is now Gulf Islands National Park Reserve). He'd take his family for the month of August. He would take students camping over long weekends, travelling in a 19-foot clinker-built (lapstrake) cedar boat called *Tuchi* that he bought from his friend Tom Genge. "It seems crazy now. I came from Horseshoe Bay over the strait. We had a few rocky rides ... We had a fire aboard once but we survived."[1579] Other times the family would travel to Saturna via the *Lady Rose* out of Steveston. Ann recalls the half-dozen summers spent on Saturna Island:

> We rented Jim Campbell's land ... only accessible by boat. It was out there. It was a two-room log cabin and we kids slept outside on the front porch and would flip a coin who would get the actual bed ... It was around then that he got his interest in the marine. Having to come up with ideas for the TV program helped him to spread out his interest sideways. The marine fit in with family; it was easy, close by and it kept him in the field. We all got taught to row, running the dredge and Garry would set these hooks and lines for skate around Campbell Bay. My job was to row him as he trawled or dredged. Garry was very influenced by this time, as he went into fisheries.[1580]

Cowan clearly had found a way to combine his love of being in the field and his education interests with being with his family. He describes the island on his first trip there in August of 1954:

I have worked along the entire length of the Island on its west side. For most of the way the coast is rocky, with bluffs or cliffs to 400 feet. The cliffs are highest near Crocker Point, and the northern tip of the Island, adjacent to Boat passage, is of low elevation and supports at least two farms ... The woods on the bluff areas have a Douglas-fir, Garry oak, *Madrone, Juniperus scopulorum* climax and an understorey dominated by red honeysuckle.[1581]

At the time, only 85 people lived on Saturna. Campbell had moved there after the war to farm and raise his children. He recalls:

Ian McTaggart Cowan was a very frequent visitor with his family that enjoyed the place a great deal and he felt from his experience that the Saturna Beach area had the widest variety of marine life of any of the locations that he knew about. So he brought over doctorate scholars in animal life that he was in charge of. They would come for 10 days or so and immediately they would go out and catch everything they could catch and put them in an aquarium and then study them and write reports on them. And he did that every year with scholars from New York to Europe – all over the country – who had come to UBC to get a doctorate in animal science.[1582]

Cowan had found a perfect outlet for Garry's marine interests and even brought him into the television programs on both the technical and the talent sides.

I hired him [Garry] to carry water and set the aquarium up on the beach. The tank was up above and we had running salt water in the aquarium. You could set up anything. I remember once a razor-shell clam, the shape of your finger, and it is very active. You put it down on the beach and you see its foot go out, penetrate the mud, swell out and pull itself down into the mud, shove it down again. It goes like a house on fire, we took hundreds of feet of film.[1583]

The Cowans' advocacy for molluscs on TV was matched only by their competitive search for mollusc diversity. Cowan developed a scientific following for his chiton work which led to the naming of the chiton after him, as was a dipperclam with which he shared no characteristics except occasional habitat.

All in all, Cowan had one vole, two molluscs and an amphipod named after him, which provides a certain notoriety, maybe with the exception of the amphipods, which are a ubiquitous family of shrimp-like crustaceans commonly described as bottom crawlers and include sand fleas. The one named after him, *Parallorchestes cowani*, is associated with brown algae on exposed and semi-protected rocky coasts, not unlike the Saturna shoreline at Boat Passage.[1585]

These naming accolades were to come later though. During the years when his children were growing up, as Ann notes, it was important to him to encourage their own interests, as his parents had done. But the rising profile of her father was not completely without its pressures:

> It was more burdensome to be Ian McTaggart Cowan's son than his daughter. As kids you aren't aware. To me he was lively and busy and always doing things but he wasn't "famous." He was on TV, which just meant that we *got* a TV.[1586]

In fact, he was becoming quite famous, since he was hosting a show that was selling around the world, from New Zealand to the United Arab Republic. Cowan admitted, "There was nothing like it on television. The only other one in the world was the BBC, based in their production office in Wales."[1587]

> I got letters from all over the world. [Joyce] and I went to New Zealand and got on the local plane in Christchurch, where I had a visiting professorship, walked up the aisle and the fellow said, "I know you, you're Dr. McTaggart-Cowan." I got in the taxi and gave our residence. "Where have I heard you before? Aren't you Dr. McTaggart-Cowan?" [The programs] were a gold mine for the CBC.[1588]

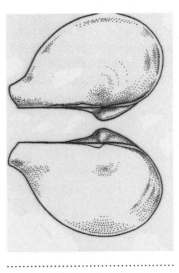

Cowan Dipperclam

Cuspidaria cowani

Shell inflated, globular. Rostrum cylindrical, very narrow, attenuate, abruptly truncate, set off by radial ridge. Off the Queen Charlotte Islands, British Columbia, in 1318 m, mud.[1584]

Living Sea aired in BC in 1957. When it sold to a US network, even before it was picked up and repeated nationally in Canada, *Vancouver Sun* TV critic Jim Gilmore wrote: "What made the series far from dull was the fathomless knowledge on the subject brought to the series by Dr. McTaggart-Cowan … He has a knack for explaining complicated things in plain, easy-to-understand and colourful terms."[1589] *The Scotsman* newspaper in Edinburgh had rave reviews for the series when it ran on Scottish television. "Dr. Ian Cowan took us on an exhilarating voyage of ocean discovery. Dolphins and porpoises were his subject, and his illustrations were real eye jerkers, especially the pictures which he showed of those fluent mammals engaged in a crack-shot game of basketball."[1590]

The success of *Living Sea* led to his best known series, *The Web of Life*, which first aired Sunday afternoons starting in October 1959 and ran for 26 episodes.[1591] It then ran nationally on Friday evenings throughout 1963. The producer was Tim Connachie, with editor John Fuller and cameraman Robert Reid. It was described as an ambitious series "dealing with special aspects of nature, animal and insect life, demonstrating the habitat and the struggle for existence among creatures which have made their home on land."[1592] Cowan went on the road with a Vancouver production team that travelled more than 30,000 miles in North America, Mexico, the Pacific Islands, Jamaica and the Florida Everglades to get the footage. The synopsis for the series noted:

> One of the purposes of this series is to illustrate that life's great capacity has been change, not just in form, but also in function; change in ability to withstand different temperatures, eat different foods and survive conditions which were formerly intolerable. Special aspects of conservation and animal husbandry are outlined.[1593]

Web of Life had themes, like the episode titled "Walking," which Cowan described as "starting out with a salamander with feet-like clubs and finishing off with the slow motion of a five-gaited horse. I had a little model made based on Gray's interesting book on the new biology – changing of weight, changing your balance points."[1594] There was also footage from African animals, which he used his network of personal contacts to obtain. "I had a friend in Africa [Bristol Foster] who was a keen cameraman and all I had to do was send him film and say Could you film some giraffes running?"[1595]

Cowan's series won awards all over the world. The Vancouver International Film Festival recognized him several years in a row. He also won the 1962 top award in the network classification for adult instruction program from Ohio State University's Institute for Education by Radio and Television; the Golden Prize in the United Arab Republic's second International Television Festival; even a glowing tribute from the Canadian Medical Association for producing a series that informed people "about how to live more happily because they were living in better health."[1596] The CBC sold *Web of Life* to Britain's Granada TV network for $200,000 in 1960 [equivalent to more than $1.6-million in 2014 according to the Bank of Canada's inflation calculator webpage], which at the time was the biggest export sale in CBC history. They did indeed make a lot of money on him. As a *Globe and Mail* article put it, "The purchase of the *Web of Life* series followed an excellent audience reaction in Britain to *The Living Sea*."[1597]

Vancouver columnist Harold Weir also had rave reviews for the series:

> The real McCoy ... or perhaps the real McTaggart would be a better way of putting it ... *The Living Sea* didn't purport to be an exhaustive course in marine biology; it was a skillfully, cheerfully, interestingly and almost breezily imparted compendium of useful and picturesque information. With a quick and unforced wit, an obvious love of his own subject and an equally obvious depth of knowledge, all the more attractive for being lightly sketched on rather than profoundly paraded, Dr. Cowan had very definitely put it over. In short, Dr. Cowan has made TV education almost nice.[1598]

Cowan described *The Living Sea* generously as "the first Suzuki film," although it would be more accurate to say Suzuki was "the second Cowan." Suzuki later admitted there was an intellectual legacy that he himself was late in acknowledging:

> I have never been much of a television watcher, especially when I first came to UBC. I didn't know Ian had a television show nor did I ever watch one, but I acknowledge that he was out there before I ever did a national TV series (my first series was a local broadcast in Edmonton when I did eight shows in 1962). While I wasn't influenced or helped by Ian's work, he really did break new ground for an academic and he did hire me, but we never talked about what I was doing and there was always a tension between arrogant young geneticists and wildlife types. We really looked down our noses at them. I gave a talk to the Ecological Society of America in Utah years ago and crawled on my belly apologizing for being such an arrogant, ignorant prick back then.[1599]

The intellectual legacy for Suzuki actually had started earlier, with ecologist Stan Rowe, a friend of Cowan's. During the Second World War, Rowe was a conscientious objector, and rather than do military service, he went to the internment camps and taught around Kaslo. David Suzuki was one of his students. Weir's assessment of Cowan's approach in 1960 would have been instructive to anyone starting out in television. "Dr. Cowan's success on this program has been due to two factors: first, his lively informality; and second, his ability to keep the thing between the Scylla of commercialism and Charybdis of stuffiness."[1600]

Cowan also did a four-part educational series with the BC Department of Education called *Patterns of Living*, which first aired in November of 1961.[1601] He was even at the forefront of colour television educational broadcasts. In 1966 the first use of colour TV was broadcast into schools in Manitoba with a half-hour film called *The Teacher and Television*.[1602] The teacher was Cowan, with Grade 6 students from Brandon, Manitoba – all in living colour.

By the time Suzuki was beginning in television, Cowan had decided to call it quits:

> You've got to be able to move ahead. And remember you shouldn't be doing it if you weren't learning, and it came to a point where I wasn't learning anymore. And you quit. After that I was asked to do half a dozen or a dozen films which were simply retrospective, recutting the other ones for the education department of the province of Manitoba. That was the end of it.[1603]

Fittingly, one of his last television shows was with Peter Scott. They cohosted an episode of *Klahanie: The Great Outdoors* in 1969 called "Wildlife in Danger."[1604] There was more to it than not learning anymore. Cowan said he had

... a need to know in a broader scene. People looking back over my research career quite rightly criticized me for hopping around. But each one of the hops was following something that I had to know ... And I couldn't find out any other way but by doing it, so I did it."[1605]

One of the seeds planted in Edinburgh in 1953 during Cowan's sabbatical year had come from his introduction to E. Max Nicholson. Nicholson was a US naturalist and ornithologist but also an astute administrator who had just started the research council called The Nature Conservancy. He fought to secure stable funding for the sciences – a goal that was nudging Cowan towards his own future role as an administrator. When asked at age 90 why he spent the last 25 years in administration, Cowan responded, "Good question. Because I liked to make things happen and that's the way to make them happen."[1606] Within two years of returning from sabbatical, Cowan had co-founded the National Research Council of Canada and become the first chairman of the Advisory Committee on Wildlife Research. It was classic Cowan to have spotted the advantage to conservation of being on the decision-making end of national research budgets. He was also following Nicholson's lead, in that once research funding was secured, conservation followed.

In 1961 he was invited to Prime Minister John Diefenbaker's national think tank, called the Resources for Tomorrow Conference, in Montreal. It was an invitational gathering of 800 of Canada's top experts on land, conservation and wildlife matters. A wildlife stamp contest was even held for the conference. Cowan was one of the keynote speakers. From whales to seabirds, Cowan argued passionately for the role of wildlife research in Canada and for the idea that understanding "the forces that interact to build, destroy and maintain an animal population is fundamental to the task."[1607] He continued, "Almost all the research to date has been outside Canada," and he pointed to research in Britain, Scandinavia and the US. His 1952–53 sabbatical had provided the fodder for his next "biopolitical campaign." It spanned the next two decades and was about raising financial support for Canadian research and scientists.

If challenging the predator bounty had seemed glacially slow for Cowan, the pace of the campaign for scientific funding was more like geological. Even by 1974, Canada's funding allocation compared with similar institutions in Britain was less than half and Cowan's tone became a little more emphatic as he wrote with fellow scientists Peter Larkin and the eminent Canadian physicist George Volkoff:

> We have lost sight of the Baconian principle that "Nature to be commanded must be obeyed." From that principle it follows that only by studying nature can we achieve technological advance and rational development. It is time we forgot Senator [Maurice] Lamontagne and remembered Newton, Faraday, Darwin, Pasteur, Rutherford, Currie and Banting.[1608]

Maurice Lamontagne was an economist politician known for what Cowan called "short-term, mission-oriented" work. There were a few slow victories, while the attacks on the biological sciences were rapid and persistent. In 1981, Ron Jeffels of the Open Learning Institute, a friend and colleague for four decades, made a tribute to Cowan when he stepped down from chair of the Academic Council of BC after six years. Jeffels characterized the struggle as being akin to wartime engagement: "He is after all the longest-endured fighter pilot in the whole history of BC education; and I can't recall an occasion when he's even been modestly wounded, let alone shot down."[1609]

Cowan had examples like Max Nicholson to follow, whose indefatigable contributions didn't end at the Scottish border. Nicholson had supported Julian Huxley (during his tenure as director general of UNESCO) in setting up the International Union for the Protection of Nature (now the International Union for the Conservation of Nature, IUCN). Cowan's professional relationship with these men landed him the distinction of being their "man in Vancouver" to sit on the many international committees. As he said in an interview in 1979, "These kinds of committees and commissions are places where you can spawn the attitude of 'living in some kind of symbiosis with the wildlife that share our planet.'"[1610] Cowan's systematic sorting through dusty drawers of specimens that year in the various museums around Europe (on his trip to Sweden and Denmark he found Great Auks, Eskimo Curlews, California Condors and Ivory-billed Woodpeckers) had sharpened his skill set on species at risk and extinctions. He became an international authority on biodiversity (though that wasn't a word yet), which landed him the vice-presidency of the IUCN for six years running.

The financing of the IUCN and the Conservation Foundation over in Washington had proven difficult, so in 1961 Nicholson, Huxley and Peter Scott co-founded the World Wildlife Fund (now the World Wide Fund for Nature) as an international fund-raising organization. They conscripted Prince Philip as their first fundraiser and collected the princely sum of $33,500 for five species at risk, including the Tule Goose in Canada, the larger and darker subspecies of the Greater White-fronted Goose that migrates with the other subspecies along the coast of British Columbia.

The British contingent looked of course to Cowan to assist in the establishment of a chapter of the WWF in Canada. He was an official scientific adviser from its start. Prior to that, in his role as chair of conservation for the Pacific Science Congresses, Cowan had been in charge of reporting the status of threatened and endangered species of the countries all around the Pacific.[1612] At this time, pressures from overhunting had long paled in comparison to the harm from expansion of dams, agriculture and industrialization. As an example, at a congress in Hawaii he suggested urbanization as the greatest threat to Canadian migratory waterfowl that utilized the Fraser Delta.

The world had come a long way from the early days of Lloyd, Taverner and Leopold, when upholding the Migratory Birds Convention Act was the biggest challenge. That year at the congress, Cowan related one good news story that linked directly back to his early mentors and the setting up of the 'B.' The wood bison population that was believed to be extinct (the herd that the 'B' first rallied around in 1925 to save from being swamped genetically by the introduced plains bison) was given a new prognosis. Cowan reported that a small, isolated relic herd had been found by the Canadian Wildlife Service and was now protected.[1613]

That Tenth Pacific Science Congress, held in Hawaii in 1960, was a milestone with the 'B' in other ways as well. The Cowans spent over a month on the islands with Starker Leopold and his family. Recalled Ann:

> It was a joint rental and we went for almost five weeks – three weeks prior to the conference for family time. I decided to take an interest in sharks and went to all the sessions on sharks ... We took a walking trip into Haleakala crater as a family for two and a half days ... it was a fantastic place.[1614]

Cowan and Leopold walked and talked, no doubt pondering such things as the vastly impoverished native Hawaiian flora and fauna, and planned for the "Future Environments of North America" conference to be held in 1965, headed up by their colleague Frank Fraser Darling.[1615]

Greater White-fronted Goose

Anser albifrons

In North America, breeds in Alaska and western arctic Canada; winters mainly from southwestern British Columbia south though California, in coastal Texas and Louisiana and in Mexico ... Timm et al. (1982) have since documented the presence of the "tule" goose in British Columbia, but they do not think that a third subspecies ... has been substantiated.[1611]

While Cowan was in Scotland, Nicholson had given him the idea of establishing a network of representative ecosystems and ecologically important areas. Nicholson had created two designations: national nature reserves, and sites of specific scientific interest. This network was the prototype for what UNESCO eventually set up called the International Biological Program, the goal of which was to identify a network of representative ecosystems around the world. Cowan visited some of these reserves in his last months in Scotland, spending several days with Nicholson to go over the minutiae of policy, operation and management.

It was right at this time that Cowan's colleague Vladimir Krajina, newly appointed to the UBC botany department and later the forestry department as well, arrived on campus fresh from leading the Czech resistance against Hitler and fleeing Stalin's regime on skis. In his biography of Krajina, author Jan Drábek tracks the Czech scientist's rather dramatic entrance on the conservation scene.[1616] As a highly trained botanist he was a natural lead on designing an ecosystem classification system based on the plants, climate and terrain (Krajina coined it the biogeoclimatic classification). Cowan's students Foster and Guiguet got involved while at the museum to ensure that areas of specific scientific interest for birds and mammals were also included. The sites that were identified "became the nucleus of our present ecological reserves system."[1617] Krajina's job was also to convince the Minister of Lands and Forests, Ray Williston, to pass the reserves into law. After facing two dictators, tackling a stubborn, pro-resource-industry minister was an easier target for Krajina, and the Ecological Reserve Act was eventually passed in 1971. It appears that it took that kind of tenacity and paranoia. A botanist colleague of Cowan's, Adolf Ceska, also a Czech emigrant, recalled that when he applied for the Ecological Reserves botany position, he was suspected of being a communist spy by Krajina and didn't get the job.[1618] Cowan had helped lay the groundwork at the national and international levels, but may well have been wise to sidestep the Cold War politics swirling at the provincial level and settle for lowly committee chair in 1971 to review proposals and issues.

Cowan's sojourn in Scotland had also ushered him into the inner circles of royalty. The summer before they left Edinburgh, he and Joyce had been invited to Holyrood Palace for the annual garden party and an introduction to Prince Philip, who had long had a keen interest in conservation. Cowan's journal doesn't mention the party; he left that to Joyce, who tracked all his honours and distinctions in scrapbooks. The journal does go into detail about his trip to the Farne Island observatory later that week, for which he had raised money by giving a public lecture at Usher Hall.

Cowan and the Prince obviously had hit it off, as the Cowans were now on the list of key invitees to functions when the royal family came to Canada. In 1967, at the Canadian Audubon Society annual banquet and fundraiser in Toronto, Cowan had given the "expression of appreciation" to Prince Philip. Curiously, they had dined on Rock Cornish hen with wild rice, neither of which was native or wild. At the 1983 Vancouver visit of Queen Elizabeth and Prince Philip (now president of the WWF), the Cowans were among the dignitaries being honoured. The *Vancouver Sun* headlined "Save Your Wildlife."[1619] When Prince Philip took his pitch to the Canadian Club, he urged Canadians

> "to preserve their wildlife heritage from extinction before it is too late." ...The prince asked his audience if they were too greedy to share the world with their fellow creatures. Or is it that we believe the whole thing is simply too unimportant to bother about?[1620]

The Cowans joined the royals aboard HMY *Britannia* for a reception, which prompted Joyce to create a large orange scrapbook of the event and Cowan to pen this note to his friend Tom Beck: "The Queen and Prince Philip are visiting UVIC in March and as chancellor and wife we are front and centre. Can you think of a better stimulus to a change of plumage?"[1621] Cowan in his 80s was to spend one last time with Prince Philip on an early morning Royal Bird-a-thon in Vancouver, during which the entourage spotted over 100 species, including a Red-breasted Nuthatch.

Nuthatches rely heavily on the supply of cones and the conifer seeds they hold, and when there are shortages, nuthatches move to find them. This was a familiar pattern for fundraisers as well. Monte Hummel, who headed up the Canadian chapter of the World Wildlife Fund from 1978 until 2004, was the organization's chief fundraiser, and not surprisingly he declared the nuthatch his favourite bird. He became a close friend of Cowan's as they scoured the landscape for funding. Hummel had grown up in the bush north of Kenora, Ontario, where his father was working on a hydro project. He claims his spirit of advocacy arose when he returned to that region years later and saw the impacts on the health of the Ojibway community from mercury contamination in fish resulting from the dam.[1623] The two collaborated for years on programs: *Whales Beneath the Ice* drew attention to the plight of the narwhals, belugas and bowheads; a project of Canada's large carnivores inspired a WWF book dedicated to the Cowans. Mostly, Cowan was a trusted reviewer of proposals for protected areas and getting species at risk off the list. Hummel was still consulting him and asking for letters of support in the summer of 1997, long after Cowan's official role as scientific adviser was over. Wrote Hummel:

Red-breasted Nuthatch

Sitta canadensis

The Red-breasted Nuthatch is one of the most widely distributed birds in the southern two-thirds of the province, but is more sparsely distributed in the far north. It is resident along the coast.[1622]

> With any luck, and your support, this fall we can obtain one of the most outstanding protected areas announcements ever in North America. I'm referring to the proposal to protect 1 million hectares in the Northern Rockies of British Columbia linked to an additional 3.3 million hectares of lands specially managed for conservation purposes ... To accomplish this, part of our strategy is to recruit an impressive display of support from the scientific community.[1624]

Ian McTaggart Cowan still elicited attention at the age of 87, and it was this unassailable credibility that Hummel marshalled with extraordinary success to convince the wealthy and influential of the value of conservation. Hummel was the salesman, while Cowan, a trusted scientific adviser, provided the reputation, rivalling Switzerland for political neutrality. In the seemingly endless tributes that flowed into the Cowan household over the years, archived by Joyce, no political party was unrepresented. Personal cards from Liberal Pierre Trudeau jostle notes from Conservative Stockwell Day and testimonials from Elizabeth May (who would become the first Green Party MP just after Cowan died). Invitations to the White House by Lyndon B. Johnson are filed next to dinner engagements with His Imperial Majesty Emperor Haile Selassie of Ethiopia and notices of talks to deliver to the local naturalist clubs or alpine garden societies. It is somewhat clear which events Cowan preferred, but he would express this only to his family and closest friends.

At the turn of the 21st century, with the dimming of Cowan's star and the close-knit network of his international connections, it was little wonder that corporate resource interests were keen to turn their guns again on the scientific community. During Cowan's watch, over 15 per cent of the province was placed out of industrial reach, and he had a role in the protection of most of the areas. More than one scientist interviewed for this book mourned deeply the loss of Cowan and his network of public servants and non-profits in defending the wilderness and their work.

For Cowan's memorial, Hummel wrote: "One of the most unforgettable evenings of my life was listening to Ian and W.O. Mitchell together giving extemporaneous after-dinner talks. The very soul of Canada was in the room that night."[1625] Hummel had reason to link Cowan with Mitchell as souls of the country. Mitchell had written the quintessential book of a boyhood in Canada that connected deeply with both the place and its people. Cowan too had that profoundly human touch, as pointed out by Edward Lyn Lewis, a polar oceanographer who had worked with him during his term with the Arctic Institute:

> He lived, as I did, in a competitive world where one's work was subject to rigorous criticism, but within this essential framework of intellectual integrity Ian created warm personal relationships. A human being first and foremost, he tried to help the less eminent.[1626]

CHAPTER 32

"We have stood tongue-tied in the presence of the dollar."

Coast to Mountains, 1953–2010

The Cowans had returned from Edinburgh to New York on RMS *Queen Mary* and wound their way back to the west coast via the United States. Cowan kept no notes from that trip; possibly he relaxed for the first time. It was also his last holiday for a while. Upon arriving back in Vancouver, they found that opportunities and responsibilities for both of them had compounded. Joyce's mother, Eileen Racey, had fallen ill and Joyce was on care duty with her brothers for both parents. Cowan's youngest sister, Pamela, had broken her leg and needed to be closer to campus, where she was a student, so she moved in with the family. Cowan had been promoted to department head. From Joyce's perspective, this translated into a growing academic herd that gathered around the salt lick of their house on 28th Avenue. Ann remembers, "There were visiting profs, colleagues, friends, grad students – people constantly filling the house ... We entertained them. I would haul my dolls around and try and get people to be interested."[1627]

Joyce had to become a hostess, a role that didn't come easily to her. It turned out she was good at it. As the daughter of Kenneth and Eileen Racey, she had grown up with a revolving door of people and wildlife. She understood and shared Cowan's deep commitment to education and conservation and she played a major role in his ability to function so highly, a fact which didn't escape any of his grad students and colleagues. One of the latter made a special tribute to Joyce at a retirement function: "Joyce ... without you he is nothing! Someone must have kept him straight across the years by love, devotion, loyalty, imagination, understanding, by bullying, cajoling and I'd guess by praying ... In honouring Ian, we honour you."[1628] Cowan's colleague and close friend Tom Beck, who spent lots of time with the couple, latterly said:

> It was a lesson for everyone who knew them to see the relationship between them. It was really something to behold ... I doubt if Ian could have accomplished what he did without Joyce. She was a very quiet and shy person but she was there for him and vice versa."[1629]

Added Joyce's close friend Shirley Beck: "One thing always amused me: Joyce was always there to remind him of what he needed to take with him. She did look after him very well."[1630]

The mountain lion's share of the management of all household tasks fell on Joyce's shoulders, but even some of the academic tasks spilled over to her as well. Cowan was starting on his nutritional studies of deer close to home with A.J. Wood, which required bringing back newborn deer to bottle feed on demand every hour. Ann recalls a Cooper's Hawk which convalesced in a cage attached to the end of the garage. In the basement there was always the processing of the hunting and gathering efforts. "It was typical to have deer and ducks hanging up and this wasn't strange. A lot of people hunted then. This made a very strong impression on me as a child."[1631] The menagerie was also expanding in the rest of the house. Garry adopted a stream of animals, starting with orphaned screech-owls for which he built a pen in his bedroom upstairs.

Baby **Western Screech-Owl**

Otus kennicottii
[*Megascops kennicottii*]

The Western Screech-Owl breeds on southern and eastern Vancouver Island, the Gulf Islands and the adjacent mainland coast, including the Fraser Lowlands ... Fledging period ... ranges from 35 to 42 days.[1632]

Back in the menagerie of academia, Cowan's administrative and graduate supervision load had tripled. When he started at UBC in 1940, not one province in Canada had a core biological staff for wildlife management. By the mid-'50s, two-thirds of the provinces had wildlife biologists and most of them were Cowan's graduates. Demands for his time as a popular lecturer were also exploding. Soon after returning from Scotland, he reported first to his base – the men on the ground in the wildlife profession – on his findings from Europe. His lecture outlined the limitations of privatized models that relied exclusively on the farming of game animals and eliminated natural ecosystems. He pointed out that legislators had failed to protect wild birds flying between countries. As he observed about a troubled postwar Europe, "They cannot get together on anything else, so you would hardly expect them to get together on waterfowl."[1633]

In an address to the same group in 1955, he warned of the impacts of hydrocarbons, DDT amongst them. Like George Spencer's and Ron Buckell's warnings ten years earlier, Cowan told his audience that these chemicals are as "capable of profoundly altering the environment more rapidly, thoroughly and insidiously than ever before," and that the corporations or "rival chemical concerns [are] so strong that demand can be created before sufficient time has been allowed for proper appraisal."[1634] In a more personal plea to North American scientists, including the

'B,' he had this to say during the winter solstice of 1955, when he was made head of the Wildlife Society:

> To gain support for our cause we have emphasized the economic values it represents and have soft-pedalled the great intangible forces of recreating the human soul, because we have not known how to talk about them in words of mutual understanding. We have stood tongue-tied in the presence of the dollar.[1635]

Cowan saw the "presence of the dollar" gathering on all fronts, especially in the rapidly urbanizing Fraser Delta. He and Joyce began casting about for a recreation place close to home, something relatively undeveloped and suitable for all the Cowans' interests. That is when they first discovered Saturna Island. When Cowan's journal entries pick up again in the summer of 1954, they have taken their first family trip there.

Juvenile **Pacific Killer Whale, or "Blackfish" [Killer Whale, Orca]**

Grampus rectipinna [Orcinus orca]

Has a voracious appetite and has been seen chasing seals and sea lions onto the beach; known to eat many kinds of fish, also sea birds, porpoises, squid and other large marine forms. Is said to attack the larger whales and to eat out their tongues as well as tearing and damaging them generally.[1636]

It was on Saturna that Cowan first encountered the Orca – then known as the Pacific Killer Whale, or Blackfish – up close.

Another major splash was about to emerge on the international scene, this time involving the "killer whale." The Orca that Cowan was watching off Saturna's East Point were actually following the Chinook Salmon migration into the Fraser. In 1955, however, the animals were only known as whale "killers" and were shot routinely by fishermen. In 1945 a Vancouver newspaper article quoting Cowan had featured the headline "Killer whale roams city inlet, 30-foot monster entertains ferry passengers with 20-foot spout."[1637] Ten years had passed with little research to disabuse people of these perceptions – until one of Cowan's students, Murray Newman, appeared on the scene.

Newman had done his master's in ichthyology at Berkeley, training with Boyd Walker in the Gulf of Mexico. He came to UBC on an H.R. MacMillan Fellowship for fisheries research and took Cowan's vertebrate zoology course. Two years after getting his PhD, with the help of MacMillan and other colleagues and philanthropists, Newman had set up the fledgling Vancouver Aquarium, where, as he observed, "I became extremely successful by being incompetent. I surrounded myself with intelligent people. Ian McTaggart Cowan was one of them. He was a fabulous naturalist."[1638] Newman's primary objective was to showcase live specimens of the undersea world to a public that had never seen them before:

I always believed that live animals are more valuable than dead animals, especially for teaching young children and changing our attitudes. There have to be people who really love the animals. I thought the public should know about them, but we believed that killer whales were too dangerous to keep in an aquarium. Our background was how vicious and dangerous they were.[1639]

Newman's idea was to have a model of a "blackfish" sculpted from a captured animal, but first he had to find one:

I went to ask [Cowan] where would be a good place to capture a whale, and he said, "East Point. This island is the most beautiful in the world." He was interested in establishing a marine biological station at East Point, where the whales come very close to land.[1640]

The story of the capture of Moby Doll and the birth of the captive whale industry is well documented.[1641] The hired team of the sculptor and a fisherman harpooned the young Orca, it was guided back to the surface by its pod, and the men decided not to fire the second, lethal shot. They took the wounded animal to Vancouver and in Newman's words, the public's reception was history-making:

We got help from various institutions like Dr. Cowan, UBC. [I] called up H.R. MacMillan, [Leigh] Stevenson and Colonel [W.] Matthews, who got interested. They got the shipyard drydock flooded, ready for the whale. Suddenly the attitude to the animal was completely different: 20,000 people visited. Moby lived three months, dying of aspergillosis. It started a worldwide industry and became pivotal in world history for changing attitudes.[1642]

The change in attitudes towards Orcas was profound and rapid for a cultural belief that had endured a century. The famous illustration of this burgeoning love affair with the Orca is the dismantling of the machine gun mounted in 1961 by fisheries managers at Seymour Narrows (narrowest spot between Vancouver Island and the mainland) intended to kill Orcas as they passed through. It was never fired. Attitudes continued to change regarding whales and whale captivity, especially amongst the scientists who worked with them. At the same time, Cowan was encouraging graduate students to use individual identification to get accurate census and behavioural data, as his wolf study had done. One of his graduate students, Mike Bigg, who had completed his PhD at UBC on harbour seals, went on to pioneer the work on Orcas. Bigg was with Cowan and Foster in QCI (Haida Gwaii) in the summer of 1961, on the water all summer amongst the whales. Foster pioneered research into the social organization of giraffes, identifying individuals by their spots. Bigg tackled the different whale societies of fish-eating residents and mammal-eating transients (now known as Bigg's Whale), using their dorsal fins and saddle patches to identify and track individuals. What Bigg's census data showed was that these distinct populations were declining and under siege.

In 1975 Bigg released his report on the live-capture killer-whale fishery, describing the population through their matrilineal lineages. This important work triggered a moratorium on Orca live captures. His approach revolutionized whale research and was carried on after he died prematurely of leukemia in 1990. In 1992, Cowan, in his capacity as chair of the national advisory committee on marine mammals, prepared a follow-up report on the capture and maintenance of cetaceans in Canada. The committee documented all deaths and health records of the captive Orca, as well as the sizes and conditions of the aquaria. They did public opinion polls and consulted Arctic indigenous people, humane societies and the top scientists, including Newman himself, Paul Spong and John Ford, the next generation of whale scientists working at the Vancouver Aquarium.

Cowan's conclusions: that live captures of Orcas should continue to be banned; that the Beluga be banned from live capture; that performance-type presentations by whales did not justify keeping animals in captivity; that present aquaria were not adequate for the care of whales; and that none of them had adequate facilities for captive breeding of Orcas. He finished with the recommendation that there are other ways for people to experience whales, such as whale watching trips in the wild, video and electronic media.[1643] Although Cowan left an opening (if the aquaria could provide high enough standards of care, cetaceans could be maintained), it was the beginning of the end for whale captivity across Canada. Newman retired in 1993 and the last captive Orca at the Vancouver Aquarium was transferred to another aquarium in 2001. Cowan was ahead of the curve in the public appetite for learning about Orcas, and he was instrumental in putting an end to the keeping of captive whales. He was 82 when he wrote the report.

Newman through all of this had fostered a relationship with H.R. MacMillan that provided two other lasting opportunities for Cowan. MacMillan in 1955 was 70 years old. He had done a master's in forestry at Yale University and in 1912 became BC's first chief forester in the newly minted BC Forest Service. In 1919 MacMillan left the civil service and, using what information he'd reaped or gleaned about BC forests, set up the MacMillan Export Company. It grew into the forest and paper giant MacMillan Bloedel, which he headed until his retirement in 1956. Like many industrial magnates, he flew to Acapulco every winter to fish marlin. He had a boat called the *Marijean* kitted up with swordfishing tackle and luxury berths for his guests. Something of the academic remained in MacMillan, and when he wasn't catching marlin, he began to take an interest in his bycatch and the natural history of the area. Newman recounts:

> The word came down from heaven for someone to go with him to Mexico to identify his fish. The profs were busy and he wanted someone immediately so I [as a doctoral student] went down with him. For 13 years I would fly down to Acapulco to the *Marijean* and would be collecting specimens for the UBC museum and the National Museum in Ottawa.[1644]

Cowan had been called upon (also from heaven) to identify the bird specimens that had come from these expeditions. In 1959 Newman couldn't go, so Cowan took his place for three weeks, leaving on February 20 along with Peter Larkin, who ran the Institute of Fisheries at UBC. His journal records an extensive list of birds, plants, fish, shells and marine mammals that he collected and photographed – more of the latter, his new "gun" was his camera. It seems MacMillan was more easily converted to research than Cowan was to some aspects of luxury travel.

Young **Black-crowned Night Heron**

Nycticorax nycticorax

The Black-crowned Night-heron has been reported from the extreme southern tip of Vancouver Island and the Fraser Lowlands east to Chilliwack...[1647]

> Spent this morning photographing ashore for two hours. Hard to get off to a good start, as breakfast is not until 8:30... A fine colony of blue-footed boobies on the beach at our anchorage. I took a lot of film, both stills and a movie. HR counted 90 nests, all the way from fresh eggs to half-grown young.[1645]

Cowan fell in love with the Sea of Cortez, especially the Tres Marías Islands, which lie 60 miles off the west coast. He put together a research project to describe the birds of the islands and discovered a breeding species to new the place, the Yellow-crowned Night Heron.[1646] This secretive night hunting bird is a very close cousin to the Black-crowned Night Heron, a species Cowan had watched shifting northward into BC with changing climates.

When asked if Cowan or the other scientists such as Larkin and himself had influenced MacMillan's interest in conservation after a career of clear-cutting forests, Newman was doubtful:

> H.R. was not sentimental. On board his ship, he liked to have people that could contribute to the conversation in things he believed in, like fisheries. He was 40 years older and I was a very junior comedian at the dinner table. He was a very strong, tough old man and most of us were afraid of him. He liked having people around, like me, who could break up the tension and entertain him.[1648]

Cowan did one more trip with MacMillan, along with UBC president Norman Mackenzie, in 1962, this time bringing Joyce with him. Perhaps this trip triggered their imagination for the opportunities for ecotourism, an industry he felt could "hard pedal" both the economic and the soulful elements of the great whales in the wild. Upon retiring, he and Joyce were some of the early naturalists working for Sven Lindblad (and his father, Lars-Eric) with his company Special Expeditions, launched in 1979. Joyce was never paid but she travelled for free, providing invaluable support to the guests. The Cowans did trips aboard *Lindblad Explorer* all through the 1980s. Photographs from this decade record their travels from Galápagos to the Sea of Cortez. One of their favourite places was Laguna San Ignacio, off Baja, where they found the shallow water specialists, the Gray Whale. "Here in the lagoons of Baja California, a large part of the eastern Pacific population of this whale comes to calve and court in waters so shallow that their tails often stir mud from the bottom."[1649]

Gray Whale

Eschrichtius glaucus
[*Eschrichtius robustus*]

This is a strongly migratory species, passing up and down the west coast twice a year en route between its winter breeding grounds in the lagoons along the coast of lower California and Mexico and its summer feeding ground in the Gulf of Alaska.[1650]

The Cowans became strongly migratory themselves during these years. Cowan kept journals and wrote some of the natural history guides for Lindblad, helping to raise the industry to a whole new standard for educational holidays. In personal files were many thank-you cards to the couple from the guests: "You are a handsome twosome who know so much and say it so nicely."[1651] At Joyce's memorial service a story was recounted about her stamina and skill for ecotourism. "[Joyce] would be motivating, encouraging and supporting an elderly lady up a steep canyon on a remote island over a mile and a half trek over steep terrain, the irony being that Joyce was much older than the elderly person!"[1652]

After 17 years of tours with Special Expeditions, which included Alaska as well, Cowan made some thoughtful observations to his son-in-law, Mikkel, about some of the limitations of the educational role ecotourism really played for the well-heeled. Again, he was always one to evaluate the relative usefulness of where he put his efforts for conservation:

> My experience is that tourists are on the trip primarily for a holiday ... They do listen with interest and ask questions about matters they encounter day to day, and a number of them carry away a slightly increased understanding of the world around them. Many if not most of them have made their money in the business world and have a preformed and fossilized view of how the natural resources world "ought" to work so that it can be exploited for gain.[1653]

Besides introducing the Cowans to the Sea of Cortez, MacMillan was also to become a major benefactor of libraries, fisheries research and zoology at UBC while Cowan was on the Senate. Cowan told the seemingly apocryphal story that he went to breakfast with MacMillan one day and asked him for a million dollars for the new library, whereupon MacMillan just wrote him a cheque. "That was the best breakfast I ever had," Cowan would often remark. Interestingly, MacMillan was rumoured to have donated far less money to the forestry department than to education generally. As Newman posited, "That was Cowan's business. H.R. was interested in the university."[1654] Towards the end of his university career, Cowan was invited to the exclusive Round Table Club in Vancouver. He left no notes about the club, just photographs of the exclusively white-male movers and shakers from UBC faculty and philanthropists. One of his original colleagues, librarian Kaye Lamb, was a member, along with Newman, Larkin and forester Peter Pearse. MacMillan appears to be amongst them in 1971, one year after he and Cowan both received their Order of Canada.

Back on Saturna in the late '50s, Cowan got his much-needed dose of pottering around in boats with Ann, Garry and Garry's friend Bill Merilees. Merilees understood that the role of Cowan's interest in molluscs did more than challenge Cowan's desire to collect:

> When he got into academia, and he had responsibilities for education and administration and then later as dean of grad studies, he didn't have time to go out in the field and spend those large blocks of time that were required to do wildlife research. So his grad students fulfilled that for him. But that's why he got interested in molluscs. He could go out on a weekend in his little boat *Tuchi*, with his dredge. He could do that in bits and pieces, and he still contributed, and at a world level. He published a lot of stuff.[1655]

Merilees was another typical Cowan student: a boy naturalist interested in seashells, especially the marine snails. He had first encountered Cowan when the biologist came to Magee High School to give a talk at a job fair. "Looking back at this job fair he came to, I bet 10 per cent of those students went on to become biologists in some fashion."[1657] Merilees was one of the inspired:

> I knew he was interested in molluscs as well; so I remember trekking out to UBC in 1957 to meet with him and ask him the identification of a clam I'd found that was causing me some trouble – it was a juvenile horse clam [a ubiquitous clam] – and he met me at his office, and you know how gracious he was, he really was a prince among men.[1658]

Merilees and both Cowan children went through high school and UBC together, sharing expeditions as members of the Varsity Outdoors Club. Merilees met the naturalists flocking around the Cowans' various habitats. His first jobs took him to remote bird colonies in BC and to the Antarctic islands before returning to Vancouver Island, where he is a highly respected naturalist, educator, biologist and author. Garry went to South America to work on tuna populations, and that is where he met his first wife, Ana. In 1968 he got a position as a fisheries biologist at Memorial University in Newfoundland. Garry's family settled there and they had two children, Mariana and Robert. Garry was a popular lecturer and for 16 years he also held a joint appointment at the Marine Sciences Research Laboratory in Logy Bay (now part of the Ocean Sciences Centre), where he specialized in sculpins and brook charr. The marriage broke up and the Cowan grandparents played a large role as the families re-established themselves, Garry having married Judy Cantwell in 1977.

White-lined Chiton

Tonicella insignis

The chiton *Tonicella insignis* was described by Reeve in 1847 ... Field collecting in the intertidal parts of the Strait of Georgia has led me to conclude that this was a rare species. Three specimens were all that had been taken in five years.[1656]

Ann met her future husband, Mikkel Schau, through the same Varsity Outdoors Club when they were both undergraduates in UBC's science faculty. Later, Garry and Mikkel received their PhDs in the same year. On stage at that UBC convocation was Cowan, their delighted father and father-in-law, now dean of the faculty of science. Shortly after, the Schaus moved to Ottawa, where the Cowans' third grandchild, Torben, was born in 1974.

Both the Cowans and their correspondence were bouncing back and forth across the country to stay connected with Ann and Garry and their growing families. When the two grandsons were graduating at opposite ends of the country, Cowan was with them on stage. When grandson Robert graduated from Memorial in May of 1990, there were – unbeknownst to him – three McTaggart Cowans there:

> My dad was on stage in full regalia and granddad was as well (black chancellor's cap and red gown). I had no idea until the girl next to me said: "Isn't that your dad up there? And wait, isn't that your granddad as well?" She had met them the night before at a shingle ceremony! I had not a clue about this ... It's also when Granddad gave me the family ring I wear every day.[1659]

Eight years later, on the other side of the country at University of Victoria, in his capacity again as former chancellor, Cowan was to see grandson Torben Schau and his granddaughter-in-law-to-be Robin Grazley receive their degrees. As Torben explained:

> Ian was on stage in regalia, but because of the route we took to the front of the stage I don't even remember being able to make eye contact. Afterwards, we took some pictures and generally had a good time, but it was low-key, in the manner of such things – after all, the BA was supposed to be just the first stop on a long academic voyage.[1660]

Both universities had special significance to Cowan, as he had turned them both down when offered their presidencies. He had had three offers of presidencies during his career – the University of Calgary was the other. The Memorial University episode started with a personal summons from Premier Joey Smallwood one Christmas. Upon arriving in the airport lobby in St. John's and meeting the departing dean of arts and sciences (who wondered why he was out there), Cowan was suspicious of the offer. Smallwood's men escorted him to one of their boss's abodes, where he was invited to imbibe with two other members of the cabinet and some junior university men. Cowan didn't drink. It started to snow. Cowan picks up the story:

> Smallwood said: "I don't want to go back to town, we better stay here." I didn't bring any gear with me. He was just a little guy and I was six foot three. His pyjamas looked like shorts on me. Anyway we slept there. In the morning he fried the eggs and bacon, we had breakfast together. His wife never showed; she had played the piano all night. On the way in [to St. John's] it was beautiful: we were driving, the snow had stopped and the sun was out … and we were admiring the scenery. I said, "By the way, where does the president live?" He said, "I don't know, don't worry about that. We'll get you that house on the hill." I was just joking but I said, "How do you know he wants to sell?" and he said, "Oh he'll sell."… I said, "When am I going to get to meet the Board of Governors?" He turned to his office boy and said, "See how many of them you can get on the phone." I was leaving that afternoon. I hadn't met anybody and I had been appointed. I said, "Well it's been so nice to see you. I've got to think about this for a little while. I want to talk to my wife about it; it is a very different place to live." I phoned him as soon as I got back and said "Sorry, b'y, no way!"[1661]

The presidency offer in Calgary was slightly less colourful but posed no less of an ethical problem for Cowan:

> I was selected by the Faculty Association … and [they] said, "There's just one more thing before it's a done deal. You go up and meet the

chairman of the board; he lives in Edmonton. So we'll fly you up there and [make] an appointment for him to see you." We went down to see the chairman of the board, and we waited and waited. He was a lawyer or something. Finally the word came down that he was sorry, he couldn't see us today. So I said, "Thanks very much, you're looking for a president, I'm not looking for a job." And I got on the plane and went home.[1662]

The newly minted University of Victoria made him an offer in 1964, but the day before it was to be announced, his brother was appointed president of Simon Fraser University. "They didn't want two brothers. The chairman of the board ... called me in, with considerable embarrassment ... The man they chose was [Malcolm G.] Taylor from Calgary."[1663] Cowan was asked if he would stay on as their vice-president and declined. "Thank god I didn't take [the presidencies]. It would have been the wrong move. At that level you can't do anything about conservation in that position. You're saddled with a juggernaut of an organization that you've got to lead. You've got to fight entirely for money."[1664]

These offers came after a period in which Cowan lost three of the people he pointed to as his greatest influences: Jim Munro died on September 29, 1958, at the home of Hoyes Lloyd in Ottawa; Kenneth Racey died at home on May 10, 1960, at the age of 78; and Cowan's mother-in-law, Eileen, died of a very aggressive cancer in 1963. The losses of his mentors hit him. At the unveiling of Munro's memorial at Summit Creek, near Creston, BC, Cowan pointed out that "the defiling of lakes and streams by pollution was a real hurt to Mr. Munro. He spoke up, almost alone, of these problems, and after many years finally found sensitive ears..."[1665] Munro's last paper was on the birds and mammals of the Creston region, where he had been pivotal in protecting the Creston Valley wetlands, one of the most important areas for migratory birds in the Pacific Flyway, such as the aptly named goldeneye ducks with their piercing gaze.[1666]

Cowan deeply missed his father-in-law, as did the many Vancouverites with whom Racey had shared his interests: "The world lost one of its greatest bird-watchers Monday morning when Kenneth Racey of this city laid aside his binoculars for the last time."[1668] Racey had been declining with a heart condition ever since Eileen died. He had stayed on at the family house on Lime Street, and his son and family had moved in to care for him. His granddaughter, Kathy (Cowan's niece by marriage), remembers her grandfather encouraging her and her siblings in natural history by getting them to collect feathers for a feather book:

Common Goldeneye

Bucephala clangula

There appears to have been an expansion of the breeding range of the Common Goldeneye in British Columbia ... the Common Goldeneye is now the most abundant of the two [goldeneye] in the Creston Valley ... This is a significant change from the 1956 breeding season in Creston Valley, when J.A. Munro observed only 1 Common Goldeneye.[1667]

My recollections of Kenneth were that he wasn't well during my short life. He went downhill after she [Eileen] died, very quickly. He was still doing some of his specimens until the day he died and was only allowed to go to "the bird room" once a day.[1669]

Racey's last entries in his field journals are from the spring of 1959 at the farm in Huntingdon. In the species accounts under Pileated Woodpecker, he notes: "A male Pileated Woodpecker heard and seen several times in woods on hill, was fairly close to us and flew from tree to tree and finally flew off across Mackenzie Road."[1670]

Another rare resident, Cowan's mother, Laura, was less lucky in the manner of her death. "My mother went from healthy and active to paraplegic in six months when a sore back (as the result of a fall) was diagnosed as the consequence of a growing spinal tumour."[1672] Laura had been a force in both her children's and her grandchildren's lives, and with her last months fraught with pain, it was difficult for Cowan to stand by and watch.

He had a high degree of expertise in medical pathologies and in physiology and anatomy, having taught in and been closely aligned with medical departments all his life. At about the time of Laura's passing he had been looking into the role of blood serum proteins in evolution, for example.[1673] He was also interested in pain management and had just published a paper on the most humane method of immobilizing animals in captivity.[1674] Cowan's frustration with the topic was still evident in 1997 when he wrote to Ann about Joyce's lengthy suffering: "I would expect any treating specialist to be knowledgeable in alleviating pain attached to the condition!"[1675]

For 1963 there are neither letters nor journal entries. The closest field journal entry is from the following autumn, when Cowan comes across a dead Harbour Porpoise: "*Phocoena phocoena*, single female on beach at Long Beach, V.I. [Vancouver Island] Length, 8 lengths of my knife."[1676]

Harbour Porpoises are shy animals and highly sensitive to noise and industrial impacts to the ocean. They are one of the "canaries" of the sea, susceptible to dying of shock if a loud engine even drives toward them, and dead animals are often found washed up on shores, victims of just such sonic killings. They also fall victim as bycatch in fishing nets set too close inshore or abandoned. In the late 1980s, as

....

Pileated Woodpecker

Dryocopus pileatus

Uncommon to rare resident in southern British Columbia, including Vancouver Island, becoming very rare throughout the remainder of the province except the northwest portion. Breeds.[1671]

....

Harbour Porpoise

Phocoena vomerina
[*Phocoena phocoena*]

The smallest of the toothed whales, it reaches a maximum length of about 6 feet. Upper surface dark grey to almost black, belly paler, no white areas on sides ... Frequents bays, harbours, inshore waters and up to 20 miles offshore.[1677]

....

chairman of the federal committee on whales and whaling, Cowan was urging the minister to curtail gill-netting on the east coast to protect the Harbour Porpoise. Nothing was done and several years later his letters, obtained by Greenpeace under access to information legislation, made headlines saying "Pity the Porpoises," which by then were already in decline.[1678]

The burgeoning family responsibilities after losing two of their parents back to back may have been another factor in the Cowans' deliberations over the offers of university presidencies. In 1964 he accepted the position of dean of graduate studies, a post that saw him through his final years at UBC, kept him in touch with students and gave him some clout at the funding tables. It also gave him some time for conservation and also for his family. As Tom Beck noted:

> He knew so many people … but there was never any doubt in your mind when you came to know them that his family was number one. Their grandchildren and eventually great-grandchildren were considered first and foremost. He stayed in touch … and he was concerned for them and watching for ways that he could help. They were always front and centre in his mind despite all his other roles. Sometimes people get busy and lose sight of their priorities, but you could never say that about Ian and Joyce.[1679]

Alison App, his niece, said of Cowan, "He made you feel as if you were the only person that mattered in the world."[1680]

The biggest challenge in Cowan's life was to come with the premature death of his son, Garry. In the winter of 1996–97, Garry was tragically struck down by cancer, dying in mid-January of 1997. Cowan confided to Bristol Foster that the hardest things he'd experienced was to see a child die. According to Garry's son, Robert, Garry had lived intensely but maintained his lasting love of teaching to the end. One of his students wrote this as her dedication for her master's:

> I'd like to dedicate this thesis to a man who greatly influenced my decision to pursue a postgraduate degree, Dr. Garry Ian McTaggart Cowan. Dr. Cowan was taken from the world by cancer on January 15, 1997, but not before he had the opportunity to show a generation of university students what it is to truly love what you do. He was a well-respected professor in biology who taught me that learning is a thing of beauty and that talent should not be wasted. He believed that every student was his equal and taught us accordingly. He lived every day to the fullest and is greatly missed. Well, Garry, I did it. Thanks for everything.[1681]

Another loss for the couple that year was to come with the death of Jim Genge. The Genges and Dennys were the Cowans' longest-standing friends, with whom they had shared holidays when they could ever since the 1930s. For Genge's memorial, Cowan wrote about the importance to them of "the tranquil bays and quiet anchorages of our central coast" and about Genge, a skilled navigator, as "a fixed point from which to navigate the shoals and deeps of life."[1682] Their daughter Alice spoke of the deep connection with all the family:

> Ian was always very thoughtful. When I took his Zoology 105 course I would sit in the aisle because there was never any room. Once I had flu and didn't turn up for two classes and he phoned my mum to make sure I was OK. He had noticed in that huge lecture hall that I wasn't there."[1683]

The Dennys too were suffering from failing health. In a letter to Ann in 1997, Cowan spoke of his concerns about their frailty. This was the second generation of close friends the Cowans had outlived. They turned to Tom and Shirley Beck, who were later additions to the intimate circle, being 20 years younger, but they provided a refuge both in their friendship and in the form of their small log cabin tucked into the Wildcat Hills of Alberta. The two couples would spend a week together each year hunting and hiking in the area. The cabin, built by the Becks themselves, had a woodstove and kerosene lanterns and water was fetched from a well, much like Alta Lake would have been for Ian and Joyce in the 1920s and '30s. Cowan described it to his family in a letter in 1999:

> A soul-restoring place, complete with birds we see only there, the song of the coyote each evening, flights of swans heading south against an evening sky and an abundance of large wildlife – even laid eyes on cougar tracks one morning, hard by the cabin in a skiff of fresh snow. But especially the time shared with close friends and a year's adventures to catch up on.[1684]

The first time they visited the cabin was in 1981. Since Cowan was considerably older and the more senior statesman, Beck had been shy to invite his colleague at first. He also hadn't had an opportunity to get to know Joyce very well. Beck described his somewhat hesitant first offer to the Cowans to join them:

> It was after a meeting and I wondered if he wanted to come hunting … The deal was clinched right on the spot: "What a great idea," [he said]. I said, "Your wife would be welcome, but the only thing is, it is a pretty rustic place with limited facilities," and he thought that would be just fine.[1685]

The cabin had two rooms and simple bunk beds. Tom Beck had to hammer an extra six inches onto the bed so that Cowan would fit. Once installed, Cowan was always "up at the crack of dawn listening for birds." The two women, both naturalists, hiked while the two men would head off at dawn and dusk to hunt (when the animals were bedding down or getting up). The best hunting was on the ridges of the hills at least a mile out from the cabin, where the deer had the broadest visibility. If a deer was shot, Tom's job was to walk back to the cabin and fetch the horse.

If there was snowcover they'd skid the deer home behind the horse. If there wasn't snow they would quarter it in the field and pack it out in the very same packhorse boxes that Cowan had used in the Rockies. Meat was taken off the shoulders, the back quarter, the back strips off each side of the spine and tenderloin, "which you can just reach in and take out; everything else is left there."[1686] Eagles, ravens and coyote would clean away all traces of the entrails by the next morning. Cowan and Beck would prepare the meat, hang it, then set some outside in a box to freeze for the Cowans to take back to the coast for their winter protein supply.

Although Cowan had always been fastidious in his approach to the law, wild game was probably the only thing that apparently would lead him to transgress. Poaching grouse as a child had been one such incident. And now, as an elderly adult completing a hunting holiday in the Wildcat Hills, he had failed to get a wild-meat export permit to take the venison back to BC. And of course, having been a forensic expert witness for detecting wildlife taken over borders illegally, he was not only well acquainted with the law, he knew how easy it was to smuggle. Beck recounts the story:

> They were flying to Victoria, so we drove them to the airport. Ian is dressed like a chancellor of a university. We got to the ticket counter at the airport and the lady wanted to know what was in the boxes and he said: Books. He looked at me and wasn't giving a clue. Off the boxes went down the conveyor belt and no one was the wiser. It was probably the only lie he ever told in his life.[1687]

The annual gathering at the cabin became as regular as the annual Christmas letter. For the Cowans, the friendship spanned the death of their son, the gradual deterioration of Joyce's health from dementia, Cowan's own troubles with his prostate, eye problems and stroke, and the profoundly challenging task of editing *Birds of BC*. As Beck noted, the letters took on the quality of a journal as Cowan tried to set down some of his thoughts about the events of the day. He writes Beck about an uncharacteristic event for him – sleeping in. It was 1998 and he and Joyce were in Tofino celebrating their 62nd anniversary:

> Though rain was promised, the sun has shone and the endless parade of breakers tolls in from the horizon as they have since time began. Today we walked the sands of Chesterman Beach, which I walked almost daily in May of 1931 when Joyce's father and I went collecting birds and mammals here. At the time, there were no other tracks on the beach; no one lived within several miles. We needed a complete break from our usual routines and no opportunity to do anything we "ought to get done." We left the patio door ajar so we could hear the waves – and did not awake until 8:30 next morning![1688]

The two men corresponded for 20 years on conservation and policy issues. In 1983 Cowan wrote, "Your new minister should be reminded that his compatriots are doing a lousy job of minding our environment and that there are thousands of voters who regard the sensitive use of environment as important."[1689] Twelve years later not much had changed, it appears: "I am concerned that many of the recent advances in conservation may be threatened as the public purse gets tighter."[1690]

Cowan loved to explore more esoteric topics as well:

> The extent of ingenious inventiveness that led to complex and elegant hunting equipment and survival equipment has always excited my imagination. The keen observation that enabled gatherers to know edible from poisonous mushrooms bespeaks remarkable attention to detail...[1691]

Lesser Snow Goose (blue phase) (Blue Goose)

Chen caerulescens

... the Lesser Snow Goose (*C. c. caerulescens*) has both white and blue colour phases ... There are 3 records of blue-phase geese in British Columbia ...[1694]

The friends also enjoyed experiences reserved only for those used to their shared Scottish heritage. Beck described one expedition when the two men were sitting at a lookout point after a morning's hard walk in the hills. It was 20 degrees below.

> The two of us sitting there with a decent fire and our lunch and talking about how cold Scotland could be in the wintertime in a north wind which would have cut you in half. We were enjoying the outdoors like a couple of enthusiastic Edinburgh schoolboys and it was a miserable day.[1692]

One indicator of Cowan's regard for Beck came in the form of gifting him with Kenneth Racey's small-gauge shotgun. "Give it to your grandson," Cowan had told him. Recounted Beck, "That gun was probably responsible for more museum specimens in Canada than any other. I don't say that lightly, because another old friend of ours was Dewey Soper and until the very end he was still collecting too, in Alberta and in the Arctic."[1693] Soper was an early biologist hired in 1934 by Hoyes Lloyd as chief migratory bird officer for the Prairies, a few years after Munro had been made the Western officer. Soper described the fabled breeding grounds of the Blue Goose (now recognized as a blue phase of the Snow Goose) after a trip of nearly 4000 kilometres by dogsled and foot on Baffin Island with Inuit guides.

Beck recounts one of Cowan's most excited last "firsts" – captured with his camera:

> It was getting late in the day ... Ian had a beautiful long-lens camera

and there was a Great Gray Owl sitting on a post up at the north end … The light was not very good at all. He got a picture of it and he was so thrilled. He has been at this all his life but still had that boyish enthusiasm in his 90s and he said it was his first live encounter with this, the Great Gray. It stuck in my mind that this was his first. A couple of weeks later, a package arrived in the post and it was labelled Great Gray on the post.[1695]

Great Gray Owl

Strix nebulosa

The distribution of the Great Gray Owl in the province is not well known. Despite its large size this elusive owl is appropriately referred to as the "phantom of the northern forests."[1696]

There was another "first" that delighted him. In 1998 their first great-grandson, Garry McTaggart Cowan, was born to Robert and Penney (Condon). The young parents had met in a comparative anatomy class at Memorial taught by Robert's father, Garry. Cowan had remarked that his grandson Robert must have been doing his comparative anatomy "by Braille."[1697] The progeny of the studious pair had fair hair and green eyes reminiscent of his grandfather, providing a special bond for the boy's great-grandmother Joyce. The two of them were thick from the start and had been out picking raspberries together when Joyce's condition started to catch up with her. She fell in the berry thicket and was unable to help herself, but Garry, a toddler, returned to his parents to alert them of her fall. Joyce's health continued to deteriorate and in 1999 Ann returned from Ottawa with Mikkel to be closer to her parents. In 2000 Cowan wrote to another elderly colleague: "It is hard to accept the limitations that age plus bad luck impose on us. My wife is having more than her share of them but so far I have been fortunate. We have been a team for more than 65 years, so the troubles of one are to some extent shared."[1698]

During these last millennial years, he was also co-writing and co-managing the fourth and final volume of *Birds of BC,* the project that had started in 1972 while Cowan was still at UBC. Wayne Campbell, hired as curator of the Cowan Vertebrate Museum at the university and later ornithologist for the Provincial Museum, had been the initial driving force behind the project, managing it until halfway through volume 3, when Cowan took over. Cowan had found a willing student and collaborator in Campbell, whose "enthusiasm for birds had difficulty in taking second place after essential studies and a job. We agreed it was time for a new look at the birds of BC."[1699] For two decades Campbell oversaw the databases and occurrence records in his capacity as provincial ornithologist, coordinating "several thousand amateur bird enthusiasts from all parts of the province..."[1700] The story of the writing of the book has received an enthusiastic treatment in itself.[1701]

Neil Dawe, who subsequently joined the project with the other five authors (John M. Cooper, Gary W. Kaiser, Andy C. Stewart, Michael C.E. McNall and G.E. John Smith, eight in all) spoke at Cowan's memorial about the contribution he had made over the course of the whole 30-year project:

> Most of us began working with Ian after *The Birds of British Columbia* project got underway, in the late 1970s. Ian had retired from UBC by then, but he had not retired. Through the completion of the four volumes, Ian mentored us by example. He was a doer; he saw a job to do and just went ahead and did it, drawing us along elegantly in his wake. Throughout the project Ian took on the tasks of analyzing data, writing species accounts, proofing galleys and, in the later years, managing the project. One might think he would have slowed a bit by the time we reached volume 4, but no. Still managing the project, he also wrote more species accounts than any other author, as well as the 46-page synopsis, the latter in his ninetieth year.
>
> We would meet at Ian and Joyce's home at least quarterly to discuss progress (or lack thereof) for whichever volume was at hand. We always looked forward to those meetings; it was such a warm and welcoming household. About halfway through our meetings, Joyce would magically appear with tea and cookies or other such goodies. It was then we'd get to hear some of Ian's wonderful stories of him and Jimmy Simpson in the Rockies or of some other time gone by. For a flock of field biologists, meetings were anathema, but meetings with Ian were relished by each of us.
>
> The summarization of the data for volumes 1 and 2 was a formidable task, each of us dealing with the information on thousands of cards that we tabulated manually. The accounts were written longhand and then given to staff at the Canadian Wildlife Service with their word-processing skills. But by the time we were to begin volume 3, the personal computer had appeared and we chose to make use of this new technology to prepare the last two volumes. This meant that most of us, including Ian, had to learn the basics of operating computers along with their word processing and database programs.
>
> John Cooper remembers the time very well: "Ian and I learned how to use a computer at about the same time. But he was 82 and I was 35! Ian would call me with questions whenever he was stumped. That lasted for about a year until it became obvious that he had passed me in computer skills and needed to call others with far more expertise." Over the last few years we'd meet with Ian each spring, bring along pizza or Chinese food for lunch and share an afternoon

with him. Our last Cowan get-together was six days before Ian left on his last great adventure. We always learned something from him and that day was no exception. Ian had someone attach a dried cattail flower head to the railing of the deck and as we had lunch we watched as an Anna's Hummingbird made repeated trips to gather cattail down for her nest. It was brilliant and beautiful to watch and we all left vowing there would soon be cattails on our decks for our hummingbirds.

Finally, it wasn't too often that Ian would miss anything but in the fourth and final volume of the "Albatross," as we affectionately called it, we had managed to include – unbeknownst to Ian – one final section: "The Last Word." It was our special thank you to him for guiding us safely through the minefield of publishing a significant ornithological work. Early in 2001 UBC Press sent us the first seven copies of volume 4 and we all gathered at Ian's home to see together, and for the first time, the results of our efforts. Because Ian assumed he had seen all the galleys, I cautioned him: "Uh, Ian, I should tell you that there's something we've included in the book that you are unaware of." His considered response: "Uh-oh!" Then we sent him to the last two pages of the final volume.

Ian was visibly moved by what he found there. What surprised us, however, was his comment that he had never before read the excerpt from a letter we had included. The letter, addressed to Hamilton Mack Laing, was from Rudolph Anderson at the National Museum. Ian was 19. The letter read, in part: "… I had only a short conversation with him last fall and was much taken by him … I think that Cowan is the real thing …"

As Ian's colleagues for over 30 years we can say in no uncertain terms: Ian McTaggart Cowan was indeed the real thing. It was comforting to know there was a person like Ian in the world: truly a most decent, remarkable and beautiful human being. We will sorely miss him.[1702]

The stresses of looking after Joyce while managing the completion of the final volume of *Birds of BC* hit Cowan hard. In mid-June of 2002, he suffered a stroke. He was in hospital for three weeks but returned home with only a minor impact to his mobility, his mental acuity hardly hampered after a period of rehabilitation. Though Ann was his main caregiver, he continued to take a role in nursing Joyce for the rest of the year until she died November 29, 2002, at the age of 90. The memorial service gathered family and friends to pay respect to the woman who had nurtured both them and their teacher. Students and colleagues also continued to check in and pay visits to Cowan. Ian Stirling had written to Cowan on the publication of his own book on the polar bear: "I'd like to put more of my time in the future into writing about wildlife and the environment."[1704] These kinds of interactions were the most effective medicine for Cowan.

In a letter to Beck in 2003, a year after Joyce's death, he was still writing about his concerns for wildlife with all the devastating wildfires and the impacts of contagious wasting disease (or chronic wasting disease) that had hit the wild ungulates:

Anna's Hummingbird

Calypte anna

Since the publication of J.A. Munro and Cowan (1947), who make no mention of the species, the Anna's Hummingbird has established itself as a resident in south-central and southwestern British Columbia, expanding its range north from California.[1703]

> Collectively it will speed up the decline in the number of hunters, and in that way greatly reduce the money ... dedicated to wildlife conservation. In the long run, that indirect impact on wildlife will probably prove much more serious to management than will the direct impact of the disease ... I very much hope I can see you again this autumn, but whether or not my vision will be up to hunting I don't know. It is certainly declining and I find it disquieting.[1705]

In a letter to Dawe a year later, after his last short visit to the mountains to see the Becks in the Wildcat Hills and his great-grandchildren in Calgary, he wrote: "... lots of deer of both species but they are not going to be preyed upon by me any further ... I continue to have problems with deteriorating vision – somewhat scary but the MDs say there is nothing can be done!"[1706]

For the next six years, Cowan concentrated on his extended family and friends and on his "hobbies." His participation in the latter, not surprisingly, reached professional calibre. His entries into the annual shows of the Rhododendron Society and the Rock and Alpine Club of Victoria were still winning awards up until about 2006. Friends made during these years in the botanical circle knew him as a master gardener with a boyish appetite for winning. He also dove competitively into his last great collection: law and revenue stamps of BC and the Yukon. Revenue stamps were stamps issued by government bodies collecting fees for hunting licences, registrations or fees on documents. He had used his contacts around BC to acquire the stamps, whether it was from small law courts shutting down in rural areas or friends sending in their old licence stamps. Many of the law stamps had been acquired earlier, in the company of Joyce, as they travelled around BC. His stamp collections won gold medals at the local and national level. These winning collections of over 100 pages each were published by the British North American Philatelic Society and comprised his last two scholarly articles. The stamp collections he left paid in part for the transcribing of the field journals for the University of Victoria.

When his eyes failed him so that he could no longer even work on the stamps, he took up the harmonica again, dusting off his old Hohner Echo. He told Ann he was going to get his lip back into shape, and he did. They shared a love of folk and country music, and sometimes played together (harmonica and concertina), remembering family campfires of long ago. He continued to play with precision and verve until just a few days before he died.

This was also a rich period for Cowan assisting with the establishment of various scholarships and endowed chairs in conservation biology. One of his greatest joys was the creation of the University of Victoria Professorship in Biodiversity and Ecological Restoration at the School of Environmental Studies in 2005. The chair was in addition to two scholarships already established at the school: one to assist undergraduates, the other (named after both himself and Joyce) to assist graduates who were specializing in endangered species recovery and ecological restoration.

On March 15, 2005, Cowan announced to a group of faculty, students, conservation group representatives, politicians, colleagues, media, family and friends round the fireplace of the Faculty Club that the funds for the professorship had been raised in total. He began his talk characteristically with an anecdote of being an "excited" freshman at UBC in 1927 describing his long association with universities, all 78 years of it:

> The experiences of these years has convinced me, as it has so many others, that the university as we know it is among the most important social inventions of our time. It has become the custodian of our knowledge of the world around us; it guides and constantly examines our attitudes and actions as we interact with our fellows and our environment. It constantly hones them to a greater relevance.[1707]

One of the student speakers offering a tribute and awarding him a gift of appreciation was a young graduate student of the school, Severn Cullis-Suzuki, whose father, David, had been hired by Cowan 50 years earlier.

In 2009 Brian Starzomski was awarded the first Ian McTaggart Cowan professorship. Starzomski met with Cowan in his home and they discussed their shared research interests, from the biodiversity of the alpine to the Great Bear Rainforest on the central coast of BC, replicating some of the baseline work on mammals and birds done by Cowan back in the 1930s, when the world was readying for war. Like Cowan, Starzomski's interests range across taxa and geography, linking theory, empirical work and community engagement. His students have been filling in some of the scientific data on coastal biodiversity in the face of pressures from oil tanker expansion, just as Cowan's students had worked on data to assess the impacts of pipelines in the North 60 years before. Starzomski has expanded the emphasis on community education with new methodologies and new bonds with indigenous elders and researchers. Cowan was delighted with the appointment.

In March 2010, at the invitation of Ann Schau, an old friend and former student, Margaret Fisher, took Cowan to visit the reconstruction of a Blue Whale being prepared for the Beaty Biodiversity Museum at UBC by conservator Mike DeRoos (a younger relative of Cowan's nephew by marriage Tom DeRoos) at a big warehouse in the Inner Harbour of Victoria. It was 73 years after he and Joyce had flensed the Minke Whale in the same spot using boiling gasoline! The reconstruction was near completion and shortly to be shipped over to Vancouver for installation and the grand opening of the museum. The Blue Whale was the final skeleton needed to complete the Cowan Tetrapod Collection. Cowan spent most of the afternoon there, talking with the crew and meeting Joanne Thomson, the artist hired on the project and a friend of Ann's, who photographed him under the giant skeleton. His niece Kathy Racey and Ann both commented on how excited he was to see the Blue Whale. Cowan remarked, "Even after all this time, it was endlessly fascinating."[1708]

He had always wanted a Blue Whale specimen for a museum collection. British Columbia boasts the smallest mammal in the world and the largest, and having the two skeletons side by side is an incomparable lesson in evolution, not to mention the biodiversity that BC offers. He had collected the smallest Pygmy Shrew in Ootsa for the collection, but there had never been an op-

Ian McTaggart Cowan in front of blue whale skeleton

Blue or Sulphur-bottom Whale [Blue Whale]

Sibbaldus musculus [Balaenoptera musculus]

The largest of the whales, reaches a length of more than 100 feet ... A weight of 120 tons is recorded for an 89-foot individual. An active, powerful whale, spout tall and columnar.[1710]

portunity for a Blue Whale. A 1945 newspaper article, describing him as "Dr. (Bring 'em back) Cowan," had quoted him as saying, "The smallest creature, about an inch and a half long, is a pigmy [sic] shrew, like a midget packrat. The largest, which space does not permit to display at UBC, is a sulphur-bottomed whale that runs around 110 feet long and weighs a ton per foot."[1709]

Viewing the Blue Whale reconstruction would be his last major outing. Ian McTaggart Cowan died of pneumonia three weeks later, on April 18, surrounded by his family, two months short of his 100th birthday. He would miss two grand celebrations: the opening of the Beaty Biodiversity Museum, and his 100th birthday party at the Lieutenant Governor's house. If Cowan were to have had a regret, it might be that he was denied these last two opportunities to don his ceremonial plumage and enthuse with an audience about how "fascinating" this world is.

AFTERWORD

"We are all walking a lonely trail, not a morose one, but a solo trail."

Is despair warranted about the state of the world?

I would ask, Is [despair] that useful? Despair implies hands over your eyes and that you have given up. You can't do that; you are part of the world … Education is trying to transfer to others what you regard as basic things that would help them be good humans. If you are successful, people recognize you as a good teacher. You're not dead when you die. You're dead when people stop thinking about you, when you stop having ideas that are no longer current or haven't given rise to improvement or modification.

Are you optimistic about the future?

I'm an optimist by intention. I find that pessimists die younger and they don't have nearly as much fun as the optimists.[1711]

ACKNOWLEDGEMENTS

It took a vibrant, healthy ecosystem to nurture and produce this book.

Thanks to Ann Schau and Rod Silver, the alphas who led the pack – for their unfailing support, hospitality, networks, editing, stories, resources and vision to see a project of this size and complexity through to completion. Also to the rest of the McTaggart Cowan clan for accepting me into the herd and sharing their stories and other support, especially Mikkel and Torben Schau, Robin Grazley, Robert McTaggart Cowan, Penny Bickford, Kathy Racey, Hilary Mackenzie and Alison App.

Thank you to Tom Sterling, Ward Stevens and Margaret Fulton, the real thing in their respective fields, who provided so much but didn't get to see the final book.

Bristol and Libby Foster, Bob and Judy Weeden, Tom and Heather Bergerud and Peter Ommundsen, being Ian's students closest to me in geography and friendship, were leaned on the hardest and never failed to support this project in every capacity. Thanks also to Lorne Hammond, Margaret Horsfield, Richard Mackie and Walter Meyer zu Erpen, historians and archivists extraordinaire, for answering all those awkward questions at the start and providing me with the confidence to take the project on. Thank you to Michael Wall for sharing part of this long journey and providing his artful images; and at RMB to Don Gorman for being a writer's dream publisher, and to Joe Wilderson for his piercing and entertaining editorial guidance.

Neil Dawe (ornithologist), Dave Nagorsen (mammalogist) and Ken Mackenzie (historian) provided expert reviewing of the entire early manuscripts, with many of those mentioned above also having tackled edits for specific sections. Thank you to Anne Parkinson for cataloguing species photographs and providing forage and feedback; Tom and Shirley Beck, Al and Mavis Brady, Don and Fiona Flook and Val and Renata Geist for providing critical winter range in Alberta and BC and sharing so much; Hilary Mackenzie for the same in Scotland; John Shields and Robin Hood for providing the salt lick in Victoria; Francis Cook, Dan Brunton, Ross Peck and Joe Bryant for filling in the details of the natural history of Cowan and his mentors in Ottawa and the North; Ben Fullalove for historical research in Alberta and for rowing expeditions; and to three generations of the Spencer/Taylor family for their history, specimen preparations, photos, transcriptions and rowing skills.

Thanks also to Don Eastman, Mark Fraker, Muriel and Trisha Guiguet, Daryll Hebert, Buzz Holling, Winifred Kessler, Wayne McCrory, Bill Merilees, Murray Newman, Art Pearson, Robert Scagel, Ian Stirling and David Suzuki, all students or colleagues of Cowan, for such invaluable, funny and frank insights

I am indebted to Don Bourdon, Rob Cannings, Michael Carter, Darren Copley, Mac Culham, Lesley Kennes, Kelly Sendall, Kelly-Ann Turkington and all the staff at the desk for digging out (like Cowan's moles) material from the Royal BC Museum and BC Archives. Similarly to Yukiko Stranger-Jones and Ildiko Szabo for giving flight to specimens at the Beaty Biodiversity Museum; Fred Bunnell and Geoff Scudder for being the real thing at UBC; and Greg Borman, Chris Conroy, Christina Fidler and William Lidicker for the same at the Museum of Vertebrate Zoology, Berkeley (and Emily Rubidge for making the introduction). Thanks also to Sam Aquila, Torrey Archer, Chanda Brietzke, Ken Cooley, Chris Darimont, Kelly Fretwell, Lisa Goddard, Katharine Mercer, Brian Starzomski, Nancy Stuart, Christine Walde and Lara Wilson, the colourful flock from UVic Library and School of Environmental Studies under the indefatigable leadership of Kathleen Matthews. And to Colin Preston, a rare but endangered species of the CBC Archives; likewise to Chantal Dussault at the Canadian Museum of Nature; Bob McGowan at the Scottish National Museum; Maria Castrillo at the National Library of Scotland; and Betty Brooks, who directed me to Ken Barton at The Allan Brooks Nature Centre.

Thank you to Robert Bateman, Thomas Berger, Jim Campbell, Susan Hannon, Steve Johnsen, Elizabeth May, Helen Moats, Helen Stewart, Andy Stewart and Tim Wahl for filling in some strategic niches in the ecosystem history; Jim Jennings and Dan Wilkins for images; Jonathan Michaels, Marylou Wakefield and Louise Wood for their communication skills; Samantha Bowen, Suzanne Hare, Dan Harrison, Steve Lawson and any others I may have missed for technical support; and to Don Gayton for planting the seed in 1999.

And of course to the funding partners, without whom none of this would have happened: the Association of Professional Biology (BC); BC Arts Council; BC College of Applied Biology; BC Conservation Data Centre; BC Conservation Foundation; BC Ministry of Environment; BC Ministry of Forests, Lands and Natural Resource Operations; BC Nature; BC Wildlife Federation; Canada Council for the Arts; Canadian Wildlife Federation; the Cowan Family (Ann and Mikkel Schau); Ducks Unlimited Canada; Habitat Conservation Trust Foundation; John P. Kelly; Kootenay Wildlife Heritage Fund; Don Krogseth; Bruce McFarlane; The Nature Trust of BC; Nature Vancouver; Private Donors; Royal BC Museum; Sylvia von Shuckman; University of British Columbia (Zoology Department); University of Victoria; Victoria Natural History Society; and the World Wildlife Fund.

I would also like to thank the people who helped make those funds happen: Tom Beck, Les Bogdan, Lynne Bonner, Aaron Bremner, Dan Buffett, Fred Bunnell, Birgit Castledine, Brian Churchill, Tim Clermont, Claudia Copley, Francis Cook, Betty Davison, Tom Ethier, Ron Erickson, Valerius Geist, Deborah Gibson, Edythe Grant, Bruce Hallsor, Blair Hammond, Gretchen Harlow, Gordon Hart, Dave Hatler, Heather Holden, Monte Hummel, Cathy Hurd, Les Husband, Pierre Iachetti, Don Krogseth, Deb Kennedy, Wini Kessler, Jasper Lament, Becky Layne, Eric Lofroth, Jeremy McCall, Al Martin, Bob Morris, Silke Neve, Sarah Otto, Carmen Purdy, Walter Quan, Clayton Rubec, Gerald Sauder, Ann Schau, Kelly Sendall, Bob Shadwick, Olav Slaymaker, Brian Springinotic, Brian Starzomski, Ron Taylor,

David Tesch, Keith Thomas, Garry and Sandra Vince, Jim Walker, John West, Robin Wilson, Nancy Wilkin and Pamela Zevit.

Finally, to my family and friends, thank you. Biggest hugs to Caroline Penn and Jeremy Carpendale, who heard me out every step of the way; my nieces and nephews, who give me so much hope; my intertidal gang, who gather around at the lows as well as the highs; and my boys, two rugged little mountain-goat kids who, during the span of this project, grew up to be large and healthy on the gifts of this beautiful land.

TABLE OF SPECIES

Alexandrian Rat   360
[Black Rat]
Rattus rattus alexandrinus

American Badger. *See* Yellow Badger.

American Beaver   124
Castor canadensis

American Black Bear   291
Ursus americanus
Image #Cowan_PH_011 courtesy University of Victoria Special Collections;
Vermilion Crossing, BC, June 27, 1943;
photograph by Ian McTaggart Cowan.

[American] Bullfrog   332
Rana catesbeiana
[*Lithobates catesbeianus*]
Image #Cowan_PH_391 courtesy University of Victoria Special Collections;
Burnaby Lake, BC, 1942; photograph by
Ian McTaggart Cowan.

American Crow   356
Corvus brachyrhynchos
Image #J-00254 courtesy Royal BC Museum, BC Archives; no date or location;
photograph by Hamilton Mack Laing.

American Moose   426
Alces alces
Image #Cowan_PH_089 courtesy University of Victoria Special Collections;
Ootsa Lake, BC, July 1936; photograph
by Ian McTaggart Cowan.

American Pika. *See* Rock Rabbit.

American Pipit   7
Anthus rubescens
Image #Cowan_PH_443 courtesy Royal
BC Museum, BC Archives; specimen
#6910, female, collected by Kenneth
Racey, Sproat Mountain, Alta Lake, BC,
September 9, 1937; photograph by Michael Wall.

American Pipit [bis]   322
Anthus rubescens

American Robin   330
Turdus migratorius
Image #J-00244 courtesy Royal BC

Museum, BC Archives; no date or location; photograph by Hamilton Mack
Laing.

American Three-toed   405
Woodpecker
Picoides tridactylus
[*Picoides dorsalis*]
Image #J-00262 courtesy Royal BC Museum, BC Archives; "Drawing of Three-toed Woodpecker," 1935; photograph by
Hamilton Mack Laing.

American White Pelican   157
Pelecanus erythrorhynchos
Image #Cowan_PH_229 courtesy University of Victoria Special Collections;
Stum Lake, BC, July 21, 1950; photograph by Ian McTaggart Cowan.

American Wigeon   374
Anas americana

Ancient Murrelet   360
Synthliboramphus antiquus

Anna's Hummingbird   458
Calypte anna

Arctic Caribou   389
[Barren-ground Caribou]
Rangifer tarandus
[*groenlandicus*]
Image #Cowan_PH_240 courtesy University of Victoria Special Collections;
photograph by Ian McTaggart Cowan.

Bald Eagle   369
Haliaeetus leucocephalus
Image #Cowan_PH_132 courtesy University of Victoria Special Collections;
Mayne Island, BC, July 1991; photograph
by Ian McTaggart Cowan.

Barrow's Goldeneye   399
Bucephala islandica

Belted Kingfisher   71
Ceryle alcyon
Image #Cowan_PH_435 courtesy Royal
BC Museum, BC Archives; illustration by
Frank L. Beebe, ca. 1955; photograph by
Michael Wall.

Bewick Wren   394
[Bewick's Wren]
Thryomanes bewickii

Bighorn Sheep   266
Ovis canadensis
Image #Cowan_PH_112 courtesy University of Victoria Special Collections; Starvation Flats, Athabasca Valley,
Jasper, Alberta, May 1943; photograph
by Ian McTaggart Cowan.

Black-crowned   444
Night Heron
Nycticorax nycticorax
Image #J-00255 courtesy Royal BC
Museum, BC Archives; no location, ca.
1937; photograph by Hamilton Mack
Laing.

Black-footed Albatross   275
Diomedea nigripes
[now *Phoebastria nigripes*]
Image #Cowan_PH_383 courtesy University of Victoria Special Collections;
From *MV Parizeau*, 1971; photograph by
Ian McTaggart Cowan.

Black-legged Kittiwake   413
[simply Kittiwake in Europe]
Rissa tridactyla
Image #Cowan_PH_203 courtesy University of Victoria Special Collections;
Ireland, May 1987; photograph by Ian
McTaggart Cowan.

Black Oystercatcher   139
Haematopus bachmani

Black Swift   233
Cypseloides niger

Blue Goose. *See* Lesser Snow
Goose (blue phase).

Blue Grouse   23
[now split into Dusky Grouse
(*D. obscurus*) and Sooty Grouse
(*D. fuliginosus*)][80]
Dendragapus obscurus
[*Dendragapus fuliginosus*]

Blue or Sulphur-bottom Whale [Blue Whale] 460
Sibbaldus musculus [Balaenoptera musculus]
Image #Cowan_PP_280 courtesy Joanne Thomson; Ian McTaggart Cowan in front of blue whale skeleton, Victoria, BC, March 2010.

Bobcat 80
Lynx rufus
Image #Cowan_PH_020 courtesy University of Victoria Special Collections; no date; photograph by Ian McTaggart Cowan.

Bob-white [Northern Bobwhite] 45
Colinus virginianus

Brant 197
Branta bernicla
Image #J-00286 courtesy Royal BC Museum, BC Archives; Comox, BC, April 6, 1955; photograph by Hamilton Mack Laing.

Brewer's Sparrow 338
taverneri subspecies (Timberline Sparrow)
Spizella breweri taverneri
Image #Cowan_PH_397 courtesy University of Victoria Special Collections; Cairn Pass, Jasper, Alberta, July 1944; photograph by Ian McTaggart Cowan.

Brown Creeper (Tree Creeper) 360
Certhia americana

Bufflehead 258
Bucephala albeola

Bushy-tailed Woodrat (Pack Rat) 97
Neotoma cinerea
Image #J-00309 courtesy Royal BC Museum, BC Archives; Creston, BC, 1929; photograph by Hamilton Mack Laing.

Cackling Goose 145
Branta canadensis minima [now considered a separate species, *Branta hutchinsii*]
Image #Cowan_PH_076 courtesy University of Victoria Special Collections; Honeymoon Bay, Cowichan, BC, November 19, 1938; photograph by Ian McTaggart Cowan.

California Bighorn [Sheep] 403
Ovis canadensis californiana

California Quail 54
Callipepla californica
Image #J-00312 courtesy Royal BC Museum, BC Archives; Comox, BC, June

30, 1931; photograph by Hamilton Mack Laing.

Calliope Hummingbird 172
Stellula calliope

Canada Jay (Whiskey Jack) [Gray Jay] 39
Perisoreus canadensis
Image #J-00297 courtesy Royal BC Museum, BC Archives; Rainbow Mountains, BC, September 8, 1938; photograph by Hamilton Mack Laing.

Canada Lynx 321
Lynx canadensis

Canada River Otter [North American River Otter] 125
Lutra canadensis [now *Lontra canadensis*]
Image #Cowan_PH_344 courtesy University of Victoria Special Collections; no date or location; photograph by Ian McTaggart Cowan.

Canadian Sandhill Crane 273
Grus canadensis rowani
Image #J-00251 courtesy Royal BC Museum, BC Archives; Comox, BC, ca. 1937; photograph by Hamilton Mack Laing.

Canvasback 394
Aythya valisineria
Image #Cowan_PH_403 courtesy University of Victoria Special Collections; Tupper Creek, BC, June 1, 1930; photograph by Ian McTaggart Cowan.

Canyon Wren 217
Catherpes mexicanus
Image #Cowan_PH_428 courtesy Royal BC Museum, BC Archives; specimen #8907, collected by Ian McTaggart Cowan, Osoyoos, BC, May 21, 1941; photograph by Michael Wall.

Cascade Hoary Marmot (Whistler) [Hoary Marmot] 79
Marmota caligata cascadensis
Image #Cowan_PH_332 courtesy University of Victoria Special Collections; no date or location; photograph by Ian McTaggart Cowan.

Cassin's Auklet 359
Ptychoramphus aleuticus

Cinereus Shrew [now Common] 270
Sorex cinereus streatori
Image #J-00301 courtesy Royal BC Museum, BC Archives; collected at Huntingdon, BC, 1927; photograph by Hamilton Mack Laing.

Clark's Nutcracker 151
Nucifraga columbiana
Image #Cowan_PH_367 courtesy

University of Victoria Special Collections; no date or location; photograph by Ian McTaggart Cowan.

Cliff Swallow 188
Hirundo pyrrhonota [now *Petrochelidon pyrrhonota*]
Image #Cowan_PH_181 courtesy University of Victoria Special Collections; Chilanko Marsh[?], BC, 1994; photograph by Ian McTaggart Cowan.

Coast Mole 86
Scapanus orarius

Coastal Tailed Frog. *See* **Tailed Toad.**

Columbian Blacktailed Deer [Columbian Black-tailed Deer] 164, 165
Odocoileus columbianus columbianus (Richardson) [*Odocoileus hemionus columbianus*]
Page 164 image #Cowan_PH_373 courtesy University of Victoria Special Collections; Tails of black and white tailed deer for Cowan BA thesis, UBC, 1932; illustration by Ian McTaggart Cowan. Page 165 image #J-00272 courtesy Royal BC Museum, BC Archives; Cowan with Black tailed Deer at Constitution Hill, near Comox, BC, November 10, 1930; photograph by Hamilton Mack Laing.

Columbian Groundsquirrel [Columbian Ground Squirrel] 109
Spermophilus columbianus columbianus
Image #J-00293 courtesy Royal BC Museum, BC Archives; Lake Louise, Alberta, August 25, 1930; photograph by Hamilton Mack Laing.

Columbian Mammoth 241
Parelephas columbi [*Mammuthus columbi*]
Image #Cowan_PH_070 courtesy University of Victoria Special Collections; photograph by Ian McTaggart Cowan.

Common Goldeneye 449
Bucephala clangula

Common Loon 76
Gavia immer
Image #Cowan_PH_329 courtesy University of Victoria Special Collections; Bow Pass, Alberta, May 1945; photograph by Ian McTaggart Cowan.

Common Murre 361
Uria aalge
Image #Cowan_PH_095 courtesy University of Victoria Special Collections;

Point Reyes, California, 1930s; photograph by Ian McTaggart Cowan.

Common Poorwill 216
Phalaenoptilus nuttallii

Common Raven 362
Corvus corax

Common Shrew.
See Cinereus Shrew.

Common Tern 413
Sterna hirundo

Common Yellowthroat 333
Geothlypis trichas

Cougar or Mountain Lion 312
Felis concolor
[*Puma concolor concolor*]
Image #Cowan_PH_376 courtesy University of Victoria Special Collections; Princeton, BC; photograph by Ian McTaggart Cowan.

Cowan Dipperclam 429
Cuspidaria cowani
Image #Cowan_PH_404 courtesy University of Victoria Special Collections; photograph by Ian McTaggart Cowan.

Coyote 323
Canis latrans
Image #Cowan_PH_037 courtesy University of Victoria Special Collections; Banff, 1944; photograph by Ian McTaggart Cowan.

Creeping Vole 284
Microtus oregoni serpens

Cuckoo [Common Cuckoo] 422
Cuculus canorus

Dawson's Caribou 204
Rangifer dawsoni [now considered an extinct subspecies, *Rangifer tarandus dawsoni*, of the Caribou from the BC mainland]
Image #Cowan_PH_027 courtesy University of Victoria Special Collections; Royal BC Museum specimen: "Queen Charlotte Islands Caribou"; photograph by Ian McTaggart Cowan.

Double-crested Cormorant 140
Phalacrocorax auritus
Image #Cowan_PH_034 courtesy University of Victoria Special Collections; Ballingall Islet, BC, 1938; photograph by Ian McTaggart Cowan.

Drummond's Meadow Mouse [Vole] 254
Microtus pennsylvanicus drummondii
Image #Cowan_PH_093 courtesy University of Victoria Special Collections;

no date or location; photograph by Ian McTaggart Cowan.

Dusky Shrew 270
Sorex obscurus longicauda [now *Sorex monticolus longicaudus*]

Eared Grebe 395
Podiceps nigricollis

Eastern Cottontail Rabbit 5
[**Eastern Cottontail**]
Sylvilagus floridanus mearnsi
[s.f. *alacer*]

Eastern Kingbird 47
Tyrannus tyrannus

Eastern Sucker 257
Catostomus commersonii commersonii

Ermine Weasel. *See* Streator's
Weasel.

European Rabbit 4
Oryctolagus cuniculus
Image #Cowan_PH_327 courtesy Greg Jones, Canadian Wildlife Service; Triangle Island, BC, June 19, 2012.

European Starling 419
Sturnus vulgaris

Fisher 124
Martes pennanti

Flesh-footed Shearwater 274
Puffinus carneipes

Fool Hen. *See* Franklin Grouse.

Fork-tailed Storm-Petrel 274
Oceanodroma furcata

Franklin Grouse 25
(**Fool Hen**) [**Spruce Grouse**]
Canachites franklinii [*Canachites canadensis franklinii*]
Image #Cowan_PH_325 courtesy University of Victoria Special Collections; Scottish National Museum (Edinburgh) type specimen: Franklin Grouse, collected by David Douglas, Athabasca Pass, Alberta, May 1, 1827; photograph by author.

Fringed Myotis 293
Myotis thysanodes thysanodes

Giant Pacific Horse 285
Equus pacificus [*Equus* sp.]
Image #Cowan_PH_386 courtesy University of Victoria Special Collections; BC Provincial Museum, no date; photograph by Ian McTaggart Cowan.

Glaucous Gull 380
Larus hyperboreus

Golden Eagle 234
Aquila chrysaetos

Golden-crowned Kinglet 51
Regulus satrapa

Golden-crowned Sparrow 126
Zonotrichia atricapilla

Golden-mantled Ground Squirrel. *See* Mantled Groundsquirrel.

Gray Jay. *See* Canada Jay
(**Whiskey Jack**).

Gray Whale 445
Eschrichtius glaucus
[*Eschrichtius robustus*]
Image #Cowan_PH_401 courtesy University of Victoria Special Collections; San Pedro Martin Island, Baja California, 1957; photograph by Ian McTaggart Cowan.

[Gray] Wolf 319
Canis lupus
Image #Cowan_PH_125 courtesy University of Victoria Special Collections; Buffalo Prairie, Jasper, Alberta, May 1945; photograph by Ian McTaggart Cowan.

Great Basin Pocket Mouse 186
Perognathus parvus
Image #G-03687 courtesy Royal BC Museum, BC Archives; Comox, BC, January 12, 1956; photograph by Hamilton Mack Laing.

Great Gray Owl 455
Strix nebulosa
Image #Cowan_PH_136 courtesy University of Victoria Special Collections; Cochrane, Alberta, 1993; photograph by Ian McTaggart Cowan.

Great Horned Owl 179
Bubo virginianus
Image #J-00307 courtesy Royal BC Museum, BC Archives; no date or location; photograph by Hamilton Mack Laing.

Greater White-fronted Goose 434
Anser albifrons
Image #Cowan_PH_286 courtesy University of Victoria Special Collections; Pitt River, BC, 1924; photograph by J.A. Munro.

Grizzly Bear 128
Ursus arctos horribilis
Image #Cowan_PH_012 courtesy University of Victoria Special Collections; Maligne Lake, Alberta, 1946; photograph by Ian McTaggart Cowan.

Harbour Porpoise 450
Phocoena vomerina
[*Phocoena phocoena*]

Harlequin Duck 341
Histrionicus histrionicus
Image #Cowan_PH_398 courtesy University of Victoria Special Collections; Southesk River, Jasper, Alberta, July 1944; photograph by Ian McTaggart Cowan.

Hermit Thrush 171
Hylocichla guttata
[now *Catharus guttatus*]
Image #Cowan_PH_120 courtesy University of Victoria Special Collections; Tupper Creek, BC, June 1938; photograph by Ian McTaggart Cowan.

Hoary Marmot. *See* **Cascade Hoary Marmot.**

Hooded Merganser 301
Lophodytes cucullatus

Horned Lark 112
Eremophila alpestris

House Finch 35
Carpodacus mexicanus
Image #Cowan_PH_427 courtesy Royal BC Museum, BC Archives; [from top] specimen #7998: Male Purple Finch, collected by Ian McTaggart Cowan, Tupper Creek, BC, May 6, 1938; specimen #13975: Male House Finch, collected by Hamilton Mack Laing, Comox, BC, December 29, 1964; Female House Finch, collected by Ian McTaggart Cowan, Victoria, BC, June 10, 1937; photograph by Michael Wall.

Hudsonian Godwit 252
Limosa haemastica
Image #Cowan_PH_362 courtesy University of Victoria Special Collections; no date or location; photograph by Ian McTaggart Cowan.

Humpback Whale 365
Megaptera novaeangliae
Image #Cowan_PH_400 courtesy University of Victoria Special Collections; no date or location; photograph by Ian McTaggart Cowan.

Keen's Mouse. *See* **Sitka Mouse.**

Keen['s] Myotis 362
Myotis keeni keeni [*Myotis keenii* no ssp. recognized]

Kermode Bear 206
Ursus americanus kermodei
Image #Cowan_PH_006 courtesy University of Victoria Special Collections; Surf Inlet, Princess Royal, 1939; photograph by Ian McTaggart Cowan.

Killdeer 107
Charadrius vociferus
Image #J-00289 courtesy Royal BC Museum, BC Archives; Comox, BC, May 3, 1931; photograph by Hamilton Mack Laing.

Large Brown Bat 256
Eptesicus fuscus

Least Chipmunk 314
Eutamias minimus selkirki
[*Neotamias minimus selkirki*]

Least Weasel 223
Mustela rixosa [now *M. nivalis*]

Lesser Snow Goose 454
(blue phase) (Blue Goose)
Chen caerulescens
Image #Cowan_PH_077 courtesy University of Victoria Special Collections; Telegraph Bay, Victoria, April 29, 1939; photograph by Ian McTaggart Cowan.

Little Brown Myotis [**Bat**] 198
Myotis lucifugus

Long-billed Curlew 136
Numenius americanus
Image #Cowan_PH_431 courtesy Royal BC Museum, BC Archives; specimen #12756: Whimbrel, collected by Hamilton Mack Laing, Comox, BC, April 26, 1927; specimen #8889: Long-billed Curlew, collected by Ian McTaggart Cowan, Oliver, BC, May 30, 1941; photograph by Michael Wall.

Long-tailed Weasel 95
Mustela frenata nevadensis
Image #J-00300 courtesy Royal BC Museum, BC Archives; Huntingdon, BC, May 25, 1927; photograph by Hamilton Mack Laing.

Magnolia Warbler 170
Dendroica magnolia
[now in the genus *Setophaga*]

Mallard 209
Anas platyrhynchos
Image #Cowan_PH_085 courtesy Mrs. Ann Taylor; Lac du Bois, BC, 1939; photograph by George J. Spencer.

Mantled Groundsquirrel 234
[**Golden-mantled Ground Squirrel**]
Citellus lateralis tescorum [*Spermophilus lateralis tescorum*]
Image #J-00252 courtesy Royal BC Museum, BC Archives; no date or location; photograph by Hamilton Mack Laing.

Marbled Murrelet 148
Brachyramphus marmoratus

Marmot, or Woodchuck 167
Marmota monax petrensis
Image #Cowan_PH_433 courtesy Royal BC Museum, BC Archives; illustration by Frank L. Beebe, ca. 1955; photograph by Michael Wall.

Marten 337
Martes americana

McCown's Longspur 118
Calcarius mccownii [now *Rhynchophanes mccownii*]
Image #Cowan_PH_432 courtesy Royal BC Museum, BC Archives; specimen BCPM #18689: collected by W. Ray Salt, Rosebud, Alberta, May 25, 1941; photograph by Michael Wall.

Merlin 169
Falco columbarius
Image #J-00299 courtesy Royal BC Museum, BC Archives; Comox, BC, November 6, 1937; photograph by Hamilton Mack Laing.

Mink 32
Mustela vison [*Neovison vison*]
Image #Cowan_PH_088 courtesy University of Victoria Special Collections; Alta Lake, BC, August 20, 1938; photograph by Ian McTaggart Cowan.

Mohave Ground Squirrel 200
Spermophilus mohavensis

Mount Baker Chipmunk 76
[**Yellow-pine Chipmunk**]
Eutamias amoenus felix
[*Neotamias amoenus felix*]
Image #Cowan_PH_022 courtesy University of Victoria Special Collections; no date or location; photograph by Ian McTaggart Cowan.

Mountain Beaver 86
Aplodontia rufa
Image #J-00248 courtesy Royal BC Museum, BC Archives; no date; illustration by Hamilton Mack Laing.

Mountain Caribou 159
Rangifer tarandus montanus
[now *R. t. caribou*]
Image #Cowan_PH_025 courtesy University of Victoria Special Collections; Poboktan Pass, Alberta, July 5, 1944; photograph by Ian McTaggart Cowan.

Mountain Cottontail 178
[**Nuttall's Cottontail**]
Sylvilagus nuttallii nuttallii

Mountain Goat 316
Oreamnos americanus
Image #Cowan_PH_073 courtesy University of Victoria Special Collections; Athabasca Lookout, Alberta, 1945; photograph by Ian McTaggart Cowan.

Mountain Hare   5
Lepus timidus

Mountain Heather-vole   126
[Western Heather Vole]
Phenacomys intermedius

Mule Deer   183
Odocoileus hemionus hemionus
Image #Cowan_PH_058 courtesy University of Victoria Special Collections;
Jasper, Alberta, 1930s; photograph by Ian McTaggart Cowan.

Musk-ox   45
[Muskox or Musk Ox]
Ovibos moschatus

Muskrat   376
Ondatra zibethica [zibethicus]
Image #Cowan_PH_314 courtesy Beaty Biodiversity Museum; Aklavik, NWT, 1947; photograph by Michael Wall.

Myrtle Warbler   253
[Yellow-rumped Warbler]
Dendroica coronata [now considered a subspecies of the Yellow-rumped Warbler, *Setophaga coronata coronata*]

Navigator Shrew   158
[American Water Shrew]
Sorex palustris

North American Opossum   194
[Virginia Opossum]
Didelphis marsupialis virginiana [*Didelphis virginiana*]

Northern Alligator Lizard   229
Gerrhonotus principis [*Elgaria coerulea principis*]
Image #Cowan_PH_084 courtesy University of Victoria Special Collections;
Cowichan River, BC, November 1939; photograph by Ian McTaggart Cowan.

Northern Bog Lemming. *See* Wrangell Bog-Lemming.

Northern Flying Squirrel   111
Glaucomys sabrinus
Image #Cowan_PH_341 courtesy University of Victoria Special Collections;
Near Quesnel, BC, no date; photograph by Ian McTaggart Cowan.

Northern Fulmar   412
Fulmarus glacialis
Image #J-00284 courtesy Royal BC Museum, BC Archives; August 12, 1924; photograph by Hamilton Mack Laing.

Northern Fur-seal   144
Callorhinus ursinus cynocephalus
Image #Cowan_PH_361 courtesy University of Victoria Special Collections;

Goose Island, BC, July 1939; photograph by Ian McTaggart Cowan.

Northern Goshawk   292
Accipiter gentilis
Image #J-00295 courtesy Royal BC Museum, BC Archives; Alaska, July 23, 1925; photograph by Hamilton Mack Laing.

Northern Pygmy-Owl   129
Glaucidium gnoma

Northern Red-legged Frog. *See* Red-legged Frog.

Northern Saw-whet Owl   362
Aegolius acadicus brooksi

Northern Sea Lion   84
[Steller's Sea Lion]
Eumetopias jubatus
Image #Cowan_PH_335 courtesy University of Victoria Special Collections;
ca. 1940s; photograph by Ian McTaggart Cowan.

Northern Shrike   189
Lanius excubitor

Northern Waterthrush   170
Seiurus noveboracensis

Northern Wheatear   9
Oenanthe oenanthe

Northwestern Salamander   276
Ambystoma gracile

Northwest Jumping Mouse   80
[Pacific Jumping Mouse]
Zapus trinotatus trinotatus
Image #J-00305 courtesy Royal BC Museum, BC Archives; Huntingdon, BC, May 25, 1927; photograph by Hamilton Mack Laing.

Olympic Meadow Mouse   66
[Long-tailed Vole]
Microtus mordax macrurus [*Microtus longicaudus macrurus*]

Olympic Phenacomys   65
[Heather Vole]
Phenacomys intermedius olympicus
Image #Cowan_PH_328 courtesy University of Victoria Special Collections;
no date or location; photograph by Ian McTaggart Cowan.

Orange-crowned Warbler   332
Vermivora celata [*Oreothlypis celata*]
Image #Cowan_PH_396 courtesy University of Victoria Special Collections;
Victoria, BC, May 26, 1993; photograph by Ian McTaggart Cowan.

Pacific Coast Newt   141
[Rough-skinned Newt]
Triturus torosus [*Taricha granulosa*]

Pacific Jumping Mouse. *See* Northwest Jumping Mouse.

Pacific Killer Whale, or   441
"Blackfish" [Killer Whale, Orca]
Grampus rectipinna [*Orcinus orca*]
Image #Cowan_PH_413 courtesy University of Victoria Special Collections;
Cherry Point, BC, September 29, 1944; photograph by Ian McTaggart Cowan.

Pacific Loon   141
Gavia pacifica

Pacific Raccoon   83
[Northern Raccoon]
Procyon lotor pacifica

Pacific Rattlesnake   290
[Northern Pacific Rattlesnake]
Crotalus viridis oreganus [*Crotalus oreganus oreganus*]

Pack Rat. *See* Bushy-tailed Woodrat.

Pallid Bat   156
Antrozous pallidus cantwelli [now *pacificus*]

Peale's Peregrine Falcon   359
Falco peregrinus pealei

Pigeon Guillemot   359
Cepphus columba

Pileated Woodpecker   450
Dryocopus pileatus

Pink-footed Shearwater   364
Puffinus creatopus

Pintail [Northern Pintail]   377
Anas acuta
Image #J-00249 courtesy Royal BC Museum, BC Archives; no date or location; photograph by Hamilton Mack Laing.

Plains Bison   46
[a subspecies of American Bison, *Bison bison*]
Bison bison bison
Image #Cowan_PH_021 courtesy University of Victoria Special Collections;
Banff, 1944; photograph by Ian McTaggart Cowan.

Pocket Gopher   104
[Northern Pocket Gopher]
Thomomys talpoides
Image #Cowan_PH_340 courtesy University of Victoria Special Collections;

Waterton Lake, Alberta, July 1945; photograph by Ian McTaggart Cowan.

Porcupine 236
Erethizon dorsatum nigrescens
Image #Cowan_PH_101 courtesy University of Victoria Special Collections; Snaring River, Alberta, July 1944; photograph by Ian McTaggart Cowan.

Puget Sound Spotted Skunk 83
[Western Spotted Skunk]
Spilogale phenax olympica
[*Spilogale gracilis*]
Image #J-00300 courtesy Royal BC Museum, BC Archives; Huntingdon, BC, May 25, 1927; photograph by Hamilton Mack Laing.

Purple Finch 35
Carpodacus purpureus
Image #Cowan_PH_427 courtesy Royal BC Museum, BC Archives; [from top] specimen #7998: Male Purple Finch, collected by Ian McTaggart Cowan, Tupper Creek, BC, May 6, 1938; specimen #13975: Male House Finch, collected by Hamilton Mack Laing, Comox, BC, December 29, 1964; Female House Finch, collected by Ian McTaggart Cowan, Victoria, BC, June 10, 1937; photograph by Michael Wall.

Purple Martin 70
Progne subis

Pygmy Horned Lizard 287
[Pygmy Short-horned Lizard]
Phrynosoma douglasii douglassii
Image #Cowan_PH_438 courtesy Royal BC Museum, BC Archives; #323-324 [pickled specimen], collected by C. de B. Green, Okanagan, BC, 1900-1912?; photograph by Michael Wall.

Pygmy Nuthatch 113
Sitta pygmaea
Image #Cowan_PH_429 courtesy Royal BC Museum, BC Archives; collected by A.C. Brooks, Okanagan, BC, December 9, 1897; photograph by Michael Wall.

Pygmy Shrew 223
Microsorex hoyi intervectus
[*Sorex hoyi*]
Image #Cowan_PH_380 courtesy University of Victoria Special Collections; no date or location; photograph by Ian McTaggart Cowan.

Red Crossbill 170
Loxia curvirostra

Red Fox 385
Vulpes fulva [*Vulpes vulpes*]

Red Squirrel 94
Tamiasciurus hudsonicus
Image #Cowan_PH_116 courtesy

University of Victoria Special Collections; Alta Lake, BC, August 1938; photograph by Ian McTaggart Cowan.

Red-backed Mouse 78
[Southern Red-backed Vole]
Clethrionomys caurinus
[*Myodes gapperi caurinus*, now a subspecies]

Red-breasted Merganser 284
Mergus serrator

Red-breasted Nuthatch 436
Sitta canadensis

Red-flecked Mopalia 13
Mopalia spectabilis Cowan & Cowan
Image #Cowan_PH_355 courtesy University of Victoria Special Collections; Mayne Island, August 1973; photograph by Ian McTaggart Cowan.

Red-legged Frog 277
[Northern Red-legged Frog]
Rana aurora aurora
Image #Cowan_PH_071 courtesy University of Victoria Special Collections; Victoria, 1940s; photograph by Ian McTaggart Cowan.

Red-shafted Flicker 395
[Northern Flicker]
Colaptes cafer [*Colaptes auratus*]
Image #J-00250 courtesy Royal BC Museum, BC Archives; no date or location; photograph by Hamilton Mack Laing.

Red-winged Blackbird 244
Agelaius phoeniceus
Image #J-00282 courtesy Royal BC Museum, BC Archives; Jasper, Alberta, July 8, 1930; photograph by Hamilton Mack Laing.

Rhinoceros Auklet 138
Cerorhinca monocerata
Image #J-00283 courtesy Royal BC Museum, BC Archives; Comox, BC, August 1922; photograph by Hamilton Mack Laing.

Richardson Vole 235
(Water Rat) [Water Vole]
Microtus richardsoni richardsoni

Ring-necked Duck 353
Aythya collaris

Ring-necked Pheasant 20
Phasianus colchicus

Rock Rabbit 79
[American Pika]
Ochotona princeps brunnescens
Image #Cowan_PH_331 courtesy University of Victoria Special Collections;

Alta Lake, BC, August 17, 1938; photograph by Ian McTaggart Cowan.

Rocky Mountain Bighorn 304
Sheep
Ovis canadensis canadensis

Rocky Mountain Elk 311
Cervus canadensis nelsoni
Image #Cowan_PH_067 courtesy University of Victoria Special Collections; Jasper, 1946; photograph by Ian McTaggart Cowan.

Rose-breasted Grosbeaks 253
Pheucticus ludovicianus

Rufous Hummingbird 173
Selasphorus rufus
Image #J-00296 courtesy Royal BC Museum, BC Archives; Stuie, BC, July 7, 1940; photograph by Hamilton Mack Laing.

Rusty Blackbird 220
Euphagus carolinus

Scammon Blackfish – 286
"Squarehead"
[Short-finned Pilot Whale]
Globicephala scammoni
[*G. macrorynchus*]

Sharp-nosed Finner, 237
Minke or Pike Whale
[Common Minke Whale]
Balaenoptera acutorostrata
Image #Cowan_PH_122 courtesy University of Victoria Special Collections; Sooke, BC, 1936; photograph by Ian McTaggart Cowan.

Sharp-tailed Grouse 20
Pedioecetes phasianellus
Image #Cowan_PH_440 courtesy Royal BC Museum, BC Archives; illustration by Frank L. Beebe, ca. 1955, for BC Provincial Museum Handbook no. 10, *Birds of BC*, vol. 4: "Upland Game Birds"; photograph by Michael Wall.

Short-finned Pilot Whale.
See Scammon Blackfish –
"Squarehead."

Short-tailed Weasel.
See Streator's Weasel.

Silver-haired Bat 166
Lasionycteris noctivagans

Sitka Mouse [Keen's Mouse] 198
Peromyscus sitkensis prevostensis
[now *P. keeni*]

Snowshoe Hare 6
Lepus americanus
Image #Cowan_PH_424 courtesy Royal

BC Museum, BC Archives; type specimen #004717, collected by Ian McTaggart Cowan, Chezacut Lake, BC, July 29, 1931; photograph by Michael Wall.

Sora   221
Porzana carolina
Image #J-00313 courtesy Royal BC Museum, BC Archives; June 23, 1930; photograph by Hamilton Mack Laing.

Spotted Bat   295
Euderma maculatum
Image #Cowan_PH_410 courtesy University of Victoria Special Collections; Okanagan Falls, BC, June 1980; photograph by Ian McTaggart Cowan.

Spotted Owl   196
Strix occidentalis
Image #Cowan_PH_425 courtesy Royal BC Museum, BC Archives; collected by Jared Hobbs, Lytton area, December 11, 2004; photograph by Michael Wall.

Spruce Grouse. *See* Franklin Grouse.

Steller's Jay   130
Cyanocitta stelleri
Image #J-00298 courtesy Royal BC Museum, BC Archives; Comox, BC, December 13, 1927; photograph by Hamilton Mack Laing.

**Steller's Sea-Lion.
See Northern Sea-lion.**

Streator's Weasel   82
[Ermine or Short-tailed Weasel]
Mustela streatori
[Mustela erminea fallenda]
Image #Cowan_PH_338 courtesy Mrs. Ann Taylor; "Weasel, Bonaparte [Short-tailed weasel]," Lac du Bois, BC, 1939; George J. Spencer photograph.

Striped Skunk   242
Mephitis mephitis hudsonica
Image #J-00260 courtesy Royal BC Museum, BC Archives; illustration by Alan Brooks.

Surf Scoter   353
Melanitta perspicillata
Image #J-00288 courtesy Royal BC Museum, BC Archives; Scoters at Comox, BC, April 17, 1939; photograph by Hamilton Mack Laing.

Swainson's Hawk   98
Buteo swainsoni
Oak Lake, Manitoba.
Image #J-00294 courtesy Royal BC Museum, BC Archives; August 9, 1921; photograph by Hamilton Mack Laing.

Swamp Sparrow   34
Melospiza georgiana

Tailed Toad   300
[Coastal Tailed Frog]
Ascaphus truei

Thick-billed Murre   419
Uria lomvia

Thinhorn Sheep   347
Ovis dalli
Image #Cowan_PH_447 courtesy University of Victoria Special Collections; illustration by Valerius Geist, ca. 1961.

**Timberline Sparrow.
See Brewer's Sparrow
taverneri subspecies.**

Townsend Mole   298
[Townsend's Mole]
Scapanus townsendi [townsendii]
Image #J-00304 courtesy Royal BC Museum, BC Archives; Huntingdon, BC, June 6, 1927; photograph by Hamilton Mack Laing.

**Townsend's Big-eared Bat.
See Western Big-eared Bat.**

Townsend's Solitaire   101
Myadestes townsendi

Townsend's Vole   143
[Cowani subspecies]
Microtus townsendii cowani
[top] #Cowan_PH_359, *Microtus townsendii cowani*, Triangle Island, BC, June 20, 2004; photograph by Moira Lemon, Canadian Wildlife Service. [bottom] #Cowan_PH_315 courtesy Beaty Biodiversity Museum; female and male, collected by Kenneth Racey, Chesterman Beach, Tofino, BC, May 18, 1931; photograph by Michael Wall.

Trowbridge Shrew   298
Sorex trowbridgii trowbridgii
Image #J-00304 courtesy Royal BC Museum, BC Archives; Huntingdon, BC, June 6, 1927; photograph by Hamilton Mack Laing.

Trumpeter Swan   250
Cygnus buccinator
Image #Cowan_PH_118 courtesy University of Victoria Special Collections; no date or location; photograph by Ian McTaggart Cowan.

Vagrant Shrew. *See* Wandering Shrew.

Vancouver Marmot   149
[Vancouver Island Marmot]
Marmota vancouverensis
Image #Cowan_PH_430 courtesy Royal BC Museum, BC Archives; specimen #5021, collected by Frank Beebe, Forbidden Plateau, Mt. Washington, BC,

August 30, 1943; photograph by Michael Wall.

Varied Thrush   77
Ixoreus naevius
Image #J-00261 courtesy Royal BC Museum, BC Archives; 1935; illustration by Hamilton Mack Laing.

Vaux's Swift   249
Chaetura vauxi

Vole. *See* Drummond's Meadow Mouse.

Wandering Shrew   96
[Vagrant Shrew]
Sorex vagrans obscurus
[Sorex vagrans vagrans]
Image #Cowan_PH_385 courtesy University of Victoria Special Collections; no date or location; photograph by Ian McTaggart Cowan.

Wandering Tattler   255
Heteroscelus incanus
[Tringa incana]
Image #Cowan_PH_384 courtesy University of Victoria Special Collections; Galápagos, 1987; photograph by Ian McTaggart Cowan.

Water Vole. *See* Richardson Vole (Water Rat).

Western Big-eared Bat   397
[now Townsend's Big-eared Bat]
Corynorhinus townsendi [townsendii]

Western Bluebird   211
Sialia mexicana

Western Blue Racer   289
[Western Yellow-bellied Racer]
Coluber constrictor mormon

Western Grebe   396
Aechmophorus occidentalis
Image #Cowan_PH_080 courtesy University of Victoria Special Collections; Williams Lake, BC, 1930s; photograph by J.A. Munro.

Western Jumping Mouse   129
Zapus princeps idahoensis

Western Meadowlark   211
Sturnella neglecta

Western Painted Turtle   289
Chrysemys picta belli

Western Red-backed Vole 299
[Southern Red-backed Vole]
Clethrionomys
occidentalis occidentalis
[*Myodes gapperi occidentalis*]

Western Sandpiper 137
Calidris mauri
Image #J-00256 courtesy Royal BC Museum, BC Archives; no date or location; photograph by Hamilton Mack Laing.

Western Screech-Owl 440
Otus kennicottii
[*Megascops kennicottii*]
Image #Cowan_PH_098 courtesy University of Victoria Special Collections; Vancouver, 1955; photograph by Ian McTaggart Cowan.

[Western] Small-footed 208
Myotis
Myotis subulatus melanorhinus
[*Myotis ciliolabrum*]

Western Spadefoot Toad 288
[Great Basin Spadefoot Toad]
Scaphiopus hammondi
[*Spea intermontana*]
Image #Cowan_PH_437 courtesy Royal BC Museum, BC Archives; [pickled specimen] #1898, collected by D. Blades, Osoyoos, BC, July 10, 1991; photograph by Michael Wall.

[Western] Spotted Skunk 301
See also Puget Sound
Spotted Skunk.
Spilogale gracilis latifrons

Western Yellow-bellied Racer.
See Western Blue Racer.

Whimbrel 136
Numenius phaeopus
Image #Cowan_PH_431 courtesy Royal BC Museum, BC Archives; specimen #12756: Whimbrel, collected by Hamilton Mack Laing, Comox, BC, April 26, 1927; specimen #8889: Long-billed Curlew, collected by Ian McTaggart Cowan, Oliver, BC, May 30, 1941; photograph by Michael Wall.

Whistling [Tundra] Swan 250
Cygnus columbianus
Image #Cowan_PH_382 courtesy University of Victoria Special Collections; no date or location; photograph by Ian McTaggart Cowan.

White-crowned Sparrow 398
[Gambel's]
Zonotrichia leucophrys

White-footed Mouse, 64
or Deer Mouse
Peromyscus maniculatus
Image #Cowan_PH_121 courtesy University of Victoria Special Collections; Kamloops, 1929; photograph by Ian McTaggart Cowan.

White-lined Chiton 447
Tonicella insignis
Image #Cowan_PH_405 courtesy University of Victoria Special Collections; UBC, September 20, 1963; photograph by Ian McTaggart Cowan.

Whitetail Deer 187
[Northwestern
White-tailed Deer]
Odocoileus virginianus ochrourus
Image #Cowan_PH_060 courtesy University of Victoria Special Collections; no date or location; photograph by Ian McTaggart Cowan.

White-tailed Jackrabbit 156
Lepus townsendi townsendi
[now *L. townsendii townsendii*]

White-tailed Ptarmigan 343
Lagopus leucurus
Image #J-00311 courtesy Royal BC Museum, BC Archives; Vancouver Island, 1931; photograph by Hamilton Mack Laing.

White-throated Swift 218
Aeronautes saxatalis

White-winged Scoter 419
Melanitta fusca

Williamson Sapsucker 114
[Williamson's Sapsucker]
Sphyrapicus thyroideus nataliae

Willow Ptarmigan 380
Lagopus lagopus

Wolverine 317
Gulo luscus [*Gulo gulo*]
Image #Cowan_PH_126 courtesy University of Victoria Special Collections; Topaz Lake, Alberta, May 1944; photograph by Ian McTaggart Cowan.

Wood Bison 46
[a subspecies of American
Bison, *Bison bison*]
Bison bison athabascae
Image #Cowan_PH_420 courtesy University of Victoria Special Collections; Elk Island, Alberta, June 1946; photograph by Ian McTaggart Cowan.

Wood Duck 38
Aix sponsa
Image #Cowan_PH_326 courtesy University of Victoria Special Collections.

Wrangell Bog-Lemming 78
[Northern Bog Lemming]
Synaptomys borealis wrangeli
[*S. b. truei*]
Image #Cowan_PH_333 courtesy University of Victoria Special Collections; Thompson Pass, Alberta, July 1945; photograph by Ian McTaggart Cowan.

Yellow Badger 105
[American Badger]
Taxidea taxus
Image #Cowan_PH_005 courtesy University of Victoria Special Collections; Newgate, BC, 1930; photograph by Ian McTaggart Cowan.

Yellow-bellied Marmot 93
Marmota flaviventris avara
Image #Cowan_PH_336 courtesy University of Victoria Special Collections; "Young groundhog [Yellow-bellied marmot]," Black Pines, BC, July 4, 1929; photograph by Ian McTaggart Cowan.

Yellow-bellied Sapsucker 256
Sphyrapicus varius varius

Yellow-headed Blackbird 33
Xanthocephalus xanthocephalus
Image #Cowan_PH_133 courtesy University of Victoria Special Collections; Okanagan River Oxbows; photograph by Ian McTaggart Cowan.

Yellow-breasted Chat 217
Icteria virens
Image #Cowan_PH_426 courtesy Royal BC Museum; specimens #5336 and #5337, collected by Ian McTaggart Cowan, Penticton, BC, June 27, 1936; photograph by Michael Wall.

Yellow-pine Chipmunk. *See*
Mount Baker Chipmunk.

Yellow Warbler 36
Dendroica aestiva
[*Setophaga petechia*]
Image #Cowan_PH_324 courtesy Beaty Biodiversity Museum, Vancouver, BC; all collected by Ian McTaggart Cowan; photograph by Michael Wall.

Yuma Myotis 300
Myotis yumanensis saturatus

NOTES

1 Ian McTaggart Cowan, interview, February 2, 2005.

2 Ian McTaggart Cowan and C.J. Guiguet, *The Mammals of British Columbia* (Victoria: BC Provincial Museum, 1956), 13. [Cited henceforth as *Mammals of BC*.]

3 Don Eastman, interview, July 11, 2002; Peter Ommundsen, personal communication, January 12, 2000.

4 Ronald D. Jakimchuk, R. Wayne Campbell and Dennis A. Demarchi, eds., *Ian McTaggart Cowan: The Legacy of a Pioneering Biologist, Educator and Conservationist* (Madeira Park, BC: Harbour Publishing, 2015).

5 Rod S. Silver, Neil K. Dawe, Brian M. Starzomski, Katherine L. Parker and David W. Nagorsen, "A Tribute to Ian McTaggart Cowan (1910–2010)," *The Canadian Field-Naturalist* 124, no. 4 (2010): 367–383. http://canadianfieldnaturalist.ca/index.php/cfn/article/view/1108/1112 (pdf accessed October 25, 2014).

6 Cowan, interview, February 26, 2001.

7 David Elliston Allen, *The Naturalist in Britain: A Social History*, 2nd ed. (Princeton, NJ: Princeton University Press, 1994).

8 Paul Lawrence Farber, *Finding Order in Nature: The Naturalist Tradition from Linnaeus to E.O. Wilson* (Baltimore: Johns Hopkins University Press, 2000).

9 Osgood Mackenzie, *A Hundred Years in the Highlands* (London: Edward Arnold, 1921), 65–66. https://archive.org/stream/hundredyearsinhioomackuoft#page/64/mode/2up (accessed October 31, 2014).

10 Mackenzie, *A Hundred Years in the Highlands*, 64.

11 Ian McTaggart Cowan, "Conservation and Man's Environment," in Paul H. Oehser, ed., *Knowledge Among Men: Eleven Essays on Science, Culture and Society* (New York: Simon and Schuster, 1966), 75.

12 David W. Nagorsen, *Rodents and Lagomorphs of British Columbia*, vol. 4 in *Mammals of BC* (Victoria: Royal BC Museum, 2005), 97–99.

13 Mackenzie, *A Hundred Years in the Highlands*, 65.

14 International Union for Conservation of Nature, *Lepus timidus*, IUCN Red List of Threatened Species, version 2015.2. www.iucnredlist.org/details/11791/0 (accessed July 10, 2015).

15 Cowan, interview, December 5, 2000.

16 Beaty Biodiversity Museum, Cowan Tetrapod Collection, specimen M006093. Vertnet UBCBBM CTC M006093. http://portal.vertnet.org/o/ubcbbm/ctc?id=m006093 (accessed October 31, 2014).

17 Cowan and Guiguet, *Mammals of BC*, 108.

18 Ian McTaggart Cowan, "The Fur Trade and the Fur Cycle 1825–1857," *The British Columbia Historical Quarterly* (January 1938): 21–22. http://is.gd/ClHlM3 (pdf pp26–27, accessed October 31, 2014).

19 Ian McTaggart Cowan, "Of Mice and Men – or the Biology of Numbers" (public lecture, Vancouver Institute, March 18, 1961). https://circle.ubc.ca/flashstreamview/bitstream/handle/2429/36425/ubc_at_010_cowan.mp3?sequence=1 (streaming audio, 78:59, accessed October 19, 2013).

20 Ian McTaggart Cowan, "Notes On the Hares of British Columbia with the Description of a New Race," *Journal of Mammalogy* 19, no. 2 (1938): 240–243. http://jmammal.oxfordjournals.org/content/19/2/240 (pdf sample accessed October 31, 2014).

21 Cowan and Guiguet, *Mammals of BC*, 100.

22 Cowan and Guiguet, *Mammals of BC*, 100.

23 Ian McTaggart Cowan, "Mammals of Point Grey," *The Canadian Field-Naturalist* 44, no. 6 (September 1930): 134. www.biodiversitylibrary.org/item/89659#page/168/mode/1up (accessed October 31, 2014).

24 Cowan, interview, December 5, 2000.

25 Cowan, interview, July 9, 2002. [A complete citation of this videotaped interview appears in the "Interviews and personal communications" section of the Bibliography.]

26 Graham Checkley, personal communication, September 1, 2013.

27 R. Wayne Campbell et al., *The Birds of British Columbia*, vol. 3. (Vancouver: UBC Press, 1997), 456. [Henceforth cited as *Birds of BC* followed by the volume number.]

28 Cowan, interview, July 9, 2002.

29 Jack Repchek, *The Man Who Found Time: James Hutton and the Discovery of the Earth's Antiquity* (Cambridge, Mass.: Perseus Publishing, 2003), 13.

30 John Playfair, "Life of Dr. Hutton," *Transactions of the Royal Society of Edinburgh* 5, pt. 3 (1805): 72–73. www.biodiversitylibrary.org/item/125770#page/490/mode/1up (accessed October 31, 2014).

31 Campbell et al., *Birds of BC*, vol. 3, 539.

32 James Hutton, *Investigation of the Principles of Knowledge and the Progress of Reason, from Sense to Science to Philosophy* (Edinburgh: Strahan & Cadell, 1794). Cited in Repchek, *The Man Who Found Time*, 23.

33 R. Bellon, "A Question of Merit: John Hutton Balfour, Joseph Hooker and the 'Concussion' over the Edinburgh Chair of Botany," *Studies in History and Philosophy of Biological and Biomedical Sciences* 36, no. 1 (March 2005): 25–54. www.ncbi.nlm.nih.gov/pubmed/16120259 (abstract accessed June 2, 2014).

34 J. Hooker to J.H. Balfour, December 7, 1842, quoted in Bellon, "A Question of Merit," 25–54.

35 Bellon, "A Question of Merit."

36 John Hutton Balfour, *Testimonials in Favour of John Hutton Balfour, MD Ed. FRSE, 1841* (Glasgow: s.n., 1841), 3.631 National Library of Scotland Special Collections.

37 Peter Ommundsen, interview, August 17, 2012.

38 Briony Penn, "Recreational Access to Land in Scotland and British Columbia," (PhD dissertation, University of Edinburgh, 1988).

39 (1885), 12 R 1051, Google Books page scans of which are at http://is.gd/6d7xIW (accessed March 1, 2015). A modern summary of the case is at Avizandum, The Scottish Law Wiki, http://scottishlaw.wikia.com/wiki/Winans_v_Macrae_(1885) (accessed March 1, 2015).

40 John Hutton Balfour, *Account of Botanical Excursions made in the Island of Arran during the Months of August and September 1869* (Edinburgh: for private circulation, 1870), 3.631 National Library of Scotland, Special Collections.

41 Ian McTaggart Cowan to James McLean, October 15, 1963, Cowan_PN_233.

42 Garry I. McTaggart Cowan and Ian McTaggart Cowan, "A New Chiton of the Genus *Mopalia* from the North East Pacific Ocean," *Syesis* 10 (1977): 45–52.

43 Roger N. Clark, "Two New Chitons of the Genus *Tripoplax* Berry, 1919 from the Monterey Sea Canyon," *American Malacological Bulletin* 25, no. 1 (2008): 77–86. http://is.gd/Tmg6pn (abstract and references accessed March 5, 2015).

44 Balfour, *Account of Botanical Excursions Made in the Island of Arran*.

45 John Hutton Balfour, *Short Syllabus of the Course of Lectures on Botany Delivered at 9 Surgeons Square Edinburgh by John Hutton Balfour, MD, Ed., FRSE* (Edinburgh, n.d.), 3.631 National Library of Scotland Special Collections.

46 Cowan, interview, July 9, 2002.

47 *The Wonders of the Microscope* (London: Tabart and Co., 1829), 1.

48 *The Wonders of the Microscope*, 131.

49 Bob Weeden, interview, July 26, 2012.

50 Diana Zink Bickford, "Notes from Laura McTaggart Cowan (Mackenzie)" (from unpublished autobiography, 1957), Cowan_PN_050.

51 Cowan, interview, November 30, 2000.

52 Bickford, "Notes from Laura McTaggart Cowan (Mackenzie)."

53 *The Broad Arrow: A Paper for the Services*, August 30, 1873, London, Cowan_PN_050.

54 Hilary Mackenzie, interview, September 7, 2013.

55 Ian McTaggart Cowan, "In the Steps of Southesk" (unpublished essay, ca. 1953), Cowan_PN_294.

56 John M. Mackenzie, *The Empire of Nature: Hunting, Conservation and British Imperialism* (Manchester: Manchester University Press, 1988).

57 Cowan, "In the Steps of Southesk," Cowan_PN_294.

58 Cowan, interview, July 9, 2002.

59 Cowan, interview, November 30, 2000.

60 Cowan, interview, July 9, 2002.

61 George Francis Burba. *Our Bird Friends: Containing Many Things Young Folks Ought to Know – and Likewise Grown-Ups.* (New

York: The Outing Publishing Company, 1908). https://archive.org/stream/ourbird-friendscoooburb#page/n7/mode/2up (accessed October 31, 2014).

62 Cowan, interview, February 2, 2005.

63 Ernest Thompson Seton, *Animal Heroes* (New York: Charles Scribner's Sons, 1905), 140–141. https://archive.org/stream/animal-heroesbeinoosetouoft#page/140/mode/2up (accessed October 31, 2014

64 J.A. Munro and Ian McTaggart Cowan, *A Review of the Bird Fauna of British Columbia* (Victoria: BC Provincial Museum Special Publication no. 2, 1947) [henceforth cited as *Bird Fauna of BC*].

65 Campbell et al., *Birds of BC*, vol. 2, 70.

66 J. Alexander Burnett, *A Passion for Wildlife: The History of the Canadian Wildlife Service* (Vancouver: UBC Press, 2003), 7–8.

67 Ernest Thompson Seton, *Life-Histories of Northern Animals: An Account of the Mammals of Manitoba*, 2 vols. (New York: Charles Scribner's Sons, 1909); *The Arctic Prairies: A Canoe Journey of 2,000 Miles in Search of the Caribou* (New York: Charles Scribner's Sons, 1911). https://archive.org/stream/lifehistoriesofn01seto#page/n9/mode/2up and https://archive.org/stream/arcticprairiesca01seto#page/n9/mode/2up (both accessed October 31, 2014).

68 (New York: Doubleday, Page & Co., 1907). https://archive.org/stream/birchbarkrollof-w00seto#page/n5/mode/2up (accessed October 31, 2014).

69 Richard Mackie, *Hamilton Mack Laing: Hunter-Naturalist* (Victoria: Sono Nis Press, 1985), 49–50. See also, e.g., *Recreation* 21, nos. 1–6 (July to December 1904). https://archive.org/stream/recreation21shie#page/n5/mode/2up (accessed October 31, 2014).

70 Cowan, interview, December 5, 2000.

71 Cowan, interview, November 30, 2000.

72 Cowan, interview, November 30, 2000.

73 Cowan, interview, November 30, 2000.

74 Cowan, interview, November 30, 2000.

75 Cowan, interview, November 30, 2000.

76 Cowan, interview, November 30, 2000.

77 Cowan, "President and Chancellor Address" at 1983 Autumn Convocation, University of Victoria, Cowan_PN_103.

78 Cowan, interview, November 30, 2000.

79 Cowan, interview, November 30, 2000

80 Since *Birds of BC* was written, the Blue Grouse has been split into two species: the Dusky Grouse (*D. obscurus*), native to the interior, and the Sooty Grouse (*D. fuliginosus*), native to the Pacific Coastal mountains and Vancouver Island.

81 Campbell et al., *Birds of BC*, vol. 2, 76–78.

82 Ian McTaggart Cowan, "Two Apparently Fatal Grouse Diseases," *Journal of Wildlife Management* 4, no. 3 (July 1940): 311–312.

83 James Hatter, *Politically Incorrect: The Life and Times of British Columbia's First Game Biologist, An Autobiography* (Victoria, BC: O & J Enterprises, 1997).

84 Fred C. Zwickel and James F. Bendell, *Blue Grouse: Their Biology and Natural History* (Ottawa: NRC Research Press, 2004).

85 Munro and Cowan, *Bird Fauna of BC*, 90.

86 Lee Straight, "Game Likes Its Logging Patchy," BC Outdoors column, *Vancouver Sun*, [ca. 1955].

87 Ian McTaggart Cowan, "Threatened Species of Mammals," in *Proceedings of the 16th International Congress of Zoology, 20–27 August 1963*, John A. Moore, ed., vol. 8 (1964): 20.

88 Zwickel and Bendell, *Blue Grouse*, 184.

89 Zwickel and Bendell, *Blue Grouse*, 184.

90 R.E. Page and A.T. Bergerud, "A Genetic Explanation for Ten-year Cycles of Grouse," *Oecologia* (Berlin) 64, no. 1 (1984): 54–60. http://link.springer.com/article/10.1007%2FBF00377543 (abstract and reference list accessed October 31, 2014).

91 Cowan, interview, November 30, 2000.

92 Ian McTaggart Cowan to Carl Clifford, September 22, 1941, GR-0111, Box 03, File 04, BCA.

93 Munro and Cowan, *Bird Fauna of BC*, 90.

94 Ian McTaggart Cowan, "The Holotype of the Franklin Grouse (*Canachites franklinii*)," *The Canadian Field-Naturalist* 78, no. 2 (1964): 127–128. www.biodiversitylibrary.org/item/89058#page/141/mode/1up (accessed October 31, 2014).

95 Cowan, interview, November 30, 2000.

96 Cowan, interview, November 30, 2000.

97 Cowan, interview, November 30, 2000.

98 McTaggart Cowan [Sr.], "Flora of BC," letter to the editor, *The Daily Province* (Vancouver), February 11, 1916, 8.

99 McTaggart Cowan [Sr.] to Francis Kermode, February 1916, GR-0111, Box 03, File 04, BCA.

100 Nancy J. Turner, *The Earth's Blanket* (Vancouver: Douglas & McIntyre, 2005), 172.

101 Ian McTaggart Cowan to Rodger Hunter, February 1997, Cowan_PN_005.

102 McTaggart Cowan [Sr.] to Jennifer Charlesworth, November 1968, Cowan_PN_504.

103 Cowan, interview, July 9, 2002.

104 Cowan, interview, July 9, 2002.

105 Cowan, interview, November 30, 2000.

106 Patrick McTaggart Cowan and Klaus Beltzner, eds., *Living with Climatic Change: Proceedings Toronto Conference Workshop, November 17–22, 1975* (Ottawa: Science Council of Canada, 1976). http://arizona.openrepository.com/arizona/bitstream/10150/303430/1/ltrr-0083.pdf (accessed October 31, 2014).

107 Gordon McBean, Michael Garstang and Donald Henderson, "Patrick McTaggart Cowan: Necrologies," *Bulletin of the American Meteorological Society,* 79, no. 1 (January 1998): 110–111. (EBSCOHost full-text pdf 216332 accessed October 31, 2014, via proxy server; please consult your local public library or a university library as to availability).

108 Cowan, *Living with Climatic Change,* 7.

109 Joanne Hatherly, "She Wanted Designs to Sing," Victoria *Times Colonist,* May 16, 2008, C4.

110 Jean Barman, *Growing up British in British Columbia: Boys in Private School, 1900–1950* (Vancouver: UBC Press, 1984).

111 Cowan, interview, November 30, 2000.

112 Cowan and Guiguet, *Mammals of BC,* 320–321.

113 Cowan, interview, November 30, 2000.

114 Cowan, interview, November 30, 2000.

115 Cowan, interview, November 30, 2000. [No evidence for this competition has been found to date in the Canadian Museum of Nature's Percy Taverner Collection: Chantal Dussault, personal communication, October 26, 2013.]

116 Ian McTaggart Cowan to Francis Kermode, October 25, 1925, BC Provincial Museum, GR-0111, Box 03, File 04, BCA.

117 Munro and Cowan, *Bird Fauna of BC.*

118 Cowan, interview, November 30, 2000.

119 James L. Baillie, "In Memoriam: James Alexander Munro," *The Auk* 86, no. 4 (1969): 624–630.

120 Campbell et al., *Birds of BC,* vol. 4, 287.

121 J.A. Munro, *An Introduction to Bird Study in British Columbia* (Victoria: Department of Education, 1931), 7.

122 Ian McTaggart Cowan to J.A. Munro, May 3, 1926, Cowan_PN_003.

123 Cowan, interview, November 30, 2000.

124 Cowan, interview, November 30, 2000.

125 Campbell et al., *Birds of BC,* vol. 4, 520.

126 Campbell et al., *Birds of BC,* vol. 4, 507.

127 J.A. Munro to I.M. Cowan, May 6, 1926, Cowan_PN_003.

128 Cowan, interview, December 5, 2000.

129 Cowan, interview, November 30, 2000.

130 Burnett, *A Passion for Wildlife,* 9.

131 J.A. Munro, "P.A. Taverner, An Appreciation: 1875–1947," *The Canadian Field-Naturalist* 62, no. 1 (January–February 1948): 35. www.biodiversitylibrary.org/item/89251#page/44/mode/1up (accessed October 31, 2014).

132 P.A. Taverner, *Birds of Western Canada,* Museum Bulletin no. 41 (Ottawa: King's Printer, 1926), 318. http://peel.library.ualberta.ca/bibliography/5112/464.html (accessed October 31, 2014).

133 John L. Cranmer-Byng, "A Life with Birds: Percy A. Taverner, Canadian Ornithologist, 1875–1947," special issue, *The Canadian Field-Naturalist* 110, no. 1 (January–March 1996): 42.

134 Ian McTaggart Cowan, "Moments from the Education of an Ornithologist: The Second Doris Huestis Speirs Lecture," *Picoides* 11, no. 2 (November 1998): 19. www.sco-soc.ca/picoides/archive/Picoides11_2_1998.pdf (pdf p21, accessed October 31, 2014). [The MS of this article, Cowan_PN_104 at p4, differs slightly from the text published in *Picoides.*]

135 Burnett, *A Passion for Wildlife,* 9.

136 C. Gordon Hewitt, *The Conservation of the Wild Life of Canada* (New York: Charles Scribner's Sons, 1921), ix. https://archive.org/stream/conservationwilo1hewigoog#page/n16/mode/2up (accessed October 31, 2014).

137 Duncan C. Scott, Memoir, Royal Society of Canada (1921), quoted in Hewitt, *The Conservation of the Wild Life of Canada,* ix.

138 Hewitt, *The Conservation of the Wild Life of Canada,* 1. https://archive.org/stream/conservationwilo1hewigoog#page/n30/mode/2up (accessed October 31, 2014).

139 Hewitt, *The Conservation of the Wild Life of Canada,* 151. https://archive.org/stream/

conservationwilo1hewigoog#page/n206/mode/2up (accessed October 31, 2014).

140 Burnett, *A Passion for Wildlife*, 9.

141 E.J. Hart, *J.B. Harkin: The Father of National Parks* (Edmonton: University of Alberta Press, 2010), 2.

142 J.B. Harkin, "Our Need for National Parks," *Canadian Alpine Journal* 9 (1918): 102. https://archive.org/stream/canadianalpine-joo9alpiuoft#page/n141/mode/2up (accessed October 31, 2014).

143 Taverner, *Birds of Western Canada*, 257–258. http://peel.library.ualberta.ca/bibliography/5112/355.html (accessed October 31, 2014).

144 Canadian Forestry Assn., *The Forests and The People*, pamphlet, n.d., 5. https://archive.org/stream/cihm_72922#page/n9/mode/2up (accessed October 31, 2014) [excerpted editorially in Victoria *Daily Colonist*, "Forests and the People," August 8, 1908, 4 at bottom of first column. http://archive.org/stream/dailycolonist19080808uvic/19080808#page/n3/mode/1up (accessed October 31, 2014)].

145 G.O. Buchanan, "Preservation of Canadian Forests," Victoria *Daily Times*, May 14, 1908.

146 *Toronto Globe*, "Ottawa Welcomes Dr. Oronhyatekha," November 26, 1903.

147 Victoria *Daily Colonist*, "Forests and the People," August 8, 1908, 4; also in Canadian Forestry Assn., *The Forests and The People*, 9. https://archive.org/stream/cihm_72922#page/n13/mode/2up (accessed October 31, 2014)

148 Hart, *J.B. Harkin*, 79–80.

149 William T. Hornaday, *Our Vanishing Wild Life: Its Extermination and Preservation* (New York: Charles Scribner's Sons, 1913), ix. https://archive.org/stream/ourvanishingwildoohorn#page/n13/mode/2up (accessed October 31, 2014).

150 Aldo Leopold Archives, University of Wisconsin Digital Collections, http://uwdc.library.wisc.edu/collections/AldoLeopold (accessed February 6, 2015).

151 Aldo Leopold, "The Conservation Ethic," *Journal of Forestry* 31, no. 6 (October 1933): 634–643.

152 Herbert L. Stoddard, *Memoirs of a Naturalist* (Norman: University of Oklahoma Press, 1969), 284.

153 Taverner, *Birds of Western Canada*, 160. http://peel.library.ualberta.ca/bibliography/5112/212.html (accessed October 31, 2014).

154 B. of V., *Lessons of the Brotherhood of Venery: Supplement*. (US: Privately printed for the use of the Order, n.d.).

155 B. of V. ed., *Some Lessons* (US: privately printed for the use of the Order by F.C. Walcott, 1939), 56–62.

156 Edward, Second Duke of York, *The Master of Game*, edited by Wm. A. and F. Baillie-Grohman with a foreword by Theodore Roosevelt, 2nd ed. (London: Chatto & Windus, 1909). https://archive.org/stream/masterofgameoldexxooedwa#page/n9/mode/2up (accessed October 31, 2014). Page images of an illuminated MS copy of the Phébus work, ca. 1485, can be viewed chez la Bibliothèque de Genève, http://is.gd/o2AQPO (accessed October 31, 2014).

157 In B. of V. ed., *Some Lessons*, 79–83.

158 In B. of V. ed., *Some Lessons: Volume 2*, 11–14; and in that same volume, "Clandeboye," 23–26; "The Geese Return," 37; "On a Monument to the Pigeon," 47–49.

159 Hoyes Lloyd, "Cavemen and their Ritual," in *Some Lessons*, ed. B. of V., 5–8.

160 Lloyd, "Cavemen and their Ritual," 7.

161 Lloyd, "Cavemen and their Ritual," 8.

162 Lloyd, "Cavemen and their Ritual," 7. (The second annual meeting was held a year later at the Hotel Pennsylvania in New York City on December 6, 1926.)

163 Hewitt, *The Conservation of the Wild Life of Canada*, 5. https://archive.org/stream/conservationwilo1hewigoog#page/n34/mode/2up (accessed October 31, 2014).

164 Janet Foster, *Working for Wildlife: The Beginning of Preservation in Canada*, 1st ed. (Toronto: University of Toronto Press, 1978); 2nd ed. (Toronto: University of Toronto Press, 1998).

165 Alan MacEachern, "Voices Crying in the Wilderness: Recent Works in Canadian Environmental History," *Acadiensis* 31, no. 2 (Spring 2002). http://is.gd/GtMVWf (accessed October 31, 2014).

166 Hewitt, *The Conservation of the Wild Life of Canada*, v. https://archive.org/stream/conservationwilo1hewigoog#page/n12/mode/2up (accessed October 31, 2014).

167 Lorne Hammond, "Introduction," in Janet Foster, *Working for Wildlife: The Beginning of Preservation in Canada*, 2nd ed. (Toronto: University of Toronto Press, 1998), xi.

168 Hammond in Foster, *Working for Wildlife*, xi.

169 Lloyd, "Cavemen and Their Ritual," 5.

170 Burnett, *A Passion for Wildlife*, 17.

171 Cowan and Guiguet, *Mammals of BC*, 387.

172 Burnett, *A Passion for Wildlife*, 17.

173 David A. Munro, "Tribute to Hoyes Lloyd, 1888–1978," *The Canadian Field-Naturalist* 93, no. 3 (July–September 1979): 332. http://is.gd/slAnK4 (accessed October 31, 2014).

174 Munro, "Tribute to Hoyes Lloyd," 331. http://is.gd/ZduFoJ (accessed October 31, 2014).

175 Burnett, *A Passion for Wildlife*, 13.

176 Burnett, *A Passion for Wildlife*, 13.

177 Hoyes Lloyd, "Field journals," August 30, 1909, unorganized collection, Royal Ontario Museum Ornithology Collection.

178 Daniel Brunton, personal communication, October 30, 2013.

179 Campbell et al., *Birds of BC*, vol. 3, 107.

180 Munro, "Tribute to Hoyes Lloyd," 332.

181 Francis Harper, letter to the editor, *Canadian Field-Naturalist* 39, no 2 (February 1925): 45. http://is.gd/DqaK7u (accessed October 31, 2014).

182 Brunton, personal communication, October 30, 2013.

183 Brunton, personal communication, October 30, 2013.

184 Harrison Lewis, "Lively: A History of the Canadian Wildlife Service, vol. 1," unpublished MS, Canadian Wildlife Service, Ottawa, R653-207-8-E [n.d.]. (The full story is described in E.J. Hart's biography of Harkin, though the trigger to create the 'B' is not covered there.)

185 Brunton, personal communication, October 30, 2013.

186 Michael W. Giese, "A Federal Foundation for Wildlife Conservation: The Evolution of the National Wildlife Refuge System, 1920–1968" (PhD dissertation, American University, 2008). http://gradworks.umi.com/33/05/3305788.html (abstract accessed October 31, 2014).

187 Giese, "A Federal Foundation for Wildlife Conservation".

188 B. of V. *Lessons of the Brotherhood of Venery: Supplement*, 4.

189 Harrison Lewis, "Editorial: The Wilderness," *The Canadian Field-Naturalist* 39, no. 2 (February 1925): 41. http://is.gd/eo3XJK (accessed October 31, 2014).

190 Lewis "Editorial: The Wilderness," 41.

191 J. Anthony Lukas, *Big Trouble: A Murder in a Small Western Town Sets Off a Struggle for the Soul of America* (New York: Simon & Schuster, 1997), 621. http://is.gd/OsRyaT (accessed October 31, 2014).

192 Timothy Egan, *The Big Burn: Teddy Roosevelt and the Fire that Saved America* (Boston: Houghton Mifflin Harcourt, 2009), 42 (quoting from Roosevelt's first State of the Union message to Congress, December 3, 1901).

193 B. of V. ed., *Some Lessons*, 68 (quoting from Viscount Grey's *Fallodon Papers* (London: Constable, 1926)).

194 Campbell et al., *Birds of BC*, vol. 3, 344–349.

195 B. of V. ed., *Some Lessons*, 68.

196 Barbara Mearns and Richard Mearns, *The Bird Collectors* (Waltham, Mass.: Academic Press, 1998).

197 Treadwell Cleveland, "NA Conservation Conference" (proceedings), *Conservation* [American Forestry Assn. magazine] 15, no. 3 (April 1909): 159–168. www.theodore-roosevelt.com/images/research/northamericanccreport.pdf (pdf accessed December 6, 2014).

198 Munro, "Tribute to Hoyes Lloyd," 331.

199 Francis Galton, "Hereditary Talent and Character," *Macmillan's Magazine* 12, no. 70 (1865): 319–320. http://galton.org/essays/1860-1869/galton-1865-hereditary-talent.pdf (pdf pp12–13, accessed October 31, 2014). Quoted in Edward J. Larson, "Biology and the Emergence of the Anglo-American Eugenics Movement," in *Biology and Ideology from Descartes to Dawkins*, ed. Denis R. Alexander and Ronald L. Numbers (Chicago: University of Chicago Press, 2010).

200 Theodore Roosevelt to Charles Davenport, January 3, 1913, Charles B. Davenport Papers, 1242, American Philosophical Society Library. http://diglib.amphilsoc.org/islandora/object/graphics:1487 (accessed October 31, 2014).

201 Angus McLaren, *Our Own Master Race: Eugenics in Canada, 1885–1945* (Toronto: McClelland & Stewart, 1990). See also, e.g., the Supreme Court of Canada decision in *E. (Mrs.) v. Eve*, [1986] 2 SCR 388, and the Alberta Queen's Bench judgment in *Muir v. Alberta*, 1996 CanLII 7287. http://canlii.ca/t/1ftqt and http://canlii.ca/t/1p6lq, respectively (accessed October 31, 2014).

202 Ian McTaggart Cowan, "The Challenge We

Take," in *Transactions of the Twentieth North American Wildlife Conference, March 14–16, 1955*. (Washington: Wildlife Management Institute, 1955), 669.

203 Cowan, "The Challenge We Take" 669.

204 Ian McTaggart Cowan, "The Penalties of Ignorance of Man's Biological Dependence," in *Our Debt to the Future: Proceedings of the Royal Society of Canada Symposium presented on the 75th Anniversary of the Society*, ed. E.G.D. Murray, 41.

205 Cowan, "Of Mice and Men." https://circle.ubc.ca/flashstreamview/bitstream/handle/2429/36425/ubc_at_010_cowan.mp3?sequence=1 (78:59 of streaming audio accessed October 19, 2013: discussion of Darwin's lecture begins at ~58:05; quoted words of Cowan begin at ~58:25).

206 Cowan, interview, February 2, 2005.

207 Ernest Thompson Seton, "Message of the Indian," in *Some Lessons*, ed. B of V., 71. (Seton's address was read to the 'B' in 1935.)

208 Egan, *The Big Burn*, 47–49.

209 Susan Flader, *Thinking Like a Mountain: Aldo Leopold and the Evolution of an Ecological Attitude Toward Deer, Wolves and Forests* (Columbia: University of Missouri Press, 1974).

210 Flader, *Thinking Like a Mountain*, 25.

211 Stanley A. Temple, Senior Fellow of Aldo Leopold Foundation, personal communication, March 2, 2015; *see also* Aldo Leopold, "Summarization of the Twelfth North American Wildlife Conference, San Antonio, Texas, February 3–5, 1947," condensed in *National Parks Magazine* 21, no. 89 (April/June 1947): 26–28.

212 Cowan, interview, December 5, 2000.

213 Leonard Wing to Aldo Leopold, July 18, 1947, Box 001, Folder 002, Professional Correspondence 1937–1948, Aldo Leopold Archives, University of Wisconsin Digital Collections. http://images.library.wisc.edu/AldoLeopold/EFacs/ALBio/ALBMCorr/reference/aldoleopold.albmcorr.i0002.pdf (pdf p96, accessed March 2, 2015).

214 Cowan, interview, December 5, 2000.

215 Campbell et al., *Birds of BC*, vol. 2, 94.

216 A. Starker Leopold et al., "Our Wildlife Refuges – A Hard Critical Look: A Report to the Secretary of the Interior from the Advisory Board on Wildlife Management," *Audubon Magazine* 70, no. 3 (1968): 8–26.

217 Ian McTaggart Cowan, "The Organic World and Its Environment," in *Future Environments of North America*, ed. Frank Fraser Darling and John P. Milton (New York: Natural History Press, 1966), 21.

218 Fred Evensen to Ian McTaggart Cowan, address on the awarding of the Wildlife Society Aldo Leopold Medal for 1970, Cowan_PN_159.

219 Bob Weeden, interview, July 26, 2012.

220 Ian McTaggart Cowan, "Small Mammals of the Western Mountains," *Canadian Geographical Journal* 47, no. 4 (1953): 130–141.

221 Hoyes Lloyd, "Man and Some of His Heritage from the Past," in *Some Lessons*, ed. B. of V., 33–34.

222 J.B. Harkin, "Canadian National Parks," in *Proceedings of the National Parks Conference Held at the National Museum, Washington, DC, January 2–6, 1917* (Washington, DC: Government Printing Office, January 5, 1917), 268. https://archive.org/stream/proceedingsofnat001917#page/268/mode/2up/search/harkin (accessed October 31, 2014).

223 Bernadette McDonald, *Brotherhood of the Rope: The Biography of Charles Houston* (Seattle: The Mountaineers Books, 2007).

224 Jessica L. Harland-Jacobs, *Builders of Empire: Freemasons and British Imperialism 1717–1927* (Chapel Hill: University of North Carolina Press, 2007), 16.

225 Harland-Jacobs, *Builders of Empire*, 17.

226 Harland-Jacobs, *Builders of Empire*, 4, 6.

227 Greg Gillespie, "The Empire's Eden: British Hunters, Travel Writing and Imperialism in Nineteenth-Century Canada," in *The Culture of Hunting in Canada*, ed. Jean L. Manore and Dale G. Miner (Vancouver: University of British Columbia Press, 2007), 44–45.

228 James B. Harkin, "Man's Brotherhood with the Wild," in *Some Lessons*, ed. B. of V., 91.

229 Tina Loo, *States of Nature: Conserving Canada's Wildlife in the Twentieth Century* (Vancouver: UBC Press, 2006).

230 Loo, *States of Nature*, 18.

231 Loo, *States of Nature*, 1.

232 Loo, *States of Nature*, 40.

233 Cowan, "Small Mammals of the Western Mountains," 137.

234 Cowan, interview, July 9, 2002.

235 Campbell et al., *Birds of BC*, vol. 1.

236 H.J. Vaux et al., "Aldo Starker Leopold, Zoology; Forestry and Conservation: Berkeley,"

University of California: In Memoriam 1985, University of California Digital Archives. http://content.cdlib.org/view?docId=hb4d-5nb20m&brand=calisphere (accessed February 3, 2014).

237 Ian McTaggart Cowan to Tom Beck, November 24, 1984, Cowan_PN_285.

238 Stew Lang, "BC-muzzled Expert Quits Ecology Post," Victoria *Times Colonist*, June 6, 1984, A1.

239 Cowan, interview, July 9, 2002.

240 Sylvia Leroy and Barry Cooper, *Off Limits: How Radical Environmentalists Are Stealing Canada's National Parks* (Vancouver: Fraser Institute, 2000). http://is.gd/77zOR8 (accessed October 31, 2014).

241 Leroy and Cooper, 14.

242 Tom Beck, interview, September 25–26, 2012.

243 Lloyd, "Cave Men and their Ritual," in *Some Lessons*, ed. B. of V., 8.

244 Cowan, interview, July 9, 2002.

245 Cowan and Guiguet, *Mammals of BC*, 109.

246 *North Vancouver High School Annual, 1927*, Cowan_PN_074.

247 Ian McTaggart Cowan, interview, February 26, 2001.

248 *North Vancouver High School Annual 1927*, Cowan_PN_074.

249 Vernon "Bert" Brink, "Brink on Davidson," interview audio and transcript at *John Davidson: The Legacy of a Canadian Botanist*, a website by UBC Botanical Garden and the Virtual Museum of Canada [n.d.], 7. www.botanyjohn.org/en/in-depth-study/brink-on-davidson?page=0,6-davidson-and-the-bc-botanists (accessed March 14, 2013). [NB: After first noting a failure of this URL to connect, on February 1, 2015, Rocky Mountain Books monitored botanyjohn.org bi-weekly for the ensuing six months, and the site was inaccessible every time. It may have been taken down altogether.]

250 Kenneth Racey and Ian McTaggart Cowan, *Mammals of the Alta Lake Region of Southwestern British Columbia* (Victoria: Report of the Provincial Museum, 1935), H18.

251 Racey and Cowan, *Mammals of the Alta Lake Region*, H25.

252 Cowan, interview, July 9, 2002.

253 Cowan, interview, July 9, 2002.

254 Racey and Cowan, *Mammals of the Alta Lake Region*, H26.

255 David Elliston Allen, "Balfour, John Hutton (1808–1884)," *Oxford Dictionary of National Biography*, Oxford University Press, 2004. www.oxforddnb.com/view/article/1192 (citation only; accessed Oct. 22, 2013; full text may be available through your local public or university library).

256 Cowan, interview, November 30, 2000.

257 Bristol Foster, interview, July 24, 2012.

258 Foster, interview, July 24, 2012.

259 Foster, interview, July 24, 2012.

260 Hatter, *Politically Incorrect*, 43.

261 Cowan, interview, November 30, 2000.

262 Cowan, interview, November 30, 2000.

263 J.V. Remsen Jr., "The Importance of Continued Collecting of Bird Specimens to Ornithology and Bird Conservation," *Bird Conservation International* 5 (1995): 145–180 at 150–153. http://is.gd/G3Q53O (pdf accessed October 31, 2014); E.H. Miller, ed., *Museum Collections: Their Roles and Future in Biological Research*, BC Provincial Museum Occasional Paper no. 25 (1985), 139–162.

264 David Nagorsen, personal communication, April 5, 2014.

265 Cowan, interview, November 30, 2000. [In curatorial parlance, "to look out" specimens means to locate them in the collection; compare "to look up" something in a book or library.]

266 BC Ornithologists Union, "The Migrant" (binder of unpublished correspondence, 1922–1924), Cowan_PN_302.

267 Campbell et al., *Birds of BC*, vol. 3, 130.

268 BC Ornithologists Union, "The Migrant."

269 BC Ornithologists Union, "The Migrant."

270 BC Ornithologists Union, "The Migrant."

271 BC Ornithologists Union, "The Migrant."

272 Campbell et al., *Birds of BC*, vol. 2, 418.

273 Mearns and Mearns, *The Bird Collectors*, 369.

274 Mearns and Mearns, *The Bird Collectors*, 370–371.

275 William Z. Lidicker Jr., "Population Ecology," in *Seventy-five Years of Mammalogy, 1919–1994*, ed. Elmer C. Birney and Jerry R. Choate (Provo, Utah: American Society of Mammalogists, 1994), 324. https://archive.org/stream/seventyfiveyears-oobirn#page/324/mode/2up (accessed October 31, 2014).

276 Lidicker, "Population Ecology," in *Seventy-five Years of Mammalogy*, 324.

277 Racey and Cowan, *Mammals of the Alta Lake Region*, H15.

278 *Montreal Daily Star*, "Cartoons of Canada According to American Movies," a series that appeared during 1923.

279 Eileen Racey to Kenneth Racey, August 23, 1923, Cowan_PN_026.

280 Campbell et al., *Birds of BC*, vol. 1, 162.

281 Joyce Racey to Kenneth Racey, August 6, 1923, Cowan_PN_026.

282 Eileen Racey to Kenneth Racey, September 6, 1923, Cowan_PN_129.

283 Racey and Cowan, *Mammals of the Alta Lake Region*, H23.

284 Joyce Racey to Kenneth Racey, July 19, 1923, Cowan_PN_026.

285 Campbell et al., *Birds of BC*, vol. 3, 422–428.

286 Ian McTaggart Cowan, "Field Journal 1932–1934," July 22, 1933, in vol. 573 at Museum of Vertebrate Zoology Archive, Berkeley [MVZA]. [Also Cowan_FN_058].

287 Cowan, "Moments from the Education of an Ornithologist," 20. www.sco-soc.ca/picoides/archive/Picoides11_2_1998.pdf (pdf p22, accessed October 31, 2014).

288 Racey family photograph albums, Cowan_PN_019, 020.

289 Cowan, interview, December 5, 2000.

290 Racey and Cowan, *Mammals of the Alta Lake Region*, H25.

291 Ann Schau, interview, October 9, 2012.

292 Racey and Cowan, *Mammals of the Alta Lake Region*, H28.

293 Joyce McTaggart Cowan to Ann Schau, September 16, 1990, Cowan_PN_504.

294 Racey and Cowan, *Mammals of the Alta Lake Region*, H22.

295 Racey and Cowan, *Mammals of the Alta Lake Region*, H25.

296 Nagorsen, *Rodents and Lagomorphs of British Columbia*, 310.

297 *Montreal Daily Star*, "Cartoons of Canada According to American Movies."

298 *Montreal Daily Star*, "Cartoons of Canada According to American Movies."

299 Racey and Cowan, *Mammals of the Alta Lake Region*, H25.

300 B. Max Götz, "Shadows of Whistler: Kenneth R. Racey and Friends in Alta Lake," *Pique* Newsmagazine, February 12, 1999. www.piquenewsmagazine.com/whistler/

natural-history/Content?oid=2137117 (accessed May 23, 2014).

301 Cowan, "Field journal for trips 1935–1961," December 29, 1935. Cowan_FN_014.

302 Cowan and Guiguet, *Mammals of BC*, 339.

303 Götz, "Shadows of Whistler."

304 Ian McTaggart Cowan, "Mammals of Point Grey," *The Canadian Field-Naturalist* 44, no. 6 (September 1930): 133. www.biodiversitylibrary.org/item/89659#page/167/mode/1up. (accessed October 31, 2014).

305 Cowan, "Mammals of Point Grey," 134.

306 Cowan, "Mammals of Point Grey," 134.

307 Ian McTaggart Cowan to BC Premier William Vander Zalm, July 6, 1987, Cowan_PN_016.

308 Cowan, "Mammals of Point Grey," 134.

309 Cowan, interview, December 5, 2000.

310 Mary N. Arai, "Charles McLean Fraser (1872–1946) – His Contributions to Hydroid Research and to the Development of Fisheries Biology and Academia in British Columbia," *Hydrobiologia* 530/531 no. 1 (2004): 3–11.

311 Cowan and Guiguet, *Mammals of BC*, 347–348.

312 Robert Scagel, interview, August 8, 2012.

313 Cowan, interview, December 5, 2000.

314 Cowan, interview, December 5, 2000.

315 Cowan, interview, December 5, 2000.

316 Beaty Biodiversity Museum, "History of the Spencer Entomological Collection." http://beatymuseum.ubc.ca/entomolgical-collection-history (accessed March 22, 2013; URL typo sic).

317 Ann Taylor, personal communication, October 27, 2013.

318 Cowan, interview, December 5, 2000.

319 Cowan, interview, December 5, 2000.

320 Cowan, interview, July 9, 2002.

321 Cowan, interview, July 9, 2002.

322 University of British Columbia Herbarium, "Fungal Collection History, Database." www.biodiversity.ubc.ca/museum/herbarium/fungi/index.html (accessed March 21, 2013).

323 "Andrew Hutchinson fonds (1888–1975)" (description of fonds in UBC Archives and UBC Special Collections). www.library.ubc.ca/archives/u_arch/hutch.pdf (pdf accessed May 24, 2014).

324 "Andrew Hutchinson fonds."

325 Cowan, interview, July 9, 2002.

326 Cowan, interview, December 5, 2000.

327 Trevor Goward, interview, March 25, 2013.

328 Cowan and Guiguet, *Mammals of BC*, 60.

329 Cowan, interview, February 2, 2005.

330 C. Andresen Hubbard, "The Fleas of California," *Pacific University Bulletin* 39, no. 8 (June 1943): 7 [specimen 88*(121)]. http://commons.pacificu.edu/casfac/22 (linked pdf p9 accessed October 31, 2014).

331 Cowan and Guiguet, *Mammals of BC*, 113–114.

332 Cowan, interview, December 5, 2000.

333 *Cariboo Observer*, "Farmers' Institutes Hold Annual Meeting [at] Canim Lake Lodge," June 29, 1946, 1, 4. www.quesnelmuseum.ca/CaribooObserverDocs/1946/19460629_Cariboo%20Observer.pdf (pdf accessed February 20, 2015).

334 George Spencer, "Obituary: Edward Ronald Buckell," *Journal of the Entomological Society of British Columbia* 60 (1963).

335 Ian McTaggart Cowan, "Chemical Sprays and Their Relation to Wildlife," *Proceedings of the Ninth Annual BC Game Convention, May 25–28, 1955*, at Nelson, BC (Victoria: Queen's Printer, 1955).

336 *Calgary Herald*, "Put Ecology First U Grads Are Told," June 1971.

337 *Calgary Herald*, "Put Ecology First U Grads Are Told."

338 *Calgary Herald*, "Put Ecology First U Grads Are Told."

339 Cowan and Guiguet, *Mammals of BC*, 119.

340 Ian McTaggart Cowan, "Note on Yellow-bellied Marmot," *The Murrelet* 10 (1929): 64.

341 Ian McTaggart Cowan, "Notes on Mammalian Ecology 1929," May 24, 1929, Cowan_FN_020.

342 Ian McTaggart Cowan, "Small Mammals of the Western Mountains," *Canadian Geographical Journal* 47, no. 4 (1953): 131.

343 Ian McTaggart Cowan, "Notes on the Distribution of the Chipmunks (*Eutamias*) in Southern British Columbia and the Rocky Mountain Region of Southern Alberta with Descriptions of Two New Races," *Proceedings of the Biological Society of Washington* 59 (October 25, 1946): 107–116. www.biodiversitylibrary.org/page/34566253#page/335/mode/1up (accessed October 31, 2014).

344 Cowan, "Notes on Mammalian Ecology," 13.

345 Cowan, "Notes on Mammalian Ecology," 12.

346 Cowan, "Notes on Mammalian Ecology," 18.

347 Cowan, "Notes on Mammalian Ecology," 18.

348 Cowan and Guiguet, *Mammals of BC*, 316.

349 Cowan, "Notes on Mammalian Ecology," 22.

350 Cowan and Guiguet, *Mammals of BC*, 149.

351 Cowan, "Notes on Mammalian Ecology," 25.

352 Ian McTaggart Cowan, "Mammals of Kamloops," 7 (unpublished field guide, 1929), Cowan_PN_381.

353 Cowan, "Mammals of Kamloops," Cowan_PN_381.

354 Cowan and Guiguet, *Mammals of BC*, 56.

355 Cowan, "Notes on Mammalian Ecology," 43.

356 Cowan and Guiguet, *Mammals of BC*, 191.

357 R.M. Anderson to H.M. Laing, December 26, 1929, H.M. Laing fonds, BCA.

358 Cowan, interview, July 9, 2002.

359 Hamilton Mack Laing, *Allan Brooks: Artist Naturalist* (Victoria: BC Provincial Museum, 1979).

360 Jean Webber, "Major Allan Brooks of Okanagan Landing," *Living Landscapes* (website), Royal BC Museum, n.d. http://142.36.5.21/thomp-ok/allan_books/major-allan.html (accessed April 10, 2014).

361 Webber, "Major Allan Brooks of Okanagan Landing."

362 Richard Mackie, *Hamilton Mack Laing: Hunter–Naturalist* (Victoria: Sono Nis Press, 1985), 137.

363 Campbell et al., *Birds of BC*, vol. 2, 32.

364 Tina Loo, *States of Nature: Conserving Canada's Wildlife in the Twentieth Century*. Vancouver: UBC Press, 2006.

365 Allan Brooks to Joseph Grinnell, March 28, 1926, MSS.0117, MVZ Historical Correspondence, MVZA.

366 Jack Miner, *Jack Miner: His Life and Religion* (Kingsville, Ont.: Jack Miner Migratory Bird Foundation, 1969).

367 Joseph Grinnell to Allan Brooks. November 9, 1930, MSS.0117, MVZ Historical Correspondence, MVZA.

368 Grinnell to Brooks, November 9, 1930, MSS.0117, MVZ Historical Correspondence, MVZA.

369 Brooks to Grinnell, July 21, 1930. MSS.0117, MVZ Historical Correspondence, MVZA.

370 Grinnell to Brooks, November 9, 1930, MVZA.

371 Cowan, "Moments from the Education of an Ornithologist," *Picoides* 11, no. 2 (November 1998): 21 [pdf 23]. www.sco-soc.ca/picoides/

archive/Picoides11_2_1998.pdf (accessed October 31, 2014).

372 Victoria *Times Colonist*, "Birdman of BC Relished Natural High," September 24, 2000, C2.

373 Campbell et al., *Birds of BC*, vol. 3, 376.

374 Cowan, interview, February 26, 2001.

375 Ian McTaggart Cowan, "Job application: Field party – Dominion Parks, with references," [ca. March] 1930, Cowan_PN_002.

376 Cowan and Guiguet, *Mammals of BC*, 163–164.

377 Cowan, "Job application," Cowan_PN_002.

378 David Campbell autograph note, ca. 1980, as attached to "Job application," Cowan_PN_002.

379 R.M. Anderson to H.M. Laing, December 26, 1929, H.M. Laing fonds, BCA.

380 Cowan, interview, December 5, 2000.

381 Loo, *States of Nature*, 20.

382 Cowan, interview, November 30, 2000.

383 Ian McTaggart Cowan, interview by Richard Mackie, July 1983, quoted in Mackie, *Hamilton Mack Laing*, 189.

384 Cowan and Guiguet, *Mammals of BC*, 324–325.

385 H.M. Laing to P. Taverner, May 6, 1936, Percy Taverner fonds, National Museum of Nature Archive, quoted in Mackie, *Hamilton Mack Laing*, 65.

386 H.M. Laing to Hoyes Lloyd, December 3, 1926, H.M. Laing fonds, Public Archives of Canada (PAC) quoted in Mackie, *Hamilton Mack Laing*, 131.

387 H.M. Laing, "Nature Diary, 1930, April 16 to November 3," April 27, 1930 [original at RBCM, File P-2 FIE-10].

388 Campbell et al., *Birds of BC*, vol. 2, 122.

389 Cowan, "Moments from the Education of an Ornithologist," 19.

390 R.M. Anderson to H.M. Laing, April 24, 1929, H.M. Laing fonds, BCA.

391 Ian McTaggart Cowan, "Field Notes 1930 British Columbia," June 2, 1930, Cowan_FN_022. [Cowan_FN_022 is Cowan's typewritten copy of the original journal, which is in the Museum of Nature, Ottawa. Cowan_FN_007 is the Field Catalogue for this trip; Cowan_FN_008 is the Specimen Catalogue.]

392 Cowan and Guiguet, *Mammals of BC*, 126.

393 Laing, "Nature Diary, 1930," April 29, 1930 [original at RBCM, File P-2 FIE-10].

394 Elizabeth Vibert, "Real Men Hunt Buffalo: Masculinity, Class and Race in British Fur Traders' Narratives," *Gender and History* 8, no. 1 (April 1996): 4. http://is.gd/XtoC7U (first-page preview accessed October 31, 2014).

395 Cowan, "Field Notes 1930," May 1, 1930, Cowan_FN_022.

396 H.M. Laing and I.M. Cowan, "Field Notes British Columbia 1930," May 1, 1930, Ornithology Collection, Canadian Museum of Nature, Cowan_FN_056.

397 David Nagorsen et al., "Conserving Mammals at Risk: The Role of Taxonomy," in *At Risk: Proceedings of a Conference on the Biology of Species and Habitats at Risk, February 15–19, 1999*, vol. 1 (Victoria: BC Ministry of Environment, Lands and Parks; Kamloops, BC: University College of the Cariboo, 2000), 41–48. http://is.gd/T1AkSq (pdf accessed October 31, 2014).

398 Laing, "Nature Diary," May 1, 1930 [original at RBCM, File P-2 FIE-10].

399 Cowan, "Notes on the Distribution of the Chipmunks (*Eutamias*)," 107–116. www.biodiversitylibrary.org/page/34566253#page/335/mode/1up (accessed October 31, 2014).

400 Cowan, *Small Mammals of the Western Mountains*, 134.

401 Cowan, "Field Notes 1930 British Columbia," June 2, 1930, Cowan_FN_022.

402 Cowan and Guiguet, *Mammals of BC*, 156–157.

403 Ian McTaggart Cowan, "Nesting Habits of the Flying Squirrel *Glaucomys sabrinus*," *Journal of Mammalogy* 17, no. 1 (1936): 58–60.

404 Judy Weeden, personal communication, July 26, 2012.

405 Laing, *Allan Brooks*, 168, quoted in Mackie, *Hamilton Mack Laing*, 101.

406 Laing, "Nature Diary," June 18, 1918 [original at RBCM, File P-2 FIE-10], quoted in Mackie, *Hamilton Mack Laing*, 101.

407 Susan Hannon, personal communication, March 21, 2014.

408 Cowan, "Field Notes 1930," May 26, 1930.

409 Cowan, "Field Notes 1930," May 26, 1930. [Sharp-tailed Grouse was the species he had thought he'd seen in Vancouver at the age of 4.]

410 Campbell et al., *Birds of BC*, vol. 3, 120–127.

411 Laing, "Nature Diary, April 16 to November 30, 1930," May 26, 1930 [original at RBCM, File P-2 FIE-10].

412 Campbell et al., *Birds of BC*, vol. 3, 286.

413 Mackie, *Hamilton Mack Laing*, 114.

414 Laing and Cowan, "Field Notes British Columbia 1930," May 26, 1930.

415 Cowan, "Moments from the Education of an Ornithologist," 19.

416 Carleton J. Phillips, "Anatomy," in *Seventy-five Years of Mammalogy 1919–1994*, ed. Elmer C. Birney and Jerry R. Choate, 244. https://archive.org/stream/seventyfiveyearsoobirn#page/244/mode/2up (accessed October 31, 2014).

417 Phillips, "Anatomy," 243. https://archive.org/stream/seventyfiveyearsoobirn#page/242/mode/2up (accessed October 31, 2014).

418 Munro and Cowan, *Bird Fauna of BC*, 142.

419 Parks Canada would do large inventories of vegetation and vertebrates in western national parks in the 1980s as well.

420 Phillips, "Anatomy," 250. https://archive.org/stream/seventyfiveyearsoobirn#page/250/mode/2up (accessed October 31, 2014).

421 R.M. Anderson to H.M. Laing, November 25, 1930. H.M. Laing fonds, BCA.

422 Nagorsen, interview, May 24, 2013.

423 Nagorsen, interview, May 24, 2013.

424 R.M. Anderson to H.M. Laing, June 4, 1930, H.M. Laing fonds, BCA.

425 Kenneth Racey to H.M. Laing, December 12, 1930, H.M. Laing fonds, BCA.

426 Racey to Laing, December 12, 1930, H.M. Laing fonds, BCA.

427 Mearns and Mearns, *The Bird Collectors*.

428 Cowan, interview, February 2, 2005.

429 R.M. Anderson to H.M. Laing, June 4, 1930. H.M. Laing fonds, BCA.

430 Cowan, interview, December 5, 2000.

431 Bob Weeden, interview, July 26, 2012.

432 "MLAs Learn about BC Game," *The Vancouver Daily Province*, February 9, 1950, 9, Cowan_PN_202.

433 Ian McTaggart Cowan to Bill Schwartz, July 6, 1993, Cowan_PN_160.

434 Cowan, "Field Notes 1930," 22.

435 Nagorsen, interview, May 24, 2013.

436 Ian McTaggart Cowan, "Distribution of the Races of the Williamson Sapsucker in British Columbia," *The Condor* 40, no. 3 (May–June 1938): 128–129. https://sora.unm.edu/sites/default/files/journals/condor/v040n03/p0128-p0129.pdf (pdf accessed October 31, 2014).

437 Cowan, "Moments from the Education of an Ornithologist," 19.

438 Campbell et al., *Birds of British Columbia*, vol. 4, 611.

439 North American Bird Conservation Initiative Canada, *The State of Canada's Birds, 2012* (Ottawa: Environment Canada, 2012), 14. www.stateofcanadasbirds.org/State_of_Canada%27s_birds_2012.pdf (pdf accessed October 31, 2014).

440 Laing's official title, as advertised on Dominion Parks Branch posters, was "Nature Guide for National Parks."

441 Cowan, "Moments from the Education of an Ornithologist," 19–20.

442 J.B. Harkin to H.M. Laing, January 9, 1930, H.M. Laing fonds, BCA.

443 Cowan, "Field Notes 1930," June 5, 1930.

444 Joe Bryant, interview, November 10, 2012.

445 Bryant, interview, November 10, 2012.

446 Hart, *J.B. Harkin*, 459.

447 J.B. Harkin to W.B. Conger, September 24, 1929, quoted in Hart, *J.B. Harkin*, 461.

448 Aldo Leopold, *Game Management* (New York: Charles Scribner's Sons, 1933).

449 Bryant, interview, November 10, 2012.

450 Bryant, interview, November 10, 2012.

451 Ian McTaggart Cowan to Joe Bryant, July 9, 1996, Cowan_PN_080.

452 Cowan and Guiguet, *Mammals of BC*, 170.

453 David F. Hatler and Alison M.M. Beal, "Furbearer Management Guidelines," Government of British Columbia, July 2003, www.env.gov.bc.ca/fw/wildlife/trapping/docs/beaver.pdf (accessed March 25, 2013).

454 Cowan and Guiguet, *Mammals of BC*, 330.

455 Ian McTaggart Cowan to Joe Bryant, July 9, 1996, Cowan_PN_080.

456 Cowan to Bryant, July 9, 1996.

457 Cowan and Guiguet, *Mammals of BC*, 305.

458 Cowan, "Field Notes 1930," 9.

459 Cowan and Guiguet, *Mammals of BC*, 209–210.

460 Cowan to Joe Bryant, July 9, 1996, Cowan_PN_080.

461 Amanda Dawn Annand, "The 1910 Fires in Alberta's Foothills and Rocky Mountain Region," unpublished undergraduate honours thesis, UVic, 2010, http://

mountainlegacy.ca/research/documents/
Annand-1910Fires-FinalReport.pdf (pdf
accessed October 31, 2014); Marie-Pierre
Rogeau, "Landscape Disturbance Project, Stand Origin Mapping 1997" (Hinton, Alta.: Foothills Model Forest, 1997),
https://foothillsri.ca/sites/default/files/null/
HLP_1997_06_Rpt_LandscapeDisturban-
ceProjectStandOriginMapping1997.pdf (pdf
accessed October 31, 2014). [700,000 hectares burned in Alberta alone.]

462 Egan, *The Big Burn*, 241.

463 Clyde Leavitt, *Forest Protection in Canada,
1912* (Ottawa: Commission of Conservation,
Committee on Forests, 1913). https://archive.
org/stream/forestprotectio00cana#page/n5/
mode/2up (accessed October 31, 2014.

464 Hart, *J.B. Harkin*, 33.

465 Peter J. Murphy, "Following the Base of the
Foothills: Tracing the Boundaries of Jasper Park and Its Adjacent Rocky Mountains
Forest Reserve," in *Culturing Wilderness in
Jasper National Park*, ed. I.S. MacLaren (Edmonton: University of Alberta Press, 2007),
71–121.

466 Cowan, "Moments from the Education of an
Ornithologist," 20.

467 Campbell et al., *Birds of BC*, vol. 4, 319.

468 Cowan, "Moments from the Education of an
Ornithologist," 20.

469 Ian McTaggart Cowan, "Roof of the World,"
Web of Life television series episode, first
aired March 18, 1964, Vancouver: CBC Television Archives.

470 Cowan and Guiguet, *Mammals of BC*, 295.

471 R.M. Anderson to H.M. Laing, August 26,
1930. H.M. Laing fonds, BCA. ["Aux" refers
to a small "auxiliary" .22 shotgun.]

472 Ian McTaggart Cowan, "Report of Wildlife
Studies in Jasper, Banff and Yoho National
Parks 1944" (unpublished, mimeographed
for National Parks Bureau, Ottawa), 43,
Cowan_PN_894.

473 Cowan, "Report of Wildlife Studies in Jasper,
Banff and Yoho National Parks 1944," 43.

474 R. Yorke Edwards, "The Preservation of Wil-
derness: Is Man a Part of Nature – or a
Thing Apart? *Canadian Audubon* (January–
February 1967): 1–7.

475 Cowan and Guiguet, *Mammals of BC*,
237–243.

476 Laing, "Nature Diary," November 8, 1930
[original at RBCM, File P-2 FIE-10].

477 Campbell et al., *Birds of BC*, vol. 2, 366.

478 Laing, "Nature Diary," November 9, 1930
[original at RBCM, File P-2 FIE-10].

479 Campbell et al., *Birds of BC*, vol. 3, 196.

480 R.M. Anderson to H.M. Laing, March 30,
1931, H.M. Laing fonds, BCA.

481 R.M. Anderson to H.M. Laing, April 21, 1931,
H.M. Laing fonds, BCA.

482 Harry S. Swarth, "Report on a Collection of
Birds and Mammals from Vancouver Island,"
*University of California Publications in Zool-
ogy* 10, no. 1 (1912): 1–2. https://archive.org/
stream/universityofcali10191213univ#page/
n11/mode/2up (accessed October 31, 2014).

483 John O. Whitaker, "University Propinquity," in *Seventy-Five Years of Mammalogy
1919–1994*, ed. Elmer C. Birney and Jerry
R. Choate (Provo, Utah: American Society of Mammalogists, 1994), 129. https://
archive.org/stream/seventyfiveyears-
oobirn#page/128/mode/2up (accessed October 31, 2014).

484 "Annie Alexander and Louise Kellogg," *Gay
Bears: The Hidden History of the Berkeley
Campus* (website), 2002. http://bancroft.
berkeley.edu/collections/gaybears/alexkel
(accessed May 23, 2014).

485 Barbara Stein, *On Her Own Terms: Annie
Montague Alexander and the Rise of Science
in the American West* (Berkeley: University
of California Press, 2001), xiii–xiv.

486 Hilda Wood Grinnell, *Annie Montague Alexander*, [typescript MS], Grinnell Naturalists
Society, MVZ, 1958.

487 Phillips, "Anatomy," 244. https://archive.org/
stream/seventyfiveyearsoobirn#page/244/
mode/2up/search/academic (accessed October 31, 2014).

488 Phillips, "Anatomy," 245.

489 Cowan, "Moments from the Education of
an Ornithologist," 18.

490 Cowan, "Moments from the Education of
an Ornithologist," 18.

491 The quote was originally attributed to "one
Indian" by an eyewitness, William J. Cleveland: "Rev. William J. Cleveland's Investigation of the Causes of the Sioux Troubles," in
*Ninth Annual Report of the Executive Com-
mittee of the Indian Rights Association for
the Year Ending December 15, 1891* (Philadelphia: Indian Rights Association, 1892), 24 at
28. http://is.gd/FOoznv (accessed October
31, 2014).

492 Hilda Wood Grinnell, "Joseph Grinnell 1877–1939," *The Condor* 42, no. 1

(January–February 1940): 3. https://sora.
unm.edu/sites/default/files/journals/con-
dor/v042n01/p0003-p0034.pdf (accessed
October 31, 2014).

493 Thomas R. Dunlap, *Saving America's Wildlife*
(Princeton, NJ: Princeton University Press,
1988), 214.

494 Stein, *On Her Own Terms*, xiv.

495 Cowan, interview, November 30, 2000.

496 Cowan, "Moments from the Education of an
Ornithologist," 18.

497 K. Racey to H.M. Laing, March 23, 1931,
H.M. Laing fonds, BCA.

498 Anthony Guppy, *The Tofino Kid: From India
to This Wild West Coast*. Nanaimo, BC: Priority Printing, 2000), 37.

499 Ian McTaggart Cowan, "Reports on Flora
of Certain Areas of BC" (unpublished, Economic Council of British Columbia, 1936),
GR-0111, Box 03, File 03, 1936–1941, BCA.

500 Ian McTaggart Cowan, "Notes Tofino, Alberni, Chezacut 1931," May 4, 1931,
Cowan_FN_010.

501 Munro and Cowan, *Bird Fauna of BC*, 104.

502 Campbell et al., *Birds of BC*, vol. 4, 156.

503 Cowan, "Notes Tofino, Alberni, Chezacut
1931," May 8, 1931, Cowan_FN_010.

504 Campbell et al., *Birds of BC*, vol. 2, 158–60.

505 Important Bird Areas Canada, "Tofino Mudflats." http://ibacanada.ca/site.jsp?siteID=B-
C002&lang=EN (accessed November 24,
2013).

506 Campbell et al., *Birds of BC*, vol. 2, 180.

507 Cowan, "Notes Tofino, Alberni, Chezacut
1931," May 9, 1931, Cowan_FN_010.

508 Campbell et al. *Birds of BC*, vol. 2, 324–327.

509 Cowan, "Notes Tofino, Alberni, Chezacut
1931," May 22, 1931, Cowan_FN_010.

510 Cowan, "Notes Tofino, Alberni, Chezacut
1931," May 22, 1931, Cowan_FN_010.

511 Campbell et al., *Birds of BC*, vol. 2, 124–129.

512 Ian McTaggart Cowan to Joyce Racey, May 13,
1931, Cowan_PN_095.

513 Cowan to Joyce Racey, May 13, 1931,
Cowan_PN_095.

514 Cowan to Joyce Racey, May 13, 1931,
Cowan_PN_095.

515 Guppy, *The Tofino Kid*, 37.

516 Popularly attributed to William Hornaday,
New York Zoological Society.

517 Cowan to Joyce Racey, May 13, 1931,
Cowan_PN_095.

518 Cowan, interview, December 5, 2000.

519 James Smith et al., *Conservation and Biology of Small Populations: The Song Sparrows
of Mandarte Island* (Oxford: Oxford University Press, 2006).

520 Campbell et al., *Birds of BC*, vol. 1, 216.

521 Cowan, "Notes Tofino, Alberni, Chezacut
1931," May 17, 1931, Cowan_FN_010.

522 Campbell et al., *Birds of BC*, vol. 1, 160.

523 Cowan, "Notes Tofino, Alberni, Chezacut
1931," May 22, 1931, Cowan_FN_010.

524 Patricia Marchak, *Green Gold: the Forest Industry in British Columbia*. (Vancouver:
UBC Press, 1983).

525 Ken Gibson, personal communication, November 22, 2013.

526 Cowan, "Notes Tofino, Alberni, Chezacut
1931," May 14, 1931, Cowan_FN_010.

527 Cowan, "Notes Tofino, Alberni, Chezacut
1931," June 3, 1931, Cowan_FN_010.

528 Margaret Horsfield, *Voices from the Sound:
Chronicles of Clayoquot Sound and Tofino
1899–1929* (Nanaimo: Salal Books, 2008),
310.

529 Horsfield, *Voices from the Sound*, 237.

530 Ian McTaggart Cowan, "A Review of the
Reptiles and Amphibians of British Colum-
bia," in *Report of the Provincial Museum of
British Columbia for the Year 1936* (Victoria:
King's Printer, 1937), K17.

531 Cowan and Guiguet, *Mammals of BC*, 223.

532 Guppy, *The Tofino Kid*, 62.

533 Crispin Guppy and Jon Shepard, *Butterflies
of British Columbia* (Vancouver and Victoria: University of British Columbia Press
and Royal British Columbia Museum, 2001).

534 Gibson, personal communication, November
22, 2013.

535 Cowan and Guiguet, *Mammals of BC*,
344–346.

536 Ian McTaggart Cowan, "Ruts and Ridges:
Some Major Issues in Wildlife Conserva-
tion," *Proceedings of the Sixth Annual BC Big
Game Convention*, May 7–10, 1952, 63–68.

537 Cowan, "Ruts and Ridges," 66.

538 David Tindall, "Twenty Years after the Protest, What We Learned from Clayoquot
Sound," *The Globe and Mail*, August 12,
2013. www.theglobeandmail.com/globe-de-
bate/twenty-years-after-the-protest-what-
we-learned-from-clayoquot-sound/arti-
cle13709014 (accessed February 4, 2015).

539 Fred Bunnell, interview, November 15, 2012.

540 Campbell et al., *Birds of BC*, vol. 1, 280–282.

541 Fred Bunnell, interview, November 15, 2012.

542 Bunnell, interview, November 15, 2012.

543 Bunnell, interview, November 15, 2012.

544 Ian McTaggart Cowan, "Room at the Top?" in *Endangered Spaces: The Future for Canada's Wilderness*, ed. Monte Hummel (Toronto: Key Porter Books, 1989), 249–266.

545 Swarth, "Report on a Collection of Birds and Mammals from Vancouver Island," 5. https://archive.org/stream/universityofca-li10191213univ#page/4/mode/2up (accessed October 31, 2014).

546 Joseph Grinnell to Annie Alexander, June 11, 1910, MSS.0117, MVZA.

547 Swarth, "Report on a Collection of Birds and Mammals from Vancouver Island," 6. https://archive.org/stream/universityofca-li10191213univ#page/6/mode/2up (accessed October 31, 2014).

548 Campbell et al., *Birds of BC*, vol. 2, 308–310.

549 N.N. Winchester, Z. Lindo and V.M. Behan-Pelletier, "Oribatid Mite Communities in the Canopy of Montane *Abies amabilis* and *Tsuga heterophylla* Trees on Vancouver Island, British Columbia," *Environmental Entomology* 37, no. 2 (April 2008): 464–471. http://is.gd/2xk7ff (abstract and cited references accessed October 20, 2014).

550 Campbell et al., *Birds of BC*, vol. 2, 308–310.

551 Cowan, interview, November 30, 2000.

552 Cowan, "Notes Tofino, Alberni, Chezacut 1931," Cowan_FN_010.

553 Cowan and Guiguet, *Mammals of BC*, 125–126.

554 Cowan, interview, November 30, 2000.

555 Cowan, interview, November 30, 2000.

556 Cowan, "Notes Tofino, Alberni, Chezacut 1931," June 21, 1930. Cowan_FN_010.

557 Cowan, "Notes Tofino, Alberni, Chezacut 1931," June 21, 1930. Cowan_FN_010.

558 Cowan, interview, November 30, 2000.

559 Cowan, "Notes Tofino, Alberni, Chezacut 1931," June 22, 1930. Cowan_FN_010.

560 Campbell et al., *Birds of BC*, vol. 3, 211.

561 Ian McTaggart Cowan, October 2006 interview by Rick Searle for Elders Council for Parks in BC, AR447, UVic Special Collections [transcription in Cowan_PN_492].

562 Cowan, interview, July 9, 2002.

563 Ian McTaggart Cowan, "Insularity in the Genus *Sorex* on the North Coast of British Columbia," *Proceedings of the Biological Society of Washington* 54 (July 1941): 95–108. www.biodiversitylibrary.org/page/34599248#page/119/mode/1up (accessed October 31, 2014).

564 Cowan, interview, November 30, 2000.

565 David W. Nagorsen and Andrea Cardini, "Tempo and Mode of Evolutionary Divergence in Modern and Holocene Vancouver Island Marmots (*Marmota vancouverensis*) (Mammalia, Rodentia)," *Journal of Zoological Systematics and Evolutionary Research* 47, no. 3 (August 2009): 258–267. www2.mcdonald.cam.ac.uk/events/conferences-workshops/GMM/Nagorsen_2009.pdf (pdf of independently paginated conference facsimile of this article accessed October 31, 2014).

566 J.H. Calaby, H. Dimpel and I. McTaggart-Cowan, "The Mountain Pigmy Possum *Burramys parvus* Broom (Marsupial) in the Kosciuszko National Park, New South Wales." Division of Wildlife Research Technical Paper 23 (Australia: Commonwealth Scientific and Industrial Research Organisation, 1971).

567 *Sydney Morning Herald*, "Rising Heat to Endanger Many Species: Study," June 13, 2013. www.smh.com.au/environment/climate-change/rising-heat-to-endanger-many-species-study-20130613-2o5br.html (accessed June 13, 2013).

568 R.M. Humphreys to Ian McTaggart Cowan, October 30, 1972, Cowan_PN_382.

569 Ian McTaggart Cowan to G. Smith, October 26, 1972, Cowan_PN_382.

570 G. Smith to Ian McTaggart Cowan, November 22, 1972, Cowan_PN_382.

571 W.T. Munro et al., *Status and Management of the Vancouver Island Marmot* (Victoria: BC Ministry of Environment, December 1983).

572 Ian McTaggart Cowan to R.J. Milko, 1981, Cowan_PN_382.

573 Jack Danylchuk, "*ForestTalk* Interviews: Dr. Ian McTaggart-Cowan," *ForesTalk* 4, no. 1 (Spring 1980): 19. http://is.gd/OmVYCt (pdf accessed October 31, 2014).

574 Danylchuk, "*ForestTalk* Interviews: Dr. Ian McTaggart-Cowan," 18–20.

575 Cowan, interview, November 30, 2000.

576 Cowan, "Moments from the Education of an Ornithologist," 20.

577 Cowan, "Moments from the Education of an Ornithologist," 20.

578 Cowan and Guiguet, *Mammals of BC*, 98.

579 D. Carter and A. Harestad, "Status of the White-Tailed Jackrabbit (*Lepus townsendii*) in British Columbia" unpublished report for Wildlife Branch, BC Ministry of Environment (1991), 39.

580 Nagorsen, *Rodents and Lagomorphs of British Columbia*, 92–95.

581 Cowan and Guiguet, *Mammals of BC*, 73.

582 *Extinct and Vanishing Mammals of the Western Hemisphere with the Marine Species of All the Oceans*, Special Publication no. 11 (Washington, DC: American Committee for International Wild Life Protection, 1942). www.biodiversitylibrary.org/item/67624#page/9/mode/1up (accessed October 31, 2014).

583 Ian McTaggart Cowan, "Extinct and Vanishing Mammals," lecture notes, ca. 1958–1959, Cowan_PN_246.

584 Campbell et al., *Birds of BC*, vol. 1, 208.

585 Cowan, "Notes Tofino, Alberni, Chezacut 1931," July 23, 1931. Cowan_FN_010.

586 Cowan and Guiguet, *Mammals of BC*, 54–56.

587 Cowan, "Notes Tofino, Alberni, Chezacut 1931," August 4, 1931. Cowan_FN_010.

588 Cowan, "Notes Tofino, Alberni, Chezacut 1931," August 8, 1931, Cowan_FN_010.

589 Ian McTaggart Cowan to Neil Dawe, March 15, 2002, Cowan_PN_289.

590 Ian McTaggart Cowan, interview, February 26, 2001.

591 Iola Knight to Ian McTaggart Cowan, June 25, 2000, Cowan_PN_081.

592 Veera Bonner, Irene Bliss and Hazel H. Litterick, *Chilcotin: Preserving Pioneer Memories* (Surrey, BC: Heritage House, 1995), 319.

593 Cowan, "Notes Tofino, Alberni, Chezacut 1931," August 28, 1931. Cowan_FN_010.

594 Cowan and Guiguet, *Mammals of BC*, 383–384.

595 Cowan, "Notes Tofino, Alberni, Chezacut 1931," August 19, 1931. Cowan_FN_010.

596 Richmond Hobson, *Grass Beyond the Mountains* (Toronto: McClelland & Stewart, 1951).

597 Robin Ridington and Jillian Ridington, *Where Happiness Dwells: A History of the Dane-zaa First Nations* (Vancouver: UBC Press, 2013).

598 A.T. Bergerud, *The Status and Management of Caribou in British Columbia* (Victoria: BC Fish and Wildlife Branch, 1978). www.env.gov.bc.ca/wld/documents/techpub/rn333.

pdf (pdf scan accessed October 31, 2014); Tom Bergerud, interview, May 22, 2013.

599 BC Wild, *Flirting with Extinction: Clear-cuts and the Demise of Southern BC's Caribou* (Smithers: Cariboo Chilcotin Resource Centre, BC Wild, 1998). www.eye-design.ca/publications/flirting.pdf (pdf accessed October 31, 2014).

600 Munro and Cowan, *Bird Fauna of BC*.

601 Ian McTaggart Cowan, "Shillaker Manuscript, 1939–1945," field notes, Cowan_PN_298.

602 Ian McTaggart Cowan, "Ecology and Northern Development," *Arctic* 22, no. 1 (1969): 1–12. http://arctic.journalhosting.ucalgary.ca/arctic/index.php/arctic/article/view/3188/3164 (accessed October 31, 2014).

603 Ian McTaggart Cowan to Tom Beck, September 3, 1994, Cowan_PN_285.

604 Cowan to Beck, September 3, 1994, Cowan_PN_285.

605 Cowan, interview, November 30, 2000.

606 Cowan, "Moments from the Education of an Ornithologist," 20.

607 *The Totem*, UBC Graduating Class of 1932 Annual (Vancouver: UBC, 1932), 98, Cowan_PN_010. www.waughfamily.ca/Waugh/UBCTotem_1932.pdf (pdf p108, accessed October 31, 2014).

608 Ian McTaggart Cowan to Francis Kermode, November 17, 1931, GR-0111, Box 03, File 04, BCA.

609 Ian McTaggart Cowan, "The Ecology and Life History of the Columbian Blacktailed Deer, *Odocoileus columbianus columbianus* (Richardson), in British Columbia," thesis for Bachelor of Arts in Zoology (UBC, 1932), 1.

610 Seton, *Lives of Game Animals* (New York: Doubleday Doran, 1929).

611 Cowan, "The Ecology and Life History of the Columbian Blacktailed Deer," 1.

612 Cowan, "The Ecology and Life History of the Columbian Blacktailed Deer," 19.

613 Cowan, "The Ecology and Life History of the Columbian Blacktailed Deer," 70.

614 Cowan, "The Ecology and Life History of the Columbian Blacktailed Deer," 72–73.

615 Cowan, "The Ecology and Life History of the Columbian Blacktailed Deer," 94.

616 Ann Schau, personal communication, May 10, 2014.

617 Ian McTaggart Cowan, "Some Notes on

the Hibernation of *Lasionycteris noctiva-gans*," *The Canadian Field-Naturalist* 47, no. 4 (April 1933): 74–75. www.biodiversitylibrary.org/item/89103#page/98/mode/1up (accessed October 31, 2014).

618 David Nagorsen and R. Mark Brigham, *Bats of British Columbia*, Royal British Columbia Museum Handbook, vol. 1 of *The Mammals of British Columbia* (Vancouver: UBC Press, 1993), 119–123.

619 Cowan and Guiguet, *Mammals of BC*, 70–73.

620 Joyce Cowan to Ann Schau, January 31, 1977, Cowan_PN_504.

621 Ian McTaggart Cowan, "The British Columbia Woodchuck *Marmota monax petrensis* Howell," *The Canadian Field-Naturalist* 47, no. 3 (March 1933): 57. www.biodiversitylibrary.org/item/89103#page/77/mode/1up (accessed October 31, 2014).

622 Cowan and Guiguet, *Mammals of BC*, 118.

623 Cowan, "The British Columbia Woodchuck," 57.

624 T.T. McCabe to Joseph Grinnell, August 28, 1929, MSS.0117, MVZ Historical Correspondence, MVZA.

625 Cowan, "Moments from the Education of an Ornithologist," 19.

626 Cowan, "Moments from the Education of an Ornithologist," 19.

627 Cowan, "Moments from the Education of an Ornithologist," 19.

628 Ian McTaggart Cowan, "Field notes on mammals of Vancouver and Cariboo, 1931–1932," May 9, 1932. Cowan_FN_021.

629 Cowan, "Field notes on mammals of Vancouver and Cariboo, 1931–1932," May 11, 1932. Cowan_FN_021.

630 Cowan, "The British Columbia Woodchuck," 57.

631 Seton, "The Message of the Indian," in *Some Lessons*, ed. B. of V, 70–72.

632 Charles Alexander Eastman (Ohiyesa), *The Soul of the Indian* (Boston: Houghton Mifflin, 1911), 89–90. https://archive.org/stream/soulindiananintooeastgoog#page/n111/mode/2up (accessed October 31, 2014).

633 Campbell et al., *Birds of BC*, vol. 2, 50–53.

634 Cowan, "Field notes on Mammals of Vancouver and Cariboo 1931–1932," May 20, 1932. Cowan_FN_021.

635 Cowan, "The British Columbia Woodchuck," 57.

636 Cowan, "Field notes on Mammals of Vancouver and Cariboo 1931–1932," June 3, 1932, Cowan_FN_021.

637 Campbell et al., *Birds of BC*, vol. 4, 48.

638 Ian McTaggart Cowan, "Journal Field Trips 1935–1961," June 30–July 1, 1932, Cowan_FN_014.

639 Ian McTaggart Cowan, "Field Notes I. McT. Cowan 1936–1937" (File M-13 FIE-29) [transcription under Cowan_FN_052].

640 Campbell et al., *Birds of BC*, vol. 4, 126.

641 Campbell et al., *Birds of BC*, vol. 4, 125.

642 Cowan, "Field Notes I. McT. Cowan 1936–1937," August 3–13, 1936 (File M-13 FIE-29) [transcription under Cowan_FN_052].

643 Campbell et al., *Birds of BC*, vol. 4, 531–537.

644 Brian Fawcett, *Virtual Clearcut, Or, The Way Things Are in My Hometown* (Toronto: Thomas Allen Publishers, 2003).

645 Munro and Cowan, *Bird Fauna of BC*, 175.

646 Campbell et al., *Birds of BC*, vol. 4, 683.

647 Campbell et al., *Birds of BC*, vol. 2, 412.

648 Campbell et al., *Birds of BC*, vol. 2, 416.

649 Rae Crossman, "One Ruby-throated Moment," unpublished poem [n.d.] read in eulogy of Ian McTaggart Cowan, Cowan_PN_291. [An excerpt from the poem appears in Rae Crossman, "Notes from the Wild: An Account in Words and Music of R. Murray Schafer's *And Wolf Shall Inherit the Moon*," posted January 25, 2007, on the website of *The New Quarterly*, www.tnq.ca/article/notes-wild-account-words-and-music-r-murray-schafers-and-wolf-shall-inherit-moon (accessed October 31, 2014).]

650 Ann Schau, "Eulogy," Cowan_PN_291.

651 Kermode to Cowan, February 16, 1932, GR-0111, Box 03, File 04, BCA.

652 Cowan, "Field Journal 1932–1934," August 27, 1932, MVZA vol. 573. (The original journal now held at Berkeley was copied by Cowan into a journal titled "Field Notes California 1934," Cowan_FN_019, but the notes are not as comprehensive. Transcription notes are referenced under Cowan_FN_058 for the original journal.)

653 Cowan and Guiguet, *Mammals of BC*, 107.

654 Cowan, "Field Journal 1932–1934," August 27, 1932, MVZA vol. 573. [Cowan_FN_058.]

655 Campbell et al., *Birds of BC*, vol. 2, 360.

656 Cowan, interview, February 26, 2001.

657 Joseph Grinnell to Annie Alexander, July 13, 1932, MSS.0117, MVZ Historical Correspondence, MVZA.

658 Grinnell to Alexander, October 24, 1932, MSS.0117, MVZ Historical Correspondence, MVZA.

659 Grinnell to Alexander, January 1, 1933, MSS.0117, MVZ Historical Correspondence, MVZA.

660 E. Raymond Hall to Annie Alexander, September 23, 1932, MSS.0117, MVZ Historical Correspondence, MVZA.

661 Cowan, interview, February 26, 2001.

662 Cowan, interview by Rick Searle for Elders Council for Parks, October 2006.

663 Lidicker, "Population Ecology," 340. https://archive.org/stream/seventyfiveyearsoobirn#page/340/mode/2up (accessed October 31, 2014).

664 Cowan, "Distribution and Variation in Deer (Genus *Odocoileus*) of the Pacific Coast Region of North America," (PhD dissertation, University of California, Berkeley, 1935).

665 Bernhard Rensch, *Das Prinzip geographischer Rassenkreise und das Problem der Artbildung* (Berlin: Gebrüder Borntraeger, 1929), 1–206. Quoted in Cowan, "Distribution and Variation in Deer."

666 Phillips, "Anatomy," 250. https://archive.org/stream/seventyfiveyearsoobirn#page/250/mode/2up (accessed October 31, 2014)

667 Joseph Grinnell, "Note to Students," September 13, 1933, Cowan_FN_019.

668 Aldo Leopold, "Wilderness," unpublished MS, ca. 1935, as quoted in Curt Meine, *Aldo Leopold: His Life and Work* (Madison: University of Wisconsin Press, 2010), 359–360.

669 T.T. McCabe to Joseph Grinnell, June 17, 1929, MSS.0117, MVZ Historical Correspondence, MVZA.

670 McCabe to Grinnell, June 17, 1929, MVZA.

671 Grinnell to McCabe, May 1, 1929, MSS.0117, MVZ Historical Correspondence, MVZA.

672 Phillips, "Anatomy," 242. https://archive.org/stream/seventyfiveyearsoobirn#page/242/mode/2up (accessed October 31, 2014).

673 Michael A. Mares and David J. Schmidly, eds., *Latin American Mammalogy: History, Biodiversity and Conservation* (Norman: University of Oklahoma Press, 1991), 63. Quoted in Phillips, "Anatomy," 243. https://archive.org/stream/seventyfiveyearsoobirn#page/242/mode/2up (accessed October 31, 2014).

674 McCabe to Grinnell, October 17, 1930, MSS.0117, MVZ Historical Correspondence, MVZA.

675 Cowan and Guiguet, *Mammals of BC*, 369.

676 Cowan and Guiguet, *Mammals of BC*, 307.

677 Phillips, "Anatomy," 244. https://archive.org/stream/seventyfiveyearsoobirn#page/244/mode/2up (accessed October 31, 2014).

678 Phillips, "Anatomy," 244.

679 Phillips, "Anatomy," 244.

680 Cowan, "Distribution and Variation in Deer," 189.

681 Olof C. Wallmo, *Mule and Black-Tailed Deer of North America* (Lincoln: University of Nebraska Press, 1981), 1–25.

682 Eastern Sierra Land Trust, "Round Valley Mule Deer and Their Migration Corridor." www.eslt.org/Pages/mule-deer-migration.html (accessed July 8, 2013).

683 Cowan and Guiguet, *Mammals of BC*, 168.

684 Cowan, interview, February 26, 2001.

685 Cowan, interview, February 26, 2001.

686 Goward, interview, March 25th, 2013.

687 Cowan and Guiguet, *Mammals of BC*, 373–375.

688 Cowan, "Distribution and Variation in Deer (Genus *Odocoileus*) of the Pacific Coast Region of North America," *California Fish and Game* 22, no. 3 (1936): 200.

689 Victor Scheffer, "A Newly Located Herd of Pacific White-Tailed Deer," *Journal of Mammalogy* 21, no. 3 (August 1940): 271–282. www.jstor.org/discover/1374754 (abstract accessed October 31, 2014).

690 Cowan, interview, February 26, 2001.

691 Campbell et al., *Birds of BC*, vol. 3, 170.

692 Cowan, "Field Journal 1932–1934," May 9, 1933, MVZA vol. 573. [Cowan_FN_058.]

693 Cowan, "Field Journal 1932–1934," May 9, 1933, MVZA vol. 573. [Cowan_FN_058.]

694 Cowan, "Field Journal 1932–1934," May 10, 1933, MVZA vol. 573. [Cowan_FN_058.]

695 Cowan, "Field Journal 1932–1934," May 10, 1933, MVZA vol. 573. [Cowan_FN_058.]

696 Cowan, "Field Journal 1932–1934," May 12, 1933, MVZA vol. 573. [Cowan_FN_058.]

697 Cowan, "Field Journal 1932–1934," May 14, 1933, MVZA vol. 573. [Cowan_FN_058.]

698 Campbell et al., *Birds of BC*, vol. 3, 481.

699 Cowan, "Field Journal 1932–1934," May 9, 1933, MVZA vol. 573. [Cowan_FN_058.]

700 Cowan, "Field Journal 1932–1934," May 9, 1933, MVZA vol. 573. [Cowan_FN_058.]

701 Ira Gabrielson, "In Memoriam: Stanley G.

Jewett," *The Murrelet* 36, no. 3 (September–December 1955): 33. www.jstor.org/discover/3534216 (accessed October 31, 2014).

702 Joseph Grinnell to Miss Wythe, October 7, 1935, MSS.0117, MVZ Historical Correspondence. MVZA.

703 Cowan, interview, February 26, 2001.

704 Cowan, interview, February 26, 2001.

705 Cowan, interview, February 26, 2001.

706 Cowan, interview, February 26, 2001.

707 Cowan, interview, February 26, 2001.

708 Cowan, interview, February 26, 2001.

709 Cowan and Guiguet, *Mammals of BC*, 40.

710 Joseph Grinnell to James K. Moffitt, August 12, 1926, MSS.0117, MVZ Historical Correspondence, MVZA.

711 David Nagorsen, *Opossums, Shrews and Moles of British Columbia*, Royal British Columbia Museum Handbook, vol. 2 in the series *The Mammals of British Columbia* (Vancouver: UBC Press, 1996), 4.

712 Cowan, "Field Journal 1932–1934," September 18, 1933, MVZA vol. 573. [Cowan_FN_058.]

713 Cowan, "Field Journal 1932–1934," September 18, 1933, MVZA vol. 573. [Cowan_FN_058.]

714 Campbell et al., *Birds of BC*, vol. 2, 372.

715 National Audubon Society, "Minutes of the Board of Directors Meeting held at the Westin Hotel, Winnipeg, Manitoba, Canada," September 21, 1986, Cowan_PN_158.

716 The Forest History Society, "The Northern Spotted Owl – Timeline" (webpage), 2010. www.foresthistory.org/ASPNET/Policy/northern_spotted_owl/index.aspx (accessed February 26, 2015).

717 E.C. Campbell and R. Wayne Campbell, "COSEWIC Status Report on the Spotted Owl *Strix occidentalis* in Canada" (Ottawa: Committee on the Status of Endangered Wildlife in Canada, 1986).

718 Brian Curtis, "James Moffitt, 1900–1943," *California Fish and Game* 29, no. 4 (October 1943): 203. https://archive.org/stream/californiafishga29_4cali#page/202/mode/2up (accessed October 31, 2014).

719 Campbell et al., *Birds of BC*, vol. 1, 272.

720 Jennifer Benito, Save the Redwoods League, personal communication, January 27, 2015.

721 Cowan, "Field Journal 1932–1934," October 25, 1933, MVZA vol. 573. [Cowan_FN_058.]

722 Benito, personal communication, January 27, 2015.

723 "Garry Oak Ecosystems," BC Ministry of Environment brochure, 1993. www.env.gov.bc.ca/wld/documents/garryoak.pdf (accessed May 24, 2014).

724 Cowan and Guiguet, *Mammals of BC*, 83.

725 Bill Merilees, interview, September 17, 2012.

726 Grinnell to Alexander, September 4, 1934, MSS.0117, MVZ Historical Correspondence, MVZA.

727 Cowan and Guiguet, *Mammals of BC*, 190.

728 Ian McTaggart Cowan, "A Distributional Study of the *Peromyscus sitkensis* Group of White-Footed Mice," *University of California Publications in Zoology* 40, no. 13 (1935): 429–438.

729 Cowan, interview, February 26, 2001.

730 Eric Damer and Herbert Rosengarten, *UBC: The First 100 Years* (Vancouver: University of British Columbia, 2009).

731 Cowan, interview, February 26, 2001.

732 Cowan, interview, February 26, 2001.

733 Joseph Grinnell and Joseph Dixon, "Natural History of the Ground Squirrels of California," *Monthly Bulletin of the State Commission of Horticulture* 7, nos. 11–12 (1918): 597–708. https://archive.org/stream/naturalhistoryofoogrin#page/n3/mode/2up (accessed October 31, 2014).

734 Jan Matějů and Lukáš Kratochvíl, "Sexual Size Dimorphism in Ground Squirrels (*Rodentia: Sciuridae: Marmotini*) Does Not Correlate with Body Size and Sociality," *Frontiers in Zoology* 10, no. 27 (2013). www.frontiersinzoology.com/content/pdf/1742-9994-10-27.pdf (accessed May 24, 2014).

735 Joyce Racey to Stewart Racey, May 23, 1935, Cowan_PN_504.

736 Peter Corley-Smith, *White Bears and Other Curiosities: The First 100 Years of the Royal British Columbia Museum* (Victoria: RBCM, 1989), 89.

737 Cowan, interview, February 26, 2001.

738 Douglas Cole, *Captured Heritage: The Scramble for Northwest Coast Artifacts* (Vancouver: UBC Press, 1995).

739 Corley-Smith, *White Bears and Other Curiosities*. See also Thomas Norris, "John Fannin," *Dictionary of Canadian Biography Online*, http://is.gd/E2NPkx (accessed May 24, 2014).

740 H. Swarth to W.A. Newcombe, July 21, 1925, MSS.0117, MVZ Historical Correspondence, MVZA.

741 Cowan, interview, November 30, 2000.

742 Cowan, interview, February 26, 2001.

743 Lorne Hammond, interview, August 7, 2013.

744 Cowan and Guiguet, *Mammals of BC*, 386.

745 Provincial Museum Act, SBC 1913, c. 50, s. 4.

746 Corley-Smith, *White Bears and Other Curiosities*, 58.

747 *Report of the Provincial Museum of Natural History for the Year 1912* (Victoria: British Columbia Legislative Assembly, 1913), 7. https://archive.org/stream/reportprovincial1912brit#page/n13/mode/2up/search/connaught (accessed October 31, 2014).

748 Corley-Smith, *White Bears and Other Curiosities*, 87.

749 Cowan, interview, November 30, 2000.

750 Cowan, interview, November 30, 2000.

751 Cowan and Guiguet, *Mammals of BC*, 294.

752 Cowan, interview, February 26, 2001.

753 Corley-Smith, *White Bears and Other Curiosities*, 80–86.

754 Ian McTaggart Cowan, interview by Peter Corley-Smith, RBCM Collection, 1985.

755 Cowan, interview by Peter Corley-Smith, RBCM Collection, 1985.

756 Cowan, interview by Peter Corley-Smith, RBCM Collection, 1985.

757 Cowan, interview, February 26, 2001.

758 Basil Stuart-Stubbs, "W.K. Lamb, 1904–1999." *BC Bookworld* (website), 2010. www.abcbookworld.com/view_author.php?id=786 (accessed April 29, 2014).

759 W. Kaye Lamb, interview, quoted in Corley-Smith, *White Bears and Other Curiosities*, 94.

760 Cowan, interview by Peter Corley-Smith, RBCM Collection, 1985.

761 Cowan, interview by Peter Corley-Smith, RBCM Collection, 1985.

762 *Report of the Provincial Museum of Natural History for the Year 1935* (Victoria: King's Printer, 1936).

763 Cowan and Guiguet, *Mammals of BC*, 85.

764 *Report of the Provincial Museum of Natural History for the Year 1935*, H8.

765 Patrick Martin to Ian McTaggart Cowan, on the occasion of his 90th birthday celebration, Cowan_PN_081.

766 Campbell et al., *Birds of BC*, vol. 1, 230.

767 *Report of the Provincial Museum of Natural History for the year 1935*, H8.

768 Cowan, "Journal Field Trips 1935–1961," November 13, 1935, Cowan_FN_014.

769 Cowan, "Journal Field Trips 1935–1961," November 13, 1935, Cowan_FN_014.

770 Campbell et al., *Birds of BC*, vol. 4, 406.

771 British Columbia Waterfowl Society fonds, "Minutes of the BCWS 1962–1967," DMAS.

772 Ian McTaggart Cowan, "Deer Study," December 29, 1935, Cowan_FN_027.

773 Cowan to Rodger Hunter, February 1997, Cowan_PN_005.

774 Roger Wiles, "Uncommon Legacy," *Lake Cowichan Gazette*, January 5, 2009, 10. [Reprinted in Cowichan Valley Rhododendron Society *Newsletter* 20, no. 2 (February 2009): 3–4. http://cowichan.rhodos.ca/newsletter-archive/CVRS Feb newsletter 2009.pdf (pdf p3, accessed February 1, 2015).]

775 Cowan, "Journal Field Trips 1935–1961," October 25, 1935, Cowan_FN_014.

776 Campbell et al., *Birds of BC*, vol. 3, 365.

777 Ian McTaggart Cowan to Secretary of the James L. Baillie Memorial Fund, Long Point Bird Observatory, January 19, 1998, Cowan_PN_016.

778 Jim Lauder, "Joyce McTaggart Cowan memorial service eulogy," December 3, 2002, Cowan_PN_058.

779 Lauder, "Joyce McTaggart Cowan memorial service eulogy," December 3, 2002, Cowan_PN_058.

780 Ian McTaggart Cowan to Francis Kermode, May 27, 1936, GR-0111, Box 03, File 04, BCA.

781 Cowan to Kermode, June 17, 1936, GR-0111, Box 03, File 04, BCA.

782 E.G. Perrault, "His Wild Life Brought Him Honours," *Vancouver Sun Magazine*, June 28, 1952, 15.

783 Perrault, "His Wild Life Brought Him Honours," 15.

784 Campbell et al., *Birds of BC*, vol. 2, 394.

785 Cowan, "Field Notes 1936–1937," June 26, 1936, Cowan_FN_052.

786 Cowan, "Journal Field Trips 1935–1961," June 21, 1936, Cowan_FN_014.

787 Campbell et al., *Birds of BC*, vol. 3, 304.

788 Cowan, "Field Notes 1936–1937," June 24, 1936, Cowan_FN_052.

789 Campbell et al., *Birds of BC*, vol. 4, 164–168.

790 Campbell et al., *Birds of BC*, vol. 4, 164–168.

791 Campbell et al., *Birds of BC*, vol. 4, 164.

792 Cowan, "Field Notes 1936–1937," June 24, 1936, Cowan_FN_052.

793 Campbell et al., *Birds of BC*, vol. 2, 402.

794 Ann Schau, interview, October 9, 2012.

795 *Penticton Herald*, "McTaggart-Cowan Lauds Park Group," October 6, 1966, Cowan_PN_186.

796 Cowan, "Journal Field Trips 1935–1961," July 1–8, 1936, Cowan_FN_014.

797 Ian McTaggart Cowan, interview by Rick Searle for Elders Council for Parks in BC, October 2006.

798 June Wood, *Home to the Nechako: The River and the Land* (Victoria: Heritage House, 2013).

799 Lady Susan Tweedsmuir, "Tweedsmuir Park: The Diary of a Pilgrimage," *National Geographic Magazine*, 73, no. 4. (April 1938): 451.

800 "Tweedsmuir South Provincial Park" (webpage), BC Parks, Ministry of Environment, n.d. www.env.gov.bc.ca/bcparks/explore/parkpgs/tweeds_s/nat_cul.html (accessed May 24, 2014).

801 Cowan, interview by Rick Searle for Elders Council for Parks in BC, October 2006.

802 Campbell et al., *Birds of BC*, vol. 4, 426–433.

803 Cowan, "Journal Field Trips 1935–1961," July 16, 1936, Cowan_FN_014.

804 Campbell et al., *Birds of BC*, vol. 4, 426–431.

805 Cowan, "Journal Field Trips 1935–1961," July 18–19, 1936, Cowan_FN_014.

806 Soren Larsen, "Collaboration Geographies: Native–White Partnerships During the Resettlement of Ootsa Lake, British Columbia, 1900–52," *BC Studies* 138/139 (Summer/Autumn 2003): 87–114. http://ojs.library.ubc.ca/index.php/bcstudies/article/view/1672/1718 (accessed October 31, 2014).

807 Cowan, interview by Rick Searle for Elders Council for Parks in BC, October 2006.

808 Cowan, "Field Notes I. McT. Cowan 1936–1937," July 28, 1936 (File M-13 FIE-29) [transcription under Cowan_FN_052].

809 Cowan, "Field Notes I. McT. Cowan 1936–1937," July 28, 1936 (File M-13 FIE-29) [transcription under Cowan_FN_052].

810 Cyril Shelford, *From War to Wilderness* (Victoria: Shelford Publishing, 1997).

811 Shelford, *From War to Wilderness*, ii.

812 Shelford, *From War to Wilderness*, 192.

813 Cyril Shelford to Ian McTaggart Cowan, January 25, 1979, Cowan_PN_276.

814 Cowan and Guiguet, *Mammals of BC*, 314.

815 Eric Collier, *Three Against the Wilderness* (New York: Irwin Publishing, 1959).

816 Eric Collier, "Address of BC Registered Trappers Association," in *Proceedings of the Ninth Annual BC Game Convention: May 25–28, 1955* (Victoria: Queen's Printer, 1955), 53.

817 *The Globe and Mail*, "Film Makes Plea for Humane Traps," February 6, 1982, E11.

818 R.D. Taber and Ian McTaggart Cowan, "Capturing and Marking Wild Animals," in *Wildlife Management Techniques*, ed. Robert H. Giles (Washington, DC: The Wildlife Society, 1969): 217–318.

819 Cowan to Kermode, July 23, 1936, GR-0111, Box 03, File 04, BCA.

820 Cowan and Guiguet, *Mammals of BC*, 58.

821 Cowan, "Small Mammals of the Western Mountains," 139.

822 Cheslatta Band, "The Cheslatta Surrender: A legal analysis of a surrender given by the Cheslatta Carrier Nation to Her Majesty in right of the government of Canada on the 21st of April, 1952," Northern BC Archives & Special Collections 2003.4.1.35. *See also* Mike Robertson, "The Story of the Surrender of the Cheslatta Reserves on April 21, 1952," Cheslatta Carrier Nation Archives, 1991. www.neef.ca/uploads/161/Story_of_the_Surrender_of_the_Cheslatta_Reserves-pdf (accessed February 28, 2015).

823 Richard L. Neuberger, "Engineers Invade Another Wilderness," *Popular Science*, November 1951, 99. http://is.gd/dPlKVQ (accessed October 31, 2014).

824 British Columbia, *Journals of the Legislative Assembly of BC*, vol. 78 (lxxviii) (March 15–21, 1949): 80; (March 21–24, 1949): 103, 107, 111, 115, 119 as linked from http://is.gd/dEt9ed (accessed February 27, 2015). The text of 1949 Bill 66 as submitted by Cabinet to the Lieutenant Governor and transmitted to the Legislature accordingly by the latter is at http://is.gd/HMPlXi (accessed February 27, 2015).

825 Ian McTaggart Cowan, "Report of the Division of Biology, 1949," in *Report of Provincial Game Commission, 1949* (Victoria: Department of Attorney-General, 1951), 54–60.

826 *Journals of the Legislative Assembly of BC*, vol. 78 (lxxviii) (March 21–24, 1949): 115, 119, as linked from http://is.gd/dEt9ed (accessed February 27, 2015).

827 *Vancouver Sun*, "Authority Sought for Aluminum Plant Deal," March 23, 1949, 13.

828 Cowan, interview, July 9, 2002.

829 *The Province*, "MLAs Learn about BC Game," February 9, 1950, 9, Cowan_PN_202.

830 Industrial Development Act, SBC 1949, c. 31, s. 3(3). http://is.gd/HMPlXi (pdf p4 of archival scan accessed February 20, 2015). See also *Vancouver Sun*, "Authority Sought for Aluminum Plant Deal," March 23, 1949, 13.

831 Peter A. Larkin, "Fisheries Research of the Game Department," in *Report of the Provincial Game Commission, 1951*, E43 (Victoria: Department of Attorney-General, 1953).

832 Cheslatta Band. "The Cheslatta Surrender: A legal analysis of a surrender given by the Cheslatta Carrier Nation to Her Majesty in right of the government of Canada on the 21st of April, 1952," Northern BC Archives & Special Collections 2003.4.1.35. *See also* Mike Robertson, "The Story of the Surrender of the Cheslatta Reserves on April 21, 1952," Cheslatta Carrier Nation Archives, 1991. www.neef.ca/uploads/161/Story_of_the_Surrender_of_the_Cheslatta_Reserves-pdf (accessed February 28, 2015).

833 *Report of the Royal Commission on Aboriginal Peoples*, vol. 1, pt. 2, c. 11, §3.4: "The Cheslatta T'en and the Kemano Hydro Project" (Ottawa: Canada Communication Group, 1996). http://is.gd/L2zUWf (accessed October 31, 2014).

834 Ian McTaggart Cowan "The Wildlife Resource in Canada: A Brief Presented to the Royal Commission on Canada's Economic Prospects," unpublished (Toronto: Canadian Conservation Association, ca. 1955), Cowan_AN_037.

835 *Transactions of the Canadian Conservation Association* (London, Ont.: Canadian Conservation Association, 1941–[195?]) [No transactions were published between 1943 and 1951].

836 Steve Johnsen, National Wildlife Federation, personal communication, February 5, 2015.

837 Donald Stainsby, "Dean of Ecology," *BC Outdoors* 35, no. 12 (December 1979), 37.

838 June Wood, *Home to the Nechako*, 31.

839 Lady Susan Tweedsmuir, "Tweedsmuir Park," 453.

840 Ian McTaggart Cowan to Francis Kermode, July 23, 1936, GR-0111, Box 03, File 04, BCA.

841 *Report of the Provincial Museum of Natural History for the Year 1939* (Victoria: King's Printer, 1940).

842 Lord Tweedsmuir, "Message to Sportsmen," *Rod and Gun in Canada*, November, 1936.

843 Editorial, "Wild Life Conservation is Everybody's Affair," *Rod and Gun in Canada* (November 1936).

844 Lady Susan Tweedsmuir, "Tweedsmuir Park," 468.

845 Mikkel Schau, interview, March 8, 2013.

846 Cowan, "A Review of the Reptiles and Amphibians of British Columbia," in *Report of the Provincial Museum of British Columbia for the Year 1936* (Victoria: King's Printer, 1937), K20.

847 No correspondence in museum files for this time.

848 Ian McTaggart Cowan, "Report on Study Trip to Eastern Museums," in *Report of the Provincial Museum of British Columbia for the Year 1937* (Victoria: King's Printer, 1938), L15.

849 Cowan, "Report on Study Trip to Eastern Museums," L18.

850 *The Daily Colonist*, "Museum Vital to Education," [ca. 1937], Cowan_PN_185.

851 Hart, *J.B. Harkin*, 481.

852 J.B. Harkin, *Banff Crag and Canyon*, April 9, 1937, as quoted in Hart, *J.B. Harkin*, 483.

853 Cowan and Guiguet, *Mammals of BC*, 91–92.

854 Ian McTaggart Cowan, "The Distribution of the Pikas (*Ochotona*) in British Columbia and Alberta," *The Murrelet* 35, no. 2 (May–August 1954): 19–24.

855 Cowan, "Small Mammals of Western Mountains," 139.

856 David J. Hafner and Andrew T. Smith, "Revision of the Subspecies of the American Pika, *Ochotona princeps* (Lagomorpha: Ochotonidae)," *Journal of Mammalogy* 91, no. 2 (April 2010): 401–417. http://is.gd/bZghXR (abstract accessed October 31, 2014).

857 Ian McTaggart Cowan to Francis Kermode, July 1, 1937, GR-0111, Box 03, File 04, 1925–1940, BCA.

858 Campbell et al., *Birds of BC*, vol. 2, 398.

859 Campbell et al., *Birds of BC*, vol. 2, 136–137.

860 Campbell et al., *Birds of BC*, vol. 2, 44.

861 Campbell et al., *Birds of BC*, vol. 2, 44.

862 Cowan, "Small Mammals of Western Mountains," 137.

863 Cowan and Guiguet, *Mammals of BC*, 133.

864 Cowan, "Field Notes 1936–1937," July 28, 1936, Cowan_FN_052.

865 Cowan and Guiguet, *Mammals of BC*, 215.

866 Daniel Ludwig, "*Microtus richardsoni*," *Mammalian Species* no. 223 (November 14, 1984): 1–6.

867 Ludwig, "*Microtus richardsoni*," 6.

868 Ludwig, "*Microtus richardsoni*," 2.

869 David Nagorsen, personal communication, May 9, 2014.

870 Cowan, interview by Rick Searle for Elders Council for Parks in BC, October 2006.

871 Ian McTaggart Cowan to Francis Kermode, July 14, 1937, GR-0111, Box 03, File 04, BCA.

872 Cowan to Kermode, July 14, 1937, GR-0111, Box 03, File 04, BCA.

873 Cowan and Guiguet, *Mammals of BC*, 245.

874 Ian McTaggart Cowan, "The Sharp-Headed Finner Whale of the Eastern Pacific," *Journal of Mammalogy* 20, no. 2 (May 1939): 215–225.

875 Cowan, interview, November 30, 2000.

876 Cowan, interview, November 30, 2000.

877 Stainsby, "Dean of Ecology," 36.

878 Cowan and Guiguet, *Mammals of BC*, 266–267.

879 Ian McTaggart Cowan, "Whales and Whaling: Some Issues of the 1980s," unpublished report to the Canadian Committee on Whales and Whaling, September 20, 1980, Cowan_PN_219.

880 Cowan, "Whales and Whaling: Some Issues of the 1980s," Cowan_PN_219.

881 Cowan, "Whales and Whaling: Some Issues of the 1980s," Cowan_PN_219.

882 Ian McTaggart Cowan, "A Report to the Canadian Committee on Whales and Whaling," presented at the 33rd Annual Meeting of the International Whaling Commission, July 20–25, 1981 (unpublished, 7 pp.), Cowan_PN_219.

883 Ian McTaggart Cowan to D. Lawrence, Rideau Hall, November 15, 1998, Cowan_PN_012.

884 Stainsby, "Dean of Ecology," 37.

885 Ian McTaggart Cowan, "Fossil and Subfossil Mammals From the Quaternary of British Columbia," *Transactions of the Royal Society of Canada*, 3rd series, vol. 35, section 4 (1941): 39–49.

886 *The Daily Colonist*, "Museum Vital to Education," [ca. 1937], Cowan_PN_185.

887 Cowan, interview by Peter Corley-Smith, October 1985.

888 Marcia Bonta, "Theodora Cope Gray: Nature's Own Child," blogpost, July 1, 2001. http://marciabonta.wordpress.com/2001/07/01/theodora-cope-gray-natures-own-child (accessed December 29, 2013).

889 Theodora Stanwell-Fletcher, *Driftwood Valley* (Boston: Little, Brown, 1946), 159.

890 Cowan and Guiguet, *Mammals of British Columbia*, 329.

891 Stanwell-Fletcher, *Driftwood Valley*, 32.

892 Stanwell-Fletcher, *Driftwood Valley*, 31.

893 Stanwell-Fletcher, *Driftwood Valley*, 95.

894 John F. Stanwell-Fletcher, "Three Years in the Wolves' Wilderness," *Natural History* 49, no. 3 (March 1942): 136–147.

895 Stanwell-Fletcher, *Driftwood Valley*, 135.

896 Stanwell-Fletcher, *Driftwood Valley*, 138.

897 Theodora C. Stanwell-Fletcher and John F. Stanwell-Fletcher, *Some Accounts of Flora and Fauna of the Driftwood Valley Region of North Central British Columbia*, Occasional Papers of the British Columbia Provincial Museum no. 4 (Victoria: King's Printer, 1943).

898 Theodora Gray to Ian McTaggart Cowan, November 9, 1999, Cowan_PN_090.

899 Campbell et al., *Birds of BC*, vol. 4, 395.

900 Lynn Woods, "Portrait of a Fracking Town: Dimock, Pennsylvania," *Chronogram* (Hudson River Valley, New York State), June 1, 2012. http://is.gd/tNhS1z (accessed February 6, 2015).

901 Ian McTaggart Cowan to Rhoda Love, December 7, 1998, Cowan_PN_090.

902 Integrated Land Management Bureau, "Fort Saint James Land and Resource Management Plan," Government of British Columbia, 1999. www.for.gov.bc.ca/tasb/slrp/pdf/LRMP/Fort St James_LRMP.pdf (pdf accessed December 5, 2014).

903 Cowan, interview by Rick Searle for Elders Council for Parks in BC, October 2006.

904 Now the Society for Northwestern Vertebrate Biology, which published the journal *The Murrelet*, now the *Northwestern Naturalist*.

905 Cowan referred to George M. Dawson, *Report on an Exploration from Port Simpson on the Pacific Coast to Edmonton on the Saskatchewan* … (Montreal: Dawson Brothers, 1881), https://archive.org/stream/

cihm_03655#page/n5/mode/2up (accessed October 31, 2014); Malcolm McLeod, ed., *Peace River: a Canoe Voyage from Hudson's Bay to Pacific by the late Sir George Simpson in 1828: Journal of the late Chief Factor Archibald McDonald, who accompanied him* (Ottawa: J. Durie & Son, 1872), https://archive.org/stream/cihm_15542#page/n7/mode/2up (accessed October 31, 2014); and Daniel W. Harmon, *A Journal of Voyages and Travels in the Interior of North America … (New York: A.S Barnes & Co., 1903), https://archive.org/stream/journalofvoyageso2harm#page/n7/mode/2up (accessed October 31, 2014).

906 *Report of the Provincial Museum of Natural History for the Year 1938* (Victoria: King's Printer, 1939), K10.

907 Ian McTaggart Cowan, "The Vertebrate Fauna of the Peace River District of British Columbia," *British Columbia Provincial Museum Occasional Paper No. 1* (1939).

908 David Nagorsen, interview, May 24, 2013.

909 Chris Siddle, "Birds of North Peace River (Fort Saint John and Vicinity): Parts 1 and 2," *Wildlife Afield* 7, nos. 1, 2 (2010): 12–123, 143–280.

910 Nagorsen, interview, May 24, 2013.

911 Ann Schau, interview, October 9, 2012.

912 Schau, interview, October 9, 2012.

913 Robie W. Tufts, "Some Common Birds of Nova Scotia," MS, Robie W. Tufts fonds, acc. 1900.433/1, Acadia University Library. Published under the same title, Kentville, NS: Kentville Publishing, 1934.

914 Campbell et al., *Birds of BC*, vol. 2, 400.

915 Ian McTaggart Cowan, "Field Notes I. McT. Cowan and P.W. Martin Peace River 1938" (File M-13 FIE-30) [transcription under Cowan_FN_053].

916 Cowan, "Field Notes … Peace River 1938," May 5–6, 1938.

917 Ian McTaggart Cowan to Francis Kermode, May 9, 1938, GR-0111, Box 03, File 04, 1925–1940 Ian McTaggart-Cowan, BCA.

918 Kenneth Racey, "K. Racey Field Notes 1924–1938," April 18, 1929. Cowan_FN_001.

919 Munro and Cowan, *Bird Fauna of BC*, 55.

920 Munro and Cowan, *Bird Fauna of BC*, 54.

921 Stanwell-Fletcher, *Driftwood Valley*, 179.

922 Leland Stowe, *Crusoe of Lonesome Lake* (New York: Random House, 1957).

923 Cowan to Kermode, May 9, 1938, BCA.

924 Campbell et al., *Birds of BC*, vol. 2, 162.

925 Campbell et al., *Birds of BC*, vol. 2, 162.

926 Cowan to Kermode, May 9, 1938, BCA.

927 Cowan, "The Vertebrate Fauna of the Peace River District of British Columbia," 49.

928 Cowan to Kermode, May 9, 1938, BCA.

929 Cowan to Kermode, May 14, 1938, GR-0111, Box 03, File 04, 1925–1940, BCA.

930 Cowan, "Field Notes … Peace River 1938," May 14, 1938, Cowan_FN_053.

931 Cowan, "Field Notes … Peace River 1938," May 14, 1938, Cowan_FN_053.

932 Cowan, "Field Notes … Peace River 1938," May 17, 1938, Cowan_FN_053.

933 Cowan, "Field Notes … Peace River 1938," May 21, 1938, Cowan_FN_053.

934 Cowan, "Field Notes … Peace River 1938," May 19, 1938 [under "Toad," 294], Cowan_FN_053.

935 Cowan to Kermode, June 4, 1938, GR-0111, Box 03, File 04, 1925–1940, BCA.

936 Campbell et al., *Birds of BC*, vol. 4, 364.

937 Ian McTaggart Cowan to Francis Kermode, May 28, 1938, GR-0111, Box 03, File 04, 1925–1940, BCA.

938 Cowan, "The Vertebrate Fauna of the Peace River District of British Columbia," 84.

939 Cowan to Kermode, June 4, 1938, BCA.

940 Munro and Cowan, *Bird Fauna of BC*, 106.

941 Cowan, "Of Mice and Men," lecture delivered March 18, 1961. https://circle.ubc.ca/flashstreamview/bitstream/handle/2429/36425/ubc_at_010_cowan.mp3?sequence=1 (streaming audio, beginning at ~44:20, accessed October 15, 2014).

942 In 1937–1938, for example, the Soviet government executed more than 100,000 Polish-Russian civilians, while nearly 30,000 more were sentenced to slower deaths in labour camps.

943 Cowan, "The Vertebrate Fauna of the Peace River District of British Columbia," 5.

944 Cowan, "The Vertebrate Fauna of the Peace River District of British Columbia," 72.

945 Cowan, "The Vertebrate Fauna of the Peace River District of British Columbia," 36.

946 Cowan, "Of Mice and Men," March 18, 1961. https://circle.ubc.ca/flashstreamview/bitstream/handle/2429/36425/ubc_at_010_cowan.mp3?sequence=1 (streaming audio, beginning at ~27:00, accessed October 15, 2014).

947 Cowan to Kermode, June 27, 1938, GR-0111, Box 03, File 04, 1925–1940 Ian McTaggart-Cowan, BCA.

948 Cowan, "The Vertebrate Fauna of the Peace River District of British Columbia," 96.

949 Ian McTaggart Cowan and James Hatter, "A Trap and Technique for the Capture of Diving Waterfowl," *Journal of Wildlife Management* 16, no. 4 (October 1952): 438–441. www.jstor.org/stable/3797492 (abstract accessed October 31, 2014).

950 Campbell et al., *Birds of BC*, vol. 1, 358.

951 E.O. Wilson, *Naturalist* (Washington, DC: Island Press, 1994), 331 [Wilson characterizing Samuelson and paraphrasing from the latter's *Newsweek* column].

952 Denis R. Alexander and Ronald L. Numbers, eds. *Biology and Ideology from Descartes to Dawkins* (Chicago: University of Chicago Press, 2010), 10.

953 Victoria Brignell, "The Eugenics Movement Britain Wants to Forget," *New Statesman*, December 9, 2010. www.newstatesman.com/society/2010/12/british-eugenics-disabled (accessed February, 6, 2015).

954 Wilson, *Naturalist*, 331.

955 Paul Weindling, "Genetics, Eugenics and the Holocaust," in Alexander and Numbers, eds., *Biology and Ideology*, 195.

956 Wilson, *Naturalist*, 328.

957 Michael Ruse, "Evolution and the Idea of Social Progress," in *Biology and Ideology from Descartes to Dawkins*, 273.

958 Wilson, *Naturalist*, 227.

959 Wilson, *Naturalist*, 225.

960 Cowan, "The Challenge We Take," 662.

961 Cowan, "Of Mice and Men," March 18, 1961. https://circle.ubc.ca/flashstreamview/bitstream/handle/2429/36425/ubc_at_010_cowan.mp3?sequence=1 (streaming audio, beginning at ~59:45, accessed October 15, 2014).

962 Ron Jeffels of Ian McTaggart Cowan, "Speech at Retirement," March 5, 1981, Cowan_PN_146.

963 Cowan to Kermode, June 27, 1938, BCA.

964 Cowan, "The Vertebrate Fauna of the Peace River District of British Columbia," 36.

965 Knut R. Fladmark, Jonathan C. Driver and Diana Alexander, "The Paleoindian Component at Charlie Lake Cave (HbRf 39), British Columbia," *American Antiquity* 53, no. 2 (April 1988): 371–384. http://is.gd/zq7XeB (abstract accessed October 31, 2014).

966 Briony Penn, "Passages from the Peace: Community Reflections on the Changing Peace Region," Suzuki Foundation and Global Forest Watch, October 2013, 2. http://is.gd/f5VMcy (pdf accessed October 31, 2014).

967 Art Napoleon, interview, June 1, 2010.

968 Hugh Brody, *Maps and Dreams* (Vancouver: Douglas & McIntyre, 1981), xi.

969 Brody, *Maps and Dreams*, xi.

970 Cowan, "Conservation and Man's Environment," in *Knowledge Among Men: Eleven Essays on Science, Culture and Society*, ed. Paul H. Oehser (New York: Simon and Schuster, 1966), 76.

971 H. Ayles, "Environmental Impact Assessment, Biological Perspective," in *National Conference on Environmental Impact Assessment: Philosophy and Methodology, Proceedings of a Conference Held November 15–16, 1973* (Winnipeg: Agassiz Centre for Water Studies, University of Manitoba, 1973), 22–29.

972 Ian McTaggart Cowan, "Environmental Impact Assessment: A Methodology for Prediction of Environmental Effects," in *National Conference on Environmental Impact Assessment: Philosophy and Methodology, Proceedings of a Conference Held November 15–16, 1973* (Winnipeg: Agassiz Centre for Water Studies, University of Manitoba, 1973), 108–132.

973 *Report of the Joint Review Panel, Site C Clean Energy Project, BC Hydro*, Ministers of Environment of Canada and British Columbia, May 2014. www.ceaa-acee.gc.ca/050/documents/p63919/99173E.pdf (accessed February 26, 2015).

974 Cowan, interview by Rick Searle for Elders Council for Parks in BC, October 2006.

975 British Columbia Ministry of Environment, "Conservation Officer Service – 100 Years: 1905–1960, The Game Wardens." www.env.gov.bc.ca/cos/100years/1905/game_warden.html (accessed January 6, 2013).

976 Cowan, interview by Rick Searle for Elders Council for Parks in BC, October 2006.

977 Harlan I. Smith, "*Materia medica* of the Bella Coola and Neighbouring Tribes of British Columbia," *National Museum of Canada Bulletin* no. 56 (1929): 47–69. www.swsbm.com/Ethnobotany/

Bella_Coola_Materia_Medica.pdf (pdf accessed October 31, 2014).

978 Corley-Smith, *White Bears and Other Curiosities*, 98.

979 Ian McTaggart Cowan, "Distribution and Variation in the Native Sheep of North America," *America Midland Naturalist* 24, no. 3 (November 1940): 505–580. www.jstor.org/stable/2420858 (abstract accessed October 31, 2014).

980 Cowan and Guiguet, *Mammals of BC*, 392.

981 Richard M. Bond to Ian McTaggart Cowan, December 14, 1938, GR-0111, Box 03, File 04, 1925–1940, BCA.

982 Leopold, "Song of the Gavilan," 11.

983 Leopold, "Song of the Gavilan," 14.

984 Ian McTaggart Cowan to Francis Kermode, June 12, 1939, GR-0111, Box 03, File 04, 1925–1940, BCA.

985 Cowan, "Moments from the Education of an Ornithologist," 19.

986 Patrick W. Martin, "Field Notes Miscellaneous 1939–1967," File M-6 FIE-3, RBCM/BCA. Transcriptions under Cowan_FN_060.

987 Ian McTaggart Cowan, "Species Index 1939–1942: Birds," Cowan_FN_015; Ian McTaggart Cowan, "Species Index 1939–1942: Mammals," Cowan_FN_016.

988 Ian McTaggart Cowan to Postmaster, Bella Bella. July 21, 1939. GR-0111, Box 03, File 04, 1925–1940, BCA.

989 *Report of the Provincial Museum of Natural History for the Year 1939* (Victoria: King's Printer, 1940), C9.

990 Cowan, "Insularity in the Genus *Sorex* on the North Coast of British Columbia," *Proceedings of the Biological Society of Washington* 54 (July 1941): 95–108. www.biodiversitylibrary.org/page/34599248#page/119/mode/1up (accessed October 31, 2014).

991 Cowan, "Insularity in the Genus *Sorex*," 97. www.biodiversitylibrary.org/page/34599248#page/121/mode/1up (accessed October 31, 2014).

992 Cowan, "Species Index 1939–1942; Mammals," *Sorex*, Cowan_FN_016.

993 Cowan, "Insularity in the Genus *Sorex*," 97.

994 Cowan, "Insularity in the Genus *Sorex*," 97.

995 Cowan, "Insularity in the Genus *Sorex*," 100.

996 Cowan and Guiguet, *Mammals of BC*, 44–45.

997 Cowan, "Insularity in the Genus *Sorex*," 104.

998 "Human Settlement," *Hakai: Science on the Coastal Margin,* Calvert Island Field Station (webpage), Hakai Institute, Tula Foundation and University of Victoria, 2014. https://hbi-calvert.wordpress.com/research-2/archaeology (accessed January 29, 2015).

999 Cowan, "Species Index 1939–1942: Mammals," P–Z, 27, Cowan_FN_016.

1000 Cowan, "Insularity in the Genus *Sorex*," 95–96.

1001 John Alroy, "The Fossil Record of North American Mammals: Evidence for a Paleocene Evolutionary Radiation," *Systematic Biology* 48, no. 1 (1999): 107–118. http://sysbio.oxfordjournals.org/content/48/1/107.full.pdf+html (accessed October 31, 2014).

1002 Nagorsen, "Opossums, Shrews and Moles of British Columbia," 28.

1003 T.T. McCabe and Ian McTaggart Cowan, "*Peromyscus maniculatus macrorhinus* and the Problem of Insularity," *Transactions of the Royal Canadian Institute* 25 (1945): 117–216. http://eurekamag.com/research/023/347/023347331.php (abstract accessed October 31, 2014).

1004 Nagorsen, interview, May 24, 2013.

1005 Cowan to Kermode, July 18, 1939, GR-0111, Box 03, File 04, 1925–1940, BCA.

1006 Ian McTaggart Cowan, personal communication, 2005.

1007 Campbell et al., *Birds of BC*, vol. 2, 110.

1008 Aldo Leopold, "Marshland Elegy," in *Some Lessons*, ed. B. of V., 79–83.

1009 Krista Roessingh and Briony Penn, "Sandhill Cranes of Coastal British Columbia: Results of Helicopter Surveys and Preliminary Observations of Habitat Use," *Proceedings of the North American Crane Workshop* 11 (2010): 7. http://is.gd/7okU4F (pdf accessed October 31, 2014).

1010 Chris Darimont, personal communication, February 24, 2005.

1011 Martin, "Field Notes Miscellaneous 1939–1967," July 8, 1939. Transcriptions under Cowan_FN_060.

1012 Campbell et al., *Birds of BC*, vol. 1, 190.

1013 Ian McTaggart Cowan, "Bird Records From British Columbia," *The Murrelet* 21, no. 3 (1940): 69–70.

1014 Campbell et al., *Birds of BC*, vol. 1, 182.

1015 Ian McTaggart Cowan, "Journal Orient Trip 1957," December 8–13, 1957, Cowan_FN_044.

1016 Cowan, "Journal Orient Trip 1957," December 8, 1957.

1017 Joseph Grinnell and Frederick H. Test,

"Geographic Variation in the Fork-Tailed Petrel," *The Condor* 41, no. 4 (July–August 1939): 170–172. https://sora.unm.edu/sites/default/files/journals/condor/v041n04/p0170-p0172.pdf (accessed October 31, 2014).

1018 Cowan, "Species Index 1939–1942: Birds," K–Q, 44, Cowan_FN_015.

1019 Campbell et al., *Birds of BC*, vol. 1, 200–203.

1020 Cowan, "A Review of the Reptiles and Amphibians of British Columbia," K19.

1021 Dorothy Abraham, *Lone Cone: A Journal of Life on the West Coast of Vancouver Island, BC* (Victoria: Tiritea, 1945).

1022 Ian McTaggart Cowan, "Longevity of the Red-Legged Frog (*Rana a. aurora*)," *Copeia* 1941, no. 1 (March 25, 1941): 48.

1023 *Victoria Daily Times,* "Birth announcements," July 11, 1940, 14.

1024 Cowan, "A Review of the Reptiles and Amphibians of British Columbia," K19.

1025 Cowan, interview by Peter Corley-Smith for RBCM, 1985.

1026 Cowan, interview by Peter Corley-Smith for RBCM, 1985.

1027 Cowan, interview by Peter Corley-Smith for RBCM, 1985.

1028 Cowan, interview, July 9, 2002.

1029 Corley-Smith, *White Bears and Other Curiosities*, 101.

1030 Cowan to Kermode, August 30, 1940, GR-0111, Box 03, File 04, 1925–1940, BCA.

1031 Cowan to Mrs. G.A. Hardy, September 6, 1940, GR-0111, Box 03, File 04, 1925–1940, BCA.

1032 Cowan to Mrs. Crummy, September 27, 1940, GR-0111, Box 03, File 04, 1925–1940, BCA.

1033 Kermode to Cowan, September 26, 1940, GR-0111, Box 03, File 04, 1925–1940, BCA.

1034 Cowan, interview by Peter Corley-Smith for RBCM, 1985.

1035 Cowan to Clifford Carl, January 15, 1942, GR-0111, Box 03, File 02, 1942, BCA.

1036 Cowan, interview, November 30, 2000.

1037 Andrew V. Suarez and Neil D. Tsutsui, "The Value of Museum Collections for Research and Society," *Bioscience* 54, no. 1 (2004): 66–74. http://nature.berkeley.edu/tsutsuilab/SuarezTsutsui2004Biosci.pdf (accessed October 31, 2014).

1038 Stainsby, "Dean of Ecology," 40.

1039 Ian McTaggart Cowan, "Land, Wildlife and People: It's Time to Put Life Back into the Wilds of BC," *Vancouver Sun*, December 26, 1972, 30.

1040 E. Bennett Metcalfe, *A Man of Some Importance: The Life of Roderick Brown* (Seattle and Vancouver: James Wood Publishers, 1985).

1041 Cowan, "Land, Wildlife and People," 30.

1042 Cowan, "Land, Wildlife and People," 30.

1043 Ian McTaggart Cowan, "Journals: Voyages along the Coast of BC with Tom and Margaret Denny 1962–1967," Cowan_FN_036.

1044 National Geographic, *Last Stand of the Great Bear,* television documentary, National Geographic Channel, aired November 3, 2004; Ian McAllister, *The Last Wild Wolves: Ghosts of the Rainforest* (Vancouver: Greystone Books, 2007).

1045 Cowan, interview, July 9, 2002.

1046 J.A. Munro and W.A. Clemens, "Waterfowl in Relation to the Spawning of Herring in British Columbia," *Bulletin of the Biological Board of Canada* 17, no. 2 (1931): 1–46.

1047 Campbell et al., *Birds of BC*, vol. 1, 366.

1048 Cowan, interview, July 9, 2002.

1049 Ian McTaggart Cowan and Margaret G. Arsenault, "Reproduction and Growth in the Creeping Vole, *Microtus oregoni serpens* Merriam," *Canadian Journal of Zoology* 32 (1954): 198–208. http://is.gd/r2rJTr (pdf accessed October 31, 2014).

1050 Cowan, interview, July 9, 2002.

1051 Cowan and Guiguet, *Mammals of BC*, 214–215.

1052 Cowan, "Fossil and Subfossil Mammals From the Quaternary of British Columbia," 42.

1053 Cowan and Guiguet, *Mammals of BC*, 258–259.

1054 G. Clifford Carl to Ian McTaggart Cowan, December 14, 1941; Cowan to Carl, December 17, 1941; both GR-0111, Box 03, File 03, 1936–1941, BCA.

1055 Cowan to Carl, December 17, 1941, BCA.

1056 Cowan to Carl, December 17, 1941, BCA.

1057 Cowan to Carl, December 17, 1941, BCA.

1058 Cowan, interview, July 9, 2002.

1059 Carl to Cowan, November 4, 1942, GR-0111, Box 03, File 02, 1942, BCA.

1060 Cowan to Carl, February 25, 1941, GR-0111, Box 03, File 03, 1936–1941, BCA.

1061 Cowan to Carl, March 17, 1941, GR-0111, Box 03, File 03, 1936–1941, BCA.

1062 G. Clifford Carl, *The Reptiles of British Columbia*, Handbook no. 3 (Victoria: BC Provincial Museum, 1944), 19–20.

1063 G. Clifford Carl, "Field Notes Carl, Cowan and Beebe, 1941–1944," May 20, 1941 (File M-6 FIE-4) [transcription under Cowan_FN_061].

1064 Ian McTaggart Cowan to Clifford Carl, August 1, 1941, GR-0111, Box 03, File 03, 1936–1941, BCA.

1065 Clifford Carl, *The Amphibians of British Columbia*, Handbook no. 2 (Victoria: BC Provincial Museum, 1943), 40–41.

1066 Ian McTaggart Cowan, "Field Notes Carl, Cowan and Beebe, 1941–1944," May 24, 1941 (File M-6 FIE-4) [transcription under Cowan_FN_061].

1067 Carl, *Reptiles of British Columbia*, 47–49.

1068 Carl, *Reptiles of British Columbia*, 28–29.

1069 Cowan, "Field Notes Carl, Cowan and Beebe 1941–44." June 2, 1941, Cowan_FN_061.

1070 Carl, *Reptiles of British Columbia*, 42–43.

1071 G.A. Mackie draft biographical sketch, University of Victoria. http://web.uvic.ca/~mackie/biography2.pdf (accessed December 15, 2013).

1072 Trisha Guiguet, interview, September 9, 2012.

1073 M.B. Harland, K.J. Nelson and P.T. Gregory, "Status of the Northern Pacific Rattlesnake in British Columbia," Ministry of Environment, Lands and Parks, Wildlife Working Report No. WR-54, 1993. www.env.gov.bc.ca/wld/documents/statusrpts/wr54.pdf (accessed October 31, 2014).

1074 Cowan and Guiguet, *Mammals of BC*, 289.

1075 Ian McTaggart Cowan, "Geographic Distribution of Color Phases of the Red Fox and Black Bear in the Pacific Northwest," *Journal of Mammalogy* 19, no. 2 (1938): 202–206.

1076 Cowan, "Field Notes, Carl, Cowan and Beebe, 1941–44," June 8, 1941, Cowan_FN_061.

1077 Charles J. Jonkel and Ian McT. Cowan, "The Black Bear in the Spruce-Fir Forest," *Wildlife Monographs* 27 (December 1971): 3–57.

1078 Cowan, interview, July 9, 2002.

1079 Ian McTaggart Cowan, "The Status and Conservation of Bears (*Ursidae*) of the World, 1970," in *Bears – Their Biology and Management: Papers and Proceedings of the International Conference on Bear Research and Management held at University of Calgary, Alberta, November 6–9, 1970*, 343–367. http://is.gd/24lXCH (pdf accessed October 31, 2014).

1080 Campbell et al., *Birds of BC*, vol. 2, 28.

1081 Ian McTaggart Cowan to G. Clifford Carl, July 30, 1941, GR-0111, Box 03, File 03, 1936–1941, BCA.

1082 Six specimens from the Chapman house were collected in 1937 by T.P. Maslin ("Fringe-tailed myotis bat in British Columbia," *Journal of Mammalogy* 19 (1938): 373) and deposited in the collections at MVZ.

1083 Ian McTaggart Cowan, "Desert Lecture," n.d., Cowan_PN_333.

1084 Cowan, "Desert Lecture," Cowan_PN_333.

1085 Cowan, interview, July 9, 2002.

1086 V.C. Brink, "The Beginnings of Wisdom," *Vancouver Natural History Society Bulletin* no. 140 (September 1968). Reprinted in Bill Merilees, *Selected Excerpts from the Vancouver Natural History Society Bulletin*, 198. http://naturevancouver.ca/sites/naturevancouver.ca/VNHS%20files/4/VNHS_Bulletin_1943-1971.pdf (pdf p202 accessed May 24, 2014).

1087 Brink, "The Beginnings of Wisdom," 198 [pdf 202].

1088 Cowan, interview, December 5, 2000.

1089 Cowan to Carl, August 1, 1941, BCA.

1090 D.A. Hlady, "South Okanagan Conservation Strategy 1990–1995," Ministry of Environment, Canadian Wildlife Service, Nature Trust of BC, Royal British Columbia Museum and University of British Columbia Wildlife Program, 1990. www.env.gov.bc.ca/wld/documents/southoka/southoka.pdf (accessed October 31, 2014).

1091 Ian McTaggart Cowan, "Spotted Bat" (handwritten draft revision [*Mammals of BC*]), 1987, Cowan_PN_271.

1092 Gregory C. Woodsworth to Ian McTaggart Cowan, February 28, 1981, Cowan_PN_271.

1093 Gary G. Gray, *Wildlife and People: The Human Dimensions of Wildlife Ecology* (Champaign-Urbana: University of Illinois Press, 1993).

1094 Lidicker, "Population Ecology," 324. https://archive.org/stream/seventyfiveyears-oobirn#page/324/mode/2up/search/distribution (accessed October 31, 2014).

1095 Lidicker, "Population Ecology," 324–325.

1096 Cowan, "Moments from the Education of an Ornithologist," 21.

1097 Ian McTaggart Cowan to Clifford Carl, September 13, 1941, GR-0111, Box 03, File 03, 1936–1941, BCA.

1098 Cowan and Guiguet, *Mammals of BC*, 59–60.

1099 Nagorsen, "Opossums, Shrews and Moles of British Columbia," 140.

1100 Ian McTaggart Cowan to Joyce Cowan, July 4–29, 1944, Cowan_PN_094.

1101 Cowan, "The Challenge We Take," 663.

1102 Mark Fraker et al., *Burns Bog Ecosystem Review: Small Mammals* (Victoria: BC Environmental Assessment Office, 1999). http://is.gd/nDgFEM (text viewed via ResearchGate, October 31, 2014).

1103 Richard J. Hebda et al., *Burns Bog Ecosystem Review: Synthesis Report for Burns Bog, Fraser River Delta, Southwestern British Columbia, Canada* (Victoria: BC Environmental Assessment Office, 2000). http://is.gd/sQaxJu (pdf accessed October 31, 2014).

1104 Cowan and Guiguet, *Mammals of BC*, 207.

1105 Vanessa Craig, Kym E. Welstead and Ross G. Vennesland, *Recovery Strategy for the Pacific Water Shrew (Sorex bendirii) in British Columbia.* (Victoria: BC Ministry of Environment, 2009). http://is.gd/16QKLz October 31, 2014.

1106 Fraker et al., *Burns Bog Ecosystem Review: Small Mammals.*

1107 "Mammal and Bird Life of Burnaby Lake," Vancouver Natural History Society *Bulletin* no. 18 (October 1945). Reprinted in Bill Merilees, *Selected Excerpts from the Vancouver Natural History Society Bulletin*, 16–17, Cowan_PN_296. http://is.gd/b9otCb (pdf pp20–21 accessed May 24, 2014).

1108 Cowan and Guiguet, *Mammals of BC*, 55.

1109 Richard Hebda, personal communication, March 2001 (also quoted in Briony Penn, "The Natural History of Ian McTaggart Cowan," *Focus* magazine, April 2001).

1110 Cowan and Guiguet, *Mammals of BC*, 88.

1111 Ian McTaggart Cowan to Clifford Carl, November 10, 1942, GR-0111, Box 03, File 02, 1942, BCA.

1112 Carl, *The Amphibians of British Columbia*, 38–39.

1113 Cowan to Carl, February 1942, GR-0111, Box 03, File 02, 1942, BCA.

1114 Cowan, "Journal Field Trips 1935–1961," September 9, 1942, Cowan_FN_014.

1115 Cowan and Guiguet. *Mammals of BC*, 326.

1116 Cowan, "Journal Field Trips 1935–1961," September 9, 1942, Cowan_FN_014.

1117 Campbell et al., *Birds of BC*, vol. 1, 360.

1118 Cowan, interview, July 9, 2002.

1119 A transcript was published under the title "Conservation of Wildlife" in a pamphlet for Kindness to Animals Week, April 20–27, 1942, by the Society for the Prevention of Cruelty to Animals, Vancouver [Cowan_AN_038].

1120 Cowan, "Conservation of Wildlife."

1121 Cowan, interview, July 9, 2002.

1122 Cowan, interview, July 9, 2002.

1123 *Report of the Provincial Game Commission*, 1956 (Victoria: Department of Attorney-General, 1957), R47.

1124 Lyn Hancock, "The Predator Hunters," in *Our Wildlife Heritage: 100 Years of Wildlife Management*, ed. A. Murray (Victoria: Centennial Wildlife Society of BC, 1987), 126–127.

1125 Cowan, interview, July 9, 2002.

1126 Cowan had been invited to officially launch the university's first PhD program in natural resources and environmental studies.

1127 Ian McTaggart Cowan, "Address to University of Northern British Columbia, May 22, 1997" (unpublished), Cowan_PN_101.

1128 Hancock, "The Predator Hunters" 127.

1129 E.J. Hart, *Jimmy Simpson*, 185.

1130 Andy O'Brien, "At 68 His Dream Trip Came Through," *Weekend Magazine* 5, no. 43 (1955): 29. http://is.gd/8AOuA8 (accessed October 31, 2014).

1131 O'Brien, "At 68 His Dream Trip Came Through," 29.

1132 Christopher Armstrong, Matthew Dominic Evenden and H.V. Nelles, *The River Returns: An Environmental History of the Bow* (Montreal: McGill-Queen's University Press, 2009), 139.

1133 C.H.D. Clarke, "Wild Life Investigation in Banff National Park, 1939" (Ottawa: National Parks Bureau and Department of Mines and Resources, ca. 1940, released for limited use), 24, Cowan_PN_497. [The Stevenson-Hamilton speech was condensed in the New Zealand magazine *Forest and Bird* in August 1939.]

1134 Cowan and Guiguet, *Mammals of BC*, 397.

1135 Cowan and Guiguet, *Mammals of BC*, 394.

1136 Austin de B. Winter, "The President's 1941 Report," Alberta Fish and Game

Association 14th Annual Convention 1942, Austin de B. Winter fonds, Glenbow Museum Archives, Calgary.

1137 R.A. Rooney to Austin de B. Winter, June 27, 1940, Alberta Fish and Game Association fonds 1940; Austin de B. Winter fonds, various papers 1934–46, Glenbow Museum Archives, Calgary.

1138 Hart, *J.B. Harkin*, 482.

1139 Clarke, *Wild Life Investigation in Banff and Jasper National Parks in 1941*, 19.

1140 Clarke, *Wild Life Investigation in Banff and Jasper National Parks in 1941*, 19.

1141 Rooney to Winter, June 27, 1940.

1142 Aldo Leopold, "The Geese Return," February 15, 1943, in *Some Lessons*, vol. 2, ed. B. of V., 37.

1143 J.B. Harkin, *The History and Meaning of the National Parks of Canada* (Saskatoon: H.R. Larson, 1957), 16.

1144 Harkin, *The History and Meaning of the National Parks of Canada*, 16.

1145 Cowan, "Address to University of Northern British Columbia, May 22, 1997," Cowan_PN_101.

1146 Ian McTaggart Cowan, "Field Notes 1943 Rocky Mtns." April 17, 1943, Cowan_FN_023.

1147 Cowan, "Field Notes 1943 Rocky Mtns." April 18, 1943, Cowan_FN_023.

1148 Cowan, "Field Notes 1943 Rocky Mtns." April 19, 1943, Cowan_FN_023.

1149 Cowan and Guiguet, *Mammals of BC*, 358–359.

1150 Ian McTaggart Cowan, "Report on Game Conditions in Banff, Jasper and Kootenay National Parks 1943" (unpublished 72 pp. mimeographed) [original with photographs, Cowan_PN_893].

1151 Cowan, "Field Notes 1943 Rocky Mtns.," June 5, 1943, Cowan_FN_023.

1152 Cowan, "Field Notes 1943 Rocky Mtns.," June 5, 1943, Cowan_FN_023.

1153 Cowan and Guiguet, *Mammals of BC*, 335–336.

1154 Cowan, "Report on Game Conditions in Banff, Jasper and Kootenay National Parks 1943," 64.

1155 Cowan, "Field Notes 1943 Rocky Mtns.," June 6, 1943, Cowan_FN_023.

1156 Ian McTaggart Cowan to Frank Butler, May 16, 1947, Cowan_PN_358.

1157 The HWI used to be part of the University of Idaho but merged with the Wildlife Conservation Society and is now based in the WCS offices in Bozeman, Montana.

1158 Maurice Hornocker to Ian McTaggart Cowan, various correspondence 1986–88, Cowan_PN_230.

1159 Daryll M. Hebert, "Forage and Serum Phosphorus Values for Bighorn Sheep," *Journal of Range Management* 25, no. 4 (1972): 292–296. https://journals.uair.arizona.edu/index.php/jrm/article/viewFile/6077/5687 (accessed October 31, 2014).

1160 Daryll Hebert, interview, September 28, 2012.

1161 Hebert, interview, September 28, 2012.

1162 Cowan, "Field Notes 1944–1945 Rocky Mtns.," August 26, 1945, Cowan_FN_024.

1163 Cowan and Guiguet, *Mammals of BC*, 135–136.

1164 Cowan, "Notes on the Distribution of the Chipmunks *Eutamias*," 107–116.

1165 Hebert, interview, September 28, 2012.

1166 Hart, *Jimmy Simpson*, 9.

1167 Cowan, interview, December 5, 2000.

1168 Cowan, "Field Notes 1943 Rocky Mtns.," June 11, 1943, Cowan_FN_023.

1169 Cowan, interview, July 9, 2002.

1170 Cowan and Guiguet, *Mammals of BC*, 388–389.

1171 Cowan, "Field Notes 1943 Rocky Mtns.," June 14, 1943, Cowan_FN_023.

1172 Cowan, interview, December 5, 2000.

1173 Cowan and Guiguet, *Mammals of BC*, 322–323.

1174 Hart, *Jimmy Simpson*, 10.

1175 Cowan, interview, December 5, 2000.

1176 Cowan, interview, July 9, 2002.

1177 Daryll Hebert and Ian McTaggart Cowan, "Natural Salt Licks as a Part of the Natural Ecology of the Mountain Goat," *Canadian Journal of Zoology* 49, no. 5 (1971): 605–610. http://is.gd/Wr3vKM (accessed October 31, 2014).

1178 Cowan, interview, December 5, 2000.

1179 Cowan, interview, December 5, 2000.

1180 Cowan and Guiguet, *Mammals of BC*, 281–282.

1181 Frank Camp, *Roots in the Rockies* (Ucluelet, BC: Frank Camp Ventures, 1993), 43.

1182 Camp, *Roots in the Rockies*, 40.

1183 Camp, *Roots in the Rockies*, 47.

1184 Cowan, interview, July 9, 2002.

1185 Cowan, interview, December 5, 2000.

1186 Cowan, interview, February 26, 2001.

1187 Cowan, interview, December 5, 2000.

1188 Cowan, interview, July 9, 2002.

1189 Cowan, interview, December 5, 2000.

1190 Lewis R. Freeman, *Down the Columbia* (New York: Dodd, Mead and Company, 1921), 25. https://archive.org/stream/down-columbia00free#page/24/mode/2up/search/biceps (accessed October 31, 2014).

1191 Cowan, "Field Notes 1943 Rocky Mtns.," June 19, 1943, Cowan_FN_023.

1192 Cowan and Guiguet, *Mammals of BC*, 342–343.

1193 Cowan, "Field Notes 1943 Rocky Mtns.," June 26, 1943.

1194 Cowan, "Field Notes 1943 Rocky Mtns.," August 4, 1943, Cowan_FN_023.

1195 Cowan, "Field Notes 1943 Rocky Mtns.," July 3, 1943, Cowan_FN_023.

1196 Cowan, "Field Notes 1943 Rocky Mtns.," July 6, 1943, Cowan_FN_023.

1197 Cowan, "Field Notes 1943 Rocky Mtns.," July 8, 1943, Cowan_FN_023.

1198 Cowan, "Field Notes 1943 Rocky Mtns.," July 14, 1943, Cowan_FN_023.

1199 Cowan, "Field Notes 1943 Rocky Mtns.," July 15, 1943, Cowan_FN_023.

1200 Campbell et al., *Birds of BC*, vol. 3, 452.

1201 Cowan, "Field Notes 1943 Rocky Mtns.," July 27, 1943, Cowan_FN_023.

1202 Cowan, "Field Notes 1943 Rocky Mtns.," August 8, 1943, Cowan_FN_023.

1203 Cowan and Guiguet, *Mammals of BC*, 276.

1204 Hart, *Jimmy Simpson*, 186.

1205 Cowan, "In the Steps of Southesk" (unpublished essay, ca. 1953), Cowan_PN_294.

1206 Cowan, interview, December 5, 2000.

1207 Ian McTaggart Cowan, "Big Game of the Mountain Province," *Canadian Geographic* 64, no. 6 (June 1952): 239. http://is.gd/exegZt (pdf p7, accessed October 31, 2014).

1208 Cowan, "Field Notes 1943 Rocky Mtns.," August 24, 1943, Cowan_FN_023.

1209 C.H.D. Clarke, "Wild Life Investigations in Banff and Jasper National Parks in 1941" (Ottawa: National Parks Bureau, 1942, released for limited use), 10, Cowan_PN_497.

1210 Cowan, "Big Game of the Mountain Province," 233.

1211 Cowan, "Report on Game Conditions in Banff, Jasper and Kootenay National Parks 1943," 32.

1212 Cowan, "Field Notes 1943 Rocky Mtns.," September 11, 1943, Cowan_FN_023.

1213 Cowan, interview, December 5, 2000.

1214 Cowan, "Report on Game Conditions in Banff, Jasper and Kootenay National Parks 1943," 1 [original with photographs, Cowan_PN_893].

1215 Cowan, interview, December 5, 2000.

1216 Cowan, interview, December 5, 2000.

1217 Cowan, "Report on Game Conditions in Banff, Jasper and Kootenay National Parks 1943," 70.

1218 Cowan, interview by Rick Searle for Elders Council for Parks in BC, October 2006.

1219 Scott Honeyman, "In Four Areas of Rockies, Park Development Opposed," *Vancouver Sun*, April 27, 1971, A10.

1220 Cowan, interview by Rick Searle for Elders Council for Parks in BC, October 2006.

1221 Honeyman, "In Four Areas of Rockies," A10.

1222 Ian McTaggart Cowan, "Research in the National Parks of Canada" (unpublished report prepared for Parks Canada, 1977), 157, Cowan_PN_898.

1223 Bill Graveland, "Controversial Glacier Skywalk Attempts to Thrill Tourists with Glass Floor," The Canadian Press, May 11, 2014. www.ctvnews.ca/business/controversial-glacier-skywalk-attempts-to-thrill-tourists-with-glass-floor-1.1816479 (accessed May 26, 2014).

1224 Cowan, "Big Game of the Mountain Province," 240.

1225 Cowan, "Big Game of the Mountain Province," 240.

1226 Cowan, "Big Game of the Mountain Province," 235.

1227 Cowan, "Big Game of the Mountain Province," 234.

1228 Ann Schau, interview, October 9, 2012.

1229 Ian McTaggart Cowan to Ann Schau, February 6, 1990, Cowan_PN_504.

1230 Hatter, *Politically Incorrect*, 28.

1231 Campbell et al., *Birds of BC*, vol. 3, 410–414.

1232 Cowan to Schau, September 12, 1988, Cowan_PN_504.

1233 Cowan to Schau, September 12, 1988, Cowan_PN_504.

1234 Stuart F. Bradley, "Mammals of UBC Area," *Vancouver Natural History Society Bulletin*

nos. 41, 42 (September 1948), Cowan_
PN_296. Reprinted in Bill Merilees, *Selected
Excerpts from the Vancouver Natural History
Society Bulletin*, 34. http://naturevancou-
ver.ca/sites/naturevancouver.ca/VNHS%20
files/4/VNHS_Bulletin_1943-1971.pdf (pdf
p38 accessed May 24, 2014).

1235 Vancouver Natural History Society, "Mammal and Bird Life of Burnaby Lake," *Bulletin* no. 18 (October 1945). Reprinted in Merilees, 17 (pdf p21).

1236 Carl, *The Amphibians of British Columbia*, 54.

1237 Vancouver Natural History Society, "Bird
Study, Seymour Mountain to Bridgeman
Park," *Vancouver Natural History Society
Bulletin* 89 (Summer 1954). Reprinted in
Merilees, 74 (pdf p78).

1238 Campbell et al., *Birds of BC*, vol. 4, 19.

1239 Ian McTaggart Cowan, "Field Notes
1944–1945 Rocky Mtns.," May 4, 1944,
Cowan_FN_024.

1240 Cowan, "Field Notes 1944–1945 Rocky
Mtns.," May 23, 1944.

1241 Campbell et al., *Birds of BC*, vol. 4, 150.

1242 Cowan to Joyce Cowan, July 4–29, 1944,
Cowan_PN_094.

1243 Cowan to Joyce Cowan, July 4–29, 1944,
Cowan_PN_094.

1244 Cowan to Joyce Cowan, July 4–29, 1944,
Cowan_PN_094.

1245 Hatter, *Politically Incorrect*, 42.

1246 Al Brady, interview, September 24, 2012.

1247 Brady, interview, September 24, 2012.

1248 Cowan, "Field Notes 1944–1945 Rocky Mtns.,"
December 18, 1944, Cowan_FN_024.

1249 Brady, interview, September 24, 2012.

1250 Brady, interview, September 24, 2012.

1251 Cowan to Joyce Cowan, July 4–29, 1944,
Cowan_PN_094.

1252 Cowan and Guiguet, *Mammals of BC*, 300.

1253 Cowan to Joyce Cowan, July 4–29, 1944,
Cowan_PN_094.

1254 Cowan and Munro, *Bird Fauna of BC*, 226.

1255 Campbell et al., *Birds of BC*, vol. 4, 212.

1256 Cowan to Joyce Cowan, July 4–29, 1944,
Cowan_PN_094.

1257 Cowan to Joyce Cowan, July 4–29, 1944,
Cowan_PN_094.

1258 Campbell et al., *Birds of BC*, vol. 1, 333–334.

1259 Cowan to Joyce Cowan, July 4–29, 1944,
Cowan_PN_094.

1260 Cowan to Joyce Cowan, July 4–29, 1944,
Cowan_PN_094.

1261 Merilees, interview, September 17, 2012.

1262 Ian McTaggart Cowan to Hamilton Mack
Laing, June 15, 1945, Hamilton Mack Laing
fonds, MS-1309, BCA.

1263 Campbell et al., *Birds of BC*, vol. 2, 84.

1264 Cowan, "Field Notes 1944–1945 Rocky Mtns.,"
July 27, 1945, Cowan_FN_024.

1265 Rick Kool, personal communication, January
13, 2014.

1266 Hatter, *Politically Incorrect*, 47.

1267 Cowan, "Field Notes 1944–1945 Rocky
Mtns.," July 6, 1945, Cowan_FN_024.

1268 Ian McTaggart Cowan, "Report of Wildlife
Studies in the Rocky Mountain National
Parks in 1945" (unpublished 63 pp. mimeographed, prepared for National Parks Bureau, Ottawa, 1945), 13, Cowan_PN_895.

1269 Cowan, "Address to University of Northern British Columbia," May 22, 1997,
Cowan_PN_101.

1270 Ian McTaggart Cowan, "The Timber Wolf
in the Rocky Mountain National Parks of
Canada," *Canadian Journal of Research* 25d,
no. 5 (October 1947): 139–174. http://is.gd/
vWpzHT (abstract accessed October 31,
2014).

1271 Cowan, "Address to University of Northern
British Columbia," May 22, 1997.

1272 Cowan, "Address to University of Northern British Columbia," May 22, 1997,
Cowan_PN_101.

1273 Gordon Haber and Marybeth Holleman,
Among Wolves (Chicago: University of Chicago Press, 2013).

1274 Cowan, "Address to University of Northern British Columbia," May 22, 1997,
Cowan_PN_101.

1275 Ian McTaggart Cowan, "Miscellaneous
Correspondence on Wolves, 1947–1999,"
Cowan_PN_276.

1276 E.O French to Ian McTaggart Cowan, January 7, 1948, questionnaire response, "Miscellaneous Correspondence on Wolves, 1947–
1999," Cowan_PN_276.

1277 Geist said he was not sure whether Johnny's
name was spelled Musco or Mosco.

1278 Valerius Geist, interview, September 17, 2012.

1279 Geist, interview, September 17, 2012.

1280 Geist, interview, September 17, 2012.

1281 Geist, interview, September 17, 2012.

1282 Cowan and Guiguet, *Mammals of* BC, 398–399.

1283 Ian McTaggart Cowan, "Foreword," in Tommy A. Walker, *Spatsizi* (Surrey: Antonson Publishing, 1976), 11–12.

1284 Geist, interview, September 17, 2012.

1285 Valerius Geist, "The Evolution of Horn-Like Organs," *Behaviour* 27, no. 1 (1966): 175–214. http://is.gd/319awq (abstract accessed October 31, 2014).

1286 Valerius Geist, "On Delayed Social and Physical Maturation in Mountain Sheep," *Canadian Journal of Zoology* 46, no. 5 (1968): 899–904. http://is.gd/u10iKS (pdf accessed October 31, 2014).

1287 Geist, interview, September 17, 2012.

1288 Valerius Geist and Ian McTaggart-Cowan, eds., *Wildlife Conservation Policy* (Calgary: Detselig Enterprises, 1995).

1289 Ian McTaggart Cowan and Wayne McCrory, "Variation in the Mountain Goat, *Oreamnos americanus*," *Journal of Mammalogy* 51, no. 1 (February 1970): 60–73. http://is.gd/bxw9hK (abstract accessed October 31, 2014).

1290 Wayne McCrory, interview, September 20, 2012.

1291 Valhalla Wilderness Society. www.vws.org (accessed May 24, 2014).

1292 Cowan, interview, July 9, 2002.

1293 Cowan, interview, July 9, 2002.

1294 William (Bill) Hoar to Ian McTaggart Cowan, March 2000, Cowan_PN_081.

1295 Cowan, interview, July 9, 2002.

1296 Muriel Guiguet, interview, September 9, 2012.

1297 Tom Sterling, interview, July 31, 2012.

1298 Sterling, interview, July 31, 2012.

1299 Sterling, interview, July 31, 2012.

1300 Sterling, interview, July 31, 2012.

1301 Sterling, interview, July 31, 2012.

1302 P.W. Martin, "A Winter Inventory of the Shoreline and Marine-Oriented Birds and Mammals of Chatham Sound," (unpublished report, British Columbia Fish and Wildlife Branch, 1978).

1303 Campbell et al., *Birds of* BC, vol. 1, 340.

1304 Sterling, interview, July 31, 2012.

1305 Sterling, interview, July 31, 2012.

1306 Campbell et al., *Birds of* BC, vol. 1, 320.

1307 Yorke Edwards, "A Tribute to Charles Joseph Guiguet, 1916–1999," *The Canadian Field-Naturalist* 114, no. 4 (October–December 2000): 712–715. http://

biodiversitylibrary.org/page/34237218 (accessed October 31, 2014).

1308 Harry R. Carter, "In Memoriam: Charles Joseph Guiguet," *Pacific Seabirds* 26, no. 2 (Fall 1999): 65: http://pacificseabirdgroup. org/publications/PacificSeabirds/VOL_26_2. PDF (pdf p7, accessed October 31, 2014).

1309 Guiguet, interview, September 9, 2012.

1310 Guiguet, interview, September 9, 2012.

1311 Ian McTaggart Cowan, "Queen Charlotte Islands," lecture notes, n.d., Cowan_PN_240.

1312 Ian McTaggart Cowan, "Migration," *Web of Life* television series episode aired January 18, 1963 (Vancouver: CBC Television Archives).

1313 Campbell et al., *Birds of* BC, vol. 3, 222–223.

1314 University of Alberta Alumni Association, "The Memorable William Rowan," *History Trails* (website), 1993. www.ualberta.ca/ ALUMNI/history/peoplep-z/93sumrowan. htm (accessed January 15, 2014).

1315 Marianne Gosztonyi Ainley, "William Rowan: Canada's First Avian Biologist," *Picoides* 1, no. 1 (1987): 6. www.sco-soc.ca/picoides/archive/Picoides1_1_1987.pdf (pdf p6 accessed October 31, 2014).

1316 Ainley, "William Rowan: Canada's First Avian Biologist," 6.

1317 University of Alberta Alumni Association, "The Memorable William Rowan."

1318 *Calgary Herald*, "Put Ecology First U Grads Are Told," June 1971.

1319 Ian McTaggart Cowan, "Field Notes 1946 Rocky Mtns. and QCI," July 10, 1946, Cowan_FN_025.

1320 C.P. Sissons to Austin de B. Winter, October 28, 1946, Austin De B. Winter personal files 1940 correspondence etc., Austin de B. Winter fonds, Glenbow Museum Archives, Calgary.

1321 Cowan, "Field Notes 1946 Rocky Mtns. and QCI," July 20, 1946.

1322 Cowan, "Field Notes 1946 Rocky Mtns. and QCI," September 3, 1946.

1323 Campbell et al., *Birds of* BC, vol. 2, 318.

1324 Ian McTaggart Cowan, "Queen Charlotte Islands," lecture notes, n.d., Cowan_PN_240.

1325 Campbell et al., *Birds of* BC, vol. 2, 56.

1326 Cowan, "Field Notes 1946 Rocky Mtns. and QCI," August 3, 1946, Cowan_FN_025.

1327 Campbell et al., *Birds of* BC, vol. 2, 304–306.

1328 Cowan, "Field Notes 1946 Rocky Mtns. and QCI," August 6, 1946.

1329 Cowan, "Field Notes 1946 Rocky Mtns. and QCI," August 6, 1946.

1330 Campbell et al., *Birds of BC*, vol. 3, 292–294.

1331 Kathleen E. Dalzell, *The Queen Charlotte Islands, vol. 2: Places and Names* (Queen Charlotte City: Bill Ellis Publisher, 1973), 267.

1332 Campbell et al., *Birds of BC*, vol. 2, 294–296.

1333 Campbell et al., *Birds of BC*, vol. 2, 312–314.

1334 R.H. Drent and C.J. Guiguet, "A Catalogue for British Columbia Sea-bird Colonies," BC Provincial Museum Occasional Paper no. 12, 1961.

1335 Cowan, "Field Notes 1946 Rocky Mtns. and QCI," August 14, 1946.

1336 Charles J. Guiguet, "Field Notes 1946–1947 QCI," August 15, 1946. Cowan_FN_059.

1337 Guiguet, "Field Notes 1946–1947 QCI," August 15, 1946, Cowan_FN_059.

1338 Guiguet, "Field Notes 1946–1947 QCI," August 15, 1946, Cowan_FN_059.

1339 Campbell et al., *Birds of BC*, vol. 3, 238.

1340 Tom Reimchen, personal communication, January 4, 2014.

1341 Cowan, interview, February 2, 2005.

1342 Cowan and Guiguet, *Mammals of BC*, 81.

1343 Campbell et al., *Birds of BC*, vol. 2, 388.

1344 Guiguet. "Field Notes 1946–1947 QCI," September 3, 1946, Cowan_FN_059.

1345 Campbell et al., *Birds of BC*, vol. 1, 188.

1346 Ian McTaggart Cowan, "Whales," *Living Sea* television episode aired January 19, 1958 (Vancouver: CBC Television Archives).

1347 Cowan, "Whales."

1348 Cowan and Guiguet, *Mammals of BC*, 268–269.

1349 Ian McTaggart Cowan, "Whales and Whaling Lectures," lecture notes, n.d., Cowan_PN_337.

1350 Cowan, "Whales and Whaling Lectures."

1351 Cowan, "Journal Field Trips 1935–1961," May 22–June 3, 1951, Cowan_FN_014.

1352 Bristol Foster, "Field Notes B. Foster, Summer 1960," May 21, 1960, Cowan_FN_054.

1353 Campbell et al., *Birds of BC*, vol. 2, 418.

1354 Campbell et al., *Birds of BC*, vol. 2, 418.

1355 Foster, "Field Notes B. Foster, Summer, 1960," May 22, 1960.

1356 Foster, "Field Notes B. Foster, Summer, 1960," May 22, 1960.

1357 Foster, interview, July 24, 2012.

1358 Foster, "Field Notes B. Foster, Summer, 1960," May 24, 1960.

1359 Foster, "Field Notes B. Foster, Summer, 1960," July 22, 1961.

1360 Foster, "Field Notes B. Foster, Summer 1960," July 21, 1961.

1361 Campbell et al., *Birds of BC*, vol. 2, 18.

1362 Elizabeth Kennedy and Ian McTaggart Cowan, "Sixteen Years with a Bald Eagle's, *Haliaeetus leucocephalus*, nest," *Canadian Field-Naturalist* 112, no. 4 (October–December 1998): 704–706. http://biodiversitylibrary.org/page/34258060 (accessed October 31, 2014).

1363 Francis Cook to Ian McTaggart Cowan, August 15, 1998, Cowan_PN_106; Francis Cook, personal communication, October 28, 2013.

1364 Mark V. Lomolino, "Body Size Evolution in Insular Vertebrates: Generality of the Island Rule," *Journal of Biogeography* 32, no. 10 (October 2005): 1683–1699. http://is.gd/hQYc8q (pdf accessed October 31, 2014).

1365 Robert H. MacArthur and Edward O. Wilson, "An Equilibrium Theory of Insular Zoogeography," *Evolution* 17, no. 4 (December 1963): 373–387. http://is.gd/2w9FoZ (pdf accessed October 31, 2014).

1366 Ted J. Case and Martin L. Cody, *Island Biogeography in the Sea of Cortez* (Berkeley: University of California Press, 1983).

1367 Ian McTaggart Cowan to Wilderness Advisory Committee, [ca. 1985], Cowan_PN_267.

1368 Ian McTaggart Cowan to Premier William Vander Zalm, July 6, 1987, Cowan_PN_016.

1369 Jim Pojar and J.B. Foster, "Natural History Theme Study of a National Area of Canadian Significance on the Queen Charlotte Islands, BC" (consultant report to Parks Canada, May 1977).

1370 Ian McTaggart Cowan to Ann Schau, July 8, 1987, Cowan_PN_504.

1371 Foster, interview, July 24, 2012.

1372 Ian McTaggart Cowan. "Nairobi," June 25, 1967, Cowan_FN_039.

1373 Cowan. "Nairobi," June 24, 1967, Cowan_FN_039.

1374 Ian McTaggart Cowan, "Preliminary Wildlife Survey of the Mackenzie Delta with Special Reference to the Muskrat" (unpublished report, Vancouver, UBC, January 30, 1948). http://is.gd/gSSq9G (pdf s.n., n.d., accessed October 31, 2014). An edited version of this paper was published as "Waterfowl

Conditions on the Mackenzie Delta – 1947":
q.v. below at n1385.

1375 Campbell et al., *Birds of BC*, vol. 1, 310.

1376 Ward Stevens, interview, November 14, 2012.

1377 Stevens, interview, November 14, 2012.

1378 Stevens, interview, November 14, 2012.

1379 Stevens, interview, November 14, 2012.

1380 Stevens, interview, November 14, 2012.

1381 Ian McTaggart Cowan, "Range Competition between Mule Deer, Bighorn Sheep and Elk in Jasper National Park," in *Transactions of the Twelfth North American Wildlife Conference, February 3–5, 1947*, ed. Ethel M. Quee (Washington, DC: Wildlife Management Institute, 1947), 223–227.

1382 Leopold, "On a Monument to the Pigeon," in *Some Lessons*, vol. 2, ed. B. of V., 47. [An annotated version appears in Leopold's *Sand County Almanac*.]

1383 Aldo Leopold, quoted in *Birds of BC*, vol. 4, 679.

1384 Stevens, interview, November 14, 2012.

1385 Ian McTaggart Cowan, "Waterfowl Conditions on the Mackenzie Delta – 1947," *The Murrelet* 29, no. 2 (May–August 1948): 21. www.jstor.org/stable/3535716 (first-page preview accessed October 31, 2014).

1386 Ian McTaggart Cowan, "Field Notes Mackenzie R. 1947," June 8, 1947, Cowan_FN_026.

1387 Cowan and Guiguet, *Mammals of BC*, 229.

1388 Cowan, "Field Notes Mackenzie R. 1947," June 29, 1947, Cowan_FN_026.

1389 Stevens, interview, November 14, 2012.

1390 Cowan, "Field Notes Mackenzie R. 1947," June 13, 1947, Cowan_FN_026.

1391 Stevens, interview, November 14, 2012.

1392 Stevens, interview, November 14, 2012.

1393 A.E. Porsild, "Birds of the Mackenzie Delta," *The Canadian Field-Naturalist* 57, nos. 2 & 3 (February–March 1943): 19–35. http://is.gd/DVSV1D (accessed October 31, 2014).

1394 Cowan, "Waterfowl Conditions on the Mackenzie Delta – 1947," 25.

1395 Cowan, "Field Notes Mackenzie R. 1947," June 20, 1947, Cowan_FN_026.

1396 Cowan, "Field Notes Mackenzie R. 1947," June 13, 1947.

1397 Cowan, "Field Notes Mackenzie R. 1947," June 13, 1947.

1398 Cowan, interview, July 9, 2002.

1399 Stevens, interview, November 14, 2012.

1400 Stevens, interview, November 14, 2012.

1401 Stevens, interview, November 14, 2012.

1402 Stevens, interview, November 14, 2012.

1403 Cowan, "Field Notes Mackenzie R. 1947," June 27, 1947, Cowan_FN_026.

1404 Campbell et al., *Birds of BC*, vol. 2, 80.

1405 Cowan, "Field Notes Mackenzie R. 1947," June 29–30, 1947.

1406 Stevens, interview, November 14, 2012.

1407 Stevens, interview, November 14, 2012.

1408 Cowan, "Field Notes Mackenzie R. 1947," July 4, 1947.

1409 Stevens, interview, November 14, 2012.

1410 Cowan, "Field Notes Mackenzie R. 1947," July 16, 1947.

1411 Cowan, "Field Notes Mackenzie R. 1947," July 18, 1947.

1412 Campbell et al., *Birds of BC*, vol. 2, 272.

1413 Cowan, interview, November 30, 2000.

1414 Bryant, interview, November 10, 2012.

1415 Cowan, "Field Notes Mackenzie R. 1947," August 9, 1947.

1416 Stevens, interview, November 14, 2012.

1417 Cowan, "Field Notes Mackenzie R. 1947," August 13, 1947.

1418 Cowan, "Field Notes Mackenzie R. 1947," August 14–15, 1947.

1419 Cowan, "Preliminary Wildlife Survey of the Mackenzie Delta with Special Reference to the Muskrat," unpublished report, January 30, 1948, 35 (pdf p41). http://is.gd/gSSq9G (pdf s.n., n.d., accessed October 31, 2014).

1420 Stevens, interview, November 14, 2012.

1421 Stevens, interview, November 14, 2012.

1422 Don Flook, interview, October 29, 2012.

1423 Brendan Kelly, "Francis Hollis Fay 1927–1994," *Arctic* 48, no. 1 (March 1995): 107. http://pubs.aina.ucalgary.ca/arctic/Arctic48-1-107.pdf (pdf accessed October 31, 2014).

1424 Burnett, *A Passion for Wildlife*, 109.

1425 Burnett, *A Passion for Wildlife*, 109.

1426 Bryant, interview, November 10, 2012.

1427 Bryant, interview, November 10, 2012.

1428 Mary Bryant to Ian McTaggart Cowan, c. 1996, Cowan_PN_081.

1429 Mary Bryant to Cowan, c. 1996, Cowan_PN_081.

1430 Joe Bryant, interview, November 10, 2012.

1431 Mary Bryant to Cowan, c. 1996, Cowan_PN_081.

1432 T.M.C. Taylor, *The Ferns and Fern-allies of British Columbia*, illustrated by Mary Bryant, Handbook no. 12 (Victoria: BC Provincial Museum, 1963).

1433 Joe Bryant, interview, November 10, 2012.

1434 Cowan and Guiguet, *Mammals of BC*, 285.

1435 Ian McTaggart Cowan, "The Ecology of the North: Knowledge is the Key to Sane Development," *Science Forum* 2, no. 1 (1969): 8 (citing Recommendation 7 from the UNESCO Biosphere Conference of 1968), Cowan_PN_897.

1436 Cowan, "The Ecology of the North," 4.

1437 Cowan, "The Ecology of the North," 6.

1438 Cowan, "The Ecology of the North," 8.

1439 Cowan, "Environmental Impact Assessment," 123.

1440 Cowan, "Environmental Impact Assessment," 123.

1441 Thomas Berger, interview, May 19, 2013.

1442 Berger, interview, May 19, 2013.

1443 Berger, interview, May 19, 2013.

1444 Berger, interview, May 19, 2013.

1445 *New Zealand Herald*, "Environment Work Funded by Canadian Government," August 6, 1975.

1446 Ecojustice, *Legal Backgrounder: Canadian Environmental Assessment Act*, May 2012. http://is.gd/gHWPh2 (accessed February 1, 2015).

1447 Cowan, "A Report to the Canadian Committee on Whales and Whaling," presented at the 33rd Annual Meeting of the International Whaling Commission, July 20–25, 1981 (unpublished), 4, Cowan_PN_219.

1448 Elizabeth May, personal communication, June 2, 2014.

1449 Porcupine Caribou Technical Committee, "Porcupine Caribou Annual Summary Report 2013" (Porcupine Caribou Management Board, November 2013), i, 7, 8 (Fig. 1), 42 (App. A). http://is.gd/Xb9AdX (pdf pp. 2, 10, 11, 45 accessed March 13, 2014).

1450 Cowan and Guiguet, *Mammals of BC*, 381–382.

1451 Tom Beck, interview, September 25–26, 2012.

1452 Tom Beck, interview, September 25–26, 2012.

1453 Tom Beck, interview, September 25–26, 2012.

1454 Tom Beck, interview, September 25–26, 2012.

1455 Tom Beck, interview, September 25–26, 2012.

1456 Tom Beck, interview, September 25–26, 2012.

1457 Tom Beck, interview, September 25–26, 2012.

1458 Cowan, interview, July 9, 2002.

1459 Munro and Cowan, *Bird Fauna of BC*, 170.

1460 Munro and Cowan, *Bird Fauna of BC*, 3.

1461 Munro and Cowan, *Bird Fauna of BC*, 10.

1462 Munro and Cowan, *Bird Fauna of BC*, 21.

1463 Campbell et al., *Birds of BC*, vol. 1, 314.

1464 Webster H. Ransom, "Miscellaneous Avifaunal Observations no. 2," *The Murrelet* 13, no. 2 (May 1932): 51.

1465 Munro and Cowan, *Bird Fauna of BC*, 138.

1466 J.A. Munro, "The Grebes," BC Provincial Museum Occasional Paper no. 3 (1941).

1467 Campbell et al., *Birds of BC*, vol. 1, 174.

1468 Nancy M. McAllister "Courtship, Hostile Behavior, Nest-establishment and Egg Laying in the Eared Grebe (*Podiceps capsicus*)," *The Auk* 75, no. 3 (July 1958): 290–310. https://sora.unm.edu/sites/default/files/journals/auk/v075n03/p0290-p0311.pdf (accessed October 31, 2014).

1469 Ann Schau, interview October 9, 2012.

1470 Campbell et al., *Birds of BC*, vol. 1, 180.

1471 Cowan, "Field Notes 1948, Anahim L. 1949, Cariboo," July 25, 1948, Cowan_FN_28.

1472 Cowan and Guiguet, *Mammals of BC*, 65.

1473 Cowan, "Field Notes 1948, Anahim L. 1949, Cariboo," August 9, 1948.

1474 Betty Copeland, personal communication, August 3, 2013.

1475 R.Y. Edwards, "Fire and the Decline of a Mountain Caribou Herd," *The Journal of Wildlife Management* 18, no. 4 (October 1954): 521–526. http://is.gd/mwFSet (pdf accessed October 31, 2014).

1476 Cowan, "Journal Field Trips, 1935–1961," May 5, 1956, Cowan_FN_014.

1477 Cowan, "Journal Field Trips, 1935–1961," May 7, 1956, Cowan_FN_014.

1478 Edwards, "The Preservation of Wilderness," 1.

1479 Cowan, "Journal Field Trips, 1935–1961," June 3, 1952, Cowan_FN_014.

1480 Ian McTaggart Cowan et al., "Westwick Lake Camp Summer 1955," May 2, 1955, Cowan_FN_018.

1481 Campbell et al., *Birds of BC*, vol. 4, 331.

1482 Cowan et al., "Westwick Lake Camp Summer 1955," May 4, 1955, Cowan_FN_018.

1483 Campbell et al., *Birds of BC*, vol. 1, 354.

1484 Cowan et al., "Westwick Lake Camp Summer 1955," May 5, 1955.

1485 Birney and Choate, eds., *Seventy-five Years of Mammalogy 1919–1994*. https://archive.org/stream/seventyfiveyears00birn#page/n5/mode/2up (accessed October 31, 2014).

1486 Ayesha E. Gill and W. Chris Wozencraft, "Committees and Annual Meetings," in *Seventy-five Years of Mammalogy 1919–1994*, ed. Elmer C. Birney and Jerry R. Choate, 164. https://archive.org/stream/seventyfiveyears00birn#page/164/mode/2up (accessed October 31, 2014).

1487 Winifred Kessler, interview, June 10, 2014.

1488 Kessler, interview, June 10, 2014.

1489 E. Margaret Fulton, interview, January 16, 2014.

1490 Scagel, interview, August 8, 2012.

1491 Marianne Gosztonyi Ainley, *Creating Complicated Lives: Women and Science at English-Canadian Universities 1880–1980* (Montreal: McGill-Queen's University Press, 2012).

1492 Cowan, "Journal Field Trips, 1935–1961," May 3, 1956, Cowan_FN_014.

1493 Geoff Scudder, interview, December 17, 2013.

1494 Scudder, interview, December 17, 2013.

1495 Ian McTaggart Cowan, mimeographed report (Vancouver: UBC, 1971); later published under same title as Australian Fauna Authorities Conference special publication no. 2 (Canberra: Australian Government Publishing Service, 1973). http://trove.nla.gov.au/work/23127344?q&versionId=45811618 (citation accessed February 25, 2015).

1496 Cowan, "The Conservation of Australian Waterfowl," 1.

1497 Cowan, "Moments from the Education of an Ornithologist," 17.

1498 Cowan and Guiguet, *Mammals of BC*, 395–397.

1499 Ian McTaggart Cowan, "Ashnola," *Klahanie: the Great Outdoors* television series episode, first aired March 15, 1973, Vancouver: CBC Television Archives).

1500 Richter Family fonds, MS-1690, BCA.

1501 Cowan, "Journal Field Trips, 1935–1961," July 8, 1951, Cowan_FN_014.

1502 Campbell et al., *Birds of BC*, vol. 2, 442.

1503 Ann Schau, interview October 9, 2012.

1504 Cowan, "Ashnola," *Klahanie* television series episode, March 15, 1973.

1505 Cowan, "Ashnola."

1506 Cowan, "Ashnola."

1507 Weeden, interview, July 26, 2012.

1508 William (Bill) Lidicker, interview, September 17, 2013.

1509 Cowan, "Journal Field Trips, 1935–1961," June 22, 1954, Cowan_FN_014.

1510 Cowan, "Of Mice and Men," March 18, 1961. https://circle.ubc.ca/flashstreamview/bitstream/handle/2429/36425/ubc_at_010_cowan.mp3?sequence=1 (streaming audio from ~16:00, accessed October 31, 2014).

1511 Ann Schau, interview, October 9, 2012.

1512 Scudder, interview, December 17, 2013.

1513 Francis X. Richter, [remarks as MLA (Social Credit) for Boundary-Similkameen in the BC Legislative Assembly, February 22, 1974 (morning sitting)], *Hansard*, 30th Parliament, 4th Session (1974), 462. http://is.gd/Tj6CN8 (accessed January 31, 2015).

1514 "Snowy Mountain Protected Area" (webpage), BC Spaces for Nature (Gibsons, BC: 2008). www.spacesfornature.org/greatspaces/snowy.html (accessed February 2, 2015).

1515 Cowan, interview, December 5, 2000.

1516 Melissa Mancini, "Science Cuts: Ottawa Views Pure Science as 'Cash Cow,' Critics Say," *Huffington Post*, May 7, 2013. www.huffingtonpost.ca/2013/05/07/science-cuts-canada_n_3228151.html (accessed May 24, 2014).

1517 "Most Federal Scientists Feel They Can't Speak Out, Even If Public Health and Safety at Risk, Says New Survey," press release, Professional Institute of the Public Service of Canada (2013). www.pipsc.ca/portal/page/portal/website/issues/science/bigchill (accessed February 2, 2015).

1518 Scudder, interview, December 17, 2013.

1519 Nancy Wilkin, "A Celebration of Life: Dr. Vernon Cuthbert Brink, OC, OBC, PhD, FAIC, November 15, 1912, to November 29, 2007," eulogy read January 31, 2008, Cowan_PN_093.

1520 Cowan, interview, December 5, 2000.

1521 Ian McTaggart Cowan, "Sabbatical Year in Scotland 1952," July 9, 1952, Cowan_FN_040.

1522 Cowan, "Sabbatical Year in Scotland 1952," July 11, 1952.

1523 Campbell et al., *Birds of BC*, vol. 1, 186.

1524 Cowan, "Sabbatical Year in Scotland 1952," July 21, 1952.

1525 Cowan, "Sabbatical Year in Scotland 1952," July 26, 1952.

1526 Cowan, "Sabbatical Year in Scotland 1952," July 25, 1952.

1527 Campbell et al., *Birds of BC*, vol. 2, 282.

1528 Cowan, "Sabbatical Year in Scotland 1952," July 29, 1952.

1529 Campbell et al., *Birds of BC*, vol. 4, 627.

1530 Ian Newton, "Vero Copner Wynne-Edwards, CBE, 4 July 1906 to 5 January 1997," *Biographical Memoirs of Fellows of the Royal Society* 44 (November 1998): 473–484. http://is.gd/GndSzD (pdf accessed October 31, 2014).

1531 Cowan, "Of Mice and Men." https://circle.ubc.ca/flashstreamview/bitstream/handle/2429/36425/ubc_at_010_cowan.mp3?sequence=1 (streaming audio from ~29:00 accessed October 31, 2014).

1532 Ian McTaggart Cowan to Mikkel Schau, September 28, 1996, Cowan_PN_504.

1533 Cowan, "Sabbatical Year in Scotland 1952," October 18, 1952.

1534 Cowan, "Sabbatical Year in Scotland 1952," Marginalia.

1535 Cowan, "Sabbatical Year in Scotland 1952," August 14, 1952.

1536 Cowan, "Sabbatical Year in Scotland 1952," July 29, 1952.

1537 Ian McTaggart Cowan, "Britain 1962, British Museum and Copenhagen Museum," May 16, 1962, Cowan_FN_042.

1538 Ann Schau, interview, October 9, 2012.

1539 Erik Smidt, "Maxwell John Dunbar," *Arctic* 46, no. 2 (June 1993): 175–177. http://is.gd/YnZ7OJ (pdf accessed October 31, 2014).

1540 "Royal Society of Edinburgh: Vertebrate Fauna of Western North America," *The Scotsman*, October 28, 1952.

1541 "Royal Society of Edinburgh: Vertebrate Fauna of Western North America," *The Scotsman*, October 28, 1952.

1542 Cowan, "Sabbatical Year in Scotland 1952," October 25, 1952.

1543 Cowan, "Sabbatical Year in Scotland 1952," October 25, 1952.

1544 Cowan, "Sabbatical Year in Scotland 1952," October 25, 1952.

1545 Cowan, "Sabbatical Year in Scotland 1952," October 25, 1952.

1546 Cowan, "Sabbatical Year in Scotland 1952," September 18, 1952.

1547 Cowan, "Sabbatical Year in Scotland 1952," September 19, 1952.

1548 Cowan, "Observations on Wildlife Conservation and Management in Britain and Norden," in *Report of Proceedings of the Eighth Annual BC Game Convention, May 26–29, 1954* (Victoria: Queen's Printer, 1954), 23.

1549 Cowan, "Sabbatical Year in Scotland 1952," September 22, 1952.

1550 Campbell et al., *Birds of BC*, vol. 3, 486–497.

1551 Cowan, "Sabbatical Year in Scotland 1952," September 24, 1952.

1552 *Scotsman*, "Edinburgh's Wild Birds," [n.d.] 1953.

1553 Campbell et al., *Birds of BC;* vol. 1, 344.

1554 Cowan, "Sabbatical Year in Scotland 1952," October 4, 1952.

1555 Campbell et al., *Birds of BC*, vol. 2, 300.

1556 Stainsby, "Dean of Ecology," *BC Outdoors* 35, no. 12 (December 1979), 40.

1557 Iain Thomson, *Isolation Shepherd* (Inverness, Scotland: Bidean Books, 1983).

1558 Andrew Jamison and Ron Eyerman, *Seeds of the Sixties* (Berkeley: University of California Press, 1994).

1559 F. Fraser Darling and John P. Milton, eds., *Future Environments of North America* (New York: Natural History Press, 1966): 296.

1560 Ian McTaggart Cowan, "Sabbatical Year in Scotland 2, 1953," May 24, 1953, Cowan_FN_041.

1561 Cowan, "Sabbatical Year in Scotland 2, 1953," May 24, 1953.

1562 "Cuckoo (*Cuculus canorus*)" (webpage, n.d.), Scottish Wildlife Trust. http://scottishwildlifetrust.org.uk/visit/wildlife/c/cuckoo (accessed May 12, 2014).

1563 "Sir Frank Fraser Darling, 1903–1979," *Navigational Aids for the History of Science, Technology & the Environment* (website), University of Edinburgh, n.d. www.nahste.ac.uk/isaar/GB_0237_NAHSTE_P2042.html (accessed March 24, 2014).

1564 Paul Weindling, "Genetics, Eugenics and the Holocaust," in *Biology and Ideology*, ed. Alexander and Numbers, 204. *See also* C. Kenneth Waters and Albert Van Helden, eds., *Julian Huxley: Biologist and Statesman of Science* (Houston, Tex.: Rice University Press, 1992).

1565 Ian McTaggart Cowan to Neil Dawe, Cowan_PN_282 (n.d.).

1566 Cowan, "Sabbatical Year in Scotland 2, 1953," May 14, 1953.

1567 Cowan, "The Challenge We Take," in *Transactions of the Twentieth North American Wildlife Conference, March 14–16, 1955* (Washington, DC: Wildlife Management Institute, 1955), 663–665.

1568 "'Exploring Minds' Topic is Growth," [n.d., c. 1957; source possibly CBUT TV, Vancouver], Cowan_PN_182.

1569 Cowan, interview, February 26, 2001.

1570 Cowan, interview, February 26, 2001.

1571 Cowan, interview, February 26, 2001.

1572 Cowan, interview, February 26, 2001.

1573 Ian McTaggart Cowan, "Synopsis for *Web of Life*," CBC Television Archives, Cowan_PN_494; also Colin Preston, CBC archivist, personal communication, November 2013.

1574 Cowan, interview, February 26, 2001.

1575 Cowan, interview, February 26, 2001.

1576 Cowan, interview, July 9, 2002.

1577 Cowan, interview, July 9, 2002.

1578 Cowan, interview, July 9, 2002.

1579 Cowan, interview, February 26, 2001.

1580 Ann Schau, interview, October 9, 2012.

1581 Cowan, "Journal Field Trips 1935–1961,"August 20, 1954, Cowan_FN_014.

1582 Jim Campbell, interview, May 25, 2013.

1583 Cowan, interview, February 26, 2001.

1584 F.R. Bernard, "*Cuspidaria cowani*, a New Septibranch Mollusc from the Northeastern Pacific," *Journal of the Fisheries Research Board of Canada* 24, no. 12 (1967): 2629–2630.

1585 Edward L. Bousfield and Edward A. Hendrycks, "The Talitroidean Amphipod Family *Hyalidae* Revised, with Emphasis on the North Pacific Fauna: Systematics and Distributional Ecology," *Amphipacifica* 3, no. 3 (2002): 17–134.

1586 Ann Schau, interview, October 9, 2012.

1587 Cowan, interview, February 26, 2001.

1588 Cowan, interview, February 26, 2001.

1589 Jim Gilmore, "US Network Bids for Local Series," *Vancouver Sun*, n.d., Cowan_PN_182.

1590 *The Scotsman*, "Sporting Dolphins are Crack-shots," August 18, 1958.

1591 Blaine Allan, "CBC Television Series 1952–1982" *Web of Life* (online database item), (Kingston, Ont.: Queen's University Department of Film and Media, 1996). www.film.

queensu.ca/cbc/W.html (accessed May 24, 2014).

1592 Cowan, "Synopsis for *Web of Life*," Cowan_PN_494.

1593 Cowan, "Synopsis for *Web of Life*," Cowan_PN_494.

1594 Cowan, interview, July 9, 2002. [He is probably referring to J. Gray's "Studies in the Mechanics of the Tetrapod Skeleton," 1944.]

1595 Cowan, interview, February 26, 2001.

1596 "Looking After Our Health," *The Globe and Mail*, February 11, 1960.

1597 *The Globe and Mail*, "CBC Sells TV Shows for $200,000 to UK," February 23, 1960, B22.

1598 Harold Weir, "Culture without Pain," *Vancouver Sun*, July 12, 1957.

1599 David Suzuki, personal communication, September 7, 2012.

1600 Weir, "Culture without Pain."

1601 Ian McTaggart Cowan, "Wings," *Patterns of Living* television series episode, first aired October 27, 1964 (Vancouver: CBC Television Archives with Canadian School Telecast).

1602 *Brandon Tribune*,"School Telecasts Lend 'Colour' to Programs," October 20, 1966, 5.

1603 Cowan, interview, July 9, 2002.

1604 "Wildlife in Danger," *Klahanie: The Great Outdoors*, television series episode first aired September 27, 1969 (Vancouver: CBC Television Archives). Cowan's last program for *Klahanie* was with Brink in "Ashnola" in 1971.

1605 Cowan, interview, December 5, 2000.

1606 Cowan, interview, December 5, 2000.

1607 Ian McTaggart Cowan, "A Review of Wildlife Research in Canada," in *Resources for Tomorrow: Conference Background Papers*, vol. 2 (Ottawa: Department of Northern Affairs and National Resources, July 1961), 892.

1608 Ian McTaggart Cowan, George M. Volkoff and Peter A. Larkin, "Basic Research Threatened by Lack of Funds," op-ed., *Vancouver Sun*, January 7, 1974.

1609 Ron Jeffels to Ian McTaggart Cowan, "The Roasting and Toasting of IMC," March 31, 1981, Cowan_PN_146.

1610 Stainsby, "Dean of Ecology," 42.

1611 Campbell et al., *Birds of BC*, vol. 1, 262.

1612 Ian McTaggart Cowan, "Conservation in Canada," in *Proceedings of the Tenth Pacific Science Congress, Honolulu, Hawaii, 1961*, ed.

Leonard D. Tuthill (Honolulu: Bishop Museum Press, 1963), 228–230.

1613 Cowan, "Conservation in Canada," 229.

1614 Ann Schau, interview, October 9, 2012.

1615 Frank Fraser Darling and John P. Milton, eds., *Future Environments of North America: Being the Record of a Conference Convened by the Conservation Foundation in April 1965 at Airlie House, Warrenton, Virginia* (New York: Natural History Press, 1966).

1616 Jan Drábek, *Vladimir Krajina: World War II Hero and Ecology Pioneer* (Vancouver: Ronsdale Press, 2012).

1617 Ecological Reserves Program, BC Parks. www.env.gov.bc.ca/bcparks/eco_reserve (accessed March 25, 2014).

1618 Adolf Ceska, personal communication, February 2, 2015.

1619 *Vancouver Sun*, "Save Your Wildlife." March 10, 1983, B1.

1620 *Vancouver Sun*, "Save Your Wildlife."

1621 Ian McTaggart Cowan to Tom Beck, February 5, 1983, Cowan_PN_285.

1622 Campbell et al., *Birds of BC*, vol. 3, 277.

1623 World Wide Fund for Nature Canada, "Monte Hummel, president emeritus," (webpage). www.wwf.ca/about_us/experts/monte_hummel.cfm (accessed May 14, 2014).

1624 Monte Hummel to Ian McTaggart Cowan, August 15, 1997, Cowan_PN_221.

1625 Monte Hummel to Ann Schau, "One hundredth birthday greetings/funeral condolences," May 4, 2010, Cowan_PN_291.

1626 Edward Lyn Lewis to Ann Schau, "One hundredth birthday greetings/funeral condolences," April 23, 2010, Cowan_PN_291.

1627 Ann Schau, interview, November 9, 2012.

1628 Jeffels to Cowan, March 31, 1981, Cowan_PN_146.

1629 Tom Beck, interview, September 25–26, 2012.

1630 Shirley Beck, interview, September 25–26, 2012.

1631 Ann Schau, interview, October 9, 2012.

1632 Campbell et al., *Birds of BC*, vol. 2, 358.

1633 Cowan, "Observations on Wildlife Conservation and Management in Britain and Norden," 23.

1634 Cowan, "Chemical Sprays and Their Relation to Wildlife" *Proceedings of the Ninth Annual BC Game Convention: May 25–28, 1955* at

Nelson, BC [first page of unpaginated article] (Victoria: Queen's Printer, 1955).

1635 Cowan, "The Challenge We Take," 669.

1636 Cowan and Guiguet, *Mammals of BC*, 257–258.

1637 *Vancouver Sun*, "Killer Whale Roams City Inlet," October 27, 1945.

1638 Murray Newman, interview, May 25, 2013.

1639 Newman, interview, May 25, 2013.

1640 Newman, interview, May 25, 2013.

1641 Murray Newman and Patrick L. McGeer, "The Capture and Care of a Killer Whale, *Orcinus orca*, in British Columbia," *Zoologica* 51, no. 5 (1966): 59–70.

1642 Newman, interview, May 25, 2013.

1643 Ian McTaggart Cowan, "Capture and Maintenance of Cetaceans in Canada: A Report Prepared by the Advisory Committee on Marine Mammals to the Minister of Fisheries and Oceans Canada, Ottawa," unpublished, 1992.

1644 Newman, interview, May 25, 2013.

1645 P.R. Grant and I. M. Cowan, "A Review of the Avifauna of the Tres Marías Islands, Nayarit, Mexico," *The Condor* 66, no. 3 (May 1964): 221–228. https://sora.unm.edu/sites/default/files/journals/condor/v066n03/p0221-p0228.pdf (accessed October 31, 2014).

1646 Ian McTaggart Cowan, "Travel to Sea of Cortez, 1959, 1962," February 22, 1959, Cowan_FN_045.

1647 Campbell et al., *Birds of BC*, vol. 1, 248.

1648 Newman, interview, May 25, 2013.

1649 Ian McTaggart Cowan, "Profile of Baja California," unpublished booklet, ca. 1985.

1650 Cowan and Guiguet, *Mammals of BC*, 263.

1651 Roger and Alli Clapp to Ian and Joyce McTaggart Cowan, July 1, 1984, Cowan_PN_013.

1652 Jim Lauder, "Joyce McTaggart Cowan memorial service eulogy," December 3, 2002, Cowan_PN_058.

1653 Ian McTaggart Cowan to Mikkel Schau, September 25, 1996, Cowan_PN_504.

1654 Newman, interview, May 25, 2013.

1655 Bill Merilees, interview, September 17, 2012.

1656 Ian McTaggart Cowan, "*Tonicella insignis* Reeve in British Columbia," *Pacific Northwest Shell News* 3, no. 5 (1963): 53.

1657 Merilees, interview, September 17, 2012.

1658 Merilees, interview, September 17, 2012.

1659 Robert McTaggart Cowan, interview, May 8, 2014.

1660 Torben Schau, personal communication, May 20, 2014.

1661 Ian McTaggart Cowan, interview, December 5, 2000.

1662 Cowan, interview, December 5, 2000.

1663 Cowan, interview, December 5, 2000.

1664 Cowan, interview, December 5, 2000.

1665 James L. Baillie, "In Memoriam: James Alexander Munro," *The Auk* 86, no. 4 (October 1969): 625. https://sora.unm.edu/sites/default/files/journals/auk/v086n04/p0624-p0630.pdf (pdf accessed October 31, 2014).

1666 James A. Munro, "The Birds and Mammals of the Creston Region, BC," BC Provincial Museum Occasional Paper no. 8 (1950): 1–90.

1667 Campbell et al., *Birds of BC*, vol. 1, 348–350.

1668 Lee Straight. "Member of Top Bird Group," *Vancouver Sun*, May 10, 1960, 14.

1669 Kathy Racey, interview, April 18, 2014.

1670 Kenneth Racey, "Field Notes 1943–1960," (Pileated Woodpecker entry in A–Z species accounts, May 5, 1958), Cowan_FN_002.

1671 Campbell et al., *Birds of BC*, vol. 2, 450.

1672 Cowan, interview, February 5, 2005.

1673 Ian McTaggart Cowan and P.A. Johnston, "Blood Serum Protein Variations at the Species and Subspecies Level in Deer of the Genus *Odocoileus*," *Systematic Zoology* 11, no. 3 (September 1962): 131–138. www.jstor.org/stable/2411876 (abstract accessed October 31, 2014).

1674 N.C. Nordan, A.J. Wood and I. McT. Cowan, "Further Studies on the Immobilization of Deer with Succinylcholine," *Canadian Journal of Comparative Medicine and Veterinary Science*, 26, no. 10 (October 1962): 246–248. www.ncbi.nlm.nih.gov/pmc/articles/PMC1583579 (full text accessed October 31, 2014).

1675 Ian McTaggart Cowan to Ann Schau, August 28, 1997, Cowan_PN_504.

1676 Cowan, "Journals: Voyages along the Coast of BC with Tom and Margaret Denny 1962–1967," Cowan_FN_036.

1677 Cowan and Guiguet, *Mammals of BC*, 260.

1678 "Pity the Porpoises," *The Gazette* (Montreal), February 24, 1993, B2. Full text at ProQuest document ID 432399556 (accessed via proxy server January 23, 2015; please consult your local public library or a university library as to availability).

1679 Tom Beck, interview, September 25–26, 2012.

1680 Alison App, interview, April 18, 2014.

1681 Marianne Michelle Stanford, "Immunoregulation in Murine Experimental Autoimmune Thyroiditis," unpublished MSc thesis, Faculty of Medicine, Memorial University, St. John's, Nfld., September 1999. http://research.library.mun.ca/974/1/Stanford_MarianneMichelle.pdf (pdf accessed October 31, 2014).

1682 Ian McTaggart Cowan, "James Robert Genge: An Appreciation," October 29, 1997, Cowan_PN_070.

1683 Alice Kubek, interview, June 12, 2014.

1684 Ian McTaggart Cowan to family and friends, December 9, 1999, Cowan_PN_504.

1685 Tom Beck, interview, September 25–26, 2012.

1686 Tom Beck, interview, September 25–26, 2012.

1687 Tom Beck, interview, September 25–26, 2012.

1688 Ian McTaggart Cowan to Tom Beck, April 21, 1998, Cowan_PN_286.

1689 Cowan to Beck, November 25, 1983, Cowan_PN_285.

1690 Cowan to Beck, December 30, 1995, Cowan_PN_286.

1691 Cowan to Beck, September 3, 1994, Cowan_PN_285.

1692 Beck, interview, September 25–26, 2012.

1693 Beck, interview, September 25–26, 2012.

1694 Campbell et al., *Birds of BC*, vol. 1, 266.

1695 Beck, interview, September 25–26, 2012.

1696 Campbell et al., *Birds of BC*, vol. 2, 376.

1697 Robert McTaggart Cowan, interview, May 8, 2014.

1698 Ian McTaggart Cowan to John J. Gaudio, September 30, 2000, Cowan_PN_001.

1699 Cowan, "Moments from an Education of an Ornithologist," 21.

1700 Cowan, "Moments from an Education of an Ornithologist," 21.

1701 Ronald D. Jakimchuk, R. Wayne Campbell and Dennis A. Demarchi, eds., *Ian McTaggart Cowan: The Legacy of a Pioneering Biologist, Educator and Conservationist* (Madeira Park, BC: Harbour Publishing, 2015), 80–105.

1702 Neil Dawe, eulogy at Cowan memorial, April 23, 2010, Cowan_PN_291.

1703 Campbell et al., *Birds of BC,* vol. 2, 408.

1704 Ian Stirling to Ian McTaggart Cowan, November 9, 1988, Cowan_PN_228.

1705 Cowan to Beck, August 24, 2002, Cowan_PN_286.

1706 Cowan to Neil Dawe (ca. autumn 2003), Cowan_PN_283.

1707 Ian McTaggart Cowan, "Address on Professorship," March 15, 2005, University of Victoria, Cowan_PN_047.

1708 Kathy Racey, interview, April 18, 2014.

1709 *Vancouver Sun,* "UBC Museum Well Stuffed But Hasn't Even One Whale," September 29, 1945, 2.

1710 Cowan and Guiguet, *Mammals of BC,* 268–269.

1711 Cowan, interview, November 30, 2000.

BIBLIOGRAPHY

Archival sources

Electronic edition readers: if a particular hyperlink doesn't work, please try copy/pasting the URL into your web browser by hand. Also, some of the publications cited here are behind paywalls but will likely be accessible at university libraries and some public libraries.

AUL Acadia University Library. Robie W. Tufts fonds (1900.433-TUF, 2008.047-TUF).

BCA British Columbia Archives:

Provincial Museum (GR-0078);

Provincial Museum Correspondence 1897–1970 (GR-0111) [includes earlier correspondence of Francis Kermode, Ian McTaggart Cowan];

Newcombe family fonds (MS-1077);

Hamilton Mack Laing fonds (MS-1309, MS-1900);

Richter family fonds (MS 1690);

Thomas A. Walker fonds (MS-2784);

Wilderness Advisory Committee Records (GR-1601);

Commission on Herbicides and Pesticides 1973 (GR-0383).

BBM Beaty Biodiversity Museum. Data on specimens accessed through Vertnet using institution code UBCBBM and collection code CTC at http://portal.vertnet.org/search (accessed October 31, 2014).

CMNA Canadian Museum of Nature Archives. Ornithology Collections, Hamilton Mack Laing and Ian McTaggart Cowan British Columbia Field Notes (1930).

DMAS Delta Museum and Archives Society. British Columbia Waterfowl Society fonds (CR-9).

GMA Glenbow Museum Archive. Austin de B. Winter fonds.

MVZA Museum of Vertebrate Zoology Archives, Berkeley, California. Historical Correspondence (MSS.0177): Annie Alexander, Allan Brooks, American Ornithologists' Union, H.A. Carr, Charles Elton, George Grinnell, Joseph Grinnell, Stanley Jewitt, Louise Kellogg, Hamilton Mack Laing, Aldo Leopold, T.T. McCabe, James K. Moffitt, J.A. Munro, W.A. Newcombe, Kenneth Racey, Theodore Roosevelt, Harry Swarth, Percy Taverner.

NBCA Northern BC Archives & Special Collections. Cheslatta Band on the Cheslatta Surrender.

PAC Public Archives of Canada. Hamilton Mack Laing fonds.

RBCM Royal British Columbia Museum:

Field Notes Miscellaneous 1939–1967 (File M-6 FIE-3) [transcription under Cowan_FN_060];

Field Notes Carl, Cowan and Beebe 1941–1944 (File M-6 FIE-4) [transcription under Cowan_FN_061];

Field Notes I. McT. Cowan 1936–1937 (File M-13 FIE-29) [transcription under Cowan_FN_052];

Field Notes I. McT. Cowan and P.W. Martin Peace River 1938 (File M-13 FIE-30) [transcription under Cowan_FN_053];

Field Notes collected by C.J. Guiguet 1946–1947 (File M-8 FIE-1) [transcription under Cowan_FN_059];

Hamilton Mack Laing Nature Diary 1930, April 16 to November 3 (File P-2 FIE-10).

ROM Royal Ontario Museum. Ornithological Collection, Hoyes Lloyd Field Notes.

SNL Scottish National Library. John Buchan Collection. See also in the bibliography below, under **Works cited**, "Balfour, John Hutton" and "Hutton, James," drawn from SNL Special Collections.

UASC University of Alberta Special Collections. William Rowan fonds (acc. 1319).

UBC RBSC University of British Columbia Rare Books and Special Collections. Andrew Hutchinson fonds (no call number available; link to summary of contents appears in bibliography below at "University of British Columbia Library"); H.R. MacMillan fonds (UBCSP-362); Burrard Field-Naturalists fonds (UBCSP-207).

UVicSC University of Victoria Special Collections. Elder Council of BC, Ian McTaggart Cowan fonds. Please note that the catalogue numbers for individual items were prepared while the collection was still in private hands and provide a finding aid for future research. These numbers are of the following types: Cowan_PN_xxx, which are personal notes, correspondence, lectures, unpublished materials, photo albums and research materials of the present author such as interviews; Cowan_PP_xxx, which comprise personal photographs of Cowan, his family, and friends and colleagues that are digitized and catalogued; Cowan_AN_xxx, which are the bound volumes and boxes of unbound materials that contain all of Cowan's published work; and Cowan_PH_xxx, which comprise the wildlife and landscape photographs Cowan took throughout his life, whether black and white prints or colour slides, many of them digitized.

UWiscDC University of Wisconsin Digital Collections. Aldo Leopold Archives (Box 001, Folder 002), Professional Correspondence 1937–1948.

Specimen sources

Beaty Biodiversity Museum, University of British Columbia, Vancouver.

Museum of Vertebrate Zoology, University of California, Berkeley.

National Museum of Scotland, Edinburgh.

Royal BC Museum, Victoria.

Field journals

Digital files *with transcriptions are available from the Ian McTaggart Cowan fonds in UVic Special Collections. The originals are also held there unless noted otherwise.*

Field notes (FN) *are in folio number order within each category.*

Cowan, Ian McTaggart

(where there are multiple journal authors, names are listed)

Cowan_FN_007, "Field Catalogue 1930 British Columbia and Alberta."

Cowan_FN_008, "Specimen Catalogue 1930"; companion volume to Cowan_FN_007.

Cowan_FN_009, "Field Catalogue December 16, 1930, to June 1, 1942."

Cowan_FN_010, "Notes Tofino, Alberni, Chezacut 1931."

Cowan_FN_011, "Specimen Catalogue from #1936–4036."

Cowan_FN_012, "Notes Mackenzie Delta 1947."

Cowan_FN_013, "Notes Mackenzie Delta 1947; companion volume bird census to Cowan_FN_012."

Cowan_FN_014, "Journal Field Trips 1935–1961" [missing 1939].

Cowan_FN_015, "Species Index 1939–1942; Birds."

Cowan_FN_016, "Species Index 1939–1942; Mammals."

Cowan_FN_017, "Field Notes 1943–1944; Sheep and elk."

Cowan_FN_018, "Westwick Lake Camp Summer 1955 Timothy Myers, Mary Jackson, Nancy Mahoney, Nancy Anderson."

Cowan_FN_019, "Field Notes California 1934."

Cowan_FN_020, "Notes on Mammalian Ecology 1929."

Cowan_FN_021, "Field Notes on Mammals of Vancouver and Cariboo 1931–1932."

Cowan_FN_022, "Field Notes 1930 British Columbia: East Kootenays, Alberta, Jasper and Banff National Parks."

Cowan_FN_023, "Field Notes 1943 Rocky Mtns."

Cowan_FN_024, "Field Notes 1944–1945 Rocky Mtns."

Cowan_FN_025, "Field Notes 1946 Rocky Mtns. & QCI"

Cowan_FN_026, "Field Notes Mackenzie R. 1947."

Cowan_FN_027, "Deer Study," December 29, 1935.

Cowan_FN_028, "Field Notes 1948, Anahim L. 1949, Cariboo," I. McT. Cowan, R.Y. Edwards, J.S. Tener.

Cowan_FN_029, "Birds Observed in Jasper Park May, June, July 1944."

Cowan_FN_033, "Beacon Hill Park Duck Census 1939."

Cowan_FN_034, "Mollusca, Saturna 1960."

Cowan_FN_035, "Bird Log and Mammals Mayne Island, BC, 1970–1990."

Cowan_FN_036, "Journals: Voyages along the Coast of BC with Tom and Margaret Denny 1962–1967."

Cowan_FN_037, "Molluscs 1958–1960."

Cowan_FN_039, "Nairobi" [journal].

Cowan_FN_040, "Sabbatical Year in Scotland" [1952 fall journal].

Cowan_FN_041, "Sabbatical Year in Scotland 2" [1953 spring–summer companion journal to Cowan_FN_040].

Cowan_FN_042, "Britain 1962 British Museum & Copenhagen Museum, Mollusca."

Cowan_FN_043, "Journal Moscow 1959; North Carolina n.d.; Baton Rouge 1963."

Cowan_FN_044, "Orient 1957; London 1958."

Cowan_FN_045, "Travel to Sea of Cortez 1959, 1962; General Notes on Faunal Differences in Plumper Sound."

Cowan_FN_046, "Field Notes 1969 Moorea, New Zealand; 1970 Australia" [1964–1970].

Cowan_FN_047, "1973 Micronesia; 1975 Rarotonga and New Zealand."

Cowan_FN_048, 1971 "Western Samoa, Fiji, Heron Island."

Cowan_FN_049, "Baja California Circumnavigated aboard MV *Pacific Northwest Explorer* Natural History Log, February, 9, 1985."

Cowan_FN_050, "List of Molluscs."

Cowan_FN_051, "Annotated Version of *A Review of the Bird Fauna of British Columbia* by J.A. Munro and I. McT. Cowan, Special Publication No. 2, 1947. British Columbia Provincial Museum" [annotated with interspersed hand notes of revisions and updates].

Cowan_FN_052, "Field Notes I. McT. Cowan 1936–1937; K. Racey Okanagan, Ootsa Lake, Monashee Pass, Mt. Revelstoke, Texas Creek" [original at RBCM, File M-13 FIE-29].

Cowan_FN_053, "Field Notes I. McT. Cowan and P.W. Martin Peace River 1938" [original at RBCM, File M-13 FIE-30].

Cowan_FN_056, "Field Notes British Columbia, East Kootenay 1930, H.M. Laing and I.M. Cowan" [Canadian Museum of Nature Archives, Ornithology Collections, unorganized].

Cowan_FN_058 "Cowan, Ian McT., 1932–1934" [California], [handwritten duplicate, with some differences, of journal in vol. 573 at Museum of Vertebrate Zoology Archives, Berkeley].

Cowan_FN_060, "Field Notes Miscellaneous 1939–1967" [Ian McTaggart Cowan and Patrick W. Martin] [original at RBCM, File M-6 FIE-3].

Cowan_FN_061, "Field Notes Carl, Cowan and Beebe 1941–1944, Carl, Clifford; Cowan, Ian McTaggart; Beebe, Frank" [original at RBCM, File M-6 FIE-4].

Foster, Bristol

Cowan_FN_054, "Field Notes B. Foster, Summer 1960." Zoology Dept. UBC (notes while with I.M. Cowan in field) [private collection but permissions granted for digitization and transcription].

Cowan_FN_055, "Field Notes B. Foster, Summer 1961" (notes while with I.M. Cowan in field); [permissions *idem*].

Grinnell, Joseph

Cowan_FN_019, "Note to Students," September 13, 1933.

Guiguet, Charles

Cowan_FN_038, "Queen Charlotte Islands May to August 1946" [bird lists].

Cowan_FN_059, "1946–1947 QCI" (notes while with I.M Cowan in field) [original at RBCM File M-8 FIE-1].

Laing, Hamilton Mack

"Nature Diary, April 16 to November 30, 1930" [original at RBCM, File P-2 FIE-10].

Racey, Kenneth

Cowan_FN_001, "K. Racey Field Notes 1924–1938."

Cowan_FN_002, "K. Racey Field Notes 1943–1960."

Cowan_FN_003, "1921–1927 Huntingdon, Sumas Prairie... Ken Racey."

Cowan_FN_004, "Alta Lake. BC 1920–1927 Notes by Kenneth Racey."

Cowan_FN_005, "K. Racey Field Notes Port Hardy 1950–51."

Cowan_FN_006, "Bird Census – Kenneth Racey."

Cowan_FN_057, "Field Catalogue Kenneth Racey, 1937."

Shillaker, F.M.

Cowan_FN_030, "Notes from Chezacut, BC by F.M. Shillaker 1943."

Cowan_FN_031, "F.M. Shillaker, Chezacut Winter 1940–41."

Cowan_FN_032, [F.M. Shillaker] "Jasper Park, Alta. May & June 1946."

Correspondence and other materials

Personal notes (PN) *are in folio number order within each category.*

Cowan, Ian McTaggart

Cowan_PN_001, to John J. Gaudio, September 30, 2000.

Cowan_PN_002, "Job application: Field party – Dominion Parks, with references," [ca. March] 1930.

Cowan_PN_003, to J.A. Munro, May 3, 1926.

from J.A. Munro, May 6, 1926.

Cowan_PN_005, to Rodger Hunter, February 1997.

Cowan_PN_012, to D. Lawrence, Rideau Hall, November 15, 1998.

Cowan_PN_013, from Roger and Alli Clapp to Ian and Joyce McTaggart Cowan, July 1, 1984.

Cowan_PN_016, to BC Premier William Vander Zalm, July 6, 1987.

to Secretary of James L. Baillie Memorial Fund, Long Point Bird Observatory, January 19, 1998.

Cowan_PN_047, "Address on Professorship," March 15, 2005, University of Victoria.

Cowan_PN_070, "James Robert Genge: An Appreciation," October 29, 1997.

Cowan_PN_080, to Joe Bryant, July 9, 1996.

Cowan_PN_081, from Mary Bryant, c. 1996.

from Patrick Martin, 2000, on the occasion of Cowan's 90th birthday celebration.

from William (Bill) Hoar, March 2000.

from Iola Knight, June 25, 2000.

Cowan_PN_090, from Theodora Gray, November 9, 1999.

to Rhoda Love, December 7, 1998.

Cowan_PN_094, to Joyce Cowan, July 4–29, 1944.

Cowan_PN_095, to Joyce Racey, May 13, 1931.

Cowan_PN_101, "Address to University of Northern British Columbia, May 22, 1997" (unpublished).

Cowan_PN_103, "President and Chancellor Address" at 1983 Autumn Convocation, University of Victoria.

Cowan_PN_104, "Moments from the Education of an Ornithologist" (MS, which differs from the published version listed below under **Works cited**, at "Cowan, Ian McTaggart"].

Cowan_PN_106, from Francis Cook, August 15, 1998.

Cowan_PN_146, from Ron Jeffels, "The Roasting and Toasting of IMC," March 31, 1981.

Cowan_PN_159, from Fred Evensen, address on the awarding of the Wildlife Society Aldo Leopold Medal for 1970.

Cowan_PN_160, to Bill Schwartz, July 6, 1993.

Cowan_PN_219, "Whales and Whaling: Some Issues of the 1980s" (unpublished report to the Canadian Committee on Whales and Whaling, September 20, 1980).

"A Report to the Canadian Committee on Whales and Whaling," presented at the 33rd Annual Meeting of the International Whaling Commission, July 20–25, 1981 (unpublished, 7 pp.) [*q.v.* below under **Works cited**, at "Cowan, Ian McTaggart"].

Cowan_PN_221, from Monte Hummel, August 15, 1997.

Cowan_PN_228, from Ian Stirling, November 9, 1988.

Cowan_PN_230, from Maurice Hornocker, various correspondence 1986–88.

Cowan_PN_233, to James McLean, October 15, 1963.

Cowan_PN_240, "Queen Charlotte Islands," lecture notes, n.d.

Cowan_PN_246, "Extinct and Vanishing Mammals," lecture notes, ca. 1958–59.

Cowan_PN_267, to Wilderness Advisory Committee, ca. 1985.

Cowan_PN_271, "Spotted Bat" (handwritten draft revision [*Mammals of BC*]), 1987.

Cowan_PN_276, "Miscellaneous Correspondence on Wolves, 1947–1999."

from E.O. French, January 7, 1948, response to questionnaire re "Miscellaneous Correspondence on Wolves, 1947–1999."

from Cyril Shelford, January 25, 1979.

Cowan_PN_282, to Neil Dawe (n.d.).

Cowan_PN_283, to Neil Dawe (ca. autumn 2003).

Cowan_PN_285, to Tom Beck, February 5, 1983.

to Tom Beck, November 25, 1983.

to Tom Beck, September 3, 1994.

to Tom Beck, November 24, 1994.

Cowan_PN_286, to Tom Beck, December 30, 1995.

to Tom Beck, April 21, 1998.

to Tom Beck, August 24, 2002.

Cowan_PN_289, to Neil Dawe, March 15, 2002.

Cowan_PN_294, "In the Steps of Southesk" (unpublished essay, ca. 1953).

Cowan_PN_298, "Shillaker Manuscript, 1939–1945," field notes.

Cowan_PN_333, "Desert Lecture," n.d.

Cowan_PN_337, "Whales and Whaling Lectures," lecture notes, n.d.

Cowan_PN_358, to Frank Butler, May 16, 1947.

Cowan_PN_381, "Mammals of Kamloops" (unpublished field guide, 1929).

Cowan_PN_382, from R.M. Humphreys, October 30, 1972.

to G. Smith, October 26, 1972.

from G. Smith, November 22, 1972.

to R.J. Milko, 1981.

Cowan_PN_494, "Synopsis for *Web of Life*," CBC Television Archives.

Cowan_PN_504, to Ann Schau, July 8, 1987.

to Ann Schau, September 12, 1988.

to Ann Schau, February 6, 1990.

to Mikkel Schau, September 25, 1996.

to Mikkel Schau, September 28, 1996.

to Ann Schau, August 28, 1997.

to family and friends, December 9, 1999.

Cowan_PN_511, "Profile of Baja California" (unpublished booklet, ca. 1985).

Cowan_PN_893, "Report on Game Conditions in Banff, Jasper and Kootenay National Parks 1943" (unpublished 72 pp. mimeographed, with photographs) [*q.v.* below under **Works cited**, at "Cowan, Ian McTaggart"].

Cowan_PN_894, "Report of Wildlife Studies in Jasper, Banff and Yoho National Parks 1944" and "Parasites, Diseases and Injuries of Game Animals in the Rocky Mountain National Parks 1942–1944" (both unpublished, mimeographed, 1944) [*q.v.* below under **Works cited**, at "Cowan, Ian McTaggart"].

Cowan_PN_895, Report of Wildlife Studies in the Rocky Mountain National Parks in 1945" prepared for National Parks Bureau, Ottawa, 1945 (unpublished 63 pp. mimeographed) [*q.v.* below under **Works cited,** at "Cowan, Ian McTaggart"].

Cowan_PN_896, "General Report upon Wildlife Studies in the Rocky Mountain National Parks in 1946" (unpublished 32 pp. mimeographed) [*q.v.* below under **Works cited,** at "Cowan, Ian McTaggart"].

Cowan_PN_897, "The Ecology of the North: Knowledge is the Key to Sane Development," *Science Forum* 2, no. 1 (1969): 8. (citing Recommendation 7 from the UNESCO Biosphere Conference of 1968) [*q.v.* below under **Works cited,** at "Cowan, Ian McTaggart"].

Cowan_PN_898, "Research in the National Parks of Canada" (unpublished report prepared for Parks Canada, 1977) [*q.v.* below under **Works cited,** at "Cowan, Ian McTaggart".

Cowan_PN_946, Map of Black-tailed Deer range from "Distribution and Variation in Deer (Genus *Odocoileus*) of the Pacific Coast Region of North America," PhD dissertation, Berkeley, 1935 [*q.v.* below under **Works cited,** at "Cowan, Ian McTaggart"].

Cowan_PN_947, Map of Central Coast from "*Peromyscus maniculatus macrorhinus* and the Problem of Insularity," February 1945 [*q.v.* below under **Works cited,** at "McCabe, T.T."].

Cowan_PN_948, Map of Jasper Park from "The Timber Wolf in the Rocky Mountain National Parks of Canada," October 1947 [*q.v.* below under **Works cited,** at "Cowan, Ian McTaggart"].

Cowan_PN_949, Map of Banff Park from "The Timber Wolf in the Rocky Mountain National Parks of Canada" October 1947 [*q.v.* below under **Works cited,** at "Cowan, Ian McTaggart"].

Miscellaneous

Cowan_AN_037, "The Wildlife Resource in Canada: A Brief Presented to the Royal Commission on Canada's Economic Prospects." Unpublished. Toronto: Canadian Conservation Association, ca. 1955.

Cowan_AN_038, "Conservation of Wildlife." Transcript of address originally given on radio under the title "In Defence of Predators." In pamphlet for Kindness to Animals Week, April 20–27, 1942. Society for the Prevention of Cruelty to Animals, Vancouver.

Cowan_PN_010, *The Totem*, UBC Graduating Class of 1932 Annual (Vancouver: UBC, 1932).

Cowan_PN_019, 020, Racey family photograph albums.

Cowan_PN_026, Joyce Racey to Kenneth Racey, July 19, 1923.

Joyce Racey to Kenneth Racey, August 6, 1923.

Eileen Racey to Kenneth Racey, August 23, 1923.

Cowan_PN_050, Diana Zink Bickford, "Notes from Laura McTaggart Cowan (Mackenzie)" (from unpublished autobiography, 1957).

The Broad Arrow: A Paper for the Services, London, August 30, 1873.

Cowan_PN_052, *Montreal Daily Star*, "Cartoons of Canada According to American Movies" series, 1923. [*q.v.* below at "*Montreal Daily Star*," under **Works cited**].

Cowan_PN_058, Jim Lauder, "Joyce McTaggart Cowan memorial service eulogy," December 3, 2002.

Cowan_PN_074, *North Vancouver High School Annual, 1927.*

Cowan_PN_093, Nancy Wilkin, "A Celebration of Life: Dr. Vernon Cuthbert Brink, OC, OBC, PhD, FAIC, November 15, 1912, to November 29, 2007," eulogy read January 31, 2008.

Cowan_PN_146, Ron Jeffels of Ian McTaggart Cowan, "Speech at Retirement," March 5, 1981.

Cowan_PN_158, National Audubon Society, "Minutes of the Board of Directors Meeting held at the Westin Hotel, Winnipeg, Manitoba, Canada," September 21, 1986.

Cowan_PN_129, Eileen Racey to Kenneth Racey, September 6, 1923.

Cowan_PN_182, Jim Gilmore, "US Network Bids for Local Series," *Vancouver Sun, n.d.*

Cowan_PN_185, *The Daily Colonist*, "Museum Vital to Education" [ca. 1937].

Cowan_PN_186, *Penticton Herald*, "McTaggart-Cowan Lauds Park Group," October 6, 1966.

Cowan_PN_202, *The Vancouver Daily Province*, "MLAs Learn about BC Game," February 9, 1950.

Cowan_PN_291, Rae Crossman, "One Ruby-throated Moment," unpublished poem [n.d.] read in eulogy of Ian McTaggart Cowan April 23, 2010.

Ann Schau, "Eulogy."

Neil Dawe, eulogy at Cowan memorial, April 23, 2010.

Lyn Lewis to Ann Schau, "One hundredth birthday greetings/funeral condolences," April 23, 2010.

Monte Hummel to Ann Schau, "One hundredth birthday greetings/funeral condolences," May 4, 2010.

Cowan_PN_296, "Mammal and Bird Life of Burnaby Lake," *Vancouver Natural History Society Bulletin* no. 18 (October 1945), reprinted in Bill Merilees, *Selected Excerpts from the Vancouver Natural History Society Bulletin*, 16–17 [*q.v.* below at both "Merilees, Bill" and "Vancouver Natural History Society," under **Works cited**].

Stuart F. Bradley, "Mammals of UBC Area," *Vancouver Natural History Society Bulletin* 41, 42 (September 1948). Reprinted in Bill Merilees, *Selected Excerpts from the Vancouver Natural History Society Bulletin*, 34 [*q.v.* below at "Bradley, Stuart," under **Works cited**]

Cowan_PN_302, "The Migrant" (binder of unpublished correspondence, 1922–1924 [*q.v.* below at "BC Ornithologists' Union," under **Works cited**].

Cowan_PN_492, Transcription of October 2006 Cowan interview by Rick Searle for Elders Council for Parks in BC. [*q.v.* below at "Clarke, C.H.D.," under **Interviews/Ian McTaggart Cowan, with**].

Cowan_PN_497, "Wild Life Investigation in Banff National Park, 1939," ca. 1940. [*q.v.* below at "Clarke, C.H.D.," under **Works cited**].

Cowan_PN_504, Joyce Racey to Stewart Racey, May 23, 1935.

McTaggart Cowan [Sr.] to Jennifer Charlesworth, November 1968.

Joyce Cowan to Ann Schau, January 31, 1977.

Joyce Cowan to Ann Schau, September 16, 1990.

Interviews

Ian McTaggart Cowan, with

by Briony Penn, November 30 and December 5, 2000; February 26, 2001; February 2, 2005.

by Val Geist, videotaped and transcribed by Briony Penn, July 9, 2002, for the Wildlife Society's "Celebrating Our Wildlife Conservation Heritage (COWCH) Project," archived with the Wildlife Society, the University of Victoria and the Habitat Conservation Trust Foundation, 1:59:07, http://vimeo.com/60839975 (accessed October 31, 2014). Excerpted as a 22-minute documentary for the series *Environ/Mental* on The New VI, CHUM TV, Victoria, BC, aired February 2, 2003. A further-edited version, "Ian McTaggart-Cowan," was posted on YouTube August 9, 2012, in two parts totalling 20:00. www.youtube.com/watch?v=IyToOaoDZSk; www.youtube.com/watch?v=kmeK4qib6a8 (both accessed October 31, 2014).

by Rick Searle, October 2006; this taped interview is part of the Elders Council for Parks in BC project, lodged in UVicSC at AR447; transcription is in the Ian McTaggart Cowan Collection, UVicSC. [*q.v.* above at Cowan_PN_492 under **Correspondence and Other Materials/Miscellaneous**].

by Peter Corley-Smith, October 1985, RBCM Collection.

Ian McTaggart Cowan, about

Alison App, April 18, 2014.

Tom Beck, September 25–26, 2012.

Shirley Beck, September 25–26, 2012.

Thomas Berger, May 19, 2013.

Tom Bergerud, May 22, 2013.

Al Brady, September 24, 2012.

Betty Brooks, October 29, 2013.

Joe Bryant, November 10, 2012.

Fred Bunnell, November 15, 2012.

Jim Campbell, May 25, 2013.

Adolf Ceska, February 2, 2015.

Francis Cook, October 28, 2013.

Betty Copeland, August 3, 2013.

Robert McTaggart Cowan, May 8, 2014.

Neil Dawe, September 18, 2012.

Chantal Dussault, October 26, 2013.

Don Eastman, July 11, 2002.

Don Flook, September 29, 2012.

Bristol Foster, July 24 and September 6, 2012.

Margaret Fulton, January 16, 2014.

Valerius Geist, September 17, 2012.

Ken Gibson, November 22, 2013.

Trevor Goward, March 25, 2013.

Muriel Guiguet, September 9, 2012.

Trisha Guiguet, September 9, 2012.

Susan Hannon, March 21, 2014.

Lorne Hammond, August 7, 2013.

Daryll Hebert, September 28, 2012.

Richard Hebda, March 2, 2001.

Steve Johnsen, February 5, 2015.

Winifred Kessler, June 10, 2014.

Rick Kool, January 13, 2014.

Alice Kubek, June 12, 2014.

William (Bill) Lidicker, September 17, 2013.

Hilary Mackenzie, September 7, 2013.

Elizabeth May, June 2, 2014.

Wayne McCrory, September 20, 2012.

Bill Merilees, September 17, 2012.

David Nagorsen, May 24, 2013; April 5 and May 9, 2014.

Murray Newman, May 25, 2013.

Art Pearson, September 29, 2012.

Kathy Racey, April 18, 2014.

Tom Reimchen, January 4, 2014.

Robert Scagel, August 8, 2012.

Ann Schau, October 9, 2012, and variously over the course of 2012–2015.

Mikkel Schau, October 9, 2012, and variously over the course of 2012–2015.

Torben Schau, May 20, 2014.

Geoff Scudder, December 17, 2013.

Rod Silver, February 24, 2014.

Tom Sterling, July 31, 2012.

Ward Stevens, November 14, 2012.

Ian Stirling, August 23, 2010.

David Suzuki, September 7, 2012.

Anne Taylor, October 27, 2013.

Stanley A. Temple, March 2, 2015.

Bob Weeden, July 26, 2012, and November 16, 2013.

Judy Weeden, July 26, 2012.

Other interviews

Jennifer Benito, January 27, 2015.

Art Napoleon, June 1, 2010.

Personal communications

Jennifer Benito, Save the Redwoods League, January 27, 2015.

Daniel Brunton, October 30, 2013.

Adolf Ceska, February 2, 2015.

Graham Checkley, September 1, 2013.

Francis Cook, October 28, 2013.

Betty Copeland, August 3, 2013.

Chris Darimont, February 24, 2005.

Chantal Dussault, Canadian Museum of Nature, October 26, 2013.

Ken Gibson, November 22, 2013.

Susan Hannon, March 21, 2014.

Richard Hebda, March 2001.

Steve Johnsen, National Wildlife Federation, February 5, 2015.

Rick Kool, January 13, 2014.

Elizabeth May, June 2, 2014.

David Nagorsen, April 5 and May 9, 2014.

Peter Ommundsen, January 12, 2000, and August 17, 2012.

Colin Preston, CBC archivist, November 2013.

Tom Reimchen, January 4, 2014.

Ann Schau, May 10, 2014.

Torben Schau, May 20, 2014.

David Suzuki, September 7, 2012.

Ann Taylor, October 27, 2013.

Stanley A. Temple, Aldo Leopold Foundation, March 2, 2015.

Judy Weeden, July 26, 2012.

Taxonomy authorities consulted

American Ornithologists' Union. *The AOU Checklist of North and Middle American Birds*. http://checklist.aou.org (accessed October 20, 2014).

Clarke, Arthur H. *The Freshwater Molluscs of Canada*. Ottawa: National Museum of Natural Sciences, National Museums of Canada, 1981.

Perrin, William F., Bernd G. Würsig and J.G.M. Thewissen, eds. Encyclopedia of Marine Mammals. 2nd ed. San Diego, Calif.: Academic Press, 2009.

Society for the Study of Amphibians and Reptiles. *Scientific and Standard English Names of Amphibians and Reptiles of North America North of Mexico*. 7th ed., Herpetological Circular no. 39. Salt Lake City, Utah: SSAR, 2012. http://ssarherps.org/wp-content/uploads/2014/07/HC_39_7thEd.pdf (accessed October 20, 2014).

Wild Species Canada 2005. [Common names at species level only.] www.wildspecies.ca/wildspecies2005/search.cfm?lang=e&sec=9 (accessed October 20, 2014).

Wilson, Don. E., and DeeAnn M. Reeder, eds. *Mammal Species of the World: A Taxonomic and Geographic Reference*. 2 vols. 3rd ed. Baltimore: Johns Hopkins University Press, 2005. An allied resource is the searchable database and taxonomic browser at *Wilson & Reeder's Mammal Species of the World*, a website of the Smithsonian National Museum of Natural History: www.vertebrates.si.edu/msw/mswcfapp/msw/index.cfm (accessed October 20, 2014).

Works cited

Abraham, Dorothy. *Lone Cone: A Journal of Life on the West Coast of Vancouver Island, BC*. Victoria: Tiritca, 1945.

Ainley, Marianne Gosztonyi. *Creating Complicated Lives: Women and Science at English-Canadian Universities 1880–1980*. Montreal: McGill-Queen's University Press, 2012.

———. "William Rowan: Canada's First Avian Biologist," *Picoides* 1, no. 1 (1987): 6–8. www.scosoc.ca/picoides/archive/Picoides1_1_1987.pdf (accessed October 31, 2014).

Aldo Leopold Archives (website). University of Wisconsin Digital Collections, 2011. http://uwdc.library.wisc.edu/collections/AldoLeopold (accessed February 6, 2015).

Alexander, Denis R., and Ronald L. Numbers, eds. *Biology and Ideology from Descartes to Dawkins*. Chicago: University of Chicago Press, 2010.

Allan, Blaine. "CBC Television Series 1952–1982" *Web of Life* (online database item). Kingston, Ont.: Queen's University Department of Film and Media, 1996. www.film.queensu.ca/cbc/W.html (accessed May 24, 2014).

Allen, David Elliston. *The Naturalist in Britain: A Social History*. 2nd ed. Princeton, NJ: Princeton University Press, 1994.

———. "Balfour, John Hutton (1808–1884)." *Oxford Dictionary of National Biography*. Oxford University Press, 2004. www.oxforddnb.com/view/article/1192 (citation only; accessed October 22, 2013; full text may be available through your local library).

Allen, Glover M. *Extinct and Vanishing Mammals of the Western Hemisphere with the Marine Species of All the Oceans*. Special Publication no. 11. Washington, DC: American Committee for International Wild Life Protection, 1942. www.biodiversitylibrary.org/item/67624#page/9/mode/1up (accessed October 31, 2014).

Alroy, John "The Fossil Record of North American Mammals: Evidence for a Paleocene Evolutionary Radiation." *Systematic Biology* 48, no. 1 (1999): 107–118. http://sysbio.oxfordjournals.org/content/48/1/107.full.pdf+html (accessed October 31, 2014).

Annand, Amanda Dawn. "The 1910 Fires in Alberta's Foothills and Rocky Mountain Region." Unpublished undergraduate honours thesis. University of Victoria, 2010. http://mountainlegacy.ca/research/documents/Annand-1910Fires-FinalReport.pdf (full text accessed October 31, 2014).

Arai, Mary N. "Charles McLean Fraser (1872–1946) – His contributions to hydroid research and to the development of fisheries biology and academia in British Columbia." *Hydrobiologia* 530/531, no. 1 (November 2004): 3–11. (EBSCOHost doc. 15417015 pdf accessed October 31, 2014, via proxy server; consult your local public library or a university as to availability.)

Armstrong, Christopher, Matthew Dominic Evenden and H.V. Nelles. *The River Returns: An Environmental History of the Bow*. Montreal: McGill-Queen's University Press, 2009.

Ayles, H. "Environmental Impact Assessment, Biological Perspective." In *Proceedings of a National Conference on Environmental Impact Assessment held November 15–16, 1973: Philosophy and Methodology*, 22–29. Winnipeg: Agassiz Centre for Water Studies, University of Manitoba, 1974.

B. of V., ed. *Some Lessons*. US: Privately printed for the use of the Order by F.C. Walcott, 1939.

———, ed. *Some Lessons*, vol. 2. US: Privately printed for the use of the Order, 1948.

———. ed. *Lessons of the Brotherhood of the Venery: Supplement*. US: Privately printed for the use of the Order [n.d.].

Baillie, James L. "In Memoriam: James Alexander Munro." *The Auk* 86, no. 4 (October 1969): 624–630. https://sora.unm.edu/sites/default/files/journals/auk/v086n04/p0624-p0630.pdf (accessed October 31, 2014).

Balfour, John Hutton. *Account of Botanical Excursions made in the Island of Arran during the Months of August and September 1869*. Edinburgh: for private circulation, 1870. 3.631 National Library of Scotland, Special Collections.

———. *Short Syllabus of the Course of Lectures on Botany Delivered at 9 Surgeons Square Edinburgh by John Hutton Balfour, MD, Ed., FRSE*. Edinburgh: n.d. 3.631 National Library of Scotland Special Collections.

———. *Testimonials in Favour of John Hutton Balfour, MD, Ed., FRSE, 1841*. Glasgow: s.n., 1841. 3.631 National Library of Scotland Special Collections.

Barman, Jean. *Growing up British in British Columbia: Boys in Private School, 1900–1950*. Vancouver: UBC Press, 1984.

BC Wild. *Flirting with Extinction: Clearcuts and the Demise of Southern BC's Caribou*. Smithers: Cariboo Chilcotin Resource Centre, BC Wild, 1998. www.eye-design.ca/publications/flirting.pdf (accessed October 31, 2014).

BC Ornithologists' Union. "The Migrant." Binder of unpublished correspondence, 1922–1924 [also Cowan_PN_302].

BC Parks. "Tweedsmuir South Provincial Parks." www.env.gov.bc.ca/bcparks/explore/parkpgs/tweeds_s/nat_cul.html (accessed May 24, 2014).

———. "Ecological Reserves Program." www.env.gov.bc.ca/bcparks/eco_reserve (accessed March 25, 2014).

Beaty Biodiversity Museum. "History of the Cowan Tetrapod Collection." http://beatymuseum.ubc.ca/tetrapod-collection-history (accessed March 22, 2013).

———. "History of the Spencer Entomological Collection." http://beatymuseum.ubc.ca/entomolgical-collection-history (accessed March 22, 2013).

Bellon, R. "A Question of Merit: John Hutton Balfour, Joseph Hooker and the 'Concussion' over the Edinburgh Chair of Botany." *Studies in History and Philosophy of Biological and Biomedical Sciences* 36, no. 1 (March 2005): 25–54. www.ncbi.nlm.nih.gov/pubmed/16120259 (abstract only, accessed June 2, 2014).

Bernard, F.R. "*Cuspidaria cowani*, a New Septibranch Mollusc from the Northeastern Pacific." *Journal of the Fisheries Research Board of Canada* 24, no. 12 (1967): 2629–2630.

Bergerud, A.T. *The Status and Management of Caribou in British Columbia*. BC Fish & Wildlife Branch, 1978. www.env.gov.bc.ca/wld/documents/techpub/rn333.pdf (scanned page image accessed October 31, 2014).

Birney, Elmer C., and Jerry R. Choate, eds. *Seventy-Five Years of Mammalogy 1919–1994*. Utah: American Society of Mammalogists, 1994. https://archive.org/stream/seventyfiveyears-oobirn#page/n5/mode/2up (accessed October 31, 2014).

Bonner, Veera, Irene Bliss and Hazel H. Litterick. *Chilcotin: Preserving Pioneer Memories*. Surrey, BC: Heritage House, 1995.

Bonta, Marcia. "Theodora Cope Gray: Nature's Own Child." Blogpost, July 1, 2001. http://marciabonta.wordpress.com/2001/07/01/theodora-cope-gray-natures-own-child (accessed May 24, 2014).

Bousfield, Edward L., and Edward A. Hendrycks. "The Talitroidean Amphipod Family *Hyalidae* Revised, with Emphasis on the North Pacific Fauna: Systematics and Distributional Ecology." *Amphipacifica* 3, no. 3 (2002): 17–134.

Bradley, Stuart F. "Mammals of UBC Area." *Vancouver Natural History Society Bulletin* nos. 41, 42 (September 1948). Reprinted in Bill Merilees, *Selected Excerpts from the Vancouver Natural History Society Bulletin*, 34. http://naturevancouver.ca/sites/naturevancouver.ca/VNHS%20files/4/VNHS_Bulletin_1943-1971.pdf (pdf p38 accessed May 24, 2014). [*q.v.* above under **Correspondence and other materials/Miscellaneous**, at Cowan_PN_296.]

Brignell, Victoria. "The Eugenics Movement Britain Wants to Forget." *New Statesman*, December 9, 2010. www.newstatesman.com/society/2010/12/british-eugenics-disabled (accessed February, 6, 2015).

Brink, Vernon "Bert." "Brink on Davidson." Transcript and streaming audio of interview by David Brownstein at *John Davidson: The Legacy of a Canadian Botanist*, a website by the UBC Botanical Garden and the Virtual Museum of Canada, n.d. www.botanyjohn.org/en/in-depth-study/brink-on-davidson?page=0,6-davidson-and-the-bc-botanists (accessed March 14, 2013). [NB: After first noting a failure of this URL to connect on February 2, 2015, Rocky Mountain Books monitored botanyjohn.org biweekly for the ensuing six months, and the site was inaccessible every time. It may have been taken down altogether.]

———. "The Beginnings of Wisdom." Vancouver Natural History Society *Bulletin* no. 140, September 14, 1968. Reprinted in *Selected Excerpts from the Vancouver Natural History Society Bulletin* (No. 1, September 1943, to No. 153, December 1971), compiled by Bill Merrilees (2005): 196–202 (pdf pp. 200–206). http://naturevan.ca/sites/naturevancouver.ca/VNHS files/4/VNHS_Bulletin_1943-1971.pdf (accessed October 31, 2014).

British Columbia. *Journals of the Legislative Assembly of the Province of* BC, vol. 78 (lxxviii). Victoria: King's Printer, 1949. As linked from http://is.gd/dEt9ed (pdfs accessed February 27, 2015).

British Columbia Ministry of Environment. "Conservation Officer Service – 100 Years: 1905–1960, The Game Wardens." www.env.gov.bc.ca/cos/100years/1905/game_warden.html *(accessed January 6, 2013)*.

Brody, Hugh. *Maps and Dreams: Indians and the British Columbia Frontier*. Vancouver: Douglas & McIntyre, 1981.

Buchanan, G.O. "Preservation of Canadian Forests." *Victoria Daily Times*. May 14, 1908.

Burba, George Francis. *Our Bird Friends: Containing Many Things Young Folks Ought to Know – and Likewise Grown-Ups*. New York: The Outing Publishing Company, 1908. https://archive.org/stream/ourbirdfriendscoooburb#page/n7/mode/2up (accessed October 31, 2014).

Burnett, J. Alexander. *A Passion for Wildlife: The History of the Canadian Wildlife Service*. Vancouver: UBC Press, 2003.

Calaby, J.H., H. Dimpel and I. McTaggart-Cowan. "The Mountain Pigmy Possum *Burramys parvus* Broom (Marsupial) in the Kosciuszko National Park, New South Wales." Division of Wildlife Research Technical Paper 23. Australia: Commonwealth Scientific and Industrial Research Organisation, 1971).

Callicott, J. Baird, ed. *Companion to* A Sand County Almanac: *Interpretive and Critical Essays*. University of Wisconsin Press, 1987.

Camp, Frank. *Roots in the Rockies*. Ucluelet, BC: Frank Camp Ventures, 1993.

Campbell, Claire Elizabeth. *A Century of Parks Canada, 1911–2011*. Canadian History and Environment Series. Calgary: University of Calgary Press, 2011.

Campbell, E.C., and R. Wayne Campbell. "COSEWIC Status Report on the Spotted Owl *Strix occidentalis* in Canada." Ottawa: Committee on the Status of Endangered Wildlife in Canada, 1986.

Campbell, R. Wayne, Neil K. Dawe, Ian McTaggart Cowan, John M. Cooper, Gary W. Kaiser and Michael C.E. McNall. *The Birds of British Columbia*. Vol. 1. Vancouver: UBC Press, 1990.

———. *The Birds of British Columbia*. Vol. 2. Vancouver: UBC Press, 1990.

Campbell, R. Wayne, Neil K. Dawe, Ian McTaggart Cowan, John M. Cooper, Gary W. Kaiser, Michael C.E. McNall and G.E. John Smith. *The Birds of British Columbia*. Vol. 3. Vancouver: UBC Press, 1997.

Campbell, R. Wayne, Neil K. Dawe, Ian McTaggart Cowan, John M. Cooper, Gary W. Kaiser, Andrew C. Stewart and Michael C.E. McNall. *The Birds of British Columbia*. Vol. 4. Vancouver: UBC Press, 2001.

Canadian Forestry Assn. *The Forests and The People*. Pamphlet, n.d., https://archive.org/stream/cihm_72922#page/n5/mode/2up (accessed October 31, 2014) [excerpted editorially by Victoria *Daily Colonist*, "Forests and the People," August 8, 1908, 4 at bottom of first column, http://archive.org/stream/dailycolonist19080808u-vic/19080808#page/n3/mode/1up (accessed October 31, 2014)].

Cariboo Observer. "Farmers' Institutes Hold Annual Meeting [at] Canim Lake Lodge." June 29, 1946, 1, 4. http://www.quesnelmuseum.ca/CaribooObserverDocs/1946/19460629_Cariboo%20Observer.pdf (accessed February 20, 2015).

Carl, G. Clifford. *The Amphibians of British Columbia*. Handbook no. 2. Victoria: BC Provincial Museum, 1943.

———. *The Reptiles of British Columbia*. Handbook no. 3. Victoria: BC Provincial Museum, 1944.

Carter, D., and A. Harestad. "Status of the White-Tailed Jackrabbit (*Lepus townsendii*) in British Columbia." Unpublished report for Wildlife Branch, BC Ministry of Environment, 1991.

Carter, Harry R. "Charles Joseph Guiguet: Recipient of Pacific Seabird Group Lifetime Achievement Award." *Pacific Seabirds* 23, no. 1 (Spring 1996): 9–10 [pdf 11–12]. http://pacificseabirdgroup.org/publications/PacificSeabirds/VOL_23_1.PDF (accessed October 31, 2014).

———. "In Memoriam Charles Joseph Guiguet." *Pacific Seabirds* 26, no. 2 (Fall 1999): 65–66 [pdf 7–8]. http://pacificseabirdgroup.org/publications/PacificSeabirds/VOL_26_2.PDF (accessed October 31, 2014).

Case, Ted J., and Martin L. Cody. *Island Biogeography in the Sea of Cortez*. Berkeley: University California Press, 1983.

Cheslatta Band. "The Cheslatta Surrender: A legal analysis of a surrender given by the Cheslatta Carrier Nation to Her Majesty in right of the government of Canada on the 21st of April, 1952." Northern BC Archives & Special Collections 2003.4.1.35.

Clark, Roger N. "Two New Chitons of the Genus *Tripoplax* Berry, 1919 from the Monterey Sea Canyon." *American Malacological Bulletin* 25, no. 1 (2008): 77–86. http://is.gd/Tmg6pn (abstract and references accessed March 5, 2015).

Clarke, Arthur H. *The Freshwater Molluscs of Canada*. Ottawa: National Museum of Natural Sciences, National Museums of Canada, 1981.

Clarke, C.H.D. "Wild Life Investigation in Banff National Park, 1939," Ottawa: National Parks Bureau, Department of Mines and Resources, ca. 1940 (released for limited use) [also Cowan_PN_497].

———. "Wild Life Investigations in Banff and Jasper National Parks 1941," Ottawa: National Parks Bureau, Department of Mines and Resources, 1942 (released for limited use.) [also Cowan_PN_497].

Cleveland, Treadwell Jr. "North American Conservation Conference" (proceedings). In *Conservation* [American Forestry Assn. magazine] 15, no. 3 (March 1909): 159–168. www.theodore-roosevelt.com/images/research/northamericanccreport.pdf (accessed December 6, 2014).

Cleveland, William J. "Rev. William J. Cleveland's Investigation of the Causes of the Sioux Troubles." In *Ninth Annual Report of the Executive Committee of the Indian Rights Association for the Year Ending December 15, 1891*, 24. Philadelphia: Indian Rights Association, 1892. http://is.gd/FOoznv (accessed October 31, 2014).

Cole, Douglas. *Captured Heritage: The Scramble for Northwest Coast Artifacts*. Vancouver: UBC Press, 1995.

Collier, Eric. "Address of BC Registered Trappers Association." In *Proceedings of the Ninth Annual BC Game Convention: May 25–28, 1955*, 46–53. Victoria: Queen's Printer, 1955.

———. *Three Against the Wilderness*. New York: Irwin Publishing, 1959.

Corley-Smith, Peter. *White Bears and Other Curiosities: The First 100 Years of the Royal British Columbia Museum*. Victoria: RBCM, 1989.

Cowan, Garry I. McTaggart, and Ian McTaggart Cowan. "A New Chiton of the Genus *Mopalia* from the Northeast Pacific Ocean." *Syesis* 10 (1977): 45–52.

Cowan, Ian McTaggart. "Ashnola." *Klahanie: The Great Outdoors* television series episode, first aired March 15, 1973. Vancouver: CBC Television Archives.

———. "Big Game of the Mountain Province." *Canadian Geographic* 64, no. 6 (June 1952): 226–241. http://is.gd/exegZt (pdf accessed October 31, 2014).

———. "Bird Records from British Columbia." *The Murrelet* 21, no. 3 (1940): 69–70.

———. "Birds and Mammals on the Queen Charlotte Islands." In *The Outer Shores: Proceedings of the Queen Charlotte Islands First International Scientific Symposium, University of British Columbia, August 1984*, 175–186. Edited by Geoffrey G.E. Scudder and Nicholas Gessler. Queen Charlotte City, BC: Queen Charlotte Islands Museum Press, 1989.

———. "The British Columbia Woodchuck, *Marmota monax petrensis* Howell." *The Canadian Field-Naturalist*, 47, no. 3 (March 1933): 57. www.biodiversitylibrary.org/item/89103#page/77/mode/1up (accessed October 31, 2014).

———. "Capture and Maintenance of Cetaceans in Canada: A Report Prepared by the Advisory Committee on Marine Mammals for the Minister of Fisheries and Oceans Canada, Ottawa." Unpublished, 1992.

———. "The Challenge We Take." In *Transactions of the Twentieth North American Wildlife Conference, March 14–16, 1955*. Washington, DC: Wildlife Management Institute (1955), 662–670.

———. "Chemical Sprays and Their Relation to Wildlife." *Proceedings of the Ninth Annual BC Game Convention: May 25–28, 1955* (at Nelson, BC). Victoria: Queen's Printer, 1955.

———. "Conservation and Man's Environment." In *Knowledge Among Men: Eleven Essays on Science, Culture and Society*, edited by Paul H. Oehser. New York: Simon and Schuster, 1966.

———. "Conservation in Canada." In *Proceedings of the Tenth Pacific Science Congress: Honolulu, Hawaii, 1961*, 228–230, edited by Leonard D. Tuthill. Honolulu: Bishop Museum Press, 1963.

———. "The Conservation of Australian Waterfowl." Mimeographed report. Vancouver: UBC, 1971. Later published under same title as Australian Fauna Authorities Conference special publication no. 2. Canberra: Australian Government Publishing Service, 1973. http://trove.nla.gov.au/work/23127344?q&versionId=45811618 (citation accessed February 25, 2015).

———. "Distribution and Variation in Deer (Genus *Odocoileus*) of the Pacific Coast Region of North America." PhD dissertation, University of California, Berkeley, 1935. [Also published; see next citation.]

———. "Distribution and Variation in Deer (Genus *Odocoileus*) of the Pacific Coastal Region of North America." *California Fish and Game* 22, no. 3 (1936): 155–246.

———. "Distribution and Variation in the Native Sheep of North America." *The American Midland Naturalist* 24, no. 3 (November 1940): 505–580. www.jstor.org/stable/2420858 (abstract accessed October 31, 2014).

———. "The Distribution of the Pikas (*Ochotona*) in British Columbia and Alberta." *The Murrelet* 35, no. 2 (May–August 1954): 19–24.

———. "Distribution of the Races of the Williamson Sapsucker in British Columbia." *The Condor* 40, no. 3 (May–June 1938): 128–129. https://sora.unm.edu/sites/default/files/journals/condor/v040n03/p0128-p0129.pdf (accessed October 31, 2014).

———. "A Distributional Study of the *Peromyscus sitkensis* Group of White-Footed Mice." *University of California Publications in Zoology* 40, no. 13 (1935): 429–438.

———. "The Ecology of the North: Knowledge is the Key to Sane Development." *Science Forum* 2, no. 1 (1969): 3–8 [*q.v.* Cowan_PN_897 above, under **Correspondence and other materials/Personal notes/Cowan**].

———. "The Ecology and Life History of the Columbian Blacktailed Deer, *Odocoileus columbianus columbianus* (Richardson), in British Columbia." Undergraduate thesis for Bachelor of Arts in the Department of Zoology, University of British Columbia, 1932.

———. "Ecology and Northern Development." *Arctic* 22, no. 1 (1969): 1–12. http://arctic.journalhosting.ucalgary.ca/arctic/index.php/arctic/article/view/3188/3164 (accessed October 31, 2014).

———. "Environmental Impact Assessment: A Methodology for Prediction of Environmental Effects." *Proceedings No. 10, National Conference on Environmental Impact Assessment: Philosophy and Methodology*. Winnipeg: Agassiz Centre for Water Studies and the University of Manitoba, 1973.

———. "Foreword." In Tommy A. Walker, *Spatsizi*. Surrey: Antonson Publishing, 1976.

———. "Fossil and Subfossil Mammals from the Quaternary of British Columbia." *Transactions of the Royal Society of Canada*, 3rd series, vol. 35, section 4 (1941): 39–49.

———. "The Fur Trade and the Fur Cycle 1825–1857." *The British Columbia Historical Quarterly* (January 1938): 19–30. http://is.gd/ClHlM3 (pdf pp24–35, accessed October 31, 2014).

———. "General Report upon Wildlife Studies in the Rocky Mountain National Parks in 1946." Prepared for National Parks Bureau, Ottawa, 1946. Unpublished 32 pp. mimeographed [original Cowan_PN_896].

———. "Geographic Distribution of Color Phases of the Red Fox and Black Bear in the Pacific Northwest." *Journal of Mammalogy* 19, no. 2 (1938): 202–206.

———. "The Holotype of the Franklin Grouse (*Canachites franklinii*)." *The Canadian Field-Naturalist* 78, no. 2 (1964): 127–128. www.biodiversitylibrary.org/item/89058#page/141/mode/1up (accessed October 31, 2014).

———. "Insularity in the Genus *Sorex* on the North Coast of British Columbia." *Proceedings of the Biological Society of Washington* 54 (July 1941): 95–108. www.biodiversitylibrary.org/page/34599248#page/119/mode/1up (accessed October 31, 2014).

———. "Land, Wildlife and People: It's Time to Put Life Back into the Wilds of BC." *Vancouver Sun*. December 26, 1972, 30.

———. "Longevity of the Red-Legged Frog (*Rana a. aurora*)." *Copeia* 1941, no. 1 (March 25, 1941): 48.

———. "Mammals of Point Grey." *The Canadian Field-Naturalist* 44, no. 6 (September 1930): 133–134. www.biodiversitylibrary.org/item/89659#page/167/mode/1up (accessed October 31, 2014).

———. "Migration." Episode in *Web of Life* television series, first aired January 18, 1963. Vancouver: CBC Television Archives.

———. "Moments from the Education of an Ornithologist: The Second Doris Huestis Speirs Lecture." *Picoides* 11, no. 2 (November 1998): 17–22. www.sco-soc.ca/picoides/archive/Picoides11_2_1998.pdf (pdf pp19–24 accessed October 31, 2014). [MS, which differs from published version, is Cowan_PN_104.]

———. "The Mule Deer of Southern California and Northern Lower California as a Recognizable Race." *Journal of Mammalogy* 14 (1933): 326–327.

———. "Nesting Habits of the Flying Squirrel *Glaucomys sabrinus.*" *Journal of Mammalogy* 17, no. 1 (1936): 58–60.

———. "Note on Yellow-bellied Marmot." *The Murrelet* 10 (1929): 64.

———. "Notes on the Distribution of the Chipmunks (*Eutamias*) in Southern British Columbia and the Rocky Mountain Region of Southern Alberta with Descriptions of Two New Races." *Proceedings of the Biological Society of Washington* 59 (October 25, 1946): 107–116. www.biodiversitylibrary.org/page/34566253#page/335/mode/1up (accessed October 31, 2014).

———. "Notes on the Hares of British Columbia with the Description of a New Race." *Journal of Mammalogy* 19, no. 2 (1938): 240–243. http://jmammal.oxfordjournals.org/content/19/2/240 (pdf sample accessed October 31, 2014).

———. "Observations on Wildlife Conservation and Management in Britain and Norden." In *Report of Proceedings of the Eighth Annual BC Game Convention, May 26–29, 1954*, 22–30. Victoria: Queen's Printer, 1954.

———. "Of Mice and Men – Or the Biology of Numbers." Lecture, Vancouver Institute, March 18, 1961. https://circle.ubc.ca/flashstreamview/bitstream/handle/2429/36425/ubc_at_010_cowan.mp3?sequence=1 (streaming audio, 78:59, accessed October 19, 2013).

———. "The Organic World and Its Environment." In *Future Environments of North America*, edited by Frank Fraser Darling and John P. Milton. New York: Natural History Press, 1966.

———. "The Penalties of Ignorance of Man's Biological Dependence." In *Our Debt to the Future: Proceedings of the Royal Society of Canada Symposium Presented on the 75th Anniversary of the Society*, edited by E.G.D. Murray, 41–50. Toronto: University of Toronto Press, 1958.

———. "Preliminary Wildlife Survey of the Mackenzie Delta with Special Reference to the Muskrat." Unpublished report, January 30, 1948. http://is.gd/gSSq9G (pdf s.n., n.d., accessed October 31, 2014). [An edited version of this paper was published as "Waterfowl Conditions on the Mackenzie Delta – 1947," *q.v.* below.]

———. "Profile of Baja California." Unpublished booklet, ca. 1985.

———. "Range Competition between Mule Deer, Bighorn Sheep and Elk in Jasper National Park." In *Transactions of the Twelfth North American Wildlife Conference, February 3–5, 1947*, edited by Ethel M. Quee. Washington, DC: Wildlife Management Institute, 1947, 223–227.

———. "Report of the Division of Biology, 1949." In *Report of Provincial Game Commission, 1949*, 54–60. Victoria: BC Department of Attorney-General, 1951.

———. "Report of Wildlife Studies in Jasper, Banff and Yoho National Parks 1944 and Parasites, Diseases and Injuries of Game Animals in the Rocky Mountain National Parks 1942–1944." Prepared for National Parks Bureau, Ottawa, 1944. Unpublished 163 pp. mimeographed [original Cowan_PN_894].

———. "Report of Wildlife Studies in the Rocky Mountain National Parks in 1945." Prepared for National Parks Bureau, Ottawa, 1945. Unpublished 63 pp. mimeographed [original Cowan_PN_895].

———. "Report on Game Conditions in Banff, Jasper and Kootenay National Parks 1943." Prepared for National Parks Bureau, Ottawa, 1943. Unpublished 72 pp. mimeographed [original with photographs, Cowan_PN_893].

———. "Report on Study Trip to Eastern Museums." In *Report of the Provincial Museum of British Columbia for the Year 1937*, L14–L18. Victoria: King's Printer, 1938.

———. "A Report to the Canadian Committee on Whales and Whaling," presented at the 33rd Annual Meeting of the International Whaling Commission, July 20–25, 1981. Unpublished, 7 pp. [original in Cowan_PN_219].

———. "Reports on Flora of Certain Areas of BC." Unpublished, Economic Council of British Columbia, 1936. GR-0111, Box 03, File 03, 1936–1941, BCA.

———. "Research in the National Parks of Canada." Prepared for Parks Canada, 1977. Unpublished 195 pp. [original Cowan_PN_898].

———. "A Review of the Reptiles and Amphibians of British Columbia." In *Report of the Provincial Museum of British Columbia for the Year 1936*, K16–K25. Victoria: King's Printer, 1937.

———. "A Review of Wildlife Research in Canada." In *Resources for Tomorrow: Conference Background Papers*. Vol. 2, 889–900. Ottawa: Department of Northern Affairs and National Resources, July 1961.

———. "Roof of the World." Episode in *Web of Life* television series, first aired March 18, 1964. Vancouver: CBC Television Archives.

———. "Room at the Top?" In *Endangered Spaces: The Future for Canada's Wilderness*, edited by Monte Hummel, 249–266. Toronto: Key Porter Books, 1989.

———. "Ruts and Ridges: Some Major Issues in Wildlife Conservation." In *Proceedings of the Sixth Annual BC Big Game Convention*, May 7–10, 1952, 63–68.

———. "The Sharp-Headed Finner Whale of the Eastern Pacific." *Journal of Mammalogy* 20, no. 2 (May 1939): 215–225.

———. "Small Mammals of the Western Mountains." *Canadian Geographical Journal* 47, no. 4 (October 1953): 130–141.

———. "Some Notes on the Hibernation of *Lasionycteris noctivagans*." *The Canadian Field-Naturalist* 47, no. 4 (April 1933): 74–75. www.biodiversitylibrary.org/item/89103#page/98/mode/1up (accessed October 31, 2014).

———. "The Status and Conservation of Bears (*Ursidae*) of the World – 1970." In *Bears – Their Biology and Management: Papers and Proceedings of the International Conference on Bear Research and Management held at University of Calgary, Alberta, November 6–9, 1970*, 343–367. http://is.gd/24lXCH (pdf accessed October 31, 2014).

———. "Threatened Species of Mammals." In *Proceedings of the 16th International Congress of Zoology, 20–27 August 1963*, edited by John A. Moore. Vol. 8, 17–21. Washington, DC, 1964.

———. "The Timber Wolf in the Rocky Mountain National Parks of Canada." *Canadian Journal of Research* 25d, no. 5 (October 1947): 139–174. http://is.gd/vWpzHT (abstract accessed October 31, 2014).

———. "*Tonicella insignis* Reeve in British Columbia," *Pacific Northwest Shell News* 3, no. 5 (1963): 53.

———. "Two Apparently Fatal Grouse Diseases." *Journal of Wildlife Management* 4, no. 3 (July 1940): 311–312.

———. "The Vertebrate Fauna of the Peace River District of British Columbia." *British Columbia Provincial Museum Occasional Paper No. 1* (1939).

———. "Waterfowl Conditions on the Mackenzie Delta – 1947." *The Murrelet* 29, no. 2 (May–August 1948): 21–26. www.jstor.org/stable/3535716 (first-page preview accessed October 31, 2014). [See also "Preliminary Wildlife Survey of the Mackenzie Delta…" above.]

———. "Whales." Episode in *Living Sea* television series, first aired January 19, 1958. Vancouver: CBC Television Archives.

———. "Wildlife in Danger." Episode in *Klahanie: The Great Outdoors* television series, first aired September 27, 1969 (Vancouver: CBC Television Archives).

———. "The Wildlife Resource in Canada: A Brief Presented to the Royal Commission on Canada's Economic Prospects." Unpublished. Canadian Conservation Association: Toronto, ca. 1955 [Cowan_AN_037].

———. "Wings." Episode in *Patterns of Living* television series, first aired October 27, 1964. Vancouver: CBC Television Archives with Canadian School Telecast.

———, and Margaret G. Arsenault. "Reproduction and Growth in the Creeping Vole, *Microtus oregoni serpens* Merriam." *Canadian Journal of Zoology* 32 (1954): 198–208. http://is.gd/r2rJTr (pdf accessed October 31, 2014).

———, and C.J. Guiguet. *The Mammals of British Columbia*. BC Provincial Museum Handbook no. 11. Victoria: British Columbia Provincial Museum (1956) [also consulted revised edition of 1965].

———, and James Hatter. "A Trap and Technique for the Capture of Diving Waterfowl." *Journal of Wildlife Management* 16, no. 4 (October 1952): 438–441. www.jstor.org/stable/3797492 (abstract accessed October 31, 2014).

———, and P.A. Johnston, "Blood Serum Protein Variations at the Species and Subspecies Level in Deer of the Genus *Odocoileus*." *Systematic Zoology* 11, no. 3 (September 1962): 131–138. www.jstor.org/stable/2411876 (abstract only, accessed October 31, 2014).

———, and Wayne McCrory. "Variation in the Mountain Goat, *Oreamnos americanus*." *Journal of Mammalogy* 51, no. 1 (February 1970): 60–73. http://is.gd/bxw9hK (abstract accessed October 31, 2014).

———, George M. Volkoff and Peter A. Larkin. "Basic Research Threatened by Lack of Funds," op-ed. *Vancouver Sun*, January 7, 1974.

Cowan, McTaggart [Sr.]. "Flora of BC." Letter to the editor. *The Daily Province (Vancouver)*. February 11, 1916, 8.

Cowan, Patrick McTaggart, and Klaus Beltzner, eds. *Living with Climatic Change: Proceedings, Toronto Conference Workshop, November 17–22, 1975*. Ottawa: Science Council of Canada, 1976. http://arizona.openrepository.com/arizona/bitstream/10150/303430/1/ltrr-0083.pdf (accessed October 31, 2014).

Craig, Vanessa, Kym E. Welstead and Ross G. Vennesland. *Recovery Strategy for the Pacific Water Shrew (Sorex bendirii) in British Columbia*. Victoria: BC Ministry of Environment, 2009. http://is.gd/16QKLz October 31, 2014.

Cranmer-Byng, John L. "A Life with Birds: Percy A. Taverner, Canadian Ornithologist, 1875–1947." Special issue, *The Canadian Field-Naturalist* 110, no. 1 (January–March 1996): 1–254 [includes index].

Crossman, Rae. "One Ruby-throated Moment." Unpublished poem excerpted in "Notes from the Wild: An Account in Words and Music of R. Murray Schafer's *And Wolf Shall Inherit the Moon*." Posted January 25, 2007, on the website of *The New Quarterly*. www.tnq.ca/article/notes-wild-account-words-and-music-r-murray-schafers-and-wolf-shall-inherit-moon (accessed October 31, 2014).

"Cuckoo (*Cuculus canorus*)." Webpage (n.d.), Scottish Wildlife Trust. http://scottishwildlifetrust.org.uk/visit/wildlife/c/cuckoo (accessed May 12, 2014).

Curtis, Brian. "James Moffitt, 1900–1943." *California Fish and Game* 29, no. 4 (October 1943): 203. https://archive.org/stream/californiafishga29_4cali#page/202/mode/2up (accessed October 31, 2014).

Dalzell, Kathleen E. *The Queen Charlotte Islands, vol. 2: Places and Names*. Queen Charlotte City: Bill Ellis Publisher, 1973.

Damer, Eric, and Herbert Rosengarten. *UBC: The First 100 Years*. Vancouver: University of British Columbia, 2009.

Danylchuk, Jack. "*ForesTalk* Interviews: Dr. Ian McTaggart Cowan." BC Ministry of Forests, *ForesTalk* 4, no. 1 (Spring 1980): 18–20. http://is.gd/OmVYCt (pdf accessed October 31, 2014).

Darling, Frank Fraser. *A Herd of Red Deer: A Study in Animal Behaviour*. London: Oxford University Press, 1936

———. *A Naturalist on Rona: Essays of a Biologist in Isolation*. Oxford: Clarendon Press, 1939.

———. *Island Years*. London: G. Bell and Sons, 1940.

———, and John P. Milton, eds. *Future Environments of North America: Being the Record of a Conference Convened by the Conservation Foundation in April 1965 at Airlie House, Warrenton, Virginia*. New York: Natural History Press, 1966.

Drábek, Jan. *Vladimir Krajina: World War II Hero and Ecology Pioneer*. Vancouver: Ronsdale Press, 2012.

Drent, R.H., and C.J. Guiguet. "A Catalogue for British Columbia Sea-bird Colonies." BC Provincial Museum Occasional Paper no. 12 (1961).

Dunlap, Thomas R. *Saving America's Wildlife*. Princeton, NJ: Princeton University Press, 1988.

Eastern Sierra Land Trust. "Round Valley Mule Deer and Their Migration Corridor." www.eslt.org/Pages/mule-deer-migration.html (accessed July 8, 2013).

Eastman, Charles Alexander (Ohiyesa). *The Soul of the Indian*. Boston: Houghton Mifflin, 1911. https://archive.org/stream/soulindianoounkngoog#page/n10/mode/2up (accessed October 31, 2014).

Ecojustice. *Legal Backgrounder: Canadian Environmental Assessment Act*, May 2012. http://is.gd/gHWPh2 (accessed on February 1, 2015).

Edward, Second Duke of York. *The Master of Game*. Edited by Wm. A. and F. Baillie-Grohman with a foreword by Theodore Roosevelt. 2nd ed. London: Chatto & Windus, 1909. https://archive.org/stream/masterofgameoldexxooedwa#page/n9/mode/2up (accessed October 31, 2014). Page images of an illuminated MS copy of the original work by Gaston Phébus, comte de Foix, ca. 1485, are linked from la Bibliothèque de Genève at http://is.gd/02AQPO (also accessed October 31, 2014).

Edwards, Yorke. "A Tribute to Charles Joseph Guiguet, 1916–1999." *The Canadian Field-Naturalist* 114, no. 4 (October–December 2000): 712–715. http://biodiversitylibrary.org/page/34237218 (accessed October 31, 2014).

———. "Fire and the Decline of a Mountain Caribou Herd." *The Journal of Wildlife Management* 18, no. 4 (October 1954): 521–526. http://is.gd/mwFSet (pdf accessed October 31, 2014).

———. "The Preservation of Wilderness: Is Man a Part of Nature – or a Thing Apart?" *Canadian Audubon* (January–February 1967): 1–7.

Edwords, Clarence E. *Camp-Fires of a Naturalist*. New York: D. Appleton, 1893. https://archive.org/details/camp-firesofnatuooedworich (accessed March 15, 2015).

Egan, Timothy. *The Big Burn: Teddy Roosevelt and the Fire that Saved America*. Boston: Houghton Mifflin Harcourt, 2009.

Fallodon, Viscount Grey. "Recreation." In *Some Lessons*, edited by B. of V. 61–68.

Farber, Paul Lawrence. *Finding Order in Nature: The Naturalist Tradition from Linnaeus to E.O. Wilson*. Baltimore: Johns Hopkins University Press, 2000.

Fawcett, Brian. *Virtual Clearcut: Or, The Way Things Are in My Hometown*. Toronto: Thomas Allen Publishers, 2003.

Flader, Susan. *Thinking Like a Mountain: Aldo Leopold and the Evolution of an Ecological Attitude Toward Deer, Wolves and Forests*. Columbia: University of Missouri Press, 1974.

Fladmark, Knut R., Jonathan C. Driver and Diana Alexander. "The Paleoindian Component at Charlie Lake Cave (HbRf 39), British Columbia." *American Antiquity* 53, no. 2 (April 1988): 371–384. http://is.gd/zq7XeB (abstract accessed October 31, 2014).

The Forest History Society. "The Northern Spotted Owl – Timeline" (webpage), 2010. www.foresthistory.org/ASPNET/Policy/northern_spotted_owl/index.aspx (accessed February 26, 2015).

Foster, Janet. *Working for Wildlife: The Beginning of Preservation in Canada*. 2nd ed. Toronto: University of Toronto Press, 1998.

Fraker, Mark, Claudio Bianchini and Ian Robertson. *Burns Bog Ecosystem Review: Small Mammals*. Victoria: BC Environmental Assessment Office, 1999. http://is.gd/nDgFEM (accessed October 31, 2014).

Freeman, Lewis R. *Down the Columbia*. New York: Dodd, Mead, 1921. https://archive.org/stream/downcolumbia00free#page/n7/mode/2up (accessed October 31, 2014).

Gabrielson, Ira N. "In Memoriam: Stanley G. Jewett." *The Murrelet* 36, no. 3 (September–December 1955): 32–34. www.jstor.org/discover/3534216 (p33 preview accessed October 31, 2014).

———. "In Memoriam: Stanley Gordon Jewett. *The Auk* 73, no. 4 (October–December 1956): 513–516. https://sora.unm.edu/sites/default/files/journals/auk/v073n04/p0513-p0516.pdf (accessed October 31, 2014).

Galton, Francis. "Hereditary Talent and Character," *Macmillan's Magazine* 12, nos. 68, 70 (1865): 157–166, 318–327. http://galton.org/essays/1860-1869/galton-1865-hereditary-talent.pdf (combined pdf accessed October 31, 2014).

"Garry Oak Ecosystems." British Columbia Ministry of Environment brochure, 1993. www.env.gov.bc.ca/wld/documents/garryoak.pdf (accessed May 24, 2014).

Giese, Michael W. "A Federal Foundation for Wildlife Conservation: The Evolution of the National Wildlife Refuge System, 1920–1968." PhD dissertation, American University, 2008. http://gradworks.umi.com/33/05/3305788.html (abstract accessed October 31, 2014).

Geist, Valerius. "On Delayed Social and Physical Maturation in Mountain Sheep." *Canadian Journal of Zoology* 46, no. 5 (1968): 899–904. http://is.gd/u10iKS (pdf accessed October 31, 2014).

———. "The Evolution of Horn-Like Organs." *Behaviour* 27, no. 1 (1966): 175–214. http://is.gd/319awq (abstract accessed October 31, 2014).

———, and Ian McTaggart-Cowan, eds. *Wildlife Conservation Policy*. Calgary: Detselig Enterprises, 1995.

Gill, Ayesha E., and W. Chris Wozencraft, "Committees and Annual Meetings." In *Seventy-five Years of Mammalogy 1919–1994*, edited by Elmer C. Birney and Jerry R. Choate, 155–170. Provo, Utah: American Society of Mammalogists, 1994. https://archive.org/stream/seventyfiveyears00birn#page/154/mode/2up (accessed October 31, 2014).

Gillespie, Greg. "The Empire's Eden: British Hunters, Travel Writing and Imperialism in Nineteenth-Century Canada." In *The Culture of Hunting in Canada*, edited by Jean L. Manore and Dale G. Miner. Vancouver: UBC Press, 2007.

Götz, B. Max. "Shadows of Whistler: Kenneth R. Racey and Friends in Alta Lake." *Pique Newsmagazine*, February 12, 1999. www.piquenewsmagazine.com/whistler/natural-history/Content?oid=2137117 (accessed May 23, 2014).

Grant, P.R., and Ian McTaggart Cowan. "A Review of the Avifauna of the Tres Marías Islands, Nayarit, Mexico." *The Condor* 66, no. 3 (May 1964): 221–228. https://sora.unm.edu/sites/default/files/journals/condor/v066n03/p0221-p0228.pdf (accessed October 31, 2014).

Graveland, Bill. "Controversial Glacier Skywalk Attempts to Thrill Tourists with Glass Floor." The Canadian Press, May 11, 2014. www.ctvnews.ca/business/controversial-glacier-skywalk-attempts-to-thrill-tourists-with-glass-floor-1.1816479 (accessed May 26, 2014).

Gray, Gary G. *Wildlife and People: The Human Dimensions of Wildlife Ecology*. Champaign–Urbana: University of Illinois Press, 1993.

Gray, J. "Studies in the Mechanics of the Tetrapod Skeleton." *Journal of Experimental Biology* 20 (June 1944): 88–116. http://is.gd/XiwsZZ (abstract accessed March 15, 2015; full-text pdf also available).

Grey, Viscount Edward of Fallodon. *Fallodon Papers*. London: Constable, 1926.

Grinnell, Hilda Wood. "Joseph Grinnell 1877–1939." *The Condor* 42, no. 1 (January–February 1940): 3–34. https://sora.unm.edu/sites/default/files/journals/condor/v042n01/p0003-p0034.pdf (accessed October 31, 2014).

———. *Annie Montague Alexander*. Typescript MS. Berkeley: Grinnell Naturalists Society, MVZ, 1958.

Grinnell, Joseph, and Joseph Dixon. "Natural History of the Ground Squirrels of California." *Monthly Bulletin of the State Commission of Horticulture* 7, nos. 11–12 (1918): 597–708. https://archive.org/stream/naturalhistoryofoogrin#page/n3/mode/2up (reprint accessed October 31, 2014).

———, and Frederick H. Test. "Geographic Variation in the Fork-Tailed Petrel." *The Condor* 41, no. 4 (July–August 1939): 170–172. https://sora.unm.edu/sites/default/files/journals/condor/v041n04/p0170-p0172.pdf (accessed October 31, 2014).

Guppy, Anthony. *The Tofino Kid: From India to This Wild West Coast*. Nanaimo, BC: Priority Printing, 2000.

Guppy, Crispin, and Jon Shepard. *Butterflies of British Columbia*. Vancouver and Victoria: UBC Press and Royal British Columbia Museum, 2001.

Haber, Gordon, and Marybeth Holleman. *Among Wolves*. Chicago: University of Chicago Press, 2013.

Hafner, David J., and Andrew T. Smith. "Revision of the Subspecies of the American Pika, *Ochotona princeps* (Lagomorpha: Ochotonidae)." *Journal of Mammalogy* 91, no. 2 (April 2010): 401–417. http://is.gd/bZghXR (abstract accessed October 31, 2014).

Hammond, Lorne. "Introduction." In Janet Foster, *Working for Wildlife: The Beginning of Preservation in Canada*. 2nd ed. Toronto: University of Toronto Press, 1998.

Hancock, Lyn. "The Predator Hunters." In *Our Wildlife Heritage: 100 Years of Wildlife Management*, edited by A. Murray. Victoria: Centennial Wildlife Society of BC, 1987.

Harkin, J.B. "Canadian National Parks." In *Proceedings of the National Parks Conference held at the National Museum, Washington, DC, January 2–6, 1917*. Washington, DC: Government Printing Office, January 5, 1917, 261–268. https://archive.org/stream/proceedingsofnatoo1917#page/260/mode/2up/search/harkin (accessed October 31, 2014).

———. *The History and Meaning of the National Parks of Canada: Extracts from the Papers of the Late Jas. B. Harkin, First Commissioner of the National Parks of Canada*. Saskatoon: H.R. Larson, 1957.

———. "Man's Brotherhood with the Wild." In B. of V., ed., *Some Lessons*, 91.

———. "Our Need for National Parks." *Canadian Alpine Journal* 9 (1918): 98–106. https://archive.org/stream/canadianalpinejoo9alpiuoft#page/n135/mode/2up/search/Harkin (accessed October 31, 2014).

———. *Crag and Canyon*, Banff, April 9, 1937. Quoted in E.J. Hart, *J.B. Harkin: Father of Canada's National Parks*. Edmonton: University of Alberta Press, 2010.

Harland, M.B., K.J. Nelson and P.T. Gregory. "Status of the Northern Pacific Rattlesnake in British Columbia." Ministry of Environment, Lands and Parks, Wildlife Working Report No. WR-54, 1993. www.env.gov.bc.ca/wld/documents/statusrpts/wr54.pdf (accessed October 31, 2014).

Harland-Jacobs, Jessica L. *Builders of Empire: Freemasons and British Imperialism 1717–1927*. Chapel Hill: University of North Carolina Press, 2007.

Harper, Francis. Letter to the editor, *Canadian Field-Naturalist* 39, no 2 (February 1925): 45. http://is.gd/DqaK7u (accessed October 31, 2014).

Hart, E.J. *J.B. Harkin: The Father of Canada's National Parks*. Edmonton: University of Alberta Press, 2010.

———. *Jimmy Simpson: Legend of the Rockies*. Banff, Alta.: Altitude Publishing, 1991.

Hatherly, Joanne. "She Wanted Designs to Sing." Victoria *Times Colonist*, May 16, 2008, C4.

Hatler, David F., and Alison M.M. Beal. "Furbearer Management Guidelines." Government of British Columbia, July 2003. www.env.gov.bc.ca/fw/wildlife/trapping/docs/beaver.pdf (accessed March 25, 2013).

Hatler, David F., David W. Nagorsen and Alison M.M. Beal. *Carnivores of British Columbia*. Royal BC Museum Handbook *Mammals of BC*, vol. 5. Victoria: RBCM, 2008.

Hatter, James. *Politically Incorrect: The Life and Times of British Columbia's First Game Biologist, An Autobiography*. Victoria, BC: O & J Enterprises, 1997.

Hayman, John, ed. Robert Brown and the Vancouver Island Exploring Expedition. Vancouver: UBC Press, 1989.

Hebda, Richard J., Kent Gustavson, Karen Golinski and Alan M. Calder. *Burns Bog Ecosystem Review: Synthesis Report for Burns Bog, Fraser River Delta, Southwestern British Columbia, Canada.* Victoria, BC: Environmental Assessment Office, 2000. www.burnsbog.org/bog/wp-content/uploads/Burns-Bog-Ecosystem-Review.pdf (accessed October 31, 2014).

Hebert, Daryll M., and Ian McTaggart Cowan. "Natural Salt Licks as a Part of the Natural Ecology of the Mountain Goat." *Canadian Journal of Zoology* 49, no. 5 (1971): 605–610. http://is.gd/Wr3vKM (accessed October 31, 2014).

———. "Forage and Serum Phosphorus Values for Bighorn Sheep." *Journal of Range Management* 25, no. 4 (1972): 292–296. https://journals.uair.arizona.edu/index.php/jrm/article/viewFile/6077/5687 (accessed October 31, 2014).

Hewitt, C. Gordon, *The Conservation of the Wild Life of Canada.* New York: Charles Scribner's Sons, 1921. https://archive.org/stream/conservationwilo1hewigoog#page/n10/mode/2up (accessed October 31, 2014).

Hlady, D.A. "South Okanagan Conservation Strategy 1990–1995." Ministry of Environment, Canadian Wildlife Service, Nature Trust of BC, Royal British Columbia Museum and University of British Columbia Wildlife Program, 1990. www.env.gov.bc.ca/wld/documents/southoka/southoka.pdf (accessed October 31, 2014).

Hobson, Richmond. *Grass Beyond the Mountains: Discovering the Last Great Cattle Frontier on the North American Continent.* Toronto: McClelland & Stewart, 1951.

Honeyman, Scott. "Park Development Opposed." *Vancouver Sun*, April 27, 1971, A10.

Hornaday, William T. *Our Vanishing Wild Life: Its Extermination and Preservation.* New York: Charles Scribner's Sons, 1913. https://archive.org/stream/ourvanishingwildoohorn#page/n7/mode/2up (accessed February 20, 2015).

Horsfield, Margaret. *Voices from the Sound: Chronicles of Clayoquot Sound and Tofino 1899–1929.* Nanaimo: Salal Books, 2008.

Hubbard, C. Andresen. "The Fleas of California." *Pacific University Bulletin* 39, no. 8 (June 1943): 1–12.

"Human Settlement." *Hakai: Science on the Coastal Margin,* Calvert Island Field Station (webpage). Hakai Institute, Tula Foundation and University of Victoria, 2014. https://hbicalvert.wordpress.com/research-2/archaeology (accessed January 29, 2015).

Hutton, James. *Investigation of the Principles of Knowledge and the Progress of Reason, from Sense to Science to Philosophy.* Edinburgh: Strahan & Cadell, 1794.

IBA (Important Bird Areas) Canada. "Tofino Mudflats," http://ibacanada.ca/site.jsp?siteID=BC002&lang=EN (accessed November 24, 2013).

Indian and Northern Affairs Canada. "The Cheslatta T'en and the Kemano Hydro Project." In *Report of the Royal Commission on Aboriginal Peoples,* vol. 1, pt. 2, c. 11, §3.4. Ottawa: Canada Communication Group, 1996. http://is.gd/L2zUWf (accessed October 31, 2014).

Industrial Development Act, SBC 1949, c. 31 [Bill 66]. http://is.gd/HMPlXi (pdf archival scan accessed February 20, 2015).

Integrated Land Management Bureau. "Fort Saint James Land and Resource Management Plan." Government of British Columbia, 1999. www.for.gov.bc.ca/tasb/slrp/pdf/LRMP/Fort St James_LRMP.pdf (accessed December 5, 2014).

International Union for Conservation of Nature. *Lepus timidus.* IUCN Red List of Threatened Species, version 2015.2. www.iucnredlist.org/details/11791/0 (accessed July 10, 2015).

Jakimchuk, Ronald D., R. Wayne Campbell and Dennis A. Demarchi, eds. *Ian McTaggart Cowan: The Legacy of a Pioneering Biologist, Educator and Conservationist.* Madeira Park, BC: Harbour Publishing, 2015.

Jamison, Andrew, and Ron Eyerman. *Seeds of the Sixties.* Berkeley: University of California Press, 1994.

Jonkel, Charles J., and Ian McTaggart Cowan. "The Black Bear in the Spruce-Fir Forest." *Wildlife Monographs* 27 (December 1971): 3–57.

Kelly, Brendan. "Francis Hollis Fay 1927–1994," *Arctic* 48, no. 1 (March 1995): 107–108. http://pubs.aina.ucalgary.ca/arctic/Arctic48-1-107.pdf (accessed October 31, 2014).

Kennedy, Elizabeth, and Ian McTaggart Cowan, "Sixteen Years with a Bald Eagle's, *Haliaeetus leucocephalus,* Nest," *Canadian Field-Naturalist* 112, no. 4 (October–December 1998): 704–706. http://biodiversitylibrary.org/page/34258060 (accessed October 31, 2014).

Laing, Hamilton Mack. *Allan Brooks: Artist–Naturalist.* Victoria: British Columbia Provincial Museum, 1979.

Lang, Stew. "BC-muzzled Expert Quits Ecology Post." Victoria *Times Colonist*, June 6, 1984, A1.

Larkin, Peter A. "Fisheries Research of the Game Department." In *Report of the Provincial Game Commission, 1951,* E43. Victoria: BC Department of Attorney-General, 1953.

Larsen, Soren. "Collaboration Geographies: Native–White Partnerships During the Resettlement of Ootsa Lake, British Columbia, 1900–52." *BC Studies* 138/139 (Summer/Autumn 2003): 87–114. http://ojs.library.ubc.ca/index.php/bcstudies/article/view/1672/1718 (accessed October 31, 2014).

Larson, Edward J. "Biology and the Emergence of the Anglo-American Eugenics Movement." In *Biology and Ideology from Descartes to Dawkins*, edited by Denis R. Alexander and Ronald L. Numbers. Chicago: University of Chicago Press, 2010.

Leavitt, Clyde. *Forest Protection in Canada, 1912*. Ottawa: Commission of Conservation, Committee on Forests, 1913. https://archive.org/stream/forestprot000cana#page/n5/mode/2up (accessed October 31, 2014.

Leopold, Aldo. "Clandeboye." In *Some Lessons*, vol. 2, edited by B. of V., 23–26.

———. "The Conservation Ethic." *Journal of Forestry* 31, no. 6 (October 1933): 634–643.

———. *Game Management*. New York: Charles Scribner's Sons, 1933.

———. "The Geese Return." In *Some Lessons*, vol. 2, edited by B. of V., 37.

———. "Marshland Elegy." In *Some Lessons*, edited by B. of V., 79–83.

———. "On a Monument to the Pigeon." In *Some Lessons*, vol. 2, edited by B. of V., 47–49.

———. "Song of the Gavilan." In *Some Lessons*, vol. 2, edited by B. of V., 11–14.

———. "Summarization of the Twelfth North American Wildlife Conference, San Antonio, Texas, February 3–5, 1947," condensed in *National Parks Magazine* 21, no. 89 (April/June 1947): 26–28.

Leopold, A. Starker, Clarence Cottam, Ian McTaggart Cowan, Ira Gabrielson and Thomas Kimball. "Our Wildlife Refuges – A Hard Critical Look: A Report to the Secretary of the Interior from the Advisory Board on Wildlife Management." *Audubon Magazine* 70, no. 3 (1968): 8–26.

Leroy, Sylvia, and Barry Cooper. *Off Limits: How Radical Environmentalists Are Stealing Canada's National Parks*. Vancouver: Fraser Institute, 2000. http://is.gd/77zOR8 (accessed October 31, 2014).

Lewis, Harrison. "Editorial: The Wilderness." *The Canadian Field-Naturalist* 39, no. 2 (February 1925): 41. http://is.gd/e03XJK (accessed October 31, 2014).

———. "Lively: A History of the Canadian Wildlife Service, vol. 1." Unpublished MS. Canadian Wildlife Service, Ottawa, R653-207-8-E [n.d.].

Lidicker, William Z. Jr. "Population Ecology." In *Seventy-Five Years of Mammalogy, 1919–1994*, edited by Elmer C. Birney and Jerry R. Choate, 323–347. Provo, Utah: American Society of Mammalogists, 1994. https://archive.org/stream/seventyfiveyears00birn#page/322/mode/2up (accessed October 31, 2014).

Lloyd, Hoyes. "Cavemen and Their Ritual." In *Some Lessons*, edited by B. of V., 5–8.

———. "Man and Some of His Heritage from the Past." In *Some Lessons*, edited by B. of V., 33–34.

Loo, Tina. *States of Nature: Conserving Canada's Wildlife in the 20th Century*. Vancouver: UBC Press, 2006.

Lomolino, Mark V. "Body Size Evolution in Insular Vertebrates: Generality of the Island Rule." *Journal of Biogeography* 32, no. 10 (October 2005): 1683–1699. http://is.gd/hQYc8q (pdf accessed October 31, 2014).

Ludwig, Daniel. "*Microtus richardsoni*." *Mammalian Species* no. 223 (November 14, 1984): 1–6.

Lukas, J. Anthony. *Big Trouble: A Murder in a Small Western Town Sets Off a Struggle for the Soul of America*. New York: Simon & Schuster, 1997.

MacArthur, Robert H. and Edward O. Wilson. "An Equilibrium Theory of Insular Zoogeography," *Evolution* 17, no. 4 (December 1963): 373–387. http://is.gd/2w9FoZ (pdf accessed October 31, 2014).

MacEachern, Alan. "Voices Crying in the Wilderness: Recent Works in Canadian Environmental History." *Acadiensis* 31, no. 2 (Spring 2002). http://is.gd/GtMVWf (accessed October 31, 2014).

Mackenzie, John M. *The Empire of Nature: Hunting, Conservation and British Imperialism*. Manchester: Manchester University Press, 1988.

Mackenzie, Osgood. *A Hundred Years in the Highlands*. London: Edward Arnold, 1921. https://archive.org/stream/hundredyearsinhi00mackuoft#page/n7/mode/2up (accessed October 31, 2014).

Mackie, Richard. *Hamilton Mack Laing: Hunter-Naturalist*. Victoria: Sono Nis Press, 1985.

Mancini, Melissa. "Science Cuts: Ottawa Views Pure Science as 'Cash Cow,' Critics Say." *Huffington Post*, May 7, 2013. www.huffingtonpost.ca/2013/05/07/science-cuts-canada_n_3228151.html (accessed May 24, 2014).

Manore, Jean L., and Dale G. Miner, eds. *Culture of Hunting in Canada*. Vancouver: UBC Press, 2007.

Marchak, Patricia. *Green Gold: The Forest Industry in British Columbia*. Vancouver: UBC Press, 1983.

Mares, Michael A., and David J. Schmidly, eds. *Latin American Mammalogy: History, Biodiversity and Conservation*. Norman: University of Oklahoma Press, 1991.

Martin, P.W. "A Winter Inventory of the Shoreline and Marine-Oriented Birds and Mammals of Chatham Sound." Unpublished report for British Columbia Fish and Wildlife Branch, 1978.

Maslin, T.P. "Fringe-tailed Myotis Bat in British Columbia," *Journal of Mammalogy* 19 (1938): 373.

Matějů, Jan, and Lukáš Kratochvíl. "Sexual Size Dimorphism in Ground Squirrels (*Rodentia: Sciuridae: Marmotini*) Does Not Correlate with Body Size and Sociality." *Frontiers in Zoology* 10, no. 27 (2013). www.frontiersinzoology.com/content/10/1/27 (accessed May 21, 2014).

McAllister, Ian. *The Last Wild Wolves: Ghosts of the Rainforest*. Vancouver: Greystone Books, 2007.

McAllister, Nancy M. "Courtship, Hostile Behavior, Nest-establishment and Egg Laying in the Eared Grebe (*Podiceps capsicus*)." *The Auk* 75, no. 3 (July 1958): 290–310. https://sora.unm.edu/sites/default/files/journals/auk/v075n03/p0290-p0311.pdf (accessed October 31, 2014).

McBean, Gordon, Michael Garstang and Donald Henderson. "Patrick McTaggart Cowan: Necrologies." *Bulletin of the American Meteorological Society* 79, no. 1 (January 1998): 110–111. (EBSCOHost full-text pdf 216332 accessed October 31, 2014, via proxy server; consult your local public or university library as to availability.)

McCabe, T.T., and Ian McTaggart Cowan. "*Peromyscus maniculatus macrorhinus* and the Problem of Insularity." *Transactions of the Royal Canadian Institute* 25 (1945): 117–216. http://eurekamag.com/research/023/347/023347331.php (abstract accessed October 31, 2014).

McDonald, Bernadette. *Brotherhood of the Rope: The Biography of Charles Houston*. Seattle: The Mountaineers Books, 2007.

McLaren, Angus. *Our Own Master Race: Eugenics in Canada, 1885–1945*. Toronto: McClelland & Stewart, 1990.

Mearns, Barbara, and Richard Mearns. *The Bird Collectors*. Waltham, Mass.: Academic Press, 1998.

Meine, Curt. *Aldo Leopold: His Life and Work*. Madison: University of Wisconsin Press, 2010.

Merilees, Bill. *Selected Excerpts from the Vancouver Natural History Society Bulletin* (No. 1, September 1943, to No. 153, December 1971) [*q.v.* below at "Vancouver Natural History Society"]. http://naturevancouver.ca/sites/naturevancouver.ca/VNHS%20files/4/VNHS_Bulletin_1943-1971.pdf (accessed May 24, 2014).

Metcalfe, E. Bennett. *A Man of Some Importance: The Life of Roderick Langmere Haig-Brown*. Seattle and Vancouver: James Wood Publishers, 1985.

Miller, E.H., ed. *Museum Collections: Their Roles and Future in Biological Research*. BC Provincial Museum Occasional Paper no. 25 (1985).

Miner, Jack. *Jack Miner: His Life and Religion*. Kingsville, Ont.: Jack Miner Migratory Bird Foundation, 1969.

Montreal Daily Star. "Cartoons of Canada According to American Movies." Series, 1923 [Cowan_PN_052].

Munro, David A. "Tribute to Hoyes Lloyd, 1888–1978." *The Canadian Field-Naturalist* 93, no. 3 (July–September 1979): 331–336. http://is.gd/ZduFoJ (accessed October 31, 2014).

Munro, J.A. *An Introduction to Bird Study in British Columbia*. Victoria: Department of Education, 1931.

———. "P.A. Taverner, An Appreciation: 1875–1947." *The Canadian Field-Naturalist* 62, no. 1 (January–February 1948): 34–35. www.biodiversitylibrary.org/item/89251#page/44/mode/1up (accessed October 31, 2014).

———. "The Birds and Mammals of the Creston Region, BC." BC Provincial Museum Occasional Paper no. 8 (1950), 1–90.

———. "The Grebes." BC Provincial Museum Occasional Paper no. 3 (1941).

———; and W.A. Clemens. "Waterfowl in Relation to the Spawning of Herring in British Columbia." *Bulletin of the Biological Board of Canada* 17, no. 2 (1931): 1–46.

———, and Ian McTaggart Cowan. *A Review of the Bird Fauna of British Columbia*. Victoria: BC Provincial Museum Special Publication no. 2, 1947.

Munro, W.T., et al. *Status and Management of the Vancouver Island Marmot*. Victoria: BC Ministry of Environment, December 1983.

Murphy, Peter J. "Following the Base of the Foothills: Tracing the Boundaries of Jasper Park and Its Adjacent Rocky Mountains Forest Reserve." In *Culturing Wilderness in Jasper National Park: Studies in Two Centuries of Human History in the Upper Athabasca River Watershed*, edited by I.S. MacLaren, 71-121. Edmonton: University of Alberta Press, 2007.

Nagorsen, David W. *Rodents and Lagomorphs of British Columbia*. Royal British Columbia Museum Handbook, vol. 4 of *The Mammals of British Columbia*. Victoria: Royal BC Museum, 2005.

———. *Opossums, Shrews and Moles of British Columbia*. Royal British Columbia Museum Handbook, vol. 2 of *The Mammals of British Columbia*. Vancouver: University of British Columbia Press, 1996.

———; and R. Mark Brigham. *Bats of British Columbia*. Royal British Columbia Museum Handbook, vol. 1 of *The Mammals of British Columbia*. Vancouver: University of British Columbia Press, 1993.

———; and Andrea Cardini. "Tempo and Mode of Evolutionary Divergence in Modern and Holocene Vancouver Island Marmots (*Marmota vancouverensis*) (Mammalia, Rodentia)." *Journal of Zoological Systematics and Evolutionary Research* 47, no. 3 (August 2009): 258–267. www2. mcdonald.cam.ac.uk/events/conferences-workshops/GMM/Nagorsen_2009.pdf (pdf of independently paginated conference facsimile of this article accessed October 31, 2014).

———, M.A. Fraker and N. Panter. "Conserving Mammals at Risk: The Role of Taxonomy." In *At Risk: Proceedings of a Conference on the Biology of Species and Habitats at Risk, February 15–19, 1999*, edited by L.M. Darling. Vol. 1, 41–48. Victoria: BC Ministry of Environment, Lands and Parks; Kamloops, BC: University College of the Cariboo, 2000. http://is.gd/T1AkSq (pdf accessed October 31, 2014).

National Geographic. *Last Stand of the Great Bear*. Television documentary, National Geographic Channel, aired November 3, 2004.

Neuberger, Richard L. "Engineers Invade Another Wilderness." *Popular Science*, November 1951, 98–99.

Newman, Murray, and Patrick L. McGeer. "The Capture and Care of a Killer Whale, *Orcinus orca*, in British Columbia." *Zoologica* 51, no. 5 (1966): 59–70.

Newton, Ian. "Vero Copner Wynne-Edwards, CBE, 4 July 1906 to 5 January 1997." *Biographical Memoirs of Fellows of the Royal Society* 44 (November 1998): 473–484. http://is.gd/GndSzD (pdf accessed October 31, 2014).

Nisbet, Jack. *The Collector: David Douglas and the Natural History of the Northwest*. Seattle: Sasquatch Books, 2009.

Nordan, N.C., A.J. Wood and I. McT. Cowan. "Further Studies on the Immobilization of Deer with Succinylcholine," *Canadian Journal of Comparative Medicine and Veterinary Science* 26, no. 10 (October 1962): 246–248. www.ncbi.nlm. nih.gov/pmc/articles/PMC1583579 (accessed October 31, 2014).

Norris, Thomas, "John Fannin." *Dictionary of Canadian Biography Online*. www.biographi.ca/ EN/009004-119.01-e.php?id_nbr=6703.

North American Bird Conservation Initiative Canada. *The State of Canada's Birds, 2012*. Ottawa: Environment Canada, 2012. www.stateofcanadasbirds.org/State_of_Canada%27s_birds_2012.pdf (accessed October 31, 2014).

O'Brien, Andy. "At 68 His Dream Trip Came Though." *Weekend Magazine* 5, no. 43 (1955): 28–29. http://is.gd/8AOuA8 (accessed October 31, 2014).

Page, R.E., and A. Thomas Bergerud, "A Genetic Explanation for Ten-year Cycles of Grouse," in *Oecologia* (Berlin) 64, no. 1 (1984): 54–60. http://link.springer.com/article/10.1007%2FBF00377543 (abstract and reference list accessed October 31, 2014).

Penn, Briony. "The Natural History of Ian McTaggart Cowan." *Focus* magazine, April 2001.

———. "Passages from the Peace: Community Reflections on the Changing Peace Region." Vancouver: Suzuki Foundation and Global Forest Watch, October 2013. http://is.gd/f5VMcy (pdf accessed October 31, 2014).

———. "Recreational Access to Land in Scotland and British Columbia." PhD dissertation, University of Edinburgh, 1988.

Perrault, E.G. "His Wild Life Brought Him Honours." *Vancouver Sun Magazine*, June 28, 1952, 15.

Phillips, Carleton J. "Anatomy." In *Seventy-Five Years of Mammalogy 1919–1994*. Edited by Elmer C. Birney and Jerry R. Choate, 234–257. Provo, Utah: American Society of Mammalogists, 1994. https://archive.org/stream/seventyfiveyears-oobirn#page/234/mode/2up (accessed October 31, 2014).

Playfair, John. "Life of Dr. Hutton." *Transactions of the Royal Society of Edinburgh* 5, pt. 3 (1805), 39–99. www.biodiversitylibrary.org/ item/125770#page/457/mode/1up (accessed October 31, 2014).

Pojar, Jim, and J.B. Foster. "Natural History Theme Study of a Natural Area of Canadian Significance on the Queen Charlotte Islands, BC." Consultant report to Parks Canada, May 1977.

Porcupine Caribou Technical Committee. "Porcupine Caribou Annual Summary Report 2013," submitted to Porcupine Caribou Management Board November 2013. http://is.gd/Xb9AdX (pdf accessed March 13, 2014).

Porsild, A.E. "Birds of the Mackenzie Delta." *The Canadian Field-Naturalist* 57, nos. 2 & 3 (February–March 1943): 19–35. http://is.gd/DVSV1D (accessed October 31, 2014).

Provincial Museum Act, SBC 1913, c. 50.

Racey, Kenneth, and Ian McTaggart Cowan. *Mammals of the Alta Lake Region of Southwestern British Columbia*. Victoria: BC Provincial Museum, 1935, H15–29.

Ransom, Webster H. "Miscellaneous Avifaunal Observations no. 2." *The Murrelet* 13, no. 2 (May 1932): 50–52. www.jstor.org/discover/10.2307/3534096 (sample first page accessed October 31, 2014).

Remsen, J.V. Jr. "The Importance of Continued Collecting of Bird Specimens to Ornithology and Bird Conservation." *Bird Conservation International* 5 (1995): 145–180. http://is.gd/G3Q53O (pdf accessed October 31, 2014).

Rensch, Bernhard. *Das Prinzip geographischer Rassenkreise und das Problem der Artbildung*. Berlin: Gebrüder Borntraeger, 1929.

Repcheck, Jack. *The Man Who Found Time: James Hutton and the Discovery of the Earth's Antiquity*. Cambridge, Mass.: Perseus Publishing, 2003.

Report of the Provincial Game Commission, 1956. Victoria: Department of Attorney-General, 1957.

Report of the Provincial Museum of Natural History for the Year 1912. Victoria: British Columbia Legislative Assembly, 1913. https://archive.org/stream/reportprovincial1912brit#page/n3/mode/2up (accessed October 31, 2014).

Report of the Provincial Museum of Natural History for the Year 1916. Victoria: British Columbia Legislative Assembly, 1917. https://archive.org/stream/reportprovincial1916brit#page/n1/mode/2up (accessed March 23, 2014).

Report of the Provincial Museum of Natural History for the Year 1935. Victoria: King's Printer, 1936.

Report of the Provincial Museum of Natural History for the Year 1936. Victoria: King's Printer, 1937.

Report of the Provincial Museum of Natural History for the Year 1937. Victoria: King's Printer, 1938.

Report of the Provincial Museum of Natural History For the Year 1938. Victoria: King's Printer, 1939.

Report of the Provincial Museum of Natural History for the Year 1939. Victoria: King's Printer, 1940.

Report of the Royal Commission on Aboriginal Peoples, vol. 1, pt. 2, c. 11, §3.4: "The Cheslatta T'en and the Kemano Hydro Project," Ottawa: Canada Communication Group, 1996. http://is.gd/L2zUWf (accessed October 31, 2014).

Richter, Francis X. [Remarks as MLA (Social Credit) for Boundary-Similkameen in the BC Legislative Assembly, February 22, 1974 (morning sitting).] *Hansard*, 30th Parliament, 4th Session (1974), 462. http://is.gd/Tj6CN8 (accessed January 31, 2015).

Ridington, Robin, and Jillian Ridington. *Where Happiness Dwells: A History of the Dane-zaa First Nations*. Vancouver: UBC Press, 2013.

Robertson, Mike. "The Story of the Surrender of the Cheslatta Reserves on April 21, 1952." Cheslatta Carrier Nation Archives, 1991. www.neef.ca/uploads/161/Story_of_the_Surrender_of_the_Cheslatta_Reserves-pdf (accessed February 28, 2015).

Roessingh, Krista, and Briony Penn. "Sandhill Cranes of Coastal British Columbia: Results of Helicopter Surveys and Preliminary Observations of Habitat Use." *Proceedings of the North American Crane Workshop* 11 (2010): 1–8. http://is.gd/70kU4F (pdf accessed October 31, 2014).

Rogeau, Marie-Pierre. "Landscape Disturbance Project, Stand Origin Mapping 1997." Hinton, Alta.: Foothills Model Forest, 1997. https://foothillsri.ca/sites/default/files/null/HLP_1997_06_Rpt_LandscapeDisturbanceProjectStandOriginMapping1997.pdf (accessed October 31, 2014).

Ruse, Michael. "Evolution and the Idea of Social Progress." In *Biology and Ideology from Descartes to Dawkins*, edited by Denis R. Alexander and Ronald L. Numbers, 247–275. Chicago: University of Chicago Press, 2010.

Scheffer, Victor. "A Newly Located Herd of Pacific White-Tailed Deer." *Journal of Mammalogy* 21, no. 3 (August 1940): 271–282. www.jstor.org/discover/1374754 (preview first page accessed October 31, 2014).

Scotsman, The [newspaper]. "Royal Society of Edinburgh: Vertebrate Fauna of Western North America," October 28, 1952.

———. "Edinburgh's Wild Birds," [n.d.] 1953.

———. "Sporting Dolphins are Crack-shots," August 18, 1958.

Seton, Ernest Thompson. *Animal Heroes*. New York: Charles Scribner's Sons, 1905. https://archive.org/stream/animalheroesbein00setouoft#page/n7/mode/2up (accessed October 31, 2014).

———. *Arctic Prairies, The: A Canoe Journey of 2,000 Miles in Search of the Caribou.* New York: Charles Scribner's Sons, 1911. https://archive.org/stream/arcticprairiesca01seto#page/n9/mode/2up (accessed October 31, 2014).

———. *Birch Bark Roll of the Woodcraft Indians, The.* New York: Doubleday, Page & Co., 1907. https://archive.org/stream/birchbarkrollofwooseto#page/n5/mode/2up (accessed October 31, 2014).

———. *Life-Histories of Northern Animals: An Account of the Mammals of Manitoba.* 2 vols. New York: Charles Scribner's Sons, 1909. https://archive.org/stream/lifehistoriesofn01seto#page/n9/mode/2up (accessed October 31, 2014).

———. *Lives of Game Animals.* New York: Doubleday, Doran, 1929.

———. "The Message of the Indian." In *Some Lessons,* edited by B. of V., 1939.

Shackleton, David. *Hoofed Mammals of British Columbia.* Royal BC Museum Handbook vol. 3. In *Mammals of British Columbia.* Revised edition. Victoria: RBCM, 2013.

Shelford, Cyril. *From War to Wilderness.* Victoria: Shelford Publishing, 1997.

Siddle, Chris. "Birds of North Peace River (Fort Saint John and Vicinity): Parts 1 and 2." *Wildlife Afield* 7, nos. 1, 2 (2010): 12–123, 143–280.

Silver, Rod S. "Renaissance Man." *Discovery: A Journal of the Vancouver Natural History Society.* Spring, 2004.

———. Neil K. Dawe, Brian M. Starzomski, Katherine L. Parker and David W. Nagorsen. "A Tribute to Ian McTaggart Cowan (1910–2010)." *The Canadian Field-Naturalist* 124, no. 4 (2010): 367–383. http://canadianfieldnaturalist.ca/index.php/cfn/article/view/1108/1112 (pdf accessed October 25, 2014).

"Sir Frank Fraser Darling, 1903–1979," *Navigational Aids for the History of Science, Technology & the Environment* (website). University of Edinburgh, n.d. www.nahste.ac.uk/isaar/GB_0237_NAHSTE_P2042.html (accessed March 24, 2014).

Smidt, Erik. "Maxwell John Dunbar," *Arctic* 46, no. 2 (June 1993): 175–177. http://is.gd/YnZ7OJ (pdf accessed October 31, 2014).

Smith, Harlan I. "*Materia medica* of the Bella Coola and Neighbouring Tribes of British Columbia." *National Museum of Canada Bulletin* no. 56 (1929): 47–68. www.swsbm.com/Ethnobotany/Bella_Coola_Materia_Medica.pdf (accessed October 31, 2014).

Smith, James, Lukas Keller, Amy Marr and Peter Arcese. *Conservation and Biology of Small Populations: The Song Sparrows of Mandarte Island.* Oxford: Oxford University Press, 2006.

"Snowy Mountain Protected Area" (webpage). BC Spaces for Nature. Gibsons, BC: 2008. www.spacesfornature.org/greatspaces/snowy.html (accessed February 2, 2015).

Society for the Study of Amphibians and Reptiles. *Scientific and Standard English Names of Amphibians and Reptiles of North America North of Mexico,* 7th ed., Herpetological Circular no. 39. Salt Lake City, Utah: SSAR, 2012. http://ssarherps.org/wp-content/uploads/2014/07/HC_39_7thEd.pdf (accessed October 20, 2014).

Society for the Prevention of Cruelty to Animals. "Kindness to Animals Week: April 20–27, 1942." Pamphlet.

Spencer, George. "Obituary: Edward Ronald Buckell." *Journal of the Entomological Society of British Columbia* 60 (1963).

Stainsby, Donald. "Dean of Ecology." *BC Outdoors* 35, no. 12 (December 1979), 36–43.

Stanford, Marianne Michelle. "Immunoregulation in Murine Experimental Autoimmune Thyroiditis." Unpublished MSc thesis, Memorial University, St. John's, Nfld., 1999. http://research.library.mun.ca/974/1/Stanford_MarianneMichelle.pdf (accessed October 31, 2014).

Stanwell-Fletcher, John F. "Three Years in the Wolves' Wilderness." *Natural History* 49, no. 3 (March 1942): 136–147.

Stanwell-Fletcher, Theodora C. *Driftwood Valley.* Boston: Little, Brown, 1946.

——— and John F Stanwell-Fletcher. *Some Accounts of Flora and Fauna of the Driftwood Valley Region of North Central British Columbia.* Occasional Papers of the British Columbia Provincial Museum, no. 4. Victoria: King's Printer, 1943.

Stein, Barbara. *On Her Own Terms: Annie Montague Alexander and the Rise of Science in the American West.* Berkeley: University of California Press, 2001.

Stoddard, Herbert L. *Memoirs of a Naturalist.* Norman: University of Oklahoma Press, 1969.

Stowe, Leland. *Crusoe of Lonesome Lake.* New York: Random House, 1957.

Straight, Lee. "Game Likes Its Logging Patchy," BC Outdoors column, *Vancouver Sun,* [ca. 1955].

———. "Member of Top Bird Group," BC Outdoors column, *Vancouver Sun,* May 10, 1960, 14.

Stuart-Stubbs, Basil. "W.K. Lamb, 1904–1999." *BC Bookworld* (website), 2010. www.abcbookworld.com/view_author.php?id=786 (accessed April 29, 2014).

Suarez, Andrew V., and Neil D. Tsutsui, "The Value of Museum Collections for Research and Society." *Bioscience* 54, no. 1 (2004): 66–74. http://nature.berkeley.edu/tsutsuilab/SuarezTsutsui2004Biosci.pdf (accessed October 31, 2014).

Swarth, Harry S. "Report on a Collection of Birds and Mammals from Vancouver Island." *University of California Publications in Zoology* 10, no. 1 (February 1912): 1–124. https://archive.org/stream/universityofcali10191213univ#page/n11/mode/2up (accessed October 31, 2014).

Sydney Morning Herald. "Rising Heat to Endanger Many Species: Study," June 13, 2013. www.smh.com.au/environment/climate-change/rising-heat-to-endanger-many-species-study-20130613-205br.html (accessed March 13, 2014).

Taber, R.D., and Ian McTaggart Cowan. "Capturing and Marking Wild Animals." In *Wildlife Management Techniques*, edited by Robert H. Giles. Washington, DC: The Wildlife Society, 1969, 217–318.

Taverner, P.A. *Birds of Western Canada*. Victoria Memorial Museum Bulletin no. 41. Ottawa: King's Printer, 1926. http://peel.library.ualberta.ca/bibliography/5112.html (accessed October 31, 2014).

Taylor, C.J. *Jasper: A History of the Place and its People*. Markham, Ontario: Fifth House Publishers, 2009.

Taylor, T.M.C. *The Ferns and Fern-allies of British Columbia*, illustrated by Mary Bryant. Handbook no. 12. Victoria: BC Provincial Museum, 1963.

Thomson, Iain. *Isolation Shepherd*. Inverness, Scotland: Bidean Books, 1983.

Tindall, David. "Twenty Years after the Protest, What We Learned from Clayoquot Sound." *The Globe and Mail,* August 12, 2013. www.theglobeandmail.com/globe-debate/twenty-years-after-the-protest-what-we-learned-from-clayoquot-sound/article13709014 (accessed February 4, 2015).

"Tofino Mudflats." *See* IBA (Important Bird Areas) Canada.

Toronto Globe, "Ottawa Welcomes Dr. Oronhyatekha," November 26, 1903.

Transactions of the Canadian Conservation Association. London, Ont.: Canadian Conservation Association, 1941–[195?]. [No transactions were published between 1943 and 1951.]

Tufts, Robie. "Some Common Birds of Nova Scotia." MS, 1934. Robie W. Tufts fonds, acc. 1900.433/1, Acadia University Library.

———. *Some Common Birds of Nova Scotia*. Kentville, NS: Kentville Publishing, 1934.

Turner, Nancy J. *The Earth's Blanket: Traditional Teachings for Sustainable Living*. Vancouver: Douglas & McIntyre, 2005.

Tweedsmuir, Lady Susan. "Tweedsmuir Park: The Diary of a Pilgrimage." *National Geographic Magazine* 73, no. 4. (April 1938): 451–476.

Tweedsmuir, Lord. "Message to Sportsmen." *Rod and Gun in Canada*, November 1936.

"Tweedsmuir South Provincial Park" (webpage). BC Parks, Ministry of Environment, n.d. www.env.gov.bc.ca/bcparks/explore/parkpgs/tweeds_s/nat_cul.html (accessed May 24, 2014).

University of Alberta Alumni Association. "The Memorable William Rowan." *History Trails* (website), 1993. www.ualberta.ca/ALUMNI/history/peoplep-z/93sumrowan.htm (accessed January 15, 2014).

University of British Columbia Herbarium. "BC Herbarium Fungal Database." www.biodiversity.ubc.ca/museum/herbarium/fungi/index.html (accessed March 21, 2013).

University of British Columbia Library. Andrew Hutchinson (1888–1975) fonds (publications from 1947–1965). http://resolve.library.ubc.ca/cgi-bin/catsearch?bid=3149746 (accessed May 24, 2014).

University of California. "Annie Alexander and Louise Kellogg." In *Gay Bears: The Hidden History of the Berkeley Campus* (website), 2002. http://bancroft.berkeley.edu/collections/gaybears/alexkel (accessed May 24, 2014).

University of Victoria. "G.A. Mackie Biography." http://web.uvic.ca/~mackie/biography2.pdf (accessed December 15, 2013).

Vancouver Natural History Society. "Mammal and Bird Life of Burnaby Lake." *Bulletin* no. 18 (October 1945). As reprinted in Bill Merilees, *Selected Excerpts from the Vancouver Natural History Society Bulletin* (No. 1, September 1943, to No. 153, December 1971), 16–17 [*q.v.* above at "Merilees"]. http://naturevancouver.ca/sites/naturevancouver.ca/VNHS%20files/4/VNHS_Bulletin_1943-1971.pdf (pdf pp20–21 accessed May 24, 2014).

———."Bird Study – Seymour Mountain to Bridgeman Park," *Bulletin* no. 89 (Summer 1954), as reprinted in Merilees at pdf pp77–78.

Vancouver Sun, "Authority Sought for Aluminum Plant Deal," March 23, 1949, 13.

———. "Killer Whale Roams City Inlet." October 27, 1945.

———. "Member of Top Bird Group." May 10, 1960, 14.

———. "Save Your Wildlife." March 10, 1983, B1.

———. "UBC Museum Well Stuffed But Hasn't Even One Whale." September 29, 1945.

Vaux, H.J., et al. "Aldo Starker Leopold, Zoology; Forestry and Conservation: Berkeley." *University of California: In Memoriam 1985*. University of California Digital Archives, http://content.cdlib.org/view?docId=hb4d5nb20m&brand=calisphere (accessed February 3, 2014).

Vibert, Elizabeth. "Real Men Hunt Buffalo: Masculinity, Class and Race in British Fur Traders' Narratives." *Gender and History* 8, no. 1 (April 1996): 4–21. http://is.gd/XtoC7U (first-page preview accessed October 31, 2014).

Victoria *Daily Colonist*. "The Forests and the People." August 8, 1908.

Victoria *Daily Times*. "Birth Announcements," July 11, 1940.

Wallmo, Olof C. *Mule and Black-Tailed Deer of North America*. Lincoln: University of Nebraska Press, 1981.

Waters, C. Kenneth, and Albert Van Helden, eds. *Julian Huxley: Biologist and Statesman of Science*. Houston, Tex.: Rice University Press, 1992.

Webber, Jean. "Major Allan Brooks of Okanagan Landing." *Living Landscapes* (website). Royal BC Museum, n.d. http://142.36.5.21/thomp-ok/allan_books/major-allan.html (accessed April 10, 2014).

Weindling, Paul. "Genetics, Eugenics and the Holocaust." In *Biology and Ideology from Descartes to Dawkins*, edited by Dennis R. Alexander and Ronald L. Numbers, 192–214. Chicago: University of Chicago Press, 2010.

Weir, Harold. "Culture without Pain." *Vancouver Sun*, July 12, 1957.

Whitaker, John O. "University Propinquity." In *Seventy-Five Years of Mammalogy 1919–1994*, edited by Elmer C. Birney and Jerry R. Choate, 121–138. Provo, Utah: American Society of Mammalogists, 1994. https://archive.org/stream/seventyfiveyears00birn#page/120/mode/2up (accessed October 31, 2014).

Wild Species Canada 2005. http://is.gd/SeNGUd (pdf accessed October 20, 2014).

Wiles, Roger. "Uncommon Legacy." *Lake Cowichan Gazette*, January 5, 2009. 10. [Reprinted in Cowichan Valley Rhododendron Society *Newsletter* 20, no. 2 (February 2009): 3–4. http://cowichan.rhodos.ca/newsletter-archive/CVRS Feb newsletter 2009.pdf (pdf p3, accessed February 1, 2015).]

Wilson, D.E., and D.M. Reeder, eds. *Mammal Species of the World: A Taxonomic and Geographic Reference*, 3rd ed. Baltimore: Johns Hopkins University Press, 2005.

Wilson, E.O. *Naturalist*. Washington: Island Press, 1994.

Winchester, N.N., Z. Lindo and V.M. Behan-Pelletier. "Oribatid Mite Communities in the Canopy of Montane *Abies amabilis* and *Tsuga heterophylla* Trees on Vancouver Island, British Columbia." *Environmental Entomology* 37, no. 2 (April 2008): 464–471. http://is.gd/2xk7ff (abstract and cited references accessed October 20, 2014).

Wonders of the Microscope, The. London: Tabart and Co., 1829.

Wood, June. *Home to the Nechako: The River and the Land*. Victoria: Heritage House, 2013.

Woods, Lynn. "Portrait of a Fracking Town: Dimock, Pennsylvania." *Chronogram* (Hudson River Valley, New York State), June 1, 2012. http://is.gd/tNhS1z (accessed February 6, 2015).

World Wide Fund for Nature Canada. "Monte Hummel, president emeritus." www.wwf.ca/about_us/experts/monte_hummel.cfm (accessed May 14, 2014).

Zwickel, Fred C., and James F. Bendell. *Blue Grouse: Their Biology and Natural History*. Ottawa: NRC Research Press, 2004.

INDEX

100 Mile House, BC 166

Aberdeen Working Man's
Natural History and Scientific
Society 65

aboriginal peoples.
See indigenous peoples

Abraham, Dorothy 276

Academic Council of BC 260,
433

Ahbau River 169

Aklavik, NWT 375

Alaksen National Wildlife Area
210

Alberta Fish and Game
Association 304–305,
327, 357. *See also* Fisher,
William "Cougar Bill"; *and
under* population ecology:
prey/predator relationships:
predation fallacy

Alberta Plateau 247

Alberta Wilderness Association
388

Alcan. *See* Kenney Dam

Alexander, Annie
Alberni expedition 135, 147
background, character 132–133
Cowan and 134, 179, 198
Grinnell and 133–134, 179, 474
patron of Merriam, Grinnell,
Cowan, as 51
philanthropy of 132, 178

Alexander, Denis 259

Alexis Creek 155

Aleza Lake 85

Alkali Lake Ranch 399

Allan Brooks Nature Centre,
Vernon, BC 101

Allen, Glover M. 156

Allen, Owen 381

Allen's Rule 368

Alpha Lake 251

Alpine Arctic Zone 78

Alpine Club of Canada 309

Alta Lake 65, 75, 173, 191, 198,
210, 301, 329, 452

Cowan's first encounter with
73
Racey family at 67, 76, 78–80

Aluminum Company of Canada.
See Kenney Dam

American Bison Society 40

American Game Protective and
Propagation Association
43, 49

American Ornithologists' Union
37, 134, 178, 267

American Society of
Mammalogists 180, 399
Racey as founding member 73

Anarchist Mountain 215

Anderson, David viii, 299

Anderson, Nancy 398

Anderson, R.M. 48, 105, 108,
115, 128, 131, 151, 178, 222,
327, 457
recommendation for Cowan
104–105

Andrews family (Cheslatta) 222

App, Alison 451

Apsassin, May 261

Arcese, Peter 141

Arctic Institute 390

Arctic Land Use Research
Advisory Committee 390

Aristazabal Island 363

Armstrong, Ed 142

Arthur's Seat 5, 8

Ashnola (district) 402, 403,
404, 405, 407
population puzzle posed by
406–407

Ashnola Mountains 402

Ashnola River 402

Association for the Protection of
Fur-Bearing Animals 223

Athabasca Pass 26

Athabasca River 123, 128, 310

Atholl, Duke of 12

Audubon Society
Beck and 390

Cowan and Canadian branch
of 435
Cowan commissions report on
spotted owl 195
lobbying for federal game
refuges 49
president a 'B' member 43. *See
also* Pearson, T. Gilbert

Aulavik National Park 390.
See also indigenous peoples:
impact of industrial land use
on: Banks Island Inuvialuit

Ayrshire, Scotland 15

Babcock, John 172

Bachelor Lake 289

Baffin Island 454

Bag Harbour 363

Bailiff, J.W. "Billy" 80

bait balls 141–142, 358

Baja California, Mexico 445

Balfour, John Hutton 3, 8, 66,
414, 416
as educator 12
"concussion" with Joseph
Hooker over botany chair at
Edinburgh 10–11
public access to land, and 12
relation to Cowan 10–11
similarity to Cowan 13–14

Balfour, Margaret 10

Balfour, Sarah 10

Bamfield, BC 400

Bamfield Biological Station 407

Banff Advisory Council 230

Banff National Park 304, 328,
342

Banks Island 270, 389

Bare Island 138, 139, 141

bark and pine beetle infestations
172

Barkerville, BC 167

Barkley, William (Bill) 279

Barnfield, Alfred 80

Barreclough, Ed 358

Barr, Jeff 404

Bass Rock, Scotland 413

Bateman, Robert viii, 98, 366

Bayliff's Range 161

BC Forest Service 19

BC Game Commission 224

BC Ornithologists Union
advocacy by 71
"collectors" vs. "observers"
71–72. *See also* Vancouver
Natural History Society: rift
with field naturalists

BC Provincial Museum
Cowan hired by, at age 25 199
Cowan letter to at age 15 32
Cowan resigns from,
recommends successor
278–279. *See also* Carl,
Clifford
Cowan's continuing
collaboration with 279–280
field work and collecting 247–
248, 249–258
fiscal austerity, and 279–280
history of 203–207. *See
also* Edwards, Yorke; Foster,
Bristol
Kermode and 204–207,
278–279
Occasional Papers series 248
rejuvenation of 206, 228–230,
240–241, 247, 279–280. *See
also* Weir, George

BC Registered Trappers
Association 223

BC Waterfowl Society 210

Beacon Hill Park, Victoria 209

Bear Lake 243

Bear Lake band 242

Beaty Biodiversity Museum,
UBC xiv, 70, 84, 85, 236,
459, 460

Beaufort Sea 375, 381

Beaver Creek 132, 147

Beck, Shirley 439, 452

Beck, Tom 60, 388, 389, 390,
435, 439, 451, 454, 458
deer hunting with Cowan in
Wildcat Hills, Alta. 452–453
on indigenous traditional
hunting ethic 162

Beebe, Frank x, 331

Bell, G.P. 295

Bendell, James 24, 25, 314

Bennett Dam. *See* W.A.C.
Bennett Dam

Bennett, J.C. 72

Berger, Thomas 60, 386–387

Bergerud, Heather 112

Bergerud, Tom 25, 160, 383, 388

Bergmann's Rule 368

Berkeley, Calif. 55, 134, 181, 184

Bigg, Mike 320, 367, 442

bighorn sheep 323–324, 325, 357
Ashnola, in 402–405, 406–407

Big Tree Trail 143

"biological species" 116

bison. *See* conservation: bison as
early rallying issue

Black Hills, South Dakota 133

Black Mountain 78, 165, 166

Black Tusk (mountain) 76

Blackwater River 160

Blood, Don 404

Bond, Richard 266

Bonta, Marcia 242

Borden, Charles 226

Borstrom, Frank 322

Botanical Society of Edinburgh
3, 10

Botany Bay (Botanical Beach
Provincial Park), Vancouver
Island 83

Boulder Creek 155

Boundary Study 115

bounty system. *See
under* population ecology:
population control

Bowen, Dan 323

Bowron Lake Provincial Park
172

Bowron River Valley
beetle infestation in 172

Boxer, Bert 377, 378

Boy, Charley 161

Boyd, Janet 167

Boynton, William H. 197

Brady, Al 335

Brady, James 335

Brady, Mavis 336

Brandon, Man. 431

Bray, Ken 426

Brazeau Lake 336, 337

Brazeau River 337

Breuil, l'Abbé Henri 44

Brewer, George 421

Brink, Bert 65, 293, 300, 309,
331, 352, 382, 402, 405, 408
Burrard Field-Naturalists,
and 293
death of 408

British American Oil Ltd. 385

British Eugenics Society 259,
422

British North American
Philatelic Society 458

Broadhead, John 370

Brody, Hugh 261

Brooks, Allan Cecil 100, 394,
397

Brooks, Major Allan Cyril x, 36,
97, 98, 99, 101, 104, 117, 134,
205, 215, 266, 288, 394
predators, and 98–100
reputation as bird artist and
collector 98–99
the 'B', and 100

Brooks, W.E. 97

Bruce, Robert the 16

Brunton, Daniel 47, 48

Bryant Creek 316

Bryant, Frank 122, 123, 124, 125,
310, 316, 384

Bryant, Joe 122, 123, 345, 381,
383, 384, 385

Bryant, Kathleen 124

Bryant, Mary (Harrington)
384–385

'B', the xiv, 99, 106, 107, 109,
114, 121, 126, 144, 166, 178,
182, 210, 225, 230, 242, 249,
267, 273, 283, 302, 303, 304,
305, 309, 328, 354, 355, 368,
373, 374, 394, 405, 421, 422,
425, 433, 434
aboriginal subsistence hunting,
and 60
Aldo Leopold and 54
allegiance to the land 60
Brooks on predators, and 98
Canadian members of 41
class, and 57
conservation advocacy 49–
50, 52, 57
egalitarian motivation for 57
political risks of 48–55
constitution of 44, 49–50
Cowan and 53, 58–59, 73, 107,
117–118, 168, 178
creation of political space 49,
55–56
English Charter of the Forest,
and 44, 49
gender, and 57–58
Harkin and Lloyd as key
instigators of 38, 45
Hornaday, and 140
Lloyd and 47–49
medieval roots of 44

Muir, and 50
Munro and influence on
    Cowan 33
national parks, and 45–46
prominent members of 43, 54
Racey's connection with 87
"reasonable extent" of
    predator-killing 122–123
Roosevelt, and 51
secret society, as 56–59
trophy hunting and 49, 51
virtue of silence, and 168
wilderness as sanctuary, and
    56–57
wildlife management, and 123
Buchanan, G.O. 39
national parks, and 45–46
Buchanan Simpson, George 210
Buchanan Simpson, Suzanne
    210
Buchan, John 21, 315. See
    also Tweedsmuir, Lord
Buckell, Ronald 91–92, 93, 289,
    404, 440
advocacy against DDT 92
Cowan's first summer job as
    biologist 85
influence on Cowan 91–92
Bunnell, Fred 144–146
Cowan, and 145–146
Burba, George F. 20
Burbridge, Mrs. 80
Burnaby Island 363
Burnaby Narrows 362, 363
Burnett, J. Alexander 20, 38
Burnham, John 43, 49, 54
Burns Bog 299
Burrard Field-Naturalists
    Society. See also
    under Vancouver Natural
    History Society
Cowan and 65, 85
influence of 72
Racey and 72, 117
Burrard Inlet 299
Butler, Frank 144, 210, 223, 225,
    265, 302, 305, 313
Byng Pass 325
Cache Creek 155
Cagney, James 421
Cairn Pass 324
Calgary Fish and Game
    Association 303. See
    also Fisher, William "Cougar
    Bill"
Calgary Power 304, 316

California Academy of Sciences
    195
Calvert Island 270, 281
Campbell, David 104
Campbell, Jim 427, 428
Campbell, R. Wayne 196
Campbell, Sir Archibald 16
Campbell, Wayne 140, 370, 455
Camp, Frank 318
Canadian Conservation
    Association 226
Canadian Environmental
    Advisory Council 390
Canadian Environmental
    Assessment Act 387. See also
    under environmental impact
    assessment
Canadian Institute of Forestry
    374
Canadian Medical Association
    430
Canadian Migration Monitoring
    Network 212
Canadian Museums Committee
    229
Canadian Nature Federation
    346
Canadian Ornithological
    Association 116
Canadian Wildlife Service 59,
    304, 351, 383, 385, 434, 456
Cannings, R.A. 98
Canoe River 26, 379
Cantwell, Judy 447
Cape Saint James 360
Carbyn, L.N. 345
Cardini, Andrea 152
Cariboo (district) 166, 171, 182,
    213, 311
Cariboo, The (region) 166
Caribou Slim 168
Carl, Clifford vii, 277, 279, 284,
    285, 286, 330
    member of the 'B' 278
Carpenter, William 11
Carr, Emily 208
Carrot Creek 311, 313
Carson, Rachel 92
Cartwright, Bert 352, 353
Cascade Creek 300
Cascade Mountain divide 187
Cascade Valley 321
Case, Ted 369

Castle Rock, Edinburgh 10
Cathedral Grove 147
Cathedral Lakes 403
Cathedral Lakes Provincial
    Park 407
Celsius, Anders 418
Centre for Applied Conservation
    Biology, UBC 144
Ceska, Adolf 435
Chagnon, Napoleon 259
Cha, Laciese 159
Chalfant, Bill 184
Charlesworth, Pamela. See
    Cowan, Pamela McTaggart
Charlie, Charlie Peter 383
Charlie Lake 255, 257, 258, 260,
    261, 272
Charlie Lake cave 261
Cheakamus Canyon 76
Cheakamus Lake 191
Cheakamus River 76
Cheslatta T'en
    Kenney Dam, and 224–226
    Ootsa Lake traditional
        territory 219
Chesterman Beach 136
Chezacut, BC 155, 157
Chezacut Lake 155
Chezacut Lake (now Chilcotin
    Lake) 157
Chief Charlie 243
Chilcotin (district) 311
Chilcotin Lake 393
Chilcotin Lake (formerly
    Chezacut Lake) 155
Chilcotin Parklands 393
Chilcotin region 155, 157, 158,
    161, 315, 345, 393
Chilcotin River 155
Chilkat Pass 251
chipmunks 110, 314
Chitty, Dennis 25, 291, 314, 423
Chitty, Dennis H. 291
Cholera Hospital, Edinburgh,
    Scotland 66
Clachnacudainn Range 232
clans 15
Clarke, C.H.D. 304, 326
Clarke, Roger 13
Clark, Sir Kenneth 262
Clay, Lucius D. 421
Clayoquot Scientific Panel 144

Cowan's contributions to 145
clear-cut logging 154. *See also* population ecology: wildlife population "sinks"
Bowron valley, in 172
caribou, and 160
grouse, and 24–25
H.R. MacMillan and 444
marmots, and 153
Meares Island, and 142–143
public protests against 144–145
South Moresby (Gwaii Haanas), at 369–370
Tetana Lake, at 245
Village Lake Louise, and 327–328
Clearwater Lake 322
Clearwater River 322
Cleland Island 138, 140
Clemens, Wilbert A. 277, 283
"climatic change" (1952) 414–415
European ornithology and 419
Coal Harbour 364
Coast Range 194, 286
Cody, Martin 369
collecting. *See* specimen collecting, preparing, curating
Collier, Eric 223
Colls, Dave 394, 396, 397
Columbia Icefield 326, 328, 329
Columbia Mountains 232
Columbia River 26, 188, 232, 320
Columbia River islands 190
Columbia River Treaty 118
Commission of Conservation 51
Committee Punchbowl, Alberta 26
Comox, BC 34, 355
Connachie, Tim 429
Connaught, Duke and Duchess of 205
conservation. *See also* national parks; Nature Conservancy, The; Nature Trust of BC, The; public access to nature; wildlife management
bison as early rallying issue 46–47, 48
dams and 118, 224–226. *See also* Cheslatta T'en; Kenney Dam; Ootsa Lake
Gordon Hewitt and 37
hunting culture and 49, 57, 227–228, 304–306
indigenous peoples, and 58.

See also indigenous peoples: cultivation of species by
lack of career opportunities in, prior to 1930 51
Laurier government and 39, 50, 58
Leopold's paradox of 273
Munro and 33
policy impetus from forest fires of 1910 125–127
politics of in US 48–50, 53–54
public advocacy for 37, 54–55
political risks of 48–54
television, and 425
the 'B' and, generally 43–60, 117
whales, of 237–238, 240. *See also* Watson, Paul
conservation biology. *See also* island biogeography; population ecology; wildlife management
curricula in retreat from '50s until '90s 406
importance of field work 181–182
importance of species naming to 116
intellectual origins of 3
Scotland's failure to implement 5, 17
specimen collection and 72, 117, 216. *See also* specimen collecting, preparing, curating
Conservation Council 328
Conservation Foundation 421
Constitution Hill, Vancouver Island 130
Cook, Francis 368
Coombs, BC (near Parksville) 148
Cooper, John M. 456
Copeland, Betty 397
Copenhagen, Denmark 416, 418
Copper Bay 363
Corley-Smith, Peter 206
COSEWIC 107, 119
marmots, and 153
Cottonwood Ranch 166, 167
cougars 311–313. *See also, generally, under* population ecology: population control *and* prey/predator relationships
Cowan, Garry McTaggart 13, 331, 341, 342, 356, 412, 415,

416, 420, 427, 428, 440, 446, 447, 451, 455
birth of 276
Cowan, Garry McTaggart (Jr.) 455
Cowan, Hugh 16
COWAN, Ian McTaggart
—Accolades—
"awards lay everywhere": in Cowan's study x
conservation advocacy
US National Wildlife Federation: International Conservationist of the Year, 1979 226
Wildlife Society: Aldo Leopold Award, 1970 55
miscellaneous 436
species names 428
television
Canadian Medical Association; Ohio State U. Institute for Education; UAR International Television Festival; Vancouver International Film Festival 430
—Character—
broad network of relations 104, 265, 390–391, 437
confirmed tea drinker 379
early life and influences. *See also under* Dickson, Frank; Fraser, Charles McLean; Hutchinson, Andrew H.; Laing, Hamilton Mack; Munday, Phyllis and Don; Munro, Jim; Racey, Eileen; Racey, Kenneth; Spencer, George J.
encouragement by both parents 28
formative reading 19–21, 28–29, 37
high school 63–64
landscape of Vancouver 21–22
modest means and xi, 17, 23–24, 31
Scotland and 5, 7–8, 24
Scouting 31–32
the 'B' 59
egalitarianism; respect for local knowledge xi, 22–23, 53, 80, 85, 122–123, 182, 260
esteem for accomplished women 112, 158–159, 399–400

fondness for early mornings
215
health 272
immigrant to Canada, as xi
open-mindedness 109
pelage 367
self-sufficiency 23–24,
122–123
sense of humour xii–xiii, 371
shy, private 212
spiritual side 173. *See also,
variously, under* 'B', the
— Family—
brother. *See* Cowan, Patrick
brothers-in-law. *See* Racey,
Alan; Racey, Stewart
daughter. *See* Schau, Ann
father. *See* Cowan,
McTaggart Sr.
father-in-law. *See* Racey,
Kenneth
grandfather, maternal.
See Mackenzie, Donald
grandfather, paternal.
See Cowan, Peter
McTaggart
grandsons. *See* Cowan, Garry
McTaggart (Jr.); Cowan,
Robert McTaggart; Schau,
Torben
illustrious ancestors.
See Balfour, John Hutton;
Hutton, James
importance of Scots lineage
15
meaning of "Cowan" in
Gaelic 16
mother. *See* Cowan, Laura
Alice (Mackenzie)
mother-in-law. *See* Racey,
Eileen (Stewart)
physical characteristics 15
sisters. *See* Cowan, Joan
McTaggart; Cowan,
Pamela McTaggart
son. *See* Cowan, Garry
McTaggart
wife. *See* Cowan, Joyce
(Racey); Racey, Joyce
wedding 212–213
—Interests—
Arctic 373–391
bear taxonomy 290–291
bighorn sheep 266–267
conservation biology 73. *See
also under* conservation
biology
deer ix, 163–165, 179–180,
183–185, 187–189, 197,
210–211

environmental advocacy
xii–xiii, 52, 369–
370, 406. *See also
under* environmentalism;
public access to nature
DDT, and 92
evolution 9–10, 180–181
islands and insularity of
species 82, 143, 151–
152, 211–212, 269–
270, 369–370. *See also
variously under* island
biogeography
genetics 15, 69–70
grouse 24–27
hunting/trapping/collecting
xiv, 16–17, 31, 130, 140,
162–163, 222–223, 452–453.
See also under 'B', the
mammalogy 94–95, 180
dentition of mammals 124
marmots 152–154, 166
molluscs 13
popularization of science
xiii–xiv, 8, 14–15, 26,
134, 384, 425, 430. *See
also under* museums and
museology
population ecology 69–70.
See also under population
ecology
rabbits 155, 177
spadefoot toads 287
teaching xi–xiii, 8, 14–15, 86,
145, 146, 186–187, 193–194,
277, 331, 351–352, 397, 431
Cowan, Joan McTaggart 15, 22,
29, 212
Cowan, Joyce (Racey) 152, 165,
191, 200, 217, 219, 231, 249,
267, 329, 330, 333, 356, 402,
404, 416, 435, 439, 444,
452, 453, 455, 456, 457. *See
also* Racey, Joyce
back to Black Mountain with
Ian, 1977 166
ecotourism, and 445
"grace and grit" 213
honeymoon in the Cariboo
167
visiting the McCabes 170–171
indispensable to Ian's success
439–440
lifelong hiker 166
love for hummingbirds 173
pregnancy complications;
grieving 248–249
wedding 212–213
Cowan, Laura Alice (Mackenzie)

7, 16, 19, 20, 26, 28, 64, 166,
199, 450
Scottish hunting culture, and
16–17
"Cowan mafia" 390
Cowan, Mariana 447
Cowan, McTaggart (Garry) 16
Cowan, McTaggart Sr. 15–16, 22
dislike for camping 27
gardener and photographer,
as 28
Garry oak, and 27–28
passion for botany 27
reasons for immigrating to
BC 19
Cowan, Pamela McTaggart 29,
65, 439
Cowan, Patrick 165
as meteorologist with early
awareness of climate change
29
Cowan, Penney (Condon) 455
Cowan, Peter McTaggart 16
Cowan, Robert McTaggart 447,
451, 455
Cowan Tetrapod Collection
84, 460
Cowan Vertebrate Museum,
UBC 399, 455
Crater Creek 403
Crater Mountain 407
creationists 33, 52. *See
also* dominionists
Creston, BC 449
Crick, Francis 423
Crocker Point 428
Crossman, Rae 173
Crown Zellerbach 152
Cullis-Suzuki, Severn 459
Cultus Lake 300
Cumshewa Inlet 358, 360
Cunningham, Jim 225, 302
curlew
Scottish culture, in 137
seen by Cowan and Racey at
Tofino 136–137
Curren, John 129
Dainard Creek 357
Dalzell, Kathleen 359
dams. *See also* indigenous
peoples: impact of industrial
land use on; Kenney Dam;
Site C dam; W.A.C. Bennett
Dam

"broken" ecosystems, and 261–263
Dane-Zaa people 261
Daniels, Frank 186, 194
Darcus, Sid 288
Darimont, Chris 273, 281, 345
Darling, Frank Fraser 55, 420, 421, 422, 434
Darwin, Charles 3, 9, 51, 53
    taxonomy and 156
Darwinists 33, 52
Davidson, John 65
Dawe, Neil 158, 196, 216, 422, 458
Dawson Creek, BC 250, 254
Dawson, George M. 247
Day, Stockwell 436
DDT 92, 169, 386, 421, 440
Death Island 142
deer 183, 197. See also under COWAN, Ian McTaggart: —Interests—: deer
deforestation 3–4
de Jong, Stan van Zyll 295
Demarchi, Ray 404
Dempster Highway 388
Denali National Park, Alaska 345
Denny, Tom and Margo 265, 452
DeRoos, Mike 459
DeRoos, Tom 459
Despard, E. 132
Detwiler, John 226, 283
Devona 310
Dickson, Frank 85
Diefenbaker, John 432
Dimock Nature Study Camp 241
Dimock, Pennsylvania 245
Dominion Entomological Branch 85, 91
Dominion Entomological Laboratory 330
dominionists 33. See also creationists
Douglas, David 3, 26
Douglas Lake Cattle Company 91
Douglas, Sir James 290
Drábek, Jan 434
Driftwood Valley 241, 244, 245
Ducks Unlimited 352, 353

Dunbar, Maxwell John 416
Duncan, Arthur 415
Dunlap, T.R. 134
Dyche, Lewis 403
Dyke, Edwin Van 180
Dymond, J.R. 283, 301
Eastman, Don x
East Pine River 260
East Point, Saturna Island 442
echinococcosis 383
Ecojustice 387
Ecological Reserve Act 435
ecology. See also population ecology
    ecological rules 368
    intellectual origins of 3
    public advocacy for 54
ecotourism 370
    Cowan on 445
Ecotrust 281
Edinburgh Botanical Gardens 416
Edinburgh Royal Society lecture 417
Edinburgh, Scotland 3, 411, 432
    as compared to Vancouver 21
Edmonton, Alberta 121
Edwards, Ralph 251
Edwards, Yorke vii, viii, 129, 279, 352, 394, 397
Edwords, Clarence 403
Egan, Timothy 126
Ehdiitat Gwich'in (Loucheux) 376, 378
elk
    re-expansion of populations during Cowan's career 161
Elkhorn Flat 161
Elton, Charles 6, 401
endangered species.
    See population ecology: species at risk
Englishman River 196
environmental impact assessment 262–263
    Mackenzie Valley pipeline hearings. See also Berger, Thomas
    1973 early prototype panel 386
    1974 Berger inquiry 386–387
    National Energy Board hearings today 387
environmentalism

Cowan's approach to xi–xii, xiv, 92–93, 146, 302
Darling on unpriced damage by energy sector 421–422
growing militancy for in 1970s 92–93. See also Watson, Paul
Erskine, Anthony 258
Esowista Peninsula 135, 138
eugenics 40
    Canada, in 52
    Cowan and 52–53
    Huxley and 42
    political utility of 52
    Roosevelt and 51–52
Eutsuk 221
Eva Lake 236
evolution. See under COWAN, Ian McTaggart: —Interests—; island biogeography
Experimental Lakes Area 407
extinction xi, 154, 157, 240, 250–251. See also population ecology: species at risk
extirpation 4–5, 82, 155, 161, 266
Fairbairn, Howard 359, 361, 362
Fannin, John 203, 228
Farley, Frank 178
Farne Island, Scotland 435
Fatu Hiva, French Polynesia 266
Fay, Francis "Bud" 383
Fenton, Brock 155, 295
Fernie, BC 108
Fernow, Bernard 40
field work. See conservation biology: importance of field work
Findhorn Valley, Scotland 4
Finnish Zoological Institute 419
First Nations. See indigenous peoples
Firth, Henry 378
Firth of Forth, Scotland 412
Fisher, Dean 144, 358
Fisher, Joseph 421
Fisher, Margaret 459
Fisher, William "Cougar Bill" 303, 304, 305, 312. See also population ecology: prey/predator relationships: predation fallacy
Fisheries Research Board 21
Fitzsimmons Creek 80
Flader, Susan 54

Flatiron (district) 403

Flatiron Range 408

Fleming, James H. 37

Flook, Don 383

Foerster, Earl 277

Ford, John 443

Ford, Peter 351

forest fires 125–126

Forest Service 50

Fort Smith, NWT 382

Fort St. John, BC 257, 260

Fort Ware, BC 261, 262

Foster, Bristol vii, viii, x, 141,
230, 272, 279, 320, 363, 366,
367, 370, 371, 397, 430, 435,
442, 451
BC government, and 59
Cowan and specimen
preparation 68
Cowan, meeting 365–367
marmots, and 153. *See
also* Haley Lake Ecological
Reserve
South Moresby (Gwaii Haanas)
activism with Cowan 370

Foster, Janet 45

Foster's Rule 368

Four Mile Creek 168

Fowlsheugh, Scotland 412, 413,
414

Fox, Rosemary 346

Fraker, Mark 299

Fraser, Charles McLean 199, 277
influence on Cowan 82–83, 84
pioneer in fisheries biology
83–84
recommendation of Cowan for
field work 103

Fraser Delta 138

Fraser, John 390

Fraser, Marian "Bobbie" 420

Fraser, Simon 247

Fraser Valley 27, 298

Freeman, Lewis R. 321

French, O.E. 346

Friday Harbour (Washington)
Marine Station 427

Fuller, John 429

Fulton, Margaret 400

Fyfe, Richard 383

Galápagos 445

Galton, Francis 51, 53

Gambier Island 26

gamekeeping 4–5

Gang Ranch 394

Garner Butte, Calif. 189

Garrod's Beach 141

Garry oak 27–28
as cultivated by indigenous
peoples 28

Garry oak ecosystem 197

Geist, Val x, 346, 347, 388

genetics 115, 116
classical zoology, and 84, 116
Cowan attending Watson and
Crick lecture 423
Cowan recruiting geneticists
for UBC 423

Genge, Jim 451

Genge, Jim and Dorothy 265

Genge, Tom 427

George C. Reifel Migratory Bird
Sanctuary 210

Gerussi, Bruno 223

Gibson, Gordon 142

Gibson, Ken 143

Gibson, Rex 309

Gillespie, Greg 57

Gilmore, Jim 429

Glacier National Park 291

Glacier Skywalk 328

Gladys Lake, BC 347

Glendenning, L.E.R. 72

Glen Strathfarrar, Scotland 421

Glen Tilt, Scotland 12

Gloger, Constantin 232

Gloger's Rule 232, 290, 368

Golden Eagle Basin 148

Goose Island 274

Goose Island Banks 275

gophers 110

Gordon Commission 226

Goward, Trevor 86, 187, 217

Grace Harbour, Gambier Island
26

Graham Island 359, 366, 368

Graham, Kenneth 235, 300

Graham, Robert 66

grasslands
conservation of 118–119
ecology of 93–97

Grassy Plains 219

Gray, Gary 295

Gray, Teddy 244, 245

Grazley, Robin 448

Great Bear Rainforest 268, 272,
281, 459

Great King Street, Edinburgh
3, 10, 16

Great Slave Lake 375

Green, Charles de Blois 286, 288

Green Mountain 148, 149, 151

Greenpeace 238

Grell Cove 221

Grey, Viscount 50–51

Grinnell, George Bird
Joseph Grinnell, Annie
Alexander, and 134
member of the 'B' 43, 54, 87
Merriam, and 182

Grinnell, Hilda Wood 133

Grinnell, Joseph
academic influence of 133,
134, 180
Annie Alexander, and 51, 132–
134, 147
as journal editor 99–100
background 133–134
Brooks and Miner on
predators, re 99–100, 134
conservation biology, and
181–182
Cowan and 87, 134, 178, 179–
180, 185, 198–199
gift of money 193
death of 267, 275
field science vs. lab science
133, 181–183, 185
hazard in parks 128–129
importance of local knowledge
182–183
indigenous peoples, and 58,
133–134
Jewett, and 190
McCabes and 171, 179, 182–183
Moffitt, and 194–195
Racey, and 178–179
science as public record xii–
xiii, 182

grizzly bear
Cowan's advice to Parks re
128–129
Jasper warden killed by 127
Mexican grizzly 156–157

grouse
communicable diseases of 27
early research interest of
Cowan's 24
missing holotype specimen
found 26
population genetics of 25

Grouse Mountain 22, 23, 354

Guiget, Muriel (Waller) 354, 365

Guiguet, Charles vii, 4, 140,

143, 195, 272, 279, 289, 351, 354, 355, 361, 365, 366, 435

Guiguet, Trisha 289

Gulf Islands 25

Gulf Islands National Park Reserve 427

Guppy, Anthony 135

Guppy, Arthur 143

Guppy, Crispin 143

Guppy, Dick
 Cowan and 140, 142–143
 family background 135
 greeting Cowan and Racey at Tofino 135
 hunting, and 135, 140

Guppy, Robert John Lechmere 135

Guppy, Tony
 on Cowan as mentor 143
 on Dick Guppy's hunting practices 140

Guujaaw 370

Gwaii Haanas 370

Gwitch'in 388

Haber, Gordon 345

Habitat Conservation Trust Foundation 49, 294, 400, 407

habitat destruction xii–xiii

Hafner, David 232

Haida Gwaii 354, 365, 368, 369, 370, 442

Haida Nation 370

Haig-Brown, Roderick 280

Haisla Nation 225

Hakai Institute 281

Haley Lake 149, 152

Haley Lake Ecological Reserve 153, 154

Hall, E. Raymond 179

Hall, Sir James 8

Hamber Provincial Park 26

Hammond, Lorne 45, 204

Hancock, Lyn 302

Hannon, Susan 112

Harbour Porpoises 450–451

Hardy, G.A. 278

Harestad, Alton 279

Hargreaves, Jack 332

Harkin, James B. 37, 38, 40, 41, 43, 45, 56, 58, 72, 121, 123, 131, 303, 304, 309, 328
 as key instigator of the 'B' 38
 early life 38–39

influenced by John Muir 38, 40

influenced by Theodore Roosevelt 40

on role of national parks 56

retirement of 230, 305

Harmon, D.W. 247

Harper, Fred 404

Harriman, E.H. 53

Harrington, Mary 384–385

Harris, Bob 351

Harris, Nancy 398

Hart, E.J. 303

Hart, John 277

Harvey, Dr. J. 379, 381

Hatter, Jim 24, 68, 330, 331, 332, 335, 351, 394

Hatzic Lake 300

Hayward, John 367

Healy Creek 315

Heard, Doug 153

Hebda, Richard 299

Hebert, Daryll 313, 314

Hecate Strait 363

Heiltsuk First Nation 281

Helmet Creek 357

Helsinki, Finland 418

Henaksiala Nation 225

Henderson, Gavin 328

Henry, J.K. 27

Henry, Mary Gibson 247

Henson, Paul 367

Henson, Peter 368

Henty, G.A. 20

Hewitt, Gordon 37, 38, 45, 47, 411
 conservation advocacy, and 37–38

Heyerdahl, Thor 266, 271

Hill, Eric 199

Hoar, Bill 351

Hobson, Rich 160

Holling, C.S. (Buzz) 145

"holotype" 26

Holyrood Palace, Edinburgh 435

Holyrood Park, Scotland 4, 7, 8

Hooker, Joseph 3, 10
 "concussion" with Balfour over botany chair at Edinburgh 10

Hooker, William 10

Hope, Thomas 9

Hornaday, William 100, 205

on hunting 140

Roosevelt, and 40

Hornocker, Maurice 313

Horseshoe Bay 31, 190, 427

Horseshoe Lake 110

Horsfield, Margaret 142

Horstadius, Sven 418

Hotspring Island 367

House Finch
 Cowan and 35–36
 example of climate change, as 36

House of All Sorts 208

Hudsonian Zone 78

Hummel, Monte 436, 437
 attacked as eccentric by business interests 60

Humphreys, R.M. 152

Hunter, Rodger 210

hunting. See also population ecology: prey/predator relationships; trapping
 class and gender aspects of 57
 conservation, and 227–228, 280
 conservation biology, and 72–73
 "good" creatures and "bad" 100
 indigenous right of 60, 385–386
 indigenous sense of kinship with prey 162
 national parks, and 49
 naturalists and 100, 117
 poaching 346–347. See also population ecology: population control: bounty system: corruption in
 sport or commercial vs. subsistence 49, 129–130
 whaling 238

Huntingdon, BC 6, 87, 297, 298, 300, 329

Hutchinson, Andrew H. 85, 103

Hutton, James 3
 "ancient earth" theory 8–10
 relation to Cowan 10

Huxley, Julian 181, 259, 395, 422, 433

hydatid disease 383

Illecillewaet River 232

Imperial Oil 327

Independent Order of Foresters 39. See also Oronhyatekha (Burning Cloud)

Indian Arm 300

Indianpoint Lake 166, 167, 170, 171

indigenous peoples
cultivation of species by 28
impact of industrial land use on. *But see* Meares Island: successful challenge to logging on
Banks Island Inuvialuit 389–390
Cheslatta T'en 224–226
Cowan on 161–162
Dempster Highway 388
Gwaii Haanas 370
Ktunaxa 118
Mackenzie Valley pipeline 385–387
Tsay Keh Dene 261–262
obliviousness of settler society toward 109, 142, 225–226, 390
right to wildlife 60, 385–386
traditional practices and conservation philosophies 162

Industrial Development Act. *See* Kenney Dam: legislation enabling

infestations 172

Ingenika 262

Ingenika Point 261

Inside Passage 268

Institute of Animal Resource Ecology, UBC 145

Institute of Fisheries, UBC 444

Institute of Oceanography (UBC) 86

International Biological Program 434

International Union for the Conservation of Nature (IUCN) 416, 433

International Whaling Commission 365
Cowan on whaling ban 237–238

Inuvialuit 376, 380–381, 389

Inverewe, Scotland 4

Invermere, BC 320

Inyo Valley, Calif. 184

Isaac Creek 337

island biogeography 82, 211, 368–369. *See also* MacArthur, Robert; University of British Columbia campus

forest: as biogeographical island; Wilson, Edward O.
Rocky Point 211–212
South Moresby (Gwaii Haanas) 369, 370
Spider Island 269–272

Island Rule. *See* Foster's Rule

Isle of Arran, Scotland 12

Isle of May, Scotland 412

Itcha Ilgachutz caribou herd 160

Itcha Mountains 159, 231

Jackson, Mary 385, 398

Jacob, Jessica Harland 57

Jacques Lake 125

Jacques Pass 124

Jasper Lake 335, 336

Jasper National Park 26, 121, 126, 336
creation of due to 1910 fire 125–126

Jeffels, Ron 260, 433

Jewett, Stanley G. 190

Jobin, Leo 249, 394

Johnson, Lyndon B. 436

Johnston, Fred 189

Joint Review Panel (re Site C dam) 263

Jonkel, Charles 291

Jordan River 148

Joslin, Paul 366

Juan Perez Sound 367

Jubilee Creek 149

Jump Creek 149

Juniper Creek 403

Kaiser, Gary W. 456

Kakawis (Christie) residential school 142

Kalela, Erkki 419

Kamloops, BC 155, 291, 404

Kamloops region 91, 94

Karppanen, Matti 419

Kaslo, BC 423

Kellogg, Louise 132, 134, 147

Kelsall, John P. 345

Kemano project. *See* Kenney Dam

Kempple, George 220

Kendall, James 417

Kenney Dam. *See also* Cheslatta T'en; Ootsa Lake
Cowans' 1936 wildlife survey as pre-dam baseline 220
legislation enabling 224–225

Quanchus Mountains, and 219

Kenney, Edward 224

Kenora, Ontario 436

Kenya 371, 382

Keremeos, BC 402

Kermode, Francis 27, 32, 48, 71, 163, 203, 204, 205, 206, 208, 213, 223, 250, 252, 257, 278, 279

Kerouard Islands 360

Kessler, Winifred 399

Kettle Valley Railway 107

Keynes, John Maynard 259

Kidluit Bay 381

King, Freeman "Skipper" vii

King, Mackenzie 46, 304

Kingsley School 31

King Solomon Basin 148

Kipling, Rudyard
influence on Cowan 21

Kitimat aluminum plant 224

Klamath River, Calif. 189

Klink, Leonard S. 277

Knight, Iola 158

Koestler, Arthur 262

Koeye Valley 281

Koocanusa reservoir 118

Kootenay Landing, BC 108

Kootenay National Park 320

Kootenay River 108, 110, 118, 320
as isolating barrier among species 110

Kosciuszko National Park, New South Wales, Australia 152

Krajina, Vladimir 347, 434
Cowan and 85

Kruger National Park (South Africa) 304

Ktunaxa people
Libby Dam, and 118
obliviousness of Laing and Cowan toward 109

Kunghit Island 359, 361

Kwadacha First Nation 261. *See also* Tsay Keh Dene

Kwakshua Channel 270, 271

Lac du Bois 289

Lac la Hache 394

Ladner, BC 250

Laguna San Ignacio 445

Laing, Ethel May (Hart) 108, 111, 112, 121, 122

Laing, Hamilton Mack 43, 47, 97, 116, 117, 119, 121, 128, 130, 131, 155, 249, 342, 354, 402, 457
attitude toward women 111–112
character and background 105–106, 114
collector, reputation as 103–105
diarist and correspondent, as 113–114
Ernest Thompson Seton and 21
influence on Cowan 113–114
Ktunaxa, and 109
"nature guide" job at Jasper 121
physical appearance 105
teacher, skill as 110
the 'B,' and 41, 106
Lake Edith 355, 356
Lake Louise 317, 328
Lake Louise Lifts 327
Lake Minnewanka 304
Lamb, W. Kaye 207, 208, 278, 446
Lame Billy 159, 161
Lamlash Bay, Scotland 12
Lamontagne, Maurice 432
Land Conservancy of BC, The 281
Langara Island 355, 361
Lang, Knud 379, 381
Lansdowne, Fenwick x, 98
Lansdowne, J. Fenwick x
Larkin, Peter 225, 432, 444, 446
Laurier, Wilfrid 38, 58
pro-conservation attitude 39, 50
Leavitt, Clyde 126
LeCompte, E. Lee 402
Leopold, Aldo xiv, 43, 44, 51, 55, 123, 156, 182, 267, 273, 309, 374, 375, 402, 433
conservation influence of 43, 54
Cowan and 54–55
public forests vs. private game reserves 54
still being attacked by business interests today 59–60
Leopold, Starker 58–59, 267, 374, 420, 421, 434
Cowan and 55
Lertzman, Ken 145
Lévi-Strauss, Claude 262
Lewis, Edward Lyn 437

Lewis, Harrison 47, 48
Libby Dam 118
Lidicker, Bill 296, 399, 406
Cowan and mammalogy, and 180
Lindblad, Lars-Eric 445
Lindblad, Sven 445
Lineham, P.D. 80
Linnaeus, Carl 418
Living Sea 364
Lloyd, Hoyes 41, 44, 45, 47, 48, 49, 51, 56, 57, 60, 99, 106, 116, 121, 123, 134, 178, 283, 328, 368, 433, 449, 454
bison issue, and 48
critic of his civil service employer, as 48
Dominion Parks Service chief ornithologist, as 46
key instigator of the 'B,' as 38
popularizer of conservation, as 47
similarity to Munro 47
Loch Shin, Scotland 422
Logier, E.B.S. 228
London, Jack 317
Lonesome Lake 251
Long Beach, Calif. 275
Long Beach Indian Reserve 142
Loo, Tina 58
Lord, John Keast 228
Loucheux (Ehdiitat Gwich'in) 376, 378
Lovat Scouts 309, 328
Love, Rhoda 245
Lulu Island 209
Lunny, Shane 223
Lyell, Charles 3, 9
Lyell Island 370
MacArthur, Robert 368
Maccarib Creek 128
MacDonald, Andrew 154
MacEachern, Alan 45
Mackay, R.H. (Ron) 251
Mackenzie, Alice 16
Mackenzie, Brian 17
Mackenzie, Daniel 415
Mackenzie Delta, NWT 9, 371, 373, 374, 375
Mackenzie District 382
Mackenzie, Donald 16
Mackenzie, Hilary 17
Mackenzie, John 17

Mackenzie, Kenneth Douglas 16
Mackenzie, Laura Alice 16
Mackenzie, Lord Donald 16
Mackenzie, Norman 352, 444
Mackenzie, Osgood 4, 5
Mackenzie River 375, 377, 378, 381
Mackie, George 288
Mackie Lake House 289
Mackie, Rev. Augustine ("Austin") Clark 288
Mackie, Richard 98, 105, 288
MacMillan Bloedel Ltd. 152, 154, 280, 443
MacMillan, H.R. 443, 444
philanthropy of 441, 442, 446
Macoun, William 48
Mahoney, Nancy 398. See also McAllister, Nancy (Mahoney)
Mailliard, John 195, 196
Mailliard, John Ward 196
Mailliard, Joseph 195
Mandarte Island 141
Mares, Michael 183
Marine Sciences Research Laboratory (Logy Bay, Nfld.) 447
marksmanship xi, 16–17
marmots 151–154, 166. See also Haley Lake Ecological Reserve
subject of Cowan's first published article (1929) 94
Marshall, Alec 160
Marsh, D.B. 376
Martin, Pat 209, 228, 249, 267, 288, 289, 339, 343, 351, 402, 411
Martin, Peter. See Oronhyatekha (Burning Cloud)
Masset, BC 148, 355, 367
Maxwell, David 426
May, Elizabeth viii, 388, 436
Maynard, Rick 404
McAllister, Ian 281
McAllister, Nancy (Mahoney) 395
McAllister, Peter 280
McArthur, Robert 82
McCabe, Elinor 166, 228
McCabe, Tom 166, 228, 361, 402
keeping Grinnell informed 167, 171

McCabe, Tom and Elinor 267
  Cowans' honeymoon 171
  environmental activism
    172–173
  influence as couple on Ian and
    Joyce 166–167
McCrory, Colleen 349
McCrory, Wayne viii, 349
McGahey, Pearl 57
McKinley, Tom 222
McLean, James 13
McNall, Michael C.E. 456
McQueen Lake 289
McTaggart-Cowan/nsək'łniw't
  Wildlife Management Area
  294
McTaggart, Elizabeth 16
McWilliams, Alice (Mackenzie)
  415
McWilliams, Jack 415
Meadow Creek 128
Meares Island 135
  successful challenge to logging
    on 142–143
Mearns, Barbara 72
Mearns, Richard 72
Mech, David 345
Meighen, Arthur 46
Memorial University, St. John's,
  Nfld. 13, 420, 447, 448
Mendocino County, Calif. 194,
  195, 197
Menzies, Harold 288
Merilees, Bill 13, 153, 446
Merriam, C. Hart 51, 132. See
  also taxonomy: speciation;
  variation: by landscape zone
  Cowan and 77, 188
Merritt, BC 395
Michelle 243
Migratory Birds Convention Act
  71, 251, 433
Migratory Bird Treaty of 1916 47
Miller, Frank 383
Millikin, Rhonda 212. See
  also island biogeography:
  Rocky Point
Miner, Jack
  evolution and 99
minke whale specimen 236–237
Minnesota Seaside Station 83
Mitchell, W.O. 437
Moat Creek 128
Moby Doll 442

Moffitt, Elizabeth 196
  Cowan and 194–195
Moffitt, James
  Cowan and 194–195
  death of 196
  opossums, and 195
molecular biologists supplanting
  field biologists 259–260. See
  also under Grinnell, Joseph:
  field science vs. lab science
Monarch Mountain 219
Monashee Pass 231
Monk, Adam 288
Monte Creek 91
Monte Creek Ranch 95
Montgomery Woods State
  Natural Reserve, Calif. 197
Montreal 79
Moore, Keith 370
Moore, W.K. 233
Moresby Island 363, 367
Morgan, J.P. 53
Morrison, Doug 404
Morton, Ted 256
Mount Assiniboine 316
Mount Begbie 166
Mount Douglas 148
Mount Dufferin 97
Mount Garibaldi 76
Mount Hebron, Calif. 189
Mount Maligne 340
Mount McCloud, Calif. 189
Mount Miller, Calif. 189
Mount Musclow 221
Mount Overlord 76
Mount Paul 95
Mount Revelstoke 231, 232
Mount Shasta, Calif. 188
Mount Tyrrell 322
Mount Waddington 23
Muir, John 3, 39, 194
  idealism contra Pinchot
    pragmatism 50
  influence on Harkin 38
  influence on Roosevelt 40
  meets Grinnell 134
  spiritual dimension to nature,
    and 15
  still being attacked by business
    interests today 59–60
Mumford, Lewis 262
Munday, Phyllis and Don 23,
  354

Munro, Alice Olive (Bunting)
  34, 212
  as member of the 'B' 57
Munro, David 47, 51, 352
Munro, Isabella (Darby) 34
Munro, Jim 34, 36, 41, 51, 57,
  58, 63, 65, 71, 100, 105, 114,
  116, 137, 141, 160, 205, 212,
  216, 242, 249, 251, 283, 288,
  330, 354, 393, 394, 395, 402,
  449, 454
  background similar to Cowan's
    33
  collector for Provincial
    Museum, as 205
  correspondence with a 15-year-
    old Cowan 33, 34–35
  educator and ornithologist,
    as 34
  over-zealous collection by 216
  similarity to Lloyd 47
Murphy, Cliff and Nellie 321
Musclow Lake 221
Musco, Johnny 346
Museum of Nature, Ottawa 36,
  70, 104, 295, 327
Museum of Vertebrate Zoology,
  Berkeley 87, 99, 100, 132,
  177, 179, 182, 185, 203, 204
museums and museology
  Cowan's improvements to BC
    Provincial Museum 240–
    241, 247–248
  Cowan's study trip and
    recommendations 229
  role of museums 70–71
Muskett, Frank 293
Myers, Timothy 398
myxomatosis 5
Nagorsen, David 70, 78, 110,
  115, 119, 248, 271, 295
  work on marmots later
    corroborating theory of
    Cowan's 152
Naismith, Dr. and Mrs. 80
Namu, BC 268
Nanaimo, BC 83, 148
Nanaimo River 148
Napoleon, Art 261
National and Provincial Parks
  Association 328
National Energy Board 387
national parks. See also
  under conservation; public
  access to nature; wildlife
  management

Canada, in
  corporate interests and 59–
    60, 304, 327–328
  Cowan on grizzly hazard in
    128–129
  Dominion Parks Branch 38.
    See also under Harkin,
    James B.
  fiscal austerity and 131
  Harkin on role of parks 56,
    309
  Harkin's legacy 230
  hunting lobbies, and 49,
    303–306
  influence of the 'B,' and
    45–46
  "nature guides" in 121
  restructuring of in 1911 126
  wildlife protection in 123
US, in
  Roosevelt and 50
National Research Council
  of Canada (now NSERC,
  the Natural Sciences and
  Engineering Research
  Council) 400, 432
natural history societies 3
Natural History Society of BC
  203
naturalists viii
  as distinct from scientists
    15, 105, 114, 133. See
    also science: lab scientists
    vs. field naturalists/
    collectors
    Thoreau tradition 114
  "collectors" vs. "observers"
    71–72, 116–117. See
    also Vancouver Natural
    History Society: rift with
    field naturalists
  Cowan as 114
  diminishing importance of
    after 1930 115, 119
  hunting, and 100
  public attitudes toward 34,
    117, 119
nature. See public access to
  nature
Nature Conservancy, The 432
Nature Trust of BC, The 161,
  196, 294
  Cowan and 118
Nechako River 219, 225. See
  also Cheslatta T'en; Kenney
  Dam; Ootsa Lake
Nelles, Alex 332
Nesatyk, George 357
Newcombe, Charles F. See

also Newcombe, William
  (Billy)
  BC Provincial Museum, and
    204–205
Newcombe, William (Billy) 206
Newgate, BC 107, 118
Newman, Murray 427, 441,
  441–444, 446
New York Zoological Society
  40, 205
NGO movement 388
Nicholson, E. Max 432, 433
Ninstints (Sgaan Gwaii) 370
Nixon, Walter 320
Nordquist, Gus 181
Norman Wells, BC 375
North American Conservation
  Commission 126
North American Conservation
  Conference 40, 51
North American Wild Life
  Conference 45, 305
North Pacific Fur Seal
  Convention (1911) 144
North Shore Mountains,
  Vancouver 145
North Vancouver 22, 31
North Vancouver High School
  63
Numa Creek 357
Numbers, Ronald 259
Ober, E.H. 184
Okanagan Falls Biodiversity
  Ranch 294
Okanagan Landing 34, 97, 100
Okanagan Mountain Provincial
  Park 407
Okanagan (region) 213, 292, 293
Okanagan Similkameen Parks
  Society 217
Oldham, E.G. 375
Oliver, BC 155, 156
Omineca Mountains 241
Ommundsen, Peter x, 11
Ontario Provincial Museum
  (now Royal Ontario
  Museum) 34
Ootsa Lake 226, 337, 346
  Cowans honeymooning at 219
  war vets and trappers at
    222–223
Open Learning Institute 260,
  433
Opitsaht people 143

Opitsaht, Vancouver Island 135
opossums 195
Orcas 441–443. See also
  under whales and whaling
Ordway, Samuel 421
ornithology 71–72, 116–117.
  See also under naturalists:
  "collectors" vs. "observers"
Oronhyatekha (Burning Cloud)
  39
Orr, Robert 197
Osborn, Henry Fairfield Jr. 421
Ottawa Field-Naturalists' Club
  47, 49, 283
overfishing 3
overhunting 4–5. See
  also extirpation; and under
  population ecology
Pacific Biological Station,
  Nanaimo, BC 72, 83, 276,
  278, 283, 400
Pacific Lime Company 19
Pacific Spirit Park, Vancouver 82
Page, R.E. 25
Pallas, Peter Simon 232
Paradise Mountain 314
Paris, France 303
Parksville, BC 132, 148
Pass Lake 289
Pattullo, Thomas Dufferin
  (Duff) 199, 228
Peace Canyon Dam 261
Peace River 256, 261
Peace River region 247
Pearse, Peter 446
Pearse, Theed 71, 288
Pearson, T. Gilbert 43, 49, 54,
  401
Peavine Lake 254
Peel Channel 384
Pelican Island, Florida 55
Pemberton Lake, BC 95
Penticton, BC 288
Penticton Indian Band 294
Perem, Mr. 216
Perry, Fred 72
Perth, Scotland 16
Perthshire, Scotland 17
Petersen, R.M. 345
Peyto, Bill 317
Pfeiffer, Bert 355, 357
Phébus, Gaston 44

Philip, Alex 80

Phillips, Carleton 183

Phillips, Charlie 310

Phillips, Panhandle 160

Pielou, Chris 145

pikas 231–232

Pinchot, Gifford 421
  pragmatism contra Muir's idealism 50, 55

Pine Ridge Reservation, South Dakota 133

Pitlochry, Scotland 421

Pitt Island 359

Playfair, John 8

Plinian Society 3

Poboktan Pass 333

Point Atkinson 31

Point Grey, Vancouver 81, 82

Polar Bears International 383

Pondosy Bay 221

population ecology. *See also* conservation; conservation biology; taxonomy: "taxonomic eye" for distinguishing traits; wildlife management
  bears, of 291
  Chitty's theory 25, 291
  Cowan and 4–5, 24–25, 52–53, 69–70, 82, 115, 146, 160–162
  "Of Mice and Men" lecture 6–7, 53, 260
  effect of clear-cut logging 24–26, 172–173. *See also* population ecology: wildlife population "sinks"

population control
  bounty system 6–7, 312
  BC Ornithologists Union and 71
  Charles McLean Fraser on 83
  corruption in 302, 318–319, 322. *See also* hunting: poaching
  Cowan's advocacy against 301–306
  "environmental resistance" 406–407
  introduced diseases 5–6
  of humans. *See also under* eugenics; Huxley, Julian; Wilson, Edward O.
  Cowan to Dawe on 422–423
  "social Darwinism" 259
  of predators 100, 123, 222, 345–346. *See*

also population ecology: prey/predator relationships
  of species 4–5, 52
  parasites the real killers, not predators 321, 326
  park wardens and 122–123, 346–347
  wildlife surveys 310–313, 319–320, 326–327. *See also under* wolves: as individuals

prey/predator relationships 6, 54, 82, 99–100, 122–123, 162, 301–306, 310–315, 361
  predation fallacy 304–305, 327, 357

reproductive strategies
  evolutionary advantage, and 413–414
  territoriality and 255, 413–414
  variation in 257–258
  "special requirements" 256–257

species at risk. *See also* COSEWIC; extinction; extirpation
  American Badger 119
  competing with industry for same territory 70
  Humpback Whale 365
  Killdeer 107
  Mountain Caribou 160
  Pacific Water-shrew 299
  Spotted Owl 195–196
  Townsend's Mole 298
  Townsend's Vole, Cowan subspecies 143
  specimen collecting and 68, 72–73, 116–117
  sympatric speciation 13
  wildlife population "sinks" 25, 153

Porcupine Caribou Management Board 388

Porsild, A.E. 377

Port Alberni, BC 132, 135

Post, Lee 376

Powell, Lord Baden 21

Prince Philip 433, 435

Prince Rupert, BC 268

Princess Patricia 205

Pritchard, Andy 277

privatization of nature. *See* public access to nature

Pruth Bay 270

public access to nature 17

Balfour and 12

Cowan and 14, 17

Darwinists vs. dominionists, and 33

Harkin and 40

Leopold and 54

pressure for privatization 50, 53–54, 126–127, 348–349

Roosevelt and Viscount Grey and 50

sport hunting lobbies and 49

Sweden, in 418

the 'B' and 49–51, 56–57

Tofino Mudflats, and 144

Quanchus Mountains 219

quantitative ecology 181

Queen Charlotte Islands (Haida Gwaii) 354, 368, 417

Queen Charlotte Islands International Symposium (1984) 369

Queen Charlotte Sound 268

Queen Elizabeth 435

Quesnel, BC 166, 167, 168

rabbits 177
  introduced 4–6

Racey, Alan 6, 67, 148, 155, 157, 212

Racey, Eileen (Stewart) 75, 155, 157, 439, 449
  influence on Cowan 67, 76

Racey, John 66

Racey, Joyce
  early interest in Ian Cowan 76, 77
  early interest in nature 75
  homeschooling, and 165
  letter from Cowan during Tofino trip 139–140
  on family expeditions to: Black Mountain 78
  Cheakamus River 76
  Chezacut Lake 155, 157–158
  See also Alta Lake: Racey family at

Racey, Kathy 460

Racey, Kenneth
  American Society of Mammalogists, and 73
  a night on Green Mountain 149, 151
  Brink influenced by 293
  Burrard Field-Naturalists, and 72, 293. *See also* Burrard Field-Naturalists' Society
  Cowan influenced by 65–66, 67, 72, 73, 76–77, 87, 94, 104

Cowan's affection for 151
death of 449
family background similar to
  Cowan's 66–67
Grinnell, and 178
husband and father, as 75
Laing, and 116–117
marmots, and 131, 151
Munro, and 34
murres, and 419–420
pikas, and 231
rabbits, and 6
shotgun given to Beck by
  Cowan 454
taxonomy and collecting,
  and 67
the 'B' and 41, 106
to the Chilcotin with the
  family 155, 157–159
to the Itcha Mountains with
  Lame Billy 160
to Tofino with Cowan 135
Racey, Stewart 67, 155, 200
Raincoast Conservation
  Foundation 273, 281
Ramsay Island 367
Ransom, W.H. 394
Rassenkreis. See Rensch,
  Bernhard
Raven, Mr. D. vii
Ray, Dixie Lee 427
Rayleigh, BC (near Kamloops)
  94
Raymont, John 423
RBCM. See Provincial Museum
  of BC
Red Cloud 133
Red Mountain 76
Reed, Chester A. 19, 34
Reef Island 360, 363
Reid, Robert 429
Reifel, George C. 210
Reimchen, Tom 145, 363
reindeer 380–381
Rensch, Bernhard 180–181, 200
Rensch's Rule 200
Restless River 340
Rexford, Montana 108
Rh factor in human pregnancy
  248–249
Rhododendron Society, Victoria
  458
Richards Island 381
Richardson, Miles 370
Richmond, BC 209

Richter, Francis 403, 407
Rio Gavilan 267
Ripley, S. Dillon 262, 421
Riske Creek 394
Roberts, Charles 20
Robinson, Don 351
Robison, John 417
Rockabella boarding house,
  Victoria 207, 208
Rock and Alpine Club of
  Victoria 458
Rockefeller, Laurance 421
Rocky Forks 339
Rocky Point (near Metchosin,
  BC) 211
Rocky River 341
Ronsin, Moses 159
Rooney, R.A. 304
Roosevelt, Theodore 44, 50, 51,
  52, 53, 54, 55, 205
background; friendship with
  Muir 40
conservation, and 40, 50–51
eugenics, and 51–52
Harkin and 40
Hornaday and 40–41
Rose Harbour 359, 361
Rose Spit 366
Round Table Club 446
Routledge, David 153, 154
Rowan, William (Bill) 305,
  355, 356
Rowe, Stan 431
Royal Botanic Gardens,
  Edinburgh 10, 417
Royal Commission on
  Aboriginal Peoples 225
Royal Medical Society,
  Edinburgh 11
Royal Society of Canada 37, 52
Royal Society of Edinburgh 3, 9
Rudbeck, Olaus 418
Russell, Bertrand 56
Saint Andrew's University,
  Perthshire, Scotland 420
Saint Cyrus, Scotland 412
Salisbury Crags, Scotland 8
Salter, F.M. 356
Sami 380, 381
Samuelson, Paul 259
Sandspit 358, 363
San Francisco Mountain 77
Sapolio 243

Saskatchewan Crossing 342
Saturna Island 427, 428, 441
Saulteux First Nation 261
Save the Redwoods League 197
Scagel, Robert 83, 400
Schau, Ann xii, 53, 78, 165, 173,
  217, 228, 248, 272, 329, 356,
  404, 407, 412, 416, 427, 428,
  434, 446, 447, 455, 457, 459
Schau, Mikkel 53, 228, 414, 445,
  447, 455
Schau, Torben 447, 448
Scheidler, J.M. 345
Schiedam Flats, BC (near
  Kamloops) 95
Schreiber, Norman 222
Schwartz, Bill 118
science
  fiscal austerity and 70–71, 115,
    248, 279–280, 295–296,
    407–408
  governments and 59, 83, 280,
    387, 390, 407, 432–433
  historical changes in approach
    115–116
  lab scientists vs. field
    naturalists/collectors 15,
    68–71, 114–115, 133, 146,
    181–183, 185, 187, 259–260,
    353. See also under Grinnell,
    Joseph: field science vs. lab
    science
  politicization of 59–60, 70,
    258–259
  whaling 237–238
  religion and 9–10, 15, 33, 99,
    259
Scotland
  conditions in 3–5, 411–412
Scott, Duncan Campbell 37
Scottish Enlightenment 3, 8, 417
Scottish hunting culture 4,
  16–17
Scottish Ornithological Society
  414
Scottish Rights of Way Society
  12. See also under public
  access to nature
Scottish romanticism 15, 17
Scott, Peter 320, 420, 431, 433
Scott, Robert 420
Scott, Sir Walter 15, 20
Scourie, Scotland 422
Scriven, Albert H. 31
Scudder, Geoff 401, 407, 408

Sea of Cortez 369, 444, 445, 446
Searle, Rick 150
Sea Shepherd Conservation Society 238
Sedgewick, Garnett 400
Selassie, Haile 436
Selkirks Range 232
Seton, Ernest Thompson ix, 37, 53, 106, 163, 168, 355
 Cowan and 181
 influence on Cowan and Laing 20–21
Severn Wildfowl Trust 420
Seymour Narrows 393, 442
Sgaan Gwaii 370
Shadow Lake 317
Shaw, D.L. 63
Shaw, George Bernard 259
Shelford, Cyril 222, 346
Shelford, Jack (father) 222
Shelford, John (son) 222
Sherman, Reuter Stinson 72
Shields, G.O. 21
Shillaker, Frank 159, 160
shrews 269–272. See also island biogeography: Spider Island
Siccar Point, Scotland 8
Siddle, Chris 248
Sierra Club 194, 280
Sierra del Nido, Mexico 156
Silver, Rod x, xii
Similkameen River 402
Simon Fraser University 449
Simpson, George Buchanan 210
Simpson, Jimmy x, 315, 317, 318, 321, 323, 324, 326, 333, 342, 348, 456
Simpson, Sir George 247
Simpson, Suzanne Buchanan 210
Sirius Peak 325
Sissons, C.P. 357
Sister Mary Celestine 397
Sister Mary Scholastica 397
Site C dam 248, 256, 261, 263
Sitka, Alaska 134
Sitkum Point 142
Sittichinli, J. Edward 379
Skaha Lake 294
Skidegate Band 370
Skidegate, BC 358

Slimbridge, England 320, 420
Slwooko, Charles and Vernon 383
Smallwood, Joey 448
Smart, James 305
Smith, Andrew 232
Smith, G.E. John 456
Smith, Gertrude 277
Smith, Glen x, 152, 351
Smith, Jamie 141
Smithsonian Institution 262
Smith, William Wright 417
Smokey the Bear 127
Smoky River 343
Snowball, A.R. 72
Snow Creek Pass 322
sociobiology 259. See also under population ecology: population control
Soda Creek 166
Soper, Dewey 454
Sorenson Lake 395
Sorenson, Sam 394
Southern Carrier people 160
Southesk, Earl of 17, 338
Southesk Lake 340
Southesk River 338
Southesk Valley 339
South Moresby (Gwaii Haanas) 370
South Moresby Wilderness 369
South Moresby Wilderness Proposal Committee 370
Spatsizi Plateau, BC 347
Special Expeditions 445
species at risk. See under population ecology
specimen collecting, preparing, curating 67–71, 86–87. See also under conservation biology; population ecology; taxonomy
 Cowan on overzealous collecting 216
 Laing and 103–105, 114
 Stanwell-Fletcher on 243
Spencer Entomological Collection 84
Spencer, George J. 276, 277, 288, 289, 301, 401, 440
 Cowan's first biology summer job, and 91
 influence on Cowan 84–85
Spider Island 269

Spong, Paul 443
Spotted Lake 287
Spray River 315
SS Maquinna 135
Stainsby, Donald 240
Stanwell-Fletcher, John 241, 242, 243, 244
Stanwell-Fletcher, Theodora "Teddy" 241, 242, 243, 244, 251
Stark, Nancy 207
Starzomski, Brian 281, 459
Stebbins, Robert 294
Stein, Barbara 132
Stenton, Ernest 311, 313
Sterling, Tom 351, 352
Stevenson, G.C. 190
Stevenson-Hamilton, Colonel James 304
Stevens, Ward 352, 373, 377, 382, 384, 385
Steveston, BC 28, 209, 427
stewardship of public lands. See under conservation; environmentalism; public access to nature
Stewart, Andy C. 456
Stewart, Charles 48
Stewart, Helen 294
Stewart, Ronald 148, 355, 360
Stirling, David 140
Stirling, Ian 383, 457
St. Lawrence Island, Alaska 383
St. Molio's Cave 12
Stoddard, Herbert L. 43–44, 100, 123, 127
Straight, Lee 24
Strawberry Canyon, Berkeley, Calif. 177, 185
strontium 90 386
Sulphur Springs 321
Sumas Lake, Abbotsford, BC 91
Summit Creek 449
Sunwapta Valley 328
Surel Creek 221
Suzuki, David viii, 115, 223, 423, 431, 459
Swan Lake 250, 251, 261
Swarth, Harry
 Annie Alexander, and 132
 Brooks and 98
 Cowan and 134
 Newcombe and 204

Sweeney, Lillian 240, 254
Swiftwater Creek 124
Swit, Loretta 223
Syilx people 294, 403
Sykes, Reverend 31
Symons, R.D. 348
systematics. *See* taxonomy
Talbot Lake 310
Tamarack Swamp (near Newgate, BC) 110
Tanzania 371
Taverner, Percy 36, 37, 38, 41, 43, 47, 48, 51, 57, 58, 98, 99, 100, 105, 106, 116, 131, 134, 178, 242, 251, 368, 411, 433
taxonomy. *See also* specimen collecting, preparing, curating
  bears, of 290–291
  common names and 66
  Darwin and 156
  genetics and 83, 116, 181, 408
  Laing and 114
  naming as cultural expression xvi
  speciation; variation
    by geography 81–82, 116, 183–185
    by landscape zone 77, 187–188
  specimen preparation for 67–69
  sympatric speciation 13
  "taxonomic eye" for distinguishing traits 181
Taylor, Ann 85
Taylor, Malcolm G. 449
Taylor, Mary 314, 399
Taylor, Tommy 426
Telegraph Creek 302
television 14
  Klahanie series (1970s) 404–405
Temple, Stanley 54
Tener, John 394
Ten Mile Lake 169, 170, 173, 218
Tetana Lake 242, 243, 245, 251
Texada Island 19
Thatcher, Margaret 415
Thompson Indian Reserve 91
Thompson Pass 344
Thomson, Joanne 460
ticks 93
Tilden, Josephine 83
Tla-o-qui-aht Nation 142
Tlell River 359

Tobacco Plains 108
Tobacco Plains Indian Band 118
Tobacco Plains Indian Reserve 109
Tofino Inlet 142
Tofino Mudflats 135, 136, 138, 144
Tofino, Vancouver Island 135, 136, 138, 276
Tomlinson ranch 109
Tompa, Frank S. 141
Tonquin Valley 125, 128, 129, 343
Torkko, Ed 148, 149, 150
Toronto Field-Naturalists 283
Tory, Henry Marshall 356
trapping 31, 63, 108, 110, 122, 123–124, 222–224, 377, 378
  Cowan's advocacy for sustainable, humane trapping 222–223
Tres Marías Islands 444
Triangle Island 4, 143, 420
Trudeau, Pierre Elliott 436
Tsay Keh Dene 261, 262
Tuck, Mrs. 207
Tufts, Robie 249
Tupper Creek 250
Tupper Creek School 254
Tweddle, Haliburton 403
Tweedsmuir, Lady 219, 226, 228
Tweedsmuir, Lord 21, 228
  hunting and conservation, on 227–228
  opening of Tweedsmuir Park, at 219
Tweedsmuir Provincial Park 219, 224, 225, 227, 354
Tyldesley, Alice 417
Tynron, Dumfriesshire, Scotland 415
Ukiah Park, Calif. 197
Ulkatcho 160
UNESCO 433, 434
UNESCO Biosphere Conference (1968) 385
United States Forest Service 40
University of Alberta 92, 355, 356
University of British Columbia 25, 81, 82, 83, 85, 86, 199, 260, 277, 278, 283, 347, 348, 352, 402, 446, 451
  campus as biogeographical

island 81, 211. *See also* island biogeography
  patriarchal culture of 400
University of Calgary 348, 448
University of California, Berkeley 198, 199
  Cowan at 177–179, 186–187, 188
University of Southampton, England. 423
University of Victoria 25, 447, 449
University of Victoria Professorship in Biodiversity and Ecological Restoration, UVic 459
Uppsala, Sweden 418
Valhalla Wilderness Society 349
Vancouver 19
  as compared to Edinburgh 21
Vancouver Aquarium 427, 441, 443
Vancouver Institute xiii, 406
Vancouver International Film Festival 430
Vancouver Island 27
Vancouver Island Rock and Alpine Garden Society vii
Vancouver Natural History Society 414. *See also* Burrard Field-Naturalists' Society
  rift with field naturalists 65, 72. *See also* naturalists: "collectors" vs. "observers"
Vancouver Society for the Prevention of Cruelty to Animals 301
van den Berghe, Pierre 259
Vanderhoof, BC 172
Vander Zalm, Bill 369
Varsity Outdoors Club, UBC 446
Vaseux Creek Canyon 155
Vaseux Lake 155, 216
  importance to Cowans as couple 217–218
Vermilion River 320
Vernon, BC 101, 288
Vernon Preparatory School 288
Vibert, Elizabeth 109
Vickers, Roy Henry viii, x
Victoria, BC 27, 28, 35, 70
Victoria College 331
Village Lake Louise 327
Volkoff, George 432

W.A.C. Bennett Dam 248, 261
Wailes, G.H. 72
Wake Island 275
Walker, Tommy and Marion 347
Wallace, Alfred 81. See
 also taxonomy: speciation;
 variation: by geography
Wallmo, Olof C. 185
Washington, DC 267
Watchman Lake 344
Watson, James Dewey 423
Watson, Paul viii
 Cowan on OC nomination of
 238–240
Watun River 366
Web of Life 14, 127, 355, 364,
 401, 429, 430
Weeden, Robert (Bob) x, 15, 55,
 117, 129, 405
Weir, George 206, 278
 Minister of Education, as 199
Weir, Harold 430
Wells, BC 354
Wells, Frank 123, 311, 344
Wells Gray Provincial Park 231,
 397
Wendle, Joe 172
Wernerian Society 3
Westham Island 210
Westwick Lake 395, 398, 399,
 401
Weyerhaeuser, Frederick 53
whales and whaling 364–365.
 See also under International
 Whaling Commission
whimbrel. See curlew
Whirlpool River, Alberta 26
Whistler, BC 67, 80
 Alta Lake, and 75
 Joyce Cowan and 78
Whistler Mountain 78
White Lake 137, 216, 287
White Lake Biodiversity Ranch
 294

Whiteman Pass 316
Whitesail River 221
Wildcat Hills, Alta. 452, 453
wilderness. See
 also conservation; public
 access to nature; hunting
 as healing sought by war
 veterans
 Frank Shillaker 159
 George Spencer 84–85
 Jack Shelford 222
 Ronald Buckell 92
 Ron Mackay 251
 Tom McCabe 167
 as sanctuary 56–57, 228
 preserving wildness of
 Cowan and Joseph Grinnell
 on 128–129
 Yorke Edwards on 398
Wilderness Advisory Committee
 (BC) 369
Wildfowl and Wetlands Trust
 320
wildlife artists 98
wildlife management.
 See also conservation;
 conservation biology
 Harkin and 122–123
 industrial agriculture and 44
 Leopold and 54
 population surveying 310–313
 pragmatism v. principle 55–56,
 117–118, 237–238
 Scotland, in 5
 sport hunting and 227–
 228, 301–306. See also
 under population ecology:
 prey/predator relationships:
 predation fallacy
 surveys. See population
 ecology: population control:
 wildlife surveys
 Sweden and Finland, in
 418–419
 the 'B' and 123
 trapping, and 223
wildlife "sinks" 25. See
 also clear-cut logging

Williams, Bryan 260
Williams Lake, BC 155, 396, 397
Williams, Syd 124
Willow Creek 325, 332
Wilson, Betty 261
Wilson, Edward O. 82, 258, 368.
 See also Wallace, Alfred
Winch, Ernest 224
Winchester, Neville 145, 148
Winch, Harold 224
Windy Bay 370
Windy Point 336
Winson, J.W. 87, 297
Winter, Austin de B. 304, 357
Wolverine Pass 357
wolves 243–244
 as individuals 318–320, 344
 wolf studies 345–346
Wood, Alec 407
Woodbourne, Pennsylvania 241,
 244, 245
Wood Buffalo National Park,
 Alberta and NWT 46
Woodhaven Terrace (Victoria,
 BC) ix, 197
Woods, Fred 80
Woodsworth, Gregory 295
woodticks 93
Woodward Island 250
World Charter for Nature 238
World Wide Fund for Nature
 433
Wright, J.P. 48
Wynne-Edwards, Vero Copner
 413
 Cowan and deer, and 414
Wythe, Margaret 190
Ya Ha Tinda Ranch 321
Young, H.E. 204
Zink, Joan. See Cowan, Joan
 McTaggart
Zwickel, Fred 24, 25

ABOUT THE AUTHOR

Briony Penn has spent the last 25 years working with a wide variety of audiences and media – from newspapers to television and field schools to lecture halls – communicating her love and knowledge of BC's ecosystems and cultures. An award-winning natural-history columnist and feature writer, from *Canadian Geographic* to *Explore* magazines, and a BC *Books* bestselling author with *A Year on the Wild Side* and *Kids Book of Canadian Geography,* she combines punchy media skills with her research affiliations at University of Victoria. She received her PhD in geography from the University of Edinburgh, Scotland. As a writer and illustrator, she has published over 400 columns on natural and cultural history in regional newspapers and magazines, including: "Wild Side" for *Monday Magazine*, Victoria, and "Natural Relations" for *Focus* magazine. She received a Western Magazine Award for Best Columnist and Feature Writer, won a Silver Environment Educator medal at the Canadian Environmental Awards and was nominated for best North American columnist in alternative weeklies. She had a television show, *Enviro/Mental*, with CHUM-TV for three years which was a runner-up for Best Magazine Show at the Canadian Broadcaster Awards.

Briony received a Canada Council grant for creative non-fiction to do research on Ian McTaggart Cowan and other pioneers of natural history and scientific research who also shared a strong ethic of education. The project was entitled *Beautiful British Columbians* and articles from it were serialized in *Focus* from 2002–2006. As part of that project, Briony conducted lengthy audio and video interviews with Ian McTaggart Cowan, which he granted her exclusive use of. In 2013 she was awarded a BC Arts Council grant for non-fiction, which assisted in the writing of *The Real Thing*.

Briony Penn has two grown sons and lives on Salt Spring Island, British Columbia.